PAUL, JUDAISM, AND THE GENTILES

PAUL, JUDAISM, AND THE GENTILES

Beyond the New Perspective

. .

REVISED AND EXPANDED EDITION

Francis Watson

WILLIAM B. EERDMANS PUBLISHING COMPANY
GRAND RAPIDS, MICHIGAN / CAMBRIDGE, U.K.

Published 2007 by

Wm. B. Eerdmans Publishing Co.

2140 Oak Industrial Drive N.E., Grand Rapids, Michigan 49505 /

P.O. Box 163, Cambridge CB3 9PU U.K.

Printed in the United States of America

12 11 10 09 08 07   7 6 5 4 3 2 1

Library of Congress Cataloging-in-Publication Data

Watson, Francis, 1956-

Paul, Judaism, and the Gentiles: beyond the new perspective /

Francis Watson. — Rev. and expanded ed.

p.   cm.

Includes bibliographical references.

ISBN 978-0-8028-4020-2 (pbk.: alk. paper)

1. Paul, the Apostle, Saint. 2. Bible. N.T. Epistles of Paul — Criticism,
interpretation, etc. 3. Christian sociology — History — Early church, ca. 30-600.
4. Law and gospel — History of doctrines — Early church, ca. 30-600.
5. Church history — Primitive and early church, ca. 30-600.
6. Judaism (Christian theology) — History of doctrines —
Early church, ca. 30-600.   I. Title

BS2655.J4W38   2007

225.9′2 — dc22

2007021104

www.eerdmans.com

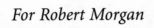

For Robert Morgan

Contents

vii

Contents

CONTENTS

Preface to the Revised Edition

During a recent meeting of the *Studiorum Novi Testamenti Societas*, I found myself seated next to a scholar well known for his contribution to the so-called "New Perspective on Paul." We had not met for a number of years, and, on my part at least, there was a slight sense of awkwardness. The scholar in question had thought well of *Paul, Judaism and the Gentiles*, my first book, but much less well of my subsequent turn towards matters theological and hermeneutical. Indeed, he had expressed himself rather forcefully on this point, in print. In my first book (he opined), I had sought to liberate exegesis from the deadening control of dogma. This had been a most promising and worthwhile contribution to the great cause. Mysteriously and disappointingly, however, my later work seemed to be headed in precisely the opposite direction. Dogma was back with a vengeance, stridently reasserting its control over exegesis. What had happened? Whatever it was, it was very much to be regretted.

Against that background, there was unlikely to be a meeting of minds. After a bare minimum of polite pleasantry, my critic turned to me with the air of one about to say something he has long wanted to say. "I have just one question to ask you," he said. "Do you still hold to the position you took in *Paul, Judaism and the Gentiles?*"

It was a fair question, but a challenging one. Looming menacingly on the horizon was the further, unspoken question: What went wrong? Unable on the spur of the moment to engage the unspoken question, to deconstruct its assumptions or unmask its hidden agendas, I could only offer the blandest of replies. I said that I felt the basic position to be sound, but that I now had reservations about some aspects of the argument. It was the stock answer that almost anyone would give if asked, a couple of decades later, about a book they had written in their twenties. I do not know whether my interrogator was satisfied; in any case the conversation proceeded no further. Yet, as far as it went, my answer was entirely truthful. I continue to believe that there was insight in this youthful work, in the midst of evident flaws and limitations.

In preparing this second, revised and expanded edition of my book, I have had the opportunity to address those flaws and limitations and to strengthen the basic argument — in the growing conviction that what I once tried to say still has a contribution to make to the ongoing debate about Paul. The rewriting has been extensive, and at some points I have retained only the empty shell of what I once argued, which I have proceeded to fill with a new content. Yet this is genuinely a second edition, a renewed book but not a new one. I have long wanted to clarify my ambivalent relationship with the New Perspective on Paul, and preparing this volume has proved the perfect opportunity to do so. I also hope that this volume can serve to complement the argument of my *Paul and the Hermeneutics of Faith* (2004). Certain perspectives on Paul's texts that are absent there are here given due attention.

A second, revised edition of a work is inevitably a hybrid, a compromise between what one wrote once and what one might wish to say now. Among other things, this affects the engagement with the secondary literature. I have retained as much as possible of the original documentation, and have updated it only selectively — not wishing the main text to be overwhelmed by a rising tide of footnotes, as in so many monographs on Pauline themes. So I must apologize to a number of scholars working in this field whose work has not received due attention.

In this edition, the subtitle no longer promises "a sociological approach," but proposes a move "beyond the New Perspective." For many years I assumed that my book could straightforwardly be aligned with the contributions of Stendahl, Sanders, Dunn, Wright, and others, who sought to replace an image of Paul derived from the Reformation with a historically oriented account focused on issues of Gentile inclusion. On further reflection, I am more impressed by the divergences among those who have adopted this general line than by the similarities. I also believe that the insistence that "Judaism is a religion of grace" has had its day, and that the extraordinary creativity and diversity of Second Temple Judaism should not be reduced to a singular soteriological scheme. In my judgment, the first edition of this book contained significant alternatives to some of the interpretative options that have since established themselves, and I have sought to highlight them here. Among other things, I propose a more nuanced account of what is and is not wrong with the type of reading that reflects the ongoing influence of Martin

Luther. The "New Perspective" was new in relation to an "Old Perspective" presided over by Luther, and it is now time to move beyond this polarity, with its depressingly entrenched positions and its all-too-predictable exegetical conclusions.

I am grateful to Michael Thomson, of Eerdmans, for the invitation to prepare this edition; to Professor John Barclay for valuable advice; to Dr. Vijay Pillai for help with the bibliography; and to Dr. Jeff Spivak for the indexes. I would also like to repeat the thanks expressed in the original preface to Professor Graham Stanton, the then editor of the SNTS monograph series in which this book first appeared.

This new edition is dedicated to Robert Morgan, in gratitude for his support and encouragement during the years when the first edition of this book was in the making. Primarily concerned with the theological interpretation of the New Testament texts, Robert Morgan has rightly and consistently emphasized that non-theological perspectives are not to be despised, but make their own distinctive contribution to the theological enterprise.

FRANCIS WATSON

Abbreviations

JAAR	*Journal of the American Academy of Religion*
JBL	*Journal of Biblical Literature*
JES	*Journal of Ecumenical Studies*
JR	*Journal of Religion*
JSJ	*Journal for the Study of Judaism*
JSNT	*Journal for the Study of the New Testament*
JSNTSup	Journal for the Study of the New Testament Supplement Series
JSOTSup	Journal for the Study of the Old Testament Supplement Series
JTS	*Journal of Theological Studies*
KEKNT	Kritisch-exegetischer Kommentar über das Neue Testament
LCL	Loeb Classical Library
LW	*Luther's Works*
MNTC	Moffatt New Testament Commentary
NCBC	New Century Bible Commentary
NICNT	The New International Commentary on the New Testament
NIGTC	New International Greek Testament Commentary
NLC	New London Commentary
NovT	*Novum Testamentum*
NovTSup	Novum Testamentum Supplement Series
NTD	Das Neue Testament Deutsch
NTS	*New Testament Studies*
PHF	F. Watson, *Paul and the Hermeneutics of Faith*
PJG[1]	F. Watson, *Paul, Judaism and the Gentiles: A Sociological Approach,* first edition
SBL Diss.	SBL Dissertation Series
SBM	Stuttgarter Biblische Monographien
SBS	Stuttgarter Bibelstudien
SBT	Studies in Biblical Theology
SBU	Symbolae Biblicae Upsalienses
SJT	*Scottish Journal of Theology*
SNTSMS	Studiorum Novi Testamenti Societas Monograph Series
SNTW	Studies in the New Testament and Its World
SP	Sacra Pagina
StEv	*Studia Evangelica*
StNT	Studien zum Neuen Testament
StTh	*Studia Theologica*
TB	*Theologische Blätter*
THKNT	Theologische Handkommentar zum Neuen Testament
TNTC	Tyndale New Testament Commentary
TSAJ	Texte und Studium zum antiken Judentum

TZ	*Theologische Zeitschrift*
WBC	Word Biblical Commentary
WMANT	Wissenschaftliche Monographien zum Alten und Neuen Testament
WUNT	Wissenschaftliche Untersuchungen zum Neuen Testament
ZBK	Züricher Bibelkommentare
ZNW	*Zeitschrift für die neutestamentliche Wissenschaft*
ZTK	*Zeitschrift für Theologie und Kirch*

Beyond the New Perspective:
Introduction to the Revised Edition of
Paul, Judaism, and the Gentiles

Published in 1986, this book was the first monograph-length response to the revolution in Pauline studies initiated by E. P. Sanders in his two magisterial works of 1977 and 1983.[1] Now, for the first time (or so it seemed), a historically credible portrayal of the Apostle to the Gentiles lay within reach. It became clear that Paul's polemical treatment of the law was no less the product of contingent historical circumstances than his discussion of food offered to idols. At the same time, a previously dominant portrayal of Paul lost credibility: the Paul of theological existentialism in its Bultmannian form, a Paul read in the light of Luther, Kierkegaard, and Heidegger, the Apostle of a divine Word that lays bare the fundamental determinants of the human condition. This sophisticated attempt to make Paul contemporary had profoundly influenced the biblical scholarship and systematic theology of the mid-twentieth century. In the work of Ernst Käsemann, it showed itself capable of adapting to the more politically oriented theological climate of the 1960s. There seemed no reason to suppose that it was on the verge of collapse.

In spite of Käsemann, it was politics as much as exegesis that proved its undoing. Integral to the Bultmannian paradigm was the assumption that human fallenness and alienation from God were definitively disclosed in the figure of the Pauline "Jew," with his "works-righteousness," his "legalism," his "boasting of his own achievements," his perversion of the law of God into a means to his own self-centered ends. During the 1970s, a new criterion of

---

1. *Paul and Palestinian Judaism* (1977) and *Paul, the Law and the Jewish People* (1983). Heikki Räisänen acknowledges that he was unable to take Sanders's *Paul, the Law and the Jewish People* fully into account in preparing his *Paul and the Law* (1983; see p. v).

1

theological discourse gradually established itself. One now began to ask whether a given theological claim was still ethically responsible "after Auschwitz." German New Testament scholars might protest that Auschwitz was irrelevant to exegesis, that the issue of "Paulus und die Juden" was a purely historical one, that theological scholarship should proceed calmly on its way as though genocide had not occurred, in living memory and at the heart of European civilization.[2] But such disclaimers were losing their persuasiveness. After Auschwitz, new language and new conceptualities would have to be found. True to the traditions of their discipline, New Testament scholars looked to history and to historically informed exegesis to undermine the old paradigm and to establish a new one in its place. E. P. Sanders's two remarkable books achieved just that. They were brilliantly executed, and they were timely. But they also left some open questions about the direction of future research.

1. Retrospective

The present book arose out of my Oxford doctoral thesis, submitted in June 1983 although not examined until January of the following year. It was written under the supervision of George Caird, with assistance from Robert Morgan, and examined by C. K. Barrett and Morna Hooker. The thesis shared the main title of the eventual book, but the subtitle was significantly different: "Universality and Exclusiveness in Paul's Understanding of the Law." In the spring of 1984, the thesis was accepted for publication in the Cambridge SNTS monograph series, after receiving a positive reader's report from J. D. G. Dunn, whose Manson Memorial lecture on "The New Perspective on Paul" had recently been published. Although I had not been aware of Dunn's lecture, my analysis of "universality and exclusiveness" was congenial to his own claim that a contrast between exclusive and inclusive understandings of the covenant lies at the heart of Paul's theology of justification. In both cases, there was a critique of "the Lutheran Paul," on grounds partly derived from Sanders. If my thesis had been published as intended, it would have been closely aligned with the "New Perspective" of Dunn and N. T. Wright. Yet the thesis was not published. Very little of it made its way into the monograph that superseded it. In order to explain why the published work took the form it did, I must say a little about its unpublished predecessor.

Unlike the final published work, the original thesis was a study in Pauline

2. See G. Klein, "Präliminarien zum Thema 'Paulus und die Juden,'" 230-33.

theology, with relatively little interest in the sociohistorical context of Paul's view of the law. It set out from the observation that "in virtually every passage where the Reformation tradition has found an attack on 'earning salvation', there is a reference to the exclusiveness of the Jewish theology of the covenant as contrasted with the universality of Paul's proclamation" ("Paul, Judaism and the Gentiles" [unpublished version], 22). A sharp distinction was to be drawn between the view of the law that Paul opposed and the view that he himself upheld. What he opposed was more or less Sanders's "covenantal nomism"; for, at every point where Paul attacked "works of law," he had in mind their distinctive covenantal context. His texts were full of references, explicit or implicit, to Jewish covenantal privileges — whose validity he now relativized (cf. Phil. 3:4-6; Rom. 2:1–3:2; 9:4-9; 2 Cor. 11:21-22). This covenantal context had been persistently overlooked or undervalued. "The Reformation tradition" (I wrote) "has misrepresented Paul by isolating his attack on 'works of the law' from its context within an attack on the Jewish theology of the covenant, generalizing the former so that it becomes a universal human error, and ignoring the latter" (30). So what was the basis of this "attack"? Not christology per se, as Sanders had argued, but rather a universalizing view of the law itself, peculiar to Paul and derived from his gospel. The law is a demand addressed to all people, observance of which is far beyond the capacity of the *sarx* shared by Jew and Gentile alike. Thus,

> the reason why Paul opposes the covenant theology of Judaism and Jewish Christianity, according to which salvation is the exclusive privilege of the Jew, is . . . that the Jew seeks by means of this theology to exempt himself from that solidarity in guilt before God which the law reveals to be the true position of all men, Jews and Gentiles alike. (32)

This distinction between the (covenantal) view of the law that Paul opposes and the (universal-condemnatory) one that he affirms was initially worked out by juxtaposing Philippians 3 with 2 Corinthians 3 (chapter 2, "The Structure of Paul's View of the Law"). It was further developed by way of "mirror readings" of Galatians and Romans 2–4, 9–10). In Galatians 3, for example, Paul asserts that "promise and law are not the exclusive property of the Jewish community, by which it is differentiated from 'Gentile sinners', but have a universal significance for all . . ." (77). Here as elsewhere, Paul's universalizing theology is directed against the "covenantal nomism" of his opponents. In Reformation-derived readings, in contrast, a construal of "works of law" as embodying a universal human error overlooks the particular focus of the Pauline polemic. But Paul was speaking about Judaism as he perceived it, *and about nothing else.* And his critique was derived not from christology as such but from a universalizing and negative view of the law derived from his christology. That explained those Pauline statements about the law that did *not* conform to the covenantal nomism model (cf. 2 Cor. 3:7-11; Rom. 3:9-20; 4:15; 5:20-21; 7:7-13; Gal. 3:13). Understood along these lines, Paul's doctrine of justification has a clear social dimension, in that it is directed against a construal of the law that serves only to *exclude* — as in the case of Cephas at Antioch. Yet this social dimension was left abstract and general, without much attention to concrete social practice.

This position was developed independently of Dunn, but has clear affinities with the "New Perspective on Paul" as he conceived it.[3] There are also significant differences. Dunn's tendency is to relativize negative statements about the law — for example, by appealing to contingent situational factors. For Dunn, Pauline "universalism" is a universalism of *the covenant,* now made comprehensive through the inclusion of Gentiles. This is not necessarily incompatible with a universalism resting on the negative significance of the law as well as the positive significance of the promise, but the emphasis falls rather differently. In addition, my argument was at this stage less exclusively focused on Sanders than was Dunn's. The "social" interpretation of justification was traced back to Baur, and its recent advocates included not only Sanders but also Markus Barth, Nils Dahl, W. D. Davies, George Howard, Ulrich Mauser, Paul Minear, Halvor Moxnes, Krister Stendahl, and N. T. Wright (22-29). This rather diverse group of scholars did not amount to "a 'school' of interpreters working with similar aims," and that made their common emphasis on the universality/exclusiveness polarity all the more striking (29). What was at stake in their work was "the social character of justification" (M. Barth), its "social function and implications" (Dahl). In contrast, Dunn's New Perspective lecture refers to none of these figures apart from Stendahl, preferring to focus on Sanders himself and on the attempt to improve on him.[4] And most of these figures no longer feature significantly in the introductory analysis of scholarly positions that opens *Paul, Judaism and the Gentiles* in its published form.

This earlier scholarship makes it possible to specify more precisely the in-

---

3. The affinities probably go back to a common indebtedness to the work of N. T. Wright, whose (unfortunately unpublished) Oxford doctoral thesis on "The Messiah and the People of God" Dunn had read and examined in 1980. In his "New Perspective" paper, Dunn acknowledges that the phrase "national righteousness" is derived from Wright (205n). The debt would seem to be more extensive than that, however — although it does not extend to christology, which is central for Wright but marginal to Dunn's new perspective.

4. Davies and Wright are referred to briefly in footnotes, however.

sight that lies at the heart of Dunn's New Perspective. Particularly illuminating in this regard is Markus Barth's unjustly neglected essay, "Jews and Gentiles: The Social Character of Justification" (1968), a revised version of a contribution to a *Festschrift* commemorating Karl Barth's eightieth birthday in 1966. In this essay, Markus Barth takes up his father's concept of *Mitmenschlichkeit* or "co-humanity" as a fundamental determinant of human existence and applies it to the Pauline doctrine of justification.[5] He notes that

> the exposition given to this doctrine from the days of Augustine to the times of the Reformation and of orthodox Protestantism has been notable indeed for great joy in the grace of God but not for special interest in the fellow human [*Mitmensch*]. . . . The actual process and procurement of justification seem to be limited to a work of God, of Jesus Christ, perhaps of the Spirit, which happens "for me," "to me," and has no use for the fellow human — except that he is treated as an *alter ego,* just another case of my own kind.[6]

Yet, Barth continues, the "social" dimension of justification is manifest in the Pauline texts. In the account of the "Antioch incident" (Gal. 2:11-21), for example, Paul's point is that Peter can only be justified along with others, i.e., Gentiles: "Every attempt at segregation . . . is branded by Paul as denial and rejection of justification through Jesus Christ" (250). The reference here to "segregation" does not mean that Barth is interested only in the general principle underlying the particularities of the Pauline text. Again following the lead of his father, and in contrast to Bultmann, he emphasizes that the Pauline Jew/Gentile issue is irreducible to any allegedly more fundamental theological anthropology. Thus, in language that recalls Stendahl, Barth insists that "Paul fights for the rights of Gentiles . . . to receive blessing through the Messiah of Israel and to believe in him without becoming Jews" (256). Yet it is not only Stendahl but also Karl Barth who is echoed in the sharp critique of the Lutheran, pseudo-Pauline demand that "every person must have a conscience crushed by the law, before he is ripe for the blessing of grace" (256).[7] In conclusion, Markus Barth states: "The two themes, justification by faith and the unity of Jew and Gentile in Christ, are for [Paul] not only inseparable

5. For Karl Barth's concept of co-humanity, see *CD* III/2, 203-85; also, my *Agape, Eros, Gender,* 237-41.
6. Markus Barth, "Jews and Gentiles," 242. Subsequent citations are given parenthetically in the text.
7. See *CD* IV/1, 358-97, a wide-ranging critique of the assumption that sin can be known independently of the gospel.

but in the last analysis identical" (258). It is also notable that "faith" is understood here as the faith of Christ (248). There is every reason to suppose that Karl Barth would have approved his son's attempt to liberate the Pauline doctrine of justification from the Lutheran straitjacket he had himself criticized so sharply.

In this "Barthian" reading, many of the exegetical possibilities later taken up by the New Perspective are already in evidence. Essentially, it is a matter of giving Romans 3:29-30 equal status with 3:27-28: the God who justifies is as such the God of Jews and Gentiles alike. At this point in Paul's argument, the presence of a "horizontal" or social dimension alongside the "vertical" or theological one is unambiguously clear — although it is still routinely missed by the New Perspective's critics. There is, however, a second essential precondition for the crystallizing of a "New Perspective," in addition to this recovery of the social dimension of justification. In *Paul and Palestinian Judaism*, E. P. Sanders updated G. F. Moore's 1921 critique of modern German Lutheran work on Judaism, extending this to the Strack-Billerbeck collection of rabbinic material and to the modern Pauline scholarship dependent on it. Moore's main targets had been F. Weber for his systematizing, Schürer for his apologetic motivations, and (more questionably) Bousset for relying on non-authoritative, non-rabbinic sources. Thus, in the case of Schürer, Moore argued that his chapter on "Life under the Law"

> was conceived, not as a chapter of the history of Judaism but as a topic of Christian apologetic; it was written to prove by the highest Jewish authority that the strictures on Judaism in the Gospels and the Pauline Epistles are fully justified. It is greatly to be regretted that Schürer's eminent merits in everything external should have led New Testament scholars generally to attach equal authority to his representation and judgment of the Jewish religion.[8]

This is essentially the critique that Sanders extended to Strack-Billerbeck. The crucial concept of "covenantal nomism" was set in polemical opposition to the familiar pejorative terminology — "legalism," "externalism," "formalism," "earning salvation," "works-righteousness," "acquiring merit," and so forth — whose overwhelmingly negative connotations eliminate from the outset all possibility of sympathetic understanding. It is easy to forget how freely and unquestioningly such terminology was used prior to Sanders, especially in the field of Pauline studies. After Sanders, the whole conceptual apparatus

---

8. Moore, "Christian Writers on Judaism," 240.

underlying this terminology would have to be dismantled. And that meant rethinking *all* the polemical Pauline antitheses: faith and works, grace and law, Spirit and letter, life and death, blessing and curse, promise and flesh.

Following the publication of *Paul and Palestinian Judaism*, Sanders was initially criticized for failing to make "covenantal nomism" fruitful for the interpretation of Paul himself. In a lengthy and generally appreciative review published in 1978, George Caird wrote:

> The chief disappointment of this fascinating book is that the expectations raised by the first part are not fulfilled by the second. What we are led to expect is the thesis that the Judaism Paul rejects is not the spurious Judaism of Weber and Bousset but the genuine Judaism expounded by Moore and Sanders. Instead we find only the lame conclusion: "This is what Paul finds wrong in Judaism: it is not Christianity" (p. 552). Yet . . . [i]f there is truth in the claim of the Shema that God is one (Rom. iii.30), then God must judge all by the same standard, and neither the ancestral possession of an air of moral superiority nor the possession of the Torah can make any difference. And is not this precisely the starting point of the argument of Romans? . . . [I]t may turn out that [the book's] greatest contribution lies in the conclusion which Sanders himself refrained from drawing.[9]

In other words, what Sanders fails to recognize is that Paul too is a witness to "covenantal nomism" — the authentic Judaism that is the target of his critique. Four years later, this criticism was echoed by J. D. G. Dunn. In his 1982 New Perspective lecture, Dunn wrote:

> The most surprising feature of Sanders' writing . . . is that he himself has failed to take the opportunity his own mould-breaking work offered. Instead of trying to explore how far Paul's theology could be explicated in relation to Judaism's "covenantal nomism," he remained more impressed by the *difference* between Paul's pattern of religious thought and that of first-century Judaism. He quickly — too quickly in my view — concluded that Paul's religion could be understood only as a basically different system from that of his fellow Jews.[10]

Unlike Caird, however, Dunn was also able to take account of Sanders's second book, *Paul, the Law, and the Jewish People* (1983), which (like myself) he had been able to read in typescript. Dunn concedes that

9. Caird, "Review of E. P. Sanders, *Paul and Palestinian Judaism*," 542-43.

10. Dunn, "New Perspective," 186. Subsequent citations are given parenthetically in the text.

[t]he picture of Judaism which emerges from this fuller study does correspond to Judaism as revealed in its own literature. Paul attacks covenantal nomism, the view that accepting and living by the law is a sign and condition of favoured status. (187)

Yet this does not satisfy Dunn. He agrees with Sanders that what Paul opposes is "covenantal nomism," but he also believes that Paul opposes this *on the basis of an expanded, inclusive, but still recognizably Jewish covenantal theology.* For Sanders the inclusivity/exclusivity schema is subordinate to Paul's "*a priori* christology." Paul criticizes Judaism because it is not Christianity, and *on that basis* contrasts inclusive and exclusive views of the scope of the divine election.[11] This emphasis on christology enables Sanders to stress that Pauline inclusivity is also in its own way exclusive: salvation is open to Jew and Gentile alike, but as such it is confined to those who are "in Christ." For Dunn, however, the inclusivity/exclusivity schema is primary rather than secondary, and it represents a debate about the scope of God's covenant with Israel. Christology plays a much less significant role than in Sanders. Thus, while acknowledging that Sanders has correctly identified the target of Paul's critique, Dunn rejects *in toto* his account of Paul's own theology. Sanders's account

is only a little better than the one rejected. . . The Lutheran Paul has been replaced by an idiosyncratic Paul who in arbitrary and irrational manner turns his face against the glory and greatness of Judaism's covenant theology and abandons Judaism simply because it is not Christianity. (187)

In this respect, Dunn argues, the 1983 book is hardly an improvement on its predecessor. In it, Sanders

still speaks of Paul breaking with the law, he still has Paul making an arbitrary jump from one system to another and posing an antithesis between faith in Christ and his Jewish heritage in such sharp, black-and-white terms that Paul's occasional defence of Jewish prerogative (as in Rom. 9.4-6) seems equally arbitrary and bewildering, his treatment of the law and of its place in God's purpose becomes inconsistent and illogical, and we are left with an abrupt discontinuity between the new movement centred in Jesus and the religion of Israel. (188)

For Dunn, Sanders's antithetical, black-and-white approach is fundamentally misguided. Right about Judaism, he is wrong about Paul.

---

11. See E. P. Sanders, *Paul, the Law and the Jewish People*, 47.

It is ironic, then, that Sanders and Dunn are both commonly seen as representatives of a single "New Perspective on Paul."[12] The reality is that a *repudiation* of Sanders's reading of Paul is integral to the New Perspective as Dunn conceived it. Sanders's "covenantal nomism" concept is an essential building block of this New Perspective, but he cannot represent a shared perspective *on Paul* when his own perspective on Paul has been so unceremoniously rejected.

My unpublished doctoral thesis occupied middle ground between Sanders and Dunn. Pauline universalism was predicated not directly on christology but on a universalizing account of the condemnatory role of the law, derived from christology and set in polemical opposition to the covenantal nomism of Paul's contemporaries. Had my thesis been published as intended, there would still have been issues to debate with Dunn. My "universal condemnatory" account of Paul's own view of the law (as opposed to the exclusionary covenantal nomism he criticizes) might or might not have proved compatible with Dunn's claim that Paul articulates an inclusive account of Jewish covenantal theology. Yet there would have been a broad consensus with Dunn (and with N. T. Wright) on the outlines of the New Perspective, based on the inclusivity/exclusivity schema and on "covenantal nomism." I and my SNTS monograph would have formed a common front with these more senior scholars.

That way of putting it indicates that I do *not* regard the actual SNTS monograph — the first edition of the present book — as representative of the New Perspective on Paul. While there is naturally still some common ground, it is essentially an *alternative* response to Sanders's challenge to rethink Paul, one that takes a far more positive view of his perspective on Paul himself. This book does not represent the New Perspective as Dunn conceived it.

My doctoral thesis was accepted for publication in the spring of 1984, but with several suggestions for strengthening the final two chapters. I did not undertake these revisions immediately, however, but chose to work instead on an article entitled "The Social Function of Mark's Secrecy Theme" (published in *JSNT* the following year). I did not return to "Paul, Judaism and the Gentiles" until the following winter. At some point in the interim — I do not recall when — it must have occurred to me that I could not proceed with the publication

---

12. While the differences between Sanders and Dunn are acknowledged, it is generally assumed that they represent a common front in spite of them: so S. Westerholm, *Perspectives Old and New on Paul*, 183; D. A. Carson, "Introduction," *Justification and Variegated Nomism*, 1:4-5; S. J. Gathercole, *Where Is Boasting?* 19.

of the thesis, and that an essentially new work would have to be written to replace it. Intellectually, the germ of the new work lay in the phrase "social function," the fruitfulness of which I had already discovered in working on Mark. Mark's messianic secret, I had argued, was not just a theological idea; rather, it articulated the Markan community's sectarian self-understanding as the privileged, elect recipient of knowledge of Jesus as the Christ that was withheld from the wider community. I had read and been impressed by John H. Elliott's sociological exegesis of 1 Peter, *A Home for the Homeless,* by Wayne Meeks's article "The Man from Heaven in Johannine Sectarianism," and by other recent work that sought to apply sociological perspectives to the New Testament texts. But the sociological impetus did not originate here but in Peter Berger and Thomas Luckmann's 1967 essay in the sociology of knowledge, *The Social Construction of Reality.* This sustained reflection on the production and role of knowledge within the life-world made as profound an impression on me as any book before or since.[13] From Berger and Luckmann I learned the concept of a "secondary socialization," supervenient on the primary process and exemplified in the "legitimations" and the "plausibility structures" erected by those whose view of reality deviates from that of the majority community. Previously, I had known texts and ideas; now those texts and ideas all had to be rethought in the light of their social dynamics. One had to ask not just the theoretical question, What does the text say? but also the pragmatic question, What does the text do? What, in other words, is its origin and destiny within the world of social, intercommunal reality? How does it shape that world, and how is it shaped by it?[14]

All this seemed directly relevant to Paul — so relevant and illuminating that "Paul, Judaism and the Gentiles" would have to be totally rewritten. In the original thesis, it now seemed to me, ideas such as "universality" or "exclusiveness" hovered in the air, semi-detached from any recognizable social reality. They needed to be brought down to earth. And when they were, their meaning and significance were altered. The term "universality" had represented the fact that, for Paul, God treats Jews and Gentiles alike, both as those condemned by the law and as recipients of the divine grace. But now the

13. Unless the *Church Dogmatics* be regarded as a single book.

14. Compare the acknowledgment of indebtedness to Berger and Luckmann in Philip Esler's *Community and Gospel in Luke-Acts,* 16-23. There are a number of affinities between Esler's extensive theoretical framework and the more modest one employed in this book. While in the process of writing it I had the opportunity to read Esler's work in typescript, and I was pleased and reassured to note the convergences with my own thinking. I believe that my version of the reform-movement/sect typology had already been developed independently, but Esler's account clearly predates mine.

question was, What do these theoretical ideas mean in practice? What is their social correlate? And the answer was that apparently universalistic language needed to be treated with a degree of caution. Paul certainly envisages a church composed of both Jews and Gentiles, but he has removed one barrier only to replace it with another. If the old boundary marker was circumcision, the new one was "faith," understood not as an inward movement of the heart but as a new orientation within the social world, characterized by baptism and ongoing participation in the life and ethos of the Christian community. Was that really "universality," or was it "exclusiveness" in a new guise? As I now wrote:

> The term "exclusiveness" is in some ways more applicable to the sectarian groups created by Paul himself than it is to the Jewish community. If in one sense it is true that Paul sought to break down the barrier between Jew and Gentile, he nevertheless did so only to re-establish exclusiveness in a new form. (*Paul, Judaism and the Gentiles* [published version], 21)

This new exclusiveness was now seen to be directed not just against the wider Gentile society but also and especially against the Jewish community, represented in the Diaspora by the institution of "the synagogue." Whatever else the great Pauline antitheses were about, they were most fundamentally about the "sectarian" separation of the Christian community from the synagogue. Terms such as "law" and "works" stood not for abstract theological principles but for a concrete form of social praxis associated with a specific minority community. The same could be said of "faith" or "grace." The claim that the Pauline antitheses are to be interpreted in the light of their social correlate lay at the heart of the contribution the new work sought to make.

Since it is Paul's talk of Christ that most fundamentally legitimates the new, sectarian social reality, Sanders's emphasis on the sheer givenness and intransigence of Paul's distinction of "Christianity" from "Judaism" seemed to be confirmed — but with a stronger emphasis on the social correlate of this distinction. Sanders had argued that the Pauline antitheses are utterly *concrete*, that the opposition between "Christ" and "Judaism" does not derive from some prior rationale such as a pessimistic anthropology or a concern about Gentile inclusion, but articulates a pure "positivism of revelation."[15] For Sanders's Paul, it just is the case that God has acted definitively for human salvation in Christ, and that salvation therefore cannot be found in Judaism. It is not that there is anything wrong with Judaism per se; it is simply that it

---

15. This phrase was famously applied by Bonhoeffer to the theology of Barth. The congruity between Barth and Sanders at this point is perceptively noted by J. L. Martyn, *Galatians*, 95n.

promotes a way of salvation other than the way of Christ. "If righteousness is through the law, then Christ died in vain" (Gal. 2:21); conversely, because Christ cannot have died in vain, righteousness cannot be through the law. In basic agreement with Sanders, my book sought to investigate the social dimension of Pauline antithesis and to offer an account of its historical origins. My position was, I think, unusual in being at least as indebted to Sanders's second Paul book as to his first. In consequence, the Paul of this book lives and thinks antithetically. He is a tactless figure. The current overemphasis on the one comparatively irenic passage (Romans 11) is notably absent here.

These decisions about the fundamental orientation of the book aligned it more closely with Sanders's *Paul, the Law and the Jewish People* than with Dunn's "New Perspective on Paul." (It is also less dependent than Dunn on "covenantal nomism" as developed in *Paul and Palestinian Judaism;* more on that below.) As a result, there are a number of points where characteristic "New Perspective" emphases are missing from my work or emerge in a quite different form.

2. Divergences

When the first edition of the present book was written in the early months of 1985, there was no "New Perspective on Paul." There was an article of that name by J. D. G. Dunn, there were two major books by E. P. Sanders, there were significant individual contributions from Heikki Räisänen and others. But these had not yet coalesced into a singular "New Perspective." It was only in retrospect, following his major commentaries and other publications, that Dunn's article became the definitive early statement of the trend in Pauline scholarship for which it also provided a label. In the mid-1980s, critique of the still prevalent "Lutheran" exegesis seemed to be the main priority. There was internal debate among those who shared this priority, but that took second place. Twenty years later, the situation has changed. What is now needed is to highlight the differences that were always present, but that can now offer viable alternatives to a number of entrenched and problematic positions. The points discussed below were all made repeatedly in my book, but it is their character as *alternatives* that must now be emphasized.

(1) In the present book, *the concept of "covenantal nomism" is used to highlight the irreducible particularity of Pauline polemic.* It is chiefly invoked in connection with Paul's own representation of Judaism, Christian or otherwise; little is said about its wider application to Second Temple Judaism. In the case of Philippians 3, for example, I argue that "what Paul renounces . . . is

his whole covenant-status as a Jew, which includes reliance on the divine gifts bestowed on Israel as well as the confirmation of those gifts by his own obedience" (*PJG¹*, 78). This reading is contrasted with the suggestion of another exegete that Philippians 3 refers to "the innate tendency on the part of the religious man to obtain a standing before God and to secure, by his own effort, approval and acceptance with Him" (*PJG¹*, 204n).[16] In my argument, covenantal nomism is deployed to prevent this reduction of Paul's Pharisaic self-understanding to allegedly innate tendencies of a generic "religious man." There is no concern to emphasize divinely bestowed privileges *at the expense of* active observance of the law — the concern underlying Dunn's warning against "making a difference in kind between the first and second halves of the catalogue in [Phil.] 3.5-6."[17] Also absent is the naïve essentialism of the typical post-Sanders claim that "Judaism is a religion of grace." While it is emphasized that "works of law" are to be understood non-generically, their soteriological significance is not denied. Pauline evidence for covenantal nomism is used to assert concretion and irreducibility rather than a particular soteriological theory.

In this account, the terms "covenantal" and "nomism" have equal weight. Paul attests a *covenantal* nomism: where he refers to "works of law," the specific context of these prescribed actions is always that of the election of Israel. Yet that which is attested is a covenantal *nomism*: for the giving and practice of the law are integral to Israel's elect identity. The demands imposed on the people of Israel at Mount Sinai are the *fulfillment* of the narrative of election that begins with the patriarchs and continues with the exodus, and not merely a secondary addendum. Thus, in Romans 9, it is "Israel" that pursues the righteousness attested in the law, mistakenly though understandably assuming that this righteous status before God is to be attained by translating the law's prescriptions into corresponding practices or "works" (vv. 31-32). "Israel" connotes the elect status of "Israelites" to whom belong "the sonship and the glory and the covenants and the legislation and the worship and the promises" (v. 4). Paul is interested in no other "works" than Israel's. But he also assumes that "works" are the natural expression of Israel's elect status, that in them individuals have appropriated their election for themselves. "Israel" is entailed in "works"; "works" are entailed in "Israel." If "works" have been emphasized at the expense of "Israel," that does not make it appropriate to emphasize "Israel" at the expense of "works," as though one could speak of "covenant status" without reference to covenant praxis.

16. Citing R. P. Martin, *Philippians*, 139-40.
17. Dunn, *Theology of Paul the Apostle*, 370.

The concept of covenantal nomism seemed valuable to me because it brought to light this interrelatedness of election and law-observance within the Judaism presupposed in Paul's texts. As a result, it retained its particularity and was in no sense a mere example of some more fundamental and universal misconstrual of the divine-human relationship. Crucially, however, this low-level application of Sanders's concept did not require me to take over the more elaborate soteriological theory that he himself associated with it. Sanders's initial definition of his concept runs as follows:

> [C]ovenantal nomism is the view that one's place in God's plan is established on the basis of the covenant and that the covenant requires as the proper response of man his obedience to the commandments, while providing the means of atonement for transgression.[18]

That seemed to fit the Pauline evidence. But the same could not be said of Sanders's attempts to demarcate the respective roles of election and law-observance in the attainment of final salvation. On this Sanders writes:

> God has chosen Israel and Israel has accepted the election. In his role as King, God gave Israel commandments which they are to obey as best they can. Obedience is rewarded and disobedience punished. In case of failure to obey, however, man has recourse to divinely ordained means of atonement, in all of which repentance is required. As long as he maintains his desire to stay in the covenant, he has a share in God's covenantal promises, including life in the world to come. The intention and effort to be obedient constitute the *condition for remaining in the covenant,* but they do not *earn* it.[19]

Although I cited this passage (*PJG¹*, 16), I did not attempt to apply its analysis of early rabbinic theology to Paul. I did not argue that, in the Judaism Paul opposes, final salvation is based on membership of the covenant, or that law-observance serves merely to maintain that communal allegiance as a kind of "default position" and has no direct part to play in attaining to final salvation.[20] This attempt to coordinate divine and human agency, in such a way as to maximize the role of divine grace, was superfluous to my requirements. I needed "covenantal nomism" only in order to underline the relationship of law-observance and election, and thus to assert the irreducible particularity

---

18. Sanders, *Paul and Palestinian Judaism,* 75.

19. Sanders, *Paul and Palestinian Judaism,* 180; italics original.

20. For the function of law-observance as "default position" in Sanders's account of Judaism, see S. J. Gathercole, *What Is Boasting?* 24.

of the Pauline critique. Covenantal nomism did not need to be a clearly artic-ulated soteriological theory to which the Pauline evidence had to conform.

This makes a considerable difference in exegetical practice. According to Paul, those who pursue "the righteousness which is by the law" do so in ac-cordance with the scriptural principle that "the one who does these things will live by them" (Rom. 10:5; Gal. 3:12). This appears to conflict with the claim that, for Second Temple Judaism, salvation is fundamentally deter-mined by a covenant status prior to the practice of the law. If Sanders is right on this point, the *prima facie* reading of this text must be wrong, and we must reinterpret it accordingly. Dunn's attempt to bring this awkward text back into line runs as follows:

> Moses did *not* say, and Paul does not understand him to say, that keeping the law was a means of earning or gaining life. . . . Rather the law prescribes the life which is to be lived by the covenant people.[21]

But it is difficult to see how a scriptural statement about the person who ob-serves the law can be transformed into a statement about the law itself — i.e., that it "prescribes the life which is to be lived by the covenant people." It is covenantal nomism *understood as a soteriological theory* that has produced this unlikely interpretation. In contrast, my own concern with Paul's Leviti-cus citation was simply to emphasize that it referred specifically to Jewish practice of the law of Moses: Paul "does not mean that faith is opposed to 'do-ing' in general, i.e. to human moral endeavour as a whole" (*PJG¹*, 67). It was the irreducible particularity of Paul's critique that needed to be emphasized. The fact that eschatological life is promised to the one who observes the com-mandments was not a cause of concern.[22]

(2) In this book, it is acknowledged that *divine agency plays a more direct and immediate role in the Pauline "pattern of religion" than in the Judaism Paul opposes*. There is no suggestion that the two systems hold similar views about the relation of divine grace to human response. The difference between the two arises from the fact that

> membership of the Jewish community is dependent on birth, whereas membership of a Pauline community is dependent on conversion. Any re-ligious group which proclaims the necessity of conversion is likely to em-phasize the distinction between the old life and the new. The old life is characterized by sin, ignorance and death, and against this dark back-

---

21. Dunn, *Romans*, 2:612.
22. For further discussion, see my *Paul and the Hermeneutics of Faith*, 315-36.

ground the nature of the new life as a miraculous divine gift will shine out all the more brightly. Rom. 5:1–6:23 is perhaps the clearest Pauline exposition of this viewpoint, which might also be illustrated from the Qumran *Hodayoth* and the literature of other conversionist groups, both ancient and modern. Such groups take a *dynamic* view of God's grace, and this contrasts with the more *static* view of grace taken by groups in which membership is determined by birth. (*PJG¹*, 66; italics original)

Yet these contrasting views of divine agency should not be allowed to harden into an opposition between soteriological theories, one ascribing salvation to divine agency alone, the other to human agency alone. Pauline "grace" transforms the human agent, making it possible and necessary to "cast off the works of darkness and put on the armour of light" (Rom. 13:12). In that sense, "the idea that salvation occurs solely through God's grace represents a deep misunderstanding of Paul" (*PJG¹*, 120) — if "solely" is taken to exclude even a human agency elicited and enabled by divine grace.[23] Jewish "works" presuppose the gift of the covenant and look to the resurrection of the dead, the eschatological divine act in which all things are made new. Far from presupposing sinlessness, they include actions prescribed in the Torah as a means to the forgiveness of sins. The two "patterns of religion" are different, but we should not conclude from Paul's juxtaposition of "grace" and "law" that they are equal and opposite. In a certain sense, they are incommensurable. We are not to imagine them as opposite ends of a spectrum, such that we might in principle start from one end and eventually arrive at the other. Pauline antithesis represents a chasm, not the opposite ends of a continuum.

If Pauline Christianity and Judaism are not essential opposites, neither are they essentially the same. This emphasis on the dynamic Pauline view of grace is incompatible with the New Perspective's claim that the two "patterns of religion" exemplify a single soteriological schema, according to which we are saved by grace but must confirm our membership in the cove-

23. What John Webster says of Barth can also be applied to Paul: "Barth seeks to underscore a conviction that the human person under grace remains an agent. This involves him in sharp divergence from Luther's anthropology, where the primary passivity of the human recipient of grace dominates" (*Barth's Ethics of Reconciliation*, 110). It is often wrongly assumed that Barth's intense focus on divine agency makes "serious consideration of human action superfluous, even, perhaps, a trespass on the sovereignty of grace" (1). Yet Barth's aim is in fact "a depiction of the world of human action as it is enclosed and governed by the creative, redemptive, and sanctifying work of God in Christ"; thus, moral life is "genuine action in analogy to prior divine action" (2). The crucial point here is that divine and human agency are not engaged in a competition in which to attribute more to the one is to attribute less to the other.

nant by obedience.[24] If there is any truth in this equation, it is at too high a level of abstraction to be interesting. When Paul looks to the Jewish community of the present, what he sees is a zealous (though misguided) practice of the law that understands itself as, first, the visible outworking of Israel's election; second, the precondition for a righteous standing before God in the present life; and third, the way that leads to the eschatological life of the age to come (cf. Rom. 9:30–10:5). A certain type of human agency stands in the foreground here. It occupies a present that spans the past of the divine electing action and an eschatological future in which election and its human outworking will reach their intended goal. On the other hand, when Paul looks to the Christian community, what he sees is the transformative power of the Spirit, the life of the risen Jesus as a present reality. He also sees certain practices that fail to reflect the presence of the Spirit, and the threat of eschatological judgment is one among his range of resources for addressing this problem. But it is still the dynamism of present divine agency that stands in the foreground here. (That is the fundamental difference between Paul and, say, the *Didache*.) To repeat: Paul's representations of divine and human agency within the two communities only look similar at an unhelpfully high level of abstraction. From a more natural perspective, one closer to Paul's own, they look very different.[25]

It is unfortunate that, in reaction against modern Lutheran readings of Paul, it is now widely assumed that all strands of Second Temple Judaism and early Christianity held broadly the same view of the relationship between "di-

24. "[B]oth Judaism and Paul saw clearly that the inter-relationship between divine grace and human response had to be maintained and expressed in daily living. Both recognized in their own ways that without the divine initiative there could be no hope of salvation, even of starting on the process. But both also believed that those in good standing with God had to meet the obligations of a law given them by their founder (Gal. 6.2). Both evidently believed that without human response ('works') there could be no grounds for judgment ('according to works') of those at present in process of being saved" (J. D. G. Dunn, *The New Perspective on Paul*, 71).

25. Compare J. L. Martyn's important critique of Dunn's reading of Galatians, which he aptly summarizes as follows: "[W]hen Paul was confronted in Galatia with a modified form of covenantal nomism combining allegiance to Christ with observance of the national and ritualistic aspects of the Law, he formulated and argued for a still more modified form of the same: faith in Christ accompanied by observance of the Law relieved of its restrictive national and ritualistic aspects" ("Events in Galatia," 163). On that account, Paul and his opponents are agreed about almost everything. Yet "attentive members" of Paul's Galatian audience "will have noted . . . that *instead* of speaking about the Law (the Teachers' major theme), Paul gives concentrated attention to Christ, to the gospel of Christ, and to the apocalypse of Christ in which God caused that gospel to happen to him, calling him to preach Christ among the Gentiles" (164; italics original).

vine grace" and "human response." Where recent scholarship finds only sameness, however, Jews of this period believed they could detect difference. Thus Josephus can differentiate the three Jewish sects by referring to their divergent views on divine and human agency. The fact that he uses inappropriate Stoic terminology to do so does not mean that the differences were unreal. Josephus writes:

> At this time there were three schools among the Jews [αἱρέσεις τῶν Ἰουδαίων], which held different views on human affairs — one being that of the Pharisees, one that of the Sadducees, and the third that of the Essenes. The Pharisees claim that some events are the work of Fate [εἱμαρμένη] but not all; in the case of other events, it is our responsibility [ἐφ᾽ ἑαυτοῖς ὑπάρχειν] whether they happen or not. The race [γένος] of the Essenes states that Fate rules over all, and that nothing befalls people except by its decree. But the Sadducees reject Fate, holding that it does not exist and that human affairs are in no way determined by it; rather, all things lie in our power [ἅπαντα δὲ ἐφ᾽ ἡμῖν αὐτοῖς κεῖσθαι], so that we ourselves are responsible for the good things that occur, and bring about the bad things by our own thoughtlessness. (*Ant.* 13.172-73)

If Josephus means "God" when he refers to Fate, his Essenes and his Sadducees constitute an almost Pauline antithesis as they ascribe significant occurrence in the world respectively to divine or to human agency. Whatever the merit of this typology, the mere fact that Josephus can use it indicates that Paul, too — on the basis of a quite different ideology and idiom — might have been capable of contrasting a gospel in which all things are ascribed to God with a practice in which all things are held to lie within our own power. With a little license, one might even take Paul's statement in 2 Corinthians 3:5 as a refutation of the claim that "all things lie in our power":

> Not that we are sufficient of ourselves [ἀφ᾽ ἑαυτῶν], to reckon anything as from ourselves [λογίσασθαί τι ὡς ἐξ ἑαυτῶν]. Rather, our sufficiency is from God.

A contrast between reliance on divine or on human agency is within Paul's repertoire, as it is within Josephus's. In Paul's case, this contrast typically takes the form of a secondary abstraction derived from the primary reality of incommensurable communal orientations towards the Law of Moses on the one hand and the gospel of Jesus Christ on the other. When, for example, "grace" and "works" are contrasted (cf. Rom. 4:1-5; 11:5-6), this antithesis derives from the association of "grace" with God's definitive saving action in

Jesus Christ (cf. Rom. 5:15-21) and of "works" with "works of law," the practice of Judaism (cf. Rom. 3:20, 28). Yet the lack of explicit reference to Christ or the Mosaic law serves to highlight the prioritizing of divine or of human agency, which, at a certain level of abstraction, is implicit within the primary opposition of Christ and law. If this opposition is *concrete*, in that it refers to the specific foundations of two different modes of communal life, it is also *asymmetrical*, in that it acknowledges contrasting construals of the relation of divine to human agency.[26]

Having established, in opposition to the prevailing New Perspective consensus, that Paul *does* on occasion thematize this difference, we should also note in passing that he normally presents his antitheses as grounded in scripture. Conversely, it is when he is engaged in scriptural argumentation that Paul thinks antithetically. Scripture is, as it were, the common ground on which he conducts his campaign against what he calls "Judaism," whether in its Christian or its non-Christian form. The opposition between the two modes of communal life is grounded in an inner-scriptural opposition between the Abrahamic promise and the law given at Sinai (cf. Gal. 3; Rom. 4). In the one case, scripture articulates the absolute, unconditional divine commitment to future saving action on behalf of Abraham and his seed, evoking faith in the addressee. In the other case, scripture prescribes a particular pattern of conduct as a precondition for future divine saving action. Pauline antithesis arises from an essentially and explicitly "sectarian" rereading of scripture.[27]

(3) It is argued in this book that *the phrase "works of law" refers to the distinctive way of life of the Jewish community, but without any necessary orientation towards "boundary markers" such as circumcision, food laws, or sabbath.* In this account, "works of law" retains its particularity, but without detriment to its comprehensiveness. As a result, there is no need to import a reference to "boundary markers" every time Paul uses the term "works." When, for example, Paul states that "by works of law shall no flesh be justified" (Rom. 3:20), he means that the practice of the law of Moses within the Jewish community is not the divinely ordained life-orientation that constitutes human "righteousness" before God.

In contrast, Dunn insists that there is

---

26. This combination of "concretion" and "asymmetry" in Pauline antithesis is acknowledged by J. Louis Martyn throughout his Galatians commentary, where it represents a creative synthesis of insights derived from Sanders and Käsemann respectively.

27. While this position is much more fully worked out in *PHF* than it is here, *PJG¹* already acknowledged that the reinterpretation of scripture is fundamental to Pauline theological discourse.

a hidden middle term in 3.20 between "works of the law" and "shall be justified" — a middle term which Reformation exegesis largely missed. . . .
The connection of thought in 3.20 does not run directly from "works of the
law" to "shall be justified" and is not aimed directly at works of the law *as a
means to achieving* righteousness and acquittal. The connection of thought
is more indirect, of works of the law *as a way of identifying the individual
with* the people whom God has chosen and will vindicate and of *maintaining his status within* that people. In a word, the hidden middle term is the
function of the law as an identity factor, the social function of the law as
marking out the people of the law in their distinctiveness (circumcision,
food laws, etc.). It is "hidden" at 3.20 simply because it could be taken for
granted in the Roman world of this period when talking about the Jews
with their religious and national peculiarities.[28]

That is an exegesis not of Romans 3:20 as it stands but of this text as it would
have been had Paul read and been persuaded by *Paul and Palestinian Judaism.*
The result is tortuous in the extreme. The text reads: "By works of law shall no
flesh be justified." It thereby appears to deny the proposition that people become righteous, or attain righteousness, by the practice of works of law. But
for Dunn the text *cannot* understand works of law "as a means to achieving
righteousness." It must not be allowed to mean that. Instead, "by works of law
shall no flesh be justified" must mean something like: by actions that identify
one with the people of God shall no one maintain his or her status within the
covenant on the basis of which God will finally vindicate his chosen people.
Rather than elucidating Paul's laconic statement, the "hidden middle term"
has overwhelmed it.

The problem is compounded when the concept of "boundary markers" is
introduced to identify those specific practices that demarcate the people of the
covenant from the rest of humanity. It is immaterial whether the phrase "works
of law" refers *solely* to the boundary markers (Dunn's original position), or
whether it refers to law-observance as a whole but *with special reference* to the
boundary markers (his revised view).[29] One way or another, these boundary
markers are essential to his argument in that they provide a rationale for the
Pauline negation other than Sanders's christological one. For Sanders, "works
of the law" refers simply and solely to actions prescribed in the law of Moses,
practiced on the assumption that they are mandated by God. For Dunn, what is
significant is not practices in themselves but the attitude that comes to expres-

---

28. Dunn, *Romans,* 1:159; italics original.
29. Dunn has now acknowledged this distinction between his original and revised formulations. See his *New Perspective on Paul,* 22-23, referring to my *PHF,* 334-35n.

sion in them: the mind-set that wishes to limit the scope of the divine concern to those *within* the boundary marked out by "circumcision, food laws, etc."[30]

The present book follows Sanders in holding it to be wrong to look for a "mind-set" where Paul speaks of practices. The phrase "works of law" refers comprehensively to the way of life prescribed for the Jewish people in the law of Moses. If so, then "observances such as circumcision, the food-laws, the Sabbath and the feast-days . . . do not exhaust the meaning of the term" (*PJG¹*, 198n). Indeed, there is no need to suppose that Paul had these "boundary markers" in mind unless the context explicitly indicates this.

(4) It is argued here that Paul *advocates a "sectarian" separation between the Christian community and "Judaism," rather than an inclusive understanding of the one people of God as encompassing even uncircumcised Gentiles.* This emphasis on separation contrasts starkly with the New Perspective's tendency to play down antithesis and controversy in quest of a more irenical account of Paul's relation to his Jewish contemporaries. But did Paul really seek to *promote* a "separation from Judaism," as argued here? Was that separation not the result of a tragic misunderstanding of his views?

I have emphasized elsewhere that Paul was a Jew, engaged in ongoing argument with his contemporaries about the true sense and significance of the scriptural texts.[31] While the communities he founded consisted largely of non-Jews, whose right to remain such he tenaciously defended, they continued to bear a more than passing resemblance to Jewish communities — in their ethical code, their attitude towards non-Jewish religion, and their concern with Jewish scripture. In the present book, however, the talk is of "separation from Judaism." Here, I argue that "[t]he social reality which underlies Paul's discussions of Judaism and the law is his creation of Gentile Christian communities in sharp separation from the Jewish community" (*PJG¹*, 19). This separation of the sectarian group from the parent religious community is accompanied by an "ideology" that legitimates its separate existence, explaining to the group's members why it is that separation is unavoidably necessary, and doing so in part on scriptural terrain shared with the group's opponents. This separation is not a mere parting of the ways within a pluralistic environment, resulting perhaps in mutual indifference. On the contrary, this is separation in the form

30. This focus on exclusivity as an underlying attitude enables Dunn to extend Paul's critique of works to cover a whole host of modern evils (denominationalism, apartheid, genocide, and so on) that "would cause Paul the same anguish and grief as he experienced in Antioch" (*New Perspective on Paul*, 31). Pauline particularity is here dissolved into generalization in a way oddly reminiscent of the Lutheran tradition. Also characteristically Lutheran is the use of Judaism as a negative symbol.

31. See my *Paul and the Hermeneutics of Faith.*

of an ongoing argument about scriptural interpretation, an attempt to show that the true sense of scripture — the one that attests the truth of the gospel — belongs to "us" rather than to "them." It is the nature of an argument that it both divides and unites. Underlying the division is the shared concern; yet precisely this shared concern is the precondition for polemical antithesis. To speak along these lines of separation or alienation from a parent religious community is fully compatible with Paul's (characteristically Jewish) scriptural argumentation. The term "separation" simply represents the distance that makes it possible and necessary for the argument to occur.

This is a separation from Judaism *in the sense in which Paul himself speaks of "Judaism."* The word itself occurs twice in a single Pauline passage, but nowhere else in Paul's writings or in the rest of the New Testament.[32] Early Christian writers can refer to the distinctive religion of the Jewish people without necessarily availing themselves of the term Ἰουδαϊσμός. Current sensitivity about the interpretation of Ἰουδαῖος (Jew, or Judean?) should also be extended to Ἰουδαϊσμός, which is *not* an unproblematically established designation of a "major world religion."[33] For Paul himself, "Judaism" appears to be virtually synonymous with "Pharisaism." It is an ideologically loaded term, not a neutral one:

> You have heard of my earlier life in Judaism [ἐν τῷ Ἰουδαϊσμῷ], that I violently persecuted the church of God and sought its destruction; and I advanced in the practice of Judaism [ἐν τῷ Ἰουδαϊσμῷ] beyond many contemporaries among my own nation, so exceptionally zealous was I for the traditions of my forebears [τῶν πατρικῶν μου παραδόσεων]. (Gal. 1:13-14)

In this usage, the word "Judaism" is bound up with the fierce loyalty to ancestral traditions that led Paul to persecute the church. As a parallel passage from Philippians indicates, this is the Judaism *of the Pharisees.* Paul describes himself as

> circumcised on the eighth day, of the nation of Israel and the tribe of Benjamin, a Hebrew born of Hebrews, as regards the law a Pharisee, as regards zeal a persecutor of the church. (Phil. 3:5-6)

32. Only with Ignatius does this term attain greater prominence in Christian usage, and then only in an antithesis between Ἰουδαϊσμός and Χριστιανισμός (*Magn.* 10.3, cf. 8.1; *Philad.* 6.1).

33. In my view, Ἰουδαῖος is more strongly correlated with Ἰουδαϊσμός than with Ἰουδαία, so that "Jew" rather than "Judean" is normally a better translation, although neither term is fully adequate. I do not agree with Philip Esler that "to translate Ἰουδαῖοι as 'Jews' removes from the designation of this ethnic group the reference to Judea, to its temple and the cult practised there" (*Conflict and Identity in Romans,* 66).

Taken together, the passages from Galatians and Philippians show that, even as a Christian, Paul continued to hold that "Judaism" is synonymous with Pharisaic orthodoxy. To make progress in Judaism, to outstrip one's contemporaries in zeal for the ancestral traditions, is to live the life of the model Pharisee.[34] Here, the Paul of the Epistles agrees with the Paul of Acts. It is generally known, Paul tells King Agrippa, "that in accordance with the strictest party [τὴν ἀκριβεστάτην αἵρεσιν] of our religion I have lived as a Pharisee" (Acts 26:5). For Luke, Pharisaism is "normative Judaism," Judaism in its strictest and purest form. Similarly for Josephus, to belong to "the party [αἵρεσις] of the Pharisees" is be in the company of "those regarded as surpassing all others in their exact knowledge [ἀκρίβεια] of the ancestral laws" (*Vita*, 191).[35]

This assumption of Pharisaic normativity underlies Paul's laconic self-description as κατὰ νόμον φαρισαῖος (Phil. 3:5). He also implies that this normativity is generally recognized among the Jewish people. Thus, in Romans 9:30–10:5 he can extend his earlier references to his own zeal for the law to "Israel" as a whole. It is not only Paul the Pharisee but Israel as such that is represented as "pursuing the law of righteousness" and as displaying a "zeal for God" (9:31; 10:2). We may conclude from this that Paul sees Pharisaic orthodoxy as holding a position of dominance throughout the entire national life. The scriptural text that articulates "Israel's" understanding of the law is therefore read in its Pharisaic sense as referring to the eternal life of the resurrection: "The one who does these things will live by them" (Lev. 18:5, cited in Rom. 10:5; Gal. 3:11). Paul no doubt knew of Sadducees and Essenes, but if so he does not see fit to mention them. "Judaism" for him is a singular, monolithic entity. Unlike Josephus (his fellow Pharisee), he never suggests that he had faced a choice about which version of Judaism to pursue (cf. *Vita*, 10-12). For Paul, there is only one Judaism. It led him to persecute the church, and he has renounced it. His own act of renunciation is to be exemplary for his Gentile converts if and when they find themselves confronted with a version of

---

34. Paul's self-descriptions presuppose a training in Jerusalem, according to Martin Hengel, *The Pre-Christian Paul*, 18-42.

35. Were Josephus, Luke, and Paul right in seeing Pharisaism as the "normative Judaism" of the later Second Temple period? E. Schürer believed that they were, holding that Pharisaism was "the legitimate and typical representative of post-exilic Judaism," and that from the first century BCE onwards "the Pharisees largely dominated Jewish public life" (*The History of the Jewish People*, 2:400, 402). More recently this view has come under attack; for an account of the debate, see R. Deines, "The Pharisees between 'Judaisms' and 'Common Judaism.'" For present purposes, all that matters is that Paul (and Josephus and Luke) could *claim* Pharisaic normativity. The truth or otherwise of this claim is a matter of perspective, then as now, and is hardly susceptible to a definite, "objective" judgment.

the Christian gospel that encourages them to "judaize" and to accept what he can only regard as the monstrosity of a Christian Ἰουδαϊσμός. That had actually happened in Galatia, and Paul fears that it may yet happen in Philippi. So violently does he repudiate this account of the gospel that he goes so far as to identify circumcision with self-castration or self-mutilation (cf. Gal. 5:12; Phil. 3:2-3). According to the evidence of Galatians, Philippians, and Romans, Pauline separation from "Judaism" is separation from Pharisaism, understood as representing a "national orthodoxy."

With its emphasis on sect-like "separation," this book parts company with the apologetic concerns characteristic of the New Perspective.[36] It does not argue that Paul remained a loyal and orthodox Jew but was misunderstood by generations of Gentile readers. It does not claim that he taught a *Sonderweg* for the Jewish people, a fast track to salvation that bypasses Jesus, a savior for Gentiles only.[37] It does not suggest that Paul's more negative utterances about the law refer purely to its effects upon Gentiles and in no way undermine its normative status among Jews.[38] It does not assume that he was motivated by a concern for social inclusion remarkably similar to our own.[39] And it does not imply that what he says in polemical contexts should be more or less discounted.[40] If, as Daniel Boyarin has persuasively argued, Paul is to be seen as "a radical Jew," then nothing is to be gained by playing down that radicalism and the controversy that inevitably attends it.

---

36. According to the New Perspective, "Paul's reflections on the relationship between the Christian faith and the Jewish law and Judaism in general spring from a highly positive attitude towards everything distinctively Jewish, an attitude that Paul had both before and after he was called to the Christ faith" (T. Engberg-Pedersen, *Paul and the Stoics,* 14).

37. So L. Gaston, *Paul and the Torah,* 147-48.

38. Following Gaston and S. Stowers, John Gager tries to solve the problem of Paul's positive and negative statements about the law by supposing them to relate to different people. On the one hand, "Paul considers the Jews still obligated to maintain the Torah" (*Reinventing Paul,* 18). On the other, "when Paul appears to say something [about the law] . . . that is unthinkable from a Jewish perspective, it is probably true that he is not talking about Jews at all. Instead we may assume that the apostle to the Gentiles is talking about the law and Gentiles" (58).

39. Barry Matlock rightly emphasizes that "we moderns are not typically concerned so much about sin and guilt as we are about notions of community, so that our theological climate is reflected here" — that is, in the shift from old to new perspective ("Almost Cultural Studies? Reflections on the 'New Perspective' on Paul," 439)

40. Compare the widespread view that Romans gives a more balanced account of the law than the earlier and more polemical Galatians. Thus, according to W. D. Davies, in Galatians "Paul views the Law with the cold eyes of an antagonist" ("Paul and the Law: Reflections on Pitfalls in Interpretation," 8). In Romans, however, "a more subtle and restrained Paul appears" (10).

As we have seen, this book diverges from the New Perspective on Paul at four main points. First, the concept of "covenantal nomism" is used to highlight the irreducible particularity of Paul's polemic against "works of law," rather than to promote a view of Judaism as "a religion of grace." Second, it is argued that divine agency plays a more direct and immediate role in the Pauline "pattern of religion" than in the Judaism Paul opposes. Third, the phrase "works of law" is here understood to refer to the distinctive way of life of the Jewish community, but without any special orientation towards "boundary markers" such as circumcision, food laws, or sabbath. Fourth, Paul is said to advocate a "sectarian" separation between the Christian community and "Judaism," rather than an inclusive understanding of the one people of God as encompassing uncircumcised Gentiles. These emphases were all central to the first edition of this book, and I now propose that they point us "beyond the New Perspective."

Scholarly positions on "Old" and "New" Perspectives are so entrenched that my proposal will probably be regarded by one party as welcome confirmation that Luther was *basically* right all along and by the other as a deplorable reversion to views that ("after Sanders") are no longer tenable.[41] In opposition to both these possible reactions, I can only insist that I propose a *forward* rather than a *backward* step. The critique of Luther's essentially allegorical interpretation of Paul's critique of works is presented here with all the emphasis I can muster. That does not mean, however, that Paul *never* looks beyond the conflict of particularities towards abstract underlying principles. Nor does the fundamental "ethnic" dimension of Paul's righteousness-by-faith conceptuality mean that questions about the relation of divine and human agency can now somehow be proscribed. I have argued for these points on exegetical grounds, and I hope they will generate renewed *exegetical* debate. To eliminate exegetical proposals on the grounds of a perceived proximity to a "Lutheran Paul" is simply to succumb to prejudice and dogmatism.[42]

This work is still directed *against* the "Lutheran Paul" as I originally con-

---

41. The respective positions are well charted by Stephen Westerholm in his *Perspectives Old and New on Paul: The "Lutheran" Paul and His Critics*. For reassertion of traditional Protestant readings of Paul over against the alleged aberrations of the New Perspective, see the various contributions to volume 2 of *Justification and Variegated Nomism* (ed. D. A. Carson et al.).

42. My apprehensions are occasioned in part by the appearance of major review articles of my *Paul and the Hermeneutics of Faith* that claim to diagnose in it a reversion to "the Lutheran Paul." Douglas Campbell finds that my book's account of Pauline soteriology is "basically the Lutheran construal of the gospel" ("An Evangelical Paul," 339). Troels Engberg-Pedersen entitles his piece, "Once More a Lutheran Paul?" Both scholars have allowed their obsession with Luther to cloud their critical judgment. I am fairly certain that each would also criticize the other's reading of Paul as "Lutheran."

strued him. This was a figure derived from Luther but reinvented by the German Protestant biblical scholarship of the mid-twentieth century. Unlike some more recent defenses of a Lutheran Paul, this image of the apostle was the product of genuine theological creativity and intellectual engagement; it was in no sense a merely "conservative" restatement of a traditional orthodoxy. Yet, however compelling it may once have seemed, this image of Paul was seriously flawed. In attempting to demolish it, my fundamental concern was to replace a conception of Paul as *thinker* with a conception of Paul as *agent.* It seemed to me (and it still does) that debates about Paul, justification, and the law are often characterized by a total lack of social realism. In interpreting the apostle's statements on these matters, one negotiates the exegetical minefield in a more or less surefooted way, arriving at conclusions that may or may not betray the continuing influence of Luther or Calvin; but it does not occur to one to ask *why* Paul sees fit to address newly founded congregations on such themes. His letters are apparently construed as papers delivered to a seminar in systematic theology. This defect is also evident in English-language scholarship, but here is a characteristic German example:

> "Rechtfertigung aus Glauben" — gerade das ist es, was zu sagen dem Paulus unbedingt am Herzen liegt. Dann aber ist in den denkerischen Bemühungen darum, also in seiner Rechtfertigungstheologie, das Eigentliche seiner Theologie zu sehen![43]

Paul here is characterized purely as "Denker." He *thinks,* and what he thinks about is "justification by faith" and its development into a "theology of justification." It is a powerful image that reflects a whole tradition of thinking about and with Paul. Yet its lack of social realism is palpable. The Pauline texts are read as self-absorbed meditations on God and the world, and they lose their character as *letters* — that is, as communicative actions that intervene decisively in the communal and individual lives of their addressees. In *thinking* about God and the world, the apostle loses his own orientation *towards* the world, and his God becomes similarly remote.

The Paul of the present book is also a thinker, but one whose thinking is at every point bound up with his action as founder of Christian communities. This view does greater justice to Paul's sense that *his own agency* is integral to the divine communicative action occurring in and through the gospel.

---

43. Hans Hübner, *Das Gesetz bei Paulus,* 15. An approximate translation: "'Justification by faith': to assert that is for Paul the one thing that matters. It is in his intellectual engagement with *this* topic, and thus in his theology of justification, that the core of his theology is to be found." (The equivalent passage occurs on p. 7 of the published English translation.)

CHAPTER 1

Paul, the Reformation, and Modern Scholarship

What is the precise focus of Paul's opposition to Judaism and judaizing Christianity? In recent Pauline scholarship, it is increasingly recognized that the answer to this question can no longer be taken for granted.

According to the account bequeathed by the Reformation, Paul opposes the idea that salvation can be earned by acts of obedience to the law, as held by his Jewish or Jewish Christian opponents. He himself preaches the gospel of salvation solely by the grace of God, and the idea that salvation is to be earned by human achievement is therefore anathema to him. Judaism is here understood as a religion of "works-righteousness," a form of Pelagianism according to which God has given us the law so that we might earn salvation by fulfilling it. Paul's gospel opposes this self-sufficiency by insisting on grace and faith alone. On this view, Paul and his opponents debate the merits of two rival answers to the question of how the human being can be accepted by God. Many scholars still believe that this interpretation of the Pauline texts is essentially correct.

But others are dissatisfied with this approach. The fundamental question is whether or not it can do justice to the socio-historical context in which Paul was writing. Paul understood himself as the apostle to the Gentiles, and the problem of the status of the Gentiles dominated his life and work. Can theological interpretations stemming from the Reformation give due weight to this highly specific historical situation? Or do they issue in a distorted view both of Paul and of the Judaism he opposed? It will be the argument of the present work that the latter is the case: the Reformation tradition's approach to Paul is seriously flawed. But before embarking on this argument, a more detailed account is needed first of the traditional "Lutheran" approach and second of the modern dissatisfaction with it.[1]

1. The Lutheran Reading of Paul

It is often said that "modern Pauline studies began with the Tübingen scholar, F. C. Baur."[2] In one sense, this is no doubt true: Baur was the first great exponent of the study of Paul by historical methods. But in another sense, the statement is misleading, for the dominant influence on the German Pauline scholarship of the twentieth century was still Martin Luther.[3] Whereas endeavors such as synoptic source criticism and the quest for the historical Jesus can be traced to quite definite beginnings in the era of the Enlightenment, we must go back to Luther to find the origin and inspiration of much of the Pauline scholarship of the modern period. This is most particularly the case when the topic is Paul's view of the law, which is our present concern. As Gerhard Ebeling has noted: "In the theology of the Reformers the problems all concentrate themselves so much on the concept of the law that the whole of theology . . . stands or falls with it."[4] Whether or not this is true of the Reformers in general, it is certainly true of Luther and of his twentieth-century reappropriation.

Luther's interpretation of Paul is dominated by opposition to the misuse of the law as a means by which sinful and deluded humans seek to attain salvation by their own moral striving. In the 1535 lectures on Galatians, Luther interprets as follows Paul's reference to ὅσοι ἐξ ἔργων νόμου (3:10):

> To want to be justified by works of the law is to deny the righteousness of faith. On this basis, when those who are self-righteous keep the law, they deny the righteousness of faith and sin against the first, second and third commandments and against the entire law, because God commands that he be worshipped by believing and fearing him. But they, on the contrary,

---

1. In this chapter, revisions to *PJG¹* are relatively modest. The discussion of Luther, Bultmann, Käsemann, and Sanders has been slightly expanded, and at a number of points I have attempted greater conceptual clarity — especially at the conclusion of the chapter. I have not incorporated any more recent literature into the main discussion, in the hope that a clear presentation of issues raised by older literature still has its merits.

2. G. Howard, *Crisis in Galatia*, 1.

3. According to Hans Hübner, in Pauline studies today just as in the sixteenth century, the great question is: "Is Luther right?" ("Pauli Theologiae Proprium," 445).

4. Ebeling, "Reflections on the Doctrine of the Law," 254.

make their works into righteousness, without faith and against faith. Therefore in their very keeping of the law they act in a manner that is most contrary to the law, and thereby sin most seriously and grievously. . . . The righteousness of the law which they think they are producing is actually nothing but idolatry and blasphemy against God. (*LW* 26:253-54)

Here and elsewhere, Luther moves away from the traditional view of sin as transgression of particular commandments and asserts that it is precisely those who keep the commandments who in doing so manifest the essence of sin, which is to rely on oneself and to reject the grace of God.

This is to presuppose that when Paul condemns "works," he means moral activity in general, and not just the Jewish "ceremonies" that are abolished by the coming of Christ. Luther considers the latter view to be a disastrous mistake. In his *De Servo Arbitrio* (1526), he speaks as follows of this reduction of "works of law" to outmoded Jewish "ceremonies":

That is the ignorant error of Jerome, which, in spite of Augustine's strenuous resistance (God having withdrawn and let Satan prevail), has spread out into the world and has persisted to the present day. It has consequently become impossible to understand Paul, and the knowledge of Christ has been inevitably obscured. Even if there had never been any other error in the Church, this one alone was pestilent and potent enough to make havoc of the gospel. (*LW* 33:258)

According to Luther, Jerome's reduction of "works" to "ceremonies" is easy to refute on exegetical grounds. When Paul states that "by works of the law shall no flesh be justified" (Gal. 2:16; Rom. 3:20), he is clearly not referring only to ceremonies. How would that help the argument that all are unrighteous and in need of grace? In the law of Moses, Luther continues, ceremonies and the Decalogue are one, equally binding. When Paul rejects righteousness by works of law, it is therefore the supposed salvific function of the whole law that he rejects. If, however, "works of law" include the observance of the Decalogue as well as circumcision and other "ceremonies," then Paul's critique cannot be confined to Judaism or the Jewish community; for Luther takes for granted a close relationship between the Decalogue and the "natural law" that is held to be binding on all people. Thus, Paul's condemnation of "works" is directed not simply against Judaism but against a general human error. It refers to "all workers and all their works," but especially to "their good and virtuous works" (*LW* 26:271-72). It is, for example, diametrically opposed to the Aristotelian account of the formation of moral character. This point is already clear in the 1516 lectures on Romans:

> The righteousness of God is so named to distinguish it from the righteous-ness of man, which comes from works, as Aristotle describes it very clearly in Book III of his *Ethics*. According to him, righteousness follows upon ac-tions and originates in them. But according to God, righteousness precedes works, and thus works are the result of righteousness. (*LW* 25:152)

Here, "works" in the potent Pauline sense may be performed by Jew or Greek alike — for at the most important points the law of Moses accessible to the Jew coincides with the law of Nature accessible also to the Greek. This exegetical conclusion is absolutely fundamental to Luther's reading of Paul. If we mis-read Paul at this point, we fatally misunderstand the gospel itself. The reason for this apparently exaggerated claim is that "faith" — the faith that justifies, on which our salvation rests — is defined on the basis of its opposition to "works." If and only if "works" stands for the quest for a righteousness estab-lished by one's own moral attainments, then "faith" will stand for the renunci-ation of such a quest on the basis of a righteousness established from beyond the self. Faith entails the recognition of one's previous entanglement in a disas-trous misuse of the law as a means of securing the self over against God.

If there is a misuse of the law, there is also a correct use. The law was given in order to reveal sin, so as to terrify the conscience and cause one to seek grace in Christ. In *The Freedom of a Christian* (1520), Luther makes this point as follows:

> We must point out that the entire scripture of God is divided into two parts: commandments and promises. Although the commandments teach things that are good, the things taught are not done as soon as they are taught, for the commandments show us what we ought to do but do not give us the power to do it. They are intended to teach man to know himself, that through them he may recognize his inability to do good and may de-spair of his own ability. . . . Now when a man has learned through the com-mandments to recognize his own helplessness and is distressed about how he might satisfy the law — since the law must be fulfilled so that not a jot or tittle shall be lost, otherwise man will be condemned without hope — then, being truly humbled and reduced to nothing in his own eyes, he finds in himself nothing whereby he may be justified or saved. Here, the second part of Scripture comes to our aid, namely, the promises of God. (*LW* 31:348)

The law is rightly understood when it reveals our helplessness and our need of grace. This does not make good works unnecessary, however, even if they contribute nothing to salvation:

> Although, as I have said, a person is abundantly and sufficiently justified by faith inwardly, in his spirit, and so has all that he needs, except insofar as this faith and these riches must grow from day to day even to the future life; yet he remains in this mortal life on earth. (*LW* 31:358)

Out of spontaneous love for God, the body must be reduced to subjection, which also enables one to serve others. And yet, one "needs none of these things for one's righteousness and salvation" (365).

Here, then, we have the ideas that were to become the second and third uses of the law in the classical Lutheran formulation.[5] In addition to its role in maintaining external civil order, the law was given to provoke despair at one's own sinfulness, so that one might flee to Christ for mercy; and it was also given to guide the earthly lives of those who are justified by faith.

We have briefly discussed Luther's interpretation of Paul's statements about the law under the two headings of the misuse of the law and its correct use.[6] Both arise from the fact that the law is a demand for total obedience: it is misused when one attempts to earn salvation by fulfilling it, for it is intended to expose one's sin so that one seeks mercy in Christ alone. In the theology of **Rudolf Bultmann**, Luther's account of the law's misuse attains still greater prominence, while the correct use recedes into the background. In an article dating from 1940, Bultmann writes:

> As for the question of being inwardly weighed down by the law, it is absolutely clear that Paul never speaks of it. In its Lutheran form, this question is entirely foreign to Judaism. . . . [Paul's] utterances about his past do not indicate that he suffered from an oppressive consciousness of sin. According to Phil. 3.4ff., he was blameless in fulfilling the law; according to Gal.

---

5. According to article VI of the *Formula of Concord* (1584), the law was given for three reasons: "first, that a certain external discipline might be preserved . . . ; second, that by the law people might be brought to an acknowledgment of their sins; third, that regenerate persons, to all of whom much that is of the flesh nevertheless still cleaves, for that very reason may have some certain rule after which they may and ought to shape their life" (P. Schaff, *Creeds of Christendom*, 3:130). See also G. Ebeling, "On the Doctrine of the Triplex Usus Legis in the Theology of the Reformation."

6. On Luther's view of the law, see further P. Althaus, *The Theology of Martin Luther*, and G. Ebeling, *Luther*.

31

1.13ff., he was a rigid zealot for the traditions of his ancestors. . . . Paul never groaned under the law. In giving it up he surrendered something which had been gain to him (Phil. 3.7): the surrender was a sacrifice for him — he gave up something that had been his pride.[7]

Bultmann warns that "Paul is easily confused with Luther," which leads us to "overlook the historical situation in which Paul is writing,"[8] one in which Jews took pride in the law and did not regard it as an intolerable burden. The Lutheran *secundus usus legis* is judged to be without historical or exegetical foundation, and significant theological consequences follow. In Luther, the *secundus usus legis* corresponds to a conventional view of "sin" as referring to acts that transgress the moral law and that it is the function of the law to expose. It is only in Luther's account of the *misuse* of the law that a more radical understanding of sin comes to light — sin as the attempt to acquire salvation by one's own moral strivings, so that one is paradoxically disobeying the law in the very act of fulfilling it.[9] While sin as transgression is of little theological interest to Bultmann, sin as self-justification is fundamental to his account of the divine word of judgment and grace that is enacted in the kerygma.[10]

This distinction is already clear in an early article entitled "Liberal Theology and the Latest Theological Movement" (1924). Bultmann writes:

> Man as such, the whole man, is called in question by God. Man stands under that question mark, whether he knows it or not. His moral transgressions are not his fundamental sin. . . . *Man's fundamental sin is his will to justify himself as man,* for thereby he makes himself God. When man becomes aware of this . . . [t]he whole world — which was *man's* world — is annihilated; nothing in it any longer has meaning and value, for everything had received this from man. But to know this judgment is also to know it as

---

7. Bultmann, "Christ the End of the Law," 39-40; italics removed.

8. Bultmann, "Christ the End of the Law," 37.

9. As Althaus notes, for Luther "[m]an's sin is twofold. First, he does not fulfil the Commandments but transgresses them. And second, he sins against the First Commandment when he attempts to fulfil the Commandments in order to win salvation, since he thereby sins against God as the only God and Creator who alone gives righteousness to men. Man is guilty in relation to God not only when he does not care but also when he is very serious about morality" (*Theology of Martin Luther,* 150).

10. Because Bultmann so emphatically dissociates himself from Luther at this point, Stendahl is wrong in assuming that Bultmann shares Luther's obsession with guilt and conscience ("Introspective Conscience," 207) — as Hübner has pointed out ("Pauli Theologiae Proprium," 446).

grace, since it is really liberation. . . . Man then knows that the question is also the answer, for it is only God who can *so* question him.[11]

Here, awareness of sin is not merely preparatory to grace; rather, it is already grace. In an equation derived from Barth's *Römerbrief,* judgment is grace and grace judgment.[12]

This view of sin as self-justification enabled by the law is fundamental to Bultmann's account of Pauline theology. Paul

> says not only that man *cannot* achieve salvation by works of the law, but that he was not even *intended* to do so. . . . But why is this the case? Because man's effort to achieve salvation by keeping the law only leads him into sin, indeed this effort itself in the end *is already sin.*[13]

Sin is a person's "self-powered striving to undergird his own existence in forgetfulness of his creaturely existence, to procure his salvation by his own strength" (*Theology,* 264), and this is precisely the nature of Jewish law observance. Thus, "[i]t is not only evil deeds already committed that make a man reprehensible in God's sight, but man's intention of becoming righteous before God by keeping the Law and thereby having his 'boast' is already sin" (267). The Pauline term for this fundamental sin is "boasting" (cf. Rom. 3:27), in radical contrast to the acceptance of God's grace as a gift, which is faith's attitude (281).

Bultmann's desire to refer as many as possible of Paul's statements about the law to its misuse as a means of achieving salvation is exemplified by his interpretation of Romans 7, a chapter that had previously served as the locus classicus for the Lutheran *secundus usus legis.*[14] In "Romans 7 and the Anthro-

---

11. Bultmann, "Liberal Theology," 46-47; italics original. This passage defies every attempt at retranslation using inclusive language.

12. This equation, later abandoned by Barth but retained by Bultmann, is identified and criticized by A. Schlatter in his review of the second edition of Barth's *Römerbrief* (reprinted in J. Moltmann, ed., *Anfänge der dialektischen Theologie,* 142-47). Schlatter is also critical of the loss of the Jew/Gentile focus and of the specifically Roman destination of Paul's letter — points that are again relevant for Bultmann.

13. *Theology of the New Testament,* 1:263-64. Page references to this work are given parenthetically in the text in the following paragraph.

14. This was the case with the previously dominant autobiographical interpretation, advocated for example by Theodor Zahn. According to Zahn, Paul is referring in vv. 7-12 to "the days of his childhood, the beginnings of his development into a moral being" (*Römer,* 343). In the guilt-inducing encounter with the commandment, the adolescent Paul finds "that something of the relative innocence and harmlessness of childhood has been lost, and becomes painfully aware in his conscience of the corresponding devaluation of his life" (344). Paul here describes

pology of Paul" (1932), he argues that this chapter is to be understood against the background of Philippians 3:6 and Romans 10:2-3, in which Paul speaks not of repentance from specific transgressions but of abandonment of zeal for the law; the essence of faith is therefore the renunciation of one's own righteousness.[15] Thus, the sin discussed in Romans 7 is the effort to achieve righteousness for oneself. "The good" in vv. 14-25 is to be understood not as what is morally good but as "life," i.e., the authentic life that is the Creator's purpose for humans. It is integral to human nature to know the possibility of authentic existence; nevertheless, one fails to attain it because one strives to achieve it through one's own efforts (152). All that one is able to procure by this means is death, which is the meaning of τὸ κακόν. One wills what is good (life), but only achieves what is evil (death). Far from helping one to overcome sin, the law awakens and evokes sin (156). Thus, Romans 7 is no longer seen as an account of the moral struggle in which the moral person is continually frustrated by a failure to overcome sin. This is not a subjective struggle at all, but a "trans-subjective" struggle underlying all human life but only disclosed in the gospel (151). Following Kümmel, Bultmann argues that Romans 7 is a retrospective analysis by the Christian of one's own past, now understood for the first time. Romans 7 becomes the test-case for the view that "sin" does not refer primarily to individual actions, but rather to the self-assertion and desire for autonomy that underlie the quest to establish one's own righteousness before God.

It would be difficult to exaggerate the importance of this whole theme in Bultmann's general theological work as well as his exegesis.[16] At its heart lies the assumption — derived from Luther — that a critique ostensibly directed at Judaism actually serves to disclose a universal human error. In their quest to establish their own righteousness, Jews are acting as representatives of humanity as such — humanity under the wrath of God. Paul

> sees that the striving of the Jews is basically motivated by the need for rec-
> ognition, and that in this connection this need to be recognized means

---

"a development which took place in many individual events on the basis of experiences which he, as the son of a pharisaic and therefore firmly law-keeping Israelite household, had had particular opportunity to encounter" (344; my translation). This reading attempts to ground the Lutheran second use of the law in the personal experience of the pre-Christian Paul.

15. "Romans 7 and the Anthropology of Paul," 148-50. Page references to this work are given parenthetically in the text that follows.

16. As Conzelmann points out, the most striking characteristic of Bultmann's theology is the harmony between his exegetical and theological work ("Die Rechtfertigungslehre des Paulus: Theologie oder Anthropologie?" 393). But Conzelmann begs the question by attributing this harmony to the agreement between Bultmann's theological concerns and those of his subject matter.

fundamentally not seeking to be accepted in the sight of other humans (though this will always be a concomitant of it), but rather to be accepted in the sight of God, the court of appeal which stands high above every human judgment. . . . A specifically human striving has merely taken on a culturally and historically specific form in Judaism. For it is in fact a universal human striving to gain recognition of one's achievement; and this generates pride.[17]

It is this pride or "boasting" that is exposed in the kergyma for the absurdity it truly is. Bultmann concludes:

Thus it is an error to think that belief in the grace of God requires a sense of sin or a confession of sin, in the sense that one must admit to oneself how much or how often and grievously one has sinned and continually is sinning. One does not need to consider frantically or artificially one's immoralities, or to contort good works into bad. One is to consider the reason for one's being, and to ask whence one's life comes: whether it is from the grace of God or from one's own powers, and whether this life is sustained by the effort to gain glory, whether one is driven this way and that by the need for recognition, or whether in the knowledge of one's vanity one has seen through the comedy of this effort and so has become conscious of one's sin in the sight of God.[18]

This is the self-knowledge disclosed in the gospel. It consists in an awareness of the perversion of human existence that occurs in the denial of radical dependency on God as the ground and source of being. This perversion is paradigmatically present in the "Judaism" that Paul opposes, and its exposure is the rationale and content of the gospel itself.[19] In Bultmann's radicalizing of Luther, it is the gospel itself that comes to expression in Pauline statements about the law.

The crucial exegetical point here is that "faith" and "works" are defined in terms of their opposition to one another. They are understood as mutually exclusive *by definition*: "faith" stands for the renunciation of "works"; "works" stands for the refusal of the decision of "faith." This has profound implications especially for christology, for "Christ" here is little more than a symbol of the kergyma's call to renounce the project of self-salvation. Indeed,

17. Bultmann, "Christ the End of the Law," 43.
18. Bultmann, "Christ the End of the Law," 48-49.
19. For reflection on the complex yet disquieting relationship between Bultmann's theology and contemporary anti-semitism, see my *Text and Truth,* 153-69.

Christ *is* that call and has no being apart from it. If "works" is abstracted from its concrete relation to Judaism, then "faith" will be abstracted from its concrete reference to the Christ *proclaimed* in the kerygma yet not simply *identified* with it.

These Bultmannian and Lutheran emphases are echoed in the work of Bultmann's successors. Thus, for **Ernst Käsemann**, the works of the law "are for Paul a higher form of godlessness than transgressions of the law, and are thus incompatible with faith."[20] Like Bultmann, Käsemann regards the Jew as exemplifying a general human phenomenon, although he is concerned to redirect Paul's critique against *homo religiosus* rather than "the need for recognition." In a broadcast talk on "Paul and Israel," published in 1961, Käsemann writes:

> The apostle's real adversary is the devout Jew . . . as the reality of the religious man. For man, whether he knows it and acts correspondingly or not, is the being who is set before God: and this fact the devout Jew acknowledges. Certainly such a profession is no protection from illusion. In fact, religion always provides man with his most thoroughgoing possibility of confusing an illusion with God. Paul sees this possibility realized in the devout Jew: inasmuch as the announcement of God's will in the law is misunderstood as a summons to human achievement and therefore as a means to a righteousness of one's own. But that is for him the root sin, because an image is set in the place of God; man, in despairing presumption, erects his own work into the criterion of the universal judgment, and God becomes an approving spectator of our doings.[21]

Paul "strikes at the hidden Jew in all of us."[22] His doctrine of the law is the "radical spearhead" of the doctrine of justification, which now needs to be directed against a complacent and conservative church. The doctrine of justification

> undoubtedly grew up in the course of the anti-Jewish struggle and stands or falls with this antithesis. But the historian must not make things easy for himself by simply, as historian, noting this incontrovertible fact. If he does, he could equally well call Jesus a pious Jew who had a memorable fate and left behind him a series of impressive sayings. Our task is to ask: what does

20. Käsemann, *Romans,* 103.

21. Käsemann, "Paul and Israel," 184-85.

22. Käsemann, "Paul and Israel," 186. Such language is obviously disturbing for more than merely exegetical reasons. It should be noted that Käsemann has borrowed the theme of "the hidden Jew" from Romans 2:29, where, however, it serves a positive role.

the Jewish nomism against which Paul fought really represent? And our answer must be: it represents the community of "good" people which turns God's promises into their own privileges and God's commandments into the instruments of self-sanctification.[23]

For Käsemann as for Bultmann, the essence of the Pauline doctrine of justification is the exposure of the attempt to earn salvation by one's own efforts. Bultmann applies this to what he sees as a tendency of human life as a whole: self-assertion, or the need for recognition. Underlying this emphasis is Bultmann's engagement with Heideggerian ontology.[24] Käsemann, uninterested in Heidegger or ontology, uses the doctrine of justification in sharply polemical fashion against various forms of theological or churchly conservatism. In spite of this difference of application, the crucial exegetical move is the same in both cases. Paul's rejection of the possibility of righteousness by works of law is given the widest possible application, and there is no interest whatsoever in what he has to say about Israel *qua* Israel.

Käsemann's polemic is also directed against Bultmann himself, whom he accuses of perpetuating a typically Lutheran individualism that overlooks the cosmic and apocalyptic scope of Pauline theology. At this point Käsemann's reading of Paul is highly distinctive, and it remains influential; and yet, even within the new framework, the particularity of "Israel" still cannot be accommodated. In this account, Paul's doctrine of justification has to do not with the individual or even with the Christian community per se, but with the Creator's claim on the godless world. That is what Paul means by δικαιοσύνη θεοῦ, the expression that encapsulates the theological argument of his letter to the Romans. Especially characteristic of Käsemann is the high value he places on Romans 9–11, a section oriented towards "salvation-history" that cannot be reduced to Lutheran or Bultmannian individualism. This section of the letter shows that "the apostle's thought and work do not circle around anthropology but around the conquest of the world" — thereby bringing to fruition the apostle's understanding of the δικαιοσύνη θεοῦ in its full apocalyptic scope.[25] Yet Käsemann's reading engages not only with Bultmann but also with F. C. Baur, who (as we shall see below) held that Romans 9–11 is no

---

23. Käsemann, "Justification and Salvation-History," 71-72.

24. See for example Bultmann's celebrated or notorious 1941 article "New Testament and Mythology: The Problem of Demythologizing the New Testament Proclamation," 21-29.

25. Käsemann, *Romans*, 296. As C. Müller succinctly puts Käsemann's point, "Romans 9–11 creates the possibility of freeing the Pauline doctrine of justification from the Procrustes-bed of individualism" (*Gottes Gerechtigkeit und Gottes Volk: Eine Untersuchung zu Römer 9-11*, 27; my translation).

mere appendix to chapters 1–8 but the climax and heart of the whole letter. According to Käsemann, Baur thereby initiated a range of "purely historical" perspectives on Pauline theology that dominated the period of "liberal" ascendancy, and that successfully marginalized the all-important doctrine of justification. Thus,

> by way of exposition of chs. 9–11, Paul, the chief witness of the evangelical churches, became first the catalyst in a radical tendency-criticism of the NT, then a Janus-like figure in the history of religion, who on the one side has been viewed in terms of eschatology as an apocalyptist, while on the other side he has been viewed in terms of the cult piety of Hellenism as a mystic.[26]

Unfortunately, in a historicizing age, no one took up Baur's challenge to rethink the *theological* significance of Romans 9–11 for Pauline interpretation as a whole and for the doctrine of justification in particular.[27] The solution, Käsemann argues, is to integrate the salvation-historical orientation of chapters 9–11 with the doctrine of justification expounded in chapters 1–8. If the δικαιοσύνη θεοῦ is seen as the theme of Romans 1–11 as a whole, then an individualistic and anthropocentric understanding of justification is no longer possible. Rather, the doctrine of justification has to do with the Creator's claim on the world as a whole. The church (rather than the individual believer) is that piece of world that hears the Creator's claim and attests it to the world. In this highly distinctive interpretation of Pauline "salvation-history," the church is understood *theocentrically:* Paul's concern is not with the church as such but with God, and with the church only in its attestation of God's action.

In all this, what becomes of Paul's apparent interest in "Israel"? According to Käsemann,

> [T]he problem of Israel must be discussed . . . as the problem of God's faithfulness to his uttered word. It can be discussed only dialectically, for here we have an example of God's faithfulness and human unfaithfulness in conflict. . . . [T]he church has to perceive in Israel the particular threat to all recipients of the promise and the gospel, and it is preserved in such a threat only if it allows the word of God which constitutes the community to be related to Christ and interprets it in terms of the message of justification.[28]

---

26. Käsemann, *Romans*, 253.
27. Käsemann, *Romans*, 254.
28. Käsemann, *Romans*, 256.

Here Käsemann gives his answer to the question why in Romans 9–11 Paul is concerned with Israel, the Jewish people. Paul has no interest in Israel per se. Rather, he sees in Israel what the church might become if it fails to grasp the message of justification and sets itself in opposition to the divine faithfulness that this message announces. While the final triumph of the divine faithfulness is certain, the opposition is real and serious, as is the threat that it might recur even and especially within the church. Once again, Käsemann is asking himself the question: What does the Jewish nomism against which Paul fought really represent? And the answer is the familiar one: that Jewish "self-righteousness" or "legalism" discloses a *general* possibility of living in opposition to the divine word that announces the justification of the ungodly. "Jewish nomism" is not just itself. Rather, it discloses and exemplifies the fundamental temptation to which Christians in particular are exposed — the temptation to assert one's own righteousness and thereby to contradict the righteousness of God. If Käsemann moves beyond Bultmann at all, he does so only by way of the familiar Bultmannian conceptuality, which always knows how to convert Pauline particularities into generalizations. Even in Romans 9–11, "Israel" must mean something other than itself.

The Bultmannian reading of Paul (exemplified by scholars such as Bornkamm, Fuchs, Conzelmann, Klein, and Hübner, as well as by Bultmann and Käsemann) should not be too lightly dismissed by those who cannot accept it. It represents much the most impressive modern attempt to reach to the heart of Paul's theology, and its theological seriousness compels respect, the more so as it has been engendered in part by the bitter experiences of modern German history.[29] Although it can sometimes lead its advocates into shortsighted polemic, on other occasions it attains a lucidity and profundity that make New Testament scholarship from other traditions seem facile and superficial by comparison. On the other hand, this does not mean that its exegesis or theology is correct. As Robert Morgan points out, "Profound theologians can be profoundly wrong."[30]

In post-Bultmannian German exegetical discussion, there has been extensive debate about the extent to which opposition to the sinful attempt to put God under an obligation by one's obedience to the law is actually to be

---

29. I leave this statement unaltered from the first edition, in spite of Daniel Boyarin's objection that "the works of Bultmann and Käsemann seem more engendered by the ideology that caused the 'bitter experiences of *German* [!] history' than by those experiences" (*A Radical Jew*, 214; italics original).

30. Morgan, "The Significance of 'Paulinism,'" 332.

found in the Pauline texts. Whereas Bultmann and his followers tend to see virtually every Pauline statement about the law in this light, others have emphasized that the traditional view of sin as transgression of the law is also of great significance to Paul.[31] U. Wilckens has rejected altogether the idea that Paul can see in "works of the law" the essence of sin, arguing that Paul does not contest the desire to fulfill the law in itself, but only the possibility of such a fulfilment.[32] In his *Law in Paul's Thought,* Hans Hübner has attempted to mediate between these two positions, arguing that Bultmann's view is to be found in Romans but not in Galatians. Thus, in Galatians 3:10 Paul denies the possibility of a "quantitative" fulfillment of the law,[33] whereas Romans 3:27 criticizes boasting in one's fulfillment of the law (116). Similarly, Abraham is described as "ungodly" in Romans 4:5 in part because he wished to be justified by works (121), whereas there is no sign of this sinful boasting in Galatians (111).

Yet other interpreters have raised more radical questions that impact on both Bultmannian and non-Bultmannian appropriations of Luther's reading of Paul. Is it really the case that at the heart of Paul's controversy with Judaism is an attack on the idea that righteousness is to be achieved by one's own efforts? Is there not a danger of reading back Luther's controversy with the Roman Catholic Church into the first century, and so of failing to understand the historical circumstances of Paul's controversy with Judaism? We must now outline the views of some of the scholars who have brought such questions to the fore.

2. Opposition to the Lutheran Reading

According to **Ferdinand Christian Baur,** Paul's polemic against Judaism was motivated by a quite different concern. Baur argued that Paul

> was the first to lay down expressly and distinctly the principle of Christian universalism as a thing essentially opposed to Jewish particularism. From the first, he set this Christian principle before him as the sole rule and standard of his apostolic activity. In his Christian consciousness, his own call to the apostolic office and the destination of Christianity to be the general

31. And to Luther: see P. Althaus, *Paulus und Luther,* 49.

32. Wilckens, "Was heisst bei Paulus: 'Aus Werken des Gesetzes wird kein Mensch gerecht'?" 94.

33. Hübner, *Law in Paul's Thought,* 38-41. Page references to this work will be given parenthetically in the following text.

principle of salvation for all people were two facts which were bound up inseparably in each other.[34]

In his conversion, Paul "broke through the barriers of Judaism and rose out of the particularism of Judaism into the universal idea of Christianity" (1:47). This contrast between universalism and particularism dominated his work. Thus, in the debates described in Galatians 2,

> The alternatives . . . were either to do away with the distinction between Jewish and Gentile Christians altogether, or to continue to be Jews, and deny to the Gentile Christians any privilege which would place them on the same level with the Jewish Christians. (1:55)

The Jerusalem apostles represented the particularist view, Paul the universalist one:

> According to the former, it is in vain to be a Christian without being a Jew also. According to the latter, it is in vain to be a Christian if, as a Christian, one chooses to be a Jew as well. (1:57)

The significance of circumcision in this debate was that, as the means of entry into the Jewish community, it is a sign of the superiority of that community. On the other hand, Paul argues that this barrier between Jew and Gentile must be removed. The main point of Galatians 3 is thus that

> all who are baptized into Christ enter . . . into a new community, in which all the causes of division between man and man, which are to be found in the outward circumstances of life, are at once removed. (1:59)

The purpose of Romans is similarly

> to do away with the last remaining portions of the Jewish exclusiveness, by taking up and representing it as the mere introduction to the Christian universalism which extended to all nations.[35]

> In the main part of the letter, from beginning to end, the theme is that each and every privilege of Jewish particularism, internal and external, is of no avail.[36]

---

34. Baur, *Church History*, 1:47. References to this work by volume and page will be given parenthetically in the following text.

35. Baur, *Paul the Apostle of Jesus Christ*, 1:322.

36. Baur, "Über Zweck und Gedankengang des Römerbriefs," 207.

In this text, the "absolute nullity" of all claims of Jewish particularism is

> the great idea which pervades the whole discussion, and which forms the
> connection between the two great sections of the Epistle (i.–viii. and ix.–
> xi.). . . . Its great significance lies not so much in its doctrinal discussions
> about sin and grace, as in its practical bearing on the most important con-
> troversy of these times, the relation between Jew and Gentile. (*Church His-
> tory*, 1:72)

Baur and his critics believed that there was a conflict between his view, according to which Paul opposes Jewish exclusivism, and the Lutheran view, according to which he opposes the Jewish attempt to earn salvation.[37]

In these later works, Baur repeats claims first developed in his earlier
study, "Über Zweck und Veranlassung des Römerbriefs und die damit
zusammenhängenden Verhältnisse der römischen Gemeinde" (1836). As the
title already indicates, the point here is to connect the letter's purpose and occasion with the situation of the Roman Christian community, which becomes
the hermeneutical key to the letter as a whole. Baur notes that, in spite of the
clear evidence in Romans 14–15 of tension between Jewish and Gentile Christians in Rome, no one has as yet related this insight to the contents of the letter as a whole.[38] The reason for this omission is that the letter has been seen as
a dogmatic handbook, the basis indeed of Protestant theology. Yet that was
not its original intention. Such a view is reminiscent of the Catholic view of
the apostles as bearers of the church's teaching, for in both, past and present
are confused (154). Baur acknowledges the apparently general character of the
letter, in which contingent circumstances seem to play a lesser part in determining the argument than in, say, 1 Corinthians; and yet it is still proper to
inquire why such a letter should be sent precisely *to Rome* (155). "It is," Baur
argues, "unthinkable that the apostle, without definite circumstances present
in the Roman congregation . . . , should have felt himself obliged to write a
letter with such a content to this congregation" (156). Another drawback of
standard post-Reformation readings of the letter is that only chapters 1–8 are
thought to be important, so that chapters 9–11 come to be regarded as an appendix of only secondary importance. In fact, this section is "der Mittelpunkt
und Kern des Ganzen" (158). Here Paul argues from his own universalistic
standpoint against the view of Jewish Christians that Gentiles could not participate in salvation until Israel accepted it (160), and he claims that in the

---

37. Cf. Baur, "Über Zweck und Gedankengang," 87-91.
38. Baur, "Über Zweck und Veranlassung," 149. Page references to this work are given parenthetically in the text in the following paragraphs. Translations are my own.

light of the success of the Gentile mission and the failure of the Jewish mission "the contrast between Jews and Gentiles, still firmly maintained by Jewish Christians, must lose its significance" (164). Contrary to the traditional view, Romans 1–8 serves as a prelude to Romans 9–11:

> Everything which the apostle develops in the first eight chapters is the necessary presupposition for cutting off at its roots the Jewish particularism which opposes the apostle's universalism not in Judaism as a whole, but in the Christian church itself. (174)

Romans 9:1 is the "true starting-point" of the letter, the moment at which the dogmatic discussions of the earlier chapters reach their intended practical application (175-76). Everywhere the same preoccupation may be seen with

> the question which goes so deeply into the essence of Pauline Christianity, embracing all of its separate parts, whether Christian salvation has an exclusive or a universal destiny, whether participation in the grace of the gospel rests on a national privilege or on a general human need. (167)

This, then, is the issue that is both specific enough to be a source of contention within the Roman church, and fundamental enough to produce a text of this scope and character.[39]

Modern interpreters in the Reformation tradition have made little use of Baur's insights in this area, despite his influence in other respects; and insofar as they have, they have assumed that Baur and the Reformation are compatible.[40] Thus, although Bultmann recognizes that Paul opposes the view that

---

39. For an important anticipation of Baur's view of Romans as concerned with the relationship of Jews and Gentiles, see John Locke's *Paraphrase and Notes on the Epistle of St Paul to the Romans* (1707), reprinted in A. W. Wainwright, ed., *Paraphrases and Notes on the Epistles of St Paul*. Locke's Pauline paraphrases were popular throughout the eighteenth century. A German translation dating from 1773 was still cited by Tholuck (1824) and Meyer (1832), though apparently not by Baur (Wainwright, *Paraphrases and Notes*, 72-73).

40. On Baur as a New Testament scholar, see Schweitzer, *Paul and His Interpreters*, 12-21; W. G. Kümmel, *The New Testament: History of the Investigation of Its Problems*, 127-37; Neill, *Interpretation*, 19-28. Neill's hostile assessment is representative of older British attitudes towards Baur. Baur is presented as an anti-Christian extremist whose work from 1833 onwards "was gravely vitiated by an irrelevant and unproven presupposition" (21), derived from his Hegelianism. Thus his historical work may be safely dismissed: "Incautious assumptions at the start lead him into error on every principal point of New Testament criticism" (23), with the result that "at very few points has investigation proved the rightness of Baur's solutions" (27). It was the work of J. B. Lightfoot to oppose "the threat presented to the Christian cause by the school of Tübingen" (31); fortunately he was "less hampered by presuppositions than the representatives of the German schools" (32).

"the condition for sharing in salvation is belonging to the Jewish people," this is allowed no real significance for Pauline theology; for "the real problem of the law" is "the problem of legalism, the problem of good works as the condition for participation in salvation."[41] In his article "Zur Geschichte der Paulus-Forschung" (1929), Bultmann commends Baur for maintaining the unity of Paul's thought and religious experience, as opposed to more recent scholars who disparage Paul's theology and seek to recover the religious experience underlying it: "For Baur, Paul's thought *is* his experience."[42] Baur thus preserves the existential character of Paul's thought. But Bultmann remains studiously silent about the fact that Baur persistently opposed the Lutheran account of Paul's controversy with Judaism — the view that Bultmann sought to revive. The idea that Paul's theology might be closely related to his historical activity was implicitly rejected.

The main reason why interpreters in the Lutheran tradition have found it so hard to make use of Baur's insights is that their position depends on the possibility of universalizing Paul's attack on Jewish "works of the law." It is held that Paul is attacking not simply Judaism but, by implication, the universal human error of trying to earn salvation by one's own efforts. There is no room here for a contrast between universality and exclusiveness, since both positions are in their own way "universal."[43] Käsemann and others rightly emphasize that it is not outside the scope of historical study to look for the general principles underlying a particular set of circumstances. But if one misunderstands the particular circumstances, one will also misunderstand the general principles.

In contrast, **Krister Stendahl** has strongly emphasized the conflict between the traditional Lutheran approach to Paul and the historical approach pioneered by Baur. He begins his well-known article "The Apostle Paul and the Introspective Conscience of the West" (1963) by comparing the introspective element in Protestantism, typified by Luther's struggles with his conscience, with the "robust" conscience displayed by Paul himself.[44] The question, "How can I find a gracious God?" was posed by late medieval piety, but it finds no echo in Paul. Paul was concerned instead with the question of the implications of the Messiah's coming for the status of the law and for the relationship between Jews and Gentiles.[45] The early church concluded that these issues

41. Bultmann, *Theology of the New Testament*, 1:55; 1.111.
42. Bultmann, "Zur Geschichte der Paulus-Forschung," 314.
43. Lutheran scholars occasionally admit that this extension of Paul's meaning is problematic (cf. Ebeling, "Reflections on the Doctrine of the Law," 261; Käsemann, *Romans*, 282).
44. Stendahl, "Introspective Conscience," 200.
45. Stendahl, "Introspective Conscience," 203.

were no longer relevant in a situation in which the separation of church and synagogue was taken for granted, and so Paul's teaching about justification and the law had little influence until the time of Augustine, when "the Pauline thought about the Law and Justification was applied in a consistent and grand style to a more general and timeless human problem." There thus arose the view (revived by Luther) that according to Paul, "Nobody can attain a true faith in Christ unless his self-righteousness has been crushed by the Law."[46] Here, Paul's concern with the problem of the inclusion of the Gentiles in the church is completely ignored. The Lutheran belief that every person has a "legalistic Jew" in his or her heart is thus a distortion of Paul's true meaning.

Stendahl returns to the attack in his book *Paul among Jews and Gentiles* (1977). In Galatians, "Paul's argument is that one does not have to go through Judaism into Christianity, but that there is a straight and direct way for the Gentiles apart from the law."[47] As regards Romans, "the real centre of gravity" is to be found in chapters 9–11, where the question of Israel is discussed (28). Romans 1–8 merely forms a preface to this, and argues that "since justification is by faith it is equally possible for both Jews and Gentiles to come to Christ" (29). All this indicates that Paul did not regard the Jewish-Gentile problem as a universally applicable paradigm illustrating the human plight and its resolution:

> The doctrine of justification by faith was hammered out by Paul for the very specific and limited purpose of defending the rights of Gentile converts to be full and genuine heirs to the promise of God to Israel. (2)

> Paul's doctrine of justification by faith has its theological context in his reflection on the relationship between Jews and Gentiles, and not within the problem of how *man* is to be saved. (26)

> When Paul speaks about the Jews, he really speaks about Jews, and not simply the fantasy Jews who stand as a symbol or as the prime example of a timeless legalism. (36-37)

It should be evident that Stendahl's position is close to that of Baur. The significance of his work is therefore that, over against the unhistorical existentialist approach of dialectical theology, he has revived Baur's insistence on the

---

46. Stendahl, "Introspective Conscience," 205-6.

47. Stendahl, *Paul among Jews and Gentiles*, 18. Page references for this book will be given parenthetically in the text.

need to relate Paul's theological reflection to his historical context and his practical concerns.

Stendahl's position is anticipated at several points by **W. D. Davies**. The main difference is that whereas Stendahl seems to regard Paul's reflection on the Jew-Gentile problem as more or less irrelevant, Davies regards it as highly significant for contemporary dialogue between the church and the Jewish community. At the heart of his position is the view that prior to Jamnia the church and the Jewish community were not separated from one another; our understanding of Paul is distorted unless we constantly bear this fact in mind.

Thus, Paul was not a convert to a new religion but "a Pharisee who had accepted Jesus as the Messiah."[48] Although he rejected the imposition of the law on Gentile converts, he continued to observe it himself, for "the observance of the law . . . was Paul's passport with Judaism." His aim in setting aside certain aspects of the law for his Gentile converts was not to distance himself from Judaism but to put into practice the universalism of parts of the Jewish scriptures, thus breaking away from the particularism of much contemporary Judaism while remaining true to Jewish tradition. He continued to believe in the unique privileges of Israel: "Despite his noble universalism, he finds it impossible not to assign a special place to his own people."[49]

Paul has thus been misunderstood because it has been forgotten that his debate with Judaism was a "family dispute" about "the true interpretation of their common Jewish tradition."[50] This disagreement was possible within Judaism because of the fluid, tolerant nature of Judaism prior to 70 CE. The fact that "between us and Paul stands the Protestant Reformation" makes it easy for us to misunderstand his view of the law.[51] As a Jew, he held that the Torah was not simply a commandment but also a gift of God's grace. He felt able to proclaim the end of the law because of the Jewish belief that the Messiah would inaugurate a new law at his coming. His statements about the law are not entirely consistent, and one should not emphasize the negative ones at the expense of the positive. Christianity was for Paul "the fulfilment and not the annulment of Judaism."[52]

For Davies, all of this has contemporary resonances. The Holocaust and the rise of the State of Israel are realities that "demand that we sit again at the feet of Paul, whose mind is a clue to the pre-Jamnian period, to learn afresh

48. Davies, *Paul and Rabbinic Judaism*, 71.
49. Davies, *Paul and Rabbinic Judaism*, 74-75.
50. Davies, "Paul and the People of Israel," 22.
51. Davies, "Paul and the Law," 6.
52. Davies, "Paul and the Law," 12.

that the debate between Jews and Christians, separated as they now are, is a familial one."[53] Paul "provided ground in his day for mutual tolerance and respect between Jew and Gentile Christian," and it is bitterly ironic that he has been so tragically misinterpreted.[54]

Much the most formidable challenge to the Reformation tradition's interpretation of Paul has come in the work of **E. P. Sanders**. In *Paul and Palestinian Judaism* (1977), Sanders claims that the modern Lutheran interpretation of Paul makes use of a quite erroneous view of Judaism derived from the misleading textbooks of Weber and Bousset.[55] These teach that, according to Judaism, humans must earn salvation by their own unaided efforts. Every good work establishes merit, and every transgression establishes demerit. Merits and demerits will be weighed at the Last Judgment, and one's destiny depends on which preponderate. Sanders is also highly critical of the Strack-Billerbeck *Kommentar zum Neuen Testament aus Talmud und Midrasch,* claiming that the selection of the material often distorts the meaning of the texts and is based on the false view of Judaism just described. Bultmann seems not to have had "substantial independent access to the literature of 'late Judaism', and particularly not to Rabbinic sources,"[56] yet his support for the Weber-Bousset view has ensured its perpetuation in the work of Braun, Rössler, Jaubert, Black, Fuller, Conzelmann, and Thyen. This view is based on "a massive perversion and misunderstanding of the material" (59), caused by "the retrojection of the Protestant-Catholic debate into ancient history, with Judaism taking the role of Catholicism and Christianity the role of Lutheranism" (57).

Sanders summarizes the true pattern of Rabbinic religion as follows:

> God has chosen Israel and Israel has accepted the election. In his role as King, God gave Israel commandments which they are to obey as best they

---

53. Davies, "Paul and the People of Israel," 37.

54. Davies, "Paul and the People of Israel," 38. Davies's work is part of a much wider movement to reexamine the relationship between Judaism and Christianity and to replace the old polemical positions with genuine understanding. See Charlotte Klein, *Anti-Judaism in Christian Theology,* for a good statement of the problem.

55. Günther Klein argues that an empirical account of Jewish law-observance cannot verify or cast doubt on Paul's critique, since it is only Christ who reveals the true nature of Judaism; otherwise the Lutheran standpoint is defenseless ("Präliminarien zum Thema 'Paulus und die Juden,'" 241). But if Paul's critique of Judaism bears no relation to the historical evidence for first-century Judaism, it is hard to see how it can be rescued by appeal to christology.

56. Sanders, *Paul and Palestinian Judaism,* 43. Page references for this book will be given parenthetically in the text.

can. Obedience is rewarded and disobedience punished. In case of failure to obey, however, man has recourse to divinely ordained means of atonement, in all of which repentance is required. As long as he maintains his desire to stay in the covenant, he has a share in God's covenantal promises, including life in the world to come. The intention and effort to be obedient constitute the *condition for remaining in the covenant,* but they do not *earn* it. (180; italics original)

Thus, obedience to the law occurs within the context of covenant and election. It cannot be seen as exemplifying a universal human tendency, as argued by Luther and Bultmann, for it is specific to a particular tradition in which God and Israel are bound to one another within a covenantal relationship. To abstract law observance from that covenantal context is inevitably to misunderstand it.

If the Judaism Paul attacked is misunderstood by the Reformation tradition, this raises the possibility that Paul himself has been misunderstood.[57] In *Paul, the Law and the Jewish People* (1983), Sanders argues that this has indeed been the case. The Judaism attacked by Paul is not the Judaism of the Lutheran caricature but Judaism as it really was; Paul attacks "the traditional understanding of the covenant and election."[58] Sanders begins his work by listing four possible interpretations of Paul's exclusion of "works of the law" (17). The first and second he describes as the "quantitative" and "qualitative" views, the positions represented by Wilckens and Bultmann respectively. The third interpretation is that of Paul's "exclusivist soteriology," and the fourth view emphasizes the setting of the controversy in the Gentile mission (Stendahl). While Sanders is sympathetic to this fourth view,[59] his own posi-

---

57. The alternative would be that Paul misunderstood Judaism — the view of H.-J. Schoeps, who argues that "the Pauline doctrine of justification . . . stems from a partial aspect of the law wrongly isolated from the saving significance of the law as a whole" (*Paul: The Theology of the Apostle in the Light of Jewish Religious History,* 196). Thus, "[a] Christian who relied on Paul for information about the meaning and purpose of the Torah as an instrument of the Jewish covenant would receive a picture that was a complete travesty" (200).

58. Sanders, *Paul, the Law and the Jewish People,* 46. Page references to this book will be given parenthetically in the text. Cf. J. D. G. Dunn, "The New Perspective on Paul," 119: "What Jewish scholars rejected as *Paul's* misunderstanding of Judaism is *itself* a misunderstanding of Paul, based on the standard Protestant (mis)reading of Paul through Reformation spectacles."

59. Thus he can write, in terms that recall Stendahl: "The subject of Galatians is not whether or not humans, abstractly conceived, can by doing good deeds earn enough merit to be declared righteous at the judgment; it is the condition on which Gentiles enter the people of God" (*Paul, the Law and the Jewish People,* 18). Sanders later attempts to coordinate this emphasis on Gentile inclusion with his primary emphasis on christology. When Paul said, "not by works of law," he meant that "God intended that entry to the body of the saved be available to all

tion is that Paul opposes Jewish exclusiveness not with a universalistic gospel but with a different form of exclusiveness, based on christology. Salvation is in Christ alone, and therefore it cannot be by the law (i.e., by membership of the Jewish people): and that is the sole content of Paul's critique of Judaism. Paul does not argue that "*since* the law cannot be entirely fulfilled, *therefore* righteousness is by faith" (23), nor does he accuse the Jews of "self-righteousness" or "legalism" — that view is "mere eisegesis which rests on long and venerated (perhaps too venerated) tradition" (155). Paul claims simply that as God's way of salvation is through faith in Christ, Judaism is automatically disqualified. He can tell us nothing about Judaism unless we share his *a priori* christology.

The contrast in Philippians 3:9 between "my own righteousness" and "the righteousness from God which depends on faith" may serve as an example:

> Paul does not say that boasting in status and achievement was wrong because boasting is the wrong attitude, but that he boasted in things that *were gain*. They *became loss* because in his black and white world, there is no second best. His criticism of his own former life is not that he was guilty of the attitudinal sin of self-righteousness, but that he put confidence in something other than faith in Jesus Christ. (44)

Sanders seeks to show that both the "quantitative" view (i.e., the view that works are wrong because it is impossible to fulfill the law in its entirety) and the "qualitative" view (i.e., the view that to attempt to fulfill the law leads to the sin of boasting in one's own achievements) are false. Paul rejects the law not because of any inherent defects in its adherents but simply because it is something other than Christ.

H. Räisänen argues that Paul's statements about the law are so full of contradictions as to be completely incoherent. He draws attention to the "uncritical praise of Paul's thought"[60] that characterizes so much Protestant scholarship: "modern Paulinism" may be described as "the theological cult of the apostle" (15). Yet, as the profound disagreement between Käsemann and Cranfield shows, "the followers of the apostle have hardly ever been able to agree on what he really wanted to say" (3). The dilemma may be stated as follows:

---

on the basis of faith in Christ. This answer can be separated out into two: Christology and the status of the Gentiles; but the fundamental unity of Paul's revised outlook must be stressed" (*Paul, the Law and the Jewish People,* 47).

60. Räisänen, *Paul and the Law,* 7. Page references to this book will be given parenthetically in the text.

On the one hand, the clarity, profundity and cogency of Paul's theological thinking is universally praised. On the other hand, it does not seem possible to reach any unanimity whatever as to what his message really was. (4)

According to Räisänen, the inconsistencies are almost endless. For example, the meaning of νόμος is often unclear; Paul may be referring to the law or to something else, and the meaning may shift even within a single passage. Paul holds that the law is abrogated but that its "decree" (Rom. 8:4) is still in force. He teaches that nobody can fulfill the law but that some non-Christian Gentiles do so. The law was given to bring "life" (Rom. 7:10), but it never had even the theoretical power to do so (Rom. 8:3; Gal. 3:21). The law was a temporary addition to the divine testament (Gal. 3:15-18), and yet a dramatic act of liberation from its power was needed (Gal. 3:13). Paul's scriptural exegesis is often arbitrary, and his view that the law calls forth sin is incredible.[61] Contrary to the common view that there is a fundamental change of stance between the polemic against the law in Galatians and the calmer and more positive tone of Romans, the real problem is the deep contradictions *within* each letter.[62] In Romans 1–3, the commonplace observation that "many live in grave sins" leads to the sweeping generalization that "all are under sin," which is "a blatant *non sequitur.*"[63] Indeed, Romans 2 is "simply a piece of propagandist denigration" *(Paul and the Law,* 101). Attempts to interpret it as a profound piece of theology are unconvincing. If this approach seems unduly negative, Räisänen's response is that a corrective is needed, since Paul is still so widely regarded as theologically authoritative.[64]

The work of Stendahl, Davies, Sanders, and Räisänen is symptomatic of a widespread dissatisfaction with the Lutheran approach to Paul. This is also apparent in the work of such scholars as M. Barth, G. Howard, J. D. G. Dunn, N. T. Wright, and (perhaps most significantly) in the important three-volume commentary on Romans by U. Wilckens.[65] The process of "purging Paul from Lutheran contaminations" (H.-J. Schoeps)[66] is already well under way. But there is as yet no consensus as to the new image of the apostle that is to replace the Lutheran one.

---

61. Räisänen, "Paul's Theological Difficulties with the Law," 304-5.
62. Räisänen, "Paul's Theological Difficulties with the Law," 302.
63. Räisänen, "Paul's Theological Difficulties with the Law," 309-10.
64. Räisänen, *Paul and the Law,* 14-15.
65. See the Bibliography for details.
66. *Paul: the Theology of the Apostle in the Light of Jewish Religious History,* 197.

3. A Sociological Approach

The scholars discussed in the previous section have criticized the "Lutheran" reading of Paul from a number of different points of view.[67] One problem that arises again and again in different forms is the relation between Paul's historical situation and his theology. The Lutheran or neo-Lutheran reading assumes that the permanent essence of the Christian gospel is to be found in Paul's teaching about justification and the law, which no doubt arose in a concrete historical situation but which must now be interpreted existentially, in relative abstraction from its historical origins. Even historically conscious scholars such as Bultmann and Käsemann argue for the legitimacy of this approach.

In opposition to this isolation of theology from context, the present discussion will adopt a sociological perspective in order to examine how Paul's theorizing is related to the concrete problems that he faced — in particular, the problems of the legitimacy of the law-free gospel for the Gentiles, and the status of the Jewish people. As we shall see, *the social reality underlying Paul's discussions of Judaism and the law is his creation of Gentile Christian communities in sharp distinction from the Jewish community. His theological reflection legitimates the separation of church from synagogue.*

Two sociological models will be used to shed light on this process; they will be presented in more detail in the final section of the following chapter. The first is *the transformation of a reform movement into a sect.*[68] New religious movements (including earliest Christianity) often begin as reform movements within an existing religious community (in this case, the Jewish community). When opposition is encountered, one possibility is that the reform movement will be transformed into a sect — i.e., a closely knit group that erects clearly defined barriers between itself and the parent community. It will be argued that this is an appropriate model for studying Paul's creation of congregations separated from a Jewish community based on institutions such as temple and synagogue. This means, for example, that the Galatian

---

67. On this see further R. Jewett, "Major Impulses in the Theological Interpretation of Romans since Barth," who shows that the ecumenical dialogue is the background to the work of Stendahl and Wilckens, whereas the dialogue with Judaism is important for Davies and Sanders.

68. This model is applied to Luke-Acts by Philip Esler, *Community and Gospel in Luke-Acts,* 65-70. Esler notes that despite the sociological interest in the development of "sects" into "churches" (H. R. Niebuhr), little work has been done on the development of reform movements into sects (50-51). He does, however, draw attention to a study of contemporary African churches that identifies "the recurrent features which characterize the passage of a reform movement within a church to an independent religious group, sectarian in nature" (52). Unlike Esler, I myself make no use of cross-cultural analogies.

controversy may be interpreted as a controversy about the nature of the church: should it continue to exist as a reform movement within the Jewish community (the view of Paul's opponents), or should it take sectarian form, clearly differentiated from the Jewish community (Paul's own view)?

The second sociological model follows from the first. If a sectarian group is to establish and maintain separation from the religious body from which it originated, it will require *an ideology legitimating its state of separation* — i.e., a theoretical justification for its separate existence, which is shared by all the group's members and which helps to maintain its cohesion.[69] This may involve, first, a *denunciation* of the group's opponents; second, the use of *antitheses,* of which the positive member (e.g., light, truth) characterizes the group's members, whereas the negative member (e.g., darkness, error) characterizes the community from which the group seeks to distance itself; and third, a *reinterpretation* of the religious traditions of the community as a whole, in the light of the belief that the sectarian group is the sole legitimate heir to those traditions. It will be argued that this is an appropriate model for interpreting Paul's theoretical reflections on Judaism and the law.

The purpose of this sociological approach is to emphasize *the close link between Paul's socio-historical context and his theological reflection:* the first model (the transformation of a reform movement into a sect) is concerned with the context as such, whereas the second model (the theoretical rationale for sectarian separation) is concerned to reread the text in the light of this construal of its context.[70] It will be argued that the social context of Paul's theology is his creation and maintaining of sectarian groups consisting largely though not exclusively of Gentiles, and separated from the Jewish community.[71] It is impor-

69. Compare Esler, *Community and Gospel,* 16-17: "Legitimation is the collection of ways in which an institution is explained and justified to its members."

70. Compare Bengt Holmberg's comments on the change of perspective required in Pauline research *(Paul,* 205). Discussing "the fallacy of idealism," he writes: "Idealism in historical research can be roughly described as the view that the determining factors of the historical process are ideas and nothing else, and that all developments, conflicts and influences are at bottom developments of, and conflicts and influences between ideas." Unconscious idealism may be traced in the work of Bultmann, Käsemann, and others. Great care is taken over historical research, "but the methodologically fateful step comes with the next stage of the work, where the historical phenomena are often interpreted as being directly formed by underlying theological structures." Paul's theology is in fact "a secondary reaction" to "primary, concrete phenomena in the social world." Holmberg's primary/secondary distinction need not exclude theology as such from the primary phenomena of the social world, if it is emphasized that "Paul's theology" exists for us only in his texts.

71. The term "theology" is retained here, alongside "ideology." J. H. Elliott advocates a move "beyond theology to ideology" (*A Home for the Homeless,* 267), on the grounds that,

tant to state that, in criticizing the Lutheran account, this approach does not claim to exclude the possibility of *any* theological interpretation of Paul. It is obvious that Paul's letters can legitimately be interpreted from a number of different standpoints.[72] This approach simply claims that one particular theological interpretation of Paul, derived from Luther, misunderstands at crucial points what the historical Paul was doing and saying.

How does the present account relate to the work of other scholars who have expressed dissatisfaction with the Lutheran approach? It endorses Baur's stress on the relationship between Paul's theological reflection and his historical activity, and it has affinities with his contrast between Pauline universalism and Jewish exclusiveness. But the latter view is not entirely satisfactory. In broad historical terms, it is no doubt true that, by "emancipating" Christianity from its origins within the Jewish community, Paul did enable it to transform itself into a "world religion." To that extent the contrast between universality and exclusiveness is justified. But it is also true that this was not what Paul himself had in mind. His eschatological expectations make it impossible that he should have foreseen or intended the way in which Christianity gradually extended its influence throughout the Roman empire until it became the official state religion, thus attaining a universality denied to Judaism. The term "exclusiveness" is in some ways more applicable to the sectarian groups created by Paul himself than it is to the Jewish community. If in one sense it is true that Paul sought to break down the barrier between Jew and Gentile, he nevertheless did so only to reestablish a new form of exclusiveness.[73]

Stendahl's renewal of Baur's insight into the relationship between Paul's theological reflection and his historical situation is to be welcomed, as is his clear perception that this is incompatible with conventional Lutheran ac-

---

"[w]hereas the 'theology' of a given author or document usually implies, or can be taken to imply, a conceptual framework which is separable or even isolated from the social matrix within which and for which it was formulated, the matter of a document's 'ideological' character does not allow such a separation. In fact, it presumes the opposite; namely, an interrelation and inseparability of social and religious frames of reference, meaning and function" (268). Elliott's terminological recommendation should be rejected, however. While "Pauline theology" is indeed often treated in abstraction from its social matrix, to abandon the term "theology" is actually to acquiesce in this usage.

72. Compare G. Theissen, "The Sociological Interpretation of Religious Traditions," 195.

73. Nils Dahl rightly criticizes "the common but simplistic notion of a contrast between Christian universalism and Jewish particularism. . . . Jewish monotheism at the time of Paul was universalistic in its own way, and Christian monotheism remained exclusive." "The One God of Jews and Gentiles (Rom. 3:29-30)," 191. Compare Sanders, *Paul, the Law and the Jewish People,* 160.

counts. But Stendahl fails to make the crucial point that Paul's view of the rights of Gentiles involved the separation of the church from the Jewish community. The debate is not simply concerned with the rights of Gentiles to enter the church, but with the nature of the church itself: should it continue as a reform movement within Judaism or become a sect over against it?

This view, with its stress on separation from Judaism, is difficult to reconcile with the view of W. D. Davies and others that Paul remained a loyal though misunderstood Jew. On the present view, Paul *criticized* fellow Christians who wished to remain loyal members of the Jewish community, insisting that the gospel required the formation of a distinct Christian identity over against Judaism. However liberal and fluid first-century Judaism may perhaps have been, most Jews would not have tolerated the claim that non–law observant Gentiles were accepted by God, whereas Jews who remained faithful to the Torah were rejected. Davies rightly sees in Paul's letters a "family dispute" about the true meaning of the shared Jewish tradition, but overlooks the potential for division and alienation precisely when disputes occur within the family.

Räisänen emphasizes the inconsistencies in Paul's discussions of the law, not only between Galatians and Romans (which would suggest development in Paul's thought — the view of Hübner and others), but also within Romans and Galatians themselves. The present treatment sees the cohesiveness of Paul's statements about the law not primarily at the theoretical level but at the level of practical strategy. It will be argued that Paul's primary aim in discussing Judaism and the law is to maintain and defend his congregations' distinctive identity over against the Jewish community. In fulfilling this aim, he makes use of various types of theoretical legitimation, which may not always be compatible with one another at the theoretical level, but which all contribute to the same pragmatic goal. In other words, in studying the Pauline texts, one should ask not simply about what Paul is *saying,* but also about what he is *doing.*[74] Arguably, what Räisänen has achieved is a *reductio ad absurdum* of the purely theoretical approach to Pauline discourse. Reconnecting Paul's discourse to social reality as he construes it will result in a more sympathetic account of his achievement.

The present discussion will seek to develop further two of the ideas stressed by Sanders. The first is the claim that the fundamental category of the Judaism that Paul opposed is not an allegedly universal error of seeking to earn salvation, but rather the covenantal relationship between God and Israel.

---

74. Compare W. Meeks, *First Urban Christians,* 142 (with specific reference to "the rituals mentioned in the Pauline letters").

The second is the claim that Paul does not oppose Judaism because of any theoretical shortcomings it may or may not have, but simply because it is not Christianity. Paul's "*a priori* christology" is the theological correlate of his equally *a priori,* non-negotiable insistence on the separation of Christian community and synagogue. That is the social reality underlying the Pauline antithesis of Christ and law.

Common to these two claims are the concepts of *particularity* and *incommensurability.* In the last resort, Pauline antithesis juxtaposes terms that represent modes of communal life that are simply and irreducibly different. One is oriented towards the law of Moses, the text that attests the unique election and vocation of the Jewish people. The other is oriented towards Christ, in whose exaltation to universal lordship Jews and Gentiles alike find salvation. Moses and Christ are particular, concrete figures, not symbols representing human achievement and its renunciation, or exclusiveness and inclusiveness. It is true, and indeed important, that comparisons may be made between the two communities: they are not simply identical in their understanding of divine in relation to human agency, or in their attitude towards Gentiles. Yet these comparisons or contrasts can be drawn only on the ground of a fundamental incommensurability between the law of Moses and the gospel of Christ as the basis for communal life. The difference cannot be reduced to an abstract propositional form in which the names of Moses and Christ have been replaced by mutually exclusive general principles. As Paul himself notes in Romans 10, Moses wrote a text that sought to define the way to righteousness, whereas Christ bestows righteousness by way of the faith elicited by the gospel, faith in his own resurrection and universal lordship. Comparisons between the two may be ventured. One is oriented towards a written text, the other towards an oral proclamation. One implies a more static view of the divine-human relationship, the other a more dynamic view. With careful qualification, such comparisons are not without value; Paul himself can sometimes make them explicit. Yet they do not exhaust the difference between the events of Sinai and of Easter. A community that identifies God by way of the one will differ fundamentally from a community that does so by way of the other, and the specific contrasts that may also come to light will illustrate that difference but will not in themselves be able to account for it.

An unexpected consequence of this perspective on Paul's texts is that it is no longer necessary to choose between the readings represented by Luther and Baur. Both readings see in Paul's antitheses an opposition between two mutually exclusive principles, relating to divine and human agency in the one case, universality and exclusiveness in the other. And both readings need to be rather drastically relativized, since they reduce Pauline antithesis to a common denominator and fail to grasp the incommensurability of patterns of communal life oriented towards two distinct and irreducible particularities: the law of Moses, the gospel of Christ. Yet the present account can in principle accommodate elements of both contrasts, if they are subordinated to the fundamental disjunction between Moses and Christ, and if they are stated in suitably qualified and nuanced form. It cannot plausibly be denied that in Pauline usage "grace" highlights a particular form of divine agency, whereas "works" highlights a particular form of human agency. Nor can it be denied that these terms are also correlated with relatively inclusive or exclusive attitudes towards non-Jews. Indeed, any number of further contrasts might be added, relating perhaps to scriptural interpretation, or to textuality as such, or to status, gender, or the body. Such contrasts and comparisons all arise out of Paul's assertion of two irreducibly different communal identities, and there is no need to choose between them. Perhaps surprisingly, particularity proves more accommodating than abstraction.

In the chapters that form Part One of this work, we shall begin by seeking to reconstruct the historical and ideological origins of Pauline Gentile communities. In the story that emerges from the fragmentary evidence of Acts and the Pauline letters, an original "reform movement" within Palestinian Judaism begins to redefine itself in "sectarian" terms, finding its identity in opposition to the majority community (Chapter 2). While Paul regards the difference as non-negotiable, it remains a construct — *his own* construct — which he both defends and further develops in opposition to fellow Christians who take a different view, in Galatians (Chapter 3) and Philippians (Chapter 4). The sociological models introduced above will shape the presentation of all this material and will make it possible to reconceptualize the issues underlying these texts. Paul's texts remain opaque so long as their pragmatic dimension is overlooked. In them, speech is *action* that intends specific and identifiable social goals.

PART ONE

Jewish Law and Gentile Mission

CHAPTER 2

The Origins of Paul's View of the Law

If we are to understand Paul's view of the law and of Judaism, our starting point should not be the complex theoretical discussions of the law found in his letters, but the situation in the history of the early church that gave rise to these discussions. There is an obvious link between Paul's statements about the law and his mission to Gentiles, and this suggests that the origins of the former are to be found in the origins of the latter.[1] In this chapter, we shall investigate the development of mission to Gentiles out of a prior mission to Jews and the corresponding reassessment of the law. As we shall see in the final part of this chapter, the historical reconstruction may be analyzed in sociological terms with the help of the reform movement/sect typology and the concept of legitimation. Pauline Gentile mission moves out of the sphere of the synagogue in order to establish Christian communities with a distinctive identity in relation to "Judaism." What must be recovered in this chapter is the logic or rationale of this fateful Pauline move.[2]

In setting up the issue in this way, I make a number of initial assumptions:

(1) Paul's appeal to his divine calling (Gal. 1:15-17) does not provide a sufficient explanation of the origins of his Gentile mission. In particular, it cannot be used to rule out the possibility that Pauline missionary strat-

---

1. Martin Hengel rightly states: "The *Sitz im Leben* of Paul's theology is the mission of the Apostle to the Gentiles" ("Die Ursprünge der christlichen Mission," 37).

2. In this chapter, chapter 2 of *PJG¹* has been substantially reworked throughout, although its basic framework has been retained.

egy (and the accompanying ideological legitimation) developed in response to contingent factors encountered in the practice of mission. As we shall see, Paul's own statements do not require us to conclude that the entire future direction of his life and thought was disclosed to him in an instant, on the Damascus Road.

(2) Mission to the Gentiles does not follow inevitably or even plausibly from a relaxed or a radical attitude towards the law.[3] Even if it could be shown that such attitudes existed within the Jesus movement, pre- and/or post-resurrection, that would not in itself produce a Gentile mission.

(3) It is *a priori* plausible that Paul's Gentile mission and his relativizing of the Torah developed in conjunction with each other, and that his statements about the Torah thus have a social correlate. This also corresponds to the nature of the evidence, since Paul's Gentile mission long predates the extant texts in which his statements about the Torah are to be found. To make this point is *not* to assign to "social reality" a priority and a determining role in relation to "theology" — as though theology did not already belong to social reality. It is simply to say that we should expect to find correlations between the two.[4]

(4) The Gentile mission cannot be explained on the basis of ideological factors distinctive to Paul as an individual.[5] Paul's activity is both constrained and enabled by the realities of its sociohistorical context.

(5) In seeking a historical reconstruction of the origins of the Gentile mission, the evidence of both Paul and Acts must be used and critically assessed. At the very least, the author of Acts is greatly preoccupied with this issue, and his account may be highly instructive even where its relation to actual historical occurrences seems tenuous or hard to determine. We should abandon the assumption that "the historicity of Acts" is an unproblematic concept that may be either asserted or denied.[6]

3. Contra G. Theissen, who writes: "Sooner or later, relativizing the Law, which began within the Jesus movement, was *bound to* relativize the distinction between Gentile and Jew" ("Legitimation and Subsistence: An Essay on the Sociology of Early Christian Missionaries," 35; italics added).

4. In *PJG¹* there is an occasional lack of methodological clarity about this issue, which led some critics to focus on the alleged "reduction" of theology to sociology and to ignore the argument for *correlating* theology and social reality that lies at the heart of the book.

5. Compare Räisänen's seven possible explanations for the origin of Paul's view of the law (*Paul and the Law*, 229-63): (1) Paul's experience under the law; (2) application of a current Jewish idea; (3) influence of scriptural prophecy; (4) influence of Jesus traditions; (5) meditation on Deuteronomy 21:23; (6) influence of Hellenists; (7) missionary experience and conflict with Judaizers. The first five of these explanations identify factors individual to Paul.

6. I make this point self-critically, since the treatment of Acts in chapter 2 of *PJG¹* is shaped

(6) Sociological models should be used retrospectively and flexibly, to assist the analysis of historical data and not to fill in gaps in our knowledge of historical causation. Pauline Gentile mission cannot be *explained* by reference to sociological laws, since quasi-natural laws simply do not exist in the social sphere. If, more cautiously, one claimed to identify a sociological *tendency* — for example, the supposed tendency of groups that experience disconfirmation of core beliefs to engage in aggressive proselytism[7] — that would at best represent an observed pattern and not an explanation of any particular instance. While a sociologically informed analysis might also identify broad historical *preconditions* for Pauline Gentile mission, this would again tell us nothing about causation.[8]

The contingent historical factors that occasioned Pauline Gentile mission are elusive and hard to identify, since adequate evidence is not forthcoming. Any concrete proposal will be part conjecture and is sure to be contested. Yet it is worth persevering with this issue, since a successful account has the potential to illuminate aspects of Paul's theology that otherwise remain deeply puzzling.

1. The Evidence of Acts

(i) The Cornelius Episode

One version of the origins of the Gentile mission is to be found in the lengthy account of the conversion of Cornelius in Acts 10:1–11:18. Unlike the otherwise comparable conversion story in Acts 8:26-40, this one is intended to have a paradigmatic significance: what is being described is not an isolated event but the origin of the Gentile mission, to whose progress much of the rest of Acts is devoted. This is clear from 11:18, where those who had initially opposed Peter's conduct confess that "to the Gentiles also God has granted repentance unto life."[9] Likewise, in Acts 15 Peter's reference to this event serves to justify

---

by this assumption. For an attempt to overcome the naïve account of "historicity" that is so deeply entrenched in biblical scholarship, see my *Text and Truth*, 33-69.

7. I here allude to John Gager's unsuccessful attempt to apply a sociological model derived from L. Festinger to early Christian history (*Kingdom and Community*, 37-49).

8. Compare Theissen's suggestion that the Roman empire required a transcending of individual ethnic identity, and that "[r]eligious movements that were well suited to break through the frontiers dividing peoples and cultures were in line with an objective task with which this society was faced" (*Social Reality and the Earliest Christians*, 221).

9. On this, see E. Haenchen, *Acts*, 359-60.

the preaching activity of Paul and Barnabas among the Gentiles: Peter reminds his audience how

> in the early days God chose among you, that through my mouth the Gentiles should hear the word of the gospel and believe; and God who knows the heart bore witness to them, giving the Holy Spirit to them just as to us. (Acts 15:7-8)

Luke here emphasizes that the origins of the Gentile mission are to be found in the conversion of Cornelius, and a discussion of this topic must take this narrative into account.

The story appears to be in some tension with Galatians 2:7-9, where Peter is seen not as the pioneer of the Gentile mission but as one entrusted with a mission to other Jews.[10] But it might be argued that, although Luke has heightened the significance of the conversion of Cornelius, this narrative nevertheless preserves genuine historical reminiscences that provide valuable information about the origins of the Gentile mission. That is the position of Dibelius, who claims that two parts of the narrative stem from pre-Lucan historical tradition: Peter's vision and the conversion of a God-fearing Gentile.[11] Dibelius believes that these two parts of the narrative were originally separate, on the grounds that the vision (10:9-16) tells of the abolition of the food laws, whereas 10:28 (cf. 11:12) applies it not to food but to humans: "God has shown me that I should not call *any person* common or unclean."[12] Dibelius further suggests that this vision may have been used by Peter or his supporters to justify his abandonment of the food laws at Antioch (Gal. 2:12). As regards the conversion of the God-fearing Gentile centurion, Dibelius concludes that it reproduces historical events, though in the style of a "legend." He writes: "We must assume that there was a period of time . . . during which such isolated cases [i.e., of the conversion of Gentiles] could have occurred, by chance and not in order to defend a principle."[13] In that case, Luke would have heightened the significance of this story, but this and other similar incidents would remain an important preliminary to the fully fledged Gentile mission.

Yet it is not clear that a pre-Lucan Cornelius tradition can confidently be identified in Acts 10. It is Luke himself who elsewhere shows a special interest

---

10. Haenchen, *Acts*, 360-61.

11. M. Dibelius, "The Conversion of Cornelius," *passim*. F. Hahn agrees that it is possible to recover an earlier narrative underlying Acts 10 (*Mission in the New Testament*, 52); this is denied by Haenchen, *Acts*, 360-62.

12. Dibelius, "The Conversion of Cornelius," 111-12.

13. Dibelius, "The Conversion of Cornelius," 121-22.

in devout centurions.[14] In his account of the healing of the centurion's servant, he adds a reference to "Jewish elders" who here convey the centurion's request to Jesus, and who testify that "he loves our nation and built our synagogue" (Luke 7:4-5).[15] The devout centurion of Capernaum corresponds closely to Cornelius of Caesarea, "a righteous and God-fearing man, commended by the whole Jewish nation" (Acts 10:22; cf. vv. 2, 4).[16] In addition, the link between Cornelius's piety and his angelophany finds an antecedent in Luke 1:8-23 (Zechariah's vision in the temple). Common features include a stress on the previous piety of the recipients of the angelophany (Luke 1:6, 13; Acts 10:2, 4), the occurrence of the angelophany during worship (Luke 1:8-11; Acts 10:3), the recipient's initial response of fear (Luke 1:12; Acts 10:4), and several features of the angel's address: use of the recipient's name (Luke 1:13; Acts 10:3), reference to previous piety (Luke 1:13; Acts 10:4), and announcement of its future consequences (Luke 1:13; Acts 10:5-6).[17] These common features suggest that in its present form the Cornelius story is a Lucan composition. If it contains pre-Lucan tradition, as it may do, this can no longer be identified as such.

As for Peter's vision (10:9-16; cf. 10:28; 11:2-12), Dibelius argues that it fits the situation presupposed in Galatians 2:12 better than its present literary context in Acts: Peter appealed to this vision to explain his disregard of dietary laws at Antioch. But a vision that features a command to "kill and eat" every kind of animal, reptile, and bird (Acts 10:12-13; 11:6) does not obviously relate to actual dietary practice. The use of animals to symbolize humans (10:28; 11:12) is not a serious enough difficulty to justify detaching the vision from its present literary context.[18] In addition, it is not clear that Peter actu-

---

14. This motif exemplifies Luke's generally favorable attitude towards Roman authority. P. Walaskay argues that Luke's political aim is not so much to commend the church to the Roman authorities (the traditional view) as to commend the empire to the church (*"And So We Came to Rome," passim*). Thus, the point of the concluding chapters of Acts is that "divine necessity brings Paul and the gospel to Rome under the aegis of Roman law" (58). In Acts 27:42-44, Julius's action on Paul's behalf shows that "the gospel was rescued by Rome" (62). Commending the empire to the church and the church to the empire are not incompatible, however.

15. *Pace* I. H. Marshall, *Luke*, 277-78, it seems clear that Luke 7:2-5 represents a (somewhat artificial) Lucan expansion of a narrative whose original opening is preserved in Matthew 8:5-6.

16. In conjunction with Acts 10:34-35, this statement would seem to support S. G. Wilson's argument that Luke justifies the salvation of the Gentiles on the pragmatic grounds that they are just as capable of piety as are Jews (*The Gentiles and the Gentile Mission in Luke-Acts*, 245).

17. Elsewhere, angels release the apostles and later Peter from prison (Acts 5:19-20; 12:7-11), guide Philip to the Ethiopian eunuch (8:26), and assure Paul of his safety when threatened with shipwreck (27:23-24).

18. So Wilson, *The Gentiles and the Gentile Mission*, 174. For the view that the vision is a Lucan composition, see Haenchen, *Acts*, 362.

ally did disregard the dietary code in eating with Gentiles at Antioch, as Dibelius assumes. What is at issue at Antioch is not the diet but the company: Peter is in the habit of eating with uncircumcised Gentiles.[19] The ensuing controversy is echoed in Acts 11:2-3, where οἱ ἐκ περιτομῆς criticize Peter for eating with the uncircumcised (cf. Gal. 2:12). In Galatians, Peter is persuaded to withdraw from table fellowship with Gentiles. In Acts, on the other hand, he defends his conduct by appealing to a vision in which the command to slaughter unclean animals corresponds to the requirement to associate with Gentiles, with a view to their conversion (11:4-12). The vision is fully integrated into the narrative. The historical kernel of the Cornelius story may consist simply in the recollection that, at Antioch and perhaps elsewhere, Peter for a while practiced table fellowship with Gentiles.

It is therefore not possible to show that independent traditions relating to the origins of the Gentile mission are preserved in Acts 10:1–11:18. Luke's purpose is to vindicate the Gentile mission and the churches that it brought into being by tracing it back ultimately not to the questionable authority of Paul[20] but to the unquestioned authority of Peter and to unmistakable supernatural signs of divine guidance (cf. Acts 15:6-12).[21]

(ii) The Origins of the Antiochene Church

Yet Luke also provides a second account of the origins of the Gentile mission. In Acts 11:19-21, he tells how some of those driven out of Jerusalem by Saul's ferocious persecution took the momentous step of preaching the gospel to non-Jews:

> Now those who were scattered by the persecution that arose over Stephen travelled as far as Phoenicia and Cyprus and Antioch, speaking the word only to Jews. But there were some of them, men of Cyprus and Cyrene, who came to Antioch and spoke also to the Greeks, preaching the Lord Jesus. And the hand of the Lord was with them, and a large number believed and turned to the Lord.[22]

19. So P. Esler, *Galatians*, 135-38.
20. On the significance of anti-Pauline tendencies for the purpose of Acts, see J. Jervell, *Luke and the People of God*, 146-47, 153-54; S. G. Wilson, *Luke and the Law*, 106-12.
21. "As Luke presents them, these divine incursions have such compelling force that all doubt in the face of them *must* be stilled" (Haenchen, *Acts*, 362).
22. Even if the original reading in v. 20 was Ἑλληνιστάς rather than Ἕλληνας, the contrast with "to Jews only" (v. 19) would make a reference to Gentiles certain (in contrast to the usage of

Luke proceeds to tell how Barnabas was sent from Jerusalem to assess the situation, how he and the newly converted Saul took over the leadership of the mixed Antiochene church, and how it was at Antioch that the term "Christian" was coined (Acts 11:22-26). Broadly speaking, Luke's account harmonizes with Galatians 2, where Paul and Barnabas again appear to be leading representatives of a church that includes significant numbers of Gentiles in its midst.

How are we to envisage this decision to proclaim the gospel "also to the Greeks"? Elsewhere, Luke assumes that the initial point of contact between non-Jews and the Christian gospel is the synagogue: there the gospel is preached, and Greeks as well as Jews are in attendance. Thus Paul's sermon in Pisidian Antioch is addressed not only to ἄνδρες Ἰσραηλῖται but also to οἱ φοβούμενοι τὸν θεόν (Acts 13:16; cf. v. 26). Its outcome is that πολλοὶ τῶν Ἰουδαίων καὶ τῶν σεβομένων προσηλύτων become adherents of Paul and Barnabas, so that the initial congregation in this location is formed from a Jewish and Gentile nucleus previously associated with the synagogue. Similarly, when the gospel is preached in the synagogue at Iconium, it is accepted by "a large number of Jews and also Greeks" (14:1). When Paul and his companions visit a προσευχή at Philippi on the sabbath, they attract to the faith a woman named Lydia, who is characterized both by her business interests and by the fact that she is a "worshipper of God [σεβομένη τὸν θεόν]" (16:13-14). In the synagogue of Thessalonica, Paul persuades Jews but also τῶν σεβομένων Ἑλλήνων πλῆθος πολύ, including "not a few" women of high social standing (17:4; cf. v. 12). At Corinth, Paul "argued in the synagogue every sabbath, and persuaded Jews and Greeks" (18:4). For Luke, non-Jews initially encounter the gospel through participation in the worship of the synagogue. A "mixed" church is therefore a natural offshoot of a "mixed" synagogue, and a mixed synagogue is itself a natural product of a mixed population. In a situation of religious pluralism, some "Greeks" may be attracted by the beliefs and practices of the "Jews" who live and worship in their midst. Luke's view is confirmed by Josephus, speaking precisely about Antioch, who states that the sizable and wealthy Jewish community there was "constantly drawing large numbers of Greeks [πολὺ πλῆθος Ἑλλήνων] to their acts of worship" (*BJ* 7.45).[23] It is true that the "Greeks" (or "Hellenists") who hear the gospel in Acts 11:20 are not explicitly linked to the synagogue, probably because Luke wishes his readers to suppose that the evangelists from Cyprus and Cyrene

---

6:1; 9:29). "Hellenists" here would refer to Syrians who had adopted the Greek way of life. On this issue, see C. K. Barrett, *Acts*, 1:550-51.

23. Note also the presence of a προσήλυτος Ἀντιοχεύς among the seven "deacons" (Acts 6:5).

took a conscious decision to preach to them. Yet the Antiochene synagogues remain the obvious point of contact between the gospel and the Gentiles.

Luke states that the "men of Cyprus and Cyrene" converted Greeks as well as Jews simply because "the hand of the Lord was with them" (11:21). He does not attribute to them any distinctive ideological position. Yet, according to Martin Hengel, a different story emerges if we probe beneath the surface of his account. In reality, Hengel argues, the "men of Cyprus and Cyrene" preached to Gentiles on the basis of the radical theological stance associated with Stephen and his circle. In Acts 6:1, Luke tells of a dispute between the "Hellenists" and the "Hebrews" in the Jerusalem church over the distribution of food, and it may be that Luke here conceals a significant theological disagreement. It has been noted that the seven individuals named in 6:5 all have Greek names and so probably belonged to the Hellenist party.[24] The only two whose activities are described — Stephen and Philip — are seen not as welfare officers, as 6:2-3 would lead us to expect, but as preachers (6:8–8:40), precisely the function supposedly reserved for the apostles alone (6:2-4). Thus (Hengel argues), the seven were leaders of a Greek-speaking wing of the Jerusalem church that was to a large extent independent of the Aramaic-speaking wing, led by the apostles. Even if it was language rather than theology that initially caused the Hellenists to separate from the Hebrews, they soon developed a radical theological stance, calling for "the eschatological abolition of Temple worship and the revision of the law of Moses in the light of the true will of God."[25] Although Luke portrays Paul's persecution as affecting the whole church (Acts 8:1), it is more likely that it affected only the Hellenists (74). It was their dispersal that eventually led them to preach to the Gentiles:

> The "Hellenists," driven out of Jewish Palestine, were gradually forced to go beyond the circle of full Jews and also to turn to Gentiles who were interested in Judaism; in other words, they paved the way for a mission to the Gentiles, which in the end had to mean disregarding the law. (75)

> It is very probable that Philip and other "Hellenists" . . . gradually and step by step went over to a mission to the Gentiles which did not involve the law: in the first instance, this "freedom from the law" will have been a matter of ignoring the requirement for circumcision and the demands of the ritual law. (79)

---

24. M. Hengel, *Acts and the History of Earliest Christianity*, 71; similar reconstructions are found in Haenchen, *Acts*, 266-69; G. Bornkamm, *Paul*, 13-14.

25. Hengel, *Acts and the History of Earliest Christianity*, 72-73. Page references to this book are given parenthetically in the text.

Thus, although the abandonment of circumcision and the whole ritual law was no doubt a gradual process, this decision was already implicit in the criticism of the law developed by the Hellenists on the basis of Jesus' own view of the law (72). For Hengel, the Hellenists bridge the gap between Jesus and Paul. In Antioch, then, these Hellenist preachers to Gentiles were motivated by a proto-Pauline theology according to which major elements of the law "had become insignificant for ultimate salvation" (89). The law-free Gentile mission was a natural and inevitable outcome of this prior theological commitment.

Hengel's reconstruction of the origins of the Gentile mission is problematic, however. Together with the majority of scholars, he does not believe that Stephen's speech in Acts 7 gives reliable information about the Hellenists' theology,[26] and the hypothesis of the Hellenists' radical view of the law must therefore rest entirely on the accusation directed against Stephen: "This man never ceases to speak words against this holy place and the law; for we have heard him say that Jesus of Nazareth will destroy this place, and will change the customs which Moses delivered to us" (Acts 6:13-14). Hengel must assume that Luke's version of the accusation against Stephen is authentic, but that its attribution to "false witnesses" is not.[27] In addition, the accusation speaks of the abolition of temple worship and the revision of the law *only at the Parousia;* until that occurs, the law presumably remains unchanged. The accusation therefore gives no basis for supposing that the Hellenists adopted a radical attitude towards the present practice of the law. In any case, Luke seems to have modeled the accusation on the charge against Jesus recorded in Mark 14:58. "False witnesses" report, "We heard him say, 'I will destroy this temple that is made with hands, and in three days I will build another, not made with hands.'" Luke omits this accusation from his account of Jesus' trial (Luke 22:66-71) and makes it the basis of Stephen's trial instead.[28] The main evidence for the hypothesis of the Hellenists' radical view of the law is therefore precarious.[29]

---

26. The historicity of Stephen's speech is asserted by M. Simon, *St Stephen,* 39-40; also by M. H. Scharlemann, for whom Stephen was "a theological genius who had grasped the divisive effect of the temple in Jerusalem," thereby showing his "insight into the problem of the Samaritans" (*Stephen: A Singular Saint,* 56). J. C. O'Neill rightly opposes commentators on Acts 7 who "have hoped to discover an esoteric theology in the seemingly harmless details of O.T. history" (*The Theology of Acts in Its Historical Setting,* 79).

27. G. N. Stanton, "Stephen in Lucan Perspective," 347, rightly emphasizes that Luke intends 6:11-14 as the accusations of false witnesses.

28. So Haenchen, *Acts,* 274.

29. There seems little evidence that "Stephen and the Hellenists must have challenged orthodox Judaism on a sensitive and fundamental point" (Wilson, *Gentile Mission,* 146). As Barrett emphasizes, "it was not Stephen's Hellenism but Stephen's Christianity that (in Luke's view) provoked opposition" (*Acts,* 1:320).

Indeed, it seems doubtful that the foundation of the mixed church of Antioch should be traced specifically to "Hellenists" from Jerusalem. The supposed tensions between "Hebrews" and "Hellenists" may simply reflect later tensions between Jerusalem and Antioch, retrojected back into the earliest days of the Jerusalem church. Additionally, or alternatively, Luke's presentation of the origins of the Gentile mission may reflect his emphasis on the centrality of Jerusalem.[30] All the main protagonists in the Gentile mission originate in Jerusalem: not only Peter, Philip, and Paul, but also the anonymous men from Cyprus and Cyrene (11:20), Barnabas (4:36-47; 11:22-24), John Mark (12:12, 25), and Silas (15:22, 27, 40). This fits the program outlined in Acts 1:8, but the historical reality may have been more complex.

The relevance of Jerusalem "Hellenists" in the origins of the Gentile mission becomes still more doubtful in the light of Luke's own understanding of this term. According to 9:29, when Paul came to Jerusalem soon after his conversion, he disputed with "Hellenists," who sought to kill him. These people are probably to be identified with the Jews from Cyrene, Alexandria, Cilicia, and Asia who disputed with Stephen (6:9), in his case successfully bringing about his death.[31] In other words, "Hellenists" are for Luke neither Gentiles,[32] nor Jews with a lax attitude towards the law,[33] nor even Greek-speaking Jews per se,[34] but Jews from the Diaspora now resident in Jerusalem.[35] If this is the case, then Luke has earlier explained the origin of the Hellenist group in the Jerusalem church.[36] In the Pentecost story, Peter's hearers consist not of native Jews but of "Jews, devout men from every nation under heaven" (Acts 2:5); a long list of their various places of origin is given in 2:9-11. It is because these many Jews from the Diaspora are converted by Peter's sermon (cf. Acts 2:41) that Luke can introduce the "Hellenists" in Acts 6:1.[37] But the presentation in Acts is determined by Luke's theological concern to underline the universal significance of the Pentecost

---

30. On this, see O'Neill, *Acts*, 68-69; Wilson, *Gentile Mission*, 239-40.

31. Saul, introduced in 7:58, was from Tarsus in Cilicia (21:3; 22:3; cf. 9:11, 30; 11:25) and is thus probably regarded by Luke as a member of the synagogue for Diaspora Jews that opposed Stephen (6:9). If the latter are identified with the Hellenists of 9:29, then the point is that Paul is disputing with his own former associates.

32. So H. J. Cadbury, "The Hellenists," 59-74.

33. So W. Schmithals, *Paul and James*, 26.

34. So M. Hengel, "Paulus und Jesus," 166.

35. So Haenchen, *Acts*, 266-67.

36. Compare M. Simon, *St Stephen*, 4-5.

37. The sudden reference to Hebrews and Hellenists in Acts 6:1 is thus not a sign that a new source or tradition is being used (against Simon, *St Stephen*, 4; S. G. Wilson, *Gentile Mission*, 129; Barrett, *Acts*, 1:305).

event.[38] Such material can tell us little about the historical origins of the Gentile mission.[39]

Like Dibelius, Hengel seeks to extract historical information on this issue from beneath the surface of the Acts narrative. Neither attempt can be regarded as successful. In contrast, Luke's own focus on the Diaspora synagogue as the primary point of contact between Gentiles and the gospel suggests a more plausible scenario.

2. The Evidence of Paul's Letters

This Lucan focus on the Diaspora synagogue is confirmed and supplemented by the picture that emerges from Paul's letters. Four main points come to light. First, at an early stage in his Christian career, Paul's missionary activity was aimed primarily at Jewish communities in the Diaspora. Second, the earliest Christian congregations inherited the issue of Gentile circumcision from the Diaspora synagogue. Third, an ideologically self-conscious Gentile mission arose from experiences of rejection by Jews and acceptance among Gentiles. Fourth, Paul's doctrine of "freedom from the law" may be traced back to his alienation from the Jewish community, stemming from his missionary experience. Paul's view of the law originates in his Gentile mission, which itself originates in a specific socio-historical situation and not in factors individual to Paul himself — his conversion experience, his psychological problems, or his insight into the existential plight of humanity. Each of these four points must now be substantiated in detail.[40]

---

38. Luke's alleged "misunderstanding" of the Pauline view of *glossolalia* (cf. Barrett, *Acts*, 1:115-16) is in fact an expression of this theological concern.

39. Speculation about the later influence of the Hellenists is therefore worthless; even within his own narrative, Luke's "Hellenists" disappear without trace. Different scholars have suggested links between the Hellenists and Paul's opponents in 2 Corinthians (G. Friedrich, "Die Gegner des Paulus im 2. Korintherbrief"), the Johannine community (O. Cullmann, *The Johannine Circle*, 87), Hebrews (W. Manson, *The Epistle to the Hebrews*, 36), the Epistle of Barnabas (L. Barnard, "St. Stephen and Early Alexandrian Christianity," 38-42), and the Pseudo-Clementine literature (H.-J. Schoeps, *Theologie und Geschichte des Judenchristentums*, 236). Compare the brief survey by Stanton, "Stephen in Lucan Perspective," 345-46.

40. This analysis differs significantly from the one presented in *PJG¹*, 28-38. In particular, the second point is entirely new.

(i) A Mission to the Diaspora

As we have seen, it is apparently Luke's view that Gentile conversions may initially be expected to occur among non-Jewish participants in synagogue worship, and that the synagogue is the primary setting for the preaching of the gospel. Neither the "men from Cyprus and Cyrene" nor Barnabas and Paul consciously intend a "Gentile mission," with a doctrine of "freedom from the law" as its ideological underpinning. "Greeks" are converted insofar as they are present alongside Jews as hearers of the message. This view has the merit of a certain *prima facie* plausibility. Yet it can hardly be the whole truth, for Luke *at no point* envisages a distinctive Pauline mission to Gentiles — unless perhaps at the very end of his work.[41] In Acts, there is little trace of a division of labor between Peter (and James and John), entrusted with a gospel for the circumcised, and Paul (and Barnabas), commissioned to evangelize the Gentiles (cf. Gal. 2:7-9).

In the light of his own evidence, it might seem impossible that Paul could *ever* have understood it as his vocation to evangelize Diaspora Jews, with the evangelization of Gentiles as a secondary consequence of that primary task. Paul himself connects his calling to preach to the Gentiles with the very beginning of his life as a Christian: for God revealed his Son to him "in order that I might proclaim him among the Gentiles" (Gal. 1:16).

Yet Paul here is reflecting on his conversion as he now understands it, in a highly charged polemical context, perhaps twenty years after the event. Here as elsewhere in Galatians 1–2, Paul is projecting his own construal of the Galatian situation back into his account of its prehistory.[42] This passage cannot be safely used as evidence for his self-understanding at the time of his conversion.[43] One should not assume that his understanding of himself as called to preach to the Gentiles was an integral part of his conversion experience,[44] any more than one should assume that the kernel of his entire theol-

---

41. Cf. J. T. Sanders, *The Jews in Luke-Acts*, 297-99.

42. On this crucial point, see J. L. Martyn, *Galatians*, 208-11, where Galatians 2:1-10 is interpreted as a "two-level drama." The point can be extended to the rest of Paul's narrative.

43. J. T. Sanders rightly argues against the assumption that Galatians 1–2 can be regarded as neutral historical reporting ("Paul's 'Autobiographical' Statements in Galatians 1–2," 336).

44. Against F. Hahn, *Mission in the New Testament*, 97; G. Lüdemann, *Paul, Apostle to the Gentiles*, 32-33. Hengel allows for development in Paul's understanding of himself as Apostle to the Gentiles ("Die Ursprünge der christlichen Mission," 21), but he too thinks that Galatians 1:15-16 and Philippians 3:4-11 prove that a law-free gospel was integral to Paul's conversion experience (22). The alternative view is taken by A. Oepke, *Galater*, 33, and W. D. Davies, "The Apostolic Age and the Life of Paul," 874.

ogy was already contained in that experience[45] — common though both views are. All we know of Paul's conversion is how he chose to understand it in polemical contexts many years later. That does not mean that Galatians 1:16 should simply be discounted, however. Even here, Paul does not actually claim that his vocation to preach to Gentiles was part of the initial disclosure, a second element alongside the revelation of the risen Jesus as God's Son. On the contrary, Paul simply states that his Gentile mission was the fundamental divine *intention* in a revelation that embraced his existence in its entirety, "from my mother's womb" (v. 15). He speaks of activity in Arabia and Damascus, Syria and Cilicia, but does not explicitly claim to have practiced an exclusive mission to Gentiles in those locations (vv. 17, 21).[46] On the contrary, Paul himself acknowledges that his vocation to the Gentiles became an issue only on the occasion of his second visit to Jerusalem, seventeen years after his conversion (cf. Gal. 2:7-9).[47]

Thus, there is no indication of a primary vocation to the Gentiles in Paul's account of his first visit to Jerusalem (Gal. 1:18-24).[48] Whatever Paul may have discussed with Cephas and James, it cannot have been the status of the Gentiles, for that did not become a problem until fourteen years later. At this stage, the Judean churches still regarded Paul's conversion as grounds for praise and thanksgiving. They did not know Paul personally, but they did hear it reported

> that "he who once persecuted us now proclaims the faith he once sought to destroy." And they praised God because of me. (Gal. 1:23-24)

The Judean churches know of Paul as a former persecutor currently active as a zealous missionary of the faith in locations such as Damascus, Arabia, and

45. So S. Kim, *The Origin of Paul's Gospel, passim;* R. Bultmann, *Theology,* 1:187-88; P. Stuhlmacher, "'Das Ende des Gesetzes': Über Ursprung und Ansatz der paulinischen Theologie," 30-31; U. Wilckens, "Die Bekehrung des Paulus als religionsgeschichtliches Problem," 15.

46. Acts, too, is cautious about linking the initial revelation with the mission to the Gentiles. In Acts 9, the newly converted Saul immediately begins to preach Jesus as God's Son, but to Jews (vv. 20-22); his future mission is disclosed to Ananias but not to Saul himself (v. 15). In Acts 22, the sending to the Gentiles occurs in an experience in the temple subsequent to the conversion (vv. 17-21). Only in Acts 26 is Paul sent to the Gentiles at the moment of his conversion (vv. 16-18); and even here he preaches to Jews first (vv. 19-20).

47. On the chronological issue, G. Lüdemann argues convincingly that the fourteen years of Galatians 2:1 date from the journey to Syria and Cilicia mentioned in 1:21; ἔπειτα in 2:1 refers back to ἔπειτα in 1:21 (*Paul, Apostle to the Gentiles,* 63).

48. Haenchen rightly remarks that Paul evidently made no great claims for himself on this first visit ("The Book of Acts as Source Material for the History of Early Christianity," 269).

"the regions of Syria and Cilicia" (1:17, 21). But there is no indication that they understand his work in those locations to be oriented primarily towards Gentiles rather than towards their fellow Jews.[49] On the contrary, it is only many years later that the leaders of the Jerusalem church recognize any such orientation in Paul's work (cf. Gal. 2:7-9).

It is therefore a mistake to conclude from the evidence of Galatians that Paul preached primarily to Gentiles from the moment of his conversion onwards.[50] Indeed, it is questionable whether Gentiles were ever the *exclusive* objects of his preaching. The motif of apostleship to the Gentiles, so prominent in Galatians and Romans, is absent from the Corinthian correspondence.[51] In 1 Corinthians, Paul contrasts himself with the other apostles on a variety of grounds: he is not accompanied by a wife, he does not accept material support from his converts, he was called later than they were, and he has worked harder than they have (9:5-6; 15:8-10). But he does not claim that he alone preaches to Gentiles, whereas they preach exclusively to Jews. On the contrary, he acknowledges the theoretical possibility that the predominantly Gentile church at Corinth might have had another apostle as its founder: "Whether then it is I or they, so we preach and so you believed" (15:11). There is no suggestion here that, as Gentiles, the Corinthians in principle *could not* have heard the gospel from (for example) Cephas (cf. 1:12; 3:22; 9:5; 15:5).

Nor is there any suggestion that Jewish communities could not have heard the gospel from Paul. In 1 Corinthians 1:22-24, the threefold reference to the Jew/Greek (or Jew/Gentile) polarity implies the opposite:

> Jews demand signs and Greeks seek wisdom, but we preach Christ crucified, a scandal to Jews and folly to Gentiles, but to those who are called, both Jews and Greeks, Christ the power of God and the wisdom of God.

49. Against Schmithals, *Paul and James*, 39-40, who thinks that Galatians 1:23-24 shows that the Judean churches approved of Paul's law-free gospel to the Gentiles. Compare Hengel, "The Attitude of Paul to the Law in the Unknown Years between Damascus and Antioch," 39-42.

50. Galatians 5:11 may even suggest that, in initial encounters with Gentiles in Diaspora synagogues, Paul himself advocated their circumcision (cf. Acts 16:3). If Paul here responds to a claim raised by his opponents, this is more likely to refer to his Christian career than to a pre-Christian, Torah-centered mission to Gentiles (the view of Terence Donaldson, *Paul and the Gentiles*, 275-84).

51. This point is widely overlooked, with the result that an apostleship to the Gentiles can be regarded as a neutral datum about Paul's Christian career in its entirety. Thus G. Theissen can argue that the original premise of Paul's mission was that Gentiles alone needed salvation, and that only as a result of experiences of Jewish or Jewish Christian opposition did he extend the need for salvation to Jews (*Social Reality and the Early Christians*, 210-11).

Paul presumably draws here on personal experience of rejection and acceptance of his gospel by Jews as well as by Greeks. This is confirmed by 1 Corinthians 9:20-22, where he writes:

> To the Jews I became as a Jew, in order to win Jews. To those under law I became as one under law — though not being myself under law — that I might win those under law. To those without law I became as one without law — not being without law toward God but under the law of Christ — that I might win those without law. To the weak I became weak, so that I might win the weak. I have become all things to all people, so that by all means I might save some.

Paul here sees his mission as comprehensive in scope, encompassing "Jews" (synonymous with "those under law"), and Gentiles, who fall into two categories: those who are "without law" (ἄνομοι), and those who are "weak" (ἀσθενεῖς). In chapter 8, the "weak" are those whose faith would be undermined by contact with idolatry (cf. 8:9, 11; in vv. 7, 10, 12, this "weakness" is located specifically in the "conscience"). In 9:22, the ἀσθενεῖς appear to be a specific and identifiable object of mission — in which case they may be Gentiles who have accepted certain observances of the law such as abstention from εἰδωλόθυτα. These would then be Gentiles with a prior connection to the synagogue, in contrast to others who are ἄνομοι, entirely outside the sphere of synagogue and law. Paul's commission extends not just to the non-Jewish world of the ἄνομοι but also to Jews and those drawn to Jewish practices. This is most plausibly understood as referring to the type of missionary practice represented in Acts.[52] Even if the Acts portrayal is unhistorical, however, Paul could hardly have written as he does in 1 Corinthians 9 if he had *always* preached exclusively to Gentiles and had *never* seen Jews as the direct objects of his missionary endeavors.[53]

If a self-conscious "Gentile mission" was a relatively late development in Paul's missionary career (as Galatians suggests), and if Paul continued to speak of Jews as objects of his preaching (as 1 Corinthians suggests), then it is plausible that at an earlier stage his preaching was addressed primarily to Jews

---

52. So S. G. Wilson, *The Gentiles and the Gentile Mission in Luke-Acts*, 250, also citing 2 Corinthians 11:24.

53. According to E. P. Sanders, the Acts portrayal is opposed by "everything that Paul says about his work except 1 Cor. 9.20" (*Paul, the Law and the Jewish People*, 187). Thus, Romans 11:13-16 suggests that Paul's work as Apostle to the Gentiles affects Jews only indirectly, through their becoming "jealous"; this seems to exclude the possibility that he continued to preach to Jews (188). 1 Corinthians 9:19-23 is therefore "hyperbolic" (186). Sanders overlooks the fact that the motif of apostleship specifically to the Gentiles is absent from the Corinthian correspondence.

and to Gentiles who attended the synagogue. Initial conversions among such Gentiles would not have raised any new ideological problems.

(ii) Gentile Circumcision and the Diaspora Synagogue

In discussions of the place of Gentiles within the synagogue, it has been conventional to differentiate between "proselytes," full converts to Judaism who (if male) have submitted to circumcision, and "God-fearers" with a looser adherence to Judaism. Appeal is made primarily to later rabbinic and inscriptional evidence.[54] Although, unlike Philo and Josephus, Acts does at least attest this dual terminology, it is less clear whether the author thinks that "proselytes" are to be *distinguished* from "those who fear God." In his sermon in the synagogue at Antioch in Pisidia, Paul addresses both ἄνδρες Ἰσραηλῖται and οἱ φοβούμενοι τὸν θεόν (Acts 13:16, 26); and in v. 43, Luke tells how πολλοὶ τῶν Ἰουδαίων καὶ τῶν σεβομένων προσηλύτων followed Paul and Barnabas. If "those who fear God" are to be *identified* with the "devout proselytes," Luke would have in mind a *single* category of Gentile adherents of the synagogue. It is possible, however, that in referring to οἱ φοβούμενοι τὸν θεόν (13:16, 26) or to οἱ σεβόμενοι (17:17; cf. 13:50; 16:4; 17:4; 18:7) he speaks of a broader category that *includes* "proselytes" but extends beyond them. This is perhaps suggested by πολλοί . . . τῶν σεβομένων προσηλύτων (13:43). In that case, all non-Jewish adherents of the synagogue could be said to "fear God," but not all would be "proselytes." That this term has an exclusive sense for Luke is suggested by the presence of proselytes but not "God-fearers" in Jerusalem (2:10; 6:5); for Luke associates Jerusalem with a hard-line view on circumcision. Cornelius the centurion is described by Luke as εὐσεβὴς καὶ φοβούμενος τὸν θεὸν (10:2), but for Peter's critics he and his devout household are simply ἄνδρας ἀκροβυστίαν ἔχοντας (11:3). No such issue arises in the case of the proselytes in Peter's audience on the day of Pentecost (2:10) or of Nikolaos the proselyte from Antioch (6:5). In these cases, at least, Luke must assume that proselytes are circumcised, in contrast to the God-fearing Cornelius. Thus Luke tends to confirm something like the conventional distinction between proselytes and God-fearers, although

---

54. See E. Schürer, *History of the Jewish People in the Age of Jesus Christ*, III.1, 160-76. The conventional distinction has been reasserted by J. Carleton Paget, who argues that "Jews were willing to sanction a multiplex form of association with Judaism on the part of Gentiles," and that "God-fearer" was "an official designation at the time of Christian origins," clearly demarcated from "proselyte" ("Jewish Proselytism at the Time of Christian Origins: Chimera or Reality?" 93).

the latter represent an inclusive category, the terminology for which varies slightly. It is not clear whether the distinction would have had any relevance to women (cf. 13:50; 17:4). In spite of remaining ambiguities, however, Luke's terminological distinction is of considerable significance in confirming that some level of Gentile adherence to the Diaspora synagogue was possible even without circumcision.

Why would one wish to be a "proselyte," and to be acknowledged as such, rather than a "God-fearer"? Like the term συναγωγή, προσήλυτος has a Septuagintal background. In the Septuagint, the συναγωγή is the *qāhāl* or *'ēdāh,* the entire people, referred to on over twenty occasions in the stereo-typed phrase, πᾶσα συναγωγὴ υἱῶν Ἰσραηλ.[55] The application of συναγωγή to the individual congregation may have been facilitated not only by etymology but also by the ambiguity of πᾶσα συναγωγή, which could be heard as a reference not to the congregation as a whole but to "every synagogue of the sons of Israel." The "synagogue" includes not only "the sons of Israel," however, but also "proselytes" — a term that occurs on sixty-three occasions in the Pentateuch to represent the *gērîm* or "sojourners" of the Hebrew text. The choice of προσήλυτος rather than πάροικος is an indication that Judaism in the Diaspora is more interested in conversion than in the status of non-Jews in Judea.[56] According to Philo, Moses uses the word "proselyte" to refer to those who have joined themselves (προσεληλυθέναι) to "the new and God-loving polity" (*Spec. leg.* 1.51). These "proselytes" are to observe the sabbath (Exod. 20:10 = Deut. 5:14) and to abstain from the consumption of blood (Lev. 17:10-13), from incest (Lev. 18:26), and from blasphemy (Lev. 24:16, 24). They may offer sacrifices (Lev. 17:8-9; 22:18). They are to be welcomed (Lev. 19:33-34), and they are entitled to hear the reading of the law (Deut. 31:12). They are required to be circumcised if (but only if) they wish to partake of the Passover (Exod. 12:48-49). To identify oneself as a "proselyte," with an acknowledged place in a "synagogue of the sons of Israel," is to enter the sphere of the Torah's address.

Is male circumcision a necessary precondition for proselyte status? In his *Questions and Answers on Exodus,* Philo offers a justification for the non-circumcision of Gentile converts to Judaism based on Exodus 23:9: "You shall

---

55. Eleven times in Exodus (12:3, 47; 16:1, 2, 6, 9, 10; 17:1; 35:1, 4, 20), twice in Leviticus (16:5, 17), and nine times in Numbers (8:9, 20; 13:26; 14:5, 7; 15:25, 33; 19:9; 26:2). Abbreviated versions of this expression are also attested (Lev. 4:13; 22:18; Num. 1:2 [?]; 16:9; 19:2; 20:1, 22).

56. Arguing against the assumption that first-century Judaism practiced mission to Gentiles, Martin Goodman claims that at this period "proselyte" can still be applied to Jews as well as to Gentile converts ("Jewish Proselytizing in the First Century," 60-63, with particular reference to Matt. 23:15). This seems unlikely in view of the Septuagintal background.

not oppress a proselyte [προσήλυτον]; for you know the soul of the proselyte, for you were proselytes in the land of Egypt." Why, his questioner asks, does Moses base his injunction on the Israelites' experiences in Egypt? In response, Moses' aim is to teach

> that the "proselyte" is one who circumcises not his foreskin but his pleasures and desires and the other passions of the soul [ὅτι προσήλυτος ἐστιν οὐχ ὁ περιτμηθεὶς τὴν ἀκροβυστίαν ἀλλ' ὁ τὰς ἡδονὰς καὶ τὰς ἐπιθυμίας καὶ τὰ ἄλλα πάθη τῆς ψυχῆς]. For in Egypt the Hebrew nation was not circumcised, but being mistreated with all manner of mistreatment by the inhabitants in their hatred of strangers, it lived with them in self-control and endurance, not by necessity but by its own free choice [οὐκ ἀνάγκῃ μᾶλλον ἢ ἐθελουσίῳ γνώμῃ], because it fled to God the saviour, who, sending his beneficent power [τὴν εὐεργέτιν δύναμιν], delivered the supplicants from their difficult and hopeless situation. Therefore he adds: "For you know the soul of the proselyte." But what is "the soul of the proselyte," if not alienation from the polytheistic belief and familiarity with the honouring of the one God and Father of all [ἀλλοτρίωσις τῆς πολυθέου δόξης, οἰκείωσις δὲ τῆς πρὸς τὸν ἕνα καὶ πατέρα τῶν ὅλων τιμῆς]? (QE, 2.2)

Philo here exploits the distinction he draws elsewhere between physical and spiritual circumcision, for which he finds scriptural warrant in the injunction of Deuteronomy 10:16 to "circumcise your hard-heartedness" (QG, 3.46; Spec. leg. 1.304-5). This circumcision of pleasure and desire does not make fleshly circumcision redundant for Jews, as Philo argues forcefully against those who take the opposite view (Migr. 92); but it does mean that fleshly circumcision should not be imposed on Gentiles.[57] The exegetical argument for this conclusion sets out from the parallel in the Exodus text between present-day proselytes and the Israelites in Egypt, who are also said to have been proselytes. Drawing perhaps on Exodus 4:24-26, according to which Moses' son was uncircumcised, Philo claims that the Israelites in Egypt were physically uncircumcised but lived in self-control and trust in God.[58] If that is what it meant to be proselytes in their case, then it must be the same for the present-day proselyte. To impose circumcision on such people would be to disobey

57. Citing this passage, P. Borgen claims that Philo's meaning is that bodily circumcision is to follow for the proselyte ("Paul Preaches Circumcision and Pleases Men," 39). That is not what the text says, however. The passage is also in some tension with E. P. Sanders's claim that "Gentiles would be expected to make a traditional conversion to Judaism and be prepared to fulfill the letter of the law" ("The Covenant as a Soteriological Category," 28).

58. Contrast Joshua 5:5, according to which it was only the generation born in the wilderness that was uncircumcised.

the scriptural injunction not to oppress them, showing the same "hatred of strangers" as the Egyptians did to the Israelites.

Philo's discussion may imply that, in some Diaspora contexts, proselytes were not required to submit to circumcision.[59] More significantly, it implies that this was a contested issue, for otherwise it would hardly have occurred to Philo to apply the Exodus text to the unrelated issue of proselyte circumcision.[60] Yet what is at issue here is not circumcision as such, but word use. The term "proselyte" confers a status as addressee of the Torah alongside the "sons of Israel." Philo argues in effect for a broader and more inclusive usage that would extend the scriptural term to include male adherents of the synagogue who have not as yet submitted to circumcision and who may never do so. The argument presupposes that there *are* people who have turned from idols to the true God, and yet remain uncircumcised: Philo recommends that the term "proselyte" be extended to include them. But it is also presupposed that "proselyte" is commonly employed in a narrower sense, referring to those who complete their conversion by submitting to circumcision. Philo wishes the scriptural term "proselyte" to be extended to the likes of Cornelius, who is uncircumcised yet fears God, gives alms, and prays constantly (Acts 10:2). Such people are already present on the fringe of the Diaspora synagogue, and Philo's aim is to enhance their status, encouraging his Jewish readers to honor them as they are, rather than making submission to circumcision a condition of acceptance.[61]

While early Christian communities appear not to have used the Torah-based terms "synagogue" and "proselyte," similar issues about Gentile participation recur in the new context. The earliest church simply *inherited* this issue from the synagogue, from where most Gentile converts would initially have been drawn. Thus, similarly to Philo, Paul can identify a circumcision that is of the heart, a rite carried out ἐν πνεύματι οὐ γράμματι, spiritually and not literally (Rom. 2:29). In both cases, Deuteronomy 10:16 has influenced the argu-

---

59. See N. J. McEleney, "Conversion, Circumcision and the Law"; opposed by J. Nolland, "Uncircumcised Proselytes?"

60. So J. Carleton Paget, "Jewish Proselytism," 95-96. Carleton Paget makes a similar point in connection with Philo's (and Josephus's) interpretation of Exodus 20:27 LXX as enjoining respect for pagan deities (79-81).

61. This interpretation is supported by statements elsewhere in which Philo expresses his admiration for converts: see *Spec. leg.* 4.178, commenting on Deuteronomy 10:17-18, where God is said to work justice "for the proselyte [Philo reads: ἐπηλύτῳ], the orphan and the widow" (cf. also *Spec. leg.* 1.309). In v. 19 it is said: "You shall love the proselyte, for you were proselytes in the land of Egypt" (cf. Exod. 22:20; 23:9). It is perhaps with this text in mind that Philo elsewhere remarks that those converted to the one God from polytheism must be regarded as "our dearest friends and kinsmen [φιλτάτους καὶ συγγενεστάτους]" (*Virt.* 179).

ment: for to enjoin that "hard-heartedness" (σκληροκαρδία) be circumcised is to postulate precisely the "circumcision of the heart" (περιτομὴ καρδίας) of which Paul here speaks. In both cases, the argument seeks to defend those Gentiles who observe the fundamental tenets of the law but without circumcision of their ἀκροβυστία (cf. Rom. 2:27). While it is less clear in Paul than in Philo that the argument concerns Gentile *converts*, this remains the most likely interpretation (on this, see Chapter 6 below). If so, then both positions presuppose a Gentile *reluctance* to undertake a painful and shaming rite and seek to facilitate conversion by arguing for an exemption.

Similar issues are debated in Josephus's account of the conversion of Izates, heir to the throne of Adiabene in northern Mesopotamia. Izates initially concludes that he cannot truly become a Jew without being circumcised (νομίζων τε μὴ ἂν εἶναι βεβαίως Ἰουδαῖος εἰ μή περιτέμοιτο [*Ant.* 20.38]), but is dissuaded on both political and religious grounds by his mother Helena and her instructor in Judaism, a merchant named Ananias. Ananias tells him that

> he could worship the deity even without circumcision [χωρὶς τῆς περιτομῆς τὸ θεῖον σέβειν], if he had fully decided to follow the traditional laws of the Jews [τὰ πάτρια τῶν Ἰουδαίων]; for this was more important than being circumcised. (*Ant.* 20.41)

Ananias's liberal view is contradicted by Eleazar from Galilee, who tells King Izates (as he now is) that he "ought not merely to read these things [i.e., the laws] but rather to do what is commanded by them" (*Ant.* 20.44). As a result, the king immediately has himself circumcised. Paul similarly claims that it is doers and not mere hearers of the law who will be justified (Rom. 2:13), but he sides with Ananias in arguing that one may "keep the decrees of the law" even in a state of uncircumcision (Rom. 2:26). From the standpoint of an Eleazar (probably a Pharisee),[62] Ananias's view is a mere pretext that evades the plain sense of scripture; Ananias, Philo, and Paul claim theological justification for their teaching, but are in fact motivated merely by an unworthy desire to make life easier for their converts.

According to Galatians 2:3, Paul's Greek companion Titus was not obliged to submit to circumcision on the occasion of their visit to Jerusalem to consult the "pillars" (2:4-5). We may perhaps conclude that the Jerusalem leaders shared the belief of Philo and Ananias that it is possible to worship God without circumcision. In the early days of the Christian mission, and

---

62. He is said to have had a reputation for strictness in relation to the law (*Ant.* 20.43), a point that Josephus elsewhere associates specifically with Pharisees (*BJ* 2.162; *Vit.* 191).

perhaps still at the Jerusalem conference, Paul and his co-workers would not have developed the complex and far-reaching theological legitimation for Gentile non-circumcision that occurs later in Galatians and Romans. At this stage, the traditional contrast between physical and literal circumcision may have sufficed.

(iii) Jewish Rejection and Gentile Mission

The Pauline Gentile mission does not follow directly from Paul's experience on the Damascus road, but represents a *reaction* to the realities of the early Christian mission. Initially, we may suppose, the gospel is preached "to the Jew first, and also to the Greek" (Rom. 1:16), with the synagogue providing access to both. As a result, some Jews and some Gentiles accept the gospel. Paul and his co-workers conclude that God's will is to "call" people "not only from among Jews but also from among Gentiles" (Rom. 9:24). But there is a disproportion. Law-observant Jews prove to be unexpectedly resistant to the divine word in which the meaning of their own scriptures is at last laid bare; and non-observant Gentiles prove to be unexpectedly receptive (cf. Rom. 9:30-33).

Openings for the gospel are found not only on the fringes of the synagogue but also in un-Jewish settings such as the lecture hall of Tyrannus (Acts 19:9). In contrast, preaching in the synagogue often proves a painful experience: "Five times I have received at the hands of Jews the forty-less-one, three times I was beaten with rods, once I was stoned . . ." (2 Cor. 11:24-25).[63] At least in the first case, a formal legal procedure is envisaged:

> If there is a dispute between men and they come to court, and the case is heard, and they acquit the innocent party and condemn the guilty one [δικαιώσωσιν τὸν δίκαιον καὶ καταγνῶσιν τοῦ ἀσεβοῦς]; then, if the guilty party deserves a flogging [πληγῶν], you shall make him lie down before the judges and they shall flog him before them according to the number fitting for his offence. Forty times they shall flog him, they shall add no more; for if they continue to flog him beyond this number of strokes, your brother will be put to shame before you. (Deut. 25:2-3)[64]

63. The ὑπό Ἰουδαίων with which 2 Corinthians 11:24 opens should probably be extended to the experiences of beating and stoning mentioned in v. 25, though obviously not to the three shipwrecks.

64. LXX refers to "the judges," whereas MT envisages a singular judge; LXX may represent legal practice in the Diaspora.

In Josephus's paraphrase, the flogging has become a punishment for transgression of laws of charity:

> Let him who acts contrary to these precepts receive forty-less-one strokes with the public lash, enduring this shameful punishment, though a free man, because by slavery to unjust gain he has offended against his own dignity. (*Ant.* 4.238)

The loose connection Josephus creates between the punishment and laws enjoining charity may imply a new context within "religious" rather than "civil" law — no longer a dispute between individuals but the infringement of the law of Moses per se. Paul claims to have undergone this ordeal on no less than five occasions, as he discharges his vocation as a "servant of Christ" (cf. 2 Cor. 11:23).

Paul appears to have evoked hostility in the synagogues he visited primarily because of his preaching of Jesus as the Christ and his success specifically among Gentiles (cf. Acts 13:45; 17:4-5).[65] The Jews, he complains, "persecute us and displease God and oppose all people, by hindering us from speaking to the Gentiles so that they may be saved" (1 Thess. 2:15-16). Jewish rejection of the gospel not only *contrasts with* Gentile acceptance of it but is also *exacerbated* by it. In the background here is no doubt a fierce competition for Gentile allegiance, whether to the old religion or to its new offshoot. The gospel proves surprisingly successful among Gentiles at or beyond the fringes of the synagogue; local Jewish communities actively resist what they take to be a perversion of their ancestral faith (as Paul himself had once done); and the outcome from a Pauline perspective is an increasing focus on Gentiles, and alienation from the Jewish community. In its opposition to the gospel, this community continues its age-old history of rebellion against God: "the Jews . . . killed both the Lord Jesus and the prophets and persecute us . . . , so as always to fill up the measure of their sins; but God's wrath has come upon them for ever!" This interpretation of Jewish resistance to the gospel as the culmination of an *Unheilsgeschichte* makes it possible to reapply scriptural polemic to the present generation. David speaks of this generation when he writes: "Let their table be a snare and a trap and a stumbling-block and a retribution for them, let their eyes be darkened so that they may not see, and bend their backs for ever!" (Ps. 68:23-24, cited in Rom. 11:9-10). Such pas-

---

65. Barrett assumes that Paul was punished for "specific offences, such as consorting with Gentiles and eating forbidden food (cf. e.g. I Cor. x.25, 27) which Paul had committed because he was a Christian" (*2 Corinthians*, 296). But Paul's argument in 2 Corinthians 11 is more effective if there is a straightforward connection between his sufferings and his apostolic preaching.

sages are both an expression of alienation from the majority Jewish community and a theological legitimation of this alienation.[66]

Jews may be said to "hinder us from speaking to the Gentiles" (1 Thess. 2:15), but in another sense it is precisely Jewish resistance to the gospel that has produced the corresponding turn to the Gentiles. In Romans 11:11, Paul writes of Israel: "Through their failure, salvation has come to the Gentiles." Israel's "failure" is the widespread Jewish rejection of the Christian gospel (cf. Rom. 9:32), and Paul acknowledges that this "failure" is the essential precondition of the Gentile mission. This point is repeated constantly in the course of Romans 11:

> If their trespass means riches for the world, and if their failure means riches for the Gentiles. . . . (11:12)

> If their rejection means the reconciliation of the world. . . . (11:15)

> If some of the branches were broken off, and you, a wild olive shoot, were grafted in their place to share the richness of the olive tree. . . . (11:17)

> You will say, "Branches were broken off so that I might be grafted in." (11:19)

> A hardening has come upon part of Israel until the full number of the Gentiles comes in. (11:25)

> As regards the gospel, they are enemies of God, for your sake. (11:28)

> You . . . have received mercy because of their disobedience. (11:30)

In each case, Gentile conversion is said to have been *occasioned by* Jewish rejection of the gospel. It is said that God has hardened the hearts of unbelieving Jews (11:8-10) because he willed to remove them from their privileged position and to install Gentiles in their place. This claim is to be understood as a secondary theological reflection on a prior socio-historical reality. When Paul states in v. 11 that salvation has come to the Gentiles, he is referring to the successful results of his own Gentile mission: thus, in v. 13 he identifies himself as "apostle to the Gentiles," hinting at his own part in the unfolding divine plan. We may therefore paraphrase the statements cited above as follows: Jewish

---

66. That Paul can cite this psalm text even in the relatively irenical Romans 11 suggests that concerns about the authenticity of 1 Thessalonians 2:14-16 are groundless. For criticism of the assumption that Romans 11 must determine what Paul can have said elsewhere, see Carol J. Schlueter, *Filling Up the Measure*, 55-64.

failure to believe the gospel has led to Paul's mission to Gentiles, and so to the salvation of many Gentiles.[67] Faced with the problem of Jewish resistance to the gospel, Paul and his colleagues increasingly turned to Gentiles — concluding that God had hardened the Jews so as to save Gentiles in their place.

It is this historical and social situation alone that can account for the remarkable series of statements in Romans 11 to the effect that Israel's unbelief has led to the salvation of the Gentiles, for it is hard to imagine how Paul could have come to such a view except through reflection on what had actually happened.[68] The "Gentile mission" began as a response to Jewish resistance to the gospel and consequent alienation from the Jewish community. Initially, it may have been a uniquely Pauline response, occasioned by the empirical reality of unforeseen success among Gentiles at or beyond the fringes of the synagogue. Although Paul claims solidarity with persecuted Christians in Judea (1 Thess. 2:14), his response to Jewish resistance proved controversial precisely in the Christian community's Judean heartland, as Galatians 2 indicates.

In Paul's early missionary activity in Syria and Asia Minor, mission is directed primarily towards Jewish communities. At this stage, the conversion of Gentiles attached to the synagogue poses no special problems, and Paul and his co-workers can avail themselves of existing exegetical arguments that legitimate male Gentile reluctance to submit to circumcision. Yet experiences of missionary success and failure create a new situation, characterized by increasing orientation towards Gentiles in consequence of increasing alienation from Jews. The crucial shift in missionary practice will have occurred during the fourteen-year period between Paul's first and second visits to Jerusalem. Following the first visit, he gains a reputation in Judea as a zealous proclaimer of the faith he once persecuted (Gal. 1:23-24). By the time of the second visit, he has become a controversial figure whose rejection of Gentile circumcision takes on new significance in a context of increasing missionary orientation towards Gentiles (cf. Gal. 2:1).

67. Schlier, *Römer*, 328, rightly explains these passages by reference to the missionary practice depicted schematically in passages such as Acts 13:45-47; 18:6-7; and 19:8-9. The Acts view is rejected as unhistorical by Sanders, *Paul, the Law and the Jewish People*, 181, who appeals to the principles enunciated by John Knox: that "the primary evidence is Paul's letters" and that "Acts should be disregarded if it is in conflict." Yet, in spite of Paul's self-designation in Romans 11:13 as "apostle to the Gentiles" (which Sanders here cites), it is not the case that Romans 11 unambiguously presents the Gentiles as the exclusive objects of Paul's entire missionary career. On the contrary, this chapter repeatedly emphasizes that mission to the Gentiles originates in (unsuccessful) mission to the Jews.

68. This view is rejected by T. Donaldson, *Paul and the Gentiles*, 271, arguing that references to the period in Arabia (Gal. 1:17; 2 Cor. 11:31-32) "indicate that Paul was involved in Gentile evangelization from the outset." Were there no synagogues in Arabia?

(iv) Freedom and Alienation

In Romans 2:25-29, as we have seen, Paul draws on a traditional Jewish defense of Gentile non-circumcision: since circumcision is a spiritual and not just a physical state, the physically uncircumcised may observe the commandments of God. The non-circumcision of the first Gentile converts to the Christian gospel was probably legitimated along precisely these lines. There is nothing in such statements to which an Ananias or a Philo would take strong exception.

In 1 Corinthians 7:19, the same distinction between circumcision and true law observance is drawn, but with a sharper polemical note: "Circumcision is nothing and uncircumcision is nothing — all that matters is keeping the commandments of God!" This claim follows the injunction that those who are circumcised should not seek to conceal their circumcised state, and those who are uncircumcised should not become circumcised. Each person, whether Jew, circumcised proselyte, or uncircumcised Gentile, should remain as they were when called by God in the gospel (7:17-18). This passage confirms that the Corinthian congregation includes former members of the synagogue, and it also suggests that Paul regarded this as normal: for, as he says, he instructs "all the churches" along the same lines (v. 17). His language suggests alienation from the synagogue. The permission to remain uncircumcised here becomes a command: "If anyone was called in a state of uncircumcision, let him not be circumcised" (v. 18). The traditional distinction between circumcision and the commandments of God is accompanied by the provocative claim that "circumcision is nothing" (v. 19). The issue is no longer whether non-circumcision debars one from participation in the life of the synagogue or church. Rather, the distinction between περιτομή and ἀκροβυστία has lost all significance, and precisely this non-signification of the difference itself signifies alienation from the synagogue, understood as the institution founded on this difference. Pauline alienation from the Jewish community comes vividly to expression in this transformation of a permission into a signifier of a new difference, the difference between the *ekklēsia* and the synagogue. As such, Paul's declaration of the nullity of circumcision represents an essential moment in the construction of Christian identity.[69] Just as circumcision can represent a "boundary marker" for the Jewish com-

---

69. Sanders regards 1 Corinthians 7:19 as "one of the most amazing sentences [Paul] ever wrote," evaluating it from an "orthodox" Jewish perspective and ignoring its social function (*Paul, the Law and the Jewish People*, 103). In reality, it represents not an inexplicable aberration but a moment of transition between a traditional Jewish argument for the non-circumcision of Gentiles and the full Pauline doctrine of freedom from the law.

munity, marking it off from the pagan world, so non-circumcision can represent a "boundary marker" for the Pauline community, marking it off from the synagogue.[70]

There are other indications in the Corinthian correspondence of this process of self-definition vis-à-vis the synagogue. Paul tells his converts to "eat whatever is sold in the meat market without discriminating on account of conscience" (1 Cor. 10:25). As the law enjoining circumcision has been declared void, so it is here with the dietary laws, abolished at a stroke on the scriptural grounds that "the earth is the Lord's and the fulness thereof" (Ps. 23:1 LXX, cited in 1 Cor. 10:26). While the primary concern in the context is whether meat remains contaminated by contact with idolatry, Paul's language implies that *all* the characteristically Jewish issues relating to dietary laws are irrelevant to the Corinthians. Equally irrelevant, it seems, is the sabbath. The congregation meets not on the sabbath but on the first day of the week (cf. 1 Cor. 16:2). This non-observance of Jewish laws relating to diet and time is not just an empirical fact about the Corinthian congregation as Paul founded it. Rather, it signifies the difference between the congregation and the synagogue. This is confirmed by the claim that "all things are lawful for me [πάντα μοι ἔξεστιν] but not all things are fitting" (1 Cor. 6:12a, repeated in 10:23a, probably without the pronoun, and with variations in 6:12b and 10:23b).[71] By means of this formulation, Paul replaces an ethic of divine command, codified in the law of Moses, with an ethic of Christian appropriateness, variously grounded in the gospel, scripture, nature, or whatever. Thus, even where the new ethos and the old law coincide materially, Paul goes to considerable lengths not to cite the law itself. The Corinthians are to "flee idolatry" because of what happens in the eucharist (1 Cor. 10:14-17). They are to avoid πορνεία because such a union would undermine their union with Christ (6:12-20).[72] For Paul, this is an ethic for the free rather

70. This interpretation of the non-observance of Jewish laws in Pauline communities replaces the claim in *PJG¹* that "[t]he abandonment of parts of the law of Moses was intended to make it easier for Gentiles to become Christians" and thereby "helped to increase the success of Christian preaching" (34). Yet, in the light of Galatians 1:10, that view cannot wholly be discounted.

71. There is no basis for the common assumption that "all things are lawful" existed as an independent Corinthian slogan, which Paul himself proceeds to qualify (so Conzelmann, *1 Corinthians*, 108-10). It is noteworthy that, in three of its four occurrences, πάντα [μοι] ἔξεστιν is immediately followed by ἀλλ' οὐ πάντα . . . (1 Cor. 6:12a; 10:23a, b); the one exception retains ἀλλ' οὐκ . . . (6:12b). This antithetical form is therefore integral to the πάντα [μοι] ἔξεστιν formulation, and there is no evidence that it ever existed without it.

72. Sanders rightly notes the material agreement between Pauline and Jewish ethics (*Paul, the Law and the Jewish People*, 94-96), but fails to observe how rarely the law is invoked as warrant for the required conduct.

than an ethic for slaves (cf. 2 Cor. 3:17; Gal. 5:1). The synagogue, at Corinth or elsewhere, is the place where the law of Moses is read and where the ethic of freedom through Christ and Spirit is suppressed (cf. 2 Cor. 3:15, 17).

It is not clear how far this ethic of freedom was already practiced within the church at Antioch. While Paul speaks of "false brothers" concerned about the practice of "freedom" there (Gal. 2:4), the only concrete example he gives is the freedom for Jewish and Gentile Christians to eat together (cf. 2:12); this need not imply any relaxation of the dietary laws.[73] Admittedly, Paul claims in Galatians 2:14 that in eating with Gentiles Peter has been living "like a Gentile" (ἐθνικῶς), and this might be taken to imply that Peter and the Jewish Christians of Antioch had abandoned the observance of the law and their Jewish identity. But this seems unlikely conduct for the apostle to the circumcision (2:7-9). It is more probable that we should understand Paul's terminology in the light of his rhetorical aim, which is to present Peter as agreeing with his own doctrines of righteousness by faith and freedom from the law, even though his actual conduct was inconsistent with this. In any case, the issue at Antioch appears to have been Gentile circumcision rather than dietary laws: for Peter's withdrawal from table fellowship with Gentiles was motivated by fear of τοὺς ἐκ περιτομῆς (2:12). While this expression may refer to "the Jewish militants to whom James's message possibly referred,"[74] the reference to "circumcision" in this context must surely allude to the reality of Antiochene Gentile non-circumcision. When Paul accuses Cephas of "compelling Gentiles to judaize" (2:14), it is no doubt circumcision that he has in mind.[75]

A fully fledged doctrine of "freedom from the law" is evident at Corinth and in Thessalonica, but the corresponding practices cannot clearly be traced back to the early history of the Antiochene church.[76] It is one thing for circumcised and uncircumcised Christians to practice table fellowship; it is another for them to buy whatever meat is available at the market, without concern for

---

73. So Dunn, "The Incident at Antioch (Galatians 2:11-18)," 29-32.

74. Bruce, *Galatians*, 131. This expression appears not to be a mere synonym for "Jews" (as in Acts 10:45; Col. 4:11), or "judaizers" (as in Acts 11:2; Tit. 1:10).

75. ἀναγκάζεις ἰουδαΐζειν (2:14) is probably synonymous with ἀνακάζουσιν περιτέμνεσθαι (6:12). On circumcision as the real issue in the "Antioch incident," see P. Esler, *Galatians*, 137-40.

76. Contra L. Goppelt, who writes: "Christians [at Antioch] had detached themselves from the Law for a reason just as obscure as that which had caused the Jewish believers in Jerusalem to continue to observe it" (*Apostolic and Post-Apostolic Times*, 66). It was only from the standpoint of the "men from James" that Antiochene Jewish Christians "had detached themselves from the law," by practicing table fellowship with the uncircumcised. Why it should be thought strange that Jerusalem Christians continued to observe the law is incomprehensible.

Jewish dietary restrictions. It is *missionary* experience that issues in the Pauline Gentile mission and in freedom from the law. In the context of mission, the Antiochene church's non-imposition of circumcision on Gentile converts is radicalized. Circumcision comes to signify the law as a whole, and non-circumcision a corresponding freedom from the law as a whole. Henceforth, Christian praxis is to be based not primarily on the law but on the gospel; in particular, laws relating to diet and to sacred days are declared invalid. If Paul's address to Cephas really represents the consensus of the Antiochene church prior to the "Antioch incident," then an advanced notion of freedom from the law was already held there (cf. Gal. 2:11-21). If, as is more likely, the address is actually directed at the Galatians themselves, its radicalism stems from developments in Paul's thought and practice after his breach with Barnabas.

3. Two Sociological Models

1. If we consider this transition from mission to Jews to mission to Gentiles from a sociological standpoint, we may describe it as *the transformation of a reform movement into a sect.* A new religious movement does not arise in a vacuum but is always related to the old religion that preceded it. Positively, it draws much of its content from what has gone before; and negatively, it rebels against other elements of the old. In many cases, it is the intention of the leader or leaders not to found a new religion but to reform the existing one. The aim may be to purge it of its present corruption and to restore its imagined original purity, or to foster new beliefs or patterns of conduct within the structure of the old religion. The reform movement intends nothing less than the transformation of the old religion; it claims the old religion for itself. Its advocates do not see themselves merely as a righteous remnant in a corrupt society. They are more ambitious than that, believing that the tremendous new impetus that has grasped them will sweep away every obstacle from its path until corruption is destroyed and reformation is complete. Thus, the religious movement initiated by Jesus was at first a movement to reform Judaism in preparation for the imminent coming of the kingdom of God; it was not a sect.[77] Even after Jesus' death, the impetus continued unabated, as his followers preached throughout Judea and Galilee in the hope of the conver-

---

77. "Earliest Christianity began as a renewal movement within Judaism brought into being through Jesus" (G. Theissen, *The First Followers of Jesus*, 1). Compare B. Holmberg: "The first Christians did not regard themselves as a sect or party within Judaism, but rather as the beginning of its total renewal" (*Paul and Power*, 183).

sion of the Jewish people to their understanding of the imminent redemption of Israel.[78]

But a reform movement is likely to encounter opposition from a very early stage.[79] Its reliance on charismatic leadership inevitably brings it into conflict with the traditional authority structures of the old religion. For a while, this conflict may help the movement to define and clarify its goals. But it may gradually become clear that the original goals of the movement are unattainable. Political power may remain firmly in the hands of the traditional authorities, and society as a whole may prove resistant to change, taking the view that "the old is good" (Luke 5:39). Slowly, the seemingly irresistible power of the original religious impulse begins to wane, as it again and again encounters resistance and rejection.

If the reform movement is able to survive the initial conflict with the traditional authority structures, it is likely that it will be gradually transformed into a sect. The distinction between the two is fluid. They represent opposite ends of the spectrum, and there are any number of possible gradations between them. The essential difference is that the reform movement adopts a hopeful attitude towards society, believing that with divine help it will be able to transform it, whereas the sect adopts a hostile and undifferentiated view of society.[80] In this perspective, there are only two categories of people, the righteous and the unrighteous (i.e., members of the sect and non-members). All distinctions of rank and status, so important to society at large, fade into insignificance by comparison with this fundamental distinction. Although missionary work may continue (for recruits still have to be found), the sect no longer believes in an irresistible divine power operating in the present, causing its message to transform society as a whole. It places its trust in a future eschatological vindication, which will prove to its opponents that, despite its

78. In the light of this distinction between reform movement and sect, it is not the case that "the community called into existence by Jesus fulfills the essential characteristics of the religious sect, as defined by recent sociological analysis" (R. Scroggs, "The Earliest Christian Communities as Sectarian Movement," 1). Jesus no more founded a sect than he founded a church.

79. The reason is that "[n]ew religious communities also exemplify the precarious status of all social worlds. By revealing that the legitimacy of the old order is not, after all, inherent in the nature of the universe, they pose a tremendous threat to that order" (J. G. Gager, *Kingdom and Community*, 110).

80. Scroggs lists seven typical characteristics of the sect: (1) It emerges out of protest. (2) It rejects the established view of reality. (3) It is egalitarian. (4) It offers love and acceptance to its members. (5) It is a voluntary group. (6) It requires total commitment. (7) It may be adventist in orientation ("The Earliest Christian Communities as Sectarian Movement"). The present discussion is concerned chiefly with the alienation from society implied by the first, second, and sixth of these points.

weak and marginal position in society, God is on the side of the sectarian group. Society outside the group is written off. It stands condemned; it is liable to God's judgment. Salvation is to be found exclusively through membership of the sect. The sect is thus differentiated from the reform movement by its alienation from society.

2. One of the sect's main needs is for *an ideology legitimating its separation from society;* an ideological barrier must be erected between the two.[81] The sect's members need to know exactly where they stand, for if they are unclear about this they may fall victim to the specious arguments of the sect's opponents (especially the traditional religious authorities). There is nothing more disastrous for the coherence or morale of a sectarian group than the apostasy of some of its members; that is why such opprobrium is heaped upon apostates. Separation may be legitimated in any or all of the following ways:

(1) *Denunciation.* The sect's opponents may be attacked either for their general moral depravity or for their crimes against the sect. Such charges may bear little resemblance to an "objective" view of reality, for the sect is not interested in "objective truth" but in its own inner coherence. To secure this, a hostile portrayal of its opponents must be perpetuated.

(2) *Antithesis.* The gulf that is perceived between the sect and society may be crystallized in the form of antitheses, characterizing the two groups as the righteous and the unrighteous, the holy and the unholy, the godly and the ungodly, and so on.[82] The antithesis may express a predestinarian outlook, distinguishing the elect from those whose hearts are hardened. The advantage of predestinarian language is that on the one hand it reinforces the sense of an elite status enjoyed by members of the sect, and on the other hand it provides an explanation for the potentially damaging fact of the unbelief of the majority.[83]

(3) *Reinterpretation.* A reform movement seeks the renewal and revitalization of the religious traditions of the whole community. In contrast, the sect regards itself as the sole legitimate possessor of those traditions and

81. Wayne Meeks notes that social cohesion requires boundaries, citing L. Festinger's definition of social cohesion as "the resultant of all the forces acting on the members to remain in the group" (Meeks, *The First Urban Christians,* 85).

82. "The complexities of moral judgments that typify a complex society are resolved into a series of binary oppositions: poor-rich, good-evil, pious-hypocrite, elect-damned" (Gager, *Kingdom and Community,* 25).

83. For a discussion of this twofold function of predestinarian language, see F. Watson, "The Social Function of Mark's Secrecy Theme."

denies the legitimacy of the claim to them made by society as a whole. The traditions must therefore be reinterpreted to apply exclusively to the sectarian group. Where tradition takes the form of written scriptures, the separation between the sectarian group and the wider community will be mirrored in the scriptural text itself, which becomes the site of two competing and opposed interpretative practices.

The sequence, reform movement–rejection–sect, is not intended as a fixed sociological law operative in all cases. Nor will a sectarian group's legitimation of separation from a parent religious community inevitably involve denunciation, antithesis, and reinterpretation. Historical phenomena rarely follow such simple models exactly; there are too many variables involved, and each case is unique. Even when these patterns do seem broadly to fit the evidence, ambiguities and complicating factors will remain. Nevertheless, one should not regard the uniqueness of each individual historical phenomenon as a reason to ignore the possibility of common underlying sociological patterns. If carefully handled, such patterns can illuminate the subject rather than distorting it. We shall attempt to apply the patterns outlined above first to the Qumran community, secondly to the Johannine community, and thirdly to Paul himself.[84] Only the broad outlines will be described, since our purpose is not the general study of sectarianism in early Judaism and Christianity but the study of Paul's alienation from Judaism as he perceives it.

(i) Qumran

1. While little is known about the origins of the Qumran community, or of the wider "Essene" movement to which it was affiliated, it has been argued that the text known as 4QMMT *(Miqsat Ma'asê ha-Tôrah)* may shed light on the formative period of the community's history.[85] This text arises from an

---

84. Compare also G. Stanton's suggestion that Matthew's community, too, "has recently parted company with Judaism after a period of prolonged hostility" ("The Gospel of Matthew and Judaism," 273). It is now "a rather beleaguered 'sect'" (277), under threat from Judaism and hostile to the Gentiles, and expressing its alienation from society by means of apocalyptic themes (274). R. Bauckham's justified claim that the Gospel of Matthew was written with a view to wide circulation ("For Whom Were Gospels Written?" 26-44) is compatible with the assumption that this text also shows signs of particular local communal experiences.

85. This discussion of 4QMMT replaces the equivalent section of *PJG¹* (41-42), which presupposed a view of the early history of the Qumran community that is now regarded as problematic. For the text of 4QMMT, see E. Qimron and J. Strugnell, DJD 10.

interpretative disagreement over "works of the law," which has led to separation from the wider community. As the author explains, "We have separated from the multitude of the people . . . and from participating in these matters" (C 7-8). The addressee is not to understand this separation as a sign of treachery or wickedness, however (C 8-9). In terms of the reform movement/sect typology, it would not be appropriate to describe the separation referred to here as "sectarian." The author is opposed to certain current temple practices, and he writes to inform his addressee of these disputed points and to persuade him to accept his community's view of them, *with a view to reform*. The "B" section lists around twenty of these "words" or "works," proposed regulations that explicitly diverge from current practice. A fragmentary line may suggest that the common theme of these regulations is priestly purity (B 3).[86]

It seems that the addressee of 4QMMT is uniquely positioned to implement the proposed reforms. He is addressed respectfully and is differentiated from the Jerusalem priests whose practice is criticized; yet he must be in a position to impose reform if the content of the letter is to be relevant to him. In endorsing the works of the law prescribed in this letter, he is to take as his role models those kings of Israel who studied the Torah and whose sins were forgiven. David is the pattern for these righteous kings of Israel, who no doubt also include Hezekiah and Josiah:

> Remember the kings of Israe[l] and reflect upon their works, how whoever of them feared [the la]w was delivered from troubles; and these were people who stu[d]ied the law and whose transgressions were forgiven. Remember David, how he was a man of pious deeds and was [de]livered from many troubles and received forgiveness. (C 23-26)

The specific reference to "the kings of Israel" suggests that the addressee is one of their successors and that the letter therefore postdates the decision of Aristobulus I to adopt the title of "king" (see Josephus, *BJ* 1.70; cf. *Ant.*

---

86. See Lawrence Schiffman, "The New Halakhic Letter (4QMMT) and the Origins of the Dead Sea Sect." Schiffman contrasts the absence of "the language of sectarian antagonism" from 4QMMT and its presence in the Damascus Document, "which was completed after the split was final and which reflects the sectarian animus that would characterize the later documents of the Qumran group" (EDSS, 1.560). The chronological relationship between 4QMMT and CD is unclear, however. These texts represent different stances in relation to the wider society — the stances of the reform movement and the sect, respectively — but they may not directly illustrate the development of one into the other.

13.301).[87] The addressee of 4QMMT might have been the anti-Pharisaic Alexander Jannaeus (103-76 BCE).[88]

Addressed to the king, the letter is concerned with the well-being not just of a sectarian group but of the wider community. The letter concludes with an appeal to the addressee to implement the proposed reforms to current priestly practice, for his own good and the good of his people:

> We have written to you a selection of the works of the law which we consider to be for your good and that of your people Isr[a]el. For we have noted in you an understanding and a knowledge of the law. Consider all these things, and seek from before him that he will make straight your counsel and keep far from you evil thoughts and the counsel of Belial. Thus you shall rejoice in the last time in finding that this selection of our words is true. And it shall be reckoned to you for righteousness when you do what is right and good before him, for your good and that of Israel. (C 26-32)

The references to a "good" that extends beyond the addressee to "your people Israel" (C 27, 32) indicate the positive outcome of the return to the Torah for which the author has earlier appealed on the basis of Deuteronomy 30:1-2 (C 12-21). Beyond the history of the blessings (David, Solomon) and the curses (Jeroboam to the exile), in which history the curses have long outweighed the blessings, there lies the possibility of a final age in which "they will return in Israel to the l[aw . . .], and not turn back" (C 21-22). This final age is what scripture calls "the last days" (C 14, 16, 21) or "the last time" (C 30), and the hope is that the addressee will help to usher in this dawning time by acting as the letter suggests, aided by his own knowledge of Torah and by the divine assistance that comes from prayer (C 27-29). The concern for the wider community is clear and explicit. The writer articulates the position of a "reform movement" and not a "sect."[89]

---

87. While Hyrcanus and his father Simon are said to have held "the rule of the nation" together with the high priestly office (1 Macc. 13:42; 14:35, 41-42; 15:2; *Ant.* 13.291, 299), they are identified primarily by their high priesthood (1 Macc. 14:27; 15:17, 21, 24; 16:24; *Ant.* 13.230, 259, 267, 282-83).

88. So O. Betz, "The Qumran Halakhah Text Miqsat Ma'asê Ha-Tôrah (4QMMT) and Sadducean, Essene, and Early Pharisaic Tradition," 195-96. Traces of a positive view of this figure are found in Qumran literature (see 4Q448 and the discussion of possible references in the pesharim in my *PHF,* 102-5).

89. "The group is determined to keep its separate identity; but, at the same time, they are convinced about having a mission for the entirety of Israel, and confident that at the end the people and the Jewish authorities would recognize the truth of their position" (G. Boccaccini, *Beyond the Essene Hypothesis,* 117). Boccaccini also notes how this outlook "could easily turn

2. The Damascus Document and the Rule of the Community reflect a different phase of community development. These texts are written by and for sectarian groups that no longer seek or expect the reform of the wider community.[90] Their attempts to legitimate their separation from the wider community may be summarized in the categories outlined above:

(1) *Denunciation.* In CD 4.12–5.11, a bitter polemic is directed against the sect's chief opponents.[91] They are guilty of fornication, in that they take a second wife while the first is still alive; they profane the Temple through intercourse during menstruation; they marry their nieces, contrary to the sect's interpretation of Leviticus 18:13. The sect describes as its enemies' constant practice what are in fact simply differences over matters of *halakah*. It denounces these differences not with a view to reform but in order to justify and perpetuate its own separate existence.

(2) *Antithesis.* Humanity is divided into two classes: "the sons of light" and "the sons of darkness" (1QS 1.9-10), "the sons of righteousness" and "the sons of wickedness" (1QS 3.20-21), "the men of the lot of God" and "the men of the lot of Belial" (1QS 2.1, 4-5). Whether one walks in righteousness or in wickedness depends on divine predestination. "From the God of knowledge comes all that is and shall be"; and God has appointed "two spirits" for humans, "the spirits of truth and falsehood" (1QS 3.15, 18-19). Thus the separation between the sect and the world is ascribed to God's own will and action. The frequent repetition of such antithetical descriptions of insiders and outsiders helps to establish and maintain the sect's alienation from the wider society.

(3) *Reinterpretation.* The sectarian group claims to be the sole legitimate possessor of the religious traditions that in fact it shares with the whole community, and it must therefore reinterpret these traditions in the light of this claim. The Qumran community's reinterpretation of scriptural traditions takes a variety of forms, only a few of which can be briefly mentioned: *(a)* Membership of the covenant through circumcision is denied to the Jewish community as a whole and claimed for the sect alone; circumcision is thus spiritualized (1QS 5.1-5). *(b)* True observance of the

---

into frustration and hatred with the negative reaction of those they wished to convert" (117), thereby transforming a reform movement into a sect.

90. The reform group/sect distinction cannot be used to establish the chronological relationship between 4QMMT on the one hand and the Damascus Document and Rule of the Community on the other. In principle a sectarian group may recover an openness to the wider society, given a particular set of internal and external circumstances.

91. On this passage, cf. Sanders, *Jesus and Judaism*, 65-66, 338.

Jewish community's holy days (sabbaths, feasts, the day of atonement) is to be found only within the sect (CD 6.18-19). *(c)* The sect alone offers true sacrifices, through obedience and prayer (1QS 9.4-5). *(d)* Scripture belongs only to the sect, and not to the community as a whole, speaking frequently of the sect and the key events in its history (1QS 8.7, 13-16; CD 3.21–4.5; the *pesharim*); indeed, the sect's formation was the climax of biblical history (CD 3.1-20).

In all these ways, the boundary between the sect and society is established, defined, and reinforced. The sect's continued existence is entirely dependent on whether its legitimation of separation remains plausible for its members. For this reason, apostates are bitterly denounced (CD 8), for in their case the ideology has proved ineffective, so that the sect's very existence is threatened.

(ii) The Johannine Community

These same two sociological phenomena — the transformation of a reform movement into a sect and the creation of an ideology legitimating separation — are also in evidence in the Fourth Gospel. While the theme of this narrative text is not the "Johannine community" as such, correlations may be found at certain points between the Johannine narrative and the experiences and perceptions of Johannine Christians.

1. The Gospel of John contains several references to expulsion from the synagogue. Jesus warns the disciples in 16:2, "They will put you out of the synagogue," and adds in v. 4, "I have said these things to you, that when their hour comes you may remember that I told you of them." This passage suggests that members of the Johannine community may have experienced expulsion from the synagogue; one way of coming to terms with this crisis was to ascribe foreknowledge of it to Jesus.[92] In the light of 15:18-25, expulsion from the synagogue may be seen as the concrete manifestation of the world's hatred towards Jesus and his community. Here, another response to the crisis of expulsion is seen: the suffering of the community at the hands of "the Jews" is not to disturb its members, since it is the logical consequence of Jewish hostility towards Jesus himself (15:18-21). Similarly, recent experiences of expulsion from the synagogue (16:2) are retrojected into the earthly life of Jesus in 9:22,

92. Suffering is also legitimated by prediction in Matthew 10:17-23 (so Gager, *Kingdom and Community*, 8).

34 and 12:42.[93] The blind man's parents "feared the Jews, for the Jews had already agreed that if any one should confess him to be the Christ, he was to be put out of the synagogue" (9:22). Here, "already" (ἤδη) is significant: expulsion from the synagogue is grounded in the Jewish attitude towards the earthly Jesus. In 9:34, the formerly blind man is duly "cast out" (i.e., expelled from the synagogue) following his confession that Jesus is "from God" (v. 33). He contrasts with the believers among the authorities who did not confess their faith "lest they be put out of the synagogue" (12:42).[94]

Thus, at an earlier stage, members of the Christian community presupposed in the Fourth Gospel had continued to participate in the life of the synagogue, hoping to persuade fellow Jews of Jesus' messiahship. This led to tensions with the traditional authorities, represented in the text as "the Pharisees" (cf. 12:42), with the result that those who openly acknowledged Jesus as the Christ were expelled from the synagogue. Those who were expelled had to reorganize themselves in sectarian separation from the Jewish community. Judging from the language of 15:18–16:4, the expulsion with its aftermath was a traumatic experience.[95]

2. In order to survive this crisis, separation had to be legitimated; an attempt had to be made to explain and justify the new position outside the Jewish community to the group's members. This may again be summed up under three headings:

(1) *Denunciation.* The Jewish leaders "receive glory from one another and do not seek the glory that comes from the only God" (5:44). Their concern for the scriptures (5:39) is thus hypocritical and self-seeking. In 7:19, the people are condemned: "None of you keeps the law." In 8:44 it is said (of those who supposedly believe, vv. 30-31) that their father is the devil, and that they carry out his desires. John 7–8 shows how the people came to share their leaders' hostility towards Jesus, initially taking his claims seriously (7:12, 15, 25-27, 31, 40-43; 8:30-31), but eventually repudiating him (8:48, 52-53, 57) and seeking to kill him (8:59). Thus, the verdict on the people as a whole at the end of Jesus' public ministry is that "though he had done so many signs before them, yet they did not believe in him"

93. Most commentators are agreed that it is the position of the Johannine community that is reflected here (Schnackenburg, 2:250; Bultmann, 335; Brown, 1:379-80; Barrett, 299-300). On this point, see especially J. Louis Martyn, *History and Theology in the Fourth Gospel.*

94. On these "crypto-Christians," see Brown, *Community of the Beloved Disciple,* 71-81.

95. W. Meeks argues convincingly that their sectarian self-understanding is articulated in their christology ("The Man from Heaven in Johannine Sectarianism," 490).

(12:37); this is in accordance with Isaiah 53:1 and 6:10 (John 12:38-40). The sectarian character of the Johannine community is thus evident in its undifferentiated hostility towards the Jewish community as a whole, and not just towards its leaders.[96] Leaders and people alike are denounced.

(2) *Antithesis.* The sect's separation from the Jewish community is articulated and justified by the use of antitheses. The structure of the gospel as a whole is antithetical. The unbelief of the Jewish community (a central theme of John 1–12) is contrasted with the true followers of Jesus, to whom private instruction is given (John 13–17).[97] Antithetical word-pairs are a vital element in John's theology, and their implied metaphysical dualism may be correlated with the sociological dualism that is the sectarian group's response to hostility from the wider community.[98] Thus, the antithesis between flesh and Spirit in 3:6 is an antithesis between the "rulers of the Jews" (cf. 3:1) and the Johannine community, those who have been "born of the Spirit" (3:5, 8). The Johannine Jews are "from below," "of this world" (8:23), "slaves" (8:32-36), in "darkness" (8:12). But Jesus is "from above," "not of this world" (8:23), and likewise his followers are "not of this world" (17:16); they are "free" (8:32-36); they have "the light of life" (8:12; cf. 12:46). The function of such antitheses is to articulate and justify the sect's separation from the Jewish community.[99]

(3) *Reinterpretation.* Reinterpretation of religious traditions denies the legitimacy of the wider community's use of these traditions and claims them exclusively for the sect. The Jewish theology of the covenant is reinterpreted in 8:54-55: the Jews claim that God is "their God," but it is Jesus and his followers who truly know him. The Jews claim to be the seed of Abraham (8:33, 37, 39), yet they deny their kinship with Abraham as they attempt to kill the one whose coming Abraham longed for (8:39-40, 56-59). The Jewish community also lays claim to Moses: "We are disciples of Moses" (9:28), "we know that God has spoken to Moses" (9:29). In fact, however, it is Moses who will convict them at the final judgment, for he

---

96. Thus, unlike the others, the fourth evangelist speaks collectively of "the Jews," from whom his own community is sharply differentiated (cf. Brown, *Community of the Beloved Disciple,* 40-43). Attempts to limit the scope of the evangelist's terminology should in my view be rejected.

97. Compare Bultmann, *The Gospel of John,* vii, x.

98. Bultmann's profound existential interpretation of Johannine dualism (e.g., *John,* 140-42, on 3:6) involves an almost complete neglect of this sociological dimension.

99. While it is true that "the Jews" are not the only group from which the Johannine community differentiates itself (Brown, *Community of the Beloved Disciple,* 59-88), they are the most important.

bears witness to Jesus (5:45-47; cf. 1:45, 3:14). The same is true of the prophets (2:17, 22b; 6:45; 12:14-16, 38-41; 15:25, etc.). The Johannine community thus claims to be the sole legitimate possessor of Jewish religious traditions.[100]

(iii) Paul

1. In this chapter, we have sought to reconstruct the origins of Paul's distinctive "Gentile mission," on the assumption that this is the social context in which his later reflections on justification and the law are rooted. If Paul's early missionary activity was aimed primarily at Jewish communities in the Diaspora, and if the issue of Gentile circumcision was simply inherited from the Diaspora synagogues, then there is no initial trace of sectarian separation from the parent religious community. Along with Cephas, Barnabas, and the unknown missionaries who brought the Christian gospel to Rome, Paul participates in a *reform movement* dedicated to the reorientation of the Jewish community and its Gentile adherents towards the confession of Jesus as Messiah. By the time that Paul wrote his extant letters, however, the social location of the communities he founded has shifted markedly. Experiences of rejection by Jewish communities and acceptance among Gentiles have led to an ideologically self-conscious Gentile mission and to the formation of communities whose alienation from the synagogue is reflected in the doctrine of "freedom from the law." Pauline Christianity now takes *sectarian* form, a shift that generated serious internal tensions within the wider Christian community, both in Galatia and in Rome.

2. Paul and his congregations seem to have been the only early Christians to have adopted an attitude of sectarian separation from the Jewish community prior to 70 CE. Like the leaders of the Qumran and Johannine communities, Paul had to develop a theoretical rationale for separation from the Jewish community as a crucial component of the new communal identity. Since most of the rest of the present work will be devoted to an exploration of the implications of this statement, only a brief summary is necessary here. Once again, the categories of denunciation, antithesis and reinterpretation are appropriate.

---

100. But note the indications of an alternative strategy in references to "your law" (8:17; 10:34) and "their law" (15:25).

(1) *Denunciation.* The clearest example is in Romans 2. In vv. 1-3, Paul turns on the Jew who, like Paul himself in the previous chapter, condemns the idolatry and immorality of the pagans; this judge is hypocritical, for he is doing exactly the same things himself. The Jewish teacher who sets himself up as an expert in the law is in fact guilty of stealing, adultery, temple robbery, and transgression in general (2:17-24). He is unconcerned about this inconsistency because he is convinced that, as one who is circumcised (2:25) and a Jew, his salvation is secure (2:4). He has a "hard and impenitent heart" (2:5). Such people will experience "wrath and fury" (2:8), "tribulation and distress" (2:9) on the day of judgment. Interpretative problems in Romans 2 are mitigated considerably when one asks what Paul is seeking to *do* in this chapter. As we shall see, the answer is that he is seeking to reinforce the barrier separating the church from the synagogue. Denunciation of the iniquity of leading representatives of the Jewish community is part of that strategy. What matters is not whether the charges can be substantiated, but whether Paul's readers are disposed to find them plausible.[101]

(2) *Antithesis.* Paul uses a variety of antithetical word-pairs in the course of controversy with "Judaism" (Christian or otherwise) as he perceives it. The following are some of the most important:

> works of law/faith of Christ Jesus (Gal. 2:16)
> works/faith (Rom. 3:27; 4:16; 9:32)
> law/Christ (Gal. 2:21)
> flesh/Spirit (Gal. 3:3; 4:29; 5:19-23)
> curse/blessing (Gal. 3:10, 13-14)
> law/promise (Gal. 3:15-18, 21)
> slavery/sonship (Gal. 4:1-7)
> slavery/freedom (Gal. 4:22–5:1)
> circumcision/Christ (Gal. 5:2)
> circumcision/cross (Gal. 5:11; 6:12)
> law/grace (Gal. 5:4; Rom. 6:14-15)
> death/life (2 Cor. 3:6)
> letter/Spirit (2 Cor. 3:6; Rom. 7:6)
> condemnation/righteousness (2 Cor. 3:9)
> confidence in the flesh/glorying in Christ Jesus (Phil. 3:4)
> a righteousness of my own based on law/righteousness from God
>   that depends on faith (Phil. 3:9; cf. Rom. 10:3)

---

101. Sanders rightly emphasizes that Pauline polemic does not convey objective information (*Jesus and Judaism*, 338).

sin/grace (Rom. 5:20-21)
works/God's call (Rom. 9:11)
works/grace (Rom. 11:6)

As in the examples from Qumran and the Fourth Gospel, the function of these antithetical contrasts is to articulate the ineradicable distinction between the sectarian group (in which salvation is to be found) and the parent religious community (where there is only condemnation).[102] The sect's members must be quite clear about the boundary separating the two groups, for to be unclear about it is to risk losing one's salvation (cf. Gal. 5:2-4). These antitheses therefore legitimate the separation of church from synagogue, rather than expressing any theoretical incompatibility between the practice of Judaism and faith in Jesus Christ. To put it in pointed form: *faith in Christ is incompatible with works of the law because the church is separate from the synagogue.*

(3) *Reinterpretation.* In Galatians 3–4, Paul focuses on the figure of Abraham. He does so not simply because Abraham was an outstanding figure in Jewish tradition, but because the relationship to Abraham was an essential element in the Jewish community's self-definition. Jews regarded themselves as "the seed of Abraham," members of God's covenant with Abraham and his descendants through the rite of circumcision, and so as heirs to the promises made to him. Paul claims that these privileges belong to the (largely Gentile) communities he himself has founded, and he denies that one can be a descendant of Abraham without participation in Christ (cf. Gal. 3:16, 29; 4:21-31). In doing so, Paul seeks to reinforce the barrier separating the church from the Jewish community.

One might expect Paul to repeat this procedure with the law — wresting it from the hands of his (Christian-)Jewish opponents and claiming that it is truly observed only in the church. He is aware of the possibility of a spiritualized interpretation of circumcision (Rom. 2:29; Phil. 3:2-3), but in general he concedes the law to his opponents, arguing that it is in fact the bringer of sin, death, and condemnation to its adherents (Gal. 3:10; 2 Cor. 3:6-9; Rom. 5:20-21; 6:14; 7:5-6). In other words, he claims that a true *understanding* of the law is to be found only in the Christian community (cf. 2 Cor. 3:14-15). If the reinterpretation of Abraham serves to emphasize the privileged position of the church in contrast to the Jewish

---

102. Compare Terence Donaldson's view: "Paul's Christ-Torah antithesis is fundamentally sociological (or, if a more theological term is required, ecclesiological) in nature. Paul perceives Christ and Torah as rival boundary markers, rival ways of determining the people of God, rival entrance requirements for the community of salvation" (*Paul and the Gentiles*, 172).

community, the reinterpretation of the law serves to emphasize the terrible plight of the Jewish community in contrast to the church. Both points serve to reinforce the barrier between the two. Paul wishes to inculcate in his converts a horror of life under the law, i.e., life as lived within the Jewish community. There, the reign of sin and death, under which the whole of humanity stands with the exception of the sect's members, is seen at its most powerful.

The reinterpretation of what are for Paul the two great themes of scripture — promise and law — is supported at every point by the use of individual texts. For Paul, scripture was not written for the benefit of the Jewish community, but "for our instruction, upon whom the end of the ages has come" (1 Cor. 10:11; cf. Rom. 15:4). Scripture is thus invoked to justify sectarian separation from the synagogue, and serves the construction of a new communal identity on that basis.

In this chapter, we have traced Paul's view of the law back to the social realities of his mission among Jews and Gentiles. It is these social realities — and especially the experiences of Jewish rejection of the gospel and Gentile openness to it — that occasion Paul's reflections on the law of Moses, the foundational document of the community that, by and large, has rejected the Christian claim that the Messiah has come in the person of Jesus of Nazareth. Jewish rejection is no less fundamental for Paul than Gentile acceptance; God's working is evident in negative as well as positive responses to the gospel. Thus, Pauline theological discourse is not an exercise in pure theory. Its theoretical dimension is always pragmatically oriented, no less so in Romans than in 1 Corinthians. The Paul of the letters is defined by his mission no less than the Paul of Acts; Paul writes out of no other context than this one. That is not to say that theory can be *reduced* to practice, however. Rather, Pauline theological theory has an inseparable *correlate* in social practice, in such a way that the theory and the practice come to be mutually constitutive. Practice needs a theoretical underpinning; theory is only pertinent if it is oriented towards practice.

In the chapters that follow, we shall investigate this correlation of theological discourse and social practice as it unfolds chronologically through Paul's texts.

CHAPTER 3

The Galatian Crisis

1. The Origins of the Crisis

We have attempted to reconstruct the process by which the Pauline mission began to transform what was originally a reform movement within Judaism into a sectarian group outside it. What has not yet been emphasized is the extent to which this decision was controversial within the Christian community itself. Not all early Christians were as ready as Paul was to conclude that most members of the Jewish community were irretrievably hard of heart, and that converts should be sought outside this community and its way of life (cf. 1 Thess. 2:14-16). The majority of Jewish Christians were not yet ready to abandon the original dream that the Jewish people as a whole would soon be united in their expectation of the coming of Jesus as the Messiah. They would have regarded Paul's preaching of freedom from the law to Gentiles as based on a false premise (that God had abandoned the Jewish people) and as gravely hindering their own mission. This disagreement came to a head in the controversy between Paul and the judaizing teachers who were achieving considerable success among his own converts in Galatia, and in the events that led up to it as described in Galatians 2. Galatians is fundamentally concerned with an issue of ecclesiology: the question whether the church should exist as a reform movement within Judaism or develop its distinctive identity on the basis of sectarian alienation.[1]

1. This is a more precise formulation of the issue than Stendahl's influential claim that for Paul "one does not have to go through Judaism into Christianity, but that there is a straight and direct way for the Gentiles apart from the law" (*Paul among Jews and Gentiles*, 18).

This view contrasts with one highly influential interpretation of Galatians. Ever since the Reformation, Paul's opponents in Galatia have been seen as the archetypal protagonists of legalistic religion.[2] Their claim that righteousness must be earned forms the dark background against which the Pauline gospel of an unearned righteousness through faith shines forth all the more brightly. Their doctrine of merit acts as a foil for Paul's doctrine of grace. Their insistence that good works must be added to faith if one is to be saved enables Paul to assert in the most uncompromising way that one is saved by faith alone. Galatians now seems to be addressing an ever-recurring problem. For example, Johannes Munck comments as follows on the Galatians' eagerness to accept judaizing ideas:

> Wherever salvation by faith without the works of the law is preached, we find people who cannot satisfy their longing for holiness (it was then called "righteousness"). They want to be doing something, they want to build up a world of holiness; they do not want to be content with the grace which they feel is debased and sullied by everyday human life, but to prepare a human vessel worthy to receive God's heavenly grace.[3]

This homiletical passage reveals the presuppositions with which scholars in the Reformation tradition still tend to approach Galatians.[4] The letter is supposed to address a general tendency to understand the divine/human relationship in a bilateral rather than a unilateral manner. The analysis in the previous chapter has already shown that this isolation of theology from sociohistorical context can only lead to fundamental misunderstanding.

In the polemical passage in 1 Thessalonians 2:14-16, "the Jews" oppose both Paul's Gentile mission and "the churches of God which are in Judea in Christ Jesus." Paul here assumes a common front with Judean Christians, over against the majority Jewish community whose age-old history of rebellion against God is now reaching its culmination. Alienation from this majority community is supposed to be the stance of the Christian community in its entirety. Yet Galatians shows that this was not straightforwardly the case. Here, solidarity with Judean Christians is strained to breaking point over the

---

2. For a recent example, see G. Ebeling's *Die Wahrheit des Evangeliums* (1981). Ebeling argues that, despite the historical differences, "the fundamental decision for which Paul fought is repeated *mutatis mutandis* in the Reformation's struggle for the truth of the gospel" (viii).

3. Munck, *Paul and the Salvation of Mankind*, 132-33.

4. Even H.-D. Betz thinks that Luther's 1535 commentary on Galatians "expresses an extraordinary and profound understanding of what Paul intended to say"; thus, "Luther speaks as Paul would have spoken had he lived at the time when Luther gave his lectures" (*Galatians*, xv).

question of the church's relation to the Jewish community as a whole. As we shall see, the issue of circumcision and "works of law" has to do with precisely that question.

(i) Mission to Gentiles: Early Debates

In the previous chapter, we saw how the practice of a law-free mission to Gentiles represented a radicalizing of the Antiochene decision to welcome Gentiles into membership of the Christian community — a radicalization occasioned in large part by missionary experience of rejection by Jews and acceptance by Gentiles. The radical view is articulated in Paul's address to Cephas at Antioch, where the issue of circumcision has come to represent the Jewish way of life, characterized by the practice of "works of law" (Gal. 2:14-21). It is not clear how far this address reports what was actually said at the time. Throughout Galatians 1–2, Paul's recollections are shaped by his perception of the current situation in Galatia, and this is true especially of the conclusion of this section, where direct address to Cephas at Antioch imperceptibly gives way to direct address to the Galatians. The main issue at Antioch is table fellowship with the uncircumcised (cf. 2:12), and the radical Pauline plea for separation from the Jewish community and its way of life is directed at the Galatians rather than at Cephas, Barnabas, and the "men from James" in Antioch. Galatians 2:1-10 may reflect a still earlier phase, where what is at issue is simply the legitimacy of missionary activity among Gentiles, without a specific focus on circumcision or on the law. It is said of the Gentile Titus, who accompanied Paul to Jerusalem, only that "he was not compelled to be circumcised" (2:3) — which does not necessarily imply that the issue of circumcision was even on the agenda. The agreement of vv. 6-9 has to do not with circumcision but with the Antiochene leaders' missionary orientation towards Gentiles per se, which the Jerusalem leaders were prepared to accept. In using the terms περιτομή (vv. 7, 8, 9) and ἀκροβυστία (v. 7) to refer to the respective spheres of mission, Paul seeks to relate the agreement in Jerusalem to the current situation in Galatia. But he also speaks of Gentiles simply as τὰ ἔθνη (vv. 8, 9), and what is actually agreed in Jerusalem is simply that he and Barnabas should continue with their missionary activity among them.[5] While it is no doubt assumed that Gentiles such as Titus will not be required to submit to circumcision, that is not the

---

5. The assumption that "the decision of the conference was that male Gentiles would not be required to undergo circumcision" (M. Slee, *The Church in Antioch*, 36) seems to stem from a harmonizing of Galatians 2:1-10 with Acts 15.

point at issue. Titus is present in Jerusalem as a representative — and presumably impressive — product of Antiochene missionary expansion, not as the possessor of a problematically intact foreskin. Thus, when circumcision does become an issue later at Antioch, Paul does not accuse Cephas (or James, or Barnabas) of reneging on the Jerusalem agreement, but simply of inconsistency with his own former practice and convictions (vv. 12, 14).[6] It is unlikely that Paul advocated the later radical policy of "freedom from the law" — that is, sectarian separation from the Jewish community and its way of life — either in Jerusalem or in Antioch. That is the issue in Galatians itself, and it is the Galatian situation that has shaped Paul's claim to have defended "our freedom which we have in Christ Jesus . . . in order that the truth of the gospel should remain for you" (vv. 4-5).[7]

Galatians 2:4 refers to "false brothers secretly brought in, who slipped in to spy out our freedom which we have in Christ Jesus." Paul's aim is clearly to present this earlier criticism or opposition as an antecedent to the current situation in Galatia, and any differences between then and now are downplayed. Yet it is plausible that a missionary activity that proved more successful among Gentiles than among Jews might have created tensions within the Antiochene Christian community; it was probably in Antioch rather than Jerusalem that these first critics of Gentile mission were located. It is true that v. 4 occurs in the context of Paul's account of his second visit to Jerusalem, and it has often been assumed that it was there that he encountered these "false brothers."[8] But this is unlikely, for vv. 3-5 should be regarded as a parenthesis. In v. 2, Paul tells how he explained his activity to "those who were of repute" in Jerusalem, and v. 6 describes their response: they had nothing to add. The intervening material is therefore a digression. In v. 3, Paul says that Titus, his companion, was not compelled to be circumcised, and v. 4 begins with the words, "But because of false brothers. . . ." Unfortunately, Paul does not tell us what it was that happened "because of false brothers," for he does not complete the sentence but merely asserts in v. 5 that he did not compromise with these people.[9] Since Paul sought and obtained in Jerusalem an en-

6. Arguing for "a complete breach of the agreement" on the part of Peter and James, Esler points to Paul's appeal to "the truth of the gospel" in v. 14, a phrase that has previously been used in v. 5 in connection with the false brothers (*Galatians*, 136-37). Yet it is precisely the appeal to the objective criterion of the gospel, rather than to the Jerusalem agreement, that makes it clear that no such breach of the agreement had occurred.

7. See J. L. Martyn's account of Galatians 2:1-10 as a "two-level drama" (*Galatians*, 208-11).

8. So Lightfoot, *Galatians*, 102; Duncan, *Galatians*, 46; and the majority of commentators.

9. Betz plausibly suggests that the omission of the negative in v. 5 in part of the textual tradition was influenced by Galatians 5:11 and Acts 16:3 (*Galatians*, 91).

dorsement of his mission to Gentiles, it was presumably this — and not Titus's uncircumcised state — that the "false brothers" challenged. Paul probably intended to say: "Because of false brothers, I had to go with Titus to Jerusalem to discuss the mission to the Gentiles." If so, v. 4 must refer to Jewish Christians at Antioch who were critical of the emphasis there on Gentile mission. While these may have been visitors from outside Antioch, it is more likely that they represent a faction within the Antiochene church itself. παρεισάκτους and παρεισῆλθεν would then refer to their *joining* the church (cf. παρεισέδυσαν τινες ἄνθρωποι, Jude 4).[10]

Several further points confirm that the encounter with false brothers occurred in Antioch rather than Jerusalem:

(1) Verse 4 says that the false brothers were "secretly brought in" and that they "slipped in to spy out our freedom." These expressions suggest an encounter at Antioch rather than Jerusalem: Antiochene freedom from the law could best be spied on in Antioch itself. If this took place in Jerusalem, the meaning is presumably that the false brothers somehow managed to infiltrate the supposedly secret meeting between Paul and "those of repute" (cf. 2:2).[11] That seems implausible, however. Paul states that he *did* meet with the Jerusalem leaders in private (κατ᾽ ἰδίαν), not that he attempted to do so but failed. κατ᾽ ἰδίαν appears to rule out the participation of anyone other than Paul, Barnabas, and Titus and James, Cephas, and John.

(2) Consistent with this is the fact that Paul reports his encounters with the "pillars" (vv. 2, 6-10) and with the "false brothers" (vv. 4-5) as though they occurred on separate occasions. The passage is most naturally read as an account of two two-sided debates rather than of one three-sided one; thus, nothing is said about any interaction between the false brothers and the pillars. Paul's account of one debate is set in the middle of his account of the other, in order to indicate that the former was the presupposition of the latter.

(3) Paul must have had some urgent reason for going up to Jerusalem, at

10. The false brothers are understood as visitors to Antioch by Hengel, *Acts and the History of Earliest Christianity,* 113. Acts 15:1-2 might be cited in support of this view; and in 15:24 the apostolic letter actually has to deny that the advocates of circumcision were sent by the apostles (so *PJG¹,* 51-52). But Paul's language in Galatians 2:4 does not imply that the false brothers originated in Jerusalem — in contrast to the later "men from James" (2:12).

11. The view of Lüdemann, *Paul, Apostle to the Gentiles,* 71; Bruce, "Galatian Problems, 1," 306. In contrast, van Dülmen, *Die Theologie des Gesetzes bei Paulus,* 13, and Betz, *Galatians,* 90, think that Galatians 2:4 refers to a later period.

least eleven years (and probably fourteen) after his previous visit. He tells us in v. 2 that he went up "by revelation," but it is likely that the context of the revelation was a crisis in the church at Antioch occasioned by missionary success among Gentiles.[12] The crisis must have been serious enough to necessitate a journey to Jerusalem to consult the "pillars" of the church there.[13] On the other hand, it was not so serious that an opposing faction felt compelled to send a delegation of their own. Paul, Barnabas, and Titus represent the whole Antiochene congregation in Jerusalem. The current crisis in Galatia has perhaps heightened Paul's hostility towards those he describes as "false brothers," just as it accounts for his disparaging remarks about the "pillars."

(4) It is true that Acts speaks of a third party at the conference itself. Paul and Barnabas are present as are Peter and James, but also present are "some believers who belonged to the party of the Pharisees," who repeat the demand for circumcision that had earlier been made at Antioch (Acts 15:5). Luke envisages the debate as occurring in the presence of "the church and the apostles and the elders" (v. 4), and it is this public setting that creates space for a third party. But there is no such space in Paul's own account of a private meeting between himself, Barnabas, and Titus on the one hand, James, Cephas, and John on the other.

Thus, Paul, Barnabas, and Titus visited the leaders of the Jerusalem church in order to resolve a crisis within the church at Antioch, occasioned by the very success of the Gentile mission. This may well have been the first time that the Jerusalem leaders were confronted with this issue.

(ii) From the Jerusalem Council to the Antioch Incident

Paul states in Galatians 2:7-9 that he and Barnabas obtained recognition for their Gentile mission. The pillars "saw that I had been entrusted with the gospel of the uncircumcision" (2:7); they "perceived the grace that was given to me," and so "gave to me and to Barnabas the right hand of fellowship, that we should go to the Gentiles" (2:9). The question is how far this recognition

---

12. Georgi rightly points out that a crisis caused by the "false brothers" and a revelation given through a prophet are fully compatible (*Die Geschichte der Kollekte des Paulus für Jerusalem*, 16).

13. Applied to James, Cephas, and John, "pillars" probably refers to their role within the "new temple" (so J. H. Schütz, *Paul and the Anatomy of Apostolic Authority*, 141). Schütz is less than convincing, however, in arguing that Paul's use of this traditional term is not disparaging.

could have extended. The "pillars" would surely not have accepted the parity of the two missions and the two corresponding apostleships. And, as we have seen, it is not clear that the non-circumcision of Gentiles was explicitly agreed or even discussed at this point. It is simply said that Titus "was not compelled to be circumcised" (v. 3), and that the pillars "added nothing to me" (v. 6). Paul and Barnabas visit Jerusalem to report their work among Gentiles and to gain approval for it, in the face of tensions at Antioch, yet there is no indication that this visit was itself the occasion of conflict and controversy. The Jerusalem leaders are more interested in the Gentile converts' financial resources than in their foreskins — an interest that Paul happily endorses (v. 10). In his disparaging references to the Jerusalem leaders as "those reputed to be something" (οἱ δοκούντες εἶναί τι, v. 6), "those reputed to be pillars" (οἱ δοκούντες στῦλοι εἶναι, v. 9), it is — once again — the current situation in Galatia that determines the presentation.[14]

Concern over circumcision first becomes explicit in the account of the "Antioch incident," which occurred during a visit of Cephas to Antioch that may have been intended as a sequel to the council in Jerusalem.[15] Cephas's initial association with Gentile Christians appears to confirm the endorsement of Gentile mission at the council. Yet it is one thing to endorse Gentile Christians at a distance, another to share the same table with them. Cephas's conduct therefore creates serious concerns in Jerusalem, with the result that James sends a delegation urging him to desist. When Paul attributes Peter's withdrawal from table fellowship with Gentiles to his "fearing those of the circumcision" (2:12), this should not be understood as a reference to a "circumcision party" within the early church.[16] In 2:7-9 the term ἡ περιτομή is used three times to refer to the whole Jewish people, the objects of the Jerusalem church's mission, and this suggests that τοὺς ἐκ περιτομῆς in 2:12 has the same sense. Peter "feared those of the circumcision" in the sense that he accepted the argument that association with uncircumcised Gentile Christians

14. So G. Klein, who draws attention to Paul's repeated use of the present participle δοκούντες ("Galater 2, 6-9 und die Geschichte der Jerusalemer Urgemeinde," 112).

15. The general assumption that the incident at Antioch took place after the Jerusalem conference is rejected by Lüdemann, *Paul, Apostle to the Gentiles*, 75-77, who argues that ὅτε δέ in Galatians 2:11 need not imply chronological continuity with the preceding narrative (77). Elsewhere in Galatians, however, this phrase does entail chronological continuity (1:15; 4:4; cf. 2:14). The view that the Antioch incident preceded the conference is also held by Munck, *Paul and the Salvation of Mankind*, 100-103, and by Hester, "The Rhetorical Structure of Galatians 1:1–2:14," 231n; opposed by Jewett, *Dating Paul's Life*, 84, and Dunn, "Incident at Antioch," 41-42.

16. The view of most exegetes (e.g., Lightfoot, *Galatians*, 116; Burton, *Galatians*, 107; Betz, *Galatians*, 109; Dunn, "The Incident at Antioch," 53). Bruce, *Galatians*, 131, and B. Reicke, "Der geschichtliche Hintergrund des Apostelkonzils und der Antiochia-Episode," 177, are exceptions.

would expose him to rejection and hostility from Jews to whom he preached. Warned by James that his conduct would damage the ἀποστολὴ τῆς περιτομῆς, he accepts the warning and acts accordingly.[17] As he now recognizes, his participation in the Antiochene church's mixed table fellowship could be taken as public endorsement of ἀκροβυστία, to the detriment of his own apostolic ministry to the circumcision (cf. vv. 8, 9). In withdrawing from table fellowship, Cephas "compels the Gentiles to judaize," that is, to accept circumcision (v. 14), in the sense that this is now seen as essential for full church membership. His action relegates Gentiles to a position on the margins of the Christian community and makes it possible to advocate circumcision as the solution to this marginalization. Indeed, it is probable that James's message to Cephas itself advocated Gentile circumcision as a condition not so much of salvation as of full church membership. In that sense, Cephas's acquiescence really did set a precedent for current events in Galatia, and Paul can accuse him of "compelling Gentiles to judaize" (2:14) just as he describes the Galatian agitators as "compelling *you* to be circumcised" (6:12).

Yet Paul does not claim that Cephas's conduct amounted to a repudiation of the Jerusalem agreement as reported in 2:7-9.[18] Cephas and Barnabas are criticized not for failing to maintain an earlier agreement but for acting contrary to their true theological convictions. James is not criticized at all: from Paul's standpoint, he was certainly wrong, but he did not act "hypocritically" (cf. 2:13) or breach an earlier agreement. The Jerusalem policy on this issue develops, but it is not self-contradictory. All along, the concern is to preserve the integrity of the primary mission to fellow Jews, and (more broadly) to ensure the well-being of "the churches of Judea which are in Christ" (Gal. 1:22). In a potentially hostile environment (cf. 1 Thess. 2:14), the Jerusalem church stood to gain from a mission to Gentiles only if the resulting conversions were not only to the messiahship of Jesus but also to the law of Moses.

The Antioch incident represented a setback for Paul and a belated victory for the "false brothers" who had raised concerns about Gentile church membership in the first place. On the other hand, the significance of the Antioch incident should not be exaggerated. Even after it, Paul could still express solidarity with the hard-pressed churches of Judea (1 Thess. 2:14). References to Cephas (1 Cor. 3:21-23; 9:5; 15:5), James (1 Cor. 15:7), and Barnabas (1 Cor. 9:6) acknowledge their significance within the wider Christian community. In

---

17. There is no evidence for Lightfoot's suggestion that "the men from James" misrepresented him (*Galatians*, 115).

18. Thus Schmithals, *Paul and James*, 68, and Betz, *Galatians*, 108-9 can actually see withdrawal from fellowship with Gentiles as a legitimate inference from the terms of the agreement.

Galatians 2, Paul heightens the significance of his confrontation with Cephas as he seeks to refute an alternative account of the social location of the Christian community. In Galatia, though not as yet in Jerusalem or Antioch, what is at issue is whether the Christian community should continue to position itself *within* the wider Jewish community, regarding this as its primary sphere of ongoing mission, or whether it should adopt a separatist stance on the basis of the radical Pauline doctrine of freedom from the law. Paul projects this overriding concern back into his account of the Antioch incident and the Jerusalem council, thereby blurring but not eradicating the differences between Jerusalem, Antioch, and Galatia.[19]

(iii) The Founding of the Galatian Churches

Modern reconstructions of Pauline chronology tend to acknowledge the general chronological reliability of Acts 16–28, but also to deny that the Jerusalem conference preceded Paul's missionary activity in Macedonia and Achaia, as Acts 15 suggests. It is argued that the conference in Jerusalem took place on the occasion of the visit to Jerusalem referred to in Acts 18:22, *after* the first visit to Greece.[20] Yet there is one point that seems to tell decisively against this view, and it concerns Paul's relationship with Barnabas. We may infer from Galatians 2:1, 9 that Barnabas was Paul's partner in his early missionary activity among the Gentiles. This partnership would seem to have come to an end with their disagreement about Gentile circumcision (2:13). According to 1 Thessalonians 1:1 and 2 Corinthians 1:19, Paul was accompanied during the initial evangelization of Greece not by Barnabas but by Silvanus and Timothy, and this suggests that the mission to Greece belongs to the period after the break with Barnabas, and so after the Jerusalem conference. The present reconstruction of the situation in Galatia therefore assumes that the chronology of Acts is substantially correct. It can be confirmed at numerous points from Paul's letters.

Soon after the break with Jerusalem and Antioch, Paul "went through Phrygia and the Galatian countryside [τὴν Φρυγίαν καὶ Γαλατικὴν χώραν]," according to Acts 16:6. Although nothing is said about his founding churches there, we are told in Acts 18:23 that at a later date Paul "went from place to

19. As in the equivalent section of *PJG¹* (53-56), this interpretation of the events narrated in Galatians 2 rejects the widespread assumption that the "pillars" reneged on the Jerusalem agreement — but without needing to criticize the veracity of Paul's own account.

20. J. Knox, *Chapters in a Life of Paul*, 68-69; R. Jewett, *Reading Paul's Life*, 95-100; G. Lüdemann, *Paul, Apostle to the Gentiles*, 144-57.

place through the Galatian countryside and Phrygia strengthening all the disciples" — i.e., consolidating the work that had been done on his first visit. These two references to "Galatia" suggest that the so-called "north Galatian" theory about the destination of Galatians is correct. Acts itself is clearly referring to north Galatia, since 16:1-6 distinguishes between "the Galatian countryside" and the (south Galatian) cities that Paul has just visited.[21] Paul, too, must have north Galatia in mind. After his second visit (Acts 18:23), he arrived at Ephesus (Acts 19:1), from where he wrote 1 Corinthians (cf. 1 Cor. 16:8). In 1 Corinthians 16:1, Paul mentions his recent instructions to the churches of Galatia about the collection for the Jerusalem Christians, and it is probable that these instructions were given during the visit to Galatia mentioned in Acts 18:23.[22] In its chronological context, 1 Corinthians 16:1 fits perfectly with Acts 18:23, and this suggests that Paul means by "Galatia" exactly what Luke means.[23] If this is correct, then Paul's defiant response to the setback in Antioch is to found new Gentile churches in Galatia.[24] Having lost one sphere of influence, he begins to establish another.

In his letter, Paul recalls the circumstances in which he founded the Galatian churches:

> You did not wrong me. You know that on account of a fleshly weakness [δι' ἀσθένειαν τῆς σάρκος] I preached the gospel to you at first; and though my condition was a trial to you, you did not scorn or despise me, but received me as an angel, as Christ Jesus. Where then is the happiness you felt? For I bear you witness that you would have pulled out your eyes and given them to me, had that been possible. (Gal. 4:12b-15)[25]

21. Luke's terminology is admittedly somewhat vague (cf. "the upper country," Acts 19:1, which, as Bruce notes [*Galatians,* 13] could refer to "more or less any part of inland Asia Minor"). But despite Bruce's argument from geography (10-18), "Galatia" in these passages cannot refer to Derbe, Lystra, Iconium, and Pisidian Antioch (i.e., "south Galatia"). In Acts 15:36, Paul announces his intention of revisiting those cities, and 16:1 mentions his arrival at Derbe and Lystra, where Timothy was circumcised (16:3). According to 16:4-5, he then went through the cities in which there were already churches, delivering the Apostolic Decree. The reference here must be to Iconium and Pisidian Antioch, for Paul had founded churches only there and in Derbe and Lystra (cf. 16:1). Thus, none of these cities can be included within the phrase, "Phrygia and the Galatian countryside" in 16:6, which marks a new phase in Paul's travels.

22. This would make it unnecessary to infer from 1 Corinthians 16:1 a lost letter ("Galatians B"), as J. L Martyn does (*Galatians,* 226).

23. The north Galatian view now seems to be accepted by the majority of scholars (e.g., Georgi, *Die Geschichte der Kollekte,* 31; Lüdemann, *Paul, Apostle to the Gentiles,* 138; and Meeks, *First Urban Christians,* 42).

24. So Georgi, *Die Geschichte der Kollekte,* 31.

25. In v. 13, τὸ πρότερον is not quite clear. It could mean "the first of two," in which case the

Paul presumably refers here to a health problem affecting his eyes, and so making travel difficult. His intention must have been to pass through Galatia on his way somewhere else (cf. Acts 16:6-7). Owing to his eye problem, however, he was delayed in Galatia, yet was able to take the opportunity to establish congregations there.[26] In these circumstances, the new congregations were probably founded not in major centers of population such as Pessinus, Ancyra, and Tavium, but in country regions. This would explain the implication that the founding of the Galatian congregations represented a deviation from Paul's normal missionary practice, occasioned by the special circumstance of his illness (Gal. 4:13). It would also explain Luke's double reference to the Galatian *countryside*.[27] On the south Galatian hypothesis, it is less easy to imagine how the founding of churches in Pisidian Antioch, Iconium, Lystra, and Derbe could be said to have been occasioned by a debilitating health problem.

From Galatia, Paul and his companions traveled on to Troas (Acts 16:8); to Philippi (16:12), Thessalonica (17:1), and Beroea (17:10) in Macedonia; and to Athens (17:15) and Corinth (18:1) in Achaea. This itinerary is confirmed in Paul's letters: Philippi and then Thessalonica (1 Thess. 2:1; Phil. 4:16), Athens (1 Thess. 3:1), and Corinth (1 Cor. 2:3; 2 Cor. 1:19; cf. Phil. 4:15). Corinth became Paul's home for eighteen months (Acts 18:11), and it may well have been there that he received news of the crisis in the Galatian churches.[28] Admittedly, the dating of Galatians is disputed, even among those who hold the north Galatian view.[29] Yet Paul himself states in Galatians 1:6 that the crisis in Galatia occurred soon after he founded the churches there: "I am astonished

---

two visits are probably those of Acts 16:6 and 18:23 (= 1 Cor. 16:1) — so Kertelge, "Gesetz und Freiheit im Galaterbrief," 385. But according to BDF 62, in Hellenistic Greek πρότερος simply means "earlier."

26. Lightfoot rightly emphasizes Paul's wording here: δι' ἀσθένειαν rather than δι' ἀσθενείας (167). It is not that, as a matter of fact, Paul happened to be unwell when he evangelized the Galatians. Rather, he did so *on account of* his health problem.

27. For χώρα in this sense, compare Acts 10:39: ἐν τῇ χώρᾳ τῶν Ἰουδαίων καὶ Ἰερουσαλήμ; also 8:1; 26:20. Advocates of the north Galatian hypothesis regularly suggest that the Galatian churches must have been located in Pessinus, Ancyra, and/or Tavium (so, e.g., Lightfoot, *Galatians*, 19). But this suggestion fails to note that Paul's missionary activity in Galatia was both occasioned and limited by his illness (Gal. 4:13). Pessinus, Ancyra, and Tavium are just about as far from each other as Pisidian Antioch, Iconium, Derbe, and Lystra; one would not expect a partially incapacitated Paul to travel such distances.

28. So Dunn, "Incident at Antioch," 70.

29. Lüdemann argues on stylistic grounds that Galatians must date from the period of 2 Corinthians and Romans (*Paul, Apostle to the Gentiles*, 85). But since many commentators have noticed a marked difference in the way Paul treats similar subjects in Galatians and Romans, such stylistic arguments are inconclusive.

that you are *so quickly* deserting him who called you." He could hardly have used this expression if a period of several years had elapsed since he had preached to them.[30] The possible objection that Galatians is unlikely to belong to the same period as 1 Thessalonians, since the two letters are so different, is unconvincing: Paul is writing to different congregations about different issues. But the Thessalonian congregation was apparently independent of the synagogue (cf. 1 Thess. 2:14-16), and this suggests that Paul had already worked out the theoretical rationale for separation that he further develops in Galatians. This early dating of Galatians means that the crisis in the Galatian churches occurred in relatively close connection to the crisis in Antioch. This has important implications for understanding the situation in Galatia.

A later dating for Galatians has been inferred from 1 Corinthians 16:1, where Paul refers to his instructions to the Galatian churches to begin collecting money for Jerusalem, and from Romans 15:26, which states that the collection was the gift of churches in Macedonia and Achaea. The failure to refer here to Galatia may suggest that the crisis there led to the abandonment of the collection project, and that 1 Corinthians 16:1 therefore *precedes* the crisis.[31] But this argument is incorrect, for in spite of Romans 15:26 it was not only the Macedonians and the Achaeans who contributed to the collection. In 2 Corinthians 9:1-5, Paul tells his readers that he has boasted to the Macedonians about the Achaeans' enthusiasm for the collection; he is therefore sending certain "brothers" to Corinth to complete the collection before he himself arrives with the Macedonian delegates, so as to avoid embarrassment. These "brothers" are clearly differentiated from the Macedonians of 9:4.[32] They are described in 8:23 as "apostles of the churches," and the nature of their apostleship is indicated in 8:19, which says of one unnamed yet gifted individual: "He has been appointed by the churches to travel with us in this gracious work." In other words, the "brothers" are the representatives of the churches that have contributed to the collection. The churches who appointed the "brothers" cannot be the churches of Macedonia (cf. 9:3-4), nor, for obvious reasons, the churches of Achaea. Thus churches other than those of Macedonia and Achaea were involved in the collection, and (in the light of 1 Cor. 16:1) the Galatians may well have been among them.[33] Macedonia and Achaea were perhaps singled out in Romans 15:26 on account of their greater prestige.

---

30. Compare Betz, *Galatians*, 47-48.

31. So Lüdemann, *Paul, Apostle of the Gentiles*, 86; Wilckens, "Über Abfassungszweck und Aufbau des Römerbriefs," 135.

32. Against Barrett, *2 Corinthians*, 228, who regards the "brother" mentioned in 8:19 as the representative of the Macedonian churches.

33. Note also the list of Paul's companions and their places of origin in Acts 20:4.

There is no evidence of a Galatian withdrawal from the collection project, and thus no reason to date the Galatian crisis and letter after 1 Corinthians.[34]

In the chronology adopted here, the founding of Pauline congregations in Galatia, Macedonia, and Achaia occurred in the aftermath of the incident at Antioch. The letters that Paul addresses to those congregations all presuppose the radical Pauline doctrine of freedom from the law and a corresponding social location independent of the synagogue. As we saw in the previous chapter, Paul legitimates this stance of sectarian separation by appealing to the general Jewish rejection of the gospel (1 Thess. 2; Rom. 9–11). In Galatians, in contrast, Paul is preoccupied with Christian rather than non-Christian Jews. Yet they, too, are at best failing to adhere to the truth of the gospel (Gal. 2:14), and at worst substituting a false gospel for the true one (1:6-9). The Jerusalem that is revered as the dwelling place of the "pillars" of the new temple becomes indistinguishable from the Jerusalem that is in abject slavery to the law (cf. 4:25). Thus it comes about that an internal debate about the social location of the church in relation to the majority Jewish community is transformed into an antithesis between Pauline Gentile-oriented communities on the one hand and Judaism (whether Christian or not) on the other. This radicalizing of an initial rejection of Gentile circumcision into the doctrine of freedom from the law will have been furthered both by the crisis in Galatia and, earlier, by the Antioch incident. Yet this radicalization does not appear to *derive* from these events within the Christian community, for its origin lies in the conviction, born of missionary experience, of a fundamental incommensurability between the gospel and the law as understood and practiced within the Jewish community. The Galatian churches were founded on this highly controversial premise.

(iv) Agitation in Galatia

What happened in Galatia following Paul's initial visit? Paul refers to the arrival of οἱ ταράσσοντες ὑμᾶς (1:7; cf. 5:10, 12), and we shall follow his usage in describing them as the Galatian "agitators."[35] To speak of these people as

34. Galatians 2:10 need not imply that a collection is already under way in Galatia. Paul speaks here of his zeal (ἐσπούδασα) in fulfilling the pillars' request for material assistance, referring presumably to a collection undertaken immediately after the Jerusalem conference — in an attempt no doubt to consolidate the favorable opinion of Gentile Christians that he hoped was taking root in Jerusalem after his visit (cf. Acts 11:29-30). D. Georgi, *Die Geschichte der Kollekte*, 30, rightly argues that Galatians 2:10 refers to an action Paul carried out in the past.

35. "Judaizers" is inaccurate, because "to judaize" is to convert to Judaism oneself, rather than to encourage others to do so (cf. 2:14).

Paul's "opponents" begs the question of their own attitude towards Paul, which was not necessarily hostile.[36] What had happened in Galatia was not only that the "agitators" had begun to agitate, but also that they seemed persuasive to many (cf. 1:6; 4:21; 5:7-8).

In Galatians 1–2, Paul gives his own account of the prehistory of the current Galatian crisis.[37] As we have seen, those in Galatia who "compel you to be circumcised" (6:12) have their antecedents in Cephas, in James and his messengers, and in the "false brothers." Indeed, it is not impossible that the Galatian agitators *were* the "men from James" (2:12), now extending their activity beyond Antioch into Paul's new mission fields.[38] Alternatively, and more probably, they may have been (Antiochene?) Jewish Christians who sought on their own initiative to make the new two-stage model for Gentile conversion the norm for other churches.[39] There is little sign that the new mission to the Galatians *originates* in Jerusalem. Yet the Galatian agitators claim allegiance to Jerusalem and to James's authoritative declaration on Gentile church membership, which has been accepted and welcomed by figures of the stature of Cephas and Barnabas.[40] Paul seems to have expected the arrival of such a mission in Galatia. In Galatians 1:9 he writes:

> *As we have said before,* so now I say again [προειρήκαμεν/λέγω]: If anyone is preaching to you a gospel contrary to the one you received, let him be accursed.

36. As was assumed in *PJG¹*, 59-61.

37. If the events narrated in Galatians 1–2 are not closely connected to the situation in Galatia, it is hard to see why these chapters have been included in the letter. The crisis in Galatia cannot therefore stem from local non-Christian Jews (J. H. Ropes, *The Singular Problem of the Epistle to the Galatians*, 45), or from among the Galatian Christians themselves (J. Munck, *Paul and the Salvation of Mankind*, 87-134), or from Gnostics (W. Schmithals, *Paul and the Gnostics*, 13-64). I would therefore withdraw my earlier qualified endorsement of Mark Nanos's restatement of J. H. Ropes's position on this (*PHF*, 216n).

38. So Dunn, "Incident at Antioch," 39 (although Dunn accepts the south Galatian theory).

39. Paul speaks of the opposition both in the plural (e.g., οἱ ἀναστατοῦντες ὑμᾶς, 5:12) and in the singular (ὁ ταράσσων ὑμας . . . , ὅστις ἐὰν ᾖ, 5:10). This suggests a group with an individual leader, analogous to Paul's own leadership of a team that includes Silvanus and Timothy. Paul may not know the identity of the leader of the opposing mission, but it is more likely that ὅστις ἐὰν ᾖ is an expression of contempt rather than of ignorance.

40. G. Klein finds evidence in Galatians 1–2 of a gradual ascendancy of James over Peter ("Galater 2, 6-9 und die Geschichte der Jerusalemer Urgemeinde"). On Paul's two visits to Jerusalem, Peter is the sole authority (110) and James is of secondary importance (111). In the reference in 2:9 to "James and Cephas and John," James is named first on account of his *present* significance, at the time when Galatians was written (111).

The phrase "As we have said before" does not merely refer back to the previous verse.[41] On several other occasions, and using very similar terminology, Paul makes it clear that he is repeating by letter what he had said when he was actually present:

I tell you, as I told you before [προλέγω/προεῖπον]. . . . (Gal. 5:21)

I told those who sinned before and all the others, and I tell them again. . . . [προείρηκα/προλέγω] (2 Cor. 13:2)

For many, of whom I have often told you and now tell you even with tears. . . . [ἔλεγον/λέγω] (Phil. 3:18)

In the light of these parallel formulations, Galatians 1:9 must refer to what Paul had earlier said to the Galatians in person. At the time when the Galatian churches were founded, he had warned his converts to beware of those who preached a different gospel from his. In the light of his experiences shortly before he founded the Galatian churches, he could have expected trouble from only one quarter: from members of the Antiochene church who shared the view on Gentile circumcision promulgated by James and accepted by Cephas, Barnabas, and just about everyone else apart from Paul. Paul is astonished that Christians in Galatia are so quickly turning aside to the gospel of circumcision (cf. 1:6), but he is not astonished that this perverted gospel is being proclaimed. Its proclaimers were not necessarily opposed to Paul. They may even have professed great admiration for him. They were merely completing what he had begun (cf. 3:3), following in his steps, building on the foundation he had laid. But Paul was opposed to them. The polemical tone of Galatians is occasioned by the need to make it unambiguously clear that he *does* oppose them, that he *does not* regard their activity as the completion and fulfillment of his own.

The agitators inform the Galatian churches that males must submit to circumcision to ensure full participation in the life of the Christian community. Paul, of course, had said nothing about this, and an account therefore had to be provided of his place within the wider Christian missionary movement. According to this account, Paul was commissioned to work among Gentiles by the Jerusalem apostles. Once the new congregations were established, Gentile converts would be given the opportunity of full church mem-

41. Against Bruce, *Galatians*, 84. Others (e.g., Duncan, *Galatians*, 19; Burton, *Galatians*, 29; Betz, *Galatians*, 53-54) rightly suggest that the reference is to what Paul had said when in Galatia.

bership through submission to circumcision: and that is what is now proposed in Galatia. Why did Paul himself not subject male Galatians to circumcision at the time of their conversion? It was because he sought to please (cf. 1:10, ἀρέσκειν × 2), making it easier for his converts by proceeding one step at a time. Yet Paul himself is in agreement with this strategy of two-stage conversion; he, too, "preaches circumcision" (5:11).

This is the story that Paul seeks to refute in Galatians 1–2. But the story has to be reconstructed from his polemical retelling of it, and the exegetical decisions underlying the reconstruction must be identified and justified.[42] It is not possible or necessary to show that his story refutes the agitators' story point by point and in detail. Paul's version is probably more detailed than theirs. All they need to do is to persuade the Galatians that they are present in Galatia in order to complete a two-stage conversion process, initiated by Paul and authorized by the apostolic authorities to whom he and they are subject. This reconstruction of their standpoint arises out of the following considerations:

(1) The narrative of Galatians 1–2 is shown to be a refutation of an alternative narrative at the very outset of the letter. Here, Paul immediately identifies himself as "an apostle neither by human commission nor from human authorities" (1:1, NRSV; cf. 1:11-12). This is most plausibly read as a denial of an actual claim to the effect that Paul did receive a commission from human authorities — a denial associated with the perversion of the gospel attacked in 1:6-9.

(2) The merely human commissioning rejected by Paul must have been attributed to the Jerusalem apostles. This is implied by Paul's remarkably emphatic denial of significant early contact with them. When God revealed his Son and entrusted Paul with the evangelization of Gentiles, "I did not confer with flesh and blood, nor did I go up to Jerusalem to those who were apostles before me" (1:15-17). When Paul did go up to Jerusalem three years later, it was to pay a private visit to Cephas; of the other apostles he saw only James (1:18-19). He adds: "In what I write to you, before God I am not lying!" (1:20). It is presumably the fact that this visit was not the occasion of a commissioning by the apostles that is here emphasized, in a manner clearly intended to refute the prior claim that (on this occasion or another) he had been so commissioned. The alleged commissioning must have been by the apostles as a whole, and not just by the

---

42. The frequent negations in Paul's narrative mean that it *demands* to be read as a refutation of the story told by his opponents. On this see J. L. Martyn's analysis of Paul's "negative travelogue" (*Galatians*, 178-79).

"pillars," for otherwise the claim not to have met apostles other than Cephas and James would be beside the point. In 2:1-10, Paul acknowledges the grain of truth in the otherwise false commissioning story: he was not commissioned by the apostles to preach to the Gentiles, but the reality of his divine calling to preach to the Gentiles was indeed acknowledged by the apostles, in the person of the "pillars."

(3) Yet the "pillars" (and especially James and Cephas) have special significance for the Galatian situation. Paul's present participles — οἱ δοκοῦντες (2:2, 6), οἱ δοκοῦντες εἶναί τι (2:6), and οἱ δοκοῦντες στῦλοι εἶναι (2:9) — must be taken seriously.[43] We may conclude from this terminology that the agitators revere these figures and are teaching the Galatians to do likewise. Reverence is due on the grounds of "what they once were" — which Paul says is of no significance to him or to God (2:6). "What they once were" must refer to their uniquely close relationship to Jesus.[44] James is "the Lord's brother" (1:19), Cephas is the leading figure among "the twelve" (cf. 1 Cor. 15:5). These were the two figures to whom the risen Lord appeared individually (1 Cor. 15:5, 7). In appealing to the authority of James and Cephas to support their view of Gentile conversion, the agitators can avail themselves of the prestige these figures derive from their relationship to Jesus.

(4) There is no need to suppose that the agitators disparaged Paul to the Galatians, accusing him of disloyalty to his commission. On the contrary, they seem to have claimed that he agreed with them, for Paul is forced to deny the accusation that he "still preaches circumcision" (5:11) just as they do.[45] In the light of this crucial point, the references to his seeking to please (1:10) are to be understood positively. Paul (they assert) accepts the two-stage model of conversion — but for reasons of pastoral sensitivity he did not feel it appropriate to mention the second stage as he sought to consolidate the first. While Paul strenuously denies that he holds a merely human commission (1:1, 11-12), the agitators will have presented

43. So G. Klein, "Galater 2, 6-9 und die Geschichte der Jerusalemer Urgemeinde," 112.

44. So Burton, *Galatians,* 87; Bruce, *Galatians,* 117-18; and the majority of commentators. Burton aptly cites 2 Corinthians 5:16 as a parallel to Galatians 2:6.

45. So rightly G. Howard: the agitators "did not themselves oppose Paul but insisted that he like them taught circumcision" (*Crisis in Galatia,* 19). Howard's account of the Galatian crisis is idiosyncratic, however. He argues that the agitators simply did not know of Paul's special commission to preach a law-free gospel; Paul had kept this secret for many years and had divulged it to the Jerusalem leaders only recently — too recently for news of it to have spread (21). But if the agitators are simply ignorant, and if Paul himself is responsible for their ignorance, why does he abuse them so violently?

his commission in a positive light, as apostolic and therefore as divinely authorized.[46] It seems to be Paul himself who makes an issue of his opposition to Cephas at Antioch, and not the agitators.[47]

(5) In his response, Paul must therefore repudiate the two-stage model of conversion: "Beginning with the Spirit, do you reach fulfillment with the flesh?" (3:3).[48] He must extricate himself from the claim to apostolic legitimacy that is made for this model by insisting on his own independence. In Galatians 1–2, the independence that he must now exercise in relation to the Galatian crisis is projected back onto his entire previous missionary career. Commissioned directly by Christ to preach the gospel to the Gentiles, he had no need of a further commissioning by the apostles. Their leading figures acknowledged this independent calling, and he was willing to oppose them when they later deviated from the truth. In his account of the Antioch incident, there is no suggestion that Paul is defending himself against accusations of insubordination. It is he, and not the agitators, who must stress his independence vis-à-vis Cephas and James. The same concern is evident in the preceding account of the Jerusalem conference. Paul's strategy is not to challenge the agitators' claim that the two-stage model is endorsed by the apostles, but to challenge the apostles themselves.

In Galatians 1–2, Paul recounts the antecedents of the current controversy in Galatia over the question whether Gentiles should submit to circumcision as the completion of the process of conversion. In doing so, he indicates that this issue has wider implications for the church's relationship with the majority non-Christian Jewish community. Should the church remain a reform movement within the Jewish community, continuing to share its traditions and patterns of conduct, with a view to its transformation? Or should it become a sect, separated from the Jewish community by a range of distinctive beliefs

---

46. They do not *criticize* Paul for dependence on Jerusalem — as W. Schmithals assumes, arguing that the agitators are to be regarded as "Gnostics" (better, "charismatics"?) who rejected all merely human transmission of authority on the basis of unmediated encounters with the divine (*Paul and the Gnostics*, 13-64; compare C. H. Talbert, "Again: Paul's Visits to Jerusalem," *passim*; J. H. Schütz, *Paul and the Anatomy of Apostolic Authority*, 125-26). For a critique of Schmithals, see J. Eckert, *Die Urchristliche Verkündigung im Streit zwischen Paulus und seinen Gegnern nach dem Galaterbrief*, 64-71.

47. As J. B. Tyson remarks with reference to Galatians 2:11-21, "It is not certain that Paul is making a specific defensive statement in this section" ("Paul's Opponents in Galatia," 247).

48. As R. Jewett rightly notes, Galatians 3:3 suggests that the agitators "planned not to oppose Paul or his theology directly but instead to offer a completion of it" ("The Agitators and the Galatian Congregation," 206).

and practices, and drawing much of its membership from among Gentiles rather than Jews? The Gentile circumcision issue signifies a decision for or against ongoing participation in the life of the wider Jewish community. Underlying the inner-ecclesial debate is the minority group's perception of itself as vulnerable to the hostile reaction of the majority Jewish community. According to one response, everything possible should be done to minimize the offence and to keep channels of communication open. According to the other, the offense is indicative of an unbridgeable ideological divide. Alienation takes the place of accommodation.

2. Paul's Response to the Crisis

In Galatians, Paul argues vehemently against the view that Gentile Christians should be incorporated into the Jewish community through submission to circumcision. He thereby opposes a view of the church that sees it as a reform movement within Judaism, arguing instead for a sectarian view of the church as alienated from Judaism. His attempt to articulate and defend this stance may be summarized under the three headings introduced in previous chapters: denunciation, antithesis, and reinterpretation.

(i) Denunciation

In Galatians, denunciation is directed primarily against the agitators, and not the Jewish community as a whole. However, the agitators are assumed to stand in close proximity to the Jewish community, so the distinction is hardly significant. There is little discernible difference between the pre-Christian Paul, whose zeal for Ἰουδαϊσμός led him to persecute the church (Gal. 1:13), and the agitators, who similarly persecute "the children of the promise" as Ishmael persecuted Isaac (4:28-29). Paul's text permits the deduction that the agitators are Christian Jews rather than non-Christian Jews — for example, in the reference to ἕτερον εὐαγγέλιον in 1:6; but at no point is this distinction *ideologically* significant.[49] On the contrary, the leader of the sectarian faction here denounces the reforming wing of the early Christian movement as indistinguishable from the parent community.

Having identified the agitators and expressed astonishment at their fa-

---

49. For the alternative view, see J. L. Martyn, *Galatians,* 35-38; and "Galatians, An Anti-Judaic Document?" in his *Theological Issues in the Letters of Paul,* 77-84.

vorable reception in Galatia, Paul proceeds to curse them twice (1:8-9). The curse is the strongest possible form of denunciation. It operates on the assumption that the deity shares the speaker's abhorrence for the person cursed, and it seeks to evoke in its hearers the sense that they are confronted with a superhuman evil that divine power will soon annihilate. Elsewhere, Paul seeks to win the Galatians over to his point of view by ridiculing the agitators and by undermining belief in their sincerity. Ridicule occurs chiefly in 5:12, where Paul suggests an analogy between circumcision and castration.[50] If only the enthusiasts for one form of genital mutilation would subject themselves to the other as well, thereby cutting off their power to reproduce themselves! In drawing this analogy, Paul encourages his readers to see circumcision as a degrading rite to which no civilized person would willingly submit. There are few passages in Paul where alienation from the Jewish community (ἡ περιτομή) is more starkly expressed.[51] The agitators' motives are also a target for denunciation. Their apparent concern for the Galatians' spiritual wellbeing is in fact a cloak for their own self-seeking (4:17). They are motivated by cowardice (6:12).[52] Their supposed zeal for the law is hypocrisy, for they are secretly transgressors of the law (6:13).[53] Paul is not interested in the slightest in an "objective" assessment of the agitators' character; thus it is mistaken to read 6:13 as evidence that they were antinomians.[54] He is concerned only that his converts should reject the call to submit to a rite that would signify their integration into the Jewish community. One way of doing this is to give a hostile assessment of the agitators' motives.

For our present purposes, the most interesting aspect of Paul's denunciations is his claim that, in seeking to impose circumcision on Gentile Christians, they are showing a cowardly unwillingness to endure persecution (6:12; cf. 2:12). Persecution is a social phenomenon requiring sociological analysis. If it is to function adequately, any society must tolerate a certain amount of variety and dissent among its members. Conversely, if it is to retain its cohesion, it must set limits to possible dissent. "Persecution" is society's reaction

---

50. Betz suggests that Paul here uses public disgust at the castration practiced in the cult of Cybele-Attis to discredit his opponents (*Galatians*, 270).

51. So Räisänen, *Paul and the Law*, 76.

52. Conversely, Paul exploits the prestige of persecution in 5:11 and 6:17 (cf. G. Shaw, *The Cost of Authority*, 41).

53. οἱ περιτεμνόμενοι may, however, refer to those Galatians who have already submitted to the agitators' demand. There is thus no need to conclude from it that Paul's opponents in Galatia were Gentile Christians (against Munck, *Paul and the Salvation of Mankind*, 87-88).

54. As Schmithals does, *Paul and the Gnostics*, 33. Räisänen, *Paul and the Law*, 96, is correct here.

to a minority group in its midst that it perceives as transgressing those limits;[55] or rather, it represents that reaction as perceived by its objects. Persecution may take a variety of forms: verbal abuse, exclusion from particular areas of life, the threat or actuality of physical violence, and so on. Persecution expresses the view that the norms of the minority group are incompatible with membership of the wider community. Any minority group faces the threat of persecution in some form, and two main responses are possible. The group may stress its continued acceptance of the norms and traditions of society as a whole, thus asserting its right to continued membership of that society. Or it may defiantly reject the old norms and traditions and accept the persecution and separation that this will entail.[56] From this second standpoint, the former response may be denounced as a cowardly accommodation. Thus Paul accuses Peter of cowardice at Antioch: Peter "feared those of the circumcision" (Gal. 2:12) — that is, he realized that his previous behavior exposed himself and others to the danger of persecution, because, from the standpoint of the majority community, he had transgressed the limits of tolerable dissent in his social relations with the uncircumcised.

Paul levels the same accusation against the agitators in Galatia:

> It is those who want to make a good impression in the flesh that would compel you to be circumcised, only so that they may not be persecuted for the cross of Christ. (6:12)

To put this point more positively, the agitators wished to circumcise the Galatians, and so to integrate them into the Jewish community, because they held that the whole church should strive for accommodation with and within that community. In the background here is perhaps the increase in nationalist militancy preceding the war that broke out in 65 CE.[57] The agitators may, however, be seen as a symptom of that militancy, and not just as a pragmatic reaction to it.[58] In denying the necessity for circumcision, Paul accepts the persecution and alienation that inevitably follow (cf. 5:11). The link between persecution and membership of a society is especially clear in 4:25-31. One

---

55. Hostility may thus reinforce the boundary between the minority group and society (so W. Meeks, *The First Urban Christians*, 96; J. H. Elliott, *A Home for the Homeless*, 117).

56. Compare Elliott, *A Home for the Homeless*, 80.

57. So R. Jewett, who finds the origins of the agitators' mission in a political situation where "persons in the villages of Judea or Galilee who maintained close relationships with Gentiles or who did not zealously seek the purity of Israel were in mortal danger" ("The Agitators and the Galatian Congregation," 204).

58. Compare J. D. G. Dunn, "Incident at Antioch," 11: Antiochene Christians would have been influenced by Jewish nationalist sentiment.

can see oneself as a member either of the community centered on "the Jerusalem above" (4:26) or of the community centered on "the present Jerusalem" (4:25). To understand oneself in terms of the former will entail exposure to persecution from those "born according to the flesh" (4:29).

(ii) Antithesis

The theological argument of Galatians is characterized by its frequent use of antitheses, especially the fundamental antithesis between "faith" and "works" that has played such an important part in Western theology since the Reformation. According to the Reformation tradition, this antithesis portrays two possible human responses to God. The way of "works" is the way of morality and/or religious observance, in which one tries to please God and earn salvation by scrupulous obedience to God's commandments. The way of "faith" is the way of submission to God's grace, which comes to us as sheer gift, quite apart from all moral attainment. It might be argued that, even if the present interpretation of Paul is correct, this would not affect the validity of the exegesis of Paul inspired by the Reformation. Whatever the attendant historical and social realities, the important thing is that Pauline alienation from Judaism was ultimately grounded in the profound theological insight expressed in the faith/works antithesis. In this way, historical and theological approaches to Paul might be reconciled.

Such a reconciliation would be illusory, however. It is the purpose of the present argument not to show that the theology which the Reformation tradition finds in Paul springs from a particular sociological context, but to show that key points in this theology are not there in Paul at all. For Paul, the expression "works (of law)" refers not to morality in general but to the practice of the law within the Jewish community; and the expression "faith (of Jesus Christ)" refers not to a willingness to receive God's grace as a free gift and to renounce reliance on one's own achievements, but to the Christian confession of Jesus as the Messiah and the social reorientation that this entails (cf. Gal. 2:16).[59] There is no theoretical reason why the practice of the Jewish law and confession of Jesus as the Messiah should be incompatible, as conservative

59. In an important monograph dating from 1932, W. Mundle rightly argues that "the Pauline antithesis against works of the law is not a protest against every kind of 'human achievement through which one might attain and merit something'; it is a much more concrete contrast with the Mosaic law and its demands" (*Der Glaubensbegriff des Paulus*, 99-100; my translation). On the "faith of Christ" issue, see note 78 below, and the extensive discussion in Chapter 7 of this work.

Jewish Christians demonstrated.[60] The antithesis between faith and works does not express a general theoretical opposition between two incompatible views of the divine-human relationship. Rather, it articulates the Pauline conviction that the church should be separate and distinct from the Jewish community. In itself, the antithesis does not provide a reason for this separation; it simply asserts its necessity.

The faith/works antithesis thus has only a limited function. It plays no part in Paul's portrayal of the inner life of his congregations; he does not play off faith against Christian behavior, as though one were saved only by means of the former. On the contrary, for Paul faith includes within itself a commitment to Christian norms of behavior.[61] From a sociological perspective, "faith" represents a radical social reorientation. It entails a breach with characteristic norms and beliefs of one's previous social environment, and the adoption of new norms and beliefs within a new social environment. The transition from the old to the new takes place in baptism. For Paul, faith is inconceivable without, for example, the abandonment of participation in idolatry (1 Thess. 1:9) or the practice of "love," i.e., commitment to the new community and its members (Gal. 5:6). It is not simply that these things inevitably *follow* from faith, so that one could theoretically distinguish them from faith. On the contrary, faith *is* the abandonment of old norms and beliefs and the adoption of new ones.[62] It is of course crucial for Paul that faith is dependent on and generated by the kerygma: for faith is a "hearing" of the message of "Jesus Christ as crucified" (Gal. 3:1, 3; cf. Rom. 10:14) and not a spontaneous decision that anyone could in principle make, entirely of their own volition.[63] Yet the genesis of faith in the kerygma does not reduce faith to passivity or eliminate its volitional dimension.

---

60. Nor is there any incompatibility between faith and the law in non-Christian Judaism. The Habakkuk pesher (1QpHab 8.1-2) applies Habakkuk 2:4 (one of Paul's main proof-texts for righteousness by faith apart from the law [Rom. 1:17; Gal. 3:11]) to "all those who observe the law" and who have "faith in the Teacher of righteousness." On this, see my *PHF*, 119-26.

61. As John Barclay notes, "If the letter is not about 'works' in general . . . , ethical exhortation no longer appears to be so misplaced" (*Obeying the Truth*, 8). Paul requires faith "not just as an 'entry-requirement'" but as "the fundamental determinant of all Christian behaviour" (237).

62. "For Paul, there is no πίστις Ἰησοῦ Χριστοῦ which does not include the ideas of baptism and joining the Christian community" (W. Mundle, *Der Glaubensbegriff des Paulus*, 84).

63. Since for Paul faith is elicited or created by the kerygma, it does not straightforwardly function as "the criterion or condition for entry [into the sphere of salvation] — a much less arduous criterion than the rigorous demand under the law for moral perfection . . . but a criterion nevertheless" (Douglas Campbell, *The Quest for Paul's Gospel*, 157; italics removed). On this view, it is the law's disclosure of one's sinful state that generates "the appropriate rational disposition" to exercise "this significantly reduced criterion for salvation" (157).

Faith for Paul is thus essentially active — an action enabled by the kergyma. There is no question of an antithesis between a passive reception of the gift of salvation followed by secondary active consequences. Paul can therefore state quite consistently that certain prohibited forms of conduct prevent people from entering the kingdom of God (Gal. 5:21), and warn:

> Do not be deceived; God is not mocked, for whatever a person sows, that he will also reap. For one who sows to the flesh will from the flesh reap corruption; but one who sows to the Spirit will from the Spirit reap eternal life. (Gal. 6:7-8)

Paul is not contradicting himself when he makes salvation dependent here on one's behavior and elsewhere on the faith generated by God's saving act in Christ, for Christian conduct is integral to faith. The faith/works antithesis is not an antithesis between faith and morality-in-general, but an antithesis between life as a Christian, with its distinctive beliefs and practices, and life as an observant Jew.

Paul does not separate faith from ethics in his account of the inner life of his congregations. Nor on the other hand does he isolate Jewish "works of the law" from their context within the divine covenant with Israel. He recognizes that his opponents in Galatia ground their appeal for submission to the law on their own understanding of the divine electing grace: God's choice of Abraham and his seed to be recipients of salvation. Abraham and the promises of salvation would hardly be so prominent a feature of his own argument in Galatians 3–4 if his opponents had not first introduced the subject.[64] In Philippians 3:4-6 and Romans 9:4-5, he again shows that on his view Jewish obedience to the law occurs in the context of divine privileges of which Jews believe themselves the beneficiaries. He does not present Judaism as a religion of pure "achievement," any more than he presents his gospel as a religion of pure passivity, i.e., the renunciation of achievement. The antithesis between faith and works asserts the separation of the church from the Jewish community; it does not provide a theoretical rationale for that separation.[65] In passages such as Galatians 2:16, the terms "faith (of Jesus Christ)" and "works (of

---

64. This is generally accepted by commentators (e.g., Burton, *Galatians,* 156-59; Duncan, *Galatians,* 83-84; Oepke, *Der Brief des Paulus an die Galater,* 69; Bring, *Commentary on Galatians,* 111; Guthrie, *Galatians,* 95). However, it is rejected by Byrne, "Sons of God," 148-49.

65. This view thus contrasts with Hübner's existentialist interpretation of the faith/works contrast in Galatians (*Das Gesetz bei Paulus,* 19). He understands this as a contrast between the "Gegründetsein in Gott" of those who understand their existence "nicht im Bedingungsgefüge immanenter Faktoren," and the reliance on the constantly increasing quantity of individual fulfillments of the law of those for whom existence is "verfügbar."

law)" are selected and opposed to one another in order to signify the church's distinct, independent existence. They encapsulate what is most characteristic of the two communities in question: the faith that acknowledges Jesus as the Christ on the one hand, the practice of the Torah on the other. Each term therefore has its own independent existence outside the antithesis. It is not the case that each is to be defined primarily by its relation to the other, as "passive" is defined by its opposition to "active." When the term "faith" is singled out in the expression "righteousness by faith," that is not to isolate faith from other, more "active" aspects of the reorientation that occurs in conversion. Rather, "faith" stands for that reorientation in its totality — a reorientation grounded in the prior divine action that faith recognizes as such. The same is true *(mutatis mutandis)* of the term "works," which stands for adherence to the Jewish way of life and membership of the Jewish community.[66] Where these terms are employed in opposition to one another, they both function as synecdoche, *pars pro toto,* standing for modes of communal life that (according to Paul) *must not* be assimilated to one another. The antithesis serves most fundamentally as an imperative.

When Paul opposes "works of law," he has in mind the distinctive way of life of the Jewish people, insofar as this is defined by the law of Moses. He is speaking of "Judaism" (Gal. 1:13, 14) and of nothing else. According to Käsemann, however,

> the exegete must not make things easier for himself by simply, as historian, noting this incontrovertible fact. . . . Our task is to ask: what does the Jewish nomism against which Paul fought really represent?[67]

Käsemann's answer to his own question is that of Luther: Paul is attacking the upright and religious person. But the assumption that for Paul the Jew represents some generic *homo religiosus* is false. An analogy may make this clearer. One might take as one's interpretative starting point Paul's opposition to the demand for circumcision and then ask: what does circumcision really represent? The answer might then be that circumcision is an external religious rite, and that in opposing it Paul is expressing his undying hostility towards all forms of sacramentalism. But one would then be faced with the difficulty that Paul sanctions the use of sacraments (baptism and the Lord's Supper) within his own congregations. The reason for this difficulty is simply that the assump-

---

66. Thus, observances such as circumcision, the food laws, the sabbath, and the feast days, which were "widely regarded as characteristically and distinctively Jewish" (J. D. G. Dunn, "The New Perspective on Paul," 107), do not exhaust the meaning of the term.

67. Käsemann, "Justification and Salvation History," 72.

tion that circumcision represents sacramentalism is incorrect. Circumcision is rather the rite of (male) entry into a particular religious community and a sign of continuing membership of that community. Similarly, it is incorrect to assume that submission to the law of Moses within the Jewish community represents the religious person's striving after moral achievement. "Works" represents nothing other than a specific communal way of life, defined in terms of the sacred text that is held to determine its distinctive characteristics and to establish its rationale. That, at least, is the *literal sense* of the term.[68] To claim that "for Paul, the Jew represents man in general"[69] is to practice a homiletical application or extension of the Pauline critique of righteousness by works of law, which one then ascribes — without supporting argumentation — to Paul himself.[70] As a result, the irreducible concreteness of the Pauline antithesis is lost. Where an abstract "works" is defined by its opposition to an equally abstract "faith," Judaism becomes a cipher for a general human attempt to secure one's being by moral attainments, and — still more disastrously — Jesus Christ becomes a cipher for the renunciation of such an attempt.

It is true, however, that Paul's view of grace is more radical than that of the (Christian) "Judaism" he opposes. It is one thing to argue for the *concreteness* of the Pauline antithesis, quite another to suggest that the communities it represents hold essentially similar views of the relation of divine to human agency — each stressing both the priority of divine agency and the need for a corresponding human response.[71] Yet the appearance of similarity emerges

68. The expression ἔργα νόμου "refers simply to observance of God's Law" (J. L. Martyn, *Galatians*, 261). Martyn cites Exodus 18:20 LXX, italicizing equivalent phrases: Moses teaches the Israelites "God's commandments and *his* Law, and makes them know *the way in which they must walk* and *the works they must do*" (261). The Galatians will not have thought "that by observing the Law they were performing totally autonomous deeds by which they could earn their own salvation, completely without the help of God" (263). They were instructed by the teachers to "celebrate a new instance of God's grace in the undisturbed context of God's gracious Law" (267n).

69. G. Bornkamm, "The Letter to the Romans as Paul's Last Will and Testament," 28.

70. Arguments for the necessity of this interpretative move are, however, offered by Bultmann, *Theology of the New Testament*, 1:283-84 (in opposition to Mundle). Bultmann appeals to the motif of "boasting" (Rom. 3:27; 4:2), to the contrast between gift and wages (Rom. 4:4-5), and to a supposed parallel between the righteousness of the law and the wisdom sought by the Greeks (cf. 1 Cor. 1:18-31). On these points, see Chapters 7 and 8 of this work.

71. See M. D. Hooker, "Paul and 'Covenantal Nomism,'" arguing that, "although 'nomism' may not be the appropriate term for Paul's 'pattern of religion', . . . his understanding of how salvation 'works' is not so far from that of Judaism as his rejection of the Law might suggest" (50). According to Hooker, Sanders fails to exploit this important implication of his own argument. The assumption that Paul and the Judaism he opposes hold similar views on the relation of divine to human agency appears to be widespread in Pauline scholarship after Sanders.

only at a high level of generality. Divine grace operates rather differently in the two "patterns of religion," and the divergent views correspond to the fact that membership of the Jewish community is dependent primarily on birth, whereas membership of a Pauline community is dependent on conversion.[72] Any religious group that proclaims the necessity of conversion is likely to emphasize the distinction between the old life and the new. The old life is characterized by sin, ignorance, and death, and against this dark background the nature of the new life as a miraculous divine gift will shine out all the more brightly.[73] Romans 5:12–6:23 is perhaps the clearest Pauline exposition of this viewpoint, which might also be illustrated from the Qumran *Hodayoth* and the literature of other conversionist groups, both ancient and modern. Such groups take a *dynamic* view of God's grace, in contrast to the more *static* view of grace in groups where membership is determined primarily by birth and upbringing. But this is by no means the same as the alleged Pauline contrast between salvation as pure gift and salvation as human achievement. Even if, in some passages, Paul does stress the idea of the miraculous divine gift, in others he stresses the human activity through which the gift is appropriated. The first group of passages has the function of reinforcing the community's belief that it originates in a supreme act of creative and gracious divine agency. The second group of passages has the function of reinforcing the norms of conduct that give the community its identity. It is a mistake to find the epitome of the Pauline gospel only in the first group of passages, implicitly commending the profound insight into the existential plight of humanity supposedly expressed in them.

It is therefore correct to say, as E. P. Sanders does, that Paul opposes Judaism not because of any inherent errors such as "self-righteousness" or "legalism," but simply *because it is not Christianity*.[74] The present discussion attempts to give a historical and sociological grounding for this viewpoint. The opposition of faith and works is contingent rather than necessary, concrete rather than abstract. The next step is to examine selected passages in Galatians in which antitheses are used and to show that the point at issue in them is not a

---

72. Compare Sanders's discussion of Paul's transfer terminology (*Paul, the Law and the Jewish People*, 5-10), emphasizing the centrality of conversion to his thought.

73. Meeks describes this as the "soteriological contrast pattern" (*First Urban Christians*, 95).

74. See Sanders, *Paul and Palestinian Judaism*, 552. J. D. G. Dunn sharply criticizes this replacement of the Lutheran Paul by "an idiosyncratic Paul who in arbitrary and irrational manner turns his face against the glory and greatness of Judaism's covenant theology and abandons Judaism simply because it is not Christianity" ("The New Perspective on Paul," 101). Chapter 2 above has attempted to show how Paul reached this position, which, from his standpoint, is not in the least arbitrary or irrational.

purely theoretical opposition but the distinctive identity of the Christian community over against the synagogue. It is important to recall here that, although Paul identifies the Galatian agitators as *Christian* Jews, his theological argument is directed against "Judaism" as such (cf. Gal. 1:13-14). Convinced as he is of the incompatibility of Christ and law, Paul cannot regard the distinction between Christian and non-Christian Judaism as significant.

(1) Galatians 2:14-16 clearly indicates the very specific context of Paul's faith/ works antithesis. Prior to the arrival of the "men from James," Cephas had "eaten with Gentiles" (μετὰ τῶν ἐθνῶν συνήσθιεν [2:12]). As we have seen, what is at issue here is not matters of diet but the *fact* of table fellowship with the uncircumcised.[75] By participating in this practice, Cephas had (according to Paul) renounced his Jewish identity by living "like a Gentile and not like a Jew" (2:14). If Jewish identity is *constituted* by the opposition of Jew and Gentile, circumcision and uncircumcision, then Cephas's previous praxis was fundamentally un-Jewish. Now, however, he has reverted to an insistence on Jewish identity as constituted by the circumcision/uncircumcision divide, thereby "building up" the barrier between Jew and Gentile that he had previously "torn down," and so admitting that in his previous course of action he had been a "transgressor" (2:18).[76] In Paul's view, the controversy at Antioch was concerned with this question: Should Jews live ἐθνικῶς, or should Gentiles live ἰουδαϊκῶς (2:14b)? Paul argues for the former. Verse 14b is parallel to vv. 15-16: "You, though a Jew . . ." (v. 14) corresponds to "We ourselves, who are Jews by birth and not Gentile sinners" (v. 15).[77] "You live like a Gentile and not like a Jew" (v. 14) corresponds to "Even we have believed in Christ Jesus, in order to be justified by faith of Christ, and not by works of law, because by works of law shall no flesh be justified" (v. 16). To seek to be justified by faith is thus synonymous with living like a Gentile, that is, as a member of

75. Thus, in asking, "What was the nature of the table-fellowship that Peter enjoyed with the Gentile believers?" Dunn poses a question that is not strictly relevant to the interpretation of Galatians 2:11-21 ("The Incident at Antioch," 4; italics removed).

76. On this view, παραβάτης refers to Peter's previous conduct seen from the Jewish standpoint (so Oepke, *Der Brief des Paulus an die Galater*, 61; Müssner, *Der Galaterbrief*, 179; Lührmann, *Der Brief an die Galater*, 45). In view of the use of ἁμαρτωλός in v. 15 in its Jewish sense, παραβάτης should be similarly understood, and not as a reference to the real sin of disloyalty to Christ and reversion to the law (the view of J. Ziesler, *The Meaning of Righteousness in Paul*, 173). In abandoning his previous praxis, Peter accepts that he has been seriously at fault.

77. Verse 15 is concessive (so Burton, *Galatians*, 119; Schlier, *Der Brief an die Galater*, 53; Müssner, *Der Galaterbrief*, 167; Ebeling, *Die Wahrheit des Evangeliums*, 168): "We, *although* we are Jews by birth. . . ." This strengthens the links with v. 14, where Ἰουδαῖος ὑπάρχων is obviously also concessive.

a Pauline congregation, in its distinctive existence over again the Jewish community. To seek to be justified by works of the law is to (re-)identify oneself with the community into which one was born (cf. ἡμεῖς φύσει Ἰουδαῖοι, v. 15) by practicing the appropriate way of life (cf. ἰουδαϊκῶς, v. 14; ἔργα νόμου, v. 16). "Works of law" does not refer to circumcision or other "characteristically and distinctively Jewish" observances per se,[78] but to the entire communal way of life that corresponds to the model of Jewish identity to which Cephas has now reverted. "Faith of Jesus Christ" represents an alternative model of communal life. It is, precisely, an *alternative,* constituted as such by the Pauline antithesis in opposition to the assimilation sought by Cephas at Antioch and the agitators in Galatia.[79]

(2) "Works of law" is abbreviated to "works" on six occasions in Romans (3:27; 4:2, 6; 9:11, 32; 11:6; full form in 3:20, 28), but nowhere in Galatians, where the full form of the expression is always used (2:16 [× 3]; 3:2, 5, 10). The "works" in question are precisely "works *of law,*" that is, the individual observances prescribed in the law of Moses, which collectively establish a pattern for Jewish communal life. There is no indication that Paul is interested here in any allegedly general human tendency merely *exemplified* in Judaism. The quest for righteousness "by works of law" (2:16) is thus identical to the soteriology Paul finds in Leviticus 18:5, "the one who does them shall live by them," which he contrasts with Habakkuk 2:4, "the one who is righteous by faith shall live" (citations in Gal. 3:11-12). In this remarkable juxtaposition of incompatible scriptural soteriologies, Paul traces back the earlier antithesis between "faith of Jesus Christ" and "works of law" to its roots in a tension within scripture itself. There is no distinction between "works" and "doing": ἔργα is to ποιεῖν as πίστις is to πιστεύειν.[80] That Paul indeed sees the

78. Against J. D. G. Dunn, "The New Perspective on Paul," 107.

79. "Faith of (Jesus) Christ" brings out the parallel with "works of law" (Gal. 2:16, × 2) better than the conventional "faith in . . . ," although καὶ ἡμεῖς εἰς Χριστὸν Ἰησοῦν ἐπιστεύσαμεν implies that "faith in . . ." is integral to the meaning. The interchangeability of the noun and the verb (cf. 3:6-9, 22) makes it difficult to accept that Paul in Galatians 2:16 is referring to Christ's own faith or faithfulness (against M. Barth, "Jews and Gentiles: The Social Character of Justification," 248; R. Hays, *The Faith of Jesus Christ,* 123-24; J. L. Martyn, *Galatians,* 269-77). "Faith of Christ" seems to have been formulated to balance "works of law": compare "hearing of faith" in 3:2, 5. For further discussion of this issue, see Chapter 7.

80. Dunn's distinction ("The New Perspective on Paul," 117) between "works of law" and Jewish "law-keeping in general" is wholly unwarranted — in spite of his sharp criticism of Sanders for identifying the two. Dunn also overlooks the fact that, in connecting law observance to "righteousness" or "life" (Gal. 2:16; 3:12), Paul is postulating a *soteriology* — and not just a nationalistic misunderstanding of the law "as a Jewish prerogative and national monopoly" (118).

two parallel texts as incompatible is evident from the thesis that they are to-gether intended to demonstrate, which is that "the law is not of faith [ἐκ πίστεως]" (3:12).[81] The two terms of this antithesis are irreducibly concrete. Paul does not mean that faith is opposed to "doing" in general, human moral endeavor as a whole.[82] The Leviticus text reads, "the one who does *them* shall live *by them*," thereby referring to the person who observes by the law of Mo-ses as a loyal member of the Jewish community. Similarly, when it is said that "the law is not of faith," this "faith" is not an attitude of pure receptivity to-wards divine grace, a renunciation of all activity intended to establish a claim on God. Rather, it refers to the total social reorientation entailed in the acceptance of Christian beliefs and norms. This reorientation or transfor-mation is, however, grounded in and enabled by the gospel message (cf. 3:2, 5: ἐξ ἀκοῆς πίστεως); and in that message it is a divine agency that is at work. Thus, "faith," though undeniably a human action, is fundamentally oriented towards the *divine* action that it acknowledges. What Paul learns from his Habakkuk citation is that "life" is to be found in the (public and comprehen-sive) *acknowledgment* of God's prior life-giving intervention in Christ. In the Leviticus citation Paul reads that "life" is to be found in an equally public and comprehensive practice, but a fundamentally different one: law obser-vance, the distinctive mode of life characteristic of the Jewish community. Here, the divine life-giving action awaits the human performance that is its precondition.[83] If others believe that the two texts can and must be harmo-nized, Paul does not. Both texts speak of the way to life in connection with an anonymous individual who represents an entire community, but one text assigns priority to divine agency, the other to human agency. To the empha-sis on the *concreteness* of the Pauline antithesis must be added a recognition of its *asymmetry*. The two different communal practices correspond to di-vergent construals of the divine/human relationship as attested in scrip-

81. In a certain sense, Paul here denies the validity of a passage of scripture (so H.-J. Schoeps, *Paul: The Theology of the Apostle in the Light of Jewish Religious History*, 177-78; E. P. Sanders, "On the Question of Fulfilling the Law in Paul and Rabbinic Judaism," 106; J. L. Martyn, *Galatians*, 328-34). Two qualifications should be added, however. First, to deny the va-lidity of a text is not necessarily to imply that it is somehow fraudulent and that it was included in scripture against the divine intention. Second, in his Leviticus citation Paul acknowledges that the Jewish pursuit of righteousness by works of law has a genuine scriptural foundation and is not to be too quickly dismissed as a mere "misunderstanding" of scripture. The paradox of a scripturally grounded form of life incompatible with the scripturally grounded gospel can only be resolved by appeal to divine predestination (cf. Rom. 9:19–10:5; 2 Cor. 3:12-15).

82. As Sanders says, everyone in Galatia was in favor of "doing" (*Paul, the Law and the Jew-ish People*, 159).

83. For a defense of this exegesis, see my *PHF*, 315-29.

ture.[84] Divine agency is more immediately present to Pauline "faith" than to Jewish law observance, and (as we shall see) the scriptural hermeneutic developed in Galatians 3 as a whole is based upon that contrast.

(3) In Galatians 5:2-12, Christ and circumcision are set in the sharpest opposition to one other. Bultmann rightly notes that the demand for circumcision means that "the condition for sharing in salvation is belonging to the Jewish people";[85] but he can still claim that Paul's discussion of circumcision brings us to the heart of "the Pauline problem of legalism," i.e., "the problem of good works as the condition for participation in salvation."[86] This mental leap from circumcision to a false understanding of good works is quite illegitimate. Paul opposes circumcision because it is the rite of entry into the Jewish people, *and for that reason alone*.[87] Thus, in an *ad hominem* attempt to deter his readers from circumcision, he can write: "I testify again to every man receiving circumcision that he is a debtor to perform the whole law" (5:3; cf. 6:13).[88] Circumcision initiates one into a community whose way of life is defined by the law as a whole. Christ is incompatible with circumcision not because "Christ" symbolizes an abstract theological principle (receiving salvation as a sheer gift) that is incompatible with the equally abstract principle underlying circumcision (earning salvation through moral achievement), but because Paul has concluded that the church is only the church when it is separate from the Jewish community. When he writes, "Now I, Paul, say to you that if you receive circumcision Christ will be of no advantage to you" (5:2),

84. Thus, there is more to Paul's claim that "the law is not of faith" than an assertion of simple incommensurability (as argued by Sanders, *Paul, the Law and the Jewish People*, 54n); more, though not less. For the broader point at issue here, see my *PHF*, 14-17, with reference both to Sanders and to J. L. Martyn. Martyn successfully retains *both* the concreteness of the two terms of the Pauline antithesis (and thus the incommensurability thesis), *and* the contrasting views of divine in relation to human agency that are found here. Pauline apocalypticism entails an overwhelming emphasis on invasive and recreative divine agency that is alien to the Teachers, with their insistence on law observance and thus a certain mode of human agency. This is not an *absolute* contrast (divine agency alone in the one case, human agency alone in the other); but there *is* a contrast here.

85. Bultmann, *Theology of the New Testament*, 1:55.

86. Bultmann, *Theology of the New Testament*, 1:111-12.

87. As John Barclay notes, circumcision may have been attractive to some in Galatia because of the possibility it offered of a positive relationship with the Jewish community: "By becoming proselytes the Galatians could hope to identify themselves with the local synagogues and thus hold a more understandable and recognizable place in society" (*Obeying the Truth*, 60).

88. This text tacitly appeals to the practical difficulty of full law observance for uninstructed Gentiles, rather than to a theological impossibility grounded in human fallenness.

not the least significant part of this sentence is the phrase, "Now I, Paul, say to you . . ." Paul here grounds his insistence on the incompatibility of allegiance to Christ with membership of the Jewish community not on further theological argumentation but on his own apostolic authority: the two things are incompatible because he says they are. Once again, it is clear that Pauline antithesis *asserts* the separation of church from synagogue, but does not *explain* theologically why such a separation is necessary. Theological arguments for the church's distinct existence occur not in Paul's antitheses per se but in his reinterpretations of scriptural traditions.

(iii) Reinterpretation

In the previous chapter, it was argued that one of the main differences between a reform movement and a sect is that the former is conscious of sharing the religious traditions of the wider group to whose reform it dedicates itself, whereas the latter regards itself as the sole legitimate possessor of those traditions and denies that they belong in any positive sense to the wider community. These two attitudes to tradition lie at the heart of the theological discussions of Galatians 3–4. The agitators appear to have claimed that the promises of salvation were originally bestowed on Abraham and his seed and that the seed or children of Abraham are those who are circumcised and law observant.[89] That is presumably the theological basis for their demand that the Galatians be circumcised. Thus, their understanding of Christ is set in the framework of the religious traditions of the Jewish community as a whole. For them, although no longer for Paul, Jesus is still a thoroughly and exclusively *Jewish* Messiah.

Galatians 3 makes best sense on the supposition that this was the agitators' message, for Paul argues here that his Gentile converts are *already* sons of Abraham, and this must be intended polemically. At the conclusion of the argument, Paul states that Jew and Greek alike are one in Christ Jesus, and that "if you are Christ's, then you are Abraham's seed" (v. 29). This transition from Christ to Abraham would be strangely anti-climactic if the Galatians were not already concerned about participation in "Abraham's seed." Thus, the question at issue is: Who is the seed of Abraham? The agitators claim that

89. Barrett writes: "At the heart of their theology was the concept of the people of God with its origin in Abraham, and the divine promise that constituted it" ("The Allegory of Abraham, Sarah and Hagar in the Argument of Galatians," 167). Barrett and other scholars are, however, over-optimistic about the possibility of reconstructing the details of the agitators' appeal to Abraham from Paul's rebuttal.

this refers to the Jewish community. But according to Paul, the Galatians must recognize that "those who are of faith, *these* are the sons of Abraham" (v. 7); οὗτοι here is emphatic, and appears to contest a contrary claim stemming from the agitators. It may be that they also made use of Genesis 12:3, which Paul reinterprets in Galatians 3:8-9 in the light of Genesis 15:6; the emphatic threefold use of the phrase ἐκ πίστεως should be noted. His opponents would have argued: "God indeed promised that he would grant salvation to the Gentiles, but only if they join themselves to the seed of Abraham — as it is written, '*In you* shall all the Gentiles be blessed.'"[90] According to Paul, this refers to a sharing by the Gentiles in the blessing with which Abraham himself was blessed, i.e., righteousness by faith (vv. 8-9, 14). The agitators claim that if the Galatians join the Jewish community, they will become heirs to the promise of salvation, for "the promises were made to Abraham and to his seed" (v. 16a). Paul argues that "seed" here refers not to the Jewish people but to Christ (v. 16b) and to those who are in Christ, Jews and Gentiles indiscriminately (vv. 26-29). In each case, the agitators are conscious of sharing religious traditions with the Jewish community as a whole, whereas Paul disinherits the Jewish community and claims that his congregations of mainly Gentile Christians are the sole legitimate possessors of these traditions.[91]

For the agitators, being a descendant of Abraham entails submission to the law. In opposition to this, Paul in Galatians 3 is concerned to drive a wedge between Abraham and law observance. The gulf between himself and his opponents reflects a gulf within scripture itself. In addition to the antithetical citation of texts from Habakkuk and Leviticus, already discussed, scripture is reinterpreted antithetically so as to make the following points:

(1) Gentile believers share in "the blessing of Abraham," but on the other hand "those who are of works of the law" are under a curse (vv. 8-10, citing Gen. 12:3 and Deut. 27:26). This is to be understood as a purely textual argument, arising from the anomaly that the same Torah that announces

---

90. J. L. Sumney argues that the absence of references to Abraham in explicit statements about the opponents "places in serious doubt the widely held view that Abraham figured prominently in the opponents' arguments"; Paul himself "could well be the one who initiates discussion of Abraham" (*'Servants of Satan', 'False Brothers' and Other Opponents of Paul*, 154). While Sumney's caveats about "mirror reading" are to be welcomed, 3:7 and 29 in particular make better sense on the supposition that the topic of Abraham and his seed was not introduced by Paul.

91. "Disinherit" will seem too strong a word only if Galatians is read from the standpoint of Romans 11, rather than (say) 1 Thessalonians 2:14-16. According to the relative dating accepted here, Galatians is chronologically closer to 1 Thessalonians than to Romans.

universal blessing at its outset threatens an almost equally universal curse at its conclusion. For Paul, the entire subsequent history of Israel stands in the shadow of that curse. The scriptural anomaly of the blessing and the curse is resolved chiastically in the cross and resurrection, where Christ endures and exhausts the law's curse and realizes the law's promise of universal blessing (Gal. 3:13-14).[92] The argument is wholly dependent on the scriptural texts; Paul's appeal to Deuteronomy does not depend on the unspoken premise that the law requires perfect obedience that is never forthcoming.[93]

(2) The law can have nothing to do with God's promises to Abraham, for that would mean that a definitive divine will or covenant had been altered or made void by the introduction of additional stipulations (Gal. 3:15-18). Paul's promise/law antithesis appeals to the incompatibility between the unconditional promise and the demands imposed at Sinai, which threaten to rewrite and to undermine the divine διαθήκη by imposing subsequent conditions. Two points should be noted here. First, the logical incompatibility of promise and demand is grounded in the text of scripture, since it has to do with the relationship between what was originally said to Abraham and what was later said to Israel at Sinai. Second, the unconditional promise is correlated not with an unconditional salvation in general but specifically with the coming of Christ, the true seed of Abraham (3:16). The universal salvation enacted in Christ is determined wholly by the God of the promise (cf. 4:4) and is not contingent upon zealous law observance or the like.[94] The correlate of the unconditional promise is the priority and present reality of the divine saving action that enables the life of faith.[95]

(3) The law marked a purely temporary phase between the promise to Abraham and the coming of Christ to fulfill it (3:19-29; 4:1-7). It is essential that the law be regarded as temporary, if its curse is to give way to blessing and if its demand is not to obstruct the realization of the promise.

---

92. See further *PHF*, 183-88, 427-34.

93. Kent Yinger rightly argues that this notion of "perfect obedience" is irrelevant both to Paul and to Second Temple Judaism generally (*Paul, Judaism, and Judgment according to Works*, 166-69). For a defense of the traditional "perfect obedience" concept in connection with Galatians 3:10, see Andrew Das, *Paul, the Law, and the Covenant*, 163-70.

94. See *PHF*, 193-202.

95. The term "unconditional" is therefore appropriate to the Pauline theme of the promise and its fulfillment, but is not in serious tension with "conditional" passages such as Galatians 5:21b or 6:7-8 — except insofar as the behavior proscribed there is itself in fundamental tension with Paul's soteriology in its entirety.

Such arguments are only relevant to the Galatian situation if the agitators had claimed that obedience to the law was the essential consequence of sonship of Abraham. They find scriptural harmony where Paul finds scriptural antithesis, in the form of two sharply opposed communities, οἱ ἐκ πίστεως and ὅσοι ἐξ ἔργων νόμου (3:9, 10). For Paul, scripture anticipates the distinctive existence of the Christian community, over against the Jewish community. For his opponents, it does no such thing: for περιτομή remains the covenant sign of the people of God, even though the majority in Israel do not yet acknowledge the messiahship of Jesus. From their perspective, the only significant scriptural antithesis is the one between περιτομή and ἀκροβυστία (cf. 2:7; 5:7; 6:15); and this antithesis, too, has two opposing communities as its social correlate.

The Galatian agitators appear to assume that the law is one of the gifts of God to the Jewish community as a whole; they do not claim to possess it exclusively. In Galatians 5:14, Paul does claim that the kernel of the law ("You shall love your neighbour as yourself") is a Christian possession, but his more characteristic view is to concede possession of the law to the Jewish community, while arguing that its effects there are negative rather than positive. Thus, in the Deuteronomy citation of Galatians 3:10, Paul grounds the separation of the church from the synagogue in the scriptural declaration of the fate of those who live under the law, which is that one inevitably falls prey to the curse it pronounces on the disobedient. Law-observant Jews, Paul claims, are wrong to imagine that the law is an instrument of blessing. It is the bringer of a curse, and the Galatians must realize that subjection to it will imperil their eternal well-being.

In one sense, Paul has conceded possession of the law to the Jewish community. In another sense, he is arguing that Christians alone possess insight into the true meaning of the law, which is exactly the opposite of what its adherents think. It is the sectarian group that truly understands the scriptural tradition to which the majority community appeals (cf. 2 Cor. 3:12-18). Radical reinterpretation of traditional views on Abraham and the law serves to justify the Pauline congregations' separation from the life of the Jewish community. In the case of the agitators, no such reinterpretation has taken place, for they desire to remain loyal members of the Jewish community as a whole and of a Christian church that exists in and with that larger community. For them, Jerusalem is the city both of the "pillars" of the church and of the Jewish people as a whole (cf. 4:25).

Returning to Käsemann's question, we may ask: What does the Jewish Christianity against which Paul fought really represent? The answer has nothing to do with "the upright and religious person," or "legalism," or "good works as the condition for participation in salvation." It represents continued participation in the religious community it was trying to reform and in the traditions and praxis of that community. That and nothing else is what is intended in the Pauline critique of "works of the law" as the way to righteousness. The critique is not occasioned by any general incompatibility between belief in Jesus as the Christ and the practice of Judaism. "Works" and "faith" are not oppositional terms that can be defined only in relation to each other, like "active" and "passive" (or indeed "exclusive" and "inclusive"). The Pauline antithesis is not so much a piece of logical analysis as an *imperative* — the call to embrace a *distinct* identity, focused on Jesus Christ and uniting Jews and Gentiles under the premise of the unimportance of the circumcision/uncircumcision divide and of the praxis corresponding to it (cf. 3:28; 5:6; 6:15). Insofar as Paul provides supporting arguments at all, his arguments are scriptural rather than theoretical. The self-differentiation of the sectarian group from the majority community takes the form of antithesis, where the separation of the communities is simply *asserted,* and of reinterpretation, where the case for separation is *argued* on shared scriptural terrain.

CHAPTER 4

Philippi, Corinth, and the
Jewish Christian Mission

As we have seen, a Jewish Christian mission to the newly founded churches in
Galatia was the occasion for a letter in which Paul outlines a radical view of
the Christian community as distinct and autonomous in relation to the majority Jewish community. The sectarian group remains "Jewish" in the sense
that it continues to engage with the Jewish scriptures. And yet scripture,
shared with the majority community, is precisely the site on which difference
is most clearly articulated. Scripture is interpreted in such a way as to legitimate the existence of largely Gentile communities in which the law is not observed and in which the distinction between circumcision and uncircumcision is declared to be null and void. If, as Paul assumes, "Judaism" entails a
communal adherence to the foundational status of the law of Moses, then the
Galatian agitators remain "Jewish" whereas Pauline Christianity does not.[1] In
that sense, it is appropriate to speak of a "Jewish Christian" mission to
Gentiles that may be distinguished from the Pauline one. The question now is
whether such a mission ever existed outside Galatia, or whether the attempt
to bring the Pauline mission to "completion" (cf. Gal. 3:3) was discontinued,
perhaps in the light of Paul's hostile response. In Philippians, Paul's opponents closely resemble the Galatian agitators. They are purely hypothetical,
however: Paul is anxious about the possibility of a renewed Galatian crisis in
Philippi, but the possibility has yet to become a reality. In Corinth, on the
other hand, an actual opposition is all too real: its leaders are denounced as
"false apostles, deceitful workers disguising themselves as apostles of Christ"

---

1. If Jewishness is otherwise defined, in terms, for example, of possession of the scriptures
(cf. Rom. 3:1), then Pauline Christianity remains thoroughly Jewish.

(2 Cor. 11:13). Yet the profile of these figures seems significantly different from that of the Galatian agitators. There is, then, no evidence of an ongoing attempt to persuade Pauline Gentile communities to submit to circumcision and to adopt the practice of the law. The Jewish Christianity presupposed in the letter to the Romans appears to lack any specific missionary orientation.

1. Philippians 3: A Postscript to Galatians

In Philippians 3 Paul expresses his anxiety that the Galatian agitators might extend their activity to other churches — or so we shall argue. In consequence, the question of the place of origin and the (relative) dating of this letter takes on a new significance. If Philippians was written from Rome, then Paul would still be preoccupied with a "Jewish Christian threat" almost a decade after the Galatian crisis.[2] That would suggest an ongoing, organized "judaizing" mission, authorized perhaps by the Jerusalem church. If Philippians was written from Ephesus, however, it would stem from the aftermath of the Galatian crisis. The tendency of such a view would be to downplay the significance of the Galatian agitators in the further development of the Pauline mission. They would belong to a particular phase of that mission, but Paul's fears of their extending their activity elsewhere would prove to be unfounded. Here as elsewhere, "introductory" issues are an important preliminary to the exegesis of the Pauline text.

(i) Place and Time of Writing

In Philippians, Paul is in prison (1:7, 13, 14) and faces the possibility of the death sentence. He believes that he will be released, because he thinks that Christ still has work for him to do (1:24-26; 2:24). But he is by no means cer-

---

2. For a recent argument in favor of a Roman place of origin, see Markus Bockmuehl, *Philippians*, 25-32, where the main points are (1) that Acts is silent about an Ephesian imprisonment (27); (2) that, for Paul as a Roman citizen, a capital charge for preaching the gospel is unlikely in Ephesus, as Acts 16:37-39 indicates (28); and (3) that ἐν ὅλῳ τῷ πραιτωρίῳ (Phil. 1:13) and οἱ ἐκ τῆς Καίσαρος οἰκίας (4:22) are historically plausible and rhetorically effective only if Paul is writing from Rome (28, 30-31). On 4:22, Bockmuehl cites the work of P. R. C. Weaver on the imperial household (1972), according to which 96 percent of the 660 individuals identified in inscriptions as *Caesaris* lived in Rome (70 percent), Italy, or North Africa (31). Bockmuehl concedes, however, that "a good many of these civil servants would be found throughout the empire" (269).

tain: death is still a possibility (1:20-33), and despite apparent confidence in release (1:24-26) he delays sending Timothy until he sees "how it will go with me" (2:23), i.e., whether or not "I am to be poured out as a libation upon the sacrificial offering of your faith" (2:17).

Like 1 Corinthians, Philippians was probably written from Ephesus during the three-year stay there that began shortly after his second visit to Galatia (Acts 19:1-41; 20:31).[3] It is true that there is no certain evidence for Paul having been imprisoned in Ephesus.[4] But in 1 Corinthians 16:9 he mentions his "many opponents" there, and in 15:32 he contemplates the possibility of "fighting with wild beasts" specifically in the theater at Ephesus. In 2 Corinthians 6:5 and 11:23, he mentions "imprisonments" among his sufferings; in Romans 16:7 he names two individuals who have been his "fellow prisoners." According to 1 Clement, Paul's many sufferings included his "seven times bearing chains" (5:6: ἑπτάκις δεσμὰ φορέσας). Evidence for an Ephesian imprisonment has also been found in 2 Corinthians 1:8-10, where Paul gives an allusive and metaphorical account of his recent experience in Asia, during which "we felt in ourselves that we had received the sentence of death [τὸ

---

3. The argument here assumes the literary unity of Philippians, which has been challenged by the claim that Philippians is a collection of two or three letters or letter fragments. Thus W. Marxsen regards 4:10-20 as the earliest letter, since Paul would not have allowed the period of time implied in 2:25-30 to elapse before thanking the Philippians for their gift (*Introduction to the New Testament*, 61). But Paul might well have delayed writing to them until Epaphroditus had recovered from a near-fatal illness (2:26). The Philippians might have heard about Epaphroditus's illness through the return of other Philippian delegates without him. Since the serenity of 4:10-20 contrasts with Paul's anxiety during Epaphroditus's illness (cf. 2:27b), 4:10-20 should not be regarded as a letter of acknowledgment dating from that time. As regards the separation of 3:1-4:1, 8-9 (so J. Gnilka, *Philipper*, 7) or 3:1-4:3, 8-9 (Marxsen, *Introduction*, 62), the following points may be made. (1) The occurrence of τὸ λοιπόν in 3:1 does not mean that this was originally the beginning of the concluding section of a letter. τὸ λοιπόν (or its variants) *may* signal the conclusion of a Pauline letter (2 Cor. 13:11; Gal. 6:17), but need not do so (1 Thess. 4:1). (2) The abruptness of the attack on opponents finds a parallel in Romans 16:17-20 (so Kümmel, *Introduction to the New Testament*, 333); the question of the original function of Romans 16 makes no difference to this point (against Gnilka, *Philipper*, 7-8). (3) The opponents are not yet present in Philippi, as 3:18 indicates, so that one would not expect references to them in Philippians 1-2 (against Gnilka, 8). (4) In 4:1, Paul calls the Philippians ἐπιπόθητοι, and 1:8 (ὡς ἐπιποθῶ πάντας ὑμᾶς; cf. 1:24-26; 2:24) indicates that this must refer to Paul's longing to visit the Philippians once he is released from prison. The *Sitz im Leben* of 3:1-4:1 is therefore the same as the rest of Philippians. Kümmel is right to find the arguments for dividing Philippians into two or three letters "totally unconvincing" (*Introduction to the New Testament*, 333).

4. Arguments in favor of an Ephesian imprisonment are given by G. S. Duncan, *St Paul's Ephesian Ministry, passim*. Duncan's arguments are criticized by Dodd, "Mind of Paul, II," 83-108. For my purposes, they are too dependent on assumptions about the historicity of Acts and the authenticity of Colossians.

ἀπόκριμα τοῦ θανάτου]" (2 Cor. 1:9). This passage does not seem merely to reflect Paul's distressed state following the dispatch of his "severe letter" to the Corinthians (cf. 2 Cor. 2:4, 12-13; 7:5-6, 8). If Paul's suffering is said to have occurred "in Asia," then it was surely occasioned by factors specific to Asia. The reference is apparently to the whole period of his recent missionary activity in Asia and is no doubt intended to set his specific problem with the Corinthian church in a broader context of apostolic suffering. While Paul's language does not *require* the threat of a literal death sentence that he faces in Philippians, it is fully compatible with it. Since there is no possibility of an extended period of imprisonment between the composition of the "severe letter" and the "letter of reconciliation," an Ephesian imprisonment would have to predate the train of events presupposed in 2 Corinthians.[5]

Two arguments for the "Ephesian hypothesis" seem particularly compelling. First, imprisonment in Ephesus is a plausible explanation for the unanticipated prolongation of Paul's stay there and the consequent delay to his proposed visit to Macedonia. Second, parallels between Philippians and Philemon serve to strengthen the connection with Ephesus.[6]

(1) According to Acts, Paul arrived at Ephesus following his second visit to Galatia (Acts 18:23; 19:1; cf. 16:6). This harmonizes well with 1 Corinthians 16:1-4, where Paul (in Ephesus, 16:8) can refer to his recent instructions to "the churches of Galatia" concerning the collection for Jerusalem. (As we have seen, Galatians itself presupposes only a single visit to date, and it may have been written during Paul's extended first visit to Corinth.) During this second visit to Galatia, Paul will have been concerned not only with arrangements for the collection but also with the after effects of the agitators' visit and his own ensuing letter. Indeed, the fact that the collection project was initiated precisely in Galatia may well be significant. Galatian Christians may have conceived the idea themselves, on the basis of Paul's statement about an earlier collection (Gal. 2:10); and Paul may have seen in this suggestion an appropriate outlet for Galatian enthusiasm for the Jerusalem church. When he arrives in Ephesus, then, the Galatian crisis is still fresh in his mind. An Ephesian origin for Philippians would explain the anxieties to which Paul gives expression in chapter 3. At this point in Paul's career, it seems only too possible that the crisis in Galatia will recur elsewhere. While there is less evi-

---

5. For a detailed reconstruction of this train of events, see my article, "2 Cor. x–xiii and Paul's Painful Letter to the Corinthians."

6. An Ephesian origin for Philippians was advocated in *PJG¹*, 73-74, but on the basis of different arguments. Otherwise, few substantive changes have been made to the present chapter.

dence in 1 Corinthians than in Philippians of a continuing preoccupation with the Galatian crisis (but note 1 Cor. 9:2; 15:56), the reason is no doubt that the Corinthian church posed a quite different set of problems.

As he writes 1 Corinthians, Paul seems to envisage only a relatively short stay in Ephesus (1 Cor. 16:8-9), followed by a visit to Macedonia and to Corinth (vv. 5-7). He will remain in Ephesus only "until Pentecost" (v. 8). The rather precise date suggests that departure is scheduled for the relatively near future.[7] Paul explains that he is staying on in Ephesus owing to missionary successes and the emergence of a powerful opposition (vv. 8-9); but that need not entail a visit of more than a few months in all. Yet, when Paul finally reaches Macedonia (cf. 2 Cor. 7:5; 8:1-5), he states that *a full year* has elapsed since the initiation of the collection project in Corinth, in the context of his earlier letter (cf. 1 Cor. 16:1-4). It is, he says, high time for them to complete what "you began *a year ago* [ἀπὸ πέρυσι] not only to do but also to desire" (2 Cor. 8:10). Paul, then, has unexpectedly had to extend his stay in Ephesus for a number of months beyond the proposed departure date at "Pentecost." On the hypothesis of an Ephesian imprisonment, there is a simple and economical explanation for this: Paul was compelled to remain in Ephesus owing to the success of his "many opponents" (1 Cor. 16:9) in having him imprisoned and under threat of the death sentence. When he writes Philippians, the imprisoned Paul still wishes to visit "Macedonia," i.e., Philippi (Phil. 1:24-26; 2:24); but the visit has been delayed, and, if the worst happens, will not take place at all.[8] In 1 Corinthians and again in Philippians, Paul hopes to visit the Philippians; in 2 Corinthians 1–9, that hope has at last been realized, after the delay caused by the imprisonment and by the crisis that occurred during his return visit to Corinth (cf. 2 Cor. 1:15–2:2).[9] The unanticipated prolongation of Paul's stay in Ephesus strongly supports the hypothesis of an Ephesian im-

---

7. Robertson and Plummer suggest that Paul is writing at Passover, appealing to 1 Corinthians 5:7 and 15:20 (*First Epistle of St Paul to the Corinthians*, 389).

8. Dodd attempts to reconcile the proposed visit to Philippi with the Roman hypothesis, suggesting that, since Paul's plan to travel to Spain depended on the support of the Roman church, and since Philippians 1:15 and 2:21 show that many in Rome were opposed to him, it is not surprising that he should have changed his plans ("The Mind of Paul: II," 96). While this may be so, it remains significant that a firm intention to revisit the Christians of Macedonia is attested from Paul's Ephesian period (1 Cor. 16:5-9).

9. In 2 Corinthians 1:15-16, Paul speaks of an intention to visit first Corinth, then Macedonia, then Corinth again. This represents a modification of the earlier plan (1 Cor. 16:5-7: first Macedonia, then Corinth), and this modified plan was itself modified: for Paul writes here to explain why, instead of visiting Corinth a third time, he sent a harsh letter instead (2 Cor. 1:23–2:4). The likelihood is that Paul also abandoned the plan of visiting Macedonia on his departure from Corinth, returning instead to Asia (cf. 2:13; 7:5-6).

prisonment, and his expressed intention to revisit the Philippians on his release fits perfectly with the evidence of the Corinthian correspondence.

(2) In discussions of the origin of Philippians, parallels with Philemon have not been given the attention they deserve. These are probably the only two "captivity epistles" that are authentically Pauline. The letter to Philemon gives no information as to the whereabouts of either its author or its addressee — except that the author is in prison (Phm. 1, 9, 10, 13, 23) and the addressee is near enough at hand for Paul to have been visited by his slave. In the context of a passage heavily dependent on Philemon (Col. 4:7-18), the later author of Colossians identifies Onesimus as "the faithful and beloved brother, who is one of yourselves" (v. 9).[10] If this link between Philemon's slave and the church of Colossae is not totally wide of the mark, it is likely that Onesimus encountered Paul in a prison in Ephesus rather than in Rome or Caesarea, and that it was from Ephesus that he was sent back to his master Philemon with a request that he be allowed to care for Paul in prison (Phm. 10-14). Indeed, even if the association of Onesimus with Colossae is a fiction, Philemon's place of residence must have been somewhere in Paul's main sphere of missionary activity in Greece and Asia Minor. Onesimus's past and future travels — to Paul, back to Philemon, and back to Paul again (vv. 10-14) — are more conceivable if we envisage a relatively short distance between Philemon's household and Paul's place of imprisonment. Also to be noted are the references to Timothy (Phm. 1) and to Aristarchus (Phm. 24). Timothy is associated exclusively with Paul's ministry in Asia Minor and Greece. Aristarchus is identified in Acts as a Christian from Thessalonica who was a co-worker of Paul's at the time of his Ephesian ministry (Acts 19:29; 20:4). While it is possible that Timothy and Aristarchus traveled with Paul to Jerusalem (cf. Rom. 16:21; Acts 20:4), there is no evidence that they later accompanied him to Rome.

There are a number of significant verbal and thematic parallels between Philemon and Philippians, which suggest that the two letters may have a common time and place of origin in the life of the apostle. These parallels include the following:

(i) Co-authorship with Timothy (Phm. 1; Phil. 1:1). Elsewhere this combination is found only in 2 Corinthians 1:1 in the authentic Pauline letters, although it is imitated by the author of Colossians.

10. Note also the message for Archippus, a co-addressee of the letter to Philemon (Phm. 2), in Colossians 4:17.

(ii) The combination of συνεργός and συστρατιώτης (Phm. 1, 2 [Philemon, Archippus]; Phil. 2:25 [Epaphroditus]).

(iii) Constant thanksgiving for the addressees (εὐχαριστῶ τῷ θεῷ μου . . . πάντοτε, Phm. 4 = Phil. 1:3-4).

(iv) References to the addressees' ἀγάπη (Phm. 5, 7; Phil. 1:9) and κοινωνία, in the context of thanksgiving (Phm. 6; Phil. 1:5).

(v) References to ἐπίγνωσις, in the context of prayers for its increase (Phm. 6; Phil. 1:9).

(vi) Repeated use of the term σπλάγχνα (Phm. 7, 12, 20; Phil. 1:8; 2:1) — employed elsewhere in Paul only in 2 Corinthians 6:12; 7:15.

(vii) The author's joy in the addressee (Phm. 7; Phil. 1:4).

(viii) The announcement that one beloved by the author is being "sent" back to the addressee (Phm. 12; Phil. 2:25, 28).

(ix) "Chains" as a reference to imprisonment, associated with the gospel or Christ: ἐν τοῖς δεσμοῖς τοῦ εὐαγγελίου (Phm. 13); τοὺς δεσμούς μου . . . ἐν Χριστῷ (Phil. 1:13).

(x) An appeal that the one sent back be given a warm reception (Phm. 17; Phil. 2:29).

(xi) Confidence in the addressees' obedience (Phm. 21; Phil. 2:12).

(xii) The announcement of a forthcoming visit on release from imprisonment (Phm. 22; Phil. 2:24).

If the two letters stem from the same context, Philemon would derive from an earlier phase in Paul's imprisonment than Philippians (cf. Phm. 23-24 with Phil. 2:19-21). Ephesus is a more likely place of origin than Rome simply by virtue of its greater proximity to Philippi and to Colossae (?). While there is no fundamental objection to Epaphroditus's journeying from Philippi to Rome and back again, it is much less plausible that Onesimus was sent back from Rome to Asia Minor to ask his master's permission to return to Rome again.[11] If the letter to Philemon cannot have been written from Rome, and if it shares a common origin with Philippians, then neither can Philippians

---

11. While Dodd rightly notes that "[w]e cannot know either what was in Onesimus's mind or what his opportunities for travel may have been" ("The Mind of Paul: II," 95), this does not make the Roman hypothesis any more plausible. Dodd continues: "[I]t is as likely that the fugitive slave, his pockets lined at his master's expense, made for Rome *because* it was distant, as that he went to Ephesus because it was near" (95; italics original). Aside from the questionable deductions from vv. 11, 15, 18 that are assumed here, it is still a problem for Dodd that Onesimus is required to make not just one long journey but three. In the scenario Dodd envisages, it is striking that Paul fails to anticipate Philemon's surprise at the (surely rather remarkable) fact that Onesimus had either sought him out in faraway Rome or met him there by pure chance.

have been written from Rome. This argument would tell equally against the theory of a Caesarean origin for Philippians.[12]

As we have noted, an Ephesian provenance for Philippians makes it possible to see the polemics of Philippians 3 as occasioned by the Galatian crisis and its aftermath. As in Galatians, a perceived Jewish Christian threat leads Paul to emphasize the radical disjunction between Judaism and the Christian gospel.

(ii) Denunciation

In Philippians Paul is serene at the prospect of death, but he is by no means serene at the prospect of Jewish Christian missionaries entering the Philippian church and trying to seduce his converts away from the gospel as he understands it (3:2-19). There is no indication that such people have actually arrived at Philippi; Paul warns of a future danger rather than describing a present reality. The people he has in mind are Christians,[13] for ἐργάτης (3:2) is an early Christian technical term for a missionary.[14] They proclaim the necessity of circumcision, for Paul refers to them in 3:2 as the κατατομή, a parody of the true περιτομή, the Pauline congregation (3:3). As in Galatians, circumcision is not regarded as an isolated act of law observance but as the rite that enacts and signifies membership of the people of God.[15] Paul's imagined opponents understand the people of God to be "the circumcision" (cf. Gal. 2:7-9), i.e., the Jewish community, which they invite Gentile Christians to join. Paul, too, understands the people of God as "the circumcision," but interprets this in a spiritualized sense (3:3). Here, he again insists on the absolute separation between the church and the majority Jewish community, in contrast to his opponents, who assume that membership of that community remains necessary for salvation. Paul also refers to his opponents as "dogs," a pejorative Jewish term for Gentiles, who are outside the covenant (cf. Matt. 15:26-27; Rev. 22:15).[16] He seems here to take up a distinction he attributes to his opponents, reversing its

---

12. For arguments in favor of a Caesarean origin for all four "captivity epistles" (Ephesians, Philippians, Colossians, and Philemon), see J. A. T. Robinson, *Redating the New Testament,* 57-67.

13. Non-Christian Jews according to G. B. Caird, *Paul's Letters from Prison,* 133; Christian Jews according to Friedrich, "Der Brief an die Philipper," 159; Michael, *Philippians,* 133; and the majority of commentators.

14. Cf. Matt. 9:37, 38 = Luke 10:2, 7; 2 Cor. 11:13; 1 Tim. 5:18; 2 Tim. 2:15; *Did.* 13.2.

15. Circumcision here is therefore not "a merely outward act" or "formalism" (against R. P. Martin, *Philippians,* 138).

16. Jewish examples in Strack-Billerbeck, 1:724-25; 3:621-52.

application:[17] Gentile Christians (together with Paul) are "the circumcision" and the Jewish Christian missionaries are "the dogs."[18]

It has been argued on the basis of 3:12-16 that these missionaries were gnostics who believed that the resurrection of the dead was a present reality.[19] But this is unlikely, for in this passage Paul is criticizing not the missionaries but (indirectly) his own congregation.[20] The first and second plural references in vv. 15-16 show that this is a purely internal matter. Philippians 3:9-11 marks a transition between Paul's rejection of his own Jewish past ("a righteousness of my own, based on law," 3:9) and a much gentler corrective to "enthusiasm" ("that if possible I may attain the resurrection from the dead," 3:11).[21] This passage has no bearing on the question of the identity of Paul's opponents — who are, we recall, hypothetical. Indeed, the passage as a whole has far more to say about the positive exemplary value of Paul's renunciation of his Jewish privileges for Christ's sake (vv. 4-17) than about the hypothetical opponents and their negative exemplary significance (vv. 2, 18-19). If, perhaps after Paul's death, missionaries of circumcision should enter the Philippian congregation, the Philippians are to recall Paul's own example in relation to his Jewish past and hold fast to Christ.

After the gentle admonitions of 3:12-16, Paul reverts in vv. 18-19 to the uncompromising polemical tone of v. 2:

> For many, of whom I have often told you and now tell you even with tears, live as enemies of the cross of Christ — whose end is destruction, whose god is the belly, and their glory is in their shame, their minds set on earthly things.

Some think that we have here a second group of opponents, who are antinomians,[22] or that the original Jewish Christian missionaries are them-

17. So Lohmeyer, *Der Brief an die Philipper,* 124; Michael, *Philippians,* 134-35; Friedrich, "Der Brief an die Philipper," 159.

18. Staab's comment is thus wide of the mark: "Er nennt sie 'Hünde', wohl deshalb, weil sie immer bellend und beissend hinter ihm herliefen" (*Gefangenschaftsbriefe,* 44).

19. Notably by W. Schmithals, *Paul and the Gnostics,* ch. 2; H. Koester, "The Purpose of the Polemic of a Pauline Fragment," for whom the opponents proclaim a "radicalized spiritualistic eschatology" (331).

20. So R. Jewett, "Conflicting Movements in the Early Church as Reflected in Philippians," 373.

21. Whereas in 3:5-8 the Pharisaic way of life is rejected, in 3:12-16 the (Pharisaic) doctrine of resurrection is used to counter "enthusiasm." (See Acts 23:8; Josephus, *BJ* 7.163; *Ant.* 18.14 for the Pharisaic belief in the resurrection.)

22. "Heretical libertinists with gnostic tendencies," according to Jewett, "Conflicting Movements," 382.

selves revealed here to be antinomians.[23] But both views read this passage in too literal a manner; we cannot conclude from it that Paul here confronts "proponents of an obviously lax lifestyle in matters of food and sex."[24] There is in fact nothing here that cannot apply to missionaries of circumcision such as the Galatian agitators. In Galatians Paul repeatedly asserts that circumcision and the law are utterly opposed to the cross (Gal. 2:21; 3:1; 5:11; 6:12-14), and it is therefore plausible that "enemies of the cross of Christ" (Phil. 3:18) also refers to the advocates of circumcision (cf. vv. 2-3). The claim that such people have "minds set on earthly things" (Phil. 3:19) recalls the implication of vv. 3-4 that they put their confidence in the flesh (vv. 3-4). The reference to "earthly things" generates a contrast with Paul and his readers, whose "citizenship is in heaven" (v. 20) — a close analogy to the contrast between the heavenly and earthly Jerusalem in Galatians 4:25-27. This leaves us with the parallel claims that their god is the belly and that their glory is in their shame.[25] "Shame" (αἰσχύνη) is probably to be understood as a euphemism for the genitals. ἀσχημόσυνη has this euphemistic sense in Exodus 20:26 and Revelation 16:15, and so too does τὰ ἀσχήμονα ἡμῶν in 1 Corinthians 12:23.[26] "Their glory is in their shame" is thus an abusive reference to circumcision. But in Philippians 3:19 Paul also states that "their god is the belly." This is probably not to be understood as a reference to the Jewish food laws,[27] for κοιλία may have the same euphemistic sense as αἰσχυνή.[28] But why then should Paul say that "*their god* is the belly"? It seems that he here alludes to phallic cults such as that of Priapus, which spread to Greece and the great Hellenistic cities after the time of Alexander, and the Dionysia, which originated in Athens but spread almost everywhere.[29] If this is correct, Paul here denounces his opponents as worshipers of the phallus. This would again be a reference to the missionaries of circumcision.

Since Paul can link circumcision with castration (Gal. 5:11) and with the

23. See note 19 above.

24. W. G. Kümmel, *Introduction to the New Testament*, 328.

25. δόξα is frequently linked in the LXX to divine manifestation (e.g., Exod. 16:7, 10; 24:16, 17; Ezek. 2:1; 3:12; 8:4); ὁ θεός and ἡ δόξα in Philippians 3:19 are thus approximate synonyms.

26. Compare the phrase ἡ περιτομὴ τῶν αἰδοίων, in Artapanus, a Hellenistic Jewish writer of the second century BCE (quoted by Eusebius in *Praep. Evan.* 9.27.10).

27. R. P. Martin, *Philippians*, 158. Other suggestions include self-interest (A. F. J. Klijn, "Paul's Opponents in Philippians III," 283) and gluttony (Koester, "The Purpose of the Polemic of a Pauline Fragment," 326).

28. I am indebted to the Rev. C. Mearns for this interpretation of κοιλία. It has this sense in the LXX of 2 Kgdms. 7:12 = 1 Chron. 17:11; 2 Kgdms. 16:11; 2 Chron. 32:31; Deut. 7:13; 28:4, 11, 18, 53; 30:9; Ps. 131:11.

29. Brief details and bibliography are in the *Oxford Classical Dictionary*, 876.

"mutilation" practiced in some forms of paganism and banned in the Old Testament (Phil. 3:2),[30] it is by no means unlikely that he should also identify it with phallic worship.[31] Paul is probably here drawing on a tradition of hostile Gentile taunts against Jews. Philo (*Spec. leg.* 1.2) and Josephus (*c. Ap.* 2.137) both indicate that circumcision could be an object of derision among non-Jews. For reasons of delicacy, neither goes into details about the nature of this derision. Paul does not share their inhibitions: he tells his Gentile converts that circumcision, the rite signifying (male) membership of the Jewish community, is simply castration, mutilation, and phallus worship. Such charges may well have been the stock-in-trade of Gentile mockery of Judaism. If so, there is a deliberate strategy underlying these crude comparisons. Paul seeks to reinforce stereotyped attitudes towards circumcision and the circumcised with which his Gentile readers have been familiar since childhood. His aim in doing so is to create an unbridgeable gulf between his congregations and the majority Jewish community, in the person of its Jewish Christian representatives.

Philippians 3:18-19 therefore denounces the same people as 3:2. There is no evidence that they were gnostics or antinomians; nor have they as yet even appeared among the Philippian congregation.[32] Paul tells the Philippians to be on the lookout for such people and to beware of them (3:2),[33] and 3:18 shows that they know of them only indirectly, through Paul's repeated warnings. He is probably referring to the people who caused the Galatian crisis. Just as he had warned the Galatians during his first visit to beware of such people (Gal. 1:9), so he here indicates that he had repeatedly warned the Philippians of the possibility of their arrival.

(iii) Antithesis

Owing to his intense anxiety about this threat, Paul in Philippians 3 once again seeks to legitimate the separation of the church from the Jewish com-

---

30. 3 Kgdms. 18:28; Hos. 7:14; Isa. 15:2; Jer. 48:37; cf. Lev. 19:28.

31. Jewett's objection to the view that vv. 18-19 refer to the opponents of v. 2, on the grounds that "the polemic would be too gross to be effective" ("Conflicting Movements," 379), is therefore not valid.

32. Against Gnilka, *Der Philipperbrief*, 8.

33. G. B. Caird (*Paul's Letters from Prison*, 133) translates βλέπετε in v. 2 not as "Beware of . . ." but as "Consider . . . ," on the grounds that βλέπειν with a direct object elsewhere means the latter (1 Cor. 1:26; 10:18; 2 Cor. 10:7; Col. 4:17). But βλέπετε τί ἀκούετε in Mark 4:24 (cited by Lightfoot, *Philippians*, 141) seems to justify the traditional interpretation. That Paul here believes himself to be faced by a real threat is suggested by his "vicious invective" (Beare, *Philippians*, 103).

munity. We have already examined one characteristic element in his strategy, which is to denounce his opponents. Reinterpretation is in evidence here only in the form of the claim to be the true circumcision (3:2-3); there is here a complete lack of the scriptural interpretation that elsewhere accompanies Paul's righteousness-by-faith terminology. In this context, the most important element in his legitimation of Christian distinctiveness is *antithesis*. Indeed, 3:2-11 as a whole is a single antithesis, designed to show that (Pharisaic) Judaism and the gospel are mutually exclusive. As in Galatians 1:13-14, Paul stresses in Philippians 3:6 that his zeal for the law had once led him to persecute the church; there could hardly be a clearer proof that "Judaism" and the gospel are irreconcilable.[34] In Philippians 3:7-11 he emphasizes the utter worthlessness of his own Jewish past from his new perspective: it is "loss" (vv. 7-8), "refuse" (σκύβαλα, v. 8). Throughout the passage, his strategy is to argue that his readers have a straight choice between ἡ περιτομή and "Christ Jesus."[35] They cannot have both at once, and the latter is infinitely preferable.

Like all the other passages in which Paul mentions the law, Philippians 3 has been pressed into the service of Lutheran readings of Paul. Thus Victor Furnish comments on this passage:

> Putting "confidence in the flesh" means regarding one's own status and achievement as the highest good and the ground of hope. It means regarding oneself as an *achiever* and in effect declaring one's independence of God.[36]

Furnish evidently has in mind here the contrast in v. 9 between "a righteousness of my own, based on law" and "that which is through faith of Christ, the righteousness from God that depends on faith"; compare v. 6, "as to righteousness under the law blameless." But the contrast here is not between two mutually exclusive principles (active achievement and passive submission to grace), but between two different ways of life in two different communities: the Jewish community, with its allegiance to the law, and the Pauline congregations, with their allegiance to Christ. As soon as one tries to make this concrete contrast abstract, problems come to light. Thus, the way of life summed up in 3:5-6 cannot simply be subsumed under the general heading of "achievement," for obedience to the law is here said to take place in the context of the unique privileges bestowed on Israel:

---

34. Cf. Beare, *Philippians*, 108-9.

35. It is this strategic intention that accounts for the "black and white" nature of Paul's statements here, to which Sanders draws attention (*Paul, the Law and the Jewish People*, 139-40).

36. Furnish, *Theology and Ethics in Paul*, 137; italics original.

Circumcised on the eighth day, of the people of Israel, of the tribe of Benjamin, a Hebrew born of Hebrews; as to the law a Pharisee, as to zeal a persecutor of the church, as to righteousness under the law blameless.[37]

What Paul renounces according to Philippians 3:7-9 is "covenantal nomism" — that is, his whole covenant status as a Jew, which includes reliance on the divine gifts bestowed uniquely on Israel as well as the confirmation of those gifts by his own obedience. On the other hand, faith oriented towards Christ cannot be regarded simply as the renunciation of achievement. If it is, then Paul is contradicting his earlier exhortation: "Work [or accomplish, or achieve] your own salvation with fear and trembling" (Phil. 2:12).[38] It is true that in 2:13 he goes on to say that "God is at work in you," but this should not be read as denying the statement of the previous verse. Paul asserts here that concurrent human and divine work are necessary to bring about salvation, being evidently unaware of the typical Protestant insistence that it is "faith alone" that saves, i.e., faith in isolation from the Christian's obedience to the appropriate ethical norms. "Faith alone" brings salvation only in the sense that for Paul "faith" comprehends not only "belief" or "trust" in the narrow sense but also the adoption of a new way of life with the social reorientation that this entails. There is, then, no tension whatsoever between the exhortation to accomplish one's own salvation (in response to divine grace and with divine help) and the stress on the efficacy of faith in 3:9. The problem arises only if faith and works are understood as abstract and logically incompatible principles, rather than as terms that encapsulate two different ways of life in two different communities. The antithesis between "law" and "faith of Christ" is to be understood not theoretically, as a logical contradiction, but practically, as an imperative.[39]

It is true that "righteousness" functions differently in the two ways of life to which Philippians 3:9 alludes. In normal Jewish usage, the "righteous" are those

37. This passage seems to confirm that righteous behavior "preserves one's place in the covenant . . . but it does not earn it" (Sanders, *Paul and Palestinian Judaism,* 205).

38. Martin's claim that σωτηρία here refers not to eschatological salvation but to "the corporate life of the Philippian church" (*Philippians,* 111) is artificial. If "corporate life" is the subject of 2:1-11, then the meaning of 2:12 is: "Behave appropriately in your corporate life, and so ensure your final salvation."

39. "Faith of Christ" in v. 9 is probably to be understood as an objective genitive: compare "the knowledge of Christ Jesus our Lord" in v. 8, and note the substitution of the unqualified "faith" at the end of v. 9. For the alternative view, see S. Stowers, "Friends and Enemies in the Politics of Heaven," 120-21, relating the phrase to the Christ hymn: "'Christ's faithfulness serves as shorthand for 'Christ's obedience unto death, Christ's servanthood and self-giving in obedience to God'" (121).

people of whom God approves, those who are pleasing to him.[40] There is an implicit contrast here with the much larger number of the "unrighteous," those of whom God disapproves. At its most general, "righteousness" is therefore that conduct which constitutes one as righteous, i.e., as approved by God. In this usage, human praxis is in the foreground, although divine agency is also presupposed, in the form of the gifts of covenant and law, understood as the means by which God establishes the possibility of righteousness in the midst of a sinful world. This is a *static* view of the divine agency, characteristic of a religious community in which membership is dependent on birth. Divine activity is essentially confined to the past (although it remains of fundamental significance), and the emphasis is on the present human response of obedience. In contrast, a community in which membership is dependent on conversion will tend to hold a more *dynamic* view of divine agency, now seen as powerfully operative in the present in bringing members of the sect from their former life of darkness and sin to their present experience of salvation. Thus, in the phrase "the righteousness from God that depends on faith," righteousness is no longer seen as human conduct but as the divine gift that transforms the convert's situation by deliverance from sin and death and bestowal of salvation and life.

This exegesis is by no means the same as the traditional Protestant contrast between salvation as human achievement and as divine gift. As we have seen, the antithesis articulates a difference between two patterns of religion, which one might perhaps label "traditional" and "conversionist" respectively.[41] Although divine and human agencies are differently conceived in the two patterns of religion, both elements are present in each of them. "Righteousness by the law" presupposes a (static) view of God's grace, to which it is a response; and the (dynamic) view of grace expressed in "the righteousness from God" is correlated with the active human response of "faith" (i.e., the reorientation of one's life according to Christian beliefs and norms). The active nature of faith is emphatically asserted in Philippians 3:12-14:

> Not that I have already attained or am already perfected, but I press on to lay hold of that for which Christ laid hold of me. My brothers and sisters, I do not consider that I have already laid hold of it. But one thing I do: forgetting what lies behind and straining towards what lies ahead, I press on to the finishing-line, for the prize of God's upward call in Christ Jesus.

40. As Sanders writes (*Paul and Palestinian Judaism*, 203): "The general view was that the righteous man was not characterized by perfection . . . but by the earnest endeavour to obey the law and by repentance and other acts of atonement in the case of transgression."

41. Cf. Elliott, *A Home for the Homeless*, 75-78, for discussion of the "conversionist response to the world."

In this metaphor from athletics, faith is seen as the strenuous human activity that is necessary to gain the prize of salvation, or "the resurrection from the dead" (3:11).[42] This is in accord with the exhortation of 2:12, "Work your own salvation" — in response, of course, to God's prior grace in Christ. Thus, Philippians 3 gives no support to the traditional contrast between "divine gift" and "human achievement" as representing mutually exclusive soteriological theories. Yet, within the Pauline antithesis, the role of divine agency as the basis for a corresponding human agency is far more emphatically asserted on one side than on the other.

The issue in Philippians 3 is the same as in Galatians. It is not: Must one do good works in order to be accepted by God? Rather, it is a matter of ecclesial self-definition. Should the church be a reform movement within the majority Jewish community or adopt a sectarian stance outside it? In order to convince the Philippians that allegiance to Christ necessitates the latter, Paul deploys strategies previously used in Galatians — especially denunciation and antithesis — to assert the community's distinctive and autonomous identity.

2. "Judaizers" at Corinth?

According to the historical reconstruction developed in this and the preceding chapter, Paul's authentic letters were composed in the following order and at the following locations:

1 Thessalonians (Athens or Corinth)
Galatians (Corinth)
1 Corinthians (Ephesus)
Philemon (Ephesus)
Philippians (Ephesus)
2 Corinthians 10–13 (Ephesus?)[43]

---

42. So Dunn, *New Perspective on Paul*, 482-83.

43. For a defense of the view that 2 Corinthians 1–9 was written later than chapters 10–13, which are to be identified with Paul's severe letter to the Corinthians, see my "2 Cor. x–xiii and Paul's Painful Letter to the Corinthians." This article opposes the view that 2 Corinthians 10–13 was written *after* chapters 1–9 (331-35), and the more complex source-analysis of Bornkamm and others (335-39), and argues that 2 Corinthians 10–13 exactly fits the description of the severe letter given and implied in 2 Corinthians 1–9 (339-46). See also the careful analysis of David Horrell, endorsing this view, in his *Social Ethos of the Corinthian Correspondence*, 281-312; and L. L. Welborn, "The Identification of 2 Corinthians 10–13 with the 'Letter of Tears.'" I remain unconvinced by the criticisms of M. E. Thrall (*2 Corinthians*, 1:18).

2 Corinthians 1–9 (Macedonia)
Romans (Corinth)

This order tends to confirm the Acts sequence, although it is dependent for the most part on the internal evidence of the letters themselves. If this order is correct, then 1 Corinthians, like Philippians, was written in the aftermath of the Galatian crisis. By analogy with Philippians 3, one might expect Paul to express anxiety about possible infiltration of the Corinthian congregation by the missionaries of circumcision. However, it is by no means clear that he does so. Although 2 Corinthians in particular has often been seen as evidence of "judaizing" activity in Corinth, it will be argued here that the problems Paul faced at Corinth were unrelated to the Galatian controversy.

(i) Jewish Christianity in 1 Corinthians?

1 Corinthians 1:12 mentions a Cephas party, and since when we last heard of him Cephas was "compelling the Gentiles to live like Jews" (Gal. 2:14), one might read this as evidence of Jewish Christian activity at Corinth. But 1 Corinthians as a whole gives no evidence of this.[44] Cephas is mentioned without any trace of hostility (1:12; 3:22; 9:5; 15:5); and the same is true of James (15:7; cf. 9:5). Outside the context of the Galatian crisis, the "Antioch incident" does not seem to have been as formative for Paul's apostolic identity as is sometimes supposed. (We recall that in 1 Thessalonians 2:14-16 he continues to express solidarity with the Judean churches.) No one at Corinth seems to share the Galatian desire to be "under law" (Gal. 4:21). It is true that in 1 Corinthians 8:7-13 the "weak" betray an anxiety about "food offered to idols" that may indicate a previous conversion to Judaism and adherence to the synagogue (cf. 1 Cor. 9:22, where "the weak" are identifiable objects of mission). The hypothetical warning that "this is ἱερόθυτον" (1 Cor. 10:28) envisages a Corinthian Christian for whom this is still a matter of conscience.[45] Yet there is no

---

44. According to Barrett, Peter had probably visited Corinth in person and may be the unnamed individual mentioned in 1 Corinthians 3:10-17 and 2 Corinthians 5:12; 10:7, 10, 11; 11:4, 19-20 ("Cephas at Corinth," 32-36). In 2 Corinthians 11:19-20, for example, "[t]he obscurity of the language, and its rapid changes, reflect the confused and embarrassing situation Paul had to deal with" (36) — i.e., the situation of having to oppose Peter. But the fact that Paul does not name his opponent is hardly a sufficient reason to identify him with Peter. For an alternative view of 2 Corinthians 10, see F. Watson, "2 Cor. x–xiii," 343-44.

45. In spite of the use of ἱερόθυτον rather than the pejorative εἰδωλόθυτα, the concern for the informant's "conscience" makes it unlikely that he is a pagan (the view taken in *PJG¹*, 81; cf. Conzelmann, *1 Corinthians*, 177; Barrett, *1 Corinthians*, 241-42).

reason to suppose that this is due to Jewish *Christian* influence.[46] In any case, the emphasis here lies on the danger of a reversion to idolatry: "the weak" are people who remain susceptible to their former sense of the reality of the god in whose honour the sacred meal is held (8:7). Opposing Christian participation in such events, Paul initially argues on pragmatic grounds, appealing to the potentially damaging impact on the weak. Their conscience will be "defiled" by such a participation (8:7, 12) — perhaps because their conscience has been formed by an earlier conversion to Judaism out of an idolatrous past. There is, however, no trace here of Jewish Christian influence, still less of a Jewish Christian *threat.*

(ii) Paul's Opponents in 2 Corinthians 10–13

At first sight, 2 Corinthians 10–13 tells a different story. The opponents whom Paul first refers to sarcastically as "superlative apostles" (11:5; cf. 12:11) and then denounces as "false apostles, deceitful workmen, disguising themselves as apostles of Christ" (11:13)[47] are clearly Jewish Christians: "Are they Hebrews? So am I. Are they Israelites? So am I. Are they descendants of Abraham? So am I." It has often been argued that these people are the same as, or at least similar to, the Galatian agitators.[48] Others, however, have rightly pointed out that nothing is said here about the question of Gentile submission to the law, which is so central to Galatians,[49] and have suggested that

46. Against Barrett, "Cephas," 33. There is little basis for Barrett's view that Peter or his adherents tried to introduce the Apostolic Decree in Corinth ("Things Sacrificed to Idols," 53).

47. Käsemann argues that the superlative apostles (11:5; 12:11) are to be differentiated from the false apostles (11:13): the former are the Jerusalem apostles, whereas the latter were actually present in Corinth ("Die Legitimität des Apostels," 42; see also Barrett, "Paul's Opponents in 2 Corinthians," 64). Whereas in 11:4 the opponents are denounced, in 11:5 Paul simply says that he is not inferior to the superlative apostles; thus, it is argued, 11:4 and 5 refer to different people. But this is unlikely, for in 11:13-15 Paul denounces the false apostles who, according to 11:12, boast of their authority, and in 11:16–12:13 attacks those who boast (11:18) by boasting himself — i.e., by means of a comparison. These two ways of attacking the same people — one direct, the other indirect — are also in evidence in 11:4-6. See Thrall, *Second Epistle to the Corinthians,* 2:667-70, for a fuller discussion that reaches the same conclusion.

48. So Käsemann, "Die Legitimität des Apostels," 43; Barrett, "Paul's Opponents in 2 Corinthians," 80.

49. Friedrich notes: "Paul's opponents in II Corinthians cannot be Judaizers like those who had emerged in Galatia. There is no sign of the characteristics of these Jewish Christian nomists, who demand circumcision, observance of the Sabbath and ritual purity. They [i.e., the opponents in 2 Corinthians] do not reproach Paul with having rejected the law, nor does Paul

Paul's opponents are representatives of a Jewish Christian "enthusiastic" spirituality.[50] Be that as it may, a good case can be made for identifying the false apostles of 2 Corinthians 10–13 with Apollos and his (unnamed) companions. It is not possible here to argue this case in detail, as this would take us too far afield; but it may be worthwhile briefly to respond to two possible objections to such a hypothesis and to note some points in its favor.

The first objection is that Paul speaks of "false apostles" in the plural, whereas nothing is said in 1 Corinthians or Acts about Apollos having had any companions. But we do not know of early Christian missionaries who worked entirely on their own. According to Mark 6:7 and Luke 10:1, Jesus sent out his disciples to preach two by two. Paul was accompanied on his so-called first missionary journey by Barnabas and Mark (according to Acts 13:2, 5), and on his second by Silas and Timothy (Acts 15:40; 16:3; 1 Thess. 1:1; 2 Cor. 1:19). Although in 1 Corinthians 2:1-5 he speaks as though he alone had preached the gospel to the Corinthians, in 2 Corinthians 1:19 he refers to "the Son of God, Jesus Christ, whom we preached among you, Silvanus, Timothy and I." It is quite possible that Apollos was accompanied by others but that Paul saw fit to name only him. This is perhaps implied by the reference in 1 Corinthians 4:5 to the Corinthians' "countless guides in Christ."

The second objection is more serious: Paul is vehemently opposed to the false apostles of 2 Corinthians 10–13, whereas he seems to have had no fundamental disagreement with Apollos.[51] It is true that in several passages in 1 Corinthians 1–4 Paul appears to be scrupulously impartial in discussing the claims of the Paul party and the Apollos party. Both parties are in the wrong, because of their "jealousy and strife" (3:3-4); Paul and Apollos should both be accepted as servants of God (3:5-9); Paul, Apollos, and Cephas belong to them all, not to separate parties (3:21-23); the Corinthians are not to press the claims of one at the expense of the other (4:6). Yet other passages in 1 Corinthians suggest that, in reality, Paul was seriously concerned about the impact of Apollos's visit to Corinth.

---

polemicize against works-righteousness as the main characteristic of their false theology" ("Die Gegner des Paulus im 2. Korintherbrief," 192; my translation). See also J. Becker, *Paul: Apostle to the Gentiles*, 222-23.

50. D. Georgi describes them as *theioi andres* (*The Opponents of Paul in Second Corinthians*, 230-38); opposed by G. Theissen, "Legitimation and Subsistence: An Essay on the Sociology of Early Christian Missionaries," 65-66.

51. Schmithals denies that Apollos was in any sense an opponent of Paul (*Paul and James*, 105); so also Holmberg, *Paul*, 45.

(1) In 1:17–2:5 Paul argues that "wisdom" and the gospel are fundamentally opposed to each other, and it is likely that this passage is directed against the Apollos party.[52] If it is addressed to all the Corinthians indiscriminately, it is hard to see what its purpose would be. Paul has criticized the church for breaking up into parties (1:10-16), and this is followed by an attack on "wisdom."[53] What is the connection? Paul's point may be that, in attributing too much importance to individual teachers, the whole church is shown to be pursuing worldly wisdom; but this seems rather a roundabout way to address the problem.[54] The critique of wisdom is unlikely to have been directed against the supporters of Peter, since it is Greeks who seek wisdom (1:22). In 2:1-5 it becomes clear that the critique of wisdom is bound up with Paul's own need to defend himself against the charge of being lacking in eloquence. The later hostile reference to his "contemptible speech" (2 Cor. 10:9) and his admission of being "unskilled in speaking" (2 Cor. 11:6) suggest that, in 1 Corinthians 1:17–2:5 as well, Paul is responding to criticism. Apollos had a reputation as ἀνὴρ λόγιος, according to Acts 18:24, and it is plausible that this criticism of Paul stemmed from members of the Apollos party (cf. 1:12; 3:4). In 1:17–2:5, then, Paul responds to the assumption that the gospel is compatible with "the wisdom of the world" — a claim that some at Corinth associated with Apollos.

(2) In 1 Corinthians 4:14-21, Paul reasserts his authority as founder of the Corinthian church, distinguishing his own unique role as "father" from the μυρίους παιδαγωγούς ἐν Χριστῷ (v. 15), who must include Apollos.[55] The Corinthians are therefore to imitate Paul (vv. 16-17); those who refuse to do so are threatened with punishment (vv. 18-21).[56] This passage indi-

cates that, despite the impression of scrupulous impartiality in some passages (1:13-16; 3:4-9; 4:6), Paul's sympathies lie with those who say, "I belong to Paul." They at least have remained loyal to their "father," whereas the others are rebels who will be punished if they do not become "imitators of me." This passage, too, indicates that Paul was seriously concerned about Apollos's influence at Corinth.

(3) In 1 Corinthians 16:12, Paul writes: "As for our brother Apollos, I strongly urged him to visit you with the other brethren, but it was not at all his will to come just now."[57] Paul had thus tried to integrate Apollos into his own team of fellow workers, but Apollos had resisted this attempt to curtail his independence.[58] The emphatic language (πολλὰ παρεκάλεσα αὐτόν and καὶ πάντως οὐκ ἦν θέλημα) may imply an already somewhat strained relationship. It is quite possible that, at a later date and in different circumstances, Paul could have denounced Apollos and his companions as "false apostles" and "servants of Satan" (2 Cor. 11:13-15).

With these objections dealt with, we may now turn to the positive evidence in favor of this identification of Paul's opponents in 2 Corinthians 10–13.

(1) Paul says in 2 Corinthians 3:1 that his opponents need letters of recommendation to and from the Corinthians. Acts 18:27 reports that Christians at Ephesus wrote a letter recommending Apollos to the Corinthian church.

(2) Paul identifies his opponents as Jews (2 Cor. 11:22) but never suggests that they had required Gentile Christians to submit to circumcision, as the Galatian agitators had done. Apollos was a Jew, according to Acts 18:24, but 1 Corinthians 1–4 gives no indication that circumcision was an issue.

(3) Paul writes in 2 Corinthians 11:5-6: "I think that I am not in the least inferior to these superlative apostles. Even if I am unskilled in speaking, I am not in knowledge; in every way we have made this plain to you in all things." It has already been argued that 1 Corinthians 1:17–2:5 answers the charge that, in comparison to Apollos, Paul was a poor speaker. At this point there is clear continuity between the two letters, for 2 Corinthians 11:5-6 reflects exactly the same charge (cf. 2 Cor. 10:10-12). If in the first

---

power as the ultimate deterrent" (*The Cost of Authority*, 69). Conzelmann asks, "Is Paul setting himself up after all as a spiritual strong man?" but answers his question unconvincingly with a negative (*1 Corinthians*, 93).

57. θέλημα could here refer to God's will; but the context suggests a reference to Apollos, whose reluctance to go to Corinth is implied by πολλὰ παρεκάλεσα αὐτόν.

58. See D. P. Ker, "Paul and Apollos — Colleagues or Rivals?" 95.

letter it is Apollos who shows up Paul's rhetorical limitations, that is probably also the case in the second letter.

(4) In 1 Corinthians 16:12, Paul announces Apollos's intention of visiting Corinth in the near future: "He will come when he has opportunity." It is clear from 2 Corinthians 10–13 that the "false apostles" visited Corinth at some time after 1 Corinthians was written, and in the light of 1 Corinthians 16:12 that is what we would have expected Apollos to have done.

These points do not prove that the false apostles of 2 Corinthians 10–13 are to be identified with Apollos and his companions. But if this identification is not correct, then the false apostles show remarkable resemblances to Apollos. Like Apollos, they come to Corinth armed with a letter of recommendation from another church. Like Apollos, they were Jewish Christians uninterested in imposing circumcision on Gentiles. Like Apollos, they were more eloquent speakers than Paul was. They visited Corinth at just the time when a visit from Apollos might have been expected. These are unlikely coincidences, and the most plausible and economical explanation is that Apollos did indeed revisit Corinth, that this second visit was still more damaging to Paul's reputation there than the first, and that Paul therefore saw fit to denounce Apollos and his companions as false apostles and as servants of Satan. This point has important implications for the interpretation of Paul's Corinthian correspondence.[59] In the present context, however, we are interested only in the negative conclusion that there is no evidence for the presence of "Judaizers" at Corinth. While Paul at one time feared that the Galatian agitators would extend their activities elsewhere (Phil. 3), there is no evidence that they ever did so.

(iii) 2 Corinthians 3 as Evidence for "Judaizers"?

The contrast in 2 Corinthians 3 between Paul's ministry of the new covenant and Moses' ministry of the old covenant is sometimes regarded as evidence of the "judaizing" tendencies of Paul's opponents at Corinth.[60] But that is to read too much into this chapter. Paul here defends the integrity of his ministry (2:17; 4:1-6) and appeals to the greatness of the commission entrusted to him, which makes petty, self-seeking aims impossible. His use of the story of

---

59. In particular, it suggests that continuities between the two Corinthian letters may have been systematically overlooked. For example, it is remarkable how little attention is given to 1 Corinthians in D. Georgi's *The Opponents of Paul in 2 Corinthians*.

60. So Barrett, "ΨΕΥΔΑΠΟΟΣΤΟΛΟΙ (2 Cor. 11.13)," 93.

Moses' shining face (Exod. 34:29-35) is not directed against "Judaizers" but is simply intended to reinforce his point about his own ministry, first by means of an *a fortiori* argument (3:7-11), and secondly by means of a contrast (3:12-18). If the divine glory was manifested in Moses' ministry, although it brought condemnation and was only temporary, how much more will it be manifested in Paul's ministry, which brings the Spirit and righteousness (3:7-11)? Thus, Paul is able to speak with complete openness and integrity, unlike Moses, who strangely concealed his face to prevent the Israelites from seeing that the glory was only transient,[61] i.e., that the law itself would eventually pass away (3:12-13).[62] This point is developed into a contrast between the Jewish and Christian communities in 3:14-18.[63] Nothing is said or implied here about the missionaries of circumcision.

However, 2 Corinthians 3 does provide valuable confirmation of some of the arguments advanced earlier. It indicates that the context of Paul's disparaging statements about the law is the need to distance the church from the Jewish community.[64] Paul speaks in 2 Corinthians 3:7-11 of the law as the bringer of death and condemnation and as being impermanent, and this is no abstract theological speculation, isolated from any significant social context. In 3:14-15 it becomes clear that this law (the "old covenant") is simply the Torah that is read every sabbath in Jewish synagogues. According to Paul, those who read and hear it do so with a veil over their minds, and (according to 3:13) the veil is that which prevents the Israelites from seeing that the glory on Moses' face fades, i.e., that the law itself is impermanent (cf. 3:11). Their misunderstanding is therefore not that they fail to understand scriptures as testimony to Christ, as is widely assumed,[65] but that they fail to perceive that, in the figure of Moses

---

61. This interpretation is rejected by P. E. Hughes on the grounds that "it attributes to Moses the practising of a subterfuge, and this to Paul would have been unthinkable" (109; cf. M. Rissi, *Studien zum zweiten Korintherbrief*, 30-32). Convictions about what "would have been unthinkable" for Paul must always be open to correction in the light of what he actually *says*.

62. According to Cranfield, "that which passes away" (v. 11) refers "not to the law or 'the whole religious system based on the law', but to the ministry of Moses at the giving of the law" ("St. Paul and the Law," 58). He argues that, for polemical reasons, Paul often discusses the law apart from Christ (61), and "it is this law-apart-from-Christ, this law that is less than its true self, which is temporary" (63). But as the law (represented by the stone tablets) is here seen purely as the bringer of condemnation, then the law itself *must* be temporary if condemnation is to give way to salvation.

63. There is no reference here to the eschatological salvation of Israel — against Munck, *Paul and the Salvation of Mankind*, 58-61.

64. So Wilckens, "Zur Entwicklung des paulinischen Gesetzesverständnisses," 163.

65. J. C. Beker, *Paul the Apostle*, 253; M. Hooker, "Beyond the Things That Are Written?" 304; E. Käsemann, "The Spirit and the Letter," 147-55; M. Rissi, *Studien zum zweiten Korinther-*

veiled, the law both conceals and reveals its own obsolescence. Rather, they regard the law as a supreme manifestation of divine electing grace, which has Israel's salvation as its aim. Becoming a Christian ("turning to the Lord," 3:16) means abandoning this fundamental conviction of the Jewish community, thus separating oneself from that community.[66] The social implications of Paul's understanding of the law are clear and explicit here.

Like other leaders of sectarian groups, Paul insists that the religious tradition that the separated group shares with the parent body must be interpreted esoterically. Only members of the sect truly understand the tradition (in this case, the law), and their reinterpretation of the tradition serves to legitimate and perpetuate sectarian alienation. According to 2 Corinthians 3:12-16, the law can be interpreted correctly only from the standpoint of faith in Christ,[67] where its hidden testimony to its own obsolescence is brought to light. Equally concealed from those who read and hear the law in the synagogue is the fact that it is the bringer of death and condemnation rather than life (3:6-11). While it is "the letter" rather than the law that is said to bring death in v. 6, τὸ γράμμα is expanded in v. 7 into ἐν γράμμασιν ἐντετυπωμένη λίθοις: the reference is to the ten commandments, inscribed on stone tablets by the finger of God (cf. Exod. 34:38; Deut. 4:13; 10:4).[68] Paul already has in mind here the story of Moses' transfiguration (Exod. 34:29-35), to which he will turn explicitly in vv. 13-18, for it is as he delivers the stone tablets of the law to the Israelites that Moses is transfigured. Nothing is said about the means by which the inscribed stone tablets "kill" (v. 6), so that Moses' ministry becomes a "ministry of death" (v. 7). Challenged to explain this, Paul might have appealed not to the intransigent reality of human fallenness but simply to the scriptural narrative — according to which the giving of the law was attended by the slaughter accompanying the Golden Calf incident (cf. 1 Cor. 10:7) and followed by the death in the wilderness of virtually the whole generation of those who stood before the Lord at Sinai.[69] If life and salvation

---

brief, 35, 37, 41; J. Collange, Énigmes de la deuxième Épître de Paul aux Corinthiens, 85; H. Windisch, Der zweite Korintherbrief, 122. This view is rightly opposed by Bultmann, Der zweite Brief an die Korinther, 90, who points out that "the παλαία διαθήκη only enters the context as the διακονία of death, of κατάκρισις, as καταργούμενον."

66. "Freedom" in v. 17 is therefore not freedom from "legalistically conceived religion" (Barrett, 2 Corinthians, 124) nor from "all the powers" (Rissi, Studien zum zweiten Korintherbrief, 38).

67. This is the one Pauline passage that explicitly makes this point (so G. Bornkamm, "Wandlungen im alt- und neutestamentlichen Gesetzesverständnis," 108).

68. Thus it is wrong to assume that "the letter" refers to some alleged Jewish perversion of the law (the view of Barrett, 2 Corinthians, 112-13).

69. On this, see my PHF, 286-91, 363-69.

are to be found in Christ alone, this makes it possible to draw from scriptural narrative the most negative conclusions about the death and condemnation that follow from the law. However, for Paul the most important thing is the fact *that* the law brings condemnation, not the question of *how* it does so, which is not discussed in 2 Corinthians 3. This view of the law serves to legitimate and reinforce the conviction that Christian congregations must be separated from the synagogue. There, each sabbath, Moses is read and heard without any awareness that, beneath the surface of the veil, the glory has departed.

PART TWO

Jews, Gentiles, and Romans

CHAPTER 5

Rome in Pauline Perspective

It has been the argument of previous chapters that there is the closest possible relationship between Paul's theological reflection and the social reality of Pauline congregations separated and distinct from the synagogue. Paul engages in theology in order to legitimate that reality. It will be the purpose of this and the following chapters to apply this claim to his letter to the Romans, which is still often interpreted without any reference to the underlying social situation within the Roman church.

1. The Question of the Purpose of Romans

Ferdinand Christian Baur was the first scholar to see Romans as a response to problems within the church at Rome. In his 1836 monograph, *Über Zweck und Veranlassung des Römerbriefs und die damit zusammenhängenden Verhältnisse der römischen Gemeinde,* he argues that "it is unthinkable that the apostle, without definite circumstances present in the Roman congregation . . . , should have felt himself obliged to write a letter with such a content to this congregation."[1] Baur argues that the church at Rome was composed mainly of Jewish Christians who denied the legitimacy of Paul's Gentile mission. Hearing of tensions between the Jewish majority in the Romans church and the Gentile minority, Paul wrote a long defense of Christian universalism over against Jewish particularism. In this way, Baur manages to relate the purpose of Romans very closely to his interpretation of its content.

---

1. Baur, *Über Zweck und Veranlassung des Römerbriefs,* 156.

Subsequent scholarship largely failed to maintain this unity of purpose and content; the content is related to the purpose only in the most general terms.[2] An exception to this is Paul S. Minear, who in his book *The Obedience of Faith* (1971) takes Romans 14–15 as his starting point for delineating the situation in Rome. He concludes from this section that there were five groups in the Roman church: the weak in faith who condemned the strong in faith; the strong in faith who despised the weak in faith; the doubters; the weak in faith who did not condemn the strong; and the strong in faith who did not despise the weak. Minear proceeds to relate this hypothesis to the contents of Romans as a whole. For example, he sees 1:18–4:25 as addressed to the weak in faith:[3] in Romans 2, Paul tries "to prove to Jewish Christians that their prideful condemnations of Gentile culture placed them on the same level in God's eyes and subject to the same penalties as the Gentiles" (51), and in Romans 4 the weak are told, "You must accept the strong in faith as children of Abraham and heirs to the promise of Abraham" (53). Although Minear's case is not always convincing, his insistence that the contents of Romans must be interpreted in the light of the situation of the Roman church is important, as is his use of Romans 14–15 as the key passage for determining that situation.[4] As Minear points out, commenting on the parallel passage in 1 Corinthians 8–10: "No one doubts that in Corinth [Paul] was wrestling directly with a specific situation. Why then should we doubt that this was also true in Rome?" (22).

In his study "The Jewish Community in Ancient Rome and the Origins of Roman Christianity," W. Wiefel attempts to relate our fragmentary knowledge of the contemporary Jewish community in Rome to the purpose of the letter to the Romans. Acts 18:2 attests both the early existence of Christians in Rome and their expulsion by Claudius, which brought the first congregation to an end.[5] Romans 16 depicts a predominantly Gentile congregation consisting of house-churches independent of the synagogue, and the letter as a whole addresses the tension between this Gentile Chris-

---

2. It is typical of this situation that M. Kettunen devotes only the last few pages of his otherwise useful monograph *Der Abfassungszweck des Römerbriefes* to Romans 1:18–11:36.

3. Minear, *The Obedience of Faith*, 46. Subsequent page references are given parenthetically in the text.

4. K. P. Donfried argues that it is not essential for Minear's case that Romans 1–4 should be *directly* addressed to Jewish Christians: "Is it not very possible that Paul can be dealing with actual problems but in so doing employs rhetorical arguments and theological perspectives of a more general nature which will aid in solving them?" ("False Presuppositions in the Study of Romans," 126).

5. Wiefel, "The Jewish Community in Ancient Rome," 110.

tian majority and returning Jewish Christians: Romans "was written to assist the Gentile Christian majority, who are the primary addressees of the letter, to live together with the Jewish Christians in one congregation, thereby putting to an end their quarrels about status."[6] In a society marked by its hostility towards Jews, Paul aims to raise the status of Jewish Christians in the eyes of Gentile Christians. This conclusion is the opposite of Baur's view that Paul's aim is to raise the status of Gentile Christians in the eyes of Jewish Christians.

J. Jervell represents a different approach. He writes: "The letter itself clearly states that its *raison d'être* does not stem from the situation of the Roman congregation, but is to be found in Paul himself at the time of writing."[7] Jervell sees Romans 1:18–11:36 as "the defense which Paul plans to give before the church in Jerusalem" (64). Here, "Paul is absorbed by what he is going to say in Jerusalem" (70), and he writes as he does because he wishes to ask the Roman congregation for its solidarity, support, and intercession (64). According to 15:15-33, "Paul wants to represent the whole Gentile world in Jerusalem, including the West" (74).[8]

Jervell is surely right to stress that in all his letters Paul is writing not just for the sake of the congregation but also for his own sake. Although we tend "to picture Paul more as a theological monument than as a human being," the fact is that "Paul needs the congregation just as much as they need him" (62). But his emphasis on Paul's own situation to the exclusion of the situation in Rome is unnecessarily one-sided. As in his other letters, it is probable that Paul is writing on account of factors *both* in the life of the congregation addressed *and* in his own situation; indeed, the two can hardly be separated. The present discussion will attempt to incorporate the emphases on the close relationship between the purpose of Romans and its content (Baur, Minear), the importance of Romans 14:1–15:13 for determining its purpose (Minear), the use of information about early Roman Christianity from other sources (Wiefel), and the significance of Paul's own situation (Jervell). It will be argued that Romans presupposes a particular social situation within the Roman church and that the contents of the theological discussions of

6. Wiefel, "The Jewish Community in Ancient Rome," 113.

7. Jervell, "The Letter to Jerusalem," 62. Subsequent page references are given parenthetically in the text.

8. Hübner's view of Romans is another attempt to understand this letter on the basis of Paul's own situation. Taking as his starting point the more reflective tone of Romans in comparison with Galatians, Hübner suggests that Paul is responding to James's objections to Galatians, moderating his views in the light of them (*Law in Paul's Thought*, 63). Hübner does not explain how James got to read Galatians, or how his critique of it reached Paul.

Romans 1–11 are determined by the letter's intended function within that social situation. The contents of Romans cannot be properly understood without an appreciation of the social realities underlying its apparently theoretical discussions.[9]

This view of the purpose of Romans may be contrasted with the approach to this letter of scholars such as Klein and Bornkamm, who reiterate Luther's conviction that in Romans Paul sets out the essence of his gospel in a universally normative manner. Klein argues that Paul "does not regard the local Christian community there [i.e., in Rome] as having an apostolic foundation."[10] The purpose of Romans is to remedy this deficiency by way of a systematic presentation of the Pauline gospel:

> The fact that Paul writes to the Romans in the form of a theological treatise is indicative of an occasion which calls for the normative message of the apostle and demands that his theological reflections be raised to a new level of general validity.[11]

It follows that the theology of Romans is supremely normative, from Paul's standpoint and also from our own. Justification is both the center of Paul's theology and the only sure foundation for the church; the theological task of historical-critical scholarship is constantly to rediscover this.

Similarly, Bornkamm argues that in Romans Paul "elevates his theology above the moment of different situations and conflicts into the sphere of the eternally and universally valid."[12] What Paul says about the Jews is an example of this universal validity, for according to Paul "the Jew represents man in general." Bornkamm continues:

> This man is indeed not somewhere outside, among believers; he is hidden within each Christian, even in Paul himself, and also in those Gentile Christians who now want to pride themselves at the expense of Israel.[13]

Once again, we note the underlying assumption that "faith" and "works" are to be defined as logical opposites rather than as incommensurables and that together they represent the two great anthropological possibilities that per-

9. Donfried aptly comments that, despite Baur, Romans has continued to be regarded as a "christianae religionis compendium"; but he also notes the increasing contemporary interest in its *Sitz im Leben* ("Romans Debate," x-xi).

10. Klein, "Paul's Purpose in Writing the Epistle to the Romans," 44.

11. Klein, "Paul's Purpose in Writing the Epistle to the Romans," 49.

12. Bornkamm, "The Letter to the Romans as Paul's Last Will and Testament," 31.

13. Bornkamm, "The Letter to the Romans as Paul's Last Will and Testament," 28-29.

meate human life in its entirety.[14] It is in *that* sense that the theology of Romans is supposed to be "eternally and universally valid."

Thus, even in consideration of a purely historical problem — the purpose of Romans — traditional Lutheran themes are once again invoked. The overwhelming authority that the Lutheran Paul still possesses is very much in evidence here.

If the Roman context of the letter to the Romans is to be taken seriously, then consideration of the fragmentary external evidence about the origins of Christianity in Rome is indispensable.[15] As we shall see, the evidence suggests a trajectory from "reform movement" to "sect," with Paul's letter located at the midpoint between the two.[16]

2. The Origins of Roman Christianity

In his account of the life of Claudius, Suetonius writes laconically of the emperor's expulsion of the Jewish community from Rome: *Iudaeos impulsore Chresto assidue tumultuantis Roma expulit* (*Cl.* 25.4).[17] There is no indication

---

14. Compare J. C. Beker's claim that Romans is "in some sense a 'dogmatics in outline', though it is not 'a timeless theological product'" (*Paul the Apostle*, 77). In spite of his emphasis on the "contingency" of the Pauline texts, Beker's reading of Romans remains heavily influenced by German Lutheran theology. Thus he can identify "the person under the law" with Luther's *homo incurvatus in se*, whose deeds "only promote the attempt to secure his existence before God" (247). Indeed, Beker can even use first-person language in paraphrasing Romans 10:3: "Although I am 'confessionally' and publicly zealously engaged in attending to God and my neighbor, I am secretly striving for my own righteousness" (247). Beker does not explain why the house-churches of first-century Rome should need such lessons in refined introspection.

15. In coordinating external and internal evidence, it is important to avoid the methodological error of "conflating the empirical and encoded reader," thereby "replac[ing] a careful analysis of the audience in the letter with a conjectural reconstruction that actually pays only scant attention to the way that the letter itself depicts its readers" (S. Stowers, *A Rereading of Romans*, 23). Yet there is no need for a rigid separation here, as though the implied audience of Romans were simply a Pauline fiction. Nor is there any special virtue in the "minimalist austerity" recommended by T. Engberg-Pedersen, who thinks that the fragmentary external information should be ignored (*Paul and the Stoics*, 353n).

16. The present interpretation of the evidence depends heavily on the references in Tacitus and Suetonius to the persecution of Christians during the reign of Nero, which make it possible to interpret Paul's letter in terms of the reform movement/sect model. The discussion in *PJG¹* (91-94) has been substantially reworked and expanded so as to take these passages into account.

17. On the Jewish community in Rome, see E. Schürer, *History of the Jewish People*, 3:73-84; J. Barclay, *Jews in the Mediterranean Diaspora*, 282-319; E. M. Smallwood, *The Jews under Roman Rule*, 201-19.

as to when this occurred, for this statement occurs in a topically rather than chronologically organized context. The historian has gathered together items of information illustrating Claudius's attitude towards foreigners, and particularly foreign cults: his courtesy towards German envoys, his prohibition of the druidic cult in Gaul, his importation from Attica of the Eleusinian mysteries, and so on. Among these other actions, he expelled the Jews from Rome because of disturbances they created "with Chrestus as instigator." It is probable that "Chrestus" is to be identified with "Christus";[18] the substitution occurred because "Chrestus" was a common personal name.[19] This substitution appears to have had wide currency. According to Tertullian, opponents of Christianity habitually mispronounce "Christianus" as "Chrestianus," which shows that "you lack even a sure knowledge of the name" (*Apol.* 3.5).[20] The Christian sect is hated, Tertullian continues, because it bears the name of its founder *(auctor)* — even though this is simply to follow the familiar precedent of the Platonists, Epicureans, and Pythagoreans (3.6). If the name of the sect is known to commemorate the founder, then "Christianus" must stem from a founder whose name was believed to have been "Chrestus." This is confirmed by Lactantius, who speaks of "the error of the ignorant who by the change of a letter are accustomed to call him 'Chrestus'" (*Inst.* 4.7.5). If Suetonius's "Chrestus" is Christ, then the disorders he mentions are likely to have occurred *within* the Roman Jewish community, as Christian Jews began to make their presence felt within the Roman synagogues.

Admittedly, Suetonius refers to Christians as "Christiani" rather than "Chrestiani." Nero, he tells us in a list of that emperor's reforms of public abuses, inflicted punishments on the *Christiani, genus hominum superstitionis novae ac maleficae* (*Nero* 16.2). Yet it is probable though not certain that Suetonius would have identified his "Chrestus" with the founder of the "Christiani." While he may erroneously have believed that "Chrestus" had been in Rome in person,[21] the compressed phrase *impulsore Chresto* is not incompatible with an awareness of the Judean origin of the disturbances in the

18. The suggestion that Chrestus was "a freedman who was advising Claudius and influenced him to expel the Judeans" (P. Esler, *Conflict and Identity in Romans*, 100) seems incompatible with Suetonius's word order. Others who doubt that Chrestus = Christus include John Barclay, *Jews in the Mediterranean Diaspora*, 304; R. Thorsteinsson, *Paul's Interlocutor in Romans 2*, 94-95.

19. So P. Lampe, *From Paul to Valentinus*, 13.

20. Note also the substitution of Χρηστιανός for Χριστιανός in the manuscript tradition (א*, in Acts 11:26; 26:28; 1 Pet. 4:16).

21. So E. M. Smallwood, *The Jews under Roman Rule*, 211; R. Jewett, *Dating Paul's Life*, 37. This widespread assumption about Suetonius's statement needs reconsideration.

Roman Jewish communities. In that case, Suetonius will have shared the view of his older contemporary Tacitus, who knows that the originator *(auctor)* of the name "Christian" was *Christus,* executed by Pontius Pilate during the reign of Tiberius. In spite of this setback, however, the "deadly superstition broke out again, not only in Judea, the origin of this evil, but even in Rome *[per urbem]*" (*Ann.* 15.44). If for Tacitus "Christus" is the originator of an evil that began in Judea but spread to Rome, then the same may be true of Suetonius's "Chrestus," the *impulsor* of disturbances in the Roman Jewish community even after his death in Judea.

If "Chrestus" is indeed "Christus," it is highly significant that he is linked with the Roman Jewish community during the time of Claudius but with a distinctive sect of "Christiani" during the time of Nero, perhaps fifteen years later. At least by the time of the fire of 64 CE, the name "Christiani" identifies a specific group of people, hated for their shameful practices *(flagitia)* and for their *odium humani generis* (Tacitus, *Ann.* 15.44).[22] In Claudius's reign, however, there are no "Christians" but only Jews who either accept or reject the claims of "Chrestus," and whose disagreement on this point leads to public disturbances and eventually to their expulsion from Rome.

Suetonius's report is confirmed by Acts 18:2, which tells how, on his arrival in Corinth, Paul

> found a certain Jew, Aquila by name, a native of Pontus, who had recently come from Italy with his wife Priscilla, because Claudius had commanded all the Jews to leave Rome.

Luke does not explain why Claudius should have commanded this, and he does not explicitly claim that Aquila and Priscilla were Christians even before they met Paul. Paul lodges with them not because they are fellow Christians but because he and Aquila practice the same trade: they are both tentmakers. When, at Ephesus, Paul encounters people who are already Christians, they are clearly identified as "disciples" (19:1). Yet neither does Luke claim that Aquila and Priscilla were converted by Paul; it is simply taken for granted that they are Christians (18:18, 26).[23] Is there a connection between Luke's failure either to give the reason for the expulsion or to mention that Aquila and Priscilla were already Christians when they met Paul? Is it the arrival of Christianity in Rome that is at both points concealed (cf. 28:15)? Luke's strangely

---

22. The reference is probably to Christian hatred of the human race rather than the human race's hatred of Christians: compare Tacitus's claim elsewhere (*Hist.* 5.5) that Jews show implacable hatred towards the rest of humankind *(adversus omnes alios hostile odium).*

23. So P. Lampe, *From Paul to Valentinus,* 11-12.

emphatic reference to "all the Jews" (πάντας τοὺς Ἰουδαίους) would be compatible with such a hypothesis: Luke knows that Christians were implicated in the events that led to expulsion from Rome but does not wish to acknowledge this. Precisely in its silences, Acts 18:2 may confirm that the Suetonius passage has to do with the arrival of the Christian gospel in the Roman synagogues.

With regard to the date of the expulsion, there are two main possibilities. Suetonius gives us no clue as to this, and most scholars have relied on the evidence of Luke and the fifth-century historian Orosius to suggest 49 CE. Luke's reference to the expulsion of the Jews from Rome implies that this event took place about two years before Gallio's proconsulship of Asia (Acts 18:11, 12), which probably lasted from July 51 to July 52.[24] This would suggest that the expulsion took place in about 49 CE, and this is confirmed by Orosius, who states that "in [Claudius's] ninth year the Jews were expelled by Claudius from the City, as Josephus reports" *(Hist. adv. pag. 7.6.15)*.[25] No such report exists in Josephus, but the apparently fortuitous agreement with Luke suggests that the report may nonetheless be reliable.[26] Even without the evidence of Orosius, however, an approximate dating of the expulsion is possible on the basis of Acts 18.

Alternatively, it can be argued that the expulsion attested in Suetonius and Acts is to be identified with a decree of Claudius that closed the Roman synagogues. Referring to an event at the start of Claudius's reign, Dio Cassius writes:

> As for the Jews, who had again increased in numbers, so that it would have been difficult to bar them from the City without provoking the mob to disorder, he did not banish them [οὐκ ἐξήλασε μεν] but, while they were to maintain their traditional way of life, he commanded them not to assemble together [μὴ συναθροίζεσθαι]. (60.6.6)

G. Lüdemann has argued that Orosius should be ignored, that in Acts 18 Luke has combined traditions relating to different visits of Paul to Corinth, and that the supposed expulsion of the Jews from Rome is to be identified with the synagogue ban attested in Dio Cassius.[27] Dio is here deliberately contradicting the statement of Suetonius or his source that the Jews *were* expelled.[28]

---

24. So R. Jewett, *Dating Paul's Life*, 38-40.

25. For the text, see E. M. Smallwood, *The Jews under Roman Rule*, 211n.

26. So Smallwood, *The Jews under Roman Rule*, 215; Jewett, *Dating Paul's Life*, 37-38.

27. Lüdemann, *Paul, Apostle to the Gentiles*, 158-75. An alternative view is represented by Stern (*Greek and Latin Authors on Jews and Judaism*, 2:116), who holds that Claudius initially issued an edict of expulsion, subsequently replaced by the ban on synagogue attendance.

28. Lüdemann, *Paul, Apostle to the Gentiles*, 164-66.

The riots that took place "at the instigation of Chrestus" could then be dated to 41 CE, which would push back the origins of Roman Christianity almost a decade. However, Lüdemann's hypothesis is unlikely to be correct. When Dio states that the Jews "had again increased in numbers" and that Claudius "did not expel them," he is not contradicting Suetonius or his source but contrasting Claudius's decision with an event mentioned earlier: the expulsion of Roman Jews during the reign of Tiberius. About this event Dio comments: "Since many Jews had come to Rome and converted many of the natives to their customs, he [Tiberius] banished most of them [τοὺς πλείονας ἐξήλασεν]" (57.18.5a).[29] When Dio later states that Claudius did not expel the Jews from the city, he is not contradicting the statement of Suetonius or his source, but explaining why Claudius did not at this point follow the precedent of Tiberius's action. Combining Dio with Suetonius, Luke, and Orosius, we may conclude that Claudius banned Jewish meetings (i.e., synagogue worship) in 41 CE and expelled the Roman Jews for disorders "at the instigation of Chrestus" in 49 CE.[30]

It is possible that the two events are connected and that the closure of the synagogues represents an initial response to an ongoing problem that culminated in the expulsion. Suetonius may hint at that when he states that the Jews were "continually" *(assidue)* creating disturbances relating to "Chrestus." Dio offers no explanation for the ban on synagogue attendance — except to say that expulsion of the whole community was not feasible as it had been in the time of Tiberius. Of the three other decrees relating to Jews that date from the first year of Claudius's reign, two are addressed to the citizens of Alexandria, where tensions between Alexandrians and Jews had escalated into virtual civil war (Josephus, *Ant.* 19.280-85; *P. Lond.* 1912), and one to "the rest of the world" (*Ant.* 19.287-91).[31] The two Alexandrian decrees differ markedly in tone. The first confirms Jewish civic rights in Alexandria and appears to resolve the longstanding quarrel of Alexandrian Greeks and Jews — attested above all in Philo — in favor of the Jews. It is said to have been written at the request of Agrippa, who played a significant part in Claudius's accession and who would shortly return to Jerusalem to take over his kingdom (*Ant.* 19.279, 292). The second, dated some months later, is written in response to an Alexandrian delegation that may well have visited Rome to appeal against the pro-

29. On this event, which is to be dated to 19 CE, see also Tacitus, *Ann.* 2.85; Suetonius, *Tib.* 36; Josephus, *Ant.* 18.81-83.

30. So E. M. Smallwood, *The Jews under Roman Rule,* 210-16; J. Barclay, *Jews in the Mediterranean Diaspora,* 305-6; A. J. M. Wedderburn, *Reasons for Romans,* 57.

31. Text of *P. Lond.* 1912 in Hunt and Edgar, *Select Papyri,* 2.212. For full discussion of the three decrees, see M. Pucci Ben Zeev, *Jewish Rights in the Roman World,* 294-342.

Jewish tenor of the first. The common denominator of the three texts is the requirement that Jews in Alexandria and elsewhere should be allowed to practice their religion without hindrance (*Ant.* 19.283-85; 290; *P. Lond* 1912, 82-88). In the background here is the mortal threat to Judaism posed by the demand that Jews too should acknowledge the deity of Gaius (Caligula), Claudius's assassinated predecessor. The new emperor assures his Jewish subjects that the threat is now past. In this generally conciliatory context, the Roman synagogue ban seems anomalous — though it, too, confirms the legitimacy of Jewish praxis, according to Dio. It is true that two of the three decrees are explicitly critical of Jews. Although in the first Alexandrian decree Claudius assumes that the Jews are the victims of Alexandrian hostility (*Ant.* 19.284), in the second he is more even-handed, criticizing the Alexandrian Jewish demand for further civic privileges, the sending of a separate Jewish delegation, and the presence in Alexandria of militants from elsewhere in Egypt and from Syria (*P. Lond.* 1912, 88-98). In the general decree, he requires Jews "to conduct themselves in a more reasonable manner, and not to reject the religious rites of other nations, but rather to keep their own laws" (*Ant.* 19.290). Yet nothing here supplies an obvious background to the Roman synagogue ban.[32]

In the Alexandrian decrees, Claudius appeals to the Jewish policy of Augustus, who permitted Jewish self-governance (*Ant.* 19.283) and freedom of religion (*P. Lond.* 1912, 85-87). According to Philo, writing specifically about the Roman Jewish community, a ban on synagogue worship was one of a number of possible anti-Jewish measures that Augustus did *not* take. Augustus, he tells us, was well aware of the sizable population of Jewish ex-slaves on the further bank of the Tiber, who met together in their houses of prayer (προσευχαί) each sabbath and sent money for sacrifices to the temple in Jerusalem (*Leg.* 155-56). Yet, in contrast to more recent events, Augustus approved of all this and desisted from the measures that were later to be taken in Rome or elsewhere:

32. W. Wiefel assumes that, in the light of Claudius's initially conciliatory attitude towards Jews, Dio Cassius's dating of the decree revoking the Roman Jews' right of assembly must be wrong; it must date instead from a time *after* the expulsion, when Jews were permitted to return to Rome but not yet to meet together ("The Jewish Community in Ancient Rome and the Origins of Roman Christianity," 110-11). Christians therefore could not assemble unless they were without ties to the synagogue; thus independent house-churches arose among Gentile Christians (cf. Rom. 16), and Paul is able to assume that they practice freedom from the law (113). But the rejection of Dio Cassius's early dating seems unnecessary, and an alternative view of the origin of Roman Gentile Christianity will be presented later in the present chapter.

He neither banished them from Rome nor deprived them of their Roman citizenship, nor took violent measures against their houses of prayer, nor prohibited them from gathering for instruction in the laws [συνάγεσθαι πρὸς τὰς τῶν νόμων ὑπηγήσεις], nor opposed their offerings of the first-fruits. (*Leg.* 157)

It is not certain that Philo has Claudius's action specifically in mind when he refers to the possibility of a synagogue ban. Yet the passage does highlight the anomaly of a synagogue ban in the aftermath of the Caligula crisis. In the broader context of a rejection of Caligula's anti-Jewish insanity and a return to Augustan norms, what special circumstances led to the closure of the Roman synagogues?[33]

While Dio Cassius's account of this measure gives no reason for it, Suetonius is more forthcoming about the harsher later measures: Jews were expelled from Rome because of continual disturbances instigated by Chrestus. If we may trace back Suetonius's *assidue* from c. 49 CE to c. 41, it is possible that such disturbances were also a significant factor in the earlier synagogue ban. If so, then the Roman Jewish community was in a state of continual unrest throughout the decade, like the Jewish communities of Asia Minor and Greece visited by Paul.

Prior to the expulsion, then, Roman Christianity was an intra-Jewish affair. If Gentiles were involved, it was on account of a prior involvement with the synagogue.[34] A decade and a half later, the situation has changed completely. Christians are no longer Jews or Jewish sympathizers who have accepted the claims of Chrestus or Christus. They are now identified wholly with those claims, and the connection with Jews and Judaism has lapsed. Now "the crowd" (*vulgus*) calls them *Christiani,* after *Christus,* their founder, and hates them for their shameful practices (Tacitus, *Ann.* 15.44). Following the fire of 64 CE, these people were put to death as Christians, and not because of any supposed role in starting the fire. While Tacitus claims that Nero's campaign against Christians was a diversionary tactic occasioned by the general

33. John Barclay suggests that Claudius's synagogue ban sought "to defuse tensions arising from Gaius' threat to the temple" (*Jews in the Mediterranean Diaspora,* 306). But it is hard to see how a punitive and provocative measure such as this would "diffuse tensions."

34. Against Hengel, *Acts and the History of Earliest Christianity,* 107-8, who suggests that the disorders were the result of "Hellenists" preaching a law-free gospel to Gentiles; see the critique of Hengel's Hellenist theory in Chapter 2, above. Like Hengel, A. J. M. Wedderburn wrongly assumes that only the preaching of a law-free gospel to Gentiles can account for the disturbances within the Roman Jewish community (*The Reasons for Romans,* 55-56). Neither scholar explains why the preaching of Jesus as Messiah would *not* have proved controversial in the Roman synagogues. Messianic claims are inherently controversial.

belief that he had ordered the fire himself, he also states that Christians were not arrested for incendiarism *(haud proinde in crimine incendii)*.[35] The link between the fire and the persecution represents Tacitus's interpretation of Nero's motive — an interpretation not shared by Suetonius, who reports the persecution (*Nero* 16.2) without reference to the fire (38.1-3). But both writers are agreed that the Christians' crime was simply that they were Christians. Although the Christians' Judean origins are known to Tacitus (certainly) and Suetonius (probably), they do not associate them with Jews. There is no indication of a campaign against Jews in the aftermath of the fire. Nor is there any suggestion that "Christians" are a subset of the wider category of "Jews."[36] Thus, the relationship of Christ-followers to the Roman Jewish community has changed fundamentally. In the terminology used in previous chapters, an original "reform movement," existing within the Roman synagogues, has given way to a sectarian separation already visible to society at large, as the new name *Christiani* makes clear. In place of an orientation towards the laws and institutions of the Jews, the new name embodies an orientation exclusively towards *Christus*.

Paul's letter to the Romans is as it were equidistant between Claudius's punitive measures against the Roman Jewish community and Nero's against the *Christiani*. Addressed to a diverse community engaged in a process of self-definition, we would expect it to show traces both of the community's Jewish past and of its Gentile future. Paul's engagement with the Roman Christian community is most explicit in Romans 14–16, and it is to these chapters that we must turn in order to orient our reading of the letter as a whole.[37]

35. This point is missed by Smallwood, *The Jews under Roman Rule*, 217-19.

36. Dunn claims that Tacitus's language is compatible with a view of the Christians as an intra-Jewish grouping, but he offers no reasons for this judgment (*Romans 1–8*, l). Nor is there any basis in Tacitus for Dunn's claim that "only in the latter years of Nero's reign . . . can we detect an awareness that Christians had become a distinct entity" (1). If the Christians whom Nero persecuted were *already* generally known and hated as "Christians," then they must have been a "distinct entity" for some time. Dunn's reading of Tacitus is strategically necessary for him, since it is fundamental to his reading of Romans that Paul here presents an enlarged theology of the covenant, rather than an argument for separation from the synagogue. (See also Mark Nanos, *The Mystery of Romans*, 68-69n.) Lampe's statement is closer to the truth: "By the time of [the letter's] composition in the second half of the 50s at the latest, urban Roman Christianity can be seen as separated from the federation of synagogues" (*From Paul to Valentinus*, 15-16). So also Barclay: "Although Jews (and the Jewish tradition) played a significant role in the earliest stages of the Christian movement in Rome, Nero's targeting of Christians after the fire of 64 CE . . . suggests a differentiation from the synagogues within a comparatively short time" (*Jews in the Mediterranean Diaspora*, 283).

37. In the following section, the concept of "a divided community" replaces the misleading reference to "the two Roman congregations" (*PJG¹*, 94-98); the change is not substantive, how-

3. A Divided Community (Romans 14:1–15:13)

The legitimacy of using Romans 14:1–15:13 as evidence of the situation of the Roman church has been disputed by R. J. Karris, in his 1973 article "Romans 14:1–15:13 and the Occasion of Romans." Karris argues that attempts to identify "weak" and "strong" parties within the Roman church have led nowhere, and that this section is rather to be interpreted as a generalized rewriting of 1 Corinthians 8–10 that eliminates everything having reference only to a concrete situation (i.e., food offered to idols).[38] In opposition to this view, I shall argue here that Romans 14:1–15:13 should not be understood as general parenesis but gives clear evidence of the situation in the Roman church as Paul understands it.[39] First, it must be shown that there is no real problem in identifying the "weak" and the "strong": the former are Christians who observe the Mosaic law, while the latter are Christians who do not. For convenience, we may refer to these two groups as "Jewish Christians" and "Gentile Christians," so long as it is remembered that the former group may have included proselytes, whereas the latter group may have included Jews like Paul himself who might be described as "Gentile-oriented Christians."

The main difficulty in identifying the "weak" with Jewish Christians who observed the law is that they are said to have abstained not simply from pork, blood, and food offered to idols, but from meat in general: "The weak man eats only vegetables" (14:2). The difficulty is increased when Paul refers to abstention from wine as well as meat (14:21; cf. 14:17).[40] Some scholars have concluded from these statements that the "weak" have been influenced by syncretistic ascetic ideas.[41] But Jewish abstention from meat and wine is mentioned in other texts. In Daniel 1:8-16, Daniel and his companions obtain permission to abstain from meat and wine, which would defile them (v. 8), and to live off vegetables and water. Judith refuses to eat and drink the food and wine provided by Holofernes (Judith 12:1-4). Esther tells how she has not eaten at Haman's table or at the king's feast, and how she has not drunk "the wine of the libations" (Es-

---

ever. More significantly, an analysis of the "implied readership" of Romans 14:1–15:13 has been added, resulting in a more nuanced account of the letter's intended impact on its Jewish or Gentile addressees.

38. So also G. Bornkamm, "Romans as Paul's Last Will and Testament," 28; J. Bassler, "Divine Impartiality in Paul's Letter to the Romans," 57n.

39. So Käsemann, *Commentary on Romans,* 366; Wilckens, *Der Brief an die Römer,* 3:79.

40. Thus, Käsemann claims that "Jewish orthodoxy can be ruled out as a source," since "general abstinence from meat and wine is not found there" (*Commentary on Romans,* 367).

41. So Barrett, *Romans,* 257-58; Schlier, *Der Römerbrief,* 405-6; Käsemann, *Commentary on Romans,* 368.

ther 14:17, LXX). Josephus commends the priests who were taken captive to Rome in 61 CE, and who did not forget their religion and so "supported themselves on figs and nuts" (*Vit.* 4). In all these examples, Jews find themselves in a Gentile environment, cut off from their community in which ceremonially pure meat and wine might be obtained. This suggests a plausible interpretation of references to "the weak" in Romans 14: abstention from meat and from wine was practiced by Roman Jewish Christians (or Christian Jews) *in the context of a predominantly Gentile environment.*[42] We might conjecture that, following the disorders in the Jewish quarter and the consequent expulsion, Christian Jews were compelled to settle in non-Jewish parts of the city.[43] Yet Paul more probably has in mind an issue arising specifically from attempts to practice table fellowship between Jewish and Gentile Christians.[44] It seems that, on such occasions, Jewish Christians acted as Daniel, Judith, Esther, and the priests did in a Gentile-dominated environment: they abstained from meat and wine. Their action was evidently the occasion of controversy within the Roman Christian community, reports of which have reached Paul.

There are further indications in Romans 14:1–15:13 that the weak are to be identified as Jewish Christians, not as ascetics or syncretists. First, in 14:14 Paul mentions the belief of the weak that certain food is κοινόν, a term used elsewhere in connection with Jewish dietary laws (Acts 10:14, 28; 11:8). In Romans 14:20, πάντα μὲν καθαρά is equivalent to οὐδὲν κοινόν in v. 14, and this language recalls Acts 10:15 and 11:9: ἃ ὁ θεὸς ἐκαθάρισεν, σὺ μὴ κοίνου (cf. Mark 7:19, καθαρίζων πάντα τὰ βρώματα). Second, Romans 14:5 speaks of a person who "esteems one day as better than another," an apparent reference to Jewish sabbaths, feasts, and fasts.[45] Third, a connection is repeatedly drawn between "eating" and "faith" (14:1, 22, 23 [× 2]) or "believing" (14:2), and this is best understood in the light of the faith/law antithesis of earlier chapters of the letter.[46] Fourth, and most significantly, 15:7-13 speaks unam-

---

42. So Byrne, *Romans*, 404-5.

43. For this conjecture, see *PJG¹*, 95, and compare Cranfield, *Romans*, 2:695. Philo (*Leg.* 155, cited above) indicates the existence of a definite "Jewish quarter" in Rome; on this see Lampe, *From Paul to Valentinus*, 38-40.

44. So Minear, *The Obedience of Faith*, 10; J. Barclay, "'Do We Undermine the Law?' A Study of Romans 14.1–15.6," 291.

45. So Schlier, *Der Römerbrief*, 407; Barrett, *Romans*, 259; Cranfield, *Romans*, 2:695; Wilckens, *Der Brief an die Römer*, 3:83. Käsemann's claim that "Christians are in view who are convinced that days stand under lucky or unlucky stars" (*Commentary on Romans*, 370) is unwarranted.

46. Note the recurrence of ἐκ πίστεως in 14:23 (× 2), an expression derived from Habakkuk 2:4 (Rom. 1:17 [× 2]) and repeated in 3:26, 30; 4:16 (× 2); 5:1; 9:30, 32; 10:6. The faith/law antithesis is explicit or implicit in all these passages.

biguously of the duty of Jews and Gentiles to welcome one another as Christ has welcomed them. While chapter 14 is concerned primarily with issues of diet whereas 15:5-13 is concerned with common worship, it is plausible that the distinction between "the circumcision" and the Gentiles in the latter passage is closely related to the distinction between the "weak" and the "strong" in the former. Thus, the opening exhortation, "Welcome the one who is weak in faith" (14:1) is echoed in the later exhortation to "welcome one another as Christ has welcomed you" (15:7). The Roman Christians are to welcome one another as Jews and as Gentiles; the strong are to welcome the weak, and the weak are not to reject their welcome; and there is every indication that the weak/strong distinction is closely related to the Jew/Gentile one.

Romans 14:1–15:13 begins with an appeal not to argue over questions of diet and concludes with a plea for common worship. Since the current disputes are mainly about food (14:2-4, 6b, 14-23) and only secondarily about sacred days (14:5-6a) and wine (14:17, 21), Paul probably has in mind here the practice of communal meals, closely associated with the common worship for which he appeals in 15:5-13. For Gentile and Jewish Christians to be able to eat and worship together in harmony, both sides must make concessions. On the one hand, Gentiles must not regard observance of the Jewish law as incompatible with Christian faith. Indeed, according to 14:13-23, they should accommodate their own eating habits to Jewish Christian sensibilities, at least in the context of table fellowship. On the other hand, Jews should not regard law observance as indispensable for Christian faith. If each side makes a concession to the other, this will further the development of a single, united Roman Christian community in which both Jews and Gentiles have an acknowledged place. Unlike the weak, Paul does not wish the community to be wholly determined by its origins within the Roman synagogues. Unlike the strong, he does not envisage a purely Gentile future. It is at this point in the letter that the situation of the Roman Christian community (as perceived by Paul) comes most clearly into focus. Paul writes to a divided community, in which problems over table fellowship and a consequent lack of common worship are symptomatic of serious ideological differences between the two groupings. In addressing the symptoms, Paul also seeks to resolve the underlying issues and to lay the foundations of a future shared communal identity.

This interpretation of Romans 14:1–15:13 helps us to identify Paul's addressees in Romans and so to clarify his reasons for writing the letter as a whole. As we have seen, F. C. Baur is in a minority in arguing for a predominantly Jewish Christian readership; the scholarly consensus is that Romans is addressed primarily to Gentiles.[47] The reality appears to be more complex, however, as we shall see by way of an examination of the shifting boundaries of the audience envisaged in this part of the letter. Paul uses second-person plural address in his opening exhortation, "Welcome the person who is weak in faith [τὸν ἀσθενοῦντα τῇ πίστει]" (14:1). If the weak person here is indeed a Jewish Christian, then the exhortation is clearly addressed to Gentile (or Gentile-oriented) Christians. In vv. 3-12, however, both parties are addressed in a series of reciprocal exhortations and affirmations. In v. 3, third-person singular imperatives are addressed not only to the person who does eat (and who is therefore "strong") but also to the one who does not (who is "weak"):

> Let the one who eats not despise the one who does not eat, and let the one who does not eat not judge the one who eats, for God has welcomed him.

It is probably both parties who are addressed in the second-person singular question that follows: "Who are you to judge another's servant?" (v. 4a). While the reference to "judging" might suggest a reference only to the non-eater (cf. v. 3b), Paul does not differentiate sharply between "judging" and "despising," as though one were uniquely characteristic of the weak and the other of the strong (cf. vv. 10, 13). He continues to address weak and strong alike in vv. 5-6, reverting to the third-person singular discourse of v. 3 and to its reciprocal references to observance and non-observance. In this context, the first-person plural usage in vv. 7-8 is clearly inclusive: we live and die not to ourselves but to the Lord, and "we" connects Paul not only to the strong (as in 15:1) but also to the weak. In v. 10, the balanced third-person singular imperatives of v. 3 are repeated in the second-person singular:

> You, why do you judge your brother? And you, why do you despise your brother? For we shall all stand before the judgment-seat of God.

Here, the comprehensiveness of the first plural verb is underlined by the addition of πάντες. In the first half of Romans 14, then, it is only in v. 1 that the "strong" are the *exclusive* objects of Paul's address; elsewhere, he addresses both sides impartially. If the weak are indeed conservative Jewish Christians, *Romans 14 is incompatible with the claim that the letter was addressed exclusively and straightforwardly to Gentiles.*[48]

---

47. So Sanday and Headlam, *Romans,* xxxiii; Barrett, *Romans,* 22; Schlier, *Der Römerbrief,* 5; Käsemann, *Commentary on Romans,* 15. Cranfield argues that both Jewish and Gentile Christians were numerous in the Roman church (*Romans,* 1:16-22).

48. Contra T. Engberg-Pedersen, who distinguishes too sharply between a "direct" address

In v. 13a, "Let us *no longer* judge one another," the μή of the corresponding exhortations in v. 3 (μὴ ἐξουθενείτω, μὴ κρινέτω) is significantly replaced by μηκέτι, confirming that Paul here addresses a concrete problem in the Roman church, rather than a merely theoretical one. In what follows, however, it is Gentile (or Gentile-oriented) Christians who are exclusively addressed, in predominantly second-person singular discourse (14:15-16, 20-22a), although the first singular (14:14), first plural (14:19; 15:1-2), and third singular (14:18, 22b-23) are also employed. Gentile Christians are to make compromises for the sake of good relations with their Jewish Christian brothers and sisters. Those who have a faith that enables them "to eat everything" (14:2) are to keep this faith to themselves (14:22a), rather than allowing this issue to perpetuate division. While the weak are the object of Paul's concern throughout 14:13b–15:3, they are not directly addressed again until the return of emphatically reciprocal language in 15:5-7:

> May the God of steadfastness and encouragement grant you to reach full agreement with one another [τὸ αὐτὸ φρονεῖν ἐν ἀλλήλοις], in harmony with Christ Jesus, so that together [ὁμοθυμαδόν] you may glorify the God and Father of our Lord Jesus Christ. Therefore welcome one another as Christ has welcomed you, to the glory of God.

In the scriptural texts that follow, the Jewish Christian is tacitly invited to appropriate the language of Psalm 17:50, "Therefore I will confess you *among the Gentiles*" (Rom. 15:9). The following two citations are addressed directly to Gentiles, who are exhorted to praise God with his people (vv. 10-11).

Thus, Romans 14:1–15:13 enables us to draw a further significant conclusion about the audience envisaged for the letter as a whole: *Paul is confident that he has access to a Gentile audience in Rome, but less confident of his access to a Jewish one.* The passages of reciprocal address (14:3-13a; 15:5-13) are offset by passages that *differentiate* the addressees from the weak (14:1; 15:1) and that call for compromise for the sake of the weak (14:13b–15:3). In the passage as a whole, Gentile Christians are *always* the objects of Paul's address, Jewish Christians *sometimes*. The circle of Paul's addressees can expand to an inclusive "we all" (14:10), but it can also contract back to the exclusive "we who are strong" (15:1). Exclusive address is, however, concerned precisely with the in-

---

to the strong and a fictive address to Jewish Christians in the diatribal second-person singular (*Paul and the Stoics*, 185). The second singular exhortations in vv. 4, 10 are not addressed only to Jewish Christians, and in any case they cannot be isolated from the other modes of address in this passage. The relationship between diatribe-style second singular address and the addressees of Romans is a variable one, as a comparison between 2:17-24 and 11:17-24 indicates.

clusion of the weak. On the evidence of this passage, Romans is addressed to Gentile Christians, but also seeks a hearing for itself in Jewish Christian circles.[49] Paul writes his letter "to *all* in Rome who are beloved of God, called to be saints" (1:7), and he both acknowledges his special relationship with Gentile Christians and seeks to move beyond it.

There is a further dimension to the situation in Rome that is presupposed in Paul's letter, crucially important though not explicit in 14:1–15:13: the relationship between the Christian community and the synagogue. In this section, the exhortation to common worship (15:5-13) also entails a call to mixed table fellowship (14:1–15:4), such as was practiced for a time in the church of Antioch (cf. Gal. 2:12). The Antiochene practice broke down, however, when a warning from James led to a general Jewish Christian withdrawal from table fellowship with the uncircumcised. According to Paul, Cephas (and presumably the others as well) withdrew because he feared τοὺς ἐκ περιτομῆς, probably (as we have seen) a reference to Jews outside rather than inside the Christian community. In other words, Jewish Christian table fellowship with Gentiles could be interpreted as a sign of alienation from the majority Jewish community; it could be seen as amounting to apostasy. Thus, reorientation within the Roman Christian community, for which Paul calls in Romans 14–15, *will have implications for the community's relationship to the Roman synagogues.* And this will affect Jewish Christians in particular. They are to practice common worship and table fellowship with those who are at best minimally law observant, thereby distancing themselves still further from the Roman Jewish community as a whole.[50] More positively, they are encouraged to embrace a common *Christian* identity, along-

49. The fact that the weak and the strong alike acknowledge Christ as Lord (14:4-9) would seem to rule out Mark Nanos's claim that the "weak" of Romans 14–15 are non-Christian Jews (*The Mystery of Romans*, 85-165). In spite of 14:8-9, Nanos assumes that the "Lord" here is God rather than Christ (108-9).

50. Compare John Barclay's nuanced account of "the social effects of Paul's advice" ("'Do We Undermine the Law?'" 303-8). On the one hand, Paul's defense of the weak ostensibly means "that those Jewish Christians in Rome who wished to retain their links with the Jewish community were enabled to do so," continuing "to attend all-important synagogue gatherings and thus [to] maintain their place in the Jewish community" (303-4). On the other hand, "Paul here requires of Christian members of the Jewish community a very significant depth of 'association' with those declining to live according to the same mode of life" — an association ultimately incompatible "with continued membership of the Jewish community, which is naturally concerned to preserve its social integrity" (307). Thus "Paul subverts the basis on which Jewish law-observance is founded and precipitates a crisis of cultural integrity among the very believers whose law-observance he is careful to protect" (308). Rather than accepting this as a "fundamental paradox" (308), I suggest that *for Paul himself* the unity of Jewish and Gentile Christians is incompatible with continuing allegiance to the majority Jewish community, though not with the option of law observance. What Barclay sees as the social *effect* of Paul's advice was actually his *intention.*

side non-Jewish fellow Christians. Already distanced from their fellow Jews as a result of the earlier intra-communal tensions, they are now to redefine themselves simply as *Christiani*. While they continue to practice traditional Jewish observances such as the dietary laws and the sabbath, they are not to demand such observances of their Gentile brothers and sisters.[51]

Romans 14–15 says nothing about the relationship between the Roman Christian community and the synagogue. As we shall see, however, much of the rest of the letter makes sense in a Roman context only if it is this relationship that is at issue. In its Roman context, the letter is to be located within a trajectory in which a Christ originally associated with *Iudaei* comes to be associated instead with *Christiani*, practitioners of what some in Rome see as "a new and evil superstition." A reform movement within the Roman Jewish synagogues has become an autonomous sect; and Paul's letter to the Romans bears witness to some of the ideological factors that led from the one communal location to the other.

In the following chapters, it will repeatedly be argued that Paul's denial of a positive soteriological role to the law functions pragmatically as an *imperative*, a call to Paul's Roman readers to finalize the ideological breach with the (Roman) synagogue, in order to promote a common Christian identity. For Paul, "the law" is not an abstract principle but a *communally authoritative text*, and to assign a negative role to this text is simultaneously to construct a sharply defined boundary between the Christian and the Jewish communities. In Paul's account of the law, one community seeks its own cohesion by defining itself over against another. This breach is the negative corollary of the call for a shared praxis of table-fellowship and worship (Rom. 14–15). If Paul's talk of "the law" finds its initial social correlate in the praxis of law-observant *Christians* in Rome, this praxis is nevertheless one that they share with the majority non-Christian Jewish community. Insofar as Roman Christians continue to insist that law-observance is obligatory, and to condemn those who take the opposite view, they remain within the ideological sphere

---

51. According to Philip Esler, Paul in Romans "seeks to establish an overarching common identity that embraces Judean [= Jewish] and Greek subgroup identities without extinguishing either" (*Conflict and Identity in Romans*, 132). Esler here draws on the social scientific finding that "recategorization from two groups to one group can be achieved by increasing the salience of existing common superordinate group membership" (30). While this model ostensibly fits Romans 14–15, it leaves the relationship between Roman Christians and the Roman synagogues entirely out of the picture. In Esler's account, the synagogues are relevant only to the prehistory of Paul's letter (86-107); thereafter they are replaced by the church. In contrast, the present discussion will assume that statements assigning a negative role to the law have the synagogue as their social correlate (as explicitly in 2 Corinthians 3).

of the synagogue — irrespective of the state of their social relations with non-Christian fellow Jews. For Paul, *a shared Christian identity based on "faith" must supersede this erroneous law-oriented definition of Christian identity,* and the entire argument of Romans 1–11 is concerned to elaborate this point.

Before we proceed to interpret the main body of the letter in the light of these findings, a discussion of other relevant material in chapters 1, 15, and 16 is necessary. This will reinforce the conclusions already reached and provide a possible answer to the historical riddle of the origins of Gentile Christianity in Rome.

4. Gentiles and Jews in Rome (Romans 16)

It has often been suggested that Romans 16 is addressed to the church not of Rome but of Ephesus, and that it is either an independent letter (in whole or in part)[52] or an appendix to a copy of Romans that was sent to Ephesus.[53] The main argument for this hypothesis is that it is thought unlikely that Paul should have known as many individuals in the Roman church as are mentioned in vv. 3-16. Ephesus is suggested because Prisca and Aquila were last heard of in connection with that city (Acts 18:19, 26) and because of the reference in v. 5 to "my beloved Epaenetus, who was the first convert in Asia for Christ." But Prisca and Aquila were only ever in Corinth (Acts 18:2-3; cf. 1 Cor. 16:19) and Ephesus (Acts 18:18-19, 26; 1 Cor. 16:19) because, along with other Jews, they had been expelled from Rome (Acts 18:2). There is no reason why they should not have returned to Rome by the time Paul wrote his letter. Some of the others named in Romans 16 may also have been Christian Jews from Rome, whom Paul met in the east as he had met Prisca and Aquila, and who have now returned to Rome as they have.[54] Even if it seems surprising that Paul should have known so many individuals in the Roman church, the view that Romans 16 is integral to the original letter is preferable to the theory that, without any break or explanation, Paul suddenly addresses the church of Ephesus, or that an unrelated letter fragment has unaccountably been attached by a later editor.[55]

---

52. So Käsemann, *Commentary on Romans,* 419; Bornkamm, *Paul,* 246; Georgi, *Die Geschichte der Kollekte des Paulus für Jerusalem,* 79-80.

53. T. W. Manson, "St. Paul's Letter to the Romans — and Others," 15.

54. So Wilckens, *Der Brief an die Römer,* 1:25.

55. The Roman destination of Romans 16 has been effectively reasserted in more recent scholarship; see especially K. Donfried, "A Short Note on Romans 16," *passim;* P. Lampe, *From Paul to Valentinus,* 153-64.

If Romans 16 can be satisfactorily explained as an integral part of the letter to the Romans, the Ephesian theory collapses automatically.

It is in fact by no means certain that Paul knew personally all the individuals who are named in Romans 16.[56] He clearly knew Prisca, Aquila, and Epaenetus (vv. 3-5), and he presumably knew those who are described as "beloved": Ampliatus (v. 8), Stachys (v. 9), and Persis (v. 12). The fact that he describes Rufus's mother as "his mother and mine" (v. 13) suggests that he knew them both. Urbanus is described as "our fellow worker [συνεργός] in Christ" (v. 9; cf. v. 3), indicating that he has worked alongside Paul; but Mary, whose labors in the Roman community are mentioned (v. 6), may be known to Paul only by reputation. It is not certain whether "those workers in the Lord, Tryphaena and Tryphosa" (v. 12) have worked alongside Paul or solely in Rome. Paul refers to Andronicus and Junia as "fellow prisoners" (v. 7), but he also describes them as "fellow countrymen," and it may be that in both expressions he simply wishes to assert his solidarity with people he has never met.[57] Like him, they are Jews, and like him, they have suffered imprisonment for the sake of Christ. Paul may or may not have known "Apelles, who is approved in Christ" (v. 10). There is nothing in vv. 10-11 to show that Paul knew personally the family of Aristobulus, or Herodion, or the family of Narcissus, and this is true also of the ten individuals who are listed in vv. 14-15, about whom nothing is said other than that they are to be greeted. This leaves nine people who are certain to have been known personally by Paul: Prisca, Aquila, Epaenetus, Ampliatus, Urbanus, Stachys, Persis, and Rufus and his mother. In other cases, Paul's sources of information about the Roman Christian community will have provided him with names of individuals he has yet to meet. The evidence of Romans 16 is hardly sufficient to suggest that it must have been sent to Ephesus. In answer to the question why Paul should have greeted people who were known to him by name and reputation only, one may point out that Romans as a whole is addressed to such people. Having written at great length to people most of whom he has never met, it is not surprising that he should send individual greetings to some who are known to him at least by name.

In discussing Romans 14:1–15:13, it was suggested that this section gives evidence of two distinct groupings within the Roman Christian community, divided over the question of the continuing practice of the law. Romans 16 sheds further light on these two groupings. We may assume that most of

---

56. So W. Meeks, *First Urban Christians*, 56.

57. So Sanday and Headlam, *Romans*, 423; Cranfield, *Romans*, 2:788-89. Others assume that imprisonment with Paul is meant (Barrett, *Romans*, 283; Käsemann, *Commentary on Romans*, 414; Wilckens, *Der Brief an die Römer*, 3:135). Schlier, *Der Römerbrief*, 444, leaves both possibilities open.

those whom Paul knew personally were associated with the "Gentile" group — which (to repeat) may have included ethnic Jews, just as the "Jewish" group may have included ethnic Gentiles. The former is presumably the case with Prisca and Aquila, of whom it is said that they "risked their lives for me, to whom not only am I thankful but also all the churches of the Gentiles" (v. 4). Greetings are also sent to τὴν κατ' οἶκον ἐκκλησίαν (v. 5), and this house-church presumably represented a Pauline, Gentile-oriented, law-free understanding of the Christian gospel. If the present interpretation of Romans 14:1–15:13 is correct, this community would have been regarded with some suspicion by other Jewish Christian members of the original community. As regards the others personally known to Paul, Epaenetus ("the first-fruits of Asia for Christ," v. 5) and Ampliatus ("my beloved in the Lord") may have been Paul's own converts; Urbanus ("our co-worker in Christ," v. 9) had worked alongside him; and Rufus ("chosen in the Lord") and his mother had shown him hospitality — hence "his mother and mine" (v. 13). Such people may be described as "Paulinists" — i.e., Christians who shared Paul's distinctive vision of the church as embracing Gentiles as well as Jews and as oriented towards Christ rather than the practice of the law. The fact that they were known to Paul personally suggests a solution to the riddle of the origin of Gentile Christianity in Rome: the Gentile group addressed especially in Romans 14:1–15:13 and in 11:13-24 may well have been founded by Paul's own converts and associates. *Gentile-oriented Christianity at Rome is therefore Pauline Christianity.*

Thus Paul can speak of himself in unqualified terms as "apostle of the Gentiles" (11:13), as commissioned to bring about "the obedience of faith among all the Gentiles" (1:5), as a "servant of Christ Jesus for the sake of the Gentiles" (15:16), without needing to acknowledge that, after all, he is not the founder of Roman Gentile-oriented Christianity. When he addresses the Roman Christian community, he is not deviating from his rule not to build on another's foundation (15:20). In encouraging Jewish Christians to worship together with Gentiles, Paul is also encouraging them to recognize the legitimacy of his own work.[58] They are to regard observance or non-observance of the law as a matter of individual choice, and the obstacle to worshiping together with Paul's Gentile Christian friends (and Paul himself, when he comes to Rome) is thus to be removed.

58. As Hübner states, "The polemical thrust of his argument is directed against those Jewish Christians who were making life difficult for the Pauline Gentile Christians" (*Law in Paul's Thought*, 68). However, Hübner also considers possible the view that the conflict in the Roman congregation was between Gentile Christians and proselytes.

Romans 16 also confirms the existence of a Jewish Christian community in Rome. In v. 7, Paul writes: "Greet Andronicus and Junia, my fellow countrymen and my fellow prisoners; they are people of note among the apostles, and they were in Christ before me." Andronicus and Junia[59] are thus linked with earliest Jewish Christianity. As "apostles," they will therefore have shared in the Jewish church's mission "to the circumcision" (cf. Gal. 2:7-9), for Paul knows of no apostle other than himself (and perhaps Barnabas) who is sent to the Gentiles.[60] For Paul, being an apostle implies, first, that one has seen the risen Lord, and second, that one has founded a congregation (cf. 1 Cor. 9:1-2), and it is therefore plausible that Paul regards Andronicus and Junia as founders of the original Jewish Christian congregation in Rome.[61] Their status as apostles no doubt makes them the most important and influential members of the Jewish section of the Roman Christian community; Paul must gain their favor if his aim of uniting a currently divided community is to be achieved.

Another member of the Jewish grouping may have been "my fellow countryman Herodion" (v. 11).[62] As in the case of Andronicus and Junia, Paul stresses the link of Jewish birth between himself and the recipient of the greeting, and in this way seeks to bridge the gap between himself and conservative Jewish Christianity. (In the case of Prisca and Aquila, also Jews according to Acts 18:2, this was not necessary, since they were already Paulinists.) If it is correct to associate τοὺς ἐκ τῶν Ἀριστοβούλου in v. 10 with a member of the Jewish royal family, then those of his household whom Paul greets may also have been prominent members of the Jewish Christian grouping.[63] While at least nine Gentile or

59. Cranfield thinks it more likely that a woman is here referred to, on the grounds that there is no evidence elsewhere for "Junias" as a male name (*Romans*, 2:788). This receives some support from Paul's statement in 1 Corinthians 9:5 that other apostles were accompanied by their wives and by his reference to another married couple (Prisca and Aquila) in Romans 16:3. On this, see also Wilckens, *Der Brief an die Römer*, 3:135.

60. Contrast Wilckens, *Der Brief an die Römer*, 3:136, who thinks that Andronicus and Junia were "Paul's co-workers in the Gentile mission."

61. M. Kettunen suggests that they may have been sent to Rome from Jerusalem (*Der Abfassungszweck des Römerbriefes*, 77). However, he regards them as members of the "Hellenist" group there (76), for whom circumcision was "in principle meaningless"; despite this, they were welcomed by many in the synagogue (80). The very existence of a Hellenistic group with views such as these is more than doubtful, and it is hard to see why Roman Jews should have welcomed people for whom the sign of the covenant had become meaningless.

62. In contrast, "Mary" (v. 6) is probably not Jewish (P. Lampe, *From Paul to Valentinus*, 175-76).

63. Precise identification is difficult, and there appear to be three main candidates. (1) The first is Aristobulus the brother of Agrippa I and Herod of Chalcis, and son of Aristobulus the

Gentile-oriented Roman Christians are personally known to Paul, it is not clear that this is the case with any of these Jewish Christians. The addressees are exhorted to convey greetings to Andronicus and Junia, Herodion, and the household of Aristobulus, but in doing so they may be *establishing* a relationship between Paul and these Jewish Christians, rather than reinforcing an existing relationship. The emphasis on shared ethnicity (συγγενεῖς/-ῆ, vv. 7, 11) and a common experience of suffering (συναιχμαλώτους, v. 7) is, as it were, a *substitute* for the warm personal relationships Paul has with a number of the "beloved" Gentile Christians (cf. vv. 5, 8, 9, 12).

Thus, Romans 16 confirms the hypothesis about the purpose of Romans derived from 14:1–15:13. The purpose of Romans is to encourage Jewish and Gentile Christians in Rome, divided over the question of the law, to set aside their differences and to worship together. The latter group are Paulinists, and it is converts and associates of Paul who have brought his message of freedom from the law and separation from the Jewish community to Rome and have established a Gentile Christian presence there. The former group represents the remnants of the original Roman Jewish Christian congregation, which regards Pauline Gentile-oriented Christianity with some suspicion. The chief purpose of Romans is to overcome this suspicion. One way in which Paul tries to do so is to include greetings for members of both sides of the community in the final part of his letter. If those known personally to Paul are Gentile or Gentile-oriented Christians, this explains why in chapters 14–15 he is more confident of a hearing from this section of the Roman Christian community than from the Jewish Christian one.

Two further features of Romans 16 support this interpretation. First, in vv. 3-16 Paul does not greet the named individuals directly. Rather, he requests his readers to greet them; the verbs are all in the imperative. (Contrast vv. 16b,

---

son of Herod the Great, executed by his father. See further references in *Ant.* 18.151-54 (which tells of his poor relationship with his brother Agrippa), *Ant.* 18.273-76 (where he plays a leading role in the campaign against Gaius's statue), and *BJ* 2.221-22 (where his death in c. 48 CE is reported). This individual is often identified with the Aristobulus of Romans 16:10 (so Sanday and Headlam, *Romans*, 425; Cranfield, *Romans*, 2:791-92; Dunn, *Romans*, 2:896; Fitzmyer, *Romans*, 740), although he appears to be resident in Palestine rather than Rome. (2) An alternative identification is with his nephew, the third son of Herod of Chalcis (*BJ* 2.221) and the second husband of Salome daughter of Herodias (*Ant.* 18.137). This is "Aristobulus the Younger," of whom Claudius speaks warmly in a letter to the Jewish people (*Ant.* 20.13). In 54 CE Nero presented him with "the kingdom of the lesser Armenia" (*BJ* 2.252; *Ant.* 20.158; Tacitus, *Ann.* 13.7). (3) Aristobulus the Younger and Salome had three sons, named, predictably enough, Herod, Agrippa, and Aristobulus (*Ant.* 18.137). The latter is the only one of the three bearers of the name who could have been resident in Rome at the time of Paul's letter. For links between the Herodians and Rome, see J. Barclay, *Jews in the Mediterranean Diaspora*, 294.

21-23, where individuals other than Paul send their own greetings to the Roman community.) Paul here in effect asks his readers in both groups to introduce themselves to one another.[64] Thus, Gentile Christians are not to "despise" Andronicus and Junia, the most important members of the Jewish Christian group. They are to regard them as "people of note among the apostles" and to bring them their greetings. Conversely, Jewish Christians are not to "pass judgment" on Prisca and Aquila; they are to be greeted as people who have greatly assisted the spread of the gospel among the Gentiles. These commands to greet named individuals are similar in function to the general command that Jewish and Gentile Christians should welcome one another (15:7).

Second, a possible reason for the abrupt polemical passage in 16:17-20 comes to light. Up to this point, Romans is notably lacking in the sharp polemic that characterizes parts of Galatians and Philippians 3.[65] Here, after concluding his greetings, Paul speaks darkly of some who are not to be welcomed or greeted, but rather avoided, since they represent a dire threat to the community:

> I appeal to you, brothers and sisters, to look out for those who create dissensions and difficulties [τὰς διχοστασίας καὶ τὰ σκάνδαλα], in opposition to the teaching in which you were instructed — and that you keep away from them. For such people do not serve our Lord Christ but their own appetites, and with specious words they deceive the hearts of the simple. (16:17-18)

Following this passionate appeal (vv. 17-20), Paul returns to the task of passing on greetings from others (vv. 21-23; cf. v. 16b). The best explanation for this remarkable outburst is that he expects opposition to his attempt to persuade Jewish Christians to accept the legitimacy of the Paulinists and to join with them for worship. Not all Jewish Christians will be convinced even by Paul's letter that law observance is a matter of personal choice and that its absence is no bar to fellowship. Paul here anticipates their objections and denounces them in advance for creating, or rather perpetuating, "divisions." As in the case of Galatians 6:13 and Philippians 3:19, to assume that Paul is speaking here of "antinomians" is to take his polemical language much too literally.[66]

---

64. According to Schlier, the imperatives make the Roman congregation the "Übermittlerin" of Paul's greetings (*Der Römerbrief,* 442-43).

65. Käsemann sees the contrast between the violence of 16:17-20 and the rest of the letter as an additional reason for separating chapter 16 (*Commentary on Romans,* 419). But Kettunen rightly points out that it fits just as badly into chapter 16 itself (*Der Abfassungszweck des Römerbriefes,* 67).

66. See Dodd, *Romans,* 244-45; Käsemann, *Commentary on Romans,* 418.

Romans 16 confirms that the letter as a whole cannot be addressed exclusively to Gentile Christians. If, in this very letter, Paul conveys greetings to Jewish as well as Gentile Christians, they are clearly included within the scope of a letter addressed "to *all* in Rome who are beloved of God, called to be saints" (1:7). We are to envisage Jewish as well as Gentile addressees of the text as a whole.[67] If Gentile Christian addressees are singled out in 11:13, Jewish Christian addressees are similarly singled out in references to "Abraham our forefather according to the flesh" (4:1) or to "our father Isaac" (9:10).[68]

5. The Evidence of Romans 1:1-17 and 15:14-33

As we have seen, there were two main groupings or factions within the Roman Christian community. One faction continued to insist on law observance whereas the other did not, with the result that common worship and table fellowship were difficult or impossible. Paul writes chiefly to persuade the two sides of the Roman Christian community to recognize one another — and especially to persuade the Jewish faction to recognize the legitimacy of the Gentile one, thereby finalizing their breach with the synagogue — with a view to a common Christian identity. The real test for this hypothesis is whether or not it sheds light on the doctrinal core of Romans (1:18–11:36): that will be the topic of the following chapters. But it is also important to ask whether the hypothesis is consistent with two passages in which Paul speaks explicitly of the Roman Christians and of his aim in writing to them (1:1-17 and 15:14-33). The first of these passages proves to be consistent with the hypothesis (1) that Romans includes Jewish Christians among its addressees, and (2) that Paul wrote his letter to unite the two groupings in a common Christian identity. In the second passage, (3) Paul indirectly acknowledges the Jewish Christian component of his readership, differentiating his addressees from the "Gentiles" who are the objects of his mission, and presenting an account of that mission that is oriented towards Jerusalem.[69]

---

67. Rightly emphasized by Esler, who criticizes the suggestion that Jewish Christians named in Romans 16 do not belong to the letter's addressees (*Conflict and Identity*, 119). The attempt to distinguish the named individuals of Romans 16 from the addressees of the letter (R. Thorsteinsson, *Paul's Interlocutor in Romans 2*, 98-99) founders on the fact that Romans is addressed to "all" Roman Christians (1:7).

68. Those who argue from 11:13 for a purely Gentile readership for the letter as a whole (e.g., S. Stowers, *A Rereading of Romans*, 21) regularly overlook "our father Isaac" in 9:10.

69. The third point is new to this edition.

(1) A purely Gentile readership for the letter is often deduced from Paul's statements in 1:5-6, according to which apostleship has been entrusted to him εἰς ὑπακοὴν πίστεως ἐν πᾶσιν τοῖς ἔθνεσιν ὑπὲρ τοῦ ὀνόματος αὐτοῦ, ἐν οἷς ἐστε καὶ ὑμεῖς κλητοὶ Ἰησοῦ Χριστοῦ.[70] Here, ἐν οἷς must mean "among whom," either in the sense that the addressees are themselves Gentiles,[71] or in the sense that they live in the midst of Gentiles.[72] If the former is the meaning, the Roman Gentile Christians are seen here as the objects of Paul's missionary activity, just like any other Gentiles. But this seems unlikely, for the addressees are *already* "called by Jesus Christ" (1:6). The key to the verse is the phrase καὶ ὑμεῖς: ". . . among whom *you too* are called by Jesus Christ."[73] "You too" probably means "you as well as me," for Paul has spoken of himself in 1:1 as having been "called," and he states in 1:5 that his call has taken him among the Gentiles. Paul is saying: "You too are called by Jesus Christ among the Gentiles, just as I am." Here, "you too" comprises the Roman Christian community in its entirety, on both its Jewish and its Gentile sides. Thus, the letter is addressed to "*all* in Rome who are beloved of God" (1:7). There is nothing here to suggest that Roman Jewish Christians such as Andronicus, Junia, and Herodion are somehow excluded.

(2) Paul wrote Romans to unite Jewish and Gentile Christians by persuading each group to accept the legitimacy of the other and to strive to create a shared Christian identity. His letter is addressed "to all in Rome who are beloved by God, called to be saints" (1:7). It may be significant that, contrary to his normal practice at the beginning of a letter, Paul does not address the recipients as an ἐκκλησία.[74] This need not be of any great importance, since the same is true of Philippians 1:1. But Romans 1:7 is at least consistent with the view that the Roman Christian community was made up of a loose network of house-churches (cf. 16:5, 10, 11, 14, 15), some oriented towards observance of the law, others towards the Pauline law-free gospel. This is strikingly confirmed by the conclusion of the letter's introductory section. In 1:13-15 Paul states that, in his capacity as apostle to the Gentiles, he wishes to preach the

70. According to Kettunen, 1:5-6, 13-15; 11:13; 15:16, 18 clearly indicate that the readers were Gentiles (*Der Abfassungszweck des Römerbriefes*, 27). But in no case is this certain. Even 11:13 could easily imply that elsewhere Paul has been speaking primarily to Jews — otherwise he would not have to single out the Gentiles for special mention.

71. So Sanday and Headlam, *Romans*, 12; Barrett, *Romans*, 22; Käsemann, *Commentary on Romans*, 15; Schlier, *Der Römerbrief*, 30.

72. So Cranfield, *Romans*, 1:20; Wilckens, *Der Brief an die Römer*, 1:67.

73. Cf. Cranfield, *Romans*, 1:67-68.

74. Compare Klein, "Paul's Purpose in Writing the Epistle to the Romans," 47.

gospel in Rome. In 1:16, however, he unexpectedly asserts that the gospel is "for the Jew first, and also for the Greek." This sudden reference to "the Jew" is comprehensible if in v. 16 Paul is still referring to the Roman situation, as in vv. 8-15. In that case, "for the Jew first" expresses Paul's acknowledgment of the priority and the preeminence of the Roman Jewish Christian community, whereas "and also for the Greek" insists on the reality and legitimacy of Pauline Gentile Christians in Rome.[75] Roman Gentile Christians must acknowledge the preeminence of Jewish fellow believers. Roman Jewish Christians must concede that salvation through Christ is not for themselves alone but "for everyone who believes" — including Gentiles.

(3) At the close of the letter, Paul differentiates the "Gentiles" who are the objects of his mission from his addressees in Rome, thereby acknowledging the diversity of the Roman Christian community. As far as the addressees are concerned, 15:14-33 is, as it were, ethnically neutral. Paul has written on the basis of his commission as "a minister of Christ Jesus to the Gentiles," which has as its goal that "the offering of the Gentiles may be acceptable, sanctified in the Holy Spirit" (15:16). It is not implied that his Roman addressees are part of that offering, however. The apostle to the Gentiles can presumably speak to Jews as well as to Gentiles about his mission (cf. Gal. 2:2). Indeed, Roman Gentile Christians are nowhere directly in view here: the passage as a whole contains four references to "the Gentiles" (Rom. 15:16 [× 2], 18, 27), none of which explicitly refers to Roman Gentile Christians.[76] Paul speaks about his mission to Gentiles in the east, but he plans to come to Rome merely to *visit* his addressees in preparation for an extension of his Gentile mission to Spain (15:23-24, 28). As for the collection, there is no suggestion that the addressees might in principle have contributed to this. It is a matter for the Macedonians and the Achaians, who seek by material means to repay a spiritual debt (15:27). This concept of Gentile indebtedness to the Jerusalem church is totally foreign to other Pauline statements about the collection (cf. 2 Cor. 8–9) and is surely introduced with a Jewish Christian audience especially in view. The same may also be true of the references to Jerusalem as the starting point of Paul's own preaching (Rom. 15:19), as the object of his own charitable concern in spite of past tensions (15:25, 31), and as the materially impoverished

75. This seems more likely than Käsemann's theological interpretation: "Paul gives Judaism precedence for the sake of the continuity of the plan of salvation" (*Commentary on Romans*, 23). The context suggests that the historical reality of the Roman church is in view.

76. It is therefore difficult to accept Ann Jervis's claim that Paul's letter "was intended specifically for the believers at Rome so that they too would become part of his 'offering' of 'sanctified' and 'obedient' Gentiles" (*The Purpose of Romans*, 163).

source of the spiritual wealth distributed among Gentiles (15:26). In stark contrast to Galatians 1–2, Paul in Romans 15 presents a thoroughly Jerusalem-oriented account of his own apostolic ministry. At present, he is occupied with a collection project intended to secure the reconciliation of Greek and Judean Christians in the eastern Mediterranean, just as his letter is intended to secure the reconciliation of similar groupings in Rome. The preceding catena, in which Jews and Gentiles are exhorted to praise God alongside each other, is relevant not only in Rome but also in Macedonia, Achaia, and Jerusalem; specifically Roman concerns are thus set within a broader international context.[77]

There is, then, nothing in the letter opening or conclusion that contradicts the thesis that Paul's letter addresses tensions within a divided Roman Christian community. Indeed, these passages provide supporting evidence for the finding that Paul writes his letter with Jewish as well as Gentile readers in mind. It should be emphasized that the letter gives expression to *Paul's own perspective* on Roman Christianity. No doubt the historical reality was more complex and diverse than his simple dichotomy between "weak" and "strong" would suggest. In principle, it is possible that Paul knew comparatively little about Christianity in Rome, or even that in certain respects he was misinformed about it. Whatever the reality, the argument here has to do with Paul's own perspective on that reality, a perspective engendered not just by developments in Rome but also by his distinctive missionary experiences in the eastern Mediterranean. In the following chapters, we shall ask how this perspective on the Roman Christian community helped to shape the entire contents of his letter.

---

77. The parallel between the letter and the collection project suggests that there is more than a grain of truth in J. Jervell's claim that in Romans Paul rehearses arguments on the Jew/Gentile question in preparation for his visit to Jerusalem ("The Letter to Jerusalem"). That does not make these arguments any less relevant to the Roman situation, however.

CHAPTER 6

The Social Function of Romans 2

1. A Sociological Approach to Romans 1–11

The two sociological models developed earlier shed light on the situation in Rome, as outlined in the previous chapter.

(1) The Roman Jewish Christian congregation originated as a reform movement within the Roman Jewish community. That is the implication of Suetonius's statement that "Chrestus" (i.e., the arrival in Rome of the Christian gospel) was the occasion of disturbances among Roman Jews. By the time of the Neronian persecution, however, there is no clear link with the Roman Jewish community. Those subject to punitive action are now no longer *Iudaei* but *Christiani*. Paul's letter to the Romans may be placed on the trajectory that leads from the one social location to the other. In chapters 14–15, the exhortation to the strong (Pauline Christians) to accommodate the weak (Jewish Christians) is accompanied by an exhortation to the weak to seek a common Christian identity in union with the strong — instead of clinging to an identity shaped by the law and so by the synagogue. Even if Roman Jewish Christians are by this time excluded from the network of Roman synagogues, they remain suspicious of the unambiguously "sectarian" Pauline standpoint, in which Christ and law seem mutually exclusive. This is evident especially in Romans 9–11, where (as we shall see) Paul defends himself against the charge that his Gentile-oriented gospel asserts a divine repudiation of the Jewish people. It is likely that he here responds to a view that he believes to be current among Roman Jewish Christians. By encouraging them to recognize the legitimacy of the Gentile Christian community rather than regarding Torah observance as non-negotiable, Paul seeks not only a single unified Christian

community but also the abandonment of the ideological link with the Roman Jewish community. In this way, a failed reform movement will adopt a sectarian stance in relation to the majority Jewish community. While Paul's letter envisages a Gentile Christian readership in Rome, it also seeks to reach out beyond them into the Roman Jewish Christian community, constructing a new identity that will encompass them both.

(2) If the argument so far is correct, this provides us with a key for interpreting the great theological argument of Romans 1–11.[1] It has long been assumed that Romans 1–11 belongs to the realm of pure theological theory.[2] Here, if anywhere, Paul rises above particular circumstances and presents his profound understanding of the gospel on a general plane.[3] Few of those who criticize this assumption have themselves succeeded in showing in detail how their perception of the situation in Rome sheds light on the argument of Romans as a whole.[4] But if Paul is indeed trying to persuade the Roman Jewish Christian congregation to accept the legitimacy of the Paulinists, thereby rejecting an initial identity as a reform movement and embracing a sectarian identity instead, then we would expect this to be apparent in Romans 1–11 as well as in chapters 14–15. The same would be true of the corresponding social reorientation required of the Paulinists, who were to extend a welcome to Christian Jews and show a willingness to compromise in matters of diet. If, both at the opening of the letter and especially in its final three chapters, Paul presupposes a community in which Jew/Gentile issues are perpetuating division, then it would be strange if he devoted the main body of the letter to quite other topics. As we shall argue, *Romans 1–11 is to be understood as the theoretical rationale for the social reorientation called for in Romans 14–15.*[5] It is not a purely theoretical discourse. If Paul's text attains to universal significance (as

---

1. It is a limitation of *PJG¹* that it omits to discuss Romans 12–13. To address this lacuna would have required an entire new chapter following Chapter 9, and I have decided to let it stand as an acknowledgment that every interpretative hypothesis has its limits.

2. For example, Conzelmann denies that Paul's views on justification and the law can be derived from his historical situation and adds: "The doctrine of the law must be understood in specifically theological terms" (*Outline of the Theology of the New Testament,* 221).

3. Thus, according to Nygren, the fact that Romans was not aimed at circumstances within the Roman congregation gives it "a uniquely objective character" (*A Commentary on Romans,* 5). Compare Dunn's methodological suggestion that "we cannot do better than take Romans as a template on which to construct our own statement of Paul's theology" (*The Theology of Paul the Apostle,* 26).

4. Minear, *The Obedience of Faith,* is an exception, and now Esler, *Conflict and Identity in Romans.*

5. Against Wilckens, "Über Abfassungszweck und Aufbau des Römerbriefs," 126, who denies any close connection between Romans 14–15 and 1–11.

its canonical status claims), it does so by *embracing* contingencies rather than erasing them. Romans 1–11 has a clear and singular pragmatic goal or social function, explaining to the Roman Christian community why and how they are to find unity in a common identity as *Christiani.* This reorientation will be more far-reaching for the "weak" than for the "strong" — who are therefore enjoined not just to "welcome" Jewish Christians but also to make whatever dietary compromises are necessary in order to ensure that shared meals are no longer the occasion of "dissensions and difficulties" (cf. 16:17).

The reading of Romans 1–11 that follows is not intended to advocate an *exclusively* pragmatic account of the letter, as though Paul's many and various arguments were *no more than* means to the end of bringing about the conduct for which he explicitly calls in chapters 14–15. A pragmatic reading that reduced the letter to a series of monotonous reiterations could not provide an adequate account of this extraordinarily rich text. The discourse of Romans may be seen not so much as a single linear argument, in which each succeeding element is grounded in what preceded it, but rather as a *series* of interrelated arguments, each with its own relative autonomy vis-à-vis the others. One need not have read Romans 4 in order to understand Romans 6. The letter is, as it were, a series of episodes rather than a single narrative. As we shall see, even the major blocks of material constructed by commentators (e.g., "1:18–3:20"; "3:21–4:25"; "9:1–11:36") are considerably less homogeneous than is often thought — not because Paul is incapable of thinking coherently but because of his preference for relatively self-contained arguments, even in large-scale works such as 1 Corinthians or Romans. In most cases, the traditional chapter divisions register the sequence of Paul's arguments more appropriately than modern renderings of the "structure" of Romans. It follows that the relationship between the individual parts of the letter and the overall pragmatic goal will be a variable and flexible one. The pragmatic goal itself allows for such variety and flexibility: for the convergence of the two factions within the Roman Christian community entails the construction of a shared Christian identity, an open-ended task that obviously requires a broad range of resources. The hypothesis of the "pragmatic goal" (or "social function") makes it possible to identify the single strategy underlying the various parts of the letter, but not in such a way as to deprive them of their distinctiveness and their internal coherence.

We should also bear in mind that Paul here prepares the way for an intended visit to Rome and that his discourse is always also *self*-presentation.[6]

---

6. As Troels Engberg-Pedersen argues, "[I]f Paul succeeded in reaching the aim of his ex-

He himself is already implicated in the Roman situation as he understands it. For that reason, he anticipates the possibility that Roman Jewish Christians may be personally hostile to him, and he responds to a number of objections — hypothetical or actual — to his work and outlook. He acknowledges that he may be accused of trying to overthrow the law through his understanding of faith (3:31). He knows of opponents who claim that he teaches, "Let us do evil that good may come" (3:8), since that is what his belief that "we are not under law but under grace" amounts to (6:14-15; cf. 6:1). By teaching that obedience to the law is incompatible with faith in Christ, he may seem to assert that "the law is sin" (Rom. 7:7) — i.e., that the conduct prescribed by the law is sinful. Such an attitude towards the divine commandments would also involve the repudiation of the rest of Israel's heritage. Paul, it is claimed, is obviously not in the least interested in the salvation of the Jewish people: 9:1-5, 10:1, and 11:11-36 should be read as denials of this charge. He teaches that God has forsaken his people (cf. 11:1, 11) and installed Gentiles in their place. At such points as these, Paul anticipates that the Roman Jewish Christians may "pass judgment" on himself and his followers in Rome (cf. 14:3-4, 10-13).[7] In outlining his rationale for a distinctive Christian identity over against the synagogue, Paul must defend *himself* against such allegations.

According to his critics, Paul's doctrine of freedom from the law is a recipe for moral chaos. Romans 1:18-32 may be read as an attempt to reassure Roman Jewish Christians on this point. There is nothing distinctively Pauline or even distinctively Christian in this passage — in this respect it is unique in the Pauline corpus. Parallels between this section and Jewish anti-Gentile polemic abound.[8] Paul denounces Gentile idolatry as a perversion of the true knowledge of God (1:18-23) and then attacks what he regards as Gentile sexual perversion (1:24-27) and moral anarchy in general (1:28-32). For Jewish Christian readers, Paul's argument will have sounded reassuringly familiar. Here, for example, is the Jewish sybil differentiating between the faithful law observance of the chosen race and the iniquitous conduct of Gentiles:

---

hortation — briefly, to generate the kind of God- and Christ-oriented unanimity in the Roman congregations that he speaks of in 15:5-6 — then he would also have prepared for his own visit in the best possible way" (*Paul and the Stoics,* 184). In that sense, Romans can be a letter of "self-recommendation" (351n) even as it addresses specifically Roman issues.

7. According to Lüdemann, *Paulus, der Heidenapostel,* 159-60, Romans 3:8 is the only definite evidence of anti-Paulinism in Romans. But the accusation explicitly acknowledged in 3:8 is closely related to the possibilities raised and ruled out in 3:31, 6:14-15, 7:7, and so on. If the first passage alludes to anti-Paulinism, so too do the others.

8. So Bornkamm, "The Revelation of God's Wrath," 50-53.

They [the Jews] are mindful of holy wedlock. Nor do they practise unholy intercourse with boys, as do Phoenicians, Egyptians and Romans, spacious Greece and many other nations, Persians and Galatians and all Asia, transgressing the holy law of immortal God, which they transgressed. Therefore the Eternal will inflict on all people disaster and famine and woes and groans and war and pestilence and lamentable ills, because they would not honour in holiness the eternal Father of all people, but honoured idols made with hands, revering them. (*Sib. Or.* 3.595-606)

Like Romans 1, this passage asserts a causal relationship between idolatry and sexual sin on the one hand and the coming "wrath of the great God" (3.556) on the other.[9] It sees in idolatry a misplaced reverence, which should have been directed instead towards the eternal God (cf. Rom. 1:23). Such polemics would have been widespread in Diaspora Jewish contexts, and Paul's argument in Romans 1 seeks to exploit their familiarity. According to some, he teaches, "Let us do evil that good may come" (3:8), and this hostile summary of his teaching may have reached the ears of Christian Jews in Rome. If Paul teaches his converts not to observe the law, does that mean that he is actually in favor of the abominations of the Gentiles? In writing here as he does, Paul reassures his non-Pauline readers that this is by no means the case. He, too, regards typical Gentile conduct as reprehensible; his doctrine of freedom from the law does not compromise this standpoint in any way. The Jewish Christians in Rome need not fear that the Paulinists there take a relaxed view of idolatry and sexual perversion. Paul's own attitude towards such things coincides exactly with that of the Roman Jewish Christians.

The function of such anti-Gentile polemic in Jewish sources is to reinforce the barrier that separates the Jewish community from the Gentile world. But in Romans, it serves as the prelude to an argument that serves *to legitimate separation from the Jewish community and identification with Gentile Christians.* That is the "social function" of Romans 2–4, whose argument may be summed up under the three headings of denunciation, antithesis, and reinterpretation, which may be applied to each of the three chapters respectively. There is some overlap: antithesis is used in Romans 4 as well as in chap-

---

9. As John Collins notes, "Sib Or 3:97-829 is generally thought to contain the oldest material in the [Sibylline] collection" (*Seers, Sibyls and Sages in Hellenistic Roman Judaism,* 187). Book 3 was evidently known to Alexander Polyhistor (writing in the first century BCE), who attributed the account of the destruction of the tower of Babel to "the sibyl" (cf. 3.97-104; Collins, *Seers, Sibyls and Sages,* 187-88). See also John Barclay, *Jews in the Mediterranean Diaspora,* 216-28, where it is argued that "book 3 of the Sibylline Oracles reflects a revival of Jewish nationalistic sentiment in the wake of the Maccabean revolt" (223).

ter 3, and reinterpretation is to be found in chapter 3 as well as in chapter 4. Nevertheless, these three headings conveniently summarize Paul's argument in this section of Romans. Throughout the discussion that follows, the aim will be to highlight the social implications of Paul's argument in the light of Jew/Gentile tensions within the Roman Christian community.

In the course of this discussion, serious weaknesses in the typical "Lutheran" interpretation of Romans will be exposed. Interpretation from the Lutheran standpoint characteristically ignores the social function of these chapters and so misunderstands them. Romans 2 has always been a particular stumbling block for the Lutheran interpretation of Paul, and the remainder of this chapter aims to show how an emphasis on its social function solves many of its interpretative problems.[10]

2. Romans 2: Denunciation

Romans 2, 3, and 4 all include arguments that promote (1) separation from the Jewish community and (2) the union of Jewish and Gentile Christians. In the light of Romans 14:1–15:13, the social function of these chapters is clear — if we focus not so much on the meaning of Paul's assertions per se, but rather on their intended impact on their Roman readers. In other words, we are concerned with the "perlocutionary" dimension of the Pauline discourse, its concealed imperative force. In Romans 2 as in the later chapters, an argument for separation from the Jewish community can be differentiated from a corresponding argument for union with Gentile Christians.

(i) Critique of the Jewish View of the Covenant

One preliminary point must be settled. While most scholars have held that Paul is addressing Jews throughout the chapter, a minority has held that he turns to a Jewish interlocutor only in 2:17, and that 2:1-6 is therefore addressed to anyone, whether a Jew or a pagan moralist, who judges the sins of his or her neighbor.[11] The indefinite ὦ ἄνθρωπε πᾶς ὁ κρίνων (2:1) might give some support to this view; but it is nevertheless unlikely. This phrase is prob-

10. The present chapter corresponds fairly closely to *PJG¹*, chapter 6, although a number of significant clarifications and expansions have been introduced.

11. So Barrett, *Romans,* 43; Leenhardt, *Romans,* 72-73; Franzmann, *Romans,* 44, 48; Pregeant, "Grace and Recompense: Reflections on a Pauline Paradox," 75; Wright, "The Messiah and the People of God," 67; Dahl, "The Missionary Theology in the Epistle to the Romans," 79.

ably to be understood in the light of ὦ ἄνθρωπε in 9:20, i.e., in terms of the gulf between the creature and the Creator. In 9:20, this phrase shows up the presumption of the creature in answering back to the Creator, whereas in 2:1 it suggests that a sinful human being is trying to usurp the function of judgment that belongs to God alone.[12] Thus, ὦ ἄνθρωπε does not exclude the possibility that the "critic" addressed in vv. 1-6 is a Jew. There is no evidence elsewhere that the figure of the (hypocritical) pagan moralist is within Paul's repertoire. It is also wrong to assume a break in the argument at 2:17, where the Jew is explicitly addressed. In fact, 2:12-24 is a single section,[13] discussing the Jew's claim to superiority over the Gentiles on the basis of possession of the law of Moses. Paul argues that Gentiles without the law nevertheless have some knowledge of the law, and that a Jew who is well instructed in the law may nevertheless fail to observe it. The phrase σὺ Ἰουδαῖος in 2:17 is introduced in order to highlight the contrast with the Gentiles of 2:14-15 and not to indicate that Paul has found himself a new addressee. A similar contrast between obedient Gentiles and disobedient Jews is found in 2:25-29; indeed, this passage builds on the earlier contrast.

Three further points confirm this interpretation:

(1) The "critic" (2:1) appears to endorse Paul's thoroughly Jewish critique of Gentile life in 1:18-32, where it is claimed that the vices characteristic of the Gentiles stem from their idolatry. The Jew addressed in 2:17-24 is said to "abhor idols" (v. 22). If the critic shares Paul's opposition to idolatry, he is probably a Jew.

(2) There are close thematic links between the two passages of second-person singular address (2:1-6, 17-24). The one who criticizes others (v. 1) is plausibly identified with the one who teaches others not to steal or commit adultery and who abhors idols (vv. 21-22). In vv. 1-6 Paul warns his interlocutor not to think that he will escape God's judgment, since he does precisely the things he condemns in others. This accusation is elaborated and made concrete in vv. 17-24. The continuity between the two passages suggests that they are addressed to the same person.

(3) In this section of his letter, Paul distinguishes consistently between "Jews and Greeks" (1:16; 2:9, 10; 3:9), between those who sin ἀνόμως and those who sin ἐν νόμῳ (2:12), and between "Gentiles" and "you, a Jew" (2:14, 17).

---

12. This seems more likely than Kuss's suggestion that Paul here addresses the Jew as "man" in order to emphasize the removal of the absolute privileges he claims (*Der Römerbrief*, 1:60).

13. Cf. Bornkamm, "Paulinische Anakoluthe im Römerbrief," 76; Dahl, "The Missionary Theology in the Epistle to the Romans," 80.

It seems that this twofold division of the human race applies throughout 1:18–3:20.[14]

For these reasons, the individual addressed in vv. 1-6 should not be differentiated from the individual addressed in vv. 17-24.[15] The person addressed in vv. 1, 3 (ὦ ἄνθρωπε πᾶς ὁ κρίνων) is more precisely identified in v. 17 (σὺ Ἰουδαῖος), for vv. 17-24 serve to substantiate the initial accusation that the critic is himself guilty of the vices that he condemns in others (vv. 1-3).

If Romans 2 is addressed from the outset to a *Jewish* interlocutor, then the chapter as a whole may plausibly be read as a critique of a Jewish covenantal theology based on possession of the law and circumcision. As such, it totally rejects the natural correlate of the traditional Jewish polemic that Paul himself reproduces in 1:18-32: that is, the assumption that, while Gentile idolatry has given rise to all manner of sexual and social vices, *the chosen nation is different.* In the passage cited above from book 3 of the *Sibylline Oracles,* those who "engage in unholy intercourse with boys" and in other such vices are contrasted with the "sacred race of pious men," who practice "the righteousness of the law of the Most High" and who surpass all others in their exemplary piety and virtue (3.573-96). In the sharpest possible contrast, Paul in Romans 2 attacks the "sacred race" ideology on the grounds that it is belied by the realities of actual conduct. If the traditional polemic serves to reinforce the Jewish community's self-image over against the surrounding world of the Gentiles, the Pauline modification creates ideological space for a community that differentiates itself *both* from the Gentiles *and* from the "sacred race," which supposes itself to be immune from Gentile impiety and vice but is not. That (as we shall argue) is the social and ideological function of this chapter, and it makes explicit an element in the Roman situation that was only implicit in chapters 14–16: the fact that the proposed union of Gentile and Jewish Christians in shared allegiance to Christ will mark a definitive breach between the Roman Christian and Jewish communities. The interpretative problems posed by this chapter can be resolved if its social function is taken into account.

Romans 2 falls into three main sections. Verses 1-11 deal in general terms with the Jew who falsely relies on his covenant status, and vv. 12-24 and vv. 25-29 deal respectively with the two components of this privileged status that distinguish Israel from the Gentiles: possession of the law and circumci-

---

14. So Cranfield, *Romans,* 1:138-39.

15. So recently S. J. Gathercole, *Where Is Boasting?* 197-200; against S. Stowers, *A Rereading of Romans,* 100-104.

sion.[16] The Jew whom Paul addresses condemns the behavior of the Gentiles (v. 1) and believes that God will ultimately confirm his opinion by passing judgment on them (v. 2). Yet, remarkably, the judge does exactly the same things himself.[17] Furthermore, he knows that he does so, but relies on "the riches of God's kindness and forbearance and patience" to secure immunity from the divine judgment that hangs over others (v. 4). It is this false presumption of immunity at the judgment that underlies Paul's insistence on divine impartiality in vv. 6-11, the purpose of which is to contradict the view that God will bestow eternal life on Jews (cf. vv. 7, 10), whereas Gentiles who do not have the law and circumcision will be condemned (cf. vv. 8, 9). At present Jews must live in the world alongside Gentiles; but, on the day when God's righteous judgment is revealed, God will destroy his enemies and vindicate Israel, whom he has chosen and destined for salvation (cf. v. 11). Paul's argument is that God's judgment is impartial, and that God therefore takes account only of people's deeds, not of their ethnicity — in opposition to the view (attributed to the non-Christian Jewish community) that the mere fact of being a Jew is a guarantee of salvation, irrespective of conduct. According to Paul, it is this false reliance on the grace of God manifested in the covenant that enables the Jew of vv. 1-5 to "sin boldly."[18]

What are the marks of this privileged status that distinguishes Jews from Gentiles? The first is possession of the law (vv. 12-24).[19] Paul's Jew regards himself as a "hearer of the law" and as such "righteous before God" (opposed in v. 13). He has "heard" the law since childhood, in the synagogue and in the home, and pities the miserable state of the Gentiles who "do not have the law" (v. 14).[20] At the same time, their existence causes the Jew to rejoice all the

16. The importance of comparison with the Gentiles in Romans 2 is rightly stressed by U. Mauser, "Galater III.20: Die Universalität des Heils," 264.

17. That is, in a quite literal sense (cf. 2:21-23) and not in the sophisticated sense suggested by Barrett, according to whom the act of judging is the same as idolatry because both cases reveal "man's ambition to put himself in the place of God" (*Romans*, 44). Paul is not against judging per se — indeed, in Romans 1:18–3:20, he seems to cast himself in the role of "God's prosecutor" (G. Shaw, *The Cost of Authority*, 149).

18. In the twofold reference in vv. 9-10 to "the Jew first and also the Greek," the intention of vv. 1-11 becomes clear: "[T]he target is Jewish presumption of priority of privilege, which, however soundly rooted in God's election of Israel . . . , has led Paul's kinsfolk to the effective conclusion that God's judgment of Israel will be on different terms from his judgment of the nations as a whole" (J. D. G. Dunn, *Romans*, 1:88).

19. Hübner, *Law in Paul's Thought*, 114, rightly points out that the Jew in 2:1–3:8 boasts of possessing the law, not of doing it.

20. Appealing to the verb ἐπονομάζῃ, R. Thorsteinsson argues that Paul here addresses "a Gentile who wants to call himself a Jew" (*Paul's Interlocutor in Romans 2*, 197). Yet (1) ἐπονομάζῃ

more in what separates him from them. Conscious of this privileged status, he is proud to call himself a Jew and regards the law as the charter of that status (v. 17). He glories in his unique relationship to God (v. 17) and in the full and complete revelation through Moses of the divine will for humanity (v. 18).[21] In the law, he has that full embodiment of knowledge and truth for which others search in vain (v. 20b), and for that reason he is conscious of his responsibility to enlighten them (vv. 19-20a). Yet, as in vv. 1-5, his pride in his privileged status is matched by a remarkable disregard for certain of the law's prohibitions in his actual conduct.[22] The Jewish teacher of righteousness to the Gentiles is himself guilty of robbery, adultery, and sacrilege (vv. 21-22). Thus he dishonors God and causes scandal even among Gentiles, to whom his hypocrisy is all too obvious (vv. 23-24).

The second characteristic that distinguishes Jews from Gentiles is circumcision (vv. 25-29). Paul here makes the value of circumcision contingent on law observance (v. 25), evidently in opposition to the claim that it is valuable in and of itself, representing a guarantee of salvation for those whom it marks out from the profane sphere of the ἀκροβυστία (cf. vv. 26-27). Through circumcision, the male Jewish child (or Gentile proselyte) receives a share in all the privileges and promises bestowed uniquely on Israel. Just as Gentiles are characterized by their lack of the law (cf. vv. 12, 14, 19), so they are also characterized by their lack of circumcision (cf. vv. 26-27): for possession of the law and circumcision are the unique marks of the Jewish people, constituting its soteriological "advantage" (3:1) over others both now and at the eschatological judgment (cf. 2:1-11).

In the chapter as a whole, Paul's argument is that his Jewish dialogue partner is falsely reliant on "the riches of [God's] kindness and forbearance and patience" (v. 4), on the priority of the Jew in regard to salvation (cf. vv. 6-11), on possession and knowledge of the law (vv. 17-24), and on circumcision (vv. 25-29). The Judaism that Paul here opposes is founded on the electing grace of God as manifested in the covenant signs of Torah and circumcision. For Paul, this position is undermined on the human side by transgression of

---

need not imply any doubt about the addressee's Jewishness, without the addition of (e.g.) ". . . but are not" (cf. Rev. 2:9); (2) even if it did imply doubt, this would be explicable on the basis of the non-ethnic redefinition of Jewishness in Romans 2:28-29.

21. καυχᾶσαι (vv. 17, 23) does not have a negative sense (against Barrett, *Romans*, 55-56). Nor does this boast seem to be "oriented toward final judgment" (Gathercole, *Where Is Boasting?* 201): that is to tie vv. 17-25 *too* closely to vv. 1-5.

22. This is, of course, polemic rather than objective description and does not provide evidence of a "terrible degradation of Jewish morals in the period preceding the Destruction of the Temple" (Dodd, *Romans*, 64).

the law and on the divine side by the impartiality of God's eschatological judgment.

If that is the argument of Romans 2, then a certain role-reversal has taken place. Theologies in the Reformation tradition have invested heavily in the view that Paul teaches salvation by grace alone, in opposition to the supposedly Jewish and Pelagian view that we are saved by our own moral strivings and attainments. In Romans 2, however, we encounter more or less the opposite of this familiar dichotomy. As Ulrich Wilckens rightly notes, "it is precisely Paul who insists on works as the single criterion for the justification of the righteous, whereas his opponent insists throughout on his salvation-historical privileges (2:12-29; 3:1ff), which Paul contests."[23] Here, in disconcerting contrast to the standard account of Paul's relation to Judaism, it is the Jewish interlocutor who is committed to salvation by grace alone, and Paul who (as we shall see) teaches salvation by obedience to the law.[24] F. Kuhr is therefore wrong when he comments on vv. 5-11: "Paul speaks from a Jewish standpoint, according to which people are justified on the basis of their works."[25] On the contrary, it is in fact the "Jewish standpoint" that Paul here attacks for its unfounded reliance on God's grace, while the theology of salvation by keeping the law is his own (cf. vv. 26, 27).[26]

Admittedly, Romans 2 is not typical, for elsewhere Paul does acknowledge the Jewish pursuit of "works of law" and does not suggest a fundamental imbalance between knowing and doing. But it is still significant that in Romans 2 Paul can accuse his interlocutor of a false reliance on divine grace. It suggests that, when he does speak of "works of law," he is not referring to the belief that salvation comes solely through one's own efforts. Rather, he understands "works of law" as the pattern of life practiced by the loyal Jew within the context of the divine election of Israel. In other words, the object of Paul's critical antitheses is utterly concrete, irreducible to a general principle contrasting divine and human agencies. Paul is speaking of *Judaism*,

23. Wilckens, *Römer*, 1:177; my translation.
24. In a somewhat desperate attempt to supply what is missing here, Barrett finds an attack on earning salvation in the term ἐριθεία (2:8), which refers to "those who are out for quick and selfish profit on their own account," i.e., "those who look on their works as achievements of their own" (47-48). That is to read a lot of theology into a single word.
25. Kuhr, "Römer 2, 14f," 253.
26. When Conzelmann states (*Outline of the Theology of the New Testament*, 249) that the theme of Romans 1–3 is "the crisis of Israel (in so far as Israel wants to exist by its own achievements)," he misses the point of Romans 2. This is well stated by N. T. Wright: "The Jews were not trying to 'earn' salvation *de novo* by good works: they were presuming upon it as an ancestral right" ("The Messiah and the People of God," 97).

which is what it is on account of its sacred text, the law of Moses. This may be seen either as the gift of the electing divine love, bestowing a soteriological advantage (cf. Rom. 2), or as engendering the distinctively Jewish mode of life summed up in the phrase "works of law" (cf. Rom. 3). Paul's critiques of these perspectives have the same object in view and the same pragmatic goal — which is to create ideological distance between the Jewish community and a Christian community composed (at least in Rome) of both Jews and Gentiles.

Would this argument have been persuasive and relevant to Roman Jewish Christians? We recall that Roman Jewish Christianity originated as a reform movement within the Roman synagogues, and that as such it failed, issuing only in a dissension that led to disaster for the whole community and (so we may speculate) an enduring legacy of bitterness. It should be noted that Romans 2 is an attack not primarily on the Jewish community as a whole but on its teachers — i.e., its leaders: for the Jew addressed here is "a guide to the blind, a light to those in darkness, an instructor of the foolish, a teacher of children" (vv. 19-20). A reform movement can expect to encounter opposition especially from the existing religious authorities. Thus, in the synoptic Gospels, Jesus' enemies are not "the Jews" (as in John, which thus betrays a sectarian standpoint) but Pharisees, Sadducees, and Herodians. It is they who are perceived as the chief opponents of the Jesus movement, not the people as a whole. If the leaders of the Roman Jewish community had been implacably opposed to the propagation of the Christian gospel in the Roman synagogues, then Paul's denunciation of such a leader might well seem persuasive and relevant to Roman Jewish Christians.[27]

That Paul is adapting his discourse to the Roman situation is also suggested by the citation in v. 24 from Isaiah 52:5: "For 'the name of God because of you [δι' ὑμᾶς] is blasphemed among the Gentiles,' as it is written." The second-person plural pronoun indicates that the individual addressed in vv. 17-23 is to be seen as a representative figure. It seems that there are others like him and that their conduct is collectively responsible for Gentile hostility to the Jewish community and its deity.[28] In Rome, that hostility has issued in the

---

27. Dunn rejects my argument that it is Jewish *leaders* who are here denounced, on the grounds that "the issue is the real meaning of 'Jew', or what being a 'Jew' involves" (*Romans,* 1:110). In the light of vv. 19-21, I do not understand how Dunn can regard vv. 17-24 as a description of a Jew per se and not specifically of a Jewish teacher. Did all Jews see it as their vocation to instruct Gentiles in their religion?

28. There is nothing here to indicate that Paul also appropriates the exilic setting of his Isaiah citation (N. T. Wright, "The Law in Romans 2," 143) — except insofar as the exilic context of scriptural prophecies of hope establishes the exile as a metaphor for the unredeemed condition of Israel and the world. Wright's reading leads to the implausible conclusion that 2:17-24 "has to

expulsion of 49 CE, which followed the precedent established by Tiberius thirty years earlier. According to Josephus (*Ant.* 18.81-84), the earlier expulsion was occasioned by a notorious incident in which a Jew who "pretended to expound the wisdom of the laws of Moses" misappropriated money donated by a wealthy female proselyte named Fulvia, which was intended for the temple in Jerusalem. This led to the expulsion of the entire Jewish community from Rome.[29] Paul's Jewish teacher is similarly involved in proselytizing activity (he is "a light to those in darkness," Rom. 2:19), and he too is accused of an act of theft that brings public opprobrium onto the entire community. As regards the further question, "Do you commit adultery?," this may also relate to proselytizing activity. In the passage referred to above, Josephus tells how Fulvia began to meet regularly with the Jewish teacher and his companions, and it is easy to see how suspicions of adultery could arise from such meetings as these.[30] If Josephus heard the story of Fulvia within the Roman Jewish community in the 80s or 90s CE, it was presumably also in circulation at the time of Paul's letter. While Paul need not have this story specifically in mind, his argument could be rhetorically effective only if it appealed to a recognizable stereotype.

Against such a background, and in the aftermath of the more recent expulsion, the relevance of Romans 2 to Roman Jewish Christians is clear. From the standpoint of the majority Jewish community, it was these Christians who disrupted the community with their proclamation of Jesus as the Messiah and who were therefore responsible for the economic and social catastrophe of the expulsion that followed. One of the functions of Romans 2:17-24 is therefore to suggest an alternative explanation of the underlying Gentile hostility towards the Jewish community: it was caused not by the Christians but by Jewish teachers who had brought the whole community into disrepute by their immoral conduct. The fact that this had been the case in the earlier expulsion under Tiberius would have given weight to the argument. Paul may

---

do with the nation as a whole" (143), showing how "[t]he nation that was to lighten the pagan world has herself succumbed to pagan darkness" (148).

29. Other writers give a more general explanation for the expulsion of 19 CE. According to Dio Cassius, Tiberius expelled the Jews because they "flocked to Rome in great numbers and were converting many of the natives to their ways" (*Hist. Rom.* 57.18.5). Converts to Judaism were expelled too, according to Suetonius (*Vit. Tib.* 36); see also Tacitus, *Ann.* 2.85.2. M. H. Williams's denial that Jewish proselytism was a factor in the expulsion ("The Expulsion of the Jews from Rome in AD 19") does not seem convincing to me.

30. Compare Martial's reference to "the lecheries of circumcised Jews" (*Epig.* 7.30.5; Stern, *Greek and Latin Authors on Jews and Judaism,* 1:524). It is not clear whether this association of circumcision and promiscuity was widespread, however.

have anticipated that such an explanation of Gentile hostility would be welcomed by the Roman Jewish Christians, and it is therefore probable that Romans 2 was written primarily for their benefit.[31] Like the rest of Romans, it seeks a hearing for itself among the Roman Jewish Christian community, beyond the limits of Paul's existing sphere of influence in Rome.

There are therefore grounds for thinking that Roman Christian Jews would have welcomed Paul's denunciation of leaders of the Roman Jewish community. These leaders had no doubt been the most implacable opponents of Christian preaching in the Roman synagogues, and the view that it was their depravity that occasioned the Gentile hostility underlying the expulsion would have seemed greatly preferable to the view that the Jewish Christians were themselves to blame. But Paul's aim is not simply to express his solidarity with the Roman Jewish Christians. Ideological distance from the rest of the Jewish community is intended to facilitate unity with Roman Gentile Christians. The motif of the obedient Gentiles in Romans 2 is to be understood against this background.

(ii) The Obedient Gentiles

In Romans 2 Paul opposes the view that Jews have a soteriological advantage by virtue of their possession of the law and their circumcision. In place of this false view, he argues for a judgment according to one's works, not according to whether one is a Jew or not. Everyone will be judged by their works, and those who have done good will receive eternal life while those who have done evil will be condemned (vv. 6-8). The familiar motif of judgment according to works is deployed here in a remarkable way: to remove the soteriological difference between Jew and Gentile.[32]

The distinctiveness of Paul's argument becomes evident when it is compared with an earlier development of this motif. In the book of *Jubilees*, the Genesis account of the angel marriages (Gen. 6:1-4) is expanded, under the

---

31. According to Minear, in Romans 2 Paul addresses a Jewish *Christian*, whose condemnation of Gentile life he rejects (*The Obedience of Faith*, 51; cf. P. Esler, *Conflict and Identity in Romans*, 151-52). But Romans 2 does not have to be directly addressed to the Roman Jewish Christians in order to be relevant to them. Kent Yinger rightly distinguishes between the addressee within the diatribe and the intended effect of the diatribe form on "Paul's Jewish-Christian addressees in Rome" (*Paul, Judaism, and Judgment according to Works*, 161-63).

32. "The analysis of works presupposed by vv. 7-8 has the important consequence of dissolving the barrier between Jew and Gentile" (Barrett, *Romans*, 48). See also van Dülmen, *Die Theologie des Gesetzes bei Paulus*, 74.

influence of the Enochic tradition, into a full-scale account of a final universal judgment:

> And the judgment of all is ordained and written on the heavenly tablets in righteousness — all who depart from the path that is ordained for them to walk in; and if they walk not therein, judgment is written for every creature and for every kind. And there is no exception in heaven or on earth, or in light or in darkness, or in Sheol or in the depth, or in the place of darkness; and all their judgments are ordained and written and engraved. In regard to all he will judge, the great according to his greatness, and the small according to his smallness, and each according to his way. And he is not one who will regard the person, nor accept anything at his hands, for he is a righteous judge. (*Jub.* 5:13-16)[33]

Like Romans 2, this passage speaks of a universal and impartial judgment. Unlike Romans 2, it proceeds to speak of a special provision made for Israel:

> And of the children of Israel it has been written and ordained: If they turn to him in righteousness, he will forgive all their transgressions and pardon all their sins. It is written and ordained that he will show mercy to all who turn from all their guilt once each year. (5:17-18)

It is assumed that the judgment is stringent enough to ensure the condemnation of most if not all Gentiles, and even many of the angels. Yet God has made provision for his elect, who repent of their sins each year on the Day of Atonement. There is to be a universal judgment according to works, yet Israel possesses a soteriological advantage.[34]

Paul allows no such soteriological advantage. In his radical reinterpretation of the traditional concepts of universality and impartiality, salvation is open to Jews and Gentiles alike. Gentiles are no less capable than Jews of doing good and receiving salvation, and Jews are no less capable than Gentiles of

---

33. I here follow the translation in *APOT* 2, adapting it slightly. On this passage, see K. Yinger, *Paul, Judaism, and Judgment according to Deeds*, 65-68. Yinger rightly notes that the judgment of the Watchers "is ultimately prototypical of the future universal judgment" (65). That also means, conversely, that the Genesis flood narrative is one of the sources for the concept of universal eschatological judgment.

34. As Yinger notes, with reference also to 5:19, "the post-Flood forgiveness of errant Jews *does* amount to a certain degree of partiality on God's part toward his covenant people. . . . The condition of repentance, however, preserves this partiality from being viewed as unfair favoritism" (*Paul, Judaism, and Judgment according to Deeds*, 67). In addition, "[j]udgment according to deeds demands not perfect obedience but covenant faithfulness, including turning back to God's path when one has strayed" (67-68).

doing evil and being condemned. Paul's association of the traditional judgment-by-works motif with the possibility of a positive as well as a negative outcome is already unusual,[35] and this distinctiveness is heightened by the insistence on the irrelevance of the Jew/Gentile distinction to these outcomes.[36] This uniquely Pauline understanding of judgment by works comes to expression especially in Romans 2:9-10:

> There will be tribulation and distress for every human being who does evil, *the Jew first and also the Greek,* but glory and honor and peace for everyone who does good, *the Jew first and also the Greek.*

Paul defends this novel interpretation of judgment by works and divine impartiality in vv. 12-15. In vv. 12-13, he defends the idea that Jews who possess the law may be condemned. Those who sinned under the law will be judged by it, for God accepts not hearers of the law but doers. The hearing/doing contrast refers initially to the Jew who hears but does not do, but it is reapplied in vv. 14-15 to Gentiles who observe the law without hearing it, and who will thereby be justified. Thus in vv. 12-15 Paul elaborates the points made in vv. 9 and 10 respectively — that Jews may be condemned as well as Greeks, and that Greeks may be saved as well as Jews. Verse 12 has spoken of those who sinned ἀνόμως, and v. 14 raises the alternative possibility of Gentiles without the law (μὴ νόμον ἔχοντα φύσει) who nevertheless observe the law (τὰ τοῦ νόμου ποιῶσιν), and who therefore qualify as "doers of the law" who "will be justified" (cf. v. 13). Thus, the possibility that Jews (as well as Greeks) will be condemned is raised in v. 9 and elaborated in vv. 12-13; the possibility that Greeks (as well as Jews) will be saved is raised in v. 10 and elaborated in vv. 14-15; and v. 13 serves initially to clarify the first point (Jews will be condemned insofar as they are hearers only, not doers) but is also used to introduce the second (Gentiles will be saved insofar as they are doers of the law, even without hearing it).[37]

The reference to the final eschatological judgment in v. 16 is difficult, but it tends to confirm that the concern with eschatological destiny in vv. 6-11 is

---

35. So Yinger, *Paul, Judaism, and Judgment according to Deeds,* 165.

36. There is, however, a partial parallel in Josephus (see my *PHF,* 348-53).

37. According to Bornkamm, v. 14 is to be linked not to v. 13 but exclusively to v. 12, on the grounds that Paul is here not interested in Gentile salvation but is concerned to show only that "the Gentiles have a knowledge of God's law, because of which they too are responsible before God" ("Gesetz und Natur," 99; see also R. Walker, "Die Heiden und das Gericht," 304). Yet Paul has shown an interest in Gentile salvation in v. 10, and it is implausible to distinguish "the doers of the law" who "will be justified" (v. 13) from the Gentiles who similarly "do the things of the law."

carried over into the statements that follow.[38] In vv. 15-16 it is stated of those who unknowingly observe the law:

> They show the work of the law written on their hearts — to which their conscience also bears witness, as do their arguments with each other, accusing or excusing — on the day when God judges the secrets of humans, according to my gospel, through Christ Jesus.

The translation presupposes the following exegetical decisions:

(1) μεταξὺ ἀλλήλων τῶν λογισμῶν appears to refer to debates between individuals, rather than to "conflicting thoughts" within the individual psyche.[39] The phrase that follows (κατηγορούντων ἤ καὶ ἀπολογουμένων) characterizes these debates as ethical in orientation, concerned to distinguish indefensible conduct from defensible.

(2) The reference to conscience and to ethical debates should be seen as a parenthesis speaking of a present and preliminary manifestation of the law written on the heart, the final and decisive manifestation of which will occur on the day of judgment.[40]

(3) Identification of the parenthesis makes it possible to connect "they show the work of the law written on their hearts" with "on the day when God judges the secrets [τὰ κρυπτά] of humans."[41] Paul speaks elsewhere of the "heart" as the location of the "secrets" that are to be exposed on the last day. According to 1 Corinthians 4:5, the Lord "will bring to light the things hidden in darkness [τὰ κρυπτὰ τοῦ σκότους] and will disclose the purposes of the heart [τὰς βουλὰς τῶν καρδιῶν]." In Romans 2:15-16, a similar disclosure of the heart and its secrets is promised for the last day.

---

38. Romans 2:16 is rejected as a gloss by R. Bultmann ("Glossen im Römerbrief," 282), followed in *PJG¹* (116-17). The present interpretation of vv. 15-16 is new to this edition.

39. So Kuss, *Der Römerbrief,* 69; Schlatter, *Gottes Gerechtigkeit,* 95. Most commentators think the reference here is to a purely internal process (so Käsemann, *Commentary on Romans,* 66; Cranfield, *Romans,* 1:162; Schlier, *Der Römerbrief,* 79-80; Wilckens, *Der Brief an die Römer,* 1:136).

40. In contrast, Cranfield argues that the demonstration of the work of the law written in the heart occurs in the Gentiles' deeds, in the present (*Romans,* 1:158), whereas the witness of conscience and the λογισμοί occurs on the day of judgment (1:161).

41. The view that v. 16 is to be linked with v. 12 or v. 13, and that the intervening material is a parenthesis (so J. Riedl, "Die Auslegung von R2,14-16 in Vergangenheit und Gegenwart," 278), is too cumbersome to be plausible. For a range of alternative construals, see R. Bell, *No One Seeks for God,* 145-62.

On this interpretation, Romans 2:12-16 is concerned not simply with Gentile accountability but with Gentile *salvation* — that is, with the possibility that there might be Gentiles who are in no sense hearers of the law but who are nevertheless doers and who will thereby be justified at the last.

As argued above, vv. 12-24 comprise a single section that contrasts Gentiles who do not know the law yet obey it with the Jew who knows the law yet transgresses it. In vv. 25-29 a similar contrast is developed, with particular reference to circumcision. This passage has the negative function of denying that circumcision is a guarantee of salvation (cf. v. 25). But it also has a positive function as an answer to a further objection that might be made to the claim of vv. 10, 13-16, that Gentiles as well as Jews may do good and so be saved. How can it be said that Gentiles may be "doers of the law" when they do not obey the fundamental commandment to be circumcised? Paul writes in v. 26: "If the uncircumcised keeps the precepts of the law, will not his uncircumcision be reckoned as circumcision?" In vv. 28-29, he argues that being circumcised and a Jew is a matter not of an external rite but of an inward disposition of the heart. It is therefore possible for Gentiles as well as Jews to do good and be saved, even without being physically circumcised. In arguing in Romans 2 against the notion that being a Jew bestows a soteriological advantage, Paul repeatedly claims that Gentiles may do good and be saved alongside obedient Jews (vv. 10, 14-15, 26-29), even though they are ignorant of the law of Moses and physically uncircumcised.[42]

Commentators are in general so concerned to find Paul in this passage apparently arguing for justification by obeying the law that they fail to do justice to the theme of Gentile obedience in Romans 2. The view of the purpose of Romans that is taken here suggests an obvious interpretation: Roman Jewish Christians are being encouraged not only to distance themselves from the Jewish community but also *to recognize the possibility and reality of genuine obedience to the law even among uncircumcised Gentile Christians.* Paul argues cautiously here, in apparently theoretical and general terms; but in the light of 14:1–15:13, his meaning is unmistakable. In order to establish this interpretation, however, a more detailed discussion is required of the problem of salvation by law observance that Romans 2 poses.

Many commentators have abandoned the attempt to find a unitary interpretation of this chapter and understand it in a piecemeal way.[43] Thus,

---

42. Contra Räisänen, *Paul and the Law*, 106, who claims that Paul has no real interest in the Gentiles of Romans 2.

43. Compare Sanders's discussion of the various interpretations of this passage (*Paul, the Law and the Jewish People*, 123-35). His own solution to its problems is that it uses material from Diaspora Judaism (127).

Käsemann argues that the reference to judgment by works (v. 6) does not contradict justification by faith, on account of the "power character" of the gift of righteousness, i.e., the fact that the gift is not only a gift but also subjects us to the lordship of Christ:

> If the gift is finally the sign and content of Christ's lordship on earth, we can no longer live by our own will and right but constantly stand in responsibility and accountability.[44]

Thus, justification by faith involves a judgment according to works: Käsemann claims that his gift/power dialectic serves to reconcile these two apparently conflicting motifs. And yet he does not extend this point into his interpretation of v. 13, with its claim that "the doers of the law will be justified"; indeed, he has little to say about this text. As for the Gentiles who "do the things of the law" (v. 15), Paul's point is simply that "there is no escaping universal judgment" (62). On vv. 25-29 Käsemann writes:

> There can no more be a Gentile who as such fulfils the Torah than there can be anyone else who of himself does what the law specifically requires. Is Paul losing himself in hypotheses? (74)

Käsemann's answer to his own question is that what had been a mere hypothesis in vv. 26-27 becomes concrete in vv. 28-29, which refers to Gentile Christians (74-77).[45] Yet he does not explain the function of these references to Christians. Neither does he explain the purpose of the "hypothesis" that Gentiles may keep the law (vv. 26-27), nor how and in what sense the hypothesis becomes reality in vv. 28-29. As with other commentators in the Lutheran tradition, for Käsemann one senses that Romans 2 is an enigma and an embarrassment.[46]

An attempt at a consistent solution to the problem of the obedient Gentiles is to be found in Cranfield's commentary, where it is argued that all these passages are about Christians.[47] Thus, "works" in v. 6 refers to "each

---

44. Käsemann, *Romans*, 58. Subsequent page references will be given parenthetically in the text. Cf. Schlier, *Der Römerbrief*, 72.

45. Schlier's comment on vv. 28-29 illustrates the confusion that results from this type of interpretation: "Here Paul has already left behind the pre-Christian moral argument. But it is still not clear from which standpoint he is judging" (*Der Römerbrief*, 90; my translation).

46. Protestant commentators' characteristic difficulties with Romans 2 are acknowledged by U. Wilckens (*Der Brief an die Römer*, 1:144).

47. Cf. also W. Mundle, "Zur Auslegung von Röm 2,13ff"; F. Flückiger, "Die Werke des Gesetzes bei der Heiden"; Barth, *Shorter Commentary*, 36-39; Minear, *The Obedience of Faith*, 47; N. T. Wright, "The Law in Romans 2," 132-39, 143-48; S. J. Gathercole, "A Law unto Themselves."

man's conduct as the expression either of faith or of unbelief."[48] But v. 6 is not to be understood in a legalistic way as referring to requital according to deserts, and the obedient Jews and Gentiles in vv. 7, 10 do not *earn* eternal life (146). The doing of the law in v. 13 is likewise explained as "that beginning of grateful obedience to be found in those who believe in Christ" (155), and it is this to which vv. 14-15 refer — a view that, as Cranfield notes, is already to be found in Ambrosiaster and Augustine (155-56). This means that τὸ ἔργον τοῦ νόμου γραπτὸν ἐν ταῖς καρδίαις αὐτῶν may be taken as a reminiscence of Jeremiah 31[38]:33, where it is said, . . . καὶ ἐπὶ καρδίαις αὐτῶν γράψω αὐτοὺς [*sc.* νόμους μου] (158-59).[49] In v. 26, the reference to the law observance of the uncircumcised entails "not a perfect fulfilment of the law's demands . . . but a grateful and humble faith in God and the life turned in the direction of obedience which is its fruit"; Paul again has the Gentile Christian in mind (173). There is thus no contradiction in Romans 2 to the doctrine of justification by faith (153).

A comparison between Cranfield and Käsemann shows the Reformed commentator to be more at home in this passage than the Lutheran one. Unlike Käsemann, Cranfield traces a consistent emphasis on the motif of obedient Gentiles, introduced in vv. 6-11 and further developed in vv. 13-16 and vv. 25-29. Yet no adequate explanation is offered as to *why* these Christian Gentiles feature so prominently in Romans 2 and why their salvation is tied to their own "doing what is good" (v. 10), "doing what the law requires" (v. 14), "keeping the precepts of the law" (v. 26), and "fulfilling the law" (v. 27) — rather than to Christ. In this chapter, Christ is referred to only once, and there

---

48. Cranfield, *Romans*, 1:151. Subsequent references to pages in volume 1 of Cranfield's commentary will be given parenthetically in the text.

49. Other Pauline allusions to the Jeremianic motif of the writing of the law on the heart are to be found in 2 Corinthians 3, where the Corinthian congregation is identified as Paul's letter of recommendation to the world, ἐγγεγραμμένη ἐν ταῖς καρδίαις ἡμῶν (v. 2), or ἐγγεγραμμένη . . . οὐκ ἐν πλαξὶν λιθίναις ἀλλ' ἐν πλαξὶν καρδίαις σαρκίναις (v. 3). The contrast between stone tablets and tablets of fleshly hearts is suggested by the contrast between the old and the new covenants in Jeremiah 38:32, as well as by the promise that τὴν καρδίαν τὴν λιθίνην will be replaced by καρδίαν σαρκίνην (Ezek. 11:19 = 36:26). It is the Jeremiah text that leads Paul to convert Ezekiel's "stony heart" into an allusion to the stone tablets of the Sinai revelation (cf. Exod. 31:18, πλάκας λιθίνας). Also to be noted is Paul's reference to the καινὴ διαθήκη (2 Cor. 3:6; cf. Jer. 38:31). In the light of the allusions to Jeremiah 31[38] in this chapter, the allusion in Romans 2:14 may be regarded as certain — although questions as to its significance remain. If, as is likely, it is Ezekiel's references to "my Spirit" (Ezek. 11:19 = 36:26) that create the association between the new covenant and the Spirit (2 Cor. 3:3, 6, 8, 17, 18), then this would shed light on the Spirit/letter contrast in Romans 2:29 and confirm that the obedient (Christian) Gentiles of vv. 14-15 are also in mind at the end of the chapter.

only as the divinely appointed judge of the world (v. 16). If Paul has Christian Gentiles in mind, as he appears to, why are they characterized in terms of the law rather than Christ? Among other things, this results in an apparently serious discrepancy between Romans 2 and 3. This discrepancy is most clearly evident if we compare 2:13b ("the doers of the law will be justified") with 3:20a ("no human being will be justified in his sight by works of the law"). There is certainly a verbal contradiction here; Paul must be working here with two different concepts of law, and we shall return to this point below. The initial question is whether and how far there is also a *conceptual* contradiction here, in the sense that chapter 2 teaches "salvation by works" while chapter 3 teaches the precise opposite, "salvation by grace."

There would seem to be no conceptual contradiction here. When Paul contrasts "faith" with "works" (Rom. 3:20-22, 27-28; 4:2-8), "works" does not refer to human moral activity in general but specifically to the Jewish way of life. And "faith" is not to be understood as the negation of "works" abstractly conceived; it is not to be defined as "the radical renunciation of achievement."[50] Rather, it stands metonymically for the totality of the life of the (Pauline) Christian community. In claiming that salvation is through faith rather than works of law, Paul is asserting that salvation is to be found in a Christian community composed of Jews and Gentiles, rather than in the non-Christian Jewish one, and that the two communities are and should be essentially separate. The faith/works antithesis is utterly concrete; it does not identify a logical impossibility but represents an assertion of incommensurability with imperative force. It is the radical renunciation not of "achievement" but of an identity formed by law observance within the Jewish community — ideally, where faith is strong, to the extent of abandoning certain of the law's stipulations. (Thus, in 14:1 the person who adheres to the law is regarded as "weak in faith," whereas true faith recognizes that "everything is indeed clean" [14:20, 22-23].) Faith may therefore be seen as thoroughly active, once one has ceased to define it by a misinterpretation of the term "works" and referred it instead to the individual and social reorientation elicited by the gospel.[51] According to Romans 10:17, "Faith stems from hearing, and hearing from the message of Christ"; yet the faith elicited by the gospel is a reorientation rather than a renunciation of human agency.[52] The link between faith and the baptismal confession in 10:9 indicates that faith is not a private, internal decision,

---

50. Bultmann, *Theology of the New Testament*, 1:316.

51. The typically Protestant anxiety lest faith should become a work (cf. D. J. Doughty, "The Priority of ΧΑΡΙΣ," 165) thus becomes superfluous.

52. "The faith which Paul preaches . . . in no sense entails a fundamental, far-reaching denial of all human activity" (Wilckens, *Der Brief an die Römer*, 1:145).

but the public renunciation of one way of life and the adoption of another.[53] It is faith in this comprehensive sense that is the *sine qua non* of salvation, since it represents the human participation intended in the divine saving action announced in the gospel. To say that such faith *earns* or *merits* salvation would be misleading, for faith is a response to the prior divine grace in Christ that aims precisely to elicit and enable such a response. Yet for Paul, God's saving agency includes human agency within its scope, establishing it on a wholly new foundation rather than excluding or eliminating it. For that reason, Paul has no difficulty in maintaining both that righteousness is by faith and that those who do good will attain to eschatological glory and honor and peace (2:10). The lack of reference to Christ's saving activity remains a problem, but the presence of a reference to human agency — divinely enabled, according to 2:15 — is not in itself problematic. Nor is it a problem that "Christ Jesus" is seen as the divinely appointed agent of judgment, for a range of statements in Romans and elsewhere confirms that this claim is indeed κατὰ τὸ εὐαγγέλιον μοῦ (2:16).

Belief in judgment by works is indeed an integral part of Paul's theology and not simply an unfortunate remnant of a Jewish outlook that the apostle has carelessly omitted to harmonize with his own distinctive theological stance. He believes that "if you live according to the flesh you will die" (Rom. 8:13), that "the one who sows to his own flesh will from the flesh reap corruption" (Gal. 6:8), and that "those who do such things [i.e., the works of the flesh] will not inherit the kingdom of God" (Gal. 5:21).[54] He also believes that "if by the Spirit you put to death the deeds of the body you will live" (Rom. 8:13), that "the one who sows to the Spirit will from the Spirit reap eternal life" (Gal. 6:8), and that Christians must "work [or accomplish, or achieve] your own salvation with fear and trembling" (Phil. 2:12). Salvation or condemnation will be decided at a judgment according to works — i.e., according to whether people have lived in the light of their Christian confession or denied it in their practical conduct (Rom. 14:10-12; 1 Cor. 4:3-5; 2 Cor. 5:10; Gal. 6:5).[55] Insofar as the eschatological revelation of what is now hidden

53. Baptism marks "an extraordinarily thorough resocialization" (W. Meeks, *First Urban Christians*, 78).

54. As Donfried argues, Paul's view is that "God can and will reject disobedient Christians" ("Justification and Last Judgment in Paul," 107). There is no need to attribute an alleged tension between justification and judgment to "the occasional nature of Paul's letters" and the difference in the addressees (so N. M. Watson, "Justified by Faith, Judged by Works — An Antinomy?" 213-14).

55. This means that justification should not be seen as an eschatological concept, except in the very general sense that virtually no Pauline idea is entirely free from eschatological over-

brings to light what is "good" as well as what is "evil" (cf. Rom. 2:9-10), this "good" is grounded in God's prior saving action, which establishes and enables an appropriately directed human agency. This is not "salvation by works" as commonly understood, that is, as a salvation attained by unaided human effort. But nor is it "salvation by grace" as commonly understood, that is, as a salvation in which the one who is saved stands in a purely passive relationship to the one who saves. Divine and human agency do not coexist on the same plane, in such a way that more of one means less of the other. Rather, God's prior grace works in and through the human agent, whose reoriented and free agency is itself the work of grace.[56]

All this helps to ease the tension between the teaching of Romans 2:6-11 that salvation depends on "patience in well-doing" (v. 7) or "doing good" (v. 10) and the teaching of Romans 3–4 that justification is by faith.[57] Where the two passages do differ is in their understanding of the law. In Romans 2, the law is evaluated thoroughly positively. The obedience of those who are to receive eternal life is seen as obedience to the law (v. 13), and the fact that Gentiles can be said to "do what the law requires" (v. 14) and to "keep the precepts of the law" even without being circumcised (v. 26) shows that living by the law is here considered in isolation from membership of the Jewish community. There is, according to Paul, a "reduced law" — a law without circumcision, dietary restrictions, cultus, or sacred days — that remains operative within the Christian community (cf. 13:8-10). Thus it can be said that "circumcision is nothing and uncircumcision is nothing — all that matters is keeping the commandments of God" (1 Cor. 7:19). A closely related point is made in Romans 2:26, where the uncircumcised can be said to keep τὰ δικαιώματα τοῦ νόμου only on the basis of a spiritualizing reinterpretation of the commandment relating to circumcision (cf. vv. 28, 29).

More commonly, however, the law is for Paul the law of Moses operative within the Jewish community; and here the emphasis is on the law's inability

---

tones: so S. Lyonnet, "Gratuité de la Justification et Gratuité du Salut," 101-2; against Bultmann, *Theology of the New Testament*, 274-79. Paul's two key righteousness-by-faith texts (Hab. 2:4; Gen. 15:6) lack any direct eschatological orientation.

56. Compare John Webster's analogous argument about Barth in contrast to Luther, *Barth's Ethics of Reconciliation*, 103-15.

57. Thus, Romans 2–3 does not arise from a constructive tension between "the logic of grace" and "the logic of recompense," which cannot be combined into a systematic unity but must both be maintained (against R. Pregeant, "Grace and Recompense: Reflections on a Pauline Paradox," 85). On this view, "it is more important that the reader experience both the event of grace and accountability for his or her deeds than to be able to order all elements of these realities into a conceptually unified whole" (87).

to secure salvation. Those who practice "works of the law" (3:28) are Jews (cf. 3:29). Because being "under law" (6:14) means being a member of a community where "law works wrath" (4:15), Christian obedience is not defined by reference to the law (6:15–7:6).[58] The main difference between Romans 2 and 3 is thus that in chapter 2 the law transcends the Jewish community and its own written embodiment, whereas in chapter 3 and elsewhere the law is inseparable from the Jewish community. Even in Romans 2, the *written* law remains the exclusive prerogative of the Jewish community (cf. vv. 12, 14, 17, 20). The move in Romans 3 to a more restrictive view of the law is also a move from a positive to a negative view of the law in its soteriological aspect, informed especially by the shift in vv. 1-20 onto distinctively *scriptural* terrain (see Chapter 7, below).

There is therefore no obstacle in the way of the view that the Gentiles of Romans 2 are Christians.[59] Paul affirms that these Gentiles do good and will receive eternal life, no less than Jewish Christians (vv. 9-10; cf. vv. 6-8).[60] He defends the possibility of Gentile obedience to the law by appealing in vv. 14-15 to the law written on the heart, and he argues that uncircumcised Gentile Christians who obey the law are true Jews and truly circumcised, in a spiritualized sense (vv. 25-29). In this chapter there is a twofold message for those Roman Christian Jews who are reached by Paul's letter. First, they must recognize the depravity of leaders of the non-Christian Jewish community, and therefore finalize their breach with that community. Second, they must acknowledge the genuine obedience to God that occurs among uncircumcised Gentile Christians on whom they have tended to "pass judgment" (14:3-4, 10) and identify themselves with these people. These Gentiles are presented in terms of their (ultimately positive) relation to the law, rather than their relation to Christ, because Roman Jewish Christians currently see in them only a negative relation to the law, which they condemn (cf. 14:3-4, 10, 13).

---

58. Isolated passages such as Romans 13:8-10 or Galatians 5:14 do not mean that it is central for Paul that "the law should be fulfilled" (as Sanders argues, *Paul, the Law and the Jewish People*, 93-122). In these passages, it is true that "in discussing the behaviour appropriate to being Christian, Paul saw no incongruity between 'living by faith' and 'fulfilling the law'" (114); yet this is not the case elsewhere. Paul might have made the law the basis for his ethical instruction, but on the whole he does not do so — preferring, for example, to ground even the prohibition of idolatry in the Christian eucharist rather than in the law (cf. 1 Cor. 10:14-22).

59. I here revert to the view of Romans 2 that I rejected — with some hesitation — in *PHF*, 352-53n. The "Gentile Christian" reading must assume that the logic of Romans 2 is significantly different from Romans 3; the "hypothetical" reading attempts to maintain a degree of continuity between the chapters.

60. Paul does not "concede" the possibility of good works in 2:7-10 (E. Jüngel, "Das Gesetz zwischen Adam und Christus," 73); he affirms it.

Reading Romans 2 with an eye to its social function has produced a very different interpretation to one that is oriented towards a Lutheran understanding of "justification by faith." Jewish leaders are here accused not of trying to earn salvation but of inappropriate reliance on the divine electing grace manifested in Torah and circumcision. Pauline Gentile Christians are presented as people who are truly concerned to obey God, and whose obedience will reap the reward of eternal life when their works are judged (2:14-16). They are the "true Jews" (2:28-29), in contrast to those who are Jews in name but who are reckoned as uncircumcised on account of their disobedience (2:25). Underlying the entire chapter is a concealed exhortation. Paul seeks to persuade Roman Jewish Christians to abandon the remaining ties that bind them to the Jewish community, which they once sought and failed to reform, and to join with his own followers in a new shared identity as "Christians."

CHAPTER 7

Pauline Antithesis and Its Social Correlate
(Romans 3)

In Chapter 5 of this work, it was argued that exegesis of Romans 14–16 provides the key to the purpose of Paul's letter to the Romans. Paul understands there to be two groupings or factions within the Roman Christian community — one Jewish Christian, oriented towards the continuing practice of the law, the other Gentile Christian, oriented towards the Pauline law-free gospel. The former represents the remnant of the original Roman Christian congregation, whereas the latter appears to have been founded by converts and associates of Paul. Paul's main purpose in writing his letter is to bring the two sides together. Writing in the first instance for a Gentile or Gentile-oriented readership, he hopes and intends that his letter will reach influential figures in the Jewish Christian faction — a strategy that the greetings of Romans 16 are intended to further. As a consequence, he also hopes and intends that Roman Jewish Christians will recognize the legitimacy of the Pauline congregations, based on the premises of freedom from the law and separation from the synagogue, and that the two factions will put aside suspicion and misunderstanding and learn to welcome one another as they have themselves been welcomed by Christ. In the preceding chapter, this hypothesis was applied to Romans 2, in which Paul denounces the leaders of the Jewish community, and so tacitly encourages Jewish Christians to distance themselves from that community, and also commends the obedience of uncircumcised Gentile Christians, with whom Jewish Christians should now identify themselves. Nowhere in Romans 2 is this social function made explicit, but the view that it was intended to have such a function resolves otherwise intractable exegetical problems.

In the present chapter, the hypothesis about the pragmatic dimension of

Paul's letter will be applied to Romans 3. Paul's attempt to legitimate separation from the synagogue in this chapter will be considered under the heading of "antithesis," and "reinterpretation" will be reserved for the discussion of Abraham in Romans 4. Paul's unfolding argument continues to manifest the same two features that we identified in Romans 2: arguments intended to promote both ideological separation from the Jewish community and the realization of Jewish and Gentile unity in Christ.[1]

Romans 3 is based on the single antithesis between "law" and "faith." In vv. 1-20, Paul argues that being a law-observant Jew is not the indispensable presupposition for salvation. Nor does law observance create an absolute separation from the Gentile world, for the law rightly understood places the Jew in the same position of guilt before God as the Gentile. In vv. 21-31, it is argued that the faith associated with Christ is God's means of salvation and that one of the chief characteristics of this faith is that Jews and Gentiles are treated in exactly the same way.[2] Roman Christians of both factions are to recognize that the law places the non-Christian Jewish community in the same position of guilt before God as the Gentiles, whereas faith has the capacity to unite Jewish and Gentile Christians in the enjoyment of salvation. Paul's argument should not be understood as an exercise in theological reflection divorced from any concrete social context. It is his concern to address a particular social context within the Roman Christian community that makes his argument what it is.

Romans 1:18–3:20 is typically seen as a single, gradually unfolding argument that aims to demonstrate the universality of sin.[3] Yet, as we have seen in the previous chapter, Romans 2 is in no sense concerned with the universality of sin. It knows of Jews and Gentiles who do what is wrong, but it also knows

---

1. In this chapter new material predominates over old. The overall argument about the social function of Romans 3 is essentially the same as in the equivalent section in *PJG¹* (123-35), but the emphasis on the textuality of the law is new, as is the defense of the centrality of "faith" in 3:21-31 and the concept of "secondary comparisons." The repeated emphasis on Paul's engagement with scripture (dependent in part on *PHF*) means that the antithesis/reinterpretation distinction is not as clear here as in *PJG¹*.

2. The phrase "the faith associated with Christ" replaces "faith in Christ" *(PJG¹)* in recognition of the open-endedness of Paul's genitival constructions (διὰ πίστεως Ἰησοῦ Χριστοῦ, v. 22; ἐκ πίστεως Ἰησοῦ, v. 26). These constructions *associate* faith and Christ, thereby delimiting the potential scope of "faith," but the context indicates that Christ may be seen not only as the object of faith but also as its origin. Nothing in the context suggests a reference to "the faithfulness of Christ" — a point to which we shall return.

3. For a recent reassertion of this traditional view, see Richard Bell, *No One Seeks for God*, 10-12 and *passim*. Bell believes that "at the time of writing of Romans . . . , Paul had worked out a fairly coherent theological system" (238-39), which he reproduces in this letter.

of Jews and Gentiles who do what is right (cf. vv. 9-10). Indeed, special emphasis is placed on the possibility of righteous Gentiles, for reasons that make good pragmatic sense within the strategy of the letter. The argument of Romans 2 works only on the premise of the *non*-universality of sin.[4] While the argument of Romans 3–4 is shaped by the same pragmatic factors as chapter 2, this section is based on different, explicitly scriptural premises. Only with Romans 3 does the motif of universal sin enter Paul's discourse, and it does so at precisely the moment at which Paul moves onto scriptural terrain and begins to interpret the λογία τοῦ θεοῦ (3:2). Romans 3:1-8 is not a somewhat cryptic digression but the key to Paul's whole argument, since here for the first time he engages with the message of scripture, which he describes as God's speech, "the words of God" (3:2).[5] The crucial exegetical point is that the references that follow to "the faithfulness of God," "the truth of God," and "the righteousness of God" all derive from the initial reference to "the words of God." In scripture God speaks, and what God speaks is an indictment of the entire human race. What is at issue is whether what God says is true, whether God is in the right in his scriptural indictment of the whole world. The scriptural indictment itself follows in vv. 9-20, and vv. 1-20 as a whole therefore represents a coherent argument about scripture or "the law" — more specifically, a scripture construed as articulating the guilt of unrighteous humankind rather than as a way to righteousness.

1. The Textuality of the Law (Romans 3:1-20)

The doctrine of the universality of sin is stated with all appropriate rhetorical force in Romans 3:9-12:

> We have already asserted that Jews and Greeks alike are all under sin, as it is written: There is no one who is righteous [οὐκ ἔστιν δίκαιος], not even one. There is no one who understands. There is no one who seeks God. All have turned away; together they have become worthless. There is no one who does good, not even one.

---

4. "The arguments of 1:18–2:29 do not aim to show the sinfulness of all humans. Rather, they seek to establish that God will accept gentiles, provided they behave toward God and neighbor as the law requires, even if they do not become Jews or live as some sort of God-fearing gentile community that possesses the law" (S. Stowers, *Rereading of Romans*, 141).

5. The "digression" view of 3:1-8 is represented by Kuss, *Der Römerbrief*, 55, 99; Schlier, *Der Römerbrief*, 97; Cranfield, *Romans*, 1:183; Bell, *No One Seeks for God*, 201.

Here, the four negative οὐκ ἔστιν statements correspond to Paul's affirmation that "Jews and Greeks alike are all under sin."[6] ("All under sin" is also echoed in the scriptural "all have turned aside.") The rhetorically impressive repetitions are in fact Paul's own creation, based on Psalm 13[14]:1-3:

1a The fool said in his heart, there is no God.
1b They are corrupted, they practice abominations,
1c there is no one who does good [ποιῶν χρηστότητα], not even one.
2a The Lord looked down from heaven upon the sons of men,
2b to see if there is anyone who understands or seeks God
 [εἰ ἔστιν συνίων ἢ ἐκζητῶν τὸν θεόν].
3a All have turned away, together they have become worthless,
3b there is no one who does good, not even one.

In Romans 3:12, Psalm 13:3 LXX is quoted verbatim (or almost so, depending on a minor textual problem), but the preceding verses of the psalm are treated selectively and are significantly modified. Paul takes the first of the psalm's two identical statements to the effect that "there is no one who does good" (Ps. 13:1c) and substitutes for it the statement that "there is no one who is righteous" (Rom. 3:10). This substitution is motivated by the desire to avoid the repetition of "there is no one who does good" (Ps. 13:1c, 3b) and to place at the beginning of his catena a term that is of fundamental importance in the argument of Romans as a whole. The second and third of the series of οὐκ ἔστιν statements are created by Paul out of a pair of participles in Psalm 13:2. The Lord looks to see if there is anyone who understands or seeks God, and the following verse describes the negative outcome of this quest. Paul reads the outcome into the quest itself, so that "if there is anyone who understands or seeks God" becomes "There is no one who understands, there is no one who seeks God." The structure of the negation in Psalm 13:1c (= v. 3b) is extended into Paul's rendering of v. 2b, by the simple device of substituting οὐκ for εἰ in the phrase εἰ ἔστιν συνίων, and by repeating the οὐκ ἔστιν (in place of ἢ) in the phrase that follows. The resulting series of identically constructed negations aptly summarizes the psalm's negative verdict on "the sons of men," and the omissions and substitutions heighten its rhetorical impact.

---

6. L. Gaston takes "as it is written" at the start of the catena to refer only to the sin of Greeks, pointing to the attacks on "Gentile sinners" in Psalms 14 and 9, from which Paul here quotes (*Paul and the Torah*, 121). Thus, in Romans 3:19-20 the law speaks to the Jewish people of the sin of the Gentile world: with the partial exception of 2:17-29, 1:18–3:20 is "an indictment of the Gentile world" (122). But there is no indication in 3:9 that the catena is to apply only to Gentiles.

In 3:13-18, further material from the Psalms and from Isaiah is assembled so as to present an analysis of sin with reference to various parts of the body: throat, tongue, lips, mouth (vv. 13-14), feet (vv. 15-17), eyes (v. 18).[7] It is, however, the material from Psalm 13 that bears the greatest weight within Paul's catena, since this passage alone asserts sin's universality — the point from which the catena set out ("Jews and Greeks alike are all under sin," v. 9) and to which it returns ("so that every mouth should be stopped and the whole world should be liable to God's judgment," v. 20). At the outset, it is Paul who first asserts sin's universal scope: "We have already charged . . ." (v. 9). At the conclusion, it is "the law" that reiterates this message, speaking in and through the psalmists whom Paul here presents as authoritative commentators on the law (v. 19).[8] That also means that Paul presents himself as another commentator, marshalling the words of his predecessors and repeating what they said in his own words. What is at stake in this passage is the law's negative verdict on humankind in general and the Jewish people in particular, and thus the true meaning of the law itself. According to Paul, the voice of the law as articulated by its later scriptural commentators rules out the more optimistic interpretation, which is that the law's true sense is to be found in the "works" — actions and abstentions — it prescribes as the way to the goal of "righteousness" (cf. v. 20). The optimistic reading of the Torah is a misreading. "Therefore by works of law shall no flesh be justified before him, for through the law comes knowledge of sin" — knowledge, that is, of sin as the final determinant of human standing before God.[9] *Romans 3:9-20 is concerned to articulate not a general doctrine of the human condition but the true meaning of a text.* The law is referred to no less than six times in vv. 19-21, confirming that Paul asserts his doctrine of sin's universality not on his own authority but only as a commentator on a text.

According to vv. 19-20, the text asserts *universal* guilt (n.b. πᾶν στόμα, πᾶς ὁ κόσμος, πᾶσα σάρξ) but is addressed specifically to Jews (τοῖς ἐν τῷ νόμῳ). As Sanders notes, Paul "offers no explanation of how what the law says

---

7. For fuller discussion of the catena, see my *PHF*, 57-66.

8. In v. 19a, ὅσα ὁ νόμος λέγει, it is possible that νόμος is given an extended sense equivalent to γραφή (cf. 1 Cor. 14:21; so Michel, *Der Brief an die Römer*, 86; Käsemann, *Commentary on Romans*, 87; Cranfield, *Romans*, 1:195). Yet the other three occurrences of νόμος in Romans 3:19-20 all refer unambiguously to the law of Moses, and it is more probable that passages from the Psalms and Isaiah are attributed to "the law" in that they are understood as commentary on the law.

9. Nothing in the context suggests that it is the law's function to *provoke* sin (the view of Bultmann, *Theology of the New Testament*, 1:264; Schlier, *Der Römerbrief*, 101; Käsemann, *Commentary on Romans*, 89-90; rightly rejected by Cranfield, *Romans*, 1:199n).

to those under it (the Jews) also applies to 'the whole world.'"[10] The problem can be resolved if we recall that "the law" is a text with specific readers or hearers, and not an abstraction representing the divine relationship to an undifferentiated humanity apart from Christ. This emphasis on the textuality of law makes it possible to differentiate the people *to* whom the law speaks from the people *of* whom it speaks. When the law says that "there is no one righteous, not even one," it speaks *of* "Jews and Greeks" alike, who are all said to be "under sin" (vv. 9-10), but it speaks specifically *to* "those who are in the law" — that is, to those who are within the sphere of the law's address. Jews are addressed by the law in the straightforward sense that they are "hearers of the law" every sabbath in the synagogue, "whenever Moses is read" (cf. Rom. 2:13; 2 Cor. 3:15). While the law places Jews in the same position before God as Gentiles, it does not do so by simply abolishing all differentiation between them, as though hearing or not hearing the law were a matter of indifference. It is no doubt true that "only through the relationship to the law can the human be convicted as a sinner," and that "the law's validity *for all* humans must therefore be demonstrated."[11] Yet at no point in Paul's argument in Romans 3 is the law abstracted from its concrete textual embodiment for the sake of its universal validity. In speaking *of* the universal human condition, it speaks locally; it speaks *to* Jews, who are distinguished from all others by the fact that to them have been entrusted "the words of God" (cf. 3:1-2). The point of v. 19 is that the law's specific address to Jews demonstrates that they too are included within its negative verdict on humanity. The verdict that "there is no one who is righteous, not even one" is truly universal and is not speaking merely of Gentiles. There are no grounds for supposing that the primary addressees of this verdict are exempted from its scope.[12]

Having established the scriptural orientation of Paul's argument, the next step is to integrate vv. 1-8 into this argument and to show that vv. 1-20 constitute a single coherent presentation of *the scriptural testimony to sin's universality*. In vv. 1-8, the later references to "the law" (vv. 19-21) are anticipated in references to "the words of God" (τὰ λογία τοῦ θεοῦ, v. 2) and to "your words" (ἐν τοῖς λόγοις σου, v. 4). These references to God's words anticipate the catena of vv. 9-18, as the subsequent references to the law summarize it. Thus, in Romans 3 scripture is explicitly at issue from the outset — in con-

---

10. Sanders, *Paul, the Law and the Jewish People*, 82.

11. E. Jüngel, "Das Gesetz zwischen Adam und Christus: Eine theologische Studie zu Röm 5,12-21," 52; my translation.

12. Against Stowers, who comments on 3:20 that "the idea of Paul saying that the law, with its divinely ordained institutions, cannot make Jews acceptable to God [is] absurd" (*Rereading of Romans*, 190); Paul intends only to exclude the law as a way of righteousness for Gentiles.

trast to chapters 1 and 2, where the fundamental statements about universal knowledge of God and divine impartiality are not presented as scriptural in origin.[13] Scripture's message is uncompromising: "There is no one righteous, not even one" (3:9). Arguments based on non-scriptural foundations help prepare the way for the annihilating scriptural judgment on humankind, but their conclusions are far less radical. When Paul states that "the advantage of the Jew" is seen first and foremost in the possession of "the words of God" (3:1-2), he signals a shift onto distinctively scriptural terrain.[14]

The link between vv. 9-20 and vv. 1-8 is implied initially in the continuation of the question-and-answer format and in the claim that "we have *already* accused [προητιασάμεθα] Jews and Greeks as all being under the power of sin" (v. 9). Paul here claims to repeat something he has said before (cf. Gal. 1:9). But he has said nothing of the kind in Romans 1–2.[15] He refers here quite specifically to his statement in 3:4, where he moves from a preceding reference to the unfaithfulness of "some" Jews to an affirmation of the falsehood of "every human":

> Let God be true and every human a liar — as it is written: ". . . so that you might be justified in your words, and overcome when you are judged." (3:4, citing Ps. 50:6 LXX)[16]

In the initial correlation of divine truth and human falsehood, it is wrong to assume that "and" (δέ) has the force of "even if" — as though Paul were merely asserting the pious truism that, *even if* falsehood is universal among humans, it cannot possibly be ascribed to God. On such an

---

13. It is true that, in Romans 2:6, ὃς ἀποδώσει ἑκάστῳ κατὰ τὰ ἔργα αὐτοῦ echoes the language of Psalm 61:13 (ὅτι σὺ ἀποδώσεις ἑκάστῳ κατὰ τὰ ἔργα αὐτοῦ) and, to a lesser extent, Proverbs 24:12 (ὃς ἀποδίδωσιν ἑκάστῳ κατὰ τὰ ἔργα αὐτοῦ). Yet neither Paul nor any other NT writer draws attention to the scriptural roots of this language (cf. Matt. 16:27; 2 Tim. 4:14; 1 Pet. 1:17; Rev. 2:23).

14. The link between Jewishness and scripture in 3:1-2 makes it impossible to accept Philip Esler's odd claim — directed against Richard Hays — that "the notion of Israel as 'a reading community' is anachronistic," given the low literacy rate in Roman Palestine (*Conflict and Identity in Romans*, 177). If Hays sees Israel as "a reading community," he is unlikely to mean that every individual in Israel was engaged in minute textual analysis. More probably, he envisages institutions such as the synagogue, in which the Torah is read and heard: "From of old Moses has in every city those who proclaim him, as he is read in the synagogues every sabbath" (Acts 15:21). In that sense, Israel is a reading-and-hearing community.

15. Against Cranfield, *Romans*, 1:191; Dunn, *Romans*, 1:148.

16. This must be Paul speaking, not his interlocutor, as Stowers claims (*Rereading of Romans*, 169; followed by Keck, *Romans*, 91-92). Whatever the case with Epictetus (to whom Stowers refers), Paul would seem to answer his own questions himself.

interpretation, πᾶς δὲ ἄνθρωπος ψεύστης would serve merely to reinforce the affirmation of the truthfulness of God.[17] In v. 7, however, the antithesis between divine truth and human falsehood is repeated in a form suggesting that divine truthfulness is somehow *dependent* on human falsehood: "If the truth of God [ἡ ἀλήθεια τοῦ θεοῦ] abounds *through* my falsehood [ἐν τῷ ἐμῷ ψεύσματι] to his glory. . . ." This premise for the question that follows is derived from v. 4 and must be taken fully into account in interpreting it. "Let God be true *even if* every human is false" would not account for the question that arises in v. 7. Rather, we should understand the δέ to have the force of "in that": "Let God be true *in that* every human is false." God's truth is manifest in universal human falsehood, just as God's righteousness is manifested in human unrighteousness (cf. v. 5). Why? Because the truthfulness of God is the truthfulness of the scriptural λογία τοῦ θεοῦ and because what God says in and through the scriptural words is that every human is false: "There is no one who is righteous, not even one. . . . With their tongues they deceive" (3:9, 13). God's truthfulness is *dependent* on human falsehood in the straightforward sense that God's words *assert* human falsehood, so that their own truth stands or falls with this assertion. This interpretation alone makes sense of v. 9, where the claim that all Jews and Gentiles have *already* been indicted as sinners before God can only refer back to v. 5.[18] Thus, Ἰουδαίους τε καὶ Ἕλληνας πάντας . . . (v. 9) paraphrases πᾶς δὲ ἄνθρωπος (v. 5).[19]

Paul's reference to universal human falsehood is itself derived from scripture. Psalm 115 LXX opens as follows:

1a I believed, therefore I spoke;
1b I was greatly humbled.
2a I said in my astonishment [ἐν τῇ ἐκστάσει μου]
2b Every human is a liar! [πᾶς ἄνθρωπος ψεύστης] (Ps. 115:1-2)

---

17. So Fitzmyer, *Romans*, 328: "For Paul, though every human being would appear before God as a liar, God's truthfulness and fidelity would shine forth."

18. "*Only at this point* does the scope of Paul's argument broaden to include all humanity. . . . It does so, moreover, solely on the basis of the cited Scripture" (Mark Seifrid, "Unrighteous by Faith: Apostolic Proclamation in Romans 1:18–3:20," 137; italics original).

19. πᾶς ἄνθρωπος thus marks a shift from "some Jews" (cf. τινες, v. 3) to "all humans without exception." D. R. Hall assumes that the emphasis falls only on the contrast between πᾶς and τινες and that in the phrase πᾶς ἄνθρωπος Paul still "has the Jews particularly in mind" ("Romans 3.1-8 Reconsidered," 186). This seems unlikely, in view of the repeated use of πᾶς elsewhere in the letter to refer comprehensively to Jews and Gentiles alike (cf. Rom. 1:16; 2:10; 3:9, 12, 19, 20, 22, 23; 4:16; 5:12, 18 [× 2]; 10:11, 12, 13; 11:32).

The affirmation "I believed, therefore I spoke" is cited in 2 Corinthians 4:13, where Paul claims to embody in his ministry "the same spirit of faith" as is expressed in the psalm text; his self-identification with a scriptural author is he. ? unusually close. The clear allusion in Romans 3:4 to the very next verse may imply that Paul finds in the psalm precisely the correlation between πίστις and universal human falsehood or guilt that is writ large in Romans 3 as a whole. The one who believes the divine word of grace also finds in that word a disclosure of universal human depravity, and it is this appalling and humiliating discovery that is emphasized both in the psalm text and in Paul's allusion to it. Even before the explicit citation from Psalm 50 LXX that follows, universal human falsehood is implicitly presented as a distinctively scriptural doctrine, counterintuitive and shattering to natural human self-esteem.

The citation from Psalm 50:6 makes explicit this focus on scripture as such; for Paul clearly connects "so that you might be justified in your words" with "the words of God" that constitute the scriptures (Rom. 3:2, 4).[20] As in the catena (3:10-18), the assumption is that the divine words as recorded in scripture constitute an indictment of the entire human race. The question was raised whether the unfaithfulness of some Jews makes it impossible for God to remain faithful to his own words (3:3). The response is that this cannot be the case, since the manifest unfaithfulness of "some" is actually a mere symptom of a universal human malaise that it is precisely the function of God's words to bring to light. The implied questioner assumes that the λόγια τοῦ θεοῦ are essentially positive in content and that Israel's unfaithfulness might pose an obstacle to their realization (v. 3). Paul's response assumes that the scriptural words of God are essentially negative in content and that Israel's unfaithfulness is actually a vindication of God's truthfulness in those words. Throughout these verses, there is the closest correlation between the faithfulness, truthfulness, or righteousness of God on the one hand and the words of scripture on the other. It is the role of the citation to make this correlation explicit, for there it is envisaged that God will be "justified in his words" — that is, that humans will come to acknowledge God's righteousness in his words, the truthfulness of the scriptural indictment of humankind. The ὅπως clause of v. 4 is similar in function and sense to the ἵνα clause of v. 19:

Let God be true, and every human false — as it is written: ". . . *so that* [ὅπως] you may be justified in your words and overcome when you are judged."

20. So Fitzmyer, *Romans*, 328.

We know that what the law says it speaks to those who are under the law, *so that* [ἵνα] every mouth may be stopped and the whole world liable to God's judgment [ὑπόδικος . . . τῷ θεῷ].

The dramatic image here is of a lawsuit in which humankind is finally compelled to concede the truth and justice of the universal divine indictment articulated in scripture. God's truth is bound up with "what the law says": God is true if and only if what the law says is true. Like Paul's own statement in 3:19, the citation from Psalm 50 is concerned with the final intention of the law's utterances, which is to persuade their addressees that the God who speaks in them is speaking the truth about the human condition. Like the word of the gospel, the voice of the law intends its own acknowledgment as true.[21]

On this reading, the question addressed in Romans 3:5-8 is whether the condemnatory divine words of scripture are really God's last word to the human race. The question is a deeply serious one; it is the question that *has* to arise at this point in the argument. To paraphrase v. 5: if our unrighteousness shows that God is indeed righteous in his words, the words of scripture that indict us, then — what next? The questioner has been led inexorably to the edge of a precipice and naturally wishes to know whether God really intends to carry out the scriptural death sentence. Paul's response is comfortless (vv. 5-6). Would God be unjust in executing his wrath, as some foolishly suppose?[22] Indeed not, for the execution of God's wrath is precisely the logic of divine judgment — a logic about which (for Paul) there is general agreement: "*We acknowledge* that the judgment of God is in truth directed against those who do such things" (Rom. 2:2). Paul's uncompromising response provokes in 3:7 a more assertive and individualized version of the question posed in 3:5. If the truth of the divine indictment is manifested in my participation in universal human falsehood, why is God not satisfied with this glorious manifestation of his truthfulness? Having conclusively vindicated his accusation, why does he still feel the need to annihilate me? Why does he not consider the option of extending his mercy? Again Paul offers no comfort but takes the op-

21. As in Romans 15:8, the truth of God has to do with the confirmation of the truth of God's words in scripture. The difference between 3:4 and 15:8 is that in the latter passage the scriptural passages in question are the patriarchal promises, whereas in the former it is the scriptural indictment summed up in the catena (3:10-18) that is in mind. Thus God's "faithfulness," "truth," and "righteousness" in Romans 3:1-8 are associated more with the covenantal threats than with the covenantal promises. For this interpretation, which highlights the connections between vv. 1-8 and vv. 9-20, see further *PHF*, 54-71.

22. The form of the question in v. 5b indicates that Paul himself is speaking, and not the objector (so Schlier, *Der Römerbrief*, 91). This does not mean that Paul has no objector in mind, however.

portunity to vindicate himself over against his critics (v. 8). If the questioner were right to imply that we have a claim on the divine mercy, the consequence would be that we could brazenly persist in our evil ways in the sure knowledge of final divine good — a claim that is slanderously attributed to Paul himself. In conclusion: we all stand unprotected and exposed before the divine judgment in which the scriptural indictment of humankind will be vindicated and executed (cf. v. 9a).[23]

This interpretation of Romans 3:1-8 rests on the identification of the λογία τοῦ θεοῦ (v. 2; cf. v. 4) with the words of the law as articulated in the catena (vv. 9-20). The great advantage of this interpretation is that Romans 3:1-20 can now be seen as a single coherent argument focused on the negative voice of scripture, which, at this point, would seem to be scripture's only voice. Thus, the θεοῦ δικαιοσύνη of v. 5 is not to be identified with the δικαιοσύνη θεοῦ of v. 21, for the one is a righteousness of God manifested in and through the law, whereas the other is a righteousness of God manifested apart from law — though attested by the law and the prophets. The divergence in word order (θεοῦ δικαιοσύνη, δικαιοσύνη θεοῦ) is already an indication that we are not here dealing with a fixed, univocal formulation. In both cases, the righteousness-of-God phraseology is constructed *ad hoc* from scriptural texts that Paul explicitly cites: Psalm 50:6 (ὅπως ἂν δικαιωθῇς, i.e., "so that your righteousness might be acknowledged") in the case of Romans 3:6; Habakkuk 2:4 in the case of Romans 1:17 and 3:21.[24] According to 3:4-5, God is justified in his speech, he is righteous and truthful, only if "every human is a liar," if humans are characterized by ἀδικία. And the logic of this assertion is derived from the *content* of the divine speech, consisting as it does in utterances to the effect that "there is no one who is righteous, not even one" and that "with their tongues they deceive" (3:10, 13).

---

23. Compare the view of D. R. Hall, for whom the divine faithfulness, truth, and righteousness in this passage all refer to God's "loyalty to his promises of salvation to his people" ("Romans 3.1-8 Reconsidered," 184). In the passage as a whole, "Paul is trying to reconcile two seemingly inconsistent ideas: on the one hand, God's faithfulness to his covenant promises to the Jewish nation; on the other hand, God's impartiality towards Jew and Gentile, both in mercy and in judgment, which he has just described in ch. 2" (183). Thus v. 5 raises the possibility that "[i]t would be unrighteous (untrue to his covenant) for God to exercise his eschatological wrath on Jew as well as Gentile" (185). In v. 6, however, Paul responds that "to deny God the freedom to condemn Jews is equivalent to denying him the freedom to be judge at all" (192). This "covenantal" interpretation of Romans 3:1-8 probably now represents the majority view, and it was followed in *PJG¹*, 124-28. The present interpretation differs from it in emphasizing that Paul's own view (as opposed to his implied questioner's) appeals not just to the concept of divine impartiality (cf. 2:11) but above all to the scriptural indictment of humankind (cf. 3:4).

24. On this, see *PHF*, 43-53.

As we have seen, the theme of Romans 3:1-20 is the scriptural indictment of humanity — the Jew first, and also the Greek. What would be the social function of such an argument, in the context of a Roman Christian community divided over the practice of the law? To answer this question, we must return to the conclusion of the argument in v. 20: "By works of law shall no flesh be justified before him, for through the law is knowledge of sin." This conclusion stems from the law's own testimony as articulated by its later scriptural commentators in the texts assembled in the catena. In the catena, scripture interprets scripture, in the sense that it is psalmists and prophets who definitively interpret the law of Moses as the divine indictment of humankind. In interpreting scripture, however, the psalmists and prophets also correct a *misinterpretation* of scripture. They refute a reading of scripture according to which "by works of law shall all flesh [πᾶσα σάρξ] be justified before him." According to the rejected reading, the law of Moses is to be understood as marking out the way of righteousness not just to Jews but potentially to "all flesh." On the view that Paul here opposes and presupposes, the law was entrusted to Israel as a gift to "all flesh," that is, to the world: the gift of an authoritative divine revelation of the way to righteousness. As the author of Wisdom puts it, it was the sons of Israel through whom "the imperishable light of the law" was "given to the world" (Wis. 18:4). Some such view seems to underlie Paul's abrupt and negative reference to "works of law" as a supposed way for humankind to attain to righteousness. The true sense of the law — that it represents the divine indictment of humankind — is set in opposition to a false one.

This helps to clarify the social function or pragmatic intention of Paul's argument. As we have seen, references to "the words of God" or to "the law" relate to a textual artifact that demarcates the social space of those who are "within the law" (Rom. 2:12; 3:19) from the surrounding space of those who are "without law" (2:12). Within this space, the law is read in public and thereby finds "hearers" (2:13) to whom it "speaks" (3:19). It speaks of prescribed or proscribed practices, with the intention that "hearers" will become "doers" and so come to be "righteous before God" (cf. 2:13; 3:20). In this focus on a particular form of human agency, however, it is not forgotten that the relevant form of life is grounded in the gracious divine revelation of knowledge and truth for which others strive in vain (cf. 2:20). Thus the Jew entrusted with this revelation relies on it and rejoices in the God who speaks in it (cf. 2:17). It is true that scripture is on occasion less obviously beneficent in intent, threatening and denouncing its hearers (cf. 3:10-18); but — for Jews other than Paul — the heart of the matter is not to be found in texts such as these. This is ultimately an optimistic rather than a pessimistic text, even if this optimism is hard-won.

It is some such phenomenological description of the role of the law within the synagogue that is implied in Paul's text; and it will apply also and especially to synagogues in Rome. We may suppose that, after years of tension marked by intracommunal disturbances, the ban on synagogue worship, and the expulsion and subsequent return, Roman Jewish Christians are in an anomalous relation to these synagogues. They were not welcomed in the early 40s CE, and they are certainly not welcome in the mid 50s. Yet, as Romans 14 indicates, they continue to observe the law and to hold themselves aloof from Gentile fellow Christians who practice the Pauline law-free gospel. Paul's letter seeks a hearing for itself among Jewish as well as Gentile Christians in Rome, and these hearers have already learned from Romans 2 to contrast the blatant transgressions of some leaders of the majority Jewish community with the genuine obedience to the (admittedly unwritten) law that may be found among Gentiles. In Romans 3:1-20, the same pragmatic argument about communal identity and social location is continued on scriptural terrain. It now transpires that the law's harsh threats and denunciations speak not only of outsiders but also of those who stand within the circle of the law's hearers and addressees. The intention and effect of Paul's argument is to create ideological distance between the hearers of his own text and of Moses', and thereby to promote the emergence of a unified community in which Jews and Gentiles find their common identity in Christ rather than in the law.[25]

The present emphasis on the textuality and social location of the law results in a quite different reading from one in which "the law" and its "works" are symbols or metaphors of more general human tendencies. Ernst Käsemann ventures the following interpretative comment on the negation of "works of law" in Romans 3:20:

> The actual law as it has been handed down does not bring about genuine obedience for the apostle, since the religious seize it and make it not only the ground of their attainment but also of their boasting. However, that is

---

25. According to Philip Esler, Paul seeks to instill in his Roman addressees a sense of their "glorious new shared identity," and in 1:18–3:20 he attempts to "persuade them of the inevitable sinfulness to which they are subject without it, yet do so in a way that is adapted to their entirely different social origins" (*Conflict and Identity*, 154). On this reading, 2:17–3:8 is addressed directly to Roman Jewish Christians (Judean Christ-followers, in Esler's terminology), just as 1:18-32 is directly addressed to Roman Gentile Christians and 3:9-20 is addressed to both parties (145-54). The Roman Jewish community as a whole plays no part in Esler's argument, as though the Judean Christ-followers were the only people in Rome to observe the law. A distinction between Christian and non-Christian Jews is, however, clear in Romans 4:12; 9:6-9; 11:1-10; 15:31.

simply sacrilege. Because Paul sees this sacrilege constantly in progress in the works of the law, he can only sharply reject it.[26]

The Pauline negation of "works of law" is here said to speak of "the religious," who seize the law, use it as a platform for their own aspirations, boast of it — and thereby make themselves guilty of "sacrilege" precisely in the pursuit of their zealous religiosity. This is supposed to describe a transhistorical reality that recurs again and again even and especially within the Christian community itself. "The law" becomes a cipher for any and every religiously sanctioned demand or ideal. Käsemann's rhetoric perfectly exemplifies a characteristically Lutheran tendency to dissolve the particularities with which Paul is concerned and to transpose his language into a supposedly more general and universal framework. The dissolution of the most elementary property of "the law" as Paul understood it — its textuality, or writtenness — is symptomatic of the interpretative violence perpetrated by this ostensibly hyper-Pauline theology of the mid-twentieth century.[27] Yet Paul does not reject "works of the law" because they represent an abstract principle of achievement that is incompatible with an equally abstract principle of submission to the lordship of the divine grace. He understands "works of the law" as the prescribed or proscribed practices that constitute the form of life of the Jewish community, the privileged inheritors of the divine election and covenant. He rejects this form of life in order to affirm another, founded on a shared allegiance to Christ and realized in a single community in which Jewish and Gentile adherents of Christ are united.[28]

26. Käsemann, *Romans*, 89.

27. For an analysis of the deep-seated prejudice against textuality that underlies this interpretation, see my *Text and Truth*, 127-76.

28. This position is also to be differentiated from that of J. D. G. Dunn, according to whom "works of law" in Romans 3:20 "must refer to the attitude attacked in chap. 2; it must denote the 'works' referred to there, particularly circumcision. That is to say, the first Roman listeners would most probably and rightly understand 'works of the law' as referring to those actions which were performed at the behest of the law, in service of the Torah; that is, those acts prescribed by the law by which a member of the covenant people identified himself as a Jew and maintained his status within the covenant" (*Romans*, 1:158). In brief, the expression "works of law" refers primarily to "circumcision, food laws, etc." (159). It does not occur to Dunn that "works of law" refers comprehensively to a communal form of life, since he rejects out of hand the view that the Pauline faith/law antithesis has a social correlate in the separation of Christian congregations from Jewish synagogues. Criticizing my own position in *PJG¹*, Dunn asserts that "Paul is arguing to maintain the bond between covenant people and Christian congregation (e.g., 3:25-26; 4:16; 11:11-32; 15:27), not for a divorce" (lvii). With the possible exception of Romans 11, however, Paul speaks in such passages of the union of Jewish and Gentile *Christians* — precisely the focus of my own argument. Dunn is prepared to concede that "the likely *effect*

Jewish and Gentile Christian readers learn from Romans 3:1-20 that membership of the Jewish community and adherence to its form of life are not a *sine qua non* of salvation. This is not a purely theoretical argument but entails an implicit call for social reorientation. Paradoxically, the law itself becomes an argument for ideological distance from the Jewish community. Paul thereby prepares the way for the positive argument for "faith" as the form of life in which Jews and Gentiles may be at one.

2. Jews, Gentiles, and Faith (Romans 3:21-31)

For Paul, "faith" has its correlate in social practice. In Romans 14:1–15:13, it is "faith" (πίστις) or "believing" (πιστεύειν) that both divides and unites the "weak" and the "strong." The "weak" person is shown to be "weak in faith" by his or her strict adherence to the law's dietary code as a precondition for table fellowship with Gentiles (14:1-2). To "eat vegetables" in such a situation, abstaining from meat and also wine, is *ipso facto* to be weak in faith. Conversely, to "believe" is — among other things — to believe that "one may eat anything" (v. 2). While this believing position is justified in itself, it is unjustified if it becomes an occasion of controversy and disunity. For the sake of unity, then, the practice that is consonant with faith should be restrained: "The faith that you have, keep to yourself, before God" (v. 22), in the recollection that, for one who eats but does so οὐκ ἐκ πίστεως, his or her action is *sin*, both subjectively and objectively (v. 23). "Faith," then, represents a sole allegiance to Jesus Christ as Lord, which in principle excludes an additional allegiance to a second lordship, that of the law. In practice, however, minor concessions may have to be made for the sake of those whose allegiance to the lordship of Jesus Christ is not yet an exclusive one. The common faith of both the strong and the weak should unite them rather than dividing them. Paul concludes his argument with a prayer that this may be so:

> May the God of hope fill you with all joy and peace *in believing* [ἐν τῷ πιστεύειν], so that you may abound in hope, in the power of the Holy Spirit. (15:13)

Here, both the weak and the strong are addressed — Christian Jews and Gentiles. Common to both parties within the Roman Christian community

---

of Paul's advocacy was a polarization of synagogue and church, as Jewish Christians found it increasingly difficult to maintain the twin loyalties to law and faith" (lvii; italics original). How can Dunn be so sure that a "likely effect" is not also an intended effect?

is the simple fact of "believing," an allegiance to Jesus Christ as Lord. When this faith becomes the basis for unity rather than an occasion of division, then the blessings of joy, peace, and hope that follow from faith will finally be realized, in the power of the Holy Spirit. Integral to this faith-based unity is the recognition that law observance is *not* a necessary precondition of unity, as the "weak" suppose. The concessions called for in vv. 13-23 are pragmatically motivated: for Paul shares with the strong the conviction that "all things are clean" (v. 20; cf. v. 14) and that allegiance to Christ is exclusive. Given the fact that not all Roman Christians have as yet grasped that insight, however, a willingness to accommodate their sensitivities is actually a requirement of exclusive allegiance to the Christ who extends his welcome to all (15:7).

That is the act of ethical imagination that Paul demands of the strong. If one subtracts the pragmatic accommodation, however, the theological situation is simple: a stark opposition between two possible allegiances, to the law or to Christ — the one expressed in the practice of "works of law," the other in the practice of "faith." It is this antithesis in its pure form, unaffected as yet by pragmatic complications, that is developed in Romans 3.

In principle, there is no reason why Jews and Gentiles should not be united in the practice of "works of law," seen as marking out the way of righteousness. The Torah itself speaks repeatedly of the προσήλυτος, the person who has joined himself or herself to the people of Israel. In Romans 3, the claim that the law is exclusive and ethnocentric plays only a limited role. Throughout vv. 1-20 it is assumed that, while the law was addressed specifically to Israel (cf. vv. 2, 19), it speaks not of Israel alone but of πᾶς ἄνθρωπος, πᾶς ὁ κόσμος and πᾶσα σάρξ (vv. 4, 19, 20). We search here in vain for any indication that Paul's concern is with a narrowly nationalistic or ethnocentric understanding of the covenant. Even in v. 29, where it is emphasized that God is the God of Gentiles as well as of Jews, the implied contrast with "works of law" (v. 28) amounts only to the fact that the Gentile Christian is deemed to have retained his or her identity as a non-Jew; it is not suggested that Gentiles are debarred from the practice of the law. In that sense it could be said of the law as well as the gospel that it is "for the Jew first, and also for the Greek" — with the proviso that the Greek who adopts the law becomes a Jew, whereas the Jew and the Greek who accept the gospel discover in it a new identity that embraces them both and relativizes the former distinction. Yet even this limited and qualified contrast between the scope of law and of gospel is absent from 3:1-20. Here, the law fails to lead its adherents to righteousness not because of its exclusiveness but because it exposes the dire reality of universal sin. That is the theological basis for the fact that, to a greater or lesser extent,

Jewish and Gentile Christians in Rome are alienated from the synagogue and must find their identity and their salvation "apart from the law" (v. 21). Their identity is constituted by "faith" and their salvation is "righteousness," and the one is the way to the other.

Having shown that an identity based on the law leads not to "righteousness" but to its opposite (vv. 1-20), Paul proceeds to argue that righteousness is attained by way of an identity based on faith (vv. 21-31).[29] The term πίστις dominates this paragraph, where it occurs eight times in formulations implying an instrumental sense: διὰ [τῆς] πίστεως (vv. 22, 25, 30, 31), διὰ νόμου πίστεως (v. 27), ἐκ πίστεως (vv. 26, 30), πίστει (v. 28). On four of these eight occasions, πίστις is correlated with δικαιοσύνη (v. 22) or δικαιοῦν (vv. 26, 28, 30), which also occurs on four further occasions (vv. 21, 25, 26 in the case of the noun, v. 24 in the case of the verb). The emphasis lies on "faith" rather than "righteousness," however, since the argument has to do with the conflict between two mutually exclusive routes (faith or law) to an agreed goal (righteousness). Thus the faith terminology noted above is closely correlated with law terminology:

διὰ [τῆς] πίστεως / διὰ νόμου (v. 20)
διὰ νόμου πίστεως / [διὰ νόμου] τῶν ἔργων (v. 27)
ἐκ πίστεως ['Ιησοῦ] / ἐφ ἔργων νόμου (v. 20)
πίστει / ἔργων νόμου (v. 28)

Paul's righteousness terminology is wholly conditioned by the faith/law antithesis. The δικαιοσύνη θεοῦ that is manifested apart from the law (v. 21) is the δικαιοσύνη θεοῦ διὰ πίστεως 'Ιησοῦ Χριστοῦ (v. 22). References to God's justifying action (v. 24) and God's righteousness (vv. 25, 26a) are summed up in a comprehensive description of God as δίκαιον καὶ δικαιοῦντα τὸν ἐκ πίστεως 'Ιησοῦ (v. 26b).

---

29. It is undeniable that in Romans 3 Paul speaks of "law" (v. 20) before he speaks of "faith" (v. 22). Douglas Campbell is critical of a Protestant exegesis in which faith "merely responds to a problem whose precise contours have already effectively dictated the shape of the solution" (*The Quest for Paul's Gospel,* 201-2n). He seeks an interpretation in which "Paul's 'faith' discussions no longer need to function in sequence with his discussion of 'works of law', thereby creating a discussion of salvific conditions and a resulting two-phase, prospective soteriology" (206; italics original). In the reading presented here, the law-faith sequence has to do with pragmatics and rhetoric rather than theological substance. Theologically, law and faith are coordinated with one another, as they must be if Paul's gospel is to be genuinely informed by his engagement with scripture. Thus, the question about the direction of Pauline thought (from plight to solution, or from solution to plight?) is misplaced.

Thus, the emphasis in this passage is on *faith* — that is, on faith as summing up in a single word the communal and individual form of life created by and oriented towards Jesus Christ, in whom is embodied the past, present, and future of the divine grace. "Righteousness" (or "the righteousness of God") is "by faith" in the sense that the form of life characterized by faith is divinely mandated and its communal expression divinely vindicated. If the aim of Romans 3 as a whole is to develop an antithesis between faith and law, then, as we have seen, this chapter has its social correlate in the three-sided and tension-laden relationship between non-Christian Jews and Jewish and Gentile Christians in Rome. The theological affirmations of this chapter have a pragmatic dimension, crucially important though widely overlooked. Its indicatives are also imperatives, as Romans 14:1–15:13 will later make explicit. Paul's concern in this faith/law antithesis is therefore not with "the individual" as such, as has often been assumed. The ἄνθρωπος of 3:28 who is "justified by faith" is no mere individual but represents the united community of Jewish and Gentile believers whose oneness corresponds to the oneness of God (cf. vv. 29-30). The "anthropocentrism" of this passage is ecclesial rather than individual in its orientation.[30] It has to do with competing communal orientations towards faith or Torah.

In spite of the focus on the ἄνθρωπος in v. 28, it is widely assumed that an "anthropocentric" reading of this passage is theologically and exegetically unacceptable. In the light of this concern, two alternative readings have been proposed, which are not necessarily mutually exclusive: it is said that this passage is primarily concerned not with human faith but with the "righteousness of God" or with the "faithfulness of Christ." In both cases, Paul's phraseology is understood to refer to divine saving action rather than to its human beneficiaries. In their opposition to "individualism," these readings would also exclude the "ecclesiocentric" or sociological reading proposed here. We must therefore engage here with each of them in turn, bringing their serious exegetical deficiencies to light.

(1) Where the theme of Romans 3:21-31 is said to be "the righteousness of God," the tendency will be to minimize its links with "faith."[31] This exegetical move is already implied in the very title of Käsemann's influential essay "'The Righteousness of God' in Paul" (1961), which overlooks the fact that the initial reference to "the righteousness of God" in Romans 3:21 is glossed in v. 22 as

---

30. Note, however, the important defense of individualism as an appropriate category for Pauline interpretation in T. Engberg-Pedersen, *Paul and the Stoics*, 40-43.

31. For the following, compare the discussion of Romans 1:16-17 in *PHF*, 47-53.

"the righteousness of God through faith of Jesus Christ." As a result of this oversight, "the righteousness of God" takes on a life of its own, referring to "God's covenant faithfulness," to "that faithfulness with which the Creator persists in his work of creation in spite of, and beyond, the falling away of his creatures,"[32] and to "God's sovereignty over the world revealing itself eschatologically in Jesus" (180). The very word "faith" is conspicuous by its virtual absence from Käsemann's essay: it occurs just eight times, of which at least four are occasioned by his interaction with more conventional Lutheran accounts of "justification by faith." "Faith" is marginalized partly because Käsemann believes — on slender evidence — that Paul takes over the phrase δικαιοσύνη θεοῦ as a preexisting formula,[33] but also on account of his polemic against the "individualism" inherent in "justification by faith" as traditionally understood. The righteousness of God is to be understood as an apocalyptic motif:

> [T]he righteousness of God does not, in Paul's understanding, refer primarily to the individual and is not to be understood exclusively in the context of the doctrine of man; but it is impossible to avoid doing these two things if its character as gift is given first priority. It is true that Paul does, for the purpose of his sharp polemic against the Jewish motif of the 'covenant people', depict the believer *[der Glaubende]*, and him alone, as the recipient of salvation. But the emergent category of the individual human being is to be seen here in immediate relation to the divine will for salvation, now directed towards the whole world and no longer limited by the confines of the law. (180-81)

In other words, Paul's references to "faith" are polemically motivated and are to be subordinated to the overarching concern not with mere individuals but with the eschatological transformation of the world. Thus, in Käsemann's commentary, Romans 3:21-26 is entitled "The Thesis," on account presumably

---

32. Käsemann, "'The Righteousness of God' in Paul," 177. Subsequent page references are given parenthetically in the text.

33. According to Käsemann, the expression δικαιοσύνη θεοῦ "appears independently [of Paul] in Matt. 6.33 and James 1.20 and can be traced back in the Old Testament to Deut. 33.21" ("'The Righteousness of God' in Paul," 172). Of these passages, only James 1:20 contains the expression δικαιοσύνη θεοῦ. Even in Paul, this expression occurs only four times (Rom. 1:17; 3:21, 22; 2 Cor. 5:21). Elsewhere we read of a θεοῦ δικαιοσύνην (Rom. 3:5), of τῆς δικαιοσύνης αὐτοῦ (3:25, 26), of τὴν τοῦ θεοῦ δικαιοσύνην (10:3), and of τὴν ἐκ θεοῦ δικαιοσύνην ἐπὶ τῇ πίστει (Phil. 3:9). Can there be a "ready-made formulation" (172) without a fixed wording? As Douglas Campbell notes, attempts by others "to broaden the lexical base for Käsemann's analysis" have been "only partially successful" (*The Rhetoric of Righteousness*, 146n).

of its fourfold reference to the divine righteousness, whereas vv. 27-31 are subordinated to the role of a "polemical development."[34]

If, however, δικαιοσύνη θεοῦ in v. 21 is not a freestanding entity but is interpreted by δικαισύνη θεοῦ διὰ πίστεως Ἰησοῦ Χριστοῦ in v. 22, then the "instrumental" sense of διὰ πίστεως implies that the righteousness of God is indissolubly linked to faith and is in some sense consequent on it.[35] As we have seen, all eight occurrences of πίστις in this passage are instrumental in form. Close parallels to the conjunction of righteousness and faith in v. 22 occur in the following passages:

δίκαιον καὶ δικαιοῦντα τὸν ἐκ πίστεως Ἰησοῦ (3:26)

λογιζόμεθα γὰρ δικαιοῦσθαι πίστει ἄνθρωπον (3:28)

ὃς δικαιώσει περιτομὴν ἐκ πίστεως καὶ ἀκροβυστίαν διὰ τῆς πίστεως (3:30)

The active or passive verbs refer to a divine act of justification *consequent on faith*. If that is the case with the verb δικαιοῦν, it will also be the case with the noun δικαιοσύνη where this, too, occurs in conjunction with an instrumental πίστις phrase — even if the righteousness in question is further qualified as the righteousness of God (v. 22). The righteousness of faith is the righteousness of God, in the sense that faith is the true righteousness, on the grounds of its validation and affirmation as such by God. As the citation from Genesis 15:6 will indicate in the following chapter, it is faith that is accounted as righteousness, and not the observance of the Torah.[36]

34. Käsemann, *Romans*, 91, 101.

35. Käsemann is dismissive of the subjective genitive reading of "through faith of [Jesus] Christ" (*Romans*, 94).

36. The broader terminological situation should be outlined at this point. In Romans 3:21-31, the noun δικαιοσύνη occurs four times, always in combination with τοῦ θεοῦ (vv. 21, 22) or αὐτοῦ (vv. 25, 26); the verb occurs five times. In 4:1-25, the noun occurs eight times, the verb only twice. In 9:30–10:21, the noun occurs ten or eleven times (twice in combination with τοῦ θεοῦ), the verb not at all. There are eleven further occurrences of the noun elsewhere in Romans, nine of the verb, giving totals for the letter of thirty-three/thirty-four and nineteen, respectively. Two conclusions may be drawn from these figures. First, four of the letter's seven references to "the righteousness of God" (or "his righteousness") occur in the passage where the verb also occurs most frequently (3:21-31). This suggests a close semantic link. Second, references to the "righteousness of God" in 10:3 occur in a context in which the noun typically occurs either on its own or in the phrase "righteousness by faith" (9:30; 10:6). This suggests that the terminological shift from "righteousness of God" / "his righteousness" (× 4 in 3:21-31) to "righteousness of faith" (4:11, 13) or "righteousness" (× 6 in 4:1-25) does not have significant semantic implications. Together, these two points suggest that Paul's righteousness terminology in Romans is of a piece. The righteousness of God is the righteousness of faith.

It seems that the righteousness terminology is intended above all to assert the *validity* before God of the new, faith-based identity, in opposition to the claim that only an individual and communal identity based on law observance is valid before God. As they are transferred from the realm of sin to the realm of grace, those who believe have their existence as believers *validated, affirmed, and vindicated.* Whatever their status in the eyes of majority Roman Jewish opinion, before God they are righteous. Paul has an authoritative, scripturally grounded decision to announce that should put to an end all disputes about the nature of "righteousness," that pattern of human conduct that conforms to the way things are. When Jews and Gentile Christians bring their conflict over true righteousness before the divine judge, the verdict is that "the one who is righteous *by faith* will live," but that (as the law itself demonstrates) "*by works of law* shall no flesh be righteous before him." This divine decision is the "righteousness of God" that is "apart from law" and yet "attested by the law and the prophets" (3:21).[37]

Also in the background here is Paul's earlier use of δικαιοῦν as an item within what Sanders has described as his "transfer terminology."[38] Thus, having listed the stereotypically Gentile vices of which some of the Corinthians had once been guilty, Paul adds: "But you were washed, but you were sanctified, but you were justified in the name of the Lord Jesus Christ and in the Spirit of our God" (1 Cor. 6:11). The divine act of sanctification or justification constitutes its human objects as ἡγιασμένοι (1 Cor. 1:2) or δικαιούμενοι (Rom. 3:24), in sharp contrast to their preceding state (cf. Rom. 5:12-21). In Romans 3, however, this transformative understanding of the divine act of justification is subordinated to a declarative understanding, *in a polemical context in which righteousness terminology serves as the common ground on which the respective claims of "faith" and "law" compete with one another.* Whatever is said about justification by faith must also be sayable about justification by works of law, even though Paul's point is that God does *not* endorse the latter. Righteousness or justification is "by faith" in the sense that faith and not law observance represents the pattern of conduct endorsed by God. Thus the righteousness of faith is also the righteousness of God. There is in this passage no reference to an act of the divine righteousness that precedes or bypasses faith. Even where Jesus' death is seen as a sign of God's righteousness (vv. 25, 26), the righteousness in question is connected to "the present time" and to the divine affirmation of "the one who

37. In this "forensic" account of Paul's doctrine of justification, δικαιοῦν would mean not so much "acquit" as "find in favor of" — as often in the Septuagint, according to P. Esler, *Conflict and Identity,* 162-63.

38. Sanders, *Paul and Palestinian Judaism,* 463-72.

is of the faith of Jesus" (v. 26). Righteousness terminology plays a quite specific and limited role in this passage.

In the faith/justification sequence, a human act is indeed followed by a divine one. Paul is less nervous about such a sequence than many of his modern commentators. Elsewhere, he can ask his readers whether they "received the Spirit by works of law or by hearing in faith" (Gal. 3:2): thus, faith precedes and conditions the giving of the Spirit just as it precedes and conditions the bestowal of righteousness. Validation and vindication are necessarily *responsive* acts. Yet the faith that is validated and vindicated is itself preceded by and comprehended within the overarching divine saving act that Paul calls "the redemption that is in Christ Jesus" (3:24). The divine righteousness consequent on faith has its prior "sign" (ἔνδειξις) in the blood of the crucified Christ (3:25, 26). While Paul does not say here what he says elsewhere, that faith itself is the creation of the divinely authorized "word" or gospel, rather than an autonomous production of human "free will" (cf. Rom. 1:1-6; 10:14-17), this view of faith's genesis is obviously presupposed. As the acknowledgment of the prior, comprehensive divine saving action in Jesus Christ, faith cannot be the self-grounded product of autonomous human agency.

Thus, the righteousness of God has to do with the divine validation of a faith-based identity as opposed to a law-based one. Käsemann's attempt to convert it into an apocalyptic victory over the world, only tenuously linked with faith, is an exegetical error. Paul's δικαιοσύνη θεοῦ usage is tightly bound up with the rest of his righteousness and faith terminology and is not to be explained as a preexisting formulation imported from elsewhere. An interpretation that severs the link between righteousness and faith will be plausible only to those who, on the basis of questionable dogmatic commitments, *cannot* accept the faith/justification sequence that Paul's language so plainly entails.

(2) *Prima facie,* it would seem that in Romans 3:21-31 a certain priority is accorded to the human act of faith in the event of justification. Theologians in the Lutheran tradition have tended to celebrate this exaltation of faith, whereas the Reformed have insisted that justification originates not in human faith but in the righteousness of Christ, which is "reckoned" or "imputed" to us.[39] (Both sides are agreed, however, that the human act of faith is

---

39. According to the Reformed, "[t]hose whom God effectually calleth he also freely justifieth; . . . [not] by imputing faith itself, the act of believing, or any other evangelical obedience to them, as their righteousness; but by imputing the obedience and satisfaction of Christ unto them, they receiving and resting on him and his righteousness by faith; which faith they have not of themselves, it is the gift of God" (*Westminster Confession* [1647], 11.1; P. Schaff, *Creeds of Christendom,* 3:626).

enabled by the Spirit through the Word.)[40] To some degree, this can be resolved into a dispute about whether the doctrine of justification is most adequately articulated in Romans 3:21-31 or 5:12-21, with their respective orientations towards faith and christology. Current interpretation of πίστις in the former passage as the "faith[fulness] of Christ" (vv. 22, 26) attempts to repristinate the old Reformed doctrine of the imputation of Christ's righteousness, boldly seeking to install this in the Lutheran heartland of Romans 3. Like Käsemann's account of the δικαιοσύνη θεοῦ, this "neo-Reformed" reading aims to extract fundamental Pauline concepts from their traditional entanglement with the present existence of "the believer" and to read the passage theocentrically rather than anthropocentrically. Indeed, the subjective genitive reading of Paul's πίστις Χριστοῦ terminology is usually grafted onto a Käsemann-derived interpretation of δικαιοσύνη θεοῦ as the divine "covenant-faithfulness."[41]

Paul's references to faith in Romans 3:21-31 all share the same instrumental form. The reason for this is simple: the passage is shaped by Paul's citation in 1:17 from Habakkuk 2:4, according to which "the one who is righteous by faith [ὁ δίκαιος ἐκ πίστεως] will live."[42] If references to faith share the same form and the same origin, it is difficult to argue that some refer to the faithfulness of Jesus, others to the faith of the contemporary believer. In the following attempt to trace the influence of the Habakkuk citation in Paul's discourse, underlining represents direct use of phraseology from the citation, and italics the use of synonymous terminology:

καθὼς γέγραπται, ὁ δὲ δίκαιος ἐκ πίστεως ζήσεται (Rom. 1:17b)

δικαιοσύνη γὰρ θεοῦ ἐν αὐτῷ ἀποκαλύπτεται ἐκ πίστεως εἰς πίστιν (1:17a)

δικαιοσύνη θεοῦ *διὰ* πίστεως Ἰησοῦ Χριστοῦ (3:22)

ὃν προέθετο ὁ θεὸς ἱλαστήριον *διὰ* τῆς πίστεως ἐν τῷ αὐτοῦ αἵματι (3:25)

---

40. According to the Augsburg Confession (1530), the Holy Spirit "worketh faith, where and when it pleaseth God, in those that hear the gospel" (art. V; Schaff, *Creeds of Christendom,* 3:10). In the French Reformed Confession of 1559, it is said: "We believe that we are enlightened in faith by the secret power of the Holy Spirit, that it is a gratuitous and special gift which God grants to whom he will" (P. Schaff, *Creeds of Christendom,* 3:371).

41. Thus, when Paul speaks of "the righteousness of God" as revealed "through faithfulness of Jesus Christ," he means that "the faithfulness of God to the promises long ago announced to Israel . . . is now revealed through the faithful Israelite, Jesus the Messiah" (N. T. Wright, *Romans,* 464).

42. See *PHF,* 71-77.

δικαίον καὶ δικαιοῦντα τὸν ἐκ πίστεως Ἰησοῦ (3:26)

λογιζόμεθα γὰρ δικαιοῦσθαι πίστει ἄνθρωπον (3:28)

ὃς δικαιώσει περιτομὴν ἐκ πίστεως καὶ ἀκροβυστίαν διὰ τῆς πίστεως (3:30)

νόμον καταργοῦμεν διὰ τῆς πίστεως; (3:31)

διὰ τοῦτο ἐκ πίστεως ἵνα κατὰ χάριν (4:16)

καὶ τῷ ἐκ πίστεως Ἀβρααμ (4:16)

δικαιωθέντες οὖν ἐκ πίστεως (5:1)

δικαιοσύνην δὲ τὴν ἐκ πίστεως (9:30)

ἡ δὲ ἐκ πίστεως δικαιοσύνη οὕτως λέγει (10:6)

Here, it is the prophetic reference to ὁ δίκαιος ἐκ πίστεως that generates (1) a series of formulations in which ἐκ πίστεως is retained while ὁ δίκαιος is replaced by δικαιοσύνη (3:22; 9:30; 10:6) or δικαιοῦν (3:26, 30; 5:1); (2) formulations in which ἐκ πίστεως is replaced by the synonymous expressions διὰ [τῆς] πίστεως (3:22, 25, 30, 31) or πίστει (3:28); (3) formulations in which ἐκ πίστεως is retained but δικ- terminology is absent (4:16, × 2).[43]

This analysis demonstrates that Paul's πίστις formulations in this passage are of a piece. The prophetic ἐκ πίστεως may be retained or it may be modified (διὰ [τῆς] πίστεως, πίστει) and/or expanded (διὰ πίστεως Ἰησοῦ Χριστοῦ, ἐκ πίστεως Ἰησοῦ); but *there is no reason to suppose that any significant semantic shift occurs within these variant formulations.*[44] If Paul's usage is consistent, either all of these passages refer to Jesus' own faith, or none of them do. The first option is not impossible, especially if one can find a reference to Jesus' faith in the Habakkuk citation itself. If for Paul it is Jesus who is ὁ δίκαιος ἐκ πίστεως, then *all* of the formulations shaped by this citation would similarly refer to the faith of Jesus. In 3:28-30, it would be said that a person is justified by Jesus' faith, without works of law, and that by Jesus' faith God will justify circumcised and uncircumcised alike.[45] But that would seem to allow the two unemphasized πίστις Χριστοῦ passages (3:22, 26) too much

43. As Schweitzer notes, it is scripture (Hab. 2:4; Gen. 15:6) that compels Paul to "formulate the doctrine of righteousness through being-in-Christ as the doctrine of righteousness by faith" (*The Mysticism of Paul the Apostle*, 208-9).

44. So rightly D. Campbell, "The Meaning of ΠΙΣΤΙΣ and ΝΟΜΟΣ in Paul," 93-96.

45. So S. Stowers, *A Rereading of Romans*, 240-41.

weight in the interpretation of the other Habakkuk-inspired formulations, occurring not just in Romans 3 but also in chapters 1, 4, 9, and 10. It is more plausible to suppose that the ten or so πίστις passages that lack a reference to Christ should determine the sense of the two passages that include one.[46]

Yet the main difficulty — the Achilles' heel — of the subjective genitive reading lies in the verb πιστεύειν, which occurs here in the phrase εἰς πάντας τοὺς πιστεύοντας (3:22; cf. παντὶ τῷ πιστεύοντι in 1:16). In 3:21-31, this is the verb's only occurrence, whereas the noun occurs eight times — under the influence, as we have seen, of Habakkuk. In general, Paul has a preference for the noun over the verb: figures for the letter as a whole are twenty-one times for πιστεύειν, thirty-seven times for πίστις.[47] The verb appears *not* to refer to the faithfulness of Christ, and advocates of the christological reading therefore argue for a semantic distinction between πιστεύειν and πίστις in Pauline usage, translating the verb as "believe" or "trust" and the noun as "faithfulness."[48] Yet the reason for the distinction is to be found in scripture rather than semantics. Paul's own use of the verb increases sharply where it is employed in his scriptural citations. πίστις occurs ten times in 4:1-25 and five times in 9:30–10:21, but the citation in 4:3 of Genesis 15:6 results in five further occurrences of the verb,[49] and the citation in 9:33 of Isaiah 28:16 produces a further six.[50] Use of the verb can be explained by reference to the scriptural citations in fourteen of its twenty-one occurrences,[51] use of the noun in all occurrences of ἐκ πίστεως (× 12) and in five or six instances of synonymous expressions[52] — thus, in seventeen of the thirty-seven occurrences in the letter. In spite of Paul's evident

46. A mediating position is possible. In v. 28, the faith that justifies is *both* the faith of ἄνθρωπος *and* "the faith of Christ," *whatever* that is taken to mean (cf. vv. 22, 25). *If* the latter refers to Jesus' own faith[fulness], then v. 28 and all other references to faith in this passage would refer to our *participation* in Jesus' faith — and thus to *our* participation in Jesus' faith, a faith that is *ours* but whose conformity to Jesus' faith can on occasion be signaled. One might then conclude that Jesus' faith belongs to the *substructure* of Paul's faith discourse in 3:27–4:25, and so circumvent the objection that it is absent from the surface of the text (cf. J. D. G. Dunn, "Once More ΠΙΣΤΙΣ ΧΡΙΣΤΟΥ," 75-76). The effect, however, would be to make this motif much less important than its adherents wish it to be.

47. Or thirty-eight if the textual variant in Romans 5:2 is included.

48. See D. Campbell, *The Quest for Paul's Gospel*, 182-88. According to Campbell, "the notion 'faithfulness', conveyed frequently in Paul by the substantive *pistis*, does not overlap significantly with the cognate verb" (187-88).

49. Rom. 4:5, 11, 17, 18, 24.

50. Rom. 10:4, 9, 10, 11, 14 (× 2). This includes a "re-citation" in 10:11.

51. That is, in the citations of Genesis 15:6, Isaiah 28:16, and Isaiah 53:1 (Rom. 10:16), and in the passages listed in the two previous notes.

52. Rom. 3:22, 25, 28, 30, 31; 5:2 (?). I have argued above that these are variants on Habakkuk's ἐκ πίστεως.

bias towards πίστις, his use of verb or noun can be explained on the basis of scriptural usage *in over half of their occurrences* (31 out of 58). If Paul's usage is shaped in large part by his citations, then the argument for a *semantic* differentiation between noun and verb is significantly weakened.

In addition to his single "faith" citation (Hab. 2:4), Paul has three citations in Romans that include the verb "believe" (Gen. 15:6; Isa. 28:16; 53:1). If the first two of these generate a number of references to "believing," all three of them also generate references to "faith." The occurrence of πιστεύειν in the citation is regularly followed by an occurrence of πίστις in Paul's interpretative comments:

(i) "Abraham *believed* [ἐπίστευσεν] and it was reckoned to him as righteousness": in other words, he "*believed* in the one who justifies the ungodly," and "his *faith* [ἡ πίστις αὐτοῦ] was reckoned as righteousness" (Rom. 4:3, 5). When he received circumcision as a sign or seal of "the righteousness of *faith*," he became "the father of all who *believe* while uncircumcised, so that righteousness might be reckoned to them, and the father of circumcision to those . . . who also walk in the steps of the *faith* of our father Abraham while uncircumcised" (4:11-12). In commenting on the scriptural usage of the verb, Paul can use either the verb or the noun. Verb and noun are simply interchangeable. An interpretation that differentiated between the senses of verb and noun, taking the one to refer to an act of belief or trust and the other to the disposition of faithfulness, would make this passage incomprehensible. Yet precisely such a distinction between verb and noun is integral to the argument for "the faithfulness of Christ" in 3:22, 26.

(ii) "Behold, I lay in Zion a stone of stumbling and a rock of offence, and the one who *believes* in him [ὁ πιστεύων ἐπ' αὐτῷ] shall not be ashamed" (Isa. 28:16 [+ 8:14]; Rom. 9:33). For Paul, those who "stumbled over the stone of stumbling" did so because they proceeded "not by *faith* but by works" (9:32). The second half of the citation is repeated in 10:11, so that 10:1-10 is as it were bracketed by the Isaianic text, which provides scriptural warrant for Paul's use of both the verb (10:4, 9, 10) and the noun (10:6, 8). Here, too, the attempt to assign different senses to the verb and to the noun would present a challenge even to the most determined of exegetes. There is "righteousness for everyone who *believes*," and the outcome is "the righteousness of *faith*" (10:4, 6). The appropriate response to "the word of *faith* that we proclaim" is to "*believe* in your heart that God raised [Jesus] from the dead" (10:8, 9).

(iii) ". . . Isaiah says: 'Lord, who *believed* our message [ἐπίστευσεν τῇ ἀκοῇ]?' Therefore *faith* is from the message [ἡ πίστις ἐξ ἀκοῆς], and the message is through the word of Christ" (Rom. 10:16-17; citing Isa. 53:1). The verb occurs in the citation but is replaced by the noun in the Pauline gloss. Thus, both the act of "believing" and the response of "faith" are elicited by the message, and these are one and the same. The terse claim that "faith is from the message" represents a semantic rule that should be applied to the vast majority of Paul's uses of πίστις and πιστεύειν. For Paul, "faith" is elicited by the gospel, as it is spoken and heard, and thus answers the God who speaks in and through the gospel. It is the human answer intended in the divine communicative action. It represents not just "an interior, individual, and mental activity"[53] but an event of personal interaction within the social world — which, as a *personal* interaction, naturally *includes* interior, individual, and mental activity even though it cannot be reduced to that. The prophetic message seeks credence, acceptance, belief, and whatever else that will entail; and, analogously, the Pauline gospel seeks "faith." No doubt this faith will entail faithfulness, as it will also entail endurance and patience, hope and love: but these entailments do not make "faithfulness" an appropriate *translation* of πίστις.

The current consensus that πίστις Χριστοῦ formulations refer to Christ's own faithfulness appears to be based on an exegetical error, reinforced by tenaciously held yet questionable theological convictions.[54] While it is entirely possible for cognate verbs and nouns to drift apart semantically, the evidence of Paul's scriptural interpretations shows that this is clearly not the case here.[55] That does not mean that the "faith of Christ" passages refer specifi-

53. Douglas Campbell, *The Quest for Paul's Gospel*, 190, arguing that the word "faith" should be used with caution, if not avoided altogether.

54. In the interests both of exegetical and theological integrity, I find myself in broad agreement here with Barry Matlock's plea for a "detheologizing" here: see his "Detheologizing the ΠΙΣΤΙΣ ΧΡΙΣΤΟΥ Debate," and his forthcoming monograph. In general, I consider that a certain theological disinvestment from Romans 3–4 would be salutary, since it seems unlikely that the heart of the Pauline gospel is to be found in a section where explicit christological affirmations are consistently subordinated to scriptural interpretation.

55. In Romans 3:22, evidence for a distinction between noun and verb has been seen in the "needless redundancy" that would ensue if the phrase διὰ πίστεως Ἰησοῦ Χριστοῦ εἰς πάντας τοὺς πιστεύοντας refers twice to "the same type of faith" (so D. Campbell, *Rhetoric of Righteousness*, 62; also R. Hays, *Faith of Jesus Christ*, 158; L. T. Johnson, "Rom 3:21-26 and the Faith of Jesus," 79; N. T. Wright, *Romans*, 470). According to Campbell, the "oscillation between prosaic brevity and verbose repetition in the same section is an embarrassment for an objective genitive

cally to "faith *in* Christ," as though by default. The genitive Ἰησοῦ [Χριστοῦ] functions almost adjectivally, to delimit the scope of πίστις, but leaves the relationship between "faith" and "Jesus [Christ]" relatively undefined. From the wider context, we might conclude that "faith" is related to "Christ" in the sense that faith has its context in "the redemption which is in Christ Jesus" (3:24), its basis in Christ's sacrificial death (3:25), and its object in the God who raised Christ from the dead (4:24). But the πίστις Χριστοῦ phraseology in itself refers simply to the faith that pertains to Christ, without further specifying the nature of that pertinence.

If, in Romans 3:21-31, δικαιοσύνη θεοῦ refers to the divine validation and vindication of those who have faith, and if the πίστις Χριστοῦ formulations identify that faith by connecting it non-specifically to Christ, then the primary concern of this passage is precisely with "faith." As presented by Paul, the divine act of justification follows the human act of faith, but both the human and the divine acts are moments within the comprehensive divine saving action that Paul here calls "redemption" (ἀπολύτρωσις). The emphasis on "faith" indicates that for Paul the divine saving action would be incomplete if it failed to secure human participation, in the form of its own acknowledgment and the communal and individual life based on that acknowledgment. It cannot plausibly be argued that anything other than the subjective genitive readings of δικαιοσύνη θεοῦ and πίστις Χριστοῦ will necessarily lead to theological disaster.[56]

This "faith," which has brought the Roman Christians into the sphere of the divine redemptive action, has a social embodiment. When Paul gives thanks to God that "your faith is proclaimed throughout the world" (1:8), he has in mind not a private occurrence within the heart of individuals but the public, visible, and social reality of a community distinguished by its "faith" from the rest of the population of Rome. Here and elsewhere in Romans,

---

reading" (62-63). Yet Campbell himself finds clear evidence of rhetorically motivated redundancy especially in the repetition of ἔνδειξις τῆς δικαιοσύνης αὐτοῦ in vv. 25-26 (95-101). If Paul can say the same thing twice in vv. 25-26, why is it an "embarrassment" to find him doing so, much more succinctly, a few lines earlier? Here at least, "the argument for the subjective reading is so weak as to qualify as one of the 'emperor has no clothes' variety" (P. Esler, *Conflict and Identity*, 157).

56. This familiar allegation is repeated uncritically by Douglas Harink, *Paul among the Postliberals* (28), a work in which exegetical decisions are constantly made on the basis of theological preferences. Harink proceeds to criticize the modern substitution of "faith" as such for "faith in Jesus Christ," in the interests of "a phenomenology of the believing subject" (29), but fails to note that a reference to Jesus Christ as ground or object of faith serves to *resist* any such anthropological reduction.

"faith" is employed in such a way as to encapsulate an entire form of communal life in a single word. The same is true of the term "law." The faith/law antithesis therefore has its social correlate in the forms of life characteristic of the Roman synagogues and of the Roman Christian communities, and it has the force not only of an indicative but also of an imperative. The existence of a community of faith is at present impaired by a disagreement about whether and in what sense it should *also* strive to be a community of the law. In *this* context, and from Paul's perspective, it is the law that creates the division and faith that points to its resolution on the basis that "there is no distinction . . . ," since "the righteousness of God" is "for *all* who believe," and since "*all* have sinned" (3:22-23).[57] From the opposite perspective, of course, it is Pauline law-free "faith" that creates the division and the law of Moses that offers the only possible basis for unity. Either way, the indicatives of Romans 3 are to be read together with the imperatives of Romans 14–15.

3. Secondary Comparisons (Romans 3:27-31)

The effect of this analysis is, once again, to stress the irreducible particularity of both terms of the faith/law antithesis. In an important sense, they are simply incommensurable. They cannot straightforwardly be placed at opposite ends of the same spectrum, with salvation ascribed maximally to divine agency at one end and to human agency at the other. Faith and law cannot be reduced to a common denominator any more than Christ and Moses can. Yet incommensurability does not rule out all possibility of comparisons or contrasts. Such comparisons will not exhaustively define the two communities, which are in the end simply different, but they will at least serve to highlight certain aspects of that difference. In Romans 3:27-31, three such comparisons are ventured:

(1) A comparison relating to *communal self-image:* "boasting" is possible within the sphere of the law but not within the sphere of faith (3:27-28; cf. 4:1-5).

---

57. On a rigorously theocentric reading, vv. 22d-24a has to be regarded as a parenthesis, since this is "the only place in the whole paragraph where the emphasis is on the import of God's rectitude for Gentiles and Jews," as opposed to "the rectifying character of God's rectitude in the event of Jesus Christ" (L. E. Keck, *Romans,* 106, 103, following the analysis of Campbell, *Rhetoric of Righteousness,* 86-95). Campbell's parenthesis requires a sharp break in v. 24 between δικαιούμενοι δωρεὰν τῇ αὐτοῦ χάριτι and διὰ τῆς ἀπολυτρώσεως τῆς ἐν Χριστῷ Ἰησοῦ — a "previously unnoticed point of syntactical transition" that makes it possible to base the analysis of vv. 22-25b on three successive διά clauses in vv. 22, 24, and 25 (*Rhetoric of Righteousness,* 94).

(2) A comparison relating to the *ethnic composition* of the two communities: in one, God is the God of the Jews, in the other of Jews and Gentiles (3:29-30).

(3) A comparison relating to a *shared scripture:* in spite of the faith/law antithesis, it is not the case that the law of Moses is disregarded or disparaged within the community of faith (3:31).

In the first comparison, issues of divine and human agency do ultimately come to the fore. Yet they do not *constitute* the difference between the communities of faith and of the law. If the community of the law found some way to exclude boasting — for example, by attributing all human acts of obedience to divine grace, as, arguably, in certain of the Qumran texts — that would bring it no closer to the community of faith. Nor would the communal divide be diminished in any way if the Roman synagogues adopted a liberal attitude towards Gentiles. Even if all such reforms and revisions were to be implemented, one community would still be oriented towards Moses, the other towards Christ: and, for Paul, *that* difference is nonnegotiable. And yet (to repeat), comparisons of a limited kind can still be made; and Paul proceeds to make them. In retracing his argument, it will be important to bear in mind the emerging distinction between the original, nonnegotiable difference signified by the names of Christ and Moses and the secondary comparisons. Where the comparisons are seen as original rather than secondary, exegetical confusion is inevitable.

(1) Romans 3:27 may be regarded as the *locus classicus* of the modern Lutheran interpretation of Paul, for which Käsemann may again serve as spokesman. According to Paul, it is characteristic of faith (or, as he puts it, "the law of faith") but not of works ("the law of works") that "boasting" is "excluded." For Käsemann, the polemical emphasis here is essential rather than merely incidental:

> It is the inalienable spearhead of justification, because it attacks the religious person and only in so doing preserves the sense of the justification of the ungodly. . . . Faith and self-boasting are incompatible, for the believer no longer lives out of or for himself. The eschatological end of the world proclaims itself anthropologically as the end of one's own ways of salvation, whereas the law throws a person back upon himself and thus into the existing world of anxiety, self-confidence, and unbroken self-assurance. To the extent that this finds expression in self-glorying it is the mark and power of the world which, even in its religiousness, does not be-

lieve. Faith puts an end to boasting, also among Gentiles according to 1 Cor 1:29.[58]

Once again, the faith/works antithesis is interpreted here in the familiar universalizing manner, as a conflict between the religious person's pursuit of achievement and the true believer's renunciation of achievement. Judaism itself has all but disappeared, and a still more specific reference to the Roman synagogues is inconceivable. Yet in spite of this, Käsemann's claim that "faith puts an end to boasting" is indeed what the text says. The question in the text is: "Where then is boasting?" It is not: "Where then is *our* boasting?" The latter question would refer exclusively to Jewish boasting, the former to a boasting-in-general of which Jewish boasting is a specific instance. In one community "boasting" can occur; in the other it is excluded. On this occasion, we must seek in the Judaism Paul here opposes the particular form of a general phenomenon. It is a specifically Jewish boasting that occasions the exclusion of boasting, but it is boasting-in-general that faith excludes.[59]

Käsemann's reference to 1 Corinthians 1:29 is entirely apposite. There, God's choice of the ignorant rather than the wise, the weak rather than the powerful, the low-born rather than the high-born is motivated by the concern that "no flesh might boast before God," which is itself the negative corollary of the citation that follows: "as it is written, 'Let the one who boasts boast in the Lord'" (1 Cor. 1:31). The citation is actually a summary of a lengthier statement from Jeremiah 9:22-23 that has also shaped the preceding antithetical statements. Here, underlining represents the citation, and italics the additional phraseology taken over by Paul:

Τάδε λέγει κυρίος *Μὴ καυχάσθω ὁ σόφος* ἐν τῇ σοφίᾳ αὐτοῦ καὶ *μὴ καυχάσθω ὁ ἰσχυρὸς ἐν τῇ ἰσχύι αὐτοῦ καὶ μὴ καυχάσθω ὁ πλούσιος ἐν τῷ πλούτῳ αὐτοῦ, ἀλλ'* ἢ ἐν τούτῳ <u>καυχάσθω ὁ καυχώμενος</u>, συνίειν καὶ γινώσκειν ὅτι ἐγώ εἰμι <u>κύριος</u> . . . (Jer. 9:22-23)

<u>ὁ</u> [δὲ] <u>καυχώμενος</u> ἐν <u>κυρίῳ καυχάσθω</u> (1 Cor. 1:31; 2 Cor. 11:17)

The citation adjusts word order and syntax for the sake of a more succinct statement. The negative imperatives (μὴ καυχάσθω, × 3) underlie Paul's "so that all flesh might not boast [μὴ καυχήσηται] before God" (1 Cor. 1:29). And

---

58. Käsemann, *Romans*, 102.

59. The translation issue is rightly noted by L. E. Keck, who contrasts NJB's "So what becomes of our boasts?" with REB's "What room then is left for human pride?" (*Romans*, 114-15). Keck himself prefers the particularizing reading.

the wise/strong/rich sequence similarly underlies Paul's reference to the divine rejection of the wise, the strong, and the "things that are" (1:27-28; cf. v. 26). In rewriting this passage, Paul retains the concluding imperative but converts the negative imperatives into antithetical affirmations about the divine election, which favors the ignorant over the wise, the weak over the strong, the nonentities over the things that are. Wisdom, power, and wealth represent claims to status, and Paul learns from Jeremiah that such claims are radically excluded by the God of the gospel.

Having drawn this exclusion-of-boasting motif from Jeremiah, Paul finds it to be applicable in a number of different contexts, and not just in connection with the divine election. When in 1 Corinthians 3:21 Paul instructs his readers not to boast in human authorities, he again echoes the language of Jeremiah (ὥστε μηδεὶς καυχάσθω ἐν ἀνθρώποις). Here, too, boasting represents a claim to status: for to announce one's allegiance to Paul, Apollos, or Cephas is to seek a share in the status accorded to these figures within the Christian community (cf. 1:12; 3:22). Closely associated with this is a claim based on one's spiritual endowments, which Paul seeks to nullify by asking:

> Who sees anything different in you? What do you have that you did not receive? And if you received, why do you boast [τί καυχᾶσαι] as though you did not receive? Already you are filled, already you are enriched, without us you reign! (1 Cor. 4:7-8)

In this occurrence of the boasting motif, Paul opposes an appeal not so much to status as to achievement: for the threefold emphasis on "receiving" as incompatible with "boasting" implies that the excluded boasting here has to do with one's own performance. The performance or achievement in question is no doubt the exercise of the *charismata*. While status and achievement are closely related and may serve to reinforce one another, they may nevertheless be distinguished. Paul could not properly put the question, "Why do you boast, as though you did not receive?" to the Jew of Romans 2, who boasts in God and in the law (vv. 17, 23). This individual boasts precisely of what he has received, basing on this a claim more to status than to achievement. A claim based on the one will often imply a corresponding claim based on the other: achievement confirms and enhances status, and status presupposes a corresponding performance. Yet the emphasis may fall on status in some contexts, performance in others. Indeed, in Philippians 3:4-6 Paul appeals to both status and performance, and to the one as corresponding to the other.[60]

60. This is rightly noted by J. D. G. Dunn in his study of Philippians 3 in *The New Perspective on Paul*, 463-83. In the case of Paul's "confidence" in his ethnic identity and tribal affiliation,

In 1 Corinthians 4:7-8 as in 3:21, Jeremiah's exhortation not to boast in anything or anyone other than the Lord remains perceptible. Its positive corollary — the exhortation to boast *only* in the Lord — returns in the repetition of the abbreviated Jeremiah citation in 2 Corinthians 10:17. The critique of boasting is now directed against the Corinthian super-apostles, who "boast according to the flesh" (11:18), not least about work actually carried out by others, i.e., by Paul himself. The reference to the opponents' "boasting in the labors of others" (10:15) again indicates that boasting may relate to achievement and not only to status. Status and achievement are, however, both in play when Paul begins to indulge in some competitive boasting of his own:

> But whatever anyone dares to boast of [τολμᾷ] . . . I too dare to boast of that [τολμῶ κἀγώ]. Are they Israelites? So am I. Are they descendants of Abraham? So am I. Are they Hebrews? So am I. Are they servants of Christ? I speak foolishly: I am a better one, with far greater labors, far more imprisonments, with countless beatings. . . . (2 Cor. 11:21b-23)

Here the shift is particularly clear from status (being an Israelite, a descendant of Abraham, a Hebrew) to achievement (work and suffering endured for Christ). The term "achievement" denotes an action as such together with the claim that it be recognized as praiseworthy or meritorious; and it is precisely this combination that is implied in this passage — subject, of course, to the qualification that "I speak as a fool" (11:21; cf. 11:16, 17; 12:11). In some passages if not others, the concept of achievement is integral to Paul's use of the scriptural boasting motif.[61]

Thus, throughout the opening chapters of the first Corinthian letter and the closing chapters of the second, "boasting . . . is excluded" (Rom. 3:27). To boast is to lay claim to a status based on education, wealth, social status, allegiance to a prestigious figure, spiritual endowment, or membership of the covenant people. It is also to claim notable achievements in the exercise of the *charismata* or in heroic apostolic labors and sufferings. Such claims are excluded not because the status or achievement is necessarily unreal but because claims based on status and achievement are inappropriate *as such*.

---

it is a matter of "*something given him* with his birth, not something achieved or merited by him" (469; italics original). In the other items listed by Paul, however, a "transition from items of ethnic identity becomes steadily more marked" (470). Thus in the references in v. 6 to zeal and righteousness, "[t]here is at least an element of self-achievement and of pride in self-achievement" (474). Dunn here retracts a statement to the contrary in his *Theology of Paul*, 370.

61. While Paul uses the boasting motif in a variety of contexts, that does not mean that "[b]oasting is the attitude of the natural man, who seeks to establish his position independently of God" (C. K. Barrett, *Romans*, 82). For Paul, boasting is simply a common phenomenon; it is not an anthropological constant.

Whatever the basis of the particular claim, it is ruled out on principle. And it is both the general principle and a further particular claim to status or achievement that confront one another when Paul asks, "Where then is boasting?" and answers: "It is excluded."[62]

The question and answer of Romans 3:27a relate to the general principle, but they must have a specific instance of boasting in mind. In the wider context, "boasting" must incorporate a distinctively Jewish claim to status, according to which to be Jewish and circumcised is to be within the sphere of salvation (cf. vv. 1-3). Also characteristic is a strong sense of the distinction between the righteous Jew and the unrighteous Gentile (cf. v. 9), so that the "boasting" of the one is at the expense of the other. This relational element in boasting is clearly evident in 11:18, where, in yet another application of the exclusion-of-boasting motif, the Gentile Christian is warned not to "boast over the branches" excised from the olive tree of God's people. Likewise in 2:17-20, calling oneself a Jew and boasting in God entails the blindness and folly of others. It would, however, be a mistake to identify this "boasting in God" or "boasting in the law" (2:17, 23) too closely with the excluded boasting of 3:27. As the Jeremiah text indicates, boasting in God is in itself entirely appropriate; Paul himself will later speak of our "boasting in God through our Lord Jesus Christ" (5:11; cf. v. 3). The boasting of Romans 2 is not in itself subject to the Pauline exclusion order, for the critique is there directed against the disparity between self-image and actual practice. It is crucially important to read the statements of Romans 3:27-28 on their own terms, without importing into them a quite different conceptuality derived from the previous chapter.[63]

Boasting is excluded on the basis not of a "law of works" but of a "law of faith" (v. 27), and this law of faith is specified in the statement that follows: "We consider that a person is justified by faith apart from works of law"

---

62. There is, however, a legitimate boasting towards God in Christ Jesus about what Christ has achieved through Paul himself (Rom. 15:17-18; cf. 1 Cor. 15:10). It seems that an appeal to Christ can make boasting acceptable.

63. As J. D. G. Dunn does, claiming that "[t]he allusion to 2:17, 23 is indisputable" (*Romans*, 1:185). Dunn continues: "Paul attacks the self-confidence of the Jew as Jew, the boasting in God as Israel's God, the pride in the law as indicating God's commitment to his people and so marking them off from other nations" (185). For Dunn, the emphasis lies on a boasting in "status" rather than "achievement." A better balance is evident in Brendan Byrne's claim (based again on the combination of Rom. 2:17, 23; 3:27) that boasting "refers to a presumption of superiority and privileged position before God based upon possession of the law and faithful fulfillment of its commands" (*Romans*, 136). Even this statement tends to elide two very different passages. In contrast, J. Fitzmyer's comment on 3:27 is unaffected by "new perspective" sensitivities: according to his paraphrase, "Self-confidence and boasting of one's achievements have no place in the new aeon, in the dispensation of divine grace and of faith" (*Romans*, 362).

(v. 28).[64] The references to the law of works or works of law clearly indicate the *source* of the particular boast that underlies the exclusion of boasting-in-general. The two expressions are closely related, as Keck notes: "[I]f 'the works of the law' are deeds prescribed by the law, 'the law of works' is the law that prescribes the deeds." Furthermore,

> Paul claims that the law that prescribes the deeds is not the means by which boasting is excluded, because that law cannot exclude boasting in Jewish identity and privilege, which is based on that same law.[65]

In other words, the law in question not only fails to exclude boasting; it actively promotes it. Yet Keck's reference to "boasting in Jewish identity and privilege" is not quite right in this context. It reflects the contemporary anxiety to avoid the term "achievement," which, however inappropriate elsewhere, is exactly right here, where the talk is not of identity or privilege but of works or deeds. As we have seen, Paul's use of the boasting motif can emphasize status or achievement or both, and in Romans 3:27-28 it is primarily achievement that is in view: that is, the combination of a specific action with the claim that the action be acknowledged as meritorious and its agent as praiseworthy. "Status" (being a Jew, being circumcised) is presupposed, confirmed, and enhanced by "achievement" (law observance), but in this passage nothing is explicitly said about status.[66]

Paul envisages Roman Jewish Christians as "boasting" in their law observance, as other Jews do, regarding it as inherently praiseworthy and as a mark of superiority over Gentiles, Christian or otherwise. It is true that Paul's language is general and non-specific; there is nothing to identify the questions Paul anticipates in 3:27–4:1 as emanating specifically from a Jewish *Christian* source.

---

64. On this interpretation, the term "law" refers to the Torah in the (implied) phrase "law of works" but not in "law of faith," which refers simply to 3:28 (so Keck, *Romans*, 116). This seems preferable to the suggestions either that νόμος in 3:27 means "principle" (Fitzmyer, *Romans*, 363), or that the law of works and the law of faith refer to the Torah from different perspectives (Dunn, *Romans*, 1:185).

65. Keck, *Romans*, 115-16.

66. Simon Gathercole finds in 3:27 a critique of the "confidence that God would vindicate Israel on the basis of both election and obedience, and that he would vindicate them both before and over against the Gentiles" (*Where Is Boasting?* 226; originally italicized). The rationale for "both election and obedience" is presumably that the same law of Moses is *both* the charter of Israel's election *and* the divine call to obedience. In the gift of the Torah, Israel is elected to be obedient: that is presumably why Paul can mention just one item ("works of law") rather than two ("election and obedience"). I am not convinced, however, that "boasting" should be understood in terms of confidence in eschatological vindication.

Yet, in the light of chapters 14–15, it is clearly a "boast" arising from the practice of the law that establishes the barrier between the two sections of the Roman Christian community. Boasting is implicit in the judgment that the law-observant pass on the non-law-observant (cf. 14:3, 10), just as it is implicit in the corresponding attitude of the latter to the former (cf. 11:17-18). Here as elsewhere in this letter, Paul's generalizing language masks a particular local application. According to his "law of faith," Roman Christians should see in themselves and in one another not just Jews or Gentiles but the "person" (ἄνθρωπος) who is justified by faith, without works of the law (3:28). That is the *social* reorientation for which Paul here calls. As he has argued in 3:21-24, faith entails the abolition of the soteriological distinction between Jews and Gentiles. "There is no difference [διαστολή]," for Jews and Gentiles are at one both in their guilt before God (v. 23) and as recipients of God's grace in Christ (v. 24). If justification is "by faith apart from works of law" (v. 28), then Jew and Gentile may be at one, whereas "works of law" separate them by enabling one to boast at the expense of the other. If Paul's Jewish Christian readers accept the νόμος πίστεως, they will abandon their "boasting" — that is, their claim to superiority on the basis of the law observance that corresponds to their status as Jews. And they will finalize their ideological separation from the majority Jewish community and unite themselves with the Pauline Gentile Christians on the ground of a common faith (cf. 15:7-13).

Thus, a particular claim to praiseworthy achievement is characteristic of the community of the law, whereas all such claims are excluded in principle in the community of faith. While there is ultimately an incommensurable difference between the two communities, certain limited and secondary comparisons can usefully be made; and contrasting attitudes towards "boasting" represent one such comparison. Were the community of the law to exclude every conceivable form of boasting from its midst, it would be no closer to the community of faith, for the faith in question is characterized by its orientation towards Jesus (cf. 3:26). Yet the comparison remains valid. While it cannot be *reduced* to a contrast between divine and human agencies, it makes a difference whether the divine/human relationship is construed as enabling or as excluding the self-affirmation of Jews, Gentiles, and indeed Christians. In the case of the (Pauline) Jews, such self-affirmation appeals not just to Jewish privileges but also and above all to the practice of "the law of works," or "works of law" (3:27, 28). It is the self-affirmation that instantiates a more general phenomenon, and not the practice itself. It is Jews alone who observe the law, but it is not only Jews who boast.

(2) In 3:28, it is ἄνθρωπος who is said to be the object of the divine justifying action. The reference is not to an individual, for in vv. 29-30 Paul speaks of

God's action as directed towards Jews and Gentiles, circumcised and uncircumcised.[67] Far from representing the individual, ἄνθρωπος is the *genus* of which Jews and Gentiles are the main *species:*

> Or is God the God of Jews only, and not of Gentiles also? Yes, of Gentiles also; for God is one, and will justify the circumcised by faith and the uncircumcised through faith.

This passage demonstrates the scope of the assertion of v. 28 that "a person is justified by faith apart from works of law." The preceding reference to "works of law" leads directly to the question whether God is the God of Jews alone, which would make membership of the elected, law-observant community a *sine qua non* for salvation.[68] Similarly, the preceding reference to "faith" leads to the claim that the soteriological distinction between Jews and Gentiles is abolished, a claim presented here as a corollary of the oneness of God. Read in the light of chapters 14–15 of this letter, the imperative concealed within this indicative statement is again clear. Roman Jewish and Gentile Christians should find a basis for unity in their common faith and should not allow issues relating to the practice of the law to divide them. Ideological separation from the synagogue will further the formation of a distinctive Christian identity based on faith.

Paul's statements imply a further comparison between two communities, to add to the preceding comparison relating to "boasting." The fundamental difference between the communities is simply that one sees itself as entrusted with the law of Moses and obligated to practice it, whereas the other seeks to live in the light of the "faith" evoked by the gospel of Christ. It is the primary function of Pauline antithesis to assert and enforce the incommensurability between the two communities. Yet, on the secondary level, comparisons may be ventured. The community of the law promotes a form of "boasting" in achievement, which is excluded on principle in the community of faith. The community of the law understands God as "the God of the Jews" — that is, as "our God," the God of the covenant. In contrast, the community of faith believes that the one God can only be the God of all humanity without distinction. Once again, it is important to note that this distinction does not exhaust the differences between the communities. The community of the law might

---

67. So Bultmann, *Theology,* 1:231; G. Klein, "Römer 4," 171n.

68. While vv. 29-30 and vv. 27-28 are closely connected, that does not mean that "the point of 3.27-30 is . . . the inclusion of Gentiles in the people of God" (H. Räisänen, *Paul and the Law,* 171; italics removed). Pauline antithesis speaks of more than just the scope of the two opposed terms.

develop its own forms of universalism — but the incommensurable orientations towards law or faith, Moses or Christ, would remain.

According to J. D. G. Dunn, however, the opposite is the case. In Dunn's
interpretation of Paul's faith/law antithesis, christology is of secondary importance, and it is the universality/exclusiveness contrast that is fundamental
to the difference between the two communities — or rather, the two competing views of the same community.[69] Commenting on vv. 29-30, Dunn writes:

> The logic of Paul's train of thought . . . is that God looks for one basic atti-
> tude and relationship with all humankind — viz., faith. In the light of 1:18ff
> faith must be another word for that responsive dependence on God as Cre-
> ator which man has failed to give; and this indeed is how Paul goes on to
> define it in 4:18-21. . . . [Faith] can also be described as faith in Jesus, be-
> cause his death both confirms that God is Redeemer as well as Creator and
> opens the scope of that redemption beyond Israel "according to the flesh."
> But here it is described simply as "faith" since it is the basic trust-reliance
> of creature on the only Creator which is in view.[70]

On this account, faith is defined as dependence on the Creator, and its
christological reference is secondary. Justification is by faith and not by works
of law because the latter serve to "mark the boundary between Jew and Gentile,"[71] reinforcing Jewish privilege at the expense of Gentiles. Faith, however,
is the abolition of that boundary, a movement *back* to a more original and
primal relationship between creature and Creator. Paul, then, addresses (non-
Christian) Jews on their own terrain and seeks to persuade them that their
own belief in the divine oneness should entail an inclusive attitude towards
Gentiles and is incompatible with their exclusionary emphasis on specifically
Jewish features of the law. *Paul's fundamental concern can thus be stated without reference to christology.* Rejecting Sanders's emphasis on the christological
orientation of the Pauline faith/law antithesis, Dunn argues that

> what Paul was concerned about was the fact that covenant promise and law
> had become too inextricably identified with ethnic Israel as such, with the
> Jewish people marked out in their national distinctiveness by the practices
> of circumcision, food laws, and sabbath in particular. . . . [W]hat Paul was
> endeavoring to do was to free both promise and law for a wider range of re-
> cipients, freed from the ethnic constraints which he saw to be narrowing

---

69. For an earlier critique of Dunn on this point, see my "The Triune Divinity Identity."
70. Dunn, *Romans*, 1:189.
71. Dunn, *Romans*, 1:188.

the grace of God and diverting the saving purpose of God out of its main channel — Christ.[72]

The concluding reference to Christ is left unexplained. According to Dunn, Paul advocates a liberal, inclusive, universalizing understanding of "promise and law" and attacks the conservative, exclusive, ethnocentric outlook that he sees among his contemporaries. It is not clear why, in this context, Paul needs Christ, and why a recovery of the universal relationship of the creature to the Creator would not fully meet his concerns. Is Christ simply an empty symbol for universalistic monotheism?[73] Or has Paul failed to integrate his christological convictions with his doctrine of justification by faith? Within the framework of this doctrine as Dunn envisages it, we would have to imagine that Paul, "concerned about" ethnocentric narrowness, would have welcomed the universalizing tendencies in a theologian such as Philo, seeing in them some tentative steps in the right direction. Yet Philo's universalizing tendencies, such as they are, bring him no closer to the Pauline gospel. Paul's faith/law antithesis is not a continuum along which one might move from an extreme Jewish ethnocentrism at one end to universalistic monotheism at the other. It does not signify a continuum at all, but rather a gulf.

When Paul speaks in v. 30 of the circumcised as justified ἐκ πίστεως, he means that they are justified ἐκ πίστεως Ἰησοῦ (cf. v. 26). When he speaks of the uncircumcised as justified διὰ τῆς πίστεως, he means that they are justified διὰ πίστεως Ἰησοῦ Χριστοῦ (v. 22). As we have seen, the christological qualification of Paul's faith terminology is intended to refer neither to "the faithfulness of Christ" nor to "faith in Christ" but, more open-endedly, to the faith that pertains to God's saving action in Christ — originating in it, participating in it, and oriented towards it. There is no reason to suppose that ἐκ πίστεως Ἰησοῦ means something fundamentally different from ἐκ πίστεως, with the former referring to "faith in Jesus," the latter to "trust-dependence on the Creator God."[74] On the contrary, the longer and shorter phrases are synonymous: the frequent omission of the christological qualification stems from Paul's dependence here on Habakkuk 2:4, the language of which underlies all his righteousness-by-faith terminology in this section of the letter (1:17 + 3:21-31).[75] The "christological reticence" of Romans 1:16–4:25 is to be explained not by Paul's desire to get back to an allegedly more basic relationship

---

72. Dunn, *Romans*, 1:lxxi-lxxii.

73. This would seem to be the case in Daniel Boyarin's *A Radical Jew,* which is heavily dependent on Dunn at this point (51-56).

74. Dunn, *Romans*, 1:189.

75. See *PHF,* 54-57, 71-77.

of creature to Creator, but rather by his attempt to develop a soteriology on the basis of scripture: for in texts such as Habakkuk 2:4 and Genesis 15:6, scripture foreshadows God's definitive saving act without naming Jesus Christ as its agent. Thus in Romans 4 Abraham's faith corresponds not to his abstract creaturehood but to his concrete existence as addressee of the divine promise of universal salvation — a salvation realized in Christ (cf. vv. 24-25). As developed here, Paul's doctrine of righteousness by faith is his attempt to expound a scriptural soteriology on the basis of specific scriptural texts. It is presumably addressed especially (though not exclusively) to Roman Jewish Christians, and it seeks to persuade them that Pauline, Gentile-oriented Christianity has *not* detached the Christian message from its true scriptural matrix.

The christological reticence of Romans 3 does not undermine the thesis that Paul's faith/law antithesis is most fundamentally concerned with a nonnegotiable difference occasioned by christology (as Sanders in particular has persuasively argued). It does not mean that Christ for Paul is a mere symbol of something supposedly more fundamental (the renunciation of achievement, dependence on the Creator) and that he lacks a concrete existence of his own. For Paul, it is impossible to imagine anything more fundamental than Jesus Christ. No other foundation can be laid than this one (cf. 1 Cor. 3:11). While the Roman Christian community can be differentiated from the synagogue by referring to its ethos (the exclusion of boasting) or its composition (the inclusion of Gentiles), such distinctions do not reach to the heart of the matter. They are inferences from the gospel, but they are not the gospel itself.

Unexpectedly, it is the Fourth Gospel that provides the best and most accurate commentary on the Pauline faith/law antithesis. One community is founded on the fact that "the law was given through Moses," the other on the fact that "grace and truth came through Jesus Christ" (John 1:17). As the proper names indicate, these are not points at extreme ends of a continuum. They are simply and irreducibly different.

(3) In Romans 3 Paul has elaborated an antithesis between faith and law, which has led into a series of comparisons between the communities that each term represents. In one community but not the other, boasting is excluded (vv. 27-28) and Gentiles are included (vv. 29-30). Comparisons in terms of communal ethos or ethnic composition have resulted in sharp contrasts that underline the original antithesis. In v. 31, however, Paul *implies* a comparison rather than asserting one and at this point discovers common ground between the communities. If the communities founded on faith and on law are incommensurably different, surely it is the case that faith negates

law, the law that presents itself rather than Christ as the divinely appointed way to righteousness and that promotes boasting and excludes Gentiles? On the contrary: the law is actually common ground between the communities — for "we uphold the law" (νόμον ἱστάνομεν). It is the law itself that tells the community of the law that "none is righteous, not even one," extending this even to those who zealously practice "works of law" (vv. 9-20). It is the law itself, together with the prophets, that bears witness to the righteousness of God (v. 21). What is at issue between the two communities is not simply whether the divine/human relationship in its definitive form is encapsulated in the term "faith" or "law." While it is true that the term "law" characterizes one community rather than the other, in the sense that it promotes "works of law" (vv. 20, 27, 28), it is also true that both communities concern themselves with the law *but differ over its interpretation.*

For one community, the law is a guide to the practice of righteousness; for the other, it exposes human guilt and testifies negatively to the need for a new divine saving act if humans are ever to be righteous. Paul acknowledges that *both* interpretations can appeal to the testimony of the law itself — and not just his own. As Galatians indicates, one interpretation is aptly summed up in the conditional promise of Leviticus 18:5, that "the one who does these things shall live by them," whereas the other is summed up in the curse of Deuteronomy 27:26 (Gal. 3:10, 12). In Romans, the Leviticus text is repeated in 10:5, where it is said that in it "Moses writes the righteousness which is of the law"; and the Deuteronomy text is replaced by the catena of 3:9-18, in which prophetic texts are understood as commentary on the law. The law negates itself as a way to righteousness, but thereby discloses human incapacity for righteousness and confirms the gospel's claim that *God* has acted to establish righteousness among Jews and Gentiles alike. Thus, Romans 3:31 is to be understood as summarizing the teaching of the entire chapter about the law. The law is the common ground upon which two interpretations form and diverge. The divergence has to do with whether (i) the practice of the Mosaic law — not necessarily the *perfect* practice, since the law itself makes provision for atonement — is capable of securing the divine approval, thereby constituting the practitioner as "righteous before God" (cf. 3:20); or (ii) the practice of the Mosaic law leaves the practitioner in that state of "unrighteousness before God" which, according to the law itself, is the position of all humanity without exception (cf. 3:19). These optimistic or pessimistic interpretations of the law articulate different accounts of *the divine decision regarding humanity, as disclosed in scripture* (cf. 3:1-20). It is God's decision (and not mere empirical reality) that determines that what passes for the practice of righteousness within the community of the law is in fact nothing but a higher unrighteousness. The divine decision is announced in scripture, which thereby confirms the gospel and is confirmed by it.[76]

This third comparison between the communities of faith and of law ostensibly identifies common ground. Yet, in the light of the chapter as a whole, this comparison too issues in a contrast. According to Paul, one community promotes boasting whereas the other excludes it. One community makes God a God of Jews only; the other sees God as God also of Gentiles. And, although both communities revere the same sacred text, one community reads it optimistically, the other pessimistically. These contrasts, located at opposite ends of a continuum, exemplify but do not constitute the difference between the communities. One might adopt a highly pessimistic reading of the Torah without becoming a member of the community of faith (as in the case of 4 Ezra). Yet these contrasts do indicate that the difference between the Roman Jewish and Christian communities is not one of pure heterogeneity. There is enough common ground here to make disagreement possible.

76. A more common interpretation refers v. 31 back to v. 21, where it is said that the righteousness of God is upheld by the law and the prophets (so Michel, *Der Brief an die Römer*, 97; Barrett, *Romans*, 84, 86; Käsemann, *Commentary on Romans*, 350; Wilckens, *Der Brief an die Römer*, 1:250; see also C. T. Rhyne, *Faith Establishes the Law*, 71-75; R. Hays, *Echoes of Scripture*, 53-54). But 3:21 understands "law" in the broader sense of "the Pentateuch" and probably refers to such passages as Genesis 15:6, discussed at length in Romans 4. In 3:31 the two occurrences of νόμος probably have the same sense, referring to the law in terms of the divine commandments: compare the repeated reference to "works [of law]," vv. 27, 28. Thus Paul "upholds the law" even where he has in mind its negative role.

CHAPTER 8

The Law and Christian Identity
(Romans 4–8)

In the previous two chapters, Paul's argument in Romans 1–3 has been interpreted as an appeal to Roman Gentile and Jewish Christians to unite with one another under the common identity encapsulated in the term "faith," thereby finalizing the ideological breach with the Roman synagogues. That is why these chapters contain a number of references to both Jewish and Gentile Christians.[1] According to Romans 1:16, the gospel is "the power of God for salvation to everyone who believes, to the Jew first and also to the Greek." In 2:10, salvation is promised to everyone who does good, "the Jew first and also the Greek." In 3:22b-24 it is said that there is no distinction between Jew and Gentile, in that both are guilty before God and redeemed through God's grace. In 3:29-30, Paul argues that, as the God of Gentiles as well as Jews, God justifies Jews and Gentiles in exactly the same way, through faith. Similar points are made in the chapter that follows. In 4:9-12 Paul argues that Abraham is the father of both Jewish and Gentile Christians; it is these two groups who are identified in 4:16-17 with "the seed of Abraham," heirs to the promised salvation. The emphasis on Jewish Christians as well as on Gentiles is very striking when one compares Romans to Galatians, in which the former play virtually no part (except as opponents). This new emphasis seems, in the light of 14:1–15:13, to be accounted for by the situation in Rome as Paul understands it. The content of the letter thus far reinforces the conclusion to which we were led by its closing chapters: that Paul writes to Christian Gentiles (some of whom are personally known to him), but also takes every possible step to ensure that its circle of readership is extended to Christian Jews.

---

1. Cf. M. Kettunen, *Der Abfassungszweck des Römerbriefes*, 76.

The letter, then, is a call for a common Christian identity that will overcome present tensions between Jewish and Gentile Christians and finalize the breach with the Roman synagogues. This imperative, hidden until chapters 14–15, will also shed light on the arguments of chapters 4–8. In particular, it explains the continuing preoccupation with the law that is evident in each of these chapters (4:13-15; 5:20-21; 6:14; 7:1–8:4).

1. Reinterpreting Abraham (Romans 4)

Romans 4 is often understood as a proof from scripture of the doctrine of justification by faith outlined in 3:21-31.[2] Thus, according to Dodd, Romans 4 is "a long digression or excursus, in which Paul illustrates and confirms his doctrine of justification 'apart from the law' by a reference to Abraham."[3] Conzelmann thinks that Abraham is chosen to illustrate justification by faith as a random example. According to Käsemann, "Paul's thesis is now shown to be vindicated by the OT."[4] Cranfield writes:

> The function of this section is to confirm the truth of what was said in the first part of 3.27. (At the same time it also adds an independent contribution of its own, particularly in vv. 17b-22, to the exposition of "by faith.")[5]

Yet such comments do not do justice to the fundamental importance of the figure of Abraham for the Judaism that Paul is opposing. Nor do they recognize the profound social implications of Paul's reinterpretation of Abraham in Romans 4, where he denies the legitimacy of the Jewish community's view of Abraham as justifying its own praxis and beliefs and asserts that Abraham in fact justifies the praxis and beliefs of mixed Jewish and Gentile congregations. In broader terms, this chapter exemplifies the sectarian group's claim to be the sole legitimate possessor of the religious traditions of the wider community — an essential part of the theoretical rationale for separation that any sectarian group requires.[6]

---

2. More specifically, it may be seen as a scriptural proof of 3:28 (Eichholz, *Paulus,* 222; Schlier, *Der Römerbrief,* 121; Hübner, *Law in Paul's Thought,* 118), or of 3:31 (W. Kümmel, *Römer 7 und die Bekehrung des Paulus,* 5-6; U. Wilckens, "Die Rechtfertigung Abrahams nach Römer 4," 41-42).

3. Dodd, *The Epistle to the Romans,* 87. Robinson, too, regards Romans 4 as an "excursus" (*Wrestling with Romans,* 52).

4. Conzelmann, *Outline,* 169, 190; Käsemann, *Commentary on Romans,* 105.

5. Cranfield, *Romans,* 1:224.

6. In this section, a brief treatment of "the Jewish view of Abraham" (*PJG¹,* 136-38) has

In Romans 4 Paul engages with a view of Abraham both as a model of obedience and as the recipient of the promise of salvation. He opposes the view that Abraham legitimates the praxis of the loyal and faithful Jew who observes the law (vv. 1-8), and he similarly opposes the view that the physical descendants of Abraham are the "seed" he was promised (vv. 9-17). Rather, Abraham is a model of the faith evoked by the divine promise (vv. 18-25). Thus, while Paul here attacks vital elements in the self-understanding of the Jewish community, he does not simply dispense with the figure of Abraham but reinterprets his significance in order to present him as a focus of unity for an ethnically and culturally diverse community with a common faith. In response to the initial question about "Abraham our forefather according to the flesh," Paul argues that, instead of regarding Abraham as a bond connecting them to the non-Christian Jewish community, Christian Jews should see him as legitimating those who share his faith even without the practice of the law and as the ground for a common hope of salvation. It is therefore these Christian Gentiles with whom they should identify themselves.[7] Understood in this way, Romans 4 becomes much more than a scriptural proof of some aspect or other of 3:21-31. It is a far-reaching reinterpretation of the figure of Abraham with important social implications, and not a purely theoretical argument opposing salvation by one's own achievements with salvation by grace alone.

It is important to note that Paul's argument takes its starting point from an anticipated *Jewish Christian* question: "What then shall we say that Abraham our forefather according to the flesh has found?"[8] As in the questions-and-answers at the end of the previous chapter, it is Paul himself who poses the question, but in such a way as to anticipate a question that might be put to him by a member of his audience in view of what he has just said. In each case, "You will say to me then . . ." is implied (9:19; cf. 11:19; 1 Cor. 15:35). At the close of Romans 3, one question is concerned with Jewish "boasting," another with whether God is the God of Gentiles as well as Jews, and a third with the

---

been omitted, in view of the much fuller treatment of this theme in *PHF*, chapter 5. Otherwise, most of the original material has been reworked, and I have added a treatment of the "implied audience" of Romans 4 and expanded the discussion of vv. 4-5.

7. The concealed imperative in Romans 4 is recognized by Paul Minear, who argues that Paul is saying to the "weak in faith": "You must accept the strong in faith as children of Abraham and heirs to the promise of Abraham" (*Obedience of Faith*, 53).

8. Richard Hays translates v. 1: "What then shall we say? Have we found Abraham to be our forefather according to the flesh?" (*Echoes of Scripture*, 54-55, summarizing his 1985 article; followed by Keck, *Romans*, 120; A. K. Grieb, *The Story of Romans*, 46). If Hays were right, one would expect further development of the κατὰ σάρκα motif in Romans 4. For the use of εὑρηκέναι in connection with the "finding" of righteousness, cf. 9:30-31; 11:7. See also the criticism of Hays's reading in T. Engberg-Pedersen, *Paul and the Stoics*, 363n.

status of the law in the face of Paul's apparently critical remarks about it.[9] Paul may have envisaged a Jewish questioner in the first and third cases (vv. 27, 31) and a Gentile questioner in the second case (v. 29), but the crucial point is that the fictitious questioners are also *Christian:* for there is no indication in the context that these questions arise from outside Paul's Christian implied audience, in contrast to the address to the Jewish teacher of the law in chapter 2. The question about "Abraham our forefather according to the flesh" is therefore raised by Paul on behalf of a Jewish Christian member of his implied audience. If so, Romans 4 in its entirety is a response to this fictitious questioner. The fiction must be plausible, however. As in the parallel case of a Gentile interlocutor in 11:17-24, it must represent the kind of thing that *might* be said by real, empirical addressees of his letter when it reaches Rome and when they hear what it has to say. If no one in Rome is likely to be interested in Abraham our forefather or in the status of believing Gentiles vis-à-vis unbelieving Jews, then Paul's fictions lose their point.[10] Here, then, it is absolutely clear that Paul seeks a hearing among the Roman Jewish Christian community. He is not writing only to Gentiles.

(i) Grace and Works

In his initial response to his imagined Jewish Christian questioner, Paul contrasts two different views of Abraham as a model of obedience (vv. 1-8). The first is the view that Abraham lived by the practice of "works" and therefore had "grounds for boasting" (v. 2). On this view, his "reward" (v. 4) — i.e., "righteousness," v. 3 — would be κατὰ ὀφείλημα, commensurate with what he had done. On the other view, Abraham was initially "ungodly" (v. 5) but was reckoned as righteous (vv. 3, 5, 6) and had his sins forgiven (vv. 7-8) by means of God's grace and the faith it evoked in him (vv. 3-5).[11] Paul will later con-

---

9. Compare Stanley Stowers's reconstruction of a single dialogue in 3:27–4:2, *Paul and the Diatribe*, 164-65. Probably rightly, Stowers assigns 4:1-2ab to Paul's interlocutor, 4:2c to Paul; I am less convinced by the attribution of 3:29c to the interlocutor, 3:29ab, 30 to Paul. The supposition that the interlocutor is to be identified with "the pretentious Jew of 2:17-24" (167) seems untenable, given the absence of all dialogical elements in 3:10-26.

10. To that extent, it is incorrect to assert that dialogical passages such as this "do not reflect the specific positions of the addressees of the letter" (Stowers, *Paul and the Diatribe*, 180). Stowers himself notes, in connection with an example from Epictetus, that "the diatribe makes no sense unless certain students . . . have the tendencies displayed by the interlocutor" (181).

11. There is nothing in the text to support Hübner's claim that Abraham was ungodly because he wanted to be justified by works (*Law in Paul's Thought*, 121).

nect Abraham's faith to its antecedent in the divine *promise*, in line with the original context in Genesis, but at this stage the emphasis is not on the occasion of his faith but on its consequence, his being "reckoned as righteous" — that is, the forgiveness of his sins. Abraham is presented as embodying David's description of the blessedness of the forgiven sinner in Psalm 31 [32 MT] (Rom. 4:6-8).

Once again, Paul is here contrasting two different "patterns of religion." The pattern he commends emphasizes the necessity of *conversion*. Prior to conversion, people are "ungodly" (v. 5), and the transition between ungodliness and blessedness (cf. vv. 7-8) occurs through an act of forgiveness on the divine side and an act of faith on the human side. The pattern that Paul opposes emphasizes the need for a certain *practice*, the attainment and maintenance of "righteousness" (a right standing with God) "by works" (ἐξ ἔργων). Here there is no explicit reference to the law. While Paul is unlikely to have believed that Abraham already practiced the law, in advance of the revelation at Mount Sinai, Abraham's "works" would still be acts of obedience to divine commands. With the exception only of his submission to circumcision, however, Paul does not specify any such acts. Instead, he focuses on the general principle they embody, and he does so by way of an analogy drawn from the world of employment and remuneration. Following the citation of Genesis 15:6, he comments:

> To the one who works [τῷ ἐργαζομένῳ] the reward is not "reckoned" as a gift but as one's due [οὐ . . . κατὰ χάριν ἀλλὰ κατὰ ὀφείλημα], whereas to the one who does not work but believes in him who justifies the ungodly his faith "is reckoned as righteousness." (Rom. 4:4-5)

The analogy from the world of work remains incomplete, for the counterpart here to the worker who earns his wages is not a person who unexpectedly receives a gift but, specifically, the person forgiven by God. Yet the contrast between κατὰ ὀφείλημα and κατὰ χάριν makes it clear how Paul's analogy would have proceeded. These expressions speak of two human possibilities, remuneration and gift, that provide contrasting models of the divine-human relationship.

It is this Pauline analogy that underlies every reference in the secondary literature to "acquiring merit" or "earning salvation" as the chief object of Paul's critique. According to H. Ridderbos,

> The predominant tendency [in Jewish sources] is the doctrine, not infrequently presented in a highly quantitative sense, of the meritoriousness of the works of the law, which eventually enable man to obtain eternal life. In

the multiplicity of the commandments is the means for gaining much merit. Every fulfilment of the law, in the sense of an act in conformity with a concrete prescription of the law, contributes to the treasury of merit, just as, conversely, every concrete transgression brings the sufficiency of merit into jeopardy.[12]

On this view, each commandment of the law represents a task whose performance must be acknowledged and rewarded by the divine employer. Unsurprisingly, Ridderbos cites Strack-Billerbeck and Bousset as authorities for this account of Jewish "legalism," but it is doubtful whether this (allegedly dominant) economic model of the divine/human relationship would have seemed so crucial to several generations of scholars had it not seemed to have a foothold in the Pauline text. The text in question offers only the slenderest support for the economic model, however. It is simply an (incomplete) analogy, like the later "slavery" image (6:15-23) according to which we have been freed from one master (Sin) in order to serve another (God) and to receive "the gift of God" (eternal life) rather than "the wages of sin" (death). In this later passage, Paul acknowledges the limitations of the image (ἀνθρώπινον λέγω, 6:19); and we should extend this qualification back to the earlier image.

On the other hand, it is equally inappropriate for more recent scholarship to deny that the economic imagery in Romans 4:4-5 does indeed contrast two quite different soteriologies, which do *not* share broadly similar conceptions about the relation of divine grace to human response. In Dunn's interpretation of this passage, the economic image has no relation at all to Judaism, and its significance dwindles away to almost nothing:

> [I]t is not necessary to assume that [Paul's] Jewish interlocutor would accept a straight equation between works of law and the payment-earning work of day-to-day life. Nor is it necessary to assume that Paul was accusing his fellow-Jews of making that equation. He simply points out that to interpret Gen 15:6 in terms of Abraham's acts (works) of covenant loyalty, leaves no room in the commonsense logic of the work-a-day world for grace.[13]

Yet Paul does appear to think that a doctrine of "righteousness by works of law" is real enough to be worth refuting (cf. Rom. 3:20, 28; 4:2) and that the wages/gift distinction can be used to highlight its difference from his own gospel (as anticipated in Gen. 15:6). Naturally, the image of work and remu-

12. Ridderbos, *Paul: An Outline of His Theology*, 133.
13. Dunn, *Romans*, 1:228.

neration is not the only or the most important thing Paul says about Judaism. Elsewhere he can speak of the people of Israel as richly endowed with divine gifts and privileges (cf. 9:4-5; 11:29). But he *does* use this image, and it highlights the contrast between an immediate presence of the transforming divine action in the event of conversion and a prescribed form of life originating in God, oriented towards God, and approved and finally vindicated by God — an ordered framework within which to live in a disordered world. With Paul, one may interject a protest ("But not before God!" 4:2) — but only on the basis of an alternative, conversionist account of the divine/human relationship, not because there is anything *inherently* wrong with the "pattern of religion" in question.

Abraham, then, is a model for the *convert*, the one who has passed from ungodliness to righteousness by a transforming event whose divine side is the forgiveness of all past sins and whose human side is simply faith in the God who acts in this way: Abraham "believes in the one who justifies the ungodly" (v. 5). He is not a model for the person committed to a lifetime of law observance. His life is most profoundly determined not by the continuity of obedience but by the disruptive divine intervention that Paul finds attested in Genesis 15:6.[14]

(ii) A Symbol of Unity

As a model for converts, Abraham is also to be a focal point of unity for Roman Gentile and Jewish Christians in their quest for a shared communal identity. All have been brought into the Christian community out of the dark background outlined in 3:9-20; all have experienced the blessedness of sins forgiven (cf. 4:6-8). But is that really the case? Abraham is "*our* forefather according to the flesh" (4:1), and — even if his righteousness is indeed the righteousness of faith — it is not clear from his story that he is a model for Gentiles *qua* Gentiles, rather than for Jews and proselytes. To reconstruct Abraham as a symbol of Pauline Jew-Gentile unity will require all Paul's exegetical acumen. His argument consists mainly of deductions from Genesis 15:6, the text that underlies the entire chapter:

τί γὰρ ἡ γραφὴ λέγει; ἐπίστευσεν δὲ Ἀβρααμ τῷ θεῷ καὶ ἐλογίσθη αὐτῷ εἰς δικαιοσύνην. (Rom. 4:3)

---

14. As Byrne notes, in the background here is the tradition of Abraham as the model proselyte (*Romans*, 149).

... πιστεύοντι δὲ ἐπὶ τὸν <u>δικαιοῦντα</u> τὸν ἀσεβῆ <u>λογίζεται</u> ἡ <u>πίστις</u> αὐτοῦ εἰς <u>δικαιοσύνην</u> (4:5)

λέγομεν γάρ, <u>ἐλογίσθη τῷ Ἀβραὰμ</u> ἡ <u>πιστις</u> εἰς δικαιοσύνην (4:9)

πατέρα πάντων τῶν <u>πιστευόντων</u> δι᾽ ἀκροβυστίας, εἰς τὸ <u>λογισθῆναι</u> καὶ αὐτοῖς τὴν <u>δικαιοσύνην</u> (4:12)

κατέναντι οὗ <u>ἐπίστευσεν</u> θεοῦ τοῦ ζωοποιοῦντος τοὺς νεκρούς (4:17)

οὐκ ἐγράφη δι᾽ αὐτὸν μόνον ὅτι <u>ἐλογίσθη αὐτῷ</u> ἀλλὰ καὶ δι᾽ ἡμᾶς, οἷς μέλλει <u>λογίζεσθαι</u>, τοῖς <u>πιστεύουσιν</u> ἐπὶ τὸν ἐγείραντα Ἰησοῦν κτλ (4:23-24)

Paul speaks of the "reckoning of righteousness" to those who "believe" because his Genesis text does so. The chapter as a whole confirms that his "doctrine of righteousness by faith" is his reading of selected texts rather than an exposition of his kerygma per se — although, of course, the reading of scripture is intended to further the exposition of the kerygma. Paul does not here attempt to extract explicit christological references from the Genesis Abraham narrative. His intention is to *reconceive* "our forefather according to the flesh" as a symbol of Jewish and Gentile unity over against the synagogue. Here as elsewhere, the sectarian group does not simply reject the traditions of the parent community (written or otherwise); rather, it *reinterprets* them, arguing that they have been misunderstood hitherto and that "we" now possess the key to their real meaning.[15]

Genesis 15:6 speaks of "righteousness by faith," but it does not speak of the unity of Jews and Gentiles. Yet Paul presses the text into the service of his own pragmatic ends in a number of ways. Having established his basic conception of Abraham as model (4:1-8), he proceeds to exploit the fact that Genesis 15 precedes Genesis 17. The diachronic sequence righteousness-of-faith/circumcision is interpreted as a sequence leading from righteousness-of-faith without circumcision to righteousness-of-faith sealed and signified by circumcision (Rom. 4:10-11a). It is then subjected to a synchronic transformation in which Abraham's two successive states (uncircumcised, circumcised) represent the two groupings within the (Roman) Christian community (4:11b-12).

The social and pragmatic dimension of Paul's appeal to Abraham is particularly clear in 4:9-12. The chapter as a whole is not an exercise in a disem-

---

15. Philip Esler rightly notes that the element of contestation is missing in some recent discussion of scriptural intertextuality (*Conflict and Identity*, 176).

bodied, merely theoretical doctrine of faith — as Ulrich Luz appears to assume when he understands 4:1-8 as an exposition of "by faith," and 4:9-16 as an exposition of "by faith *alone*."[16] Paul does not regard circumcision as a mere example of a meritorious "work," as this suggests, but as the rite that defines the male Jew or convert as a member of the Jewish community.[17] In v. 9 Paul poses the question: Which is the community in which the blessing of righteousness and forgiveness is to be found? Is it to be found only within the περιτομή, the Jewish community? Or is it also to be found among the ἀκροβυστία, the Pauline Gentile Christian congregations? Paul claims that since Abraham enjoyed righteousness by faith both before and after he was circumcised, he aptly symbolizes the union of Gentile and Jewish Christians (vv. 10-12). In v. 12, it becomes clear that righteousness is not to be found among the περιτομή as such (as v. 9 had seemed to imply), but only among those Jews and Gentiles who like Abraham have faith.[18] The message to the Roman Jewish and Gentile Christians is that they should each recognize the legitimacy of the other, irrespective of ἀκροβυστία or περιτομή. In particular, Jewish Christians should recognize that Abraham, righteous by faith although uncircumcised, has spiritual descendants who are similarly righteous by faith although uncircumcised; and they should learn to regard this righteousness-by-faith as more fundamental than circumcision to their own identity as descendants of Abraham. The old view of Abraham as the ideal Jew is abandoned, as Abraham comes to serve instead as a figurehead for a mixed community of Jewish and Gentile Christians.

In a Jewish context, Abraham is also the recipient of the promise of salvation for the community of the law that comprises his descendants. Paul claims in 4:13-15 that this cannot be the case, and he does so on the basis of the view of the law set forth in 3:9-20. There he argued that the law, correctly understood, places Israel in exactly the same position of guilt before God as the Gentiles. Thus, it can be said in 4:14b-15 that the promise of salvation cannot

---

16. Luz, *Das Geschichtsverständnis bei Paulus,* 175: cf. Bultmann, *Theology of the New Testament,* 1:112. D. Zeller's analysis is more satisfactory: vv. 1-8 answer the question of v. 1, and vv. 9-25 are concerned with the question, "To whom?" (*Juden und Heiden in der Mission des Paulus,* 100).

17. As Sanders points out, Paul in 4:9-12 attacks not self-righteousness but privileged status (*Paul, the Law and the Jewish People,* 34).

18. In 4:12, πατέρα περιτομῆς τοῖς οὐκ ἐκ περιτομῆς μόνον ἀλλὰ καὶ τοῖς στοιχοῦσιν κτλ suggests as it stands that two separate groups of Jewish Christians are referred to: (i) those who are not of circumcision alone, and (ii) those who follow in Abraham's footsteps. This seems unlikely, and the second τοῖς is commonly regarded as a mistake, either by Paul or by his copyist (so Kuss, *Der Römerbrief,* 186; Schlier, *Der Römerbrief,* 128; Cranfield, *Romans,* 1:237; Wilckens, *Der Brief an die Römer,* 1:266).

be fulfilled through the law, since the law merely accentuates condemnation. In other words, membership of the Jewish community is neither necessary nor desirable. Law-observant Jews are not as such the true seed of Abraham that is heir to the promise of salvation (v. 14); the true seed consists of Jewish and Gentile Christians (vv. 16-17). The unity of Christian Jews and Gentiles has as its corollary the alienation of the Christian community from the synagogue. If Paul is arguing *only* the positive point, without any such negative corollary, it is hard to see why he here so emphatically disinherits οἱ ἐκ νόμου (v. 14).[19]

Admittedly, in vv. 16-17 the definition of the "seed" to whom the promise is "sure" is ambiguous. Paul states that the promise is by grace and by faith,

εἰς τὸ εἶναι βεβαίαν τὴν ἐπαγγελίαν παντὶ τῷ σπέρματι, οὐ τῷ ἐκ τοῦ νόμου μόνον ἀλλὰ καὶ τῷ ἐκ πίστεως Ἀβρααμ. . . .

It is "by faith, so as to be according to grace" that the promise is sure to Abraham's entire seed — "not only to that which is of the law but also to that which is of the faith of Abraham" (v. 16). The difficulty is that the promise is here said to be sure to that seed which is ἐκ τοῦ νόμου (although not exclusively so), whereas in v. 14 it is expressly denied that οἱ ἐκ νόμου are heirs of the promise at all. The solution to this difficulty is probably that the law represents common ground between non-Christian and Christian Jews and that the former are at this point excluded from the scope of the promise, whereas the latter are included.[20] In v. 16, in contrast to v. 14, the reference to those who are ἐκ τοῦ νόμου occurs in the context of the affirmation: Διά τοῦτο ἐκ πίστεως ἵνα κατὰ χάριν. This is the case not only for observers of the law but also for those who (merely) share Abraham's faith. For the law-observant and for the non-observant who share Abraham's faith, the promise is sure only "by faith, so that it might be according to grace." The distinction within the

---

19. Alienation from the network of Roman synagogues does not constitute "the abandonment of an existing ethnic identity" (so P. Esler, in criticism of *PJG¹; Conflict and Identity*, 178). The criticism suggests that "ethnic identity" is being misunderstood along essentialist lines. Esler speaks of Paul as using the figure of Abraham "to recategorize the Judean and non-Judean subgroups of the Christ-movement in Rome into a new common group identity" (177-78) but remains strangely reticent about the impact of Paul's views on relations between "Judean Christ-followers" and the wider "Judean" community in Rome.

20. So Käsemann, *Commentary on Romans*, 121; Cranfield, *Romans*, 1:242; Wilckens, *Der Brief an die Römer*, 1:271-72. In opposition to this, Michel, *Der Brief an die Römer*, 123, and Schlier, *Der Römerbrief*, 131, take the phrase οὐ τῷ ἐκ τοῦ νόμου μόνον as a reference to Jews in general; but this seem out of keeping with a context in which the law-observant are threatened with exclusion (v. 14).

single seed of Abraham between those oriented towards law and faith and those oriented towards faith alone corresponds closely to the distinction between the weak and the strong in chapters 14–15.

At the start of the chapter, Abraham is "our forefather according to the flesh"; Paul and his imaginary interlocutor appear to occupy a purely Jewish environment. By v. 12, he has become "our father Abraham" in the sense that he is father of uncircumcised and circumcised alike. In vv. 16-17, he is "father of us all," in fulfillment of the scriptural promise that "I will make you father of many Gentiles/nations" (Gen. 17:5). At this point the gap between Genesis 15 and 17, so crucial in the earlier discussion of faith and circumcision, disappears entirely as the promise of Genesis 17 is conflated with that of 15:5, "So shall your seed be." Thus, what Abraham believed on the occasion of his justification was the divine promise that "I will make you father of many Gentiles." Faith in this promise became the guiding light of his entire life thereafter and was focused initially on the divine gift of a child in spite of the reproductive deadness of his and Sarah's bodies. Abraham was "reckoned as righteous" by way of his faith in the God who gives life to the dead, a faith that prefigures Christian faith in the God who gave life to the deadness of Jesus. Thus at its opening Romans 4 presents Abraham as a model of the forgiven sinner and, at its close, as a model of the life of faith, as one whose whole life is oriented towards the life-giving God of the promise. Through Paul's exegetical virtuosity, "our forefather according to the flesh" has shifted his communal location and now points the way towards a united community of Christian Jews and Gentiles.

2. Christ, Hope, and Reconciliation (Romans 5)

In Romans 5, the Jew/Gentile issue that has dominated the letter to this point disappears completely. Conversely, explicit christological statements are to the fore, replacing the scriptural orientation of the exposition of righteousness by faith — both in the law/faith antithesis in chapter 3 and in the reinterpretation of Abraham in chapter 4. Yet chapter 5 does not simply introduce a new theme. The preoccupation with "righteousness" is maintained here; indeed, a wider range of righteousness terminology is employed here than in the previous chapter, associated now no longer with faith (after v. 1) but with Christ (vv. 9, 18, 19) and with grace (vv. 16, 17, 21).[21] In Romans 3–4, Paul presents himself as an interpreter of scripture, in Romans 5 as apostle of Christ. The two roles are

---

21. δικαιοσύνη (4:3, 5, 6, 9, 11 [× 2], 13, 22; 5:17, 21); δικαιοῦν (4:2, 5; 5:1, 9); δικαίωσις (4:25; 5:18); δικαίωμα (5:16, 18); δίκαιος (5:7, 19).

intimately connected, for at the very opening of the letter it is said that "the gospel of God" was "promised beforehand through his prophets in the holy scriptures" (1:1-2). Yet the two roles may be distinguished in Romans 3–5, owing to the remarkable lack of christological material in the scripturally oriented chapters 3–4 (confined to 3:22-26; 4:24-25). In the light of v. 1, it might be said that Romans 5 unfolds the scriptural doctrine of righteousness by faith in the light of its final realization through Christ. If so, it is a serious mistake to find the heart of the Pauline gospel in earlier righteousness-by-faith formulations such as 3:28 or 4:5, as though Pauline christology were reducible to statements of theological anthropology. The preliminary scriptural exposition of chapters 3–4 comes to fruition only in chapter 5. However significant Abraham may be, it is Christ and not Abraham who will provide the ultimate focus for the faith of the Roman Christian community.[22] Scripture is not absent here, however: for, as we shall see, the christology Paul develops here is decisively shaped by another character from Genesis.

What of the crucial pragmatic dimension of Paul's argument, which we have traced through chapters 1–4 but which seems less evident in a context where the Jew/Gentile issue is no longer explicit? In general terms, we may say that chapters 1–4 address a problem — division within the Roman Christian community — that arises from its members' diverse origins. In that sense, chapters 1–4 have to do with *the past*. In chapter 5, however, the problem has disappeared: for what now comes into view is the community's *future*. This point must now be established exegetically and its social significance brought to light.[23]

(i) The Social Significance of Hope

There is some disagreement about the theme that binds together Romans 5:1-11. In v. 1, Paul announces his intention to draw further conclusions from the

22. Contrast Bultmann, who extends his anthropologically oriented reading of Romans 3 into chapter 5 by arguing that the Adam-christology here is a reinterpretation of Gnostic mythology along anthropological lines ("Adam and Christ according to Romans 5," 158). Among the various resulting exegetical oddities is the claim that the sin that the law increases (according to 5:20) is that of "boasting" (3:27). Karl Barth (against whom Bultmann's argument is directed) is closer to the mark here in arguing that this chapter "has nothing to do with a general idea of God and of man," but that it is concerned with "a particular fact, the fact of the person of Jesus Christ" (*Shorter Commentary*, 57).

23. Here, the discussion of Romans 5:1-11 corresponds closely to *PJG¹*, 143-46; the discussion of 5:12-21 has been expanded.

fact of justification by faith, as established in previous chapters: "Therefore, since we are justified by faith. . . ." Since Paul goes on to say, "we have peace with God through our Lord Jesus Christ,"[24] it could be argued that "peace with God" is the theme of vv. 1-11 as a whole, and this would receive some support from the emphasis on reconciliation in vv. 10-11.[25] But a comparison between vv. 9 and 10, which have a very similar structure, suggests that being "reconciled to God by the death of his Son" (v. 10) is not so much a consequence of being "justified by his blood" (v. 9) as another way of speaking of the same thing.[26] In any case, in spite of vv. 1, 10, and 11, "peace" does not seem to be prominent enough in vv. 1-11 to be seen as the theme of the whole passage.

It is better to interpret the passage as a meditation on *hope*. Although ἐλπίς occurs only in vv. 2, 4, and 5, the idea is expressed throughout the passage and also connects it back to the preceding discussion of the promise, which evokes in Abraham a "hope against hope" (4:18). According to 5:1-2, the consequence of justification, peace, and grace is that "we rejoice in hope of the glory of God." Suffering, too, gives rise to hope, in that it produces "steadfastness," δοκιμή, and an eschatological hope confirmed by the transforming reality of the divine love poured into our hearts by the Holy Spirit (vv. 3-5).[27] The death of Christ for our sins shows God's love for us (vv. 6-8) and assures us that, being justified and reconciled, we shall finally be saved (vv. 9-10). This affirmation about hope's realization is to give rise to joy (v. 11). Thus, the various themes of the passage — justification, reconciliation, suffering, the Holy Spirit, the death of Christ — all converge on hope. Hope is the theme that binds all these subordinate topics together.[28]

How is this meditation on hope related to the situation of the Roman Christians and Paul's purpose in writing to them? Romans 15 suggests an answer. In 15:4, Paul mentions parenthetically that it is the purpose of the scriptures to kindle hope, and then prays in vv. 5-6 that the Jewish and Gentile Christians of Rome may live in harmony with one another so as to be able to worship together. In vv. 7-12, texts from the Psalms and Isaiah show that it is

---

24. See Nygren, *A Commentary on Romans*, 193-94, on the textual problem here.

25. See Cranfield, *Romans*, 1:256-57.

26. So Nygren, *A Commentary on Romans*, 205; Käsemann, *Commentary on Romans*, 138.

27. Most commentators take ἡ ἀγάπη τοῦ θεοῦ as a subjective genitive (Barrett, *Romans*, 105; Schlier, *Der Römerbrief*, 150; Käsemann, *Commentary on Romans*, 135; Cranfield, *Romans*, 1:262; Wilckens, *Der Brief an die Römer*, 1:293). But v. 5 must imply that we are the *subjects* of the love of God poured into our hearts, just as we are the subjects of the peace of God that guards our hearts (Phil. 4:7). In both cases, the genitive in question is a genitive of origin.

28. So Bultmann, *Theology of the New Testament*, 1:252; E. Jüngel, "Das Gesetz zwischen Adam und Christus," 49.

God's purpose that Jews should worship God alongside Gentiles, that Gentiles should worship together with Jews, and that the Messiah should come for the salvation of Gentiles as well as Jews. After this appeal to the Jewish and Gentile groups to join together for worship, Paul writes in v. 13: "May the God of *hope* fill you with all joy and peace in believing, so that by the power of the Holy Spirit you may abound in *hope*." This prayer is surely not unrelated to the preceding verses.[29] Paul is not simply expressing pious aspiration but is indicating that a consequence of the united worship of Jewish and Gentile Christians will be that, through the Spirit, they will abound in hope.

Why should shared worship and a common identity lead them to abound in hope? A sociological interpretation of hope suggests a possible answer. "Hope" refers to the subjective confidence of the community and its individual members in the reality of the future salvation for which they long. That salvation is "unseen" (Rom. 8:24-25), and its reality is explicitly or implicitly denied by society at large. This makes hope peculiarly vulnerable. The massive, visible reality of everyday life makes subjective confidence in an unseen, greater, future reality hard to maintain.[30] Thus in Romans 4:18-22 Abraham is praised because he overcame precisely this difficulty. The problem becomes acute in the event of "suffering" occasioned by the hostility of the surrounding society, stemming from resentment at a sectarian group that rejects its norms and beliefs and adheres to alien norms and beliefs of its own. Although suffering can enhance hope (cf. Rom. 5:3-4), it also threatens it, for there is a danger that members of the group will decide that the price of separation is too great, and so "fall away" (cf. Mark 4:17; 1 Thess. 3:5).[31] Nothing is so damaging to the group's confidence as the defection of its own members, and "suffering" is one of the main causes of such defections. Thus, "hope" (subjective confidence in the reality of the future salvation) is constantly under threat, and since it is precisely "hope" that gives the group its *raison d'être* and its cohesion, its maintenance is a matter of great importance.

29. So Käsemann, *Commentary on Romans*, 387. However, on Käsemann's view, 15:9-13 has to do with turning away from liturgy to everyday life — an anti-ecclesial reading that is surely alien to Paul.

30. See W. Meeks, *First Urban Christians*, 162.

31. Compare J. H. Elliott's comments on the group addressed by 1 Peter: "The severity of the polarization with outsiders was endangering the sect's social cohesion, the self-esteem of its members, their conviction that they possessed a new status conferred by God, their common commitment to the unique religious values, social values, ideals and goals of the group, and their vision of a common salvation to which even current anti-Christian opponents would one day be won" (*A Home for the Homeless*, 101).

How is hope to be maintained? Above all, *hope requires social support*. If hope is threatened by everyday reality and by the hostility of outsiders, the group's meetings become all the more important as the place at which hope is rekindled. This takes place through constantly renewed articulation of the group's beliefs and aspirations in hymns, prayers, readings from scripture (cf. Rom. 15:4), teaching, and exhortations (cf. 15:14).[32] Through participation in communal worship, the individual is able to reappropriate the norms and beliefs of the group and to defy the threat to his or her confidence posed by everyday reality. Paul attributes increase in hope to "the power of the Holy Spirit" (15:13), and the dwelling place of the Holy Spirit is precisely the Christian community.[33]

If hope is dependent on social support, that may explain why Paul believes that the union of Jews and Gentiles in worship will enable them all to "abound in hope" (15:13). In the current fragmented state of the Roman Christian community, each group represents part of the threat to the "hope" of the other. When they "despise" or "pass judgment on" one another (cf. Rom. 14:3-4, 10-13), they each betray an anxiety about their own standing that runs counter to joy, peace, and hope. Thus, the antipathy between Jewish and Gentile Christians in Rome is damaging to both parties. Conversely, their union will increase hope by providing the additional social support that will enable it to flourish. That is why it can be said in Romans 15:7-13 that the union of the two communities will lead to an abundance of hope.

(ii) The Universal Christ

The focus on hope is maintained in 5:12-21, which highlights the "life" that through Christ is the object or content of hope, set against the background of the death inherited from Adam. Those who receive the gift of righteousness will reign in life (v. 17); Jesus Christ's act of righteousness brings justification that leads to life (v. 18); Christ has established a reign of grace "through righteousness to eternal life" (v. 21). Each of these statements opens with a reference to sin and concludes with a reference to life (cf. also v. 10). In spite of sin, the free gift of grace leads initially to justification (vv. 16, 19) and ultimately to eternal life (vv. 17, 18, 21). In vv. 1-11, Paul has described hope as it is or should

32. See Meeks's comments about the way in which ritual speech and music, the reading of scripture, and preaching promote social cohesiveness (*First Urban Christians*, 145-46).

33. The communal focus of this passage is also evident in the use of the first-person plural, in contrast to the impersonality of the preceding chapters: on this see P. McDonald, "Romans 5.1-11 as a Rhetorical Bridge."

be experienced within the congregation. In vv. 12-21, he gives a broader description of the grounds for hope by means of a portrayal of salvation history in terms of two antithetical realms: the realm of Adam, sin, death, law, and condemnation, and the realm of Christ, grace, righteousness, and life.

There is, however, more to this passage than antithesis, an "Adam-Christ contrast." Formally, the emphasis lies not on the contrast but on the analogy, introduced as such by the ὥσπερ of v. 12 and resumed in the ὡς/ὥσπερ . . . οὕτως formulations of vv. 18-19, following the qualifications of vv. 13-14 and the disanalogies of vv. 15-17 (n.b. οὐχ ὡς . . . οὕτως, v. 15). Yet it is the disanalogies that bear the greatest rhetorical weight. Rather than simply reversing the effects of Adam's action, Christ's impact on "the many" far outweighs Adam's (v. 15). If Christ's act is compared not with Adam's but with the divine judgment that followed it, a further anomaly comes to light: one transgression issues in universal condemnation, many transgressions in universal justification (v. 16). Death reigns over the human race in the one case, but it is the human race that itself reigns in life in the other (v. 17). The disanalogies are not just contrasts, as though Paul were merely pointing out that death and life, sin and righteousness are opposites rather than synonyms. Rather, they highlight the disproportion or excess of grace, signified by repeated references to "abundance" (ἡ χάρις . . . ἐπερίσσευσεν, v. 15; ἡ περισσεία τῆς χάριτος, v. 17; ὑπερεπερίσσευσεν ἡ χάρις, v. 21). Far from merely counteracting Adam's action with a saving act that restores the disrupted status quo, the divine grace enacted in Jesus Christ is characterized by prodigality, extravagance, and excess. It goes far beyond what is needful and proper; it lacks economy and restraint. Only in vv. 18 and 19 is the suspended analogy of v. 12 finally resumed, by which point Paul's own linguistic excess has reduced it to the status of an appendix. Even here, however, he is ostensibly speaking about a salvation for all through Christ that is just as universal in its scope as the condemnation for all occasioned by Adam. Any implication of a restriction — for example, to the minority who practice the Abraham-like life of faith — would be utterly at odds with the logic of this remarkably inclusive passage.[34]

How and why has Paul arrived at such a conclusion about the scope of the divine saving act? It is somehow derived from Genesis 3, where Adam's disobedience subjects his descendants to the reign of death and sin. (Eve is omitted here as Adam is in 2 Corinthians 11:3, to ensure the balance of the analogy.) Adam's act thus has consequences not just for some but for all, *and it is in that respect that he is a "type of the Coming One"* (v. 14). Paul here re-

---

34. Since the scope of Christ's act is as universal as Adam's, Paul cannot here be employing "social stereotypes" with a view to "group differentiation" (P. Esler, *Conflict and Identity*, 202).

reads Genesis retrospectively, in the light of Christ — in contrast to the prospective reading of Genesis in the previous chapter. As he does so, the direction of the reading is reversed as Christ is in turn illuminated by the scriptural text. In the figure of the single individual whose act has ultimate consequences for everyone, Paul beholds a faint but perceptible foreshadowing of Christ. That, it seems, is the moment of exegetical and theological insight that determines the entire passage, and especially its "universalism."[35]

As a result, Paul can here present a messianic figure attested in Jewish scripture whose work is nevertheless universal in its scope. The situation he came to remedy is not the oppression of Israel but the fallen state of the world, which has succumbed to sin, death, and condemnation. Those who are under the law (i.e., the Jewish community) are merely a part of that fallen world.[36] Indeed, the law has intensified the reign of sin (vv. 20-21). At no point in this passage is there a question of a significant difference between Jew and Gentile. Paul here leads his readers beyond a restricted view of Jesus as the Messiah of Israel; even though a particularistic christology retains some validity (cf. 9:5; 15:8), the emphasis is now on a Christ who is "Lord of all" (10:12). What is remarkable in Romans 5 is that there is no place here even for a Christian particularism. If Adam is a type of Christ, then Christ's act can hardly be narrower in its scope than Adam's. It is not only Roman Jewish Christians who will have their horizons broadened by Paul's christological interpretation of Genesis 3.

Since the universal transformation of which Paul here speaks is not yet universally manifest, it can only be the object of hope. This is a hope that transcends the limits of the individual and the community within which Romans 5:1-11 remained confined. In Romans 8 this hope without limit will be further extended to embrace not just humankind but the entire cosmos. The newly united Roman Christian community is to be a preliminary sign of the coming universal reconciliation of all things.

3. Grace, Law, and Sin (Romans 6–7)

Paul's announcement of the universal triumph of grace is intended to evoke unlimited hope, but it may equally well elicit only objections and contradic-

35. As Dunn notes, Christ is the type or pattern of Christ "in that each begins an epoch, and the character of that epoch is established by their action. That their actions are very different and the outcomes markedly disproportionate . . . does not alter that basic similarity" (*Romans*, 1:277).

36. Nothing in this passage implies that the sphere of the law is universal (against Jüngel, "Das Gesetz zwischen Adam und Christus," 52).

tions. By the end of Romans 5, the law has been completely sidelined as a code of conduct and way of life. Before the law, sin is not reckoned (5:13), but with the coming of the law sin is increased (5:20). The law of Moses — which Paul himself will shortly acknowledge to be "holy and just and good" (7:12) — serves only to intensify human profanity and injustice and evil, and has now been overtaken by the superabundance bestowed by Paul's remarkably prodigal deity. What place is left for the pursuit of the righteousness laid down in the law's commandments? Is Moses no longer to be "a guide to the blind, a light to those in darkness, an educator of the ignorant" (2:19-20)? Does Paul in fact teach: "Let us do evil that good may come" (3:8)? He has certainly made some deeply disturbing statements. The law discloses sins without remedying them (cf. 3:20). The practice of the law is irrelevant for righteousness (cf. 3:28). The Gentile foreskin signifies descent from the uncircumcised Abraham (4:9-12). The law makes the human condition worse rather than better (5:20). There is, perhaps, a simple explanation for all this. If the law inculcates a hatred of sin, then hatred of the law can only stem from love of sin. Is Paul an antinomian, perverting the authentic scriptural teaching of forgiveness (cf. Ps. 32) into a doctrine of license? "Should we remain in sin, so that grace may abound?" The questioner in 6:1 does not explicitly mention the law (in contrast to 6:15) but has correctly grasped that the abundance of grace is premised on a negation of the law (cf. 5:20). Paul no doubt has an anticipated Jewish Christian reader in mind here, although he also has in mind his intended Gentile Christian readership who need to know exactly *why* they live by faith, hope, and grace and not by the law.[37]

(i) Two Communal Identities

Paul's strategy in Romans 6–7 is to insist that he, too, is resolutely opposed to human sin and arbitrariness, but that it is precisely in the sphere of grace rather than law that *effective* opposition is to be found. The realized human obedience of chapter 6 occurs within the sphere of grace and of Christ's death and resurrection. The agonizing failure of chapter 7 occurs within the sphere of the law — which, of course, Paul knows at first hand and can speak of in the first person. Thus, Romans 6–7 constitutes a single, two-part argument about the basis for righteous conduct: is it to be grace or the law? As regards grace, the intention is to show, first, that grace does not promote arbitrariness, since it is oriented

37. In the following sections, the pairing of Romans 6 and 7 is new to this edition, and the discussion of the Genesis background to Romans 7 has been considerably expanded.

towards a sin-free eschatological future already attained by the crucified and risen Christ (6:2-14); and second, that the sphere of grace has its own traditional τύπος διδαχῆς (6:17), which demands total obedience to the dictates of righteousness and total rejection of a truly arbitrary pre-Christian past (6:15-23).[38] As regards the law, the intention is to show, first, that Jesus' death and resurrection consigns to the past not only sin but also the law itself (7:1-6); and second, that to live under the law, as though there were no such thing as grace, is to become still more deeply enmeshed in precisely the sins that, instructed by the law, one longs to escape (7:7-25). Romans 6–7 is to be seen as an antithetically constructed diptych, contrasting Christ and law, righteousness and sin, light and darkness. Readers, in Rome or elsewhere, must make a choice here. If they choose rightly, they will recognize that to be free from the law is an essential prerequisite for the fruits of righteousness and obedience (cf. 6:14, 22; 7:4).

Why does Paul persist in taking such a negative view of the law? It is often supposed that he does so for purely theological reasons. Thus Cranfield comments on 6:14b ("you are not under law but under grace") that "the meaning of this sentence is that believers are not under God's condemnation pronounced by the law but under His undeserved favour."[39] This comment is inadequate because it overlooks the link that Paul everywhere assumes between the law and its primary social context, the Jewish community, whose way of life is determined by the law.[40] When Paul claims that the law increases the trespass (5:20), he means that this has taken place within the Jewish community. When he tells his readers that they are free from the law (6:14-15; 7:1-6), this entails their independence from the community whose identity is determined by the law and its practice. In other words, Paul's negative statements about the law are to be understood in the light of the pragmatic intention of the letter as a whole, which is to persuade Jewish and Gentile Christians to unite around a common Christian identity clearly demarcated from the Jewish identity constituted by the law.[41] If he can convince his Jewish Christian

38. "Righteousness" in Romans 6 refers to conduct approved by God. The view that righteousness here is "the power of God which has come on the scene in Christ" (Käsemann, *Commentary on Romans,* 177) is an unwarranted deduction from the "slavery" metaphor (cf. 6:19a). Still less apposite is Hübner's claim that righteousness in Romans 6 cannot be "even only in part a deed or achievement of man" — that is, "unless we wish to reverse the whole drift of Pauline theology" (*Law in Paul's Thought,* 131).

39. Cranfield, *Romans,* 1:320.

40. As B. N. Kaye notes, "throughout the letter law is the possession of the Jew" (*The Thought Structure of Romans with Special Reference to Chapter 6,* 110).

41. Romans 7 is therefore not concerned with "man's situation" but with the Jewish situation (against Kümmel, *Römer 7 und die Bekehrung des Paulus,* 134; Bornkamm, *Paul,* 126; Hahn, "Das Gesetzesverständnis im Römer- und Galaterbrief," 57). As Esler rightly remarks, "Such

readers that the effect of the law in the Jewish community is simply to intensify the dominion of sin, an important part of his purpose will have been achieved.[42]

We note once more that this crucially important pragmatic dimension of Paul's argument has been persistently neglected, on account of the post-Reformation tendency to view Romans as a syllabus of necessary dogmatic topics — a tendency that has survived even F. C. Baur's devastating critique. Such a reading of this letter makes it seem natural that Paul should communicate to the Romans his authoritative thoughts on sin and fallenness, justification and sanctification, law and grace, election and freedom — without any need to see a context within the Roman Christian community as determining the form and content of the communication. It was assumed that what Paul had once said to the Romans coincided at all essential points with what early Protestants still wanted to say, to the Romans and to each other. In this way, what was actually a creative rereading of Paul's letter, within a specific early modern European context, was able to pass itself off as the *sensus literalis*. To highlight the pragmatic, contextual dimension of Paul's argument is not to undermine the Lutheran or Reformed interpretation, but simply to call for hermeneutical self-awareness. Here as elsewhere, the use of scripture in theological construction is a matter of creative rereading rather than mere appeal to an authoritarian norm.

When Paul states that "sin will have no dominion over you, for you are not under law but under grace," he has in mind two communal identities that represent competing solutions to the reality of sin, which (it is agreed) holds sway everywhere else. From the perspective of one community, the other's appeal to grace perversely legitimates the dominion of sin (cf. 6:1). Paul's aim is to show that the reverse is the case: that it is precisely where the law determines communal identity that the dominion of sin is most powerfully exposed. Roman Jewish Christians occupy an anomalous social location between the two identities and must be helped to complete the transition from the one to the other. Roman Gentile Christians represent the social embodiment of "grace" but must be helped to understand *why* they

---

views stumble over the fact that the law of Moses was given not to humanity in general, but to Israel" (*Conflict and Identity*, 236).

42. That Romans 7 is addressed especially to Jewish Christians is recognized by Minear, *Obedience of Faith*, 62; Bläser, *Das Gesetz bei Paulus*, 29-30; Wright, "The Messiah and the People of God," 147; Esler, *Conflict and Identity*, 224-27. This is preferable to the view of Scroggs that Romans 7 rejects a possible solution to the problem of enthusiasm ("Paul as Rhetorician," 288). Nor is there any indication that Paul here adopts the persona of the Gentile constitutionally incapable of observing the law (Stowers, *Rereading Romans*, 258-84).

have not converted to Judaism. In this context, Paul's strategy is to persuade members of both groupings that their common baptism represents a destruction of old, sinful identities and the creation of a new identity grounded in the death and resurrection of Christ, and that this is the case irrespective of whether or not the pre-baptismal life was a life "under the law," within the Jewish community. For that reason, there are striking parallels between the depiction of conversion as a "dying to sin" in 6:1-14 and as a "dying to the law" in 7:1-6. The unusual use of the dative in the sense "in relation to" is common to both (ἀπεθάνομεν τῇ ἁμαρτίᾳ, 6:2; ἐθανατώθητε τῷ νόμῳ, 7:4). In both cases, the death that occurs in baptism and conversion is a dying in union with Christ's death: the detailed outworking of this point in 6:3-7 is alluded to in the reference in 7:4 to dying to the law "through the body of Christ." In both cases, the self that dies is an other: ὁ παλαιὸς ἡμῶν ἄνθρωπος, τὸ σῶμα τῆς ἁμαρτίας in 6:6, the "husband" of 7:2-3. In both cases, union with Christ in his death also entails union with him in his resurrection: here, too, the later passage alludes to the fuller statements in the earlier one ("that you may belong to another, to him who has been raised from the dead," 7:4; cf. 6:4, 5, 8-11). Both passages employ the same double-sided images of oldness and newness (6:4-5; 7:6), slavery (6:16-23; 7:6), and fruitfulness (6:21-22; 7:4, 5). The purpose of these parallels is to present "dying to the law" as a subset of the more comprehensive category of "dying to sin." All Paul's addressees have experienced in baptism a dying to sin, and for some but not others this dying to sin also entailed a dying to the law. Why? Because, as chapter 7 will proceed to show, it is precisely where the law holds sway that sin's dominion is experienced most intensely.

(ii) The Genesis of Sin

In baptism, the law itself is nullified as the determinant of identity. Paul addresses himself in 7:1 to "brothers and sisters" who "know the law," and that can only be a reference to Christian Jews (or proselytes). The law, he reminds these fellow Jews, is binding on people only during their lifetimes; this is of course true of any law (v. 1). Since as Christians these fellow Jews have "died" in baptism, the Jewish law no longer applies to them (vv. 4-6). As an analogy for this death of the self-as-other, Paul develops the image of the woman who is legally bound to her husband as long as he lives (v. 2), but who cannot be stigmatized as an adulteress if she remarries after her husband's death (v. 3). Similarly, those who were once "under the law" but now realize their new baptismal identity in Christ cannot be charged with "adultery," that is, with apostasy. Only if death had not taken place (Christ's death and their own) would such a charge be justified. But in fact this inclusive death *has* taken place, and those who have experienced it have passed beyond the sphere of the law's jurisdiction. Developing earlier hints in 5:20 and 6:14, Paul now says that the law operates *within* the dominion of sin: "While we were living in the flesh, our sinful passions, *aroused by the law,* were working in our members to bear fruit for death" (7:5).[43] If such a view of the law is correct, then salvation must involve salvation from the law itself and thus ideological separation from the Jewish community.

The law increases the trespass and arouses sinful passions. The obvious conclusion is that the law is sin (v. 7) — that the law arouses sin in the sense that the conduct prescribed by the law is sinful, so that obedience to the law is disobedience to God. Nevertheless, Paul repudiates this conclusion in vv. 7-12, drawing a distinction between the content of the law (which is of divine origin and therefore good) and its effect: through the machinations of Sin (a quasi-demonic power), the law gives rise to sin and death.[44] The argument of vv. 7-12 is not simply that the law reveals sin, but that the effect of the law is somehow to *evoke* sin; the whole passage elaborates the reference in v. 5 to "our sinful passions, aroused by the law." When in v. 7 Paul says that "without the law I should not have known sin" and that "I should not have known desire," he means not that he would not have *understood* sin or desire without the law, but rather that he would not have *experienced* sin or desire.[45] This is clear from the sequel: "But sin, finding opportunity in the commandment, wrought in me every kind of desire" (v. 8). Without the law, the speaker would not have known desire (v. 7), whereas with the coming of the law desire was formed in him (v. 8): in order for these two statements to correspond, the "knowledge" of v. 7 must be experiential rather than theoretical. Sin used the commandment prohibiting desire precisely to elicit the prohibited desire. This point is repeated in vv. 9-12 with the addition of a new element, the fact that in the hands of Sin the law becomes the instrument producing not only sin but also its penalty — death. Thus, "Sin worked death in me through what is good" — that is, through the law (v. 13).

43. Minear's view, that the sin aroused by the law is the sin of condemning one's Christian brothers (*Obedience of Faith,* 67), is unlikely, since in 7:7-8 "sin" is identified with "desire."

44. This marks a new phase in Paul's account of the law. Hübner, *Law in Paul's Thought,* 71-72, rightly stresses the active nature of sin and the passive nature of the law in this passage and proceeds to contrast this with Galatians 3:19 (78). Yet Hübner denies that at this point Romans 7:7-12 also contrasts with 4:15 and 5:20 (79-83), thereby emphasizing differences between Romans and Galatians at the expense of differences within Romans itself.

45. So Käsemann, *Commentary on Romans,* 193, and others.

However this strange argument is to be interpreted, Paul's strategy seems reasonably clear. The "sin" focused on is that of "desire" (ἐπιθυμία); the abbreviated citation of the tenth commandment (v. 7) eliminates all reference to specific objects of desire (the neighbor's wife, house, or whatever) in order to focus on the phenomenon of prohibited desire in itself. Paul traces desire back to its origin and tells how it was aroused *by the law* — the very law that also prohibited it. He hastens to add that the law is good in itself and only had this appalling effect because it fell into the hands of Sin; but this qualification does little to mitigate the radical nature of Paul's claim. His strategy is clear: he wishes to evoke in his readers a horror of life under the law. They should retain their belief in the law's essential goodness, but they must also recognize that its effect in practice has been to arouse the desire it prohibits. To allow one's identity to be determined by the law is to fall victim to the exorbitance of desire, which the law cannot quell and which it even exacerbates.

How can Paul make such a claim about the law and expect it to be credible? It has been argued that he is referring to the tendency of any authoritative commandment to provoke resentment and rebellion,[46] or to the way in which the law leads to the sin of "legalism," seeking to establish one's own righteousness.[47] Neither view is very plausible. Throughout Romans 7:7-25, sin is seen as a cruel fate against which the subject protests, rather than as a deliberate act of rebellion springing from resentment. The view that "desire" here means the desire to earn salvation is based on the misunderstanding of Paul's faith/works antithesis that it has been one of the main aims of the present work to expose. In addition, the identification of ἐπιθυμία with "legalism" is arbitrary and receives no support from Pauline usage elsewhere.[48]

An alternative solution is that the persuasiveness of Paul's claim about sin and the law depends in large part on its scriptural echoes. Many interpreters have noted that the narrative of Genesis 2–3 is alluded to in Romans 7.[49] It is, however, not quite true to say with Käsemann that "a story is told in vv. 9-11 and that the event depicted can refer strictly only to Adam."[50] The complex

---

46. Cranfield, *Romans*, 1:337-38; H. Räisänen, *Paul and the Law*, 142.

47. Bultmann, "Romans 7 and the Anthropology of Paul," 155; G. Bornkamm, "Sin, Law and Death: An Exegetical Study of Romans 7," 96; H. Conzelmann, *Outline of the Theology of the New Testament*, 227; Käsemann, *Commentary on Romans*, 194; Hübner, *Law in Paul's Thought*, 72-78.

48. See the full discussion of this point in H. Räisänen, "Zum Gebrauch von *EPITHYMIA und EPITHYMEIN bei Paulus*."

49. Accepted by most recent commentators, but opposed by W. Kümmel, *Römer 7 und die Bekehrung des Paulus*, 86-87; P. Bläser, *Das Gesetz bei Paulus*, 114-15; R. Gundry, "The Moral Frustration of Paul," 231; D. Moo, *Romans*, 423-41; P. Esler, *Conflict and Identity*, 233-36.

50. Käsemann, *Commentary on Romans*, 196.

event depicted here includes the coming of the commandment (v. 9), and the commandment in question is, "You shall not desire" (v. 7). The citation of the tenth commandment in abbreviated form can refer strictly only to the event of Sinai. There it is that the commandment "came" (ἐλθούσης, 7:9): for it was at Sinai that the law "came in alongside" (παρεισῆλθεν, 5:20). The use of the first-person singular suggests a recapitulation of the Sinai event in individual experience.[51] Yet allusions to Genesis 2–3 are unmistakable. In Romans 7:7-12, it seems that the (individualized) Sinai event is interpreted with the help of motifs borrowed from Genesis. Events in the garden are superimposed on events in the wilderness that are themselves made contemporary and individualized.[52] Detailed correspondences between Romans 7 and Genesis are as follows:

(1) "I was once alive apart from the law [χωρὶς νόμου]" (Rom. 7:9). In Genesis 2:7-15 the Lord God forms man out of the dust and places him in Eden, where he is able to partake of "the tree of life in the midst of the garden." Elsewhere in Romans it is said of the pre-Sinai period that "where the law is not [οὗ οὐκ ἔστιν νόμος], there is no transgression" (4:15) and that "sin is not reckoned in the absence of law [μὴ ὄντος νόμου]" (5:13). Yet, "death reigned from Adam until Moses" (5:14). Thus, the claim that "I was once alive apart from the law" projects the Genesis motif of "original life" onto the pre-Sinai experience of Israel or the individual Israelite.[53] The place of this "original life" is named not only "Eden" but also "Paradise" (ὁ παράδεισος, Gen. 2:8, etc.), which — whatever its original location — is now to be found in the third heaven (2 Cor. 12:2, 4). Paul may here allude to the myth of the soul's fall from an original heavenly life into embodied existence, applying it specifically to Jew-

51. The focus on the individual "I" should not be played down — as it is by N. T. Wright, *Climax of the Covenant*, 197-98, where it is identified with "Israel"; cf. also D. Moo, "Israel and Paul in Romans 7.7-12," on which see my *PHF*, 360n. The individual focus is entirely consistent with the pragmatic aim of this chapter, which is to dissuade Roman Christians from the practice of a communally normative mode of life.

52. For an interpretation of this passage oriented more towards Sinai and its aftermath than towards Adam, see *PHF*, 356-80; the Genesis background is also acknowledged, however (359-60; 508n).

53. R. Gundry objects that "the command came to light after the creation and setting of man in Eden: there is no hint of an interval without law" ("Moral Frustration of Paul," 231). But Paul exercises a degree of interpretative freedom here, extending the barely perceptible interval between the arrival in paradise and the giving of the commandment (Gen. 2:15, 16), while eliminating the subsequent intervals between commandment and transgression (Gen. 2:16–3:7) and between transgression and death (Gen. 3:8–5:5).

ish existence under the law.[54] Alternatively or additionally, he may have childhood in mind.[55]

(2) "But when the commandment came . . ." (Rom. 7:9). According to Genesis 2:16-17, "the Lord God commanded [ἐνετείλατο] Adam, saying, 'From every tree of the garden you shall eat food. . . .'" The commandment (ἐντολή, Rom. 7:8-13 × 6) was "unto life" (Rom. 7:10) in that its aim was the preservation of access to the tree of life, just as its contravention meant separation from the tree of life (cf. Gen. 3:22-24). In Romans 7 the reference is ostensibly to the tenth commandment, and thus to Sinai rather than Eden. Yet ἐντολή here is synonymous with νόμος, and after vv. 7-8 the link with the tenth commandment becomes tenuous. Both points suggest that ἐντολή includes an allusion to the ἐνετείλατο of Genesis 2:16.

(3) The result of the coming of the commandment was that "sin came to life and I died" (Rom. 7:9). This is a highly compressed statement, needing to be broken down into its component parts. The first stage is that sin "found opportunity in the commandment" (Rom. 7:8, 11). In Genesis 3:1-5, the serpent finds opportunity in the commandment to bring about an action that will (eventually) kill the perpetrator. Paul's personification of Sin can derive only from Genesis, and the same is true of his repeated claim that the commandment provided an ἀφορμή for Sin (Rom. 7:8, 11). If we ask *how* Sin "found opportunity in the commandment," the answer would be that the category of the "sinful act" is actually the *creation* of the commandment and does not exist prior to the commandment.[56]

(4) Through the commandment, "sin . . . deceived me" (ἐξηπάτησέν με, Rom. 7:11). Eve, too, complains that the serpent, using the commandment, "deceived me" (ἠπάτησέν με, Gen. 3:13). The "man under the law" of Romans 7 is Eve as well as Adam. Paul warns of a similar reenactment of the Fall on the part of the Corinthians: "I fear lest, as the serpent deceived [ἐξηπάτησεν] Eve by his cunning, so your thoughts will be corrupted from the integrity and purity which is in Christ" (2 Cor. 11:3). After Sinai as in the Garden, Sin uses the commandment to "deceive" by arguing persuasively for the benefits of transgression.

(5) The serpent's use of the commandment to deceive generates desire: "Sin . . . wrought in me every kind of desire" (Rom. 7:8).[57] This may be linked

54. Compare E. Fuchs, *Die Freiheit des Glaubens: Römer 5-8 ausgelegt*, 58-60.

55. See *PHF*, 378-79.

56. This point is rightly noted by T. Engberg-Pedersen, *Paul and the Stoics*, 241-42, although without reference to Genesis 2–3.

57. "The work of the law as a spur to sin can be demonstrated only by Adam" (Käsemann, *Commentary on Romans*, 196).

with the desirability of the tree (Gen. 3:6) or, more probably, with the sexual awakening consequent on eating its fruit (3:7).[58] This is confirmed by the sexual orientation of the tenth commandment in both of its Septuagintal forms (Exod. 20:17; Deut. 5:21). The "desire" motif also evokes strong echoes of Sinai and its aftermath: for, as Paul recognizes elsewhere, the immediate post-Sinai history of Israel is a history of illicit desire, which comes to fruition in actions such as idolatry or πορνεία (cf. 1 Cor. 10:6-10).[59] Yet the Genesis narrative still underlies the claim that Sin has used the commandment to arouse sinful desire. Sin, initially externalized in the form of the serpent, has taken up residence within the human frame.

(6) The outcome is simply death: "I died" (Rom. 7:9). Thus, "the command-ment . . . proved to be death to me" (7:10; cf. v. 13); or rather, "Sin, finding opportunity in the commandment, . . . by it killed me" (7:11). In Genesis, the effect of the sin that has arisen through the commandment is mortal-ity rather than immediate death (cf. Gen. 3:19, 22-24; 5:5). Again, echoes of the history of Israel are readily perceptible, for Paul — reflecting no doubt on the annihilation of the Sinai generation in the wilderness — argues elsewhere that "the letter kills," referring to the inscribed stone tablets and their consequences (2 Cor. 3:6-11). Yet the connection between command-ment, transgression, and death also unmistakably recalls Genesis.

(7) It is Genesis rather than the post-Sinai narrative that underlies the first-person narration here: for Adam (or Adam/Eve) is better placed to serve as a representative figure than the Israelite after Sinai. Adam is ὁ πρῶτος ἄνθρωπος, the man formed of earth, and what is true of him is also true of his descendants: οἷος ὁ χοϊκός, τοιοῦτοι καὶ οἱ χοϊκοί (1 Cor. 15:47, 48). It is a short step from this typological relationship to the first-person narration of Romans 7, in which life under the law is interpreted in the light of the Genesis and Sinai narratives that are here conflated.

In Romans 7:7-12, the Genesis narrative makes possible a highly pessimistic account of life under the law. Far from providing a defense against sin, the law is deeply implicated in sin's origins. It is primarily the Genesis story that ac-counts for Paul's presentation of a personified Sin that finds its opportunity to reproduce itself in the good commandment of God. This account of sin's etiology arises not from psychological observation but from scriptural exege-sis. As has already been stated, Paul's purpose is to distance his Jewish Chris-

---

58. So D. Boyarin, A Radical Jew, 162-64, citing PJG¹, 152.
59. See PHF, 363-69.

tian readers from the law and from the community in which it is practiced, in order that, together with Gentile Christians, they may seek their identity instead in the death and resurrection of Christ.

There is more to come, however. The first-person narration continues, in spite of repeated references to the speaker's death (vv. 10, 11, 13). The continuation is characterized not only by a change of tense (from past to present) but also by a change of vocabulary. Verses 7-12 are determined by the polarity of life and death, vv. 13-25 by the polarity of good and evil. These four coordinates may be traced back to Moses' great farewell appeal, where they summarize the contents and the possible outcomes of the Torah:

> Behold I have set before your face this day life and death, good and evil [τὴν ζωὴν καὶ τὸν θάνατον, τὸ ἀγαθὸν καὶ τὸ κακόν]. (Deut. 30:15)[60]

In Romans 7, τὸ ἀγαθόν is the law (v. 13 [× 2]), but it is also what I do *not* find in myself (v. 18a), what I will to do but do not (vv. 19a, 21); Paul also uses the synonym καλός to make closely related points about the law (v. 16) and about myself (vv. 18b, 21). As for τὸ κακόν, this is what I actually do, although unwillingly (vv. 19b, 21). Thus, the Mosaic good/evil polarity has gone awry. Moses offers good or evil, but I have sought the good yet realized the evil. The same is true of the life/death polarity. I have sought the life attained by way of the commandments, but I have realized only death (vv. 7-12). How is it that unsought-for death and evil are found precisely in the quest for life and the good? In the case of the life/death polarity, it is the narrative of Genesis 2–3 that explains how the commandment that promised life was manipulated by Sin to bring forth illicit desire and death. Moses' appeal at the conclusion of the Torah has already been subverted by the parable of the law's advent at its opening. The question is whether the Genesis narrative can also shed light on the subversion of the good/evil polarity.

In this connection we recall for the first time the *content* of the commandment in Genesis 2. Adam and Eve are to refrain from the fruit of the tree of the knowledge of good and evil: τὸ ξύλον τοῦ εἰδέναι γνωστὸν καλοῦ καὶ πονηροῦ (2:9), [τὸ ξύλον] τοῦ γινώσκειν καλὸν καὶ πονηρόν (2:17). Is the tree a symbol of the Torah itself, the holy and just and good law of God in which the knowledge of good and evil is to be found?

The absence of the term πονηρόν from Romans 7 is not a problem for this reading. If the ἀγαθόν of Deuteronomy 30 can on occasion be replaced by καλόν (the term used in Genesis 2), there is no difficulty in seeing κακόν and

---

60. See *PHF*, 506-8.

πονηρόν as interchangeable. Nor is it a problem that the Torah is identified *both* with the giving of the commandment (Rom. 7:7-12) *and* with the knowledge that the commandment prohibits (7:13-25). On the contrary, it is precisely this disjunction that would explain the difference between the two passages (together with Deuteronomy 30). It is, then, the Torah itself that is the tree of the knowledge of good and evil — a knowledge that ought to be entirely positive and beneficial, but is not. Thus, verbs of knowing or perceiving recur constantly:

> *I did not know* [οὐκ ἔγνων] sin except through the law. (7:7)
> *We know* [οἴδαμεν] that the law is spiritual. (7:14)
> For what I accomplish *I do not know* [οὐ γινώσκω]. (7:15)
> *I agree* with the law that it is good. (7:16)
> *I know* [οἶδα] that nothing good dwells in me, that is, in my flesh. (7:18)
> *I find* then the law that, in my willing the good, evil is present to me. (7:21)
> *I delight in* the law of God . . . , but *I see* another law in my members. (7:22-23)

This is the knowledge of good and evil accessible through the law of Moses and attained by Adam and Eve — to their own destruction. Once again, the Genesis narrative is projected onto the Torah as a whole, subverting the gracious offer of life rather than death, good rather than evil, by revealing that death is the outcome of the quest for life and that evil is the outcome of the quest for the good.[61]

The knowledge of good and evil sounds utterly simple and straightforward as Moses calls us to accept one and reject the other. But it is in fact highly problematic, full of contradictions, tension, and anomalies. My knowledge of the good is limited to my acknowledgment that the law itself is good, my desire to realize this goodness in practical conduct, and my despairing recognition that I am quite unable to do so owing to the lack of the good within me. My knowledge of the evil is not a theoretical knowledge of what to avoid but an experiential knowledge of every kind of prohibited desire and of practices that continue to reproduce themselves in defiance of the law's opposition and my mind's endorsement of that opposition. The Torah is the tree of the knowledge of good and evil, and eating its fruit has left me entangled in

61. The importance of the cognitive dimension of the encounter with the law narrated in Romans 7 is emphasized by T. Engberg-Pedersen, *Paul and the Stoics*, 243. I would add that this stems from an identification of the Torah with the tree of the knowledge of good and evil.

insoluble contradictions. The Mosaic coordinates collapse in on one another, and there is no firm ground on which to stand.

The tree and its fruit are good in themselves, and Paul therefore emphasizes the goodness of the law (Rom. 7:12, 13, 14, 16, 22) as well as its evil effects. This has led some scholars to regard the whole section as an "apologia for the law."[62] But that is surely an exaggerated claim, since there is a far greater emphasis on the evil results of the law's coming than on its own essential goodness.[63] It is also frequently claimed that Paul's appreciation of the goodness of the law shows that his thought has developed and matured since the allegedly angry and intemperate discussions of the law in Galatians.[64] But as with other differences between Galatians and Romans, the explanation is to be sought in the different audiences addressed rather than in Paul's own theological development. Galatians is addressed to Gentiles who have in many cases only recently become acquainted with the law, whereas Romans 7 is addressed primarily to Jewish Christians or proselytes ("those who know the law," v. 1), for whom the goodness and holiness of the law is second nature. While the remarkable appeal to Genesis may possibly indicate a profounder level of theological reflection than in Galatians, it is important not to lose sight of the pragmatic intent of Paul's argument. He wishes to persuade Jewish Christians to find their identity exclusively in Christ, and not in the Torah, and his Genesis-inspired argument in Romans 7 aims to persuade his readers that life under the law leads only to insoluble contradiction as the quest for life issues in death and the quest for the good issues in evil. Even in this extraordinary passage, Paul is no disembodied theorizer.[65]

---

62. W. G. Kümmel, *Römer 7 und die Bekehrung des Paulus*, 8; J. C. Beker, *Paul the Apostle*, 238. Räisänen more appropriately calls this chapter "an apology for [Paul's] theology of the law" (*Paul and the Law*, 67).

63. So Käsemann, *Commentary on Romans*, 192.

64. So H.-J. Schoeps, *Paul: The Theology of the Apostle*, 183; H. Hübner, *Law in Paul's Thought, passim;* W. D. Davies, "Paul and the Law," 8-9.

65. This view of the purpose of Romans 7 makes discussion of the extent to which "man under the law" is aware of his "desperate plight" (Hübner, *Law in Paul's Thought*, 76-78) redundant. As an abstract issue of theological anthropology, this question is of no interest to Paul. Speaking ὡς ὑπὸ νόμον, μὴ ὢν αὐτὸς ὑπὸ νόμον (1 Cor. 9:20), Paul's first-person narration exposes the sinister reality of life under law in order to persuade Christian Jewish readers that an identity determined by Christ *and* the law is no longer feasible.

4. Law and Spirit (Romans 7–8)

As we have seen, Romans 6 and 7 represent two sides of a single argument, arising out of the grace/law opposition introduced in 5:20 and repeated in 6:14-15. Both chapters are concerned with the realization of "righteousness" or "obedience" (cf. 6:12-23), with "doing the good" (7:18, 19, 21). If the good as defined by the law differs from the traditional Christian pattern of conduct (cf. 6:17), Paul does not here reflect on that difference. In the end, it seems that the two accounts of the good converge (cf. 13:8-10). Thus, both are concerned with mastering the imperious demands of "desire" (6:12; 7:7). Where they diverge as sharply as ever is not in their content but in their context or ethos, determined in one case by the death and resurrection of Christ and in the other by the text (γράμμα, 7:6) known as "the law of Moses." In the one context, righteousness is realizable; in the other, firsthand testimony indicates that it is not. The anthropological optimism of chapter 6 gives way to the deep pessimism of the first-person singular narration of chapter 7. If the Christian and Jewish communities are seen as competing with one another to realize the good, one will be the clear winner and the other the equally clear loser: for one community pursues the good in the context of the reality of the divine saving action in Christ, whereas the other remains entrenched in what has been an anachronism since the resurrection of Christ. That at least is what is implied in Paul's contrast between "the newness of the Spirit" and "the oldness of the letter" (7:6). Like Moses, Paul sets before his readers life and death, blessing and curse (cf. Deut. 30:19): but now the life is the risen life of Christ, and the death is the living death of one for whom the spirituality of the law merely exposes the depths of his own carnality (cf. 7:14). There is a particular message here to those Roman Jewish Christians among whom Paul's letter finds an audience, singled out here as "those who know the law" (7:1). They are to choose life within the reign of grace rather than death within the realm of the law. Above all, they are to learn to recognize the difference. But Roman Gentile Christians must also be convinced of the difference. As Paul has learned from his Galatian experience, the law can still exercise a powerful attraction on Gentiles. Newness is not self-evidently preferable to oldness (cf. Rom. 7:6; Luke 5:39). If, listening in to Paul's narration as outsiders to the law, they learn that life under the law is the nightmare of permanent exclusion from paradise — then so much the better.[66]

---

66. The concluding section of this chapter consists largely of new material, replacing *PJG¹*, 153-59, although drawing on some of the exegetical conclusions reached there.

(i) "To those under law as one under law . . ."

On this reading, Romans 7 is a seamless whole. The point is worth emphasizing, since the rhetorical power and the interpretive problems of the first-person narrative have often led to an isolation of vv. 7-25 (or vv. 14-25) from vv. 1-6, which is then seen as an unimportant postscript to chapter 6. As a result, one fails to grasp that the first-person narrative is still determined by the law/grace antithesis announced in 6:14-15 and given definitive form in 7:1-6, where its christological logic is strongly emphasized. The first-person narrative grows out of the claim in v. 5 that "when we were in the flesh, the passions of sins *that came about through the law* were operative in our members to bear fruit for death." Where the first-person narrative (or the latter part of it) becomes detached from the law/grace antithesis, the tendency is to see it as introductory to chapter 8 and to overlook entirely its connection to chapter 6.

To separate out the present-tense narration of 7:14-25 and to apply it to the experience of the *Christian* is highly implausible. The present tense indicates that Paul is now describing the "living death" that arises out of the primal event described in vv. 7-12. It does not mean that he is now analyzing the Christian experience of sin.[67] The thanksgiving of v. 25a is hardly a valid argument in favor of identifying the speaker as a Christian, since it may plausibly be seen as an interjection anticipating the liberation from the law of sin announced in 8:1-2.[68] The claim that the delight in the law portrayed in 7:22 is incompatible with Paul's view of "unredeemed humanity" overlooks the fact

67. As argued still by Cranfield, *Romans*, 1:344-47; Dunn, *Romans*, 1:403-4. Dunn's reading of Romans 7 is summarized in the matching titles he provides for vv. 1-6 and vv. 7-25 respectively: "The Believer Has Been Released from the Law Which Condemned to Death" (1:357), "But the Law Is Still Exploited by Sin and Death, As Experience Demonstrates" (1:374). On this account, vv. 7-25 simply cancel out vv. 1-6. Cranfield's reading is unduly dependent on the judgment that vv. 14-25 express an authentically Christian consciousness of "continuing sinfulness" and "stubborn all-pervasive egotism" (1:347). There is a failure here to distinguish this text's contextual meaning within Romans from its appropriation by Christian piety, which has assimilated it to penitential psalms such as Psalm 51. Also to be noted is the view that Romans 7:14-25 and 8:1-17 describe *successive* phases of the Christian life. Thus F. F. Bruce comments enthusiastically on αὐτὸς ἐγώ in 7:25: "[I]t is 'I by myself' who experience this defeat and frustration, but 'I', as a Christian, am not left to 'myself': 'the law of the Spirit of life in Christ Jesus' has come to dwell within me, and His presence and power make an almighty difference" (*Romans*, 156). In the background here are certain evangelical preoccupations with the attaining of "holiness," "sanctification," and "perfection," traceable to John Wesley. Later Christian usage is again confused with contextual meaning.

68. Against Dunn, "Rom. 7,14-25 in the Theology of Paul," 262; Cranfield, *Romans*, 1:345. Bultmann considers both 7:25b and 8:1 to be glosses ("Glossen im Römerbrief," 279); Dodd, *Romans*, 132, places v. 25b immediately after v. 23. Such expedients are unnecessary.

that Paul elsewhere acknowledges a genuine zeal for the law among his Jewish contemporaries (Rom. 10:2; cf. Phil. 3:6).[69]

The speaker here should not be seen as a Christian but as a Jew. Or rather, the speaker is Paul himself, adopting the persona of one who is under the law, exactly as he elsewhere says he does:

. . . τοῖς ὑπὸ νόμον ὡς ὑπὸ νόμον, μὴ ὢν αὐτὸς ὑπὸ νόμον, ἵνα τοὺς ὑπὸ νόμον κερδήσω. (1 Cor. 9:20)

There is a fictive element in Paul's placing himself under the law, for in reality he is not under the law. Yet his own Jewish roots give the "fiction" its plausibility and integrity: this is no mere play-acting but a reengagement for the sake of others with Paul's own pre-Christian identity.[70] This speech ὡς ὑπὸ νόμον is so compelling and so poignant that generations of readers have assumed that Paul must be articulating his present experience as a Christian. Yet, in its context, the passage can only be speaking of life under another regime than that of grace.[71] The question whether Paul in his pre-Christian period ever experienced the tensions he here describes is unanswerable. All we can say is that he may well have done so. The possibility cannot be ruled out by appeal to Paul's claim to have attained a "blameless" righteousness as defined by the law (Phil. 3:6) — as though life under the law were such a simple and straightforward matter that only one thing could ever be said about it.[72] The attempt to eliminate all trace of autobiography from Romans 7 led to the remarkable conclusion that it is not specifically about Jewish life at all, but that it "describes the struggle and the longing for redemption of the non-Christian."[73] Against this familiar universalizing of Paul's view of the law, we recall that the law in this passage is summed up not only in the term ἐντολή

69. Against Cranfield, *Romans*, 1:346; J. I. Packer, "Wretched Man That I Am," 625-26.

70. Stowers's concept of *prosopopoiia* or "speech-in-character" (*Rereading Romans*, 264-69) seems to continue the tradition stemming from Kümmel, which seeks to distance the "I" of Romans 7 as far as possible from Paul himself. In Stowers's case, the reason is that Romans 7 is said to depict the *non*-Jew's experience of the law (273-84).

71. Such an exegetical conclusion is frequently rejected on the grounds that it betrays a deficiency in that consciousness of sin that is integral to the workings of grace. (For an impassioned statement along these lines, see Cranfield, *Romans*, 1:365-66.) While graceless exegesis probably does exist, confident identifications of specific examples should be treated with some skepticism.

72. The Philippians text became a kind of trump card for the anti-autobiographical reading of Romans 7: see W. G. Kümmel, *Römer 7 und die Bekehrung des Paulus*, 117. For criticism of Kümmel on this point, see G. Theissen, *Psychological Aspects of Pauline Theology*, 234-43; and, from a different standpoint, my *PHF*, 374-80, which finds here a "representative autobiography."

73. Kümmel, *Römer 7 und die Bekehrung des Paulus*, 118.

(7:7-12), which underlines its singularity, but also in the term γράμμα (7:6), which underlines its written character. The γράμμα (cf. 2 Cor. 3:6) is the final form of the Mosaic text that originated in a divine writing, "written . . . on stone tablets" (3.3; cf. v. 7). Life under the law refers concretely to a life determined by the law of Moses. The pragmatic goal of Paul's argument in Romans 7 is to dissuade his Roman addressees from a specific textually mandated, communally normative praxis.

(ii) A Conflict of Jurisdictions

Romans 6–7 must be seen as forming a single, two-part argument that makes good pragmatic sense within Paul's overall strategy. Yet it is also the case that Romans 7–8 forms a single, two-part argument. Romans 7 faces in two directions at once. It completes the law/grace antithesis (cf. 6:14-15) and initiates a law/Spirit antithesis. If the death-and-resurrection conceptuality of 7:1-6 ties this passage to chapter 6, the reference to the Spirit (7:6) anticipates chapter 8. Indeed, the reference to a service of God "in newness of the Spirit and not in oldness of the letter" states precisely the antithesis on which chapters 7–8 are founded, just as the reference to grace and law in 6:14-15 states the antithesis on which chapters 6–7 are founded. To serve God "in oldness of the letter" — that is, under the old regime of the law of Moses — is to experience the divine commandment as the occasion for sin to gain entrance and to become "sin dwelling within me" (vv. 17, 20), "bearing fruit for death" (v. 5). The alternative is to serve God "in newness of the Spirit" (7:6), and this is developed in 8:1-17 by associating the Spirit with *life* (8:2, 6, 10, 11, 13), which counteracts the *death* that has dominated the preceding analysis of life under the law (7:5, 10, 11, 13, 24). The antithesis of law (or letter) and Spirit is simultaneously an antithesis of death and life. Thus Romans 7–8 elaborates the double antithesis of 2 Corinthians 3:6: "The letter kills, but the Spirit gives life." Death and life are the respective outcomes of the service of God "in oldness of the letter" and "in newness of the Spirit" (Rom. 7:6).

Within this broad antithesis is to be found a more elaborate antithesis between "the law of the Spirit of life" and "the law of sin [and death]" (cf. 8:2). This antithesis occurs at the juncture of the two chapters (7:21–8:4), a passage characterized by repeated and diverse use of the term νόμος. This term occurs eleven times in this section, as opposed to twice in the preceding section (7:13-20: vv. 14, 16) and once in the one that follows (8:5-17: v. 7). Also highly distinctive here is the juxtaposition of positive and negative uses of the term. "Law" here is "the law of the Spirit of life in Christ Jesus" (8:2); it is "the decree of the law" that is "fulfilled in us" (8:4); it is "the law of God" (7:22, 25) and "the law of my mind" (7:23). But it is also "the law of sin and death" (8:2), "the law of sin" (7:25), "the law of sin that is in my members," the "other law" that is contrasted with "the law of God" (7:22-23), the "law" that "in my willing to do the good, evil is present" (7:21). We also read of a law that is "weak through the flesh" (8:3). Disentangling this complex usage will prove to be the key to the law/Spirit antithesis that Paul unfolds in these chapters. As we shall see, the liberation from "the law of sin and death," announced in 8:2, is a liberation from the situation analyzed in 7:7-25 in its entirety.

To clarify the usage of νόμος here, it is best to work backwards from 8:2, according to which "the law of the Spirit of life in Christ Jesus freed you/me from the law of sin and death." Whichever pronoun represents the original reading, the link with the preceding first-person narration is clear. The speaker (Paul, speaking ὡς ὑπὸ νόμον, μὴ ὢν αὐτὸς ὑπὸ νόμον) now tells himself or is told by another that the nightmare of self-incomprehension and despair has been brought to an end. There is now no condemnation; his warfare is ended and his iniquity is pardoned. The link with chapter 7 is further strengthened by the reference to "the law of sin and death," which clearly recalls and expands "the law of sin" (7:25).[74] In turn, "the law of sin" recalls "the law of sin in my members," which is itself closely identified with the "other law in my members" (7:23). Wishing to submit fully to the authority of the law of God,

> I see another law in my members, fighting against the law of my mind and making me captive to the law of sin in my members.

While this appears to distinguish a second ("other") law from a third ("the law of sin in my members"), the two expressions are virtually synonymous — as is indicated by the phrase ἐν τοῖς μέλεσίν μου, common to both. This "law" is "other" in relation to "the law of God" (v. 22), which is also "the law of my mind" (v. 23). In order to specify more clearly the nature of its otherness, it is also identified as "the law of sin in my members," standing over against the law of God. If the other law is *not* the law of sin, then there must be not one but two malevolent laws in my members — which would seem unlikely.[75]

---

74. If "law of sin" means the sinful principle in humans, whereas "law of sin and death" refers to the perversion of the Torah (the view of Hübner, *Law in Paul's Thought*, 145-46), then Paul has made life unnecessarily difficult for his readers by failing to make such distinctions clear.

75. Daniel Boyarin suggests that the "other law" is "the command to procreate [Gen. 1:28], and the desire that it produces in the members" (*A Radical Jew*, 159). I find this suggestion bril-

Setting aside the law of the Spirit for the moment, we appear to have just two laws under the various designations: the law of God on the one hand, the law of sin on the other. It has been suggested that "the law of sin and death" is an appropriate description of the law of God that sin usurped in order to deceive and kill (cf. 7:7-12).[76] If so, then the two laws of 7:22-25 are the same law in its original and its perverted forms. Yet νόμος has a singular sense in vv. 7-12: the law usurped by sin remains holy (vv. 11-12). In addition, it would be confusing to speak of "another law in my members" and of "the law of my mind" when what is meant is the same law from different perspectives and in different locations. Instead, Paul here combines literal and metaphorical uses of νόμος, in a straightforward and rhetorically effective way. If the "law of my mind" is the law of God, whose authority my mind acknowledges, then the "law of sin in my members" is the opposing set of imperatives whose authority is acknowledged by my body. If I am "sold under Sin" (7:14), then Sin's word is law. The law of sin is parasitic on the law of God, which it subjects to a process of textual emendation in which prohibitions become requirements and requirements prohibitions.

Continuing to work back through chapter 7, we find a further play on the word "law." Paul discovers "the law that, as I will to do good, evil is present at hand" (v. 21). This "law" is not identical to the law of sin, but there is a close relationship between them. Whenever one seeks the good, one comes up against one's own evil: this is the law that Paul discovers, and it is a "law" in the sense that it states what is invariably and necessarily the case given a certain set of conditions. This is a law of Paul's own nature, discovered by self-observation: "I find the law that. . . ." This usage of νόμος differs from the "law of sin" formulation in that it is descriptive rather than prescriptive. Yet the law that evil is at hand is a proof that the law of sin holds sway. The law Paul discovers does not state merely that evil is always close at hand, *even when* I seek the good. Rather, it states that evil is close at hand *precisely as* I seek the good: and, since v. 21 summarizes vv. 13-20, this is the point of the entire pas-

---

liant and implausible in equal measure. This interpretation of the "other law" leads to an encratite interpretation of Romans 7 as a whole: "Adam's double bind, commanded on the one hand to procreate and on the other to avoid eating of the fruit of the tree of (carnal) knowledge, is the type of Jewish humanity under the flesh, commanded to procreate but also to not have lustful desires, let alone act on them. The Christian, however, having been released from procreation and thus from sexuality, can conquer her desires and bear fruit for God" (165). Boyarin may, however, have shown that Romans 7 is at least open to an encratite reading, especially in conjunction with 1 Corinthians 7.

76. Cf. Wilckens, *Der Brief an die Römer*, 2:90; Dunn, *Romans*, 1:409; Fitzmyer, *Romans*, 476; rightly rejected by Byrne, *Romans*, 232.

sage. Once again, sin works "through the good" (v. 13). In other words, the relation between willing the good and doing the evil is not a merely contingent one. Rather, Paul's law is that willing the good has doing the evil as its necessary consequence. The attempt to make one's conduct conform to God's law, in full recognition that what the law prescribes is holy and just and good, generates only evil: that is the desperate situation of the person who is under the law of Moses and who delights in it and acknowledges its goodness.

It is to the credit of the Bultmannian reading of Romans 7 that it emphasizes the necessary and non-contingent relation between willing the good and doing the evil, recognizing that in this chapter sin consistently operates through the law (vv. 5, 7), the commandment (v. 11), or the good (v. 13). Yet, on this reading, doing the evil is typically restricted to the "boasting" that is excluded in 3:27, or to the quest to "establish one's own righteousness" (10:3). Thus, according to Käsemann: "Standing under the law repeats the situation of Adam, namely, that through the law a person is driven to desire self-assertion, self-glory and pious ungodliness."[77] It follows that "the moral person is precisely the one who is most deeply engulfed in the power of sin"; Paul here is not "simply bewailing our lack of will-power."[78] Käsemann here repeats Bultmann's insistence that sin comes to expression not merely in specific transgressions but above all in "boasting" (Rom. 3:27), in which one puts God under an obligation and so subverts the creature's relation of absolute dependence on the Creator.[79] As we have seen in the previous chapter, a specifically Jewish "boasting" is in 3:27 subjected to a ban on boasting as such; the boasting generated by the law is indeed an example of a more widely instantiated phenomenon. Yet Paul never describes boasting as "sin," nor does he see it as an expression of "desire."[80] If we are to import material from elsewhere in Romans into chapter 7, it would be more appropriate to appeal to the catena in 3:9-20: for the law of sin is located "in my members," and the earlier passage attributes sins of the throat, tongue, lips, mouth, feet, and eyes to "those who are in the law" and who seek righteousness "by works of law." In Romans 7, however, the evil consequent on the pursuit of the good is left general and non-specific.

77. Käsemann, *Commentary on Romans*, 197.

78. Käsemann, *Commentary on Romans*, 200-201.

79. For the original version of this reading, see Bultmann's article "Romans 7 and the Anthropology of Paul." Neither Bultmann nor Käsemann sees how the "law" of v. 21, asserting a necessary and non-contingent relationship between willing the good and producing the evil, might strengthen their position.

80. On this point, see Räisänen, "Zum Gebrauch von EPITHUMIA und EPITHUMEIN bei Paulus."

"Paul's law" (v. 21) is related to the "law of sin" but is to be differentiated from it. More closely related to the law of sin is "sin dwelling within me," which produces evil when I strive for the good (vv. 17, 20). Indeed, the "law of sin in my members" simply adds a further metaphorical layer to "sin dwelling within me," where the background is the phenomenon of demonic posses-sion.[81] How, though, has it come about that my very own agency has been usurped by this external power that has taken up residence within me? Pur-suing the law of sin back to its source, we find ourselves back in the Garden of Eden on the fateful occasion when the prohibition that preserved access to the tree of life became the occasion of death. Compliance with the law of sin is enforced by sin's own agency, and it was the law of God that provided the occasion for this usurpation of my own agency *and that continues to do so*. It was the case then, and it is still the case now, that sin reproduces itself in me "through the law" (vv. 5, 7), "through the commandment" (vv. 11, 13), and "through the good" (v. 13): for sin operates now in and through my willing what the law defines as the good. While later references to sin's agency use more dramatic imagery (ἀντιστρατευόμενον, αἰχμαλωτίζοντα, v. 23), Paul has earlier preferred the term κατεργάζεσθαι:

ἀφορμὴν δὲ λαβοῦσα ἡ ἁμαρτία διὰ τῆς ἐντολῆς κατειργάσατο ἐν ἐμοὶ πᾶσαν ἐπιθυμίαν. (v. 8)

. . . ἀλλὰ ἡ ἁμαρτία, ἵνα φανῇ ἁμαρτία, διὰ τοῦ ἀγαθοῦ μοι κατεργαζομένη θάνατον, ἵνα γένηται καθ' ὑπερβολὴν ἁμαρτωλὸς διὰ τῆς ἐντολῆς. (v. 13)

ὃ γὰρ κατεργάζομαι οὐ γινώσκω . . . νυνὶ δὲ οὐκέτι ἐγὼ κατεργάζομαι αὐτὸ ἀλλὰ ἡ οἰκοῦσα ἐν ἐμοὶ ἁμαρτία. (v. 17)

εἰ δὲ ὃ οὐ θέλω τοῦτο ποιῶ, οὐκέτι ἐγὼ κατεργάζομαι αὐτὸ ἀλλὰ ἡ οἰκοῦσα ἐν ἐμοὶ ἁμαρτία. (v. 20)

What sin did once — working evil through what is good — sin still does to this day. The transition from a primal event to an ongoing present is indicated in the present participle and the ἵνα clause in v. 13. The malevolent agency em-powered by the law is identified first as "sin" (vv. 7-14, × 9), then as "sin dwell-ing within me" (vv. 17, 20), then as "the law of sin in my members" (v. 23; cf. v. 25) — but it is the same agency that is referred to on each occasion.

Romans 7 is a seamless garment, and there is no room at all for a new speaker or theme from v. 14 onwards. Sin works through the law, and there is

81. So Käsemann, *Commentary on Romans,* 204.

no access to a law of God that has not already been commandeered by the law of sin. Majestic in its holiness and spirituality, the law's effect in the realm of the flesh is uniformly disastrous. From a pragmatic perspective, Paul's argument functions as a *warning* to his Roman addressees to avoid further entanglement with the law of Moses and the individual and communal praxis that it sanctions.[82]

(iii) Rehabilitating the Law

This, then, is "the law of sin and death." Those held captive by it can be liberated only by "the law of the Spirit of life in Christ Jesus" (8:2). Deliverance from "the law of sin and death" (8:2) is also deliverance from "the law of sin in my members" (7:23), from "sin dwelling within me" (7:17, 20), and from "sin" itself (cf. 7:7-12): for these different expressions all speak of the same reality. In this reference to "the law of the Spirit of life" and "the law of sin and death," the relationship between Romans 7 and 8 is brought into the sharpest focus. These chapters develop a complex antithesis between death and life, law and the Spirit, representing two regimes established within two distinct communal contexts. The communal dimension is, however, more explicit in the other Pauline exposition of this antithesis, in 2 Corinthians 3, where the references to the reading of "the old covenant" or of "Moses" provide an unusually vivid glimpse of synagogue worship. There is nothing of the kind in Romans 7, since Roman Jewish Christians are to some degree alienated from Roman synagogues although not from the law itself. In vv. 1-6, it is assumed that life under the law is a shared communal experience: Paul wishes to persuade the Jewish Christian readers he here envisages (cf. v. 1) that this experience lies now in the past. In the rest of the chapter, it is a solitary individual who speaks; only in v. 14 is the communal dimension again briefly acknowledged ("*We know* that the law is spiritual . . ."). Indeed, not the least significant difference between chapters 7 and 8 is the contrast between the first-person singular usage of 7:7-25 and the predominance of the first-person plural in chapter 8 (especially in the second half of the chapter). In Romans 7, reviving his past persona as one whose identity is determined by the law, Paul depicts himself as engaged in an isolated and failing struggle with hostile powers who are too much for him. In chapter 8, he joins himself with his readers in articulating a common identity in Christ, realized through the Spirit:

82. It is not just "a systematically developed negative foil" to the account of life in the Spirit that follows, as argued by T. Engberg-Pedersen, *Paul and the Stoics,* 368n.

So then, brothers and sisters, *we* are debtors, not to the flesh to live according to the flesh. . . . (8:12)

When *we* cry, "Abba, Father," the Spirit himself bears witness with *our* spirit that *we* are children of God. (8:17)

. . . *we ourselves,* who have the firstfruits of the Spirit, groan inwardly as we await adoption, the redemption of *our* bodies. For in this hope *we* were saved. (8:23-24)

We know that for those who love God all things work together for good. (8:28)

If God is for *us,* who is against *us?* (8:31)

In all these things *we* are more than conquerors through him who loved *us.*" (8:37)

Second-person plural address is also to be found here (8:9-11, 13-15a), but from v. 15b the first-person plural is used consistently until the end of the chapter.

In v. 15 it is said both that "*you* received the Spirit of adoption" and that "*we* cry, 'Abba, Father,'" and the rhetorical difference between the two modes of address is considerable. Where discourse is addressed to "you," its hearers understand themselves solely as the speaker's object, and the sense of community with one another is weak. Where "you" becomes "we," the inclusion of the speaker converts an objectified "you" into a communal subject. This is of course not an absolute distinction; the rhetorical effect of first- or second-person plural discourse will be shaped by a range of contextual factors. When Paul states his desire "that *you* may *together* glorify the God and Father of our Lord Jesus Christ" (15:6), the second-person address refers explicitly to their communal existence. Nevertheless, in itself "we" gives much clearer expression to community than "you." In the letter as a whole, first-person plural language is infrequent in chapters 1–4 and 9–16, although it does occur from time to time (e.g., 1:5; 3:9; 4:24-25; 9:24; 12:4-7; 13:12-13; 14:10-12; 15:1-4). It is, however, the dominant mode of address in major sections of chapters 5–8, of which the second half of chapter 8 is much the most extensive (5:1-11; 6:1-8; 7:5-6; 8:15b-39).[83]

---

83. The shift from "I" in Romans 7 to "we" in Romans 8 fits the "I→X→S model" of conversion that Troels Engberg-Pedersen finds in both Stoic and Pauline thought (*Paul and the Stoics*, 33-44), where "I" represents the initial self-centered stage, "S" the subsequent other-oriented state, and "X" the intentional object (logos, or Christ) that enables the transition from one to the other. In the case of Romans 7, in which X = the law, the point is that "the I→X movement can never be completed" (246).

It is (we have been arguing) the major purpose of Paul's letter to build community among the Jewish and Gentile Christians of Rome; and we have seen that the distinction between them is still to the fore as Paul writes chapters 6–7. In both chapters, his readers are said to have experienced a conversion that participates in the pattern of Christ's own death and resurrection, dying to the old life and rising to the new. In one case, the old life is characterized as a slavery to sin; in the other more complex case, as an enslavement to sin operative in and through the law. The diverse origins of the two groupings within the Roman Christian community are acknowledged here but are also relativized by the shared experience of transformation through Christ's death and resurrection. In the depiction in chapter 8 of the regime of "the Spirit of life," there is no longer any trace of the difference of origin. The first-person plural address constitutes the readers as the single community that experiences now the firstfruits of the life of the age to come, which is the risen life of Jesus Christ. Throughout the chapter, "we" means "us whom [God] called, not only from Jews but also from Gentiles" (9:24). Yet in chapter 8 the first-person plural address does not draw attention to this comprehensive overcoming of difference. Paul constructs for his readers a shared identity determined by their *future*, which is also the future of God and the world. They do not always need to be reminded of a past difference that has now been transcended.

Remarkably, the law — apparently consigned to the past in chapter 7 — is now to be found at the heart of that shared identity. In the first passage of first-person plural address in this chapter, Paul writes:

> For what was impossible for the law, since it was weak through the flesh, God [has done]: sending his own Son in the likeness of flesh of sin and as a sin-offering, he condemned sin in the flesh, so that the law's righteousness/decree [τὸ δικαίωμα τοῦ νόμου] might be fulfilled in *us*, who walk not according to the flesh but according to the Spirit. (8:3-4)

The law, rendered impotent by sin, was quite unable to accomplish the condemnation or destruction of "sin in the flesh" — that is, "the law of sin," or "sin dwelling within me." That we already know from chapter 7. Now, we learn that God has accomplished this act of destruction in the death of his Son, with a view to a *fulfilling of the law through the Spirit*. The speaker in 7:7-25 is right: the law is holy and just and good, and one should strive to obey it. The task lies beyond the power of human flesh, but that power has now been overthrown by the greater power of the Spirit. In spite of the antitheses of faith and works, grace and law, Spirit and law, it is here most unexpectedly stated that the purpose of the incarnation is the fulfillment of the law.[84]

What is τὸ δικαίωμα τοῦ νόμου? In chapter 5, the term δικαίωμα is the opposite of κατάκριμα (v. 16) and παράπτωμα (v. 18): it appears to mean "righteousness" or "righteous act." In that case, τὸ δικαίωμα τοῦ νόμου might refer to "the righteousness of the law," that is, to the law's requirement envisaged as a singular whole (cf. RSV's "the just requirement of the law"). Also relevant here is the reference in 2:26 to the Gentile who keeps τὰ δικαιώματα τοῦ νόμου in spite of remaining uncircumcised. Such a Gentile has experienced a circumcision of heart, ἐν πνεύματι οὐ γράμματι (2:29) — precisely the antithesis that recurs programmatically in 7:6. This is a keeping of the law's demands in which the law is no longer identical with the written text (γράμμα). Here, the law's demands remain plural, and the phraseology remains close to the Septuagint.[85] The singular δικαίωμα τοῦ νόμου of 8:4 might then refer to an individual commandment, such as the one enjoining love of neighbor (cf. 13:8-10).[86] According to 13:10, love is "the fulfilling of the law" (πλήρωμα νόμου), and the fulfilling of the law is precisely the concern in 8:4. Yet in the Septuagint δικαίωμα is rarely used in connection with a single commandment, and, where it is, the commandment in question is clearly specified (cf. Exod. 21:9; Num. 31:21).[87] There is no reference to love of neighbor in Romans 8, and even the citation of the tenth commandment in Romans 7:7 is too far distant from 8:4 for a reader to make the connection. Yet the concept of the "fulfilling of the law" remains highly relevant. In this formulation, Paul construes the law not as a multiplicity of demands but as a singular, comprehensive demand, attested in the text but not identical to the text: thus there can be a fulfilling of the law or

84. This entails "the possibility of actual sinless practice," according to Engberg-Pedersen, *Paul and the Stoics,* 255. Asking how Paul might conceive this to operate, Engberg-Pedersen bypasses *religionsgeschichtliche* explanations (247) and appeals to the "self-understanding" that Paul's own text seeks to engender in its addressees. In Romans 8:4, "Paul is *describing* the Christian way of life *as part of* making an underlying *appeal* to his addressees. His aim is that they should come to *see themselves* in the light of his 'description'. Later (8:12-13), he will then make the implicit appeal of 8:4 explicit" (251; italics original). Engberg-Pedersen's emphasis on the cognitive dimension of Pauline theology is important not least because it is so unfashionable.

85. In 2:26, ἐὰν . . . τὰ δικαιώματα τοῦ νόμου φυλάσσῃ echoes the language especially of Deuteronomy: e.g., φυλάξασθε τὰ δικαιώματα αὐτοῦ (Deut. 4:40).

86. So S. Lyonnet, "Gratuité de la Justification et Gratuité du Salut," 108; A. J. Bandstra, *The Law and the Elements of the World,* 107; L. E. Keck, "Justification of the Ungodly and Ethics," 202.

87. Exodus 21:9 states that a slave girl intended for one's son should be treated κατὰ τὸ δικαίωμα τῶν θυγατέρων. Numbers 31:21 uses the exact phrase τὸ δικαίωμα τοῦ νόμου in connection with the laws of warfare. Also possibly relevant to Paul's usage is Numbers 15:16, νόμος εἷς ἔσται καὶ δικαίωμα ἓν ἔσται ὑμῖν καὶ προσηλύτῳ τῷ προσκειμένῳ ἐν ὑμῖν.

of the δικαίωμα of the law, but there is no fulfilling of the γράμμα. Even in Romans 2, the appearance of multiplicity (τὰ δικαιώματα τοῦ νόμου, v. 26) rapidly resolves itself into a unity (τὸν νόμον τελοῦσα, v. 27). Thus, putting the evidence together, in 8:4 the law is understood (1) as a singular demand (cf. 2:27; 13:10), (2) as overlapping with the written text but not identical to it (cf. 2:29), and (3) as open to fulfillment by Gentiles who do not submit to the rite of circumcision enjoined in the written text (cf. 2:26-29). This is the law that is put into effect by the Spirit, within the Christian community; it is "the law of the Spirit of life in Christ Jesus" (8:2). It is not identical to the law of Moses ("the letter"), but neither is it entirely dissimilar.[88]

Here, then, is a law around which Jewish and Gentile Christians can unite. In speaking as he does of the fulfillment of the law's requirement as the goal of the incarnation, Paul goes as far as he can to accommodate the Jewish Christian loyalty to the law, which (as Romans 14 will show) is the major barrier to unity. If this passage is read in abstraction from its intended social function, it will seem difficult to reconcile with the sharp antitheses of preceding chapters. It will appear that Paul is simply contradicting himself, veering to and fro between more or less "positive" or "negative" statements about the law. As Räisänen puts it, Paul somehow teaches both that "the law has been abrogated" and that "nevertheless its 'just requirement' (Rom. 8:4) is still in force and is met by Christians." He teaches that "[n]obody can fulfill the law, and yet its requirements are fulfilled even by some non-Christian Gentiles." In addition, "[t]he concept of law oscillates between the Torah and something else."[89] Yet, as we have seen, Paul's divergent claims cohere with one another once their pragmatic dimension is brought to light. Roman Christians need to develop a common identity based on their allegiance to Christ, thereby differentiating themselves from those whose identity is still determined by the law of Moses. Yet a place must nevertheless be found for the law within the Christian community, partly out of a pragmatic concern for Jewish Christian sensibilities, but more importantly because Paul refuses to abandon his own conviction that the law remains the law of God. Within the Christian community, the law is attested by the written text but no longer identical with it. It is certainly remarkable that Paul chooses to address the problems of the Roman Christian community from such diverse perspectives. Yet, in their different ways and with their different emphases, these all aim at a single pragmatic goal.

---

88. For the identification of "the law of the Spirit of life" with the law of God, see the persuasive arguments of J. L. Martyn, "*Nomos* plus Genitive Noun in Paul: The History of God's Law."

89. Räisänen, "Paul's Theological Difficulties with the Law," 8.

CHAPTER 9

Election: Reimagining the Scriptural Witness
(Romans 9–11)

It has been argued in previous chapters that close attention to the situation of the Roman Christians and to Paul's purpose in writing to them is much more important for the interpretation of the epistle than is commonly thought. That does not mean that an interest in the situation behind the text has replaced a concern for the text itself. It is the text itself that identifies and defines the situation it is addressing, especially in its final three chapters. Everywhere, it is *Paul's construal* of the Roman situation that determines how he writes. His letter *constructs* the issue it seeks to address. Quite different perspectives on the Roman situation were presumably possible, and the individual Roman Christians named in chapter 16 would no doubt have given a more nuanced and diverse account of Roman Christianity in the mid-50s CE than we find in Paul's letter, oriented as it is to the single issue on which (for Paul) all else hangs: the issue of Jewish and Gentile unity, the creation of a common Christian identity. Insofar as we have had to attend to realities behind or ahead of the text, it is because the text itself directs its readers to an existing situation and to its future transformation; and the former is as much a construct of the text as the latter. The boundary between what is internal to the text and what is external cannot be precisely drawn. What characterizes a reading oriented towards the text's "social function" is simply that it can give a better account of the coherence of the letter as a whole than one in which chapters 14–16 are an unimportant postscript.

The supposition that Romans presupposes an existing social situation, and was intended to function in particular ways within that situation, has proved more fruitful than the common view that in Romans Paul the theologian rises above the concrete situations he has dealt with in other letters, and

301

at last sets forth his gospel in a definitive and universally valid manner. This view derives its apparent plausibility not only from the relative lack of explicit contextual references in Romans, but also and above all from the peculiar role that the letter has played in Protestant theologies since the Reformation. If, following Luther, one holds that "this epistle is really the chief part of the New Testament, and is truly the purest gospel,"[1] then its treatment of sin and righteousness, faith and works, grace and law will inevitably seem to break free from the contextual limitations of other Pauline letters. It will appear that Paul "wanted in this one epistle to sum up briefly the whole Christian and evangelical doctrine."[2] Everything necessary is found here, and in the appropriate order:

> Concern yourself first with Christ and the gospel, that you may recognize your sin and his grace. Then fight your sin, as the first eight chapters here have taught. Then, when you have reached the eighth chapter, and are under the cross and suffering, this will teach you correctly of predestination in chapters 9, 10 and 11, and how comforting it is.[3]

The letter to the Romans treats of justification by faith alone, and election by grace alone, because the gospel itself does so. Thus this letter is "truly the purest gospel," a unique textual articulation of the gospel's essential dynamics. The argument is circular, however. We know that the letter is the purest gospel on the basis of its content, and we know that its content is the purest gospel on the basis of the letter. We proceed in Romans 9–11 to a treatment of "predestination" on account of this topic's position within the logic of the gospel.

Modern scholarship has been readier to concede a contextual determination in the case of Romans 9–11 than in the first half of the letter. Even where these chapters are still understood in terms of "predestination," the inspiration may now be the Israel-centered and universalizing account of predestination developed by Karl Barth, rather than the double predestination of Augustine, Luther, and Calvin.[4] The discovery that Paul here is genuinely concerned with the Jewish people ("Israel"), and not with abstractions, marks a genuine step

---

1. *LW* 35:365.

2. *LW* 35:380.

3. *LW* 35:378.

4. Barth's radical reworking of the Reformed doctrine of predestination occurs in *CD* II/2, 1-506; Romans 9–11 is the basis for §34, "The Election of the Community" (195-305). An exegetically sharper version of the same basic position is found in Cranfield's commentary, where indebtedness to Barth at this point is explicitly and emphatically acknowledged (*Romans*, 2:448-50). See also M. Barth, *The People of God*.

forward. Yet the assumption that the starting point here is simply "Israel's fail-ure to accept the gospel," which is then explained by way of an appeal to elec-tion, is too superficial to be of much help. Rather, it is *Paul's own understand-ing* of Israel's failure to accept the gospel that is at stake here. Paul anticipates that he is known to Roman Jewish Christians as the founder of communities in which Jesus is seen as Messiah for non–law-observant Gentiles, and so as one who has renounced his own people along with the law of Moses — and as one whose God has done likewise. Paul must therefore show, on scriptural ter-rain, how his Gentile-oriented missionary activity reflects the ongoing divine work of election. Also to be noted at the outset is the fact that, for Roman read-ers, "Israel" is concretely embodied in local communities and their syna-gogues, as well as in faraway Jerusalem and Judea.[5]

1. Orientation (Romans 9:1-5)

In Romans 9:1-3, Paul briefly but emphatically becomes the theme of his own discourse. If we discount the "representative autobiography" of 7:7-25, this is virtually the first time he has spoken of himself since the letter's opening (1:1-17). After chapter 8 has concluded with an ecstatic expression of hope in the triumph of the divine love, chapter 9 opens jarringly with a grief so intense that salvation itself might willingly be forfeited in order to put right what is amiss. Located at the juncture between two major divisions of the letter (Rom. 1–8, 9–11), Paul's sudden recourse to first-person singular discourse is highly significant.

The subjects discussed in Romans 1–8 are many and various, but they are held together by a single pragmatic purpose: to persuade Gentile and Jewish Christians to strive to create a single, shared communal identity oriented to-wards Christ, over against the non-Christian Jewish community whose iden-tity is determined by the law. Paul teaches his readers that the Jewish leaders are corrupt, and that true obedience to God is rather to be found among uncircumcised Gentiles (chapter 2). Far from separating Israel from the Gentiles, the law places Israel in exactly the same position of guilt before God as the Gentiles, whereas faith unites Jews and Gentiles in the salvation brought about through Christ (chapter 3). The church of Jewish and Gentile believers is the true seed of Abraham, heirs to the promised salvation, rather than the members of the community of the law (chapter 4). Christian hope and Chris-

---

5. This chapter is dependent on the equivalent chapter of *PJG¹* only for its basic orienta-tion, but incorporates some material from this chapter in its first, third, and fourth sections.

tian obedience are independent of the law that remains normative within the Jewish community (chapters 5–6); for the law entangles its adherents in sin and death, and God can be truly served only in the community where a transformed law operates within the regime of the Spirit of life (chapters 7–8).

What would Jewish Christian readers have made of these arguments? As we have seen, there are a number of indications in Romans that Paul expects and intends his letter to be read and heard beyond the limits of the Pauline, Gentile-oriented section of Roman Christianity (cf. 1:16; 4:1; 7:1; 14:3-4; 15:9; 16:7, 11). Paul was quite capable of persuading Roman Jewish Christians to accept his standpoint, as the case of Prisca and Aquila probably shows; and he no doubt hopes and intends that many more Jewish Christian readers in Rome will accept the social reorientation for which he calls in Romans 1–8. Yet, at the opening of chapter 9, he also takes into account the possibility of a more negative reaction. In rejecting the law as the basis of communal identity, and in advocating the inclusion of non-observant Gentiles, Paul may seem to have turned his back on his own people. He has denied the validity of Israel's unique God-given privileges, claiming that they belong by right to the small breakaway groups founded by himself, where the membership is largely Gentile and where law observance is actively discouraged. Is Paul concerned only with Gentiles and indifferent to the fate of Israel? Does he not care that they are perishing?

The strangely emphatic and emotional language of 9:1-5 seems to anticipate this accusation of indifference.[6] Paul asserts the reality, the depth, and the extent of his sorrow in vv. 2-3, and he introduces this assertion by claiming emphatically that it is the truth and not a lie: "I am speaking the truth in Christ, I am not lying, as my conscience bears me witness in the Holy Spirit" (v. 1). This remarkably emphatic opening anticipates the possibility that some readers may react with incredulity to his profession of sorrow, believing him to be indifferent to the fate of his own people. This personal involvement in the argument is also evident in 10:1-2, where Paul expresses his "heart's desire and prayer to God for them," which is "that they may be saved," also attesting the reality of their "zeal for God." In 11:1, Paul is himself the proof that God has not rejected his people: "For I myself am an Israelite, of the seed of Abraham, of the tribe of Benjamin."[7] Such statements serve to anticipate and disarm Roman Jewish Christian suspicion of Paul himself, rather than address-

6. So Michel, *Der Brief an die Römer,* 223; Wilckens, *Der Brief an die Römer,* 2:189-90; Dunn, *Romans,* 2:530-31; Byrne, *Romans,* 285; opposed by Cranfield, *Romans,* 2:453-54.

7. According to Esler, "The most striking stylistic feature of chaps. 9–11 is that each of these three chapters begins with a statement by Paul expressing his concern for Israel" (*Conflict and Identity,* 270).

ing the Gentile anti-Jewish "boasting" criticized in Paul's later olive tree analogy (11:16-24). Romans 9–10 clearly presupposes a Jewish as well as a Gentile Christian audience.[8] In Romans 11, in contrast, second-person plural or singular discourse *is* ostensibly addressed to Gentiles only (vv. 13, 25, 28, 30-31 [pl.]; vv. 17-22 [sing.]). The restriction is announced in 11:13 (ὑμῖν δὲ λέγω τοῖς ἔθνεσιν) and corresponds to the earlier restriction to Jewish Christian readers announced in 7:1 (γινώσκουσιν γὰρ νόμον λαλῶ). In both cases, a distinction is drawn between the indeterminate circle of readers addressed in the preceding discourse and the specific sub-group to which Paul now turns.[9] Where these distinctions are not drawn, we should assume that Paul addresses "you Gentiles" and "those who know the law" indiscriminately. That is explicitly the case in 9:24, where Paul associates himself with his readers in speaking of "us whom he called, not only from Jews but also from Gentiles." Indeed, this phraseology suggests a certain priority for Jews: it recalls "to the Jew first but also to the Greek" (1:16). In principle, both passages might refer to Jewish Christians in general, rather than specifically in Rome (cf. 11:1-6). Yet that is ruled out by the passing reference to Isaac as "our father" (9:10). As in the earlier reference to Abraham as "our forefather according to the flesh," it is clear that Paul here aligns himself with the Jewish Christian readers he hopes and intends to reach with his letter. Like chapter 7, chapter 9 as a whole is written primarily with a Jewish Christian readership in mind, although Gentiles are by no means excluded.[10]

The emotional outburst at the start of Romans 9 must therefore be understood in terms of its intended rhetorical effect on the Jewish Christian readers whom Paul here envisages. It is not an expression of Paul's own psychological state, as though he had experienced a severe mood swing following the exultant conclusion to the previous chapter. C. K. Barrett's psychologizing account of this transition envisages the letter as an interior monologue rather than an act of communication:

8. It is unhelpful to generalize about the intended audience of chapters 9–11 on the basis of the olive tree passage — as W. D. Davies does when he argues that these chapters as a whole "reveal a Paul conscious of an emerging anti-Judaism among Gentile Christians that could draw on the endemic hostilities of the Graeco-Roman world to help it" ("Paul and the People of Israel," 22).

9. It is remarkable how frequently appeal is made to Romans 11:13 to demonstrate a purely Gentile readership for the letter as a whole (so S. Stowers, *A Rereading of Romans*, 287: "Paul speaks so explicitly on this point that there should be no need to argue it"). If 11:13 does *not* announce a delimitation within Paul's audience, then it is necessary to explain why he chooses to refer to his addressees at precisely this point.

10. In these chapters, "Paul is largely addressing the concerns of Judean/Israelite members of the Christ-movement in Rome" (P. Esler, *Conflict and Identity*, 268-69).

In the last verses of Ch. viii [Paul] sings with moving eloquence the love of God bestowed freely and invincibly upon sinful man from foreknowledge to glory. The dictation is ended; and in the silence he reflects: He came unto his own, and they that were his own received him not. Disappointed and bitter, he continues: "I am speaking the truth in Christ, it is no lie. . . ."[11]

Why, if he is merely recording his own emotions, does Paul so vehemently insist that his expression of grief is genuine rather than a fake? Who needs to be persuaded of this, and why? A psychological interpretation of the passage forgets that a text is written in order to be read, and with a view to its intended readers.

Equally inadequate is the view that Paul here addresses the quasi-objective problem of "Israel's unbelief." According to J. A. Fitzmyer, Paul here responds to

> the obvious objection that the mass of his own fellow coreligionists [*sic*] had resisted his gospel, had rejected the power of God that it unleashed for the salvation of all, Jew and Greek alike, and had not acknowledged the freedom that it announced.[12]

Fitzmyer does not indicate who is responsible for this "obvious objection," or why Paul here sees fit to address it, or what moves him to substitute a statement about the reality of his grief for the explicit statement about Israel's unbelief that one might have expected. Underlying this passage is Paul's image of his intended readers, and of their image of him. As Keck writes:

> Chapters 9–11 were not set afoot by either a repressed criticism of Peter's unsuccessful mission or by an unstated desire to exonerate him. Rather, the vehemence with which Paul begins (9:1-5) suggests that he knows he has been accused of being a major factor in the Jewish refusal. Not because he took the gospel to *Gentiles*, but because of the *gospel he took* — one that insisted that Gentiles must not be required to become converts to Judaism in order to enjoy the full benefits of salvation in Christ, the Messiah. So one reason the Jews' No is Paul's problem is that law-observant Christian Jews *made* it his problem by blaming him for preaching a gospel to Gentiles that made it unacceptable to most Jews who were convinced that he dissolved the significance of Judaism.[13]

11. Barrett, *Romans*, 175.
12. Fitzmyer, *Romans*, 539.
13. Keck, *Romans*, 224-25; italics original.

That is exactly right. Roman Jewish Christians are critical of their Gentile Christian counterparts, and Paul himself is implicated in their criticisms.

If Paul has turned from his own people towards Gentiles, so too has his God. According to his critics, his God has abandoned the people of the covenant in order to create a new people from among the Gentiles: and this is incredible, because it would mean that God's scriptural promise to be *Israel's* God had been invalidated. It would mean that God had responded to the faithlessness of some among his own people by a corresponding faithlessness of his own (cf. 3:3). This, then, is the challenge addressed in Romans 9–11: if, as Paul claims, God has turned from Jews to Gentiles, does this not invalidate the scriptural doctrine of election, according to which God will remain the God of this people in perpetuity, no matter what? When Paul states, "It is not as though the word of God has failed" (9:6), the "failure" in question is specific to his own view of the ongoing divine engagement with the world. That is why each of his two denials relates to an alleged indifference to the covenant, on his own part and on God's (9:1, 6). Suspected of denying the scriptural doctrine of the election of Israel, Paul affirms of his own people that

> they are Israelites, and theirs is the sonship and the glory and the covenants and the lawgiving and the worship and the promises. Theirs are the fathers and from them as regards the flesh is the Christ, who is God over all, blessed for ever. (9:4-5)

Paul here concedes to Jewish Christian readers that they are right to see Jesus as the Jewish Messiah, sent in the first instance to the Jewish people as the fulfillment rather than the annulment of their scriptural traditions — the "lawgiving" included (cf. 15:8). They are also right to emphasize the greatness and glory of Israel's privileges as attested by scripture and to understand their practice of the law within this covenantal context. Yet the fact that this affirmation of the covenant is *made by Paul* is at least as significant as the affirmation itself. Romans 9:1-5 presupposes the existence of Jewish Christians who have not yet severed their links with the majority Jewish community, whose reform and renewal they seek. These Christians look askance at a sectarian Gentile-oriented Christianity that seems to envisage the abolition of the divine covenant attested by scripture. Such Jewish Christian critics exist at least in Paul's own mind as he writes, for the opening of chapter 9 can only be read as addressed to some such implied readership.

Romans 9–11 retraces much of the ground covered in Romans 1–8. Once again, Paul speaks of the patriarchs, of righteousness by faith rather than works, of Jesus' resurrection, of grace and reconciliation and universal salvation. Yet there is an essential difference. In chapters 1–8, the emphasis lies on *the new community,* in its scriptural basis, its orientation towards Christ and his Spirit, and its differentiation from the old. In the sequel, the emphasis lies on *the old community* as an inadequate embodiment of the scriptural promise definitively realized in the new (chapters 9–10), but also as divinely ordained to coexist with the new community in ways that further the final salvation of both (chapter 11).

2. The Pattern of Election (Romans 9:6-29)

According to Paul, the God of the gospel has chosen Gentiles at the expense of Jews. Branches have been broken off the olive tree, and a wild olive has been grafted in (11:17). That is the starting point from which the discussion sets out. Gentile Christian readers will not object, but Jewish Christians may well be resistant to such a claim. It seems that the God who eternally elects Israel to be his people, and whose faithfulness to his own electing purpose has been confirmed in Jesus the Messiah, has been replaced by a capricious deity who has evidently changed his mind and decided that, after all, he prefers Gentiles. This is, surely, a deity fashioned by Paul in his own self-image, wholly at odds with the scriptural portrayal of the God of Israel?

In Romans 9 as in chapter 4, Paul engages in scriptural reinterpretation in order to legitimate the existence of a Christian community consisting of Gentiles and Jews.[14] He does so in a piece of scriptural argumentation whose extraordinary artistry has been insufficiently appreciated (9:6-29). As we shall see, the artistry is integral to the message. In the first instance, Paul displays his exegetical virtuosity by constructing a scriptural argument that preserves the scriptural sequence across an extensive selection of material from Genesis and Exodus, Hosea and Isaiah. Beginning with the Genesis account of Abraham's two sons (Gen. 16–21), Paul proceeds to speak of Isaac's two sons (Gen. 25), with a little help from Malachi, before finding a third contrasting pair in Moses and Pharaoh (Exod. 33:19; 9:16).[15] This completes what we may de-

14. In approaching this material, "we must be alert to the possibility that the close, at times almost seamless, connection between social and theological factors already observed in earlier parts of the letter will also be found here" (P. Esler, *Conflict and Identity,* 275).

15. As Byrne rightly states, Romans 9:14-18 concerns "the elective pattern shown in Moses and Pharaoh" (*Romans,* 295; upper case removed); this follows directly from 9:6-13, "the elective pattern shown in the patriarchs" (291). Such an analysis is greatly preferable to propositional accounts such as that of Fitzmyer, for whom 9:14-23 demonstrates that "God's sovereign freedom even uses indocility to his purpose" (*Romans,* 563; upper case removed).

scribe as the "narrative sequence," in which Paul finds intimations of the divine electing purpose in three pairs of contrasting figures drawn from the narratives of Genesis and Exodus.

The first two pairings (Isaac and Ishmael, Jacob and Esau) are well known, but the third (Moses and Pharaoh) is created by Paul himself. For this pairing to be effective, it is essential that the statement about divine mercy ("I will have mercy on whom I have mercy, and I will have compassion on whom I have compassion," v. 15) be addressed to Moses as clearly as the statement about divine power is addressed to Pharaoh ("For this purpose I raised you up, so as to show my power in you and so that my name may be proclaimed in all the earth," v. 17). Thus Paul provides the two citations with matching introductions: τῷ Μωϋσεῖ γὰρ λέγει (v. 15), λέγει γὰρ ἡ γραφὴ τῷ Φαραώ (v. 17). Paul has rightly noted that in Exodus 33:18-23 Moses' request for a theophany concerns himself alone. In this dialogue with God, he is neither the leader (cf. 33:12-17) nor the lawgiver (cf. 34:1-4), but a purely individual figure. As a result, however, the two scriptural citations remain asymmetrical, since Moses is seen as the *object* of divine mercy whereas Pharaoh is seen as the *instrument* whereby divine power is displayed to the world. This asymmetry is deftly removed in v. 18, where, drawing a general conclusion from the cases of Moses and of Pharaoh, Paul states that God "has mercy on whom he wills and hardens whom he wills." As Moses is the object of the divine mercy, so Pharaoh is the object of the divine hardening: the parallel is now exact. Paul has drawn the reference to hardening from the immediate context of the statement about divine power (Exod. 9:16), for the first of five identically worded statements on the divine hardening occurs in Exodus 9:12: ἐσκλήρυνεν δὲ κύριος τὴν καρδίαν φαραω is obviously the inspiration for Paul's ὃν δὲ θέλει σκληρύνει.[16] Pharaoh thus typifies one kind of divine intentional object, Moses the other. The pairing of Moses and Pharaoh is no less effective than the preceding pairings of Isaac and Ishmael, Jacob and Esau.

Although Paul does not make the point, the third pairing even preserves the familial context of the other two, since Moses himself had been a member of the Egyptian royal household (cf. Acts 7:21-22). In each case, then, the members of each pair are actually very similar. They are made dissimilar only

---

16. The other four occurrences are in Exodus 10:20, 27; 11:10; 14:8. References to the divine hardening also occur in the first-person singular aorist (Exod. 10:1), in the first singular future (4:21; 7:3; 14:4, 17), and in the third singular aorist passive (7:22?; 8:15; 9:35). Pharaoh may himself be the subject of the hardening (7:22?; 13:15). As Ross Wagner argues, "Here we have a clear case of Paul's awareness of the larger context of a quotation [i.e., Exod. 9:16] and his exegetical interest in elements of the narrative not explicitly cited" (*Heralds of the Good News,* 54).

by the divine words recorded in scripture, through which they are sharply divided from one another:

A *Isaac and Ishmael*
   1 "In Isaac shall your seed be called" (Gen. 21:12; Rom. 9:7)
   2 "At this time I shall come and Sarah shall have a son" (Gen. 18:10 + 14; Rom. 9:9)
B *Jacob and Esau*
   1 "The greater will serve the lesser" (Gen. 25:23; Rom. 9:12)
   2 "Jacob I loved, Esau I hated" (Mal. 1:2-3; Rom. 9:13)
C *Moses and Pharaoh*
   1 "I will have mercy on whom I have mercy, and I will have compassion on whom I have compassion" (Exod. 33:19; Rom. 9:15)
   2 "For this purpose I raised you up, so as to show my power in you and so that my name may be proclaimed in all the earth" (Exod. 9:16; Rom. 9:17)

In each case, God is the speaker, and in each case the divine utterances enact a division, within the original context *(A)*, explicitly *(B)*, or in conjunction with each other *(C)*.

In *A1*, the context in Genesis is the divine endorsement of Sarah's harsh demand that her husband "cast out this slave girl and her son, for the son of this slave girl shall not inherit with my son Isaac" (Gen. 21:10; cited in Gal. 4:30, where it is attributed not to Sarah but to the voice of scripture). *A2* provides the background to this confirmation of Isaac's position at the expense of Ishmael's. Isaac was born in fulfillment of a divine promise, which Paul contrasts with the natural, fleshly birth of Ishmael: "The one who was from the slave girl was born according to the flesh" (Gal. 4:23). Thus Ishmael and Isaac are types of "the children of the flesh" and "the children of the promise" respectively (Rom. 9:8; cf. Gal. 4:23, 28).

In Galatians, it is the Gentile readers who are said to be κατὰ Ἰσαὰκ ἐπαγγελίας τέκνα (Gal. 4:28). In Romans 9, however, the same promise/flesh distinction is used to make a distinction *within* Israel.[17] Paul refers to Jews as "Israelites," who possess a range of scripturally attested privileges (vv. 4-5),

---

17. According to Elizabeth Johnson, Romans 9 does *not* refer to two classes of people, the elected and the rejected, but argues "that God's redemptive word of election . . . has not collapsed with the inclusion of Gentiles because that inclusion has been accomplished on precisely the same terms as God's call to Israel" ("Romans 9–11: The Faithfulness and Impartiality of God," 227). On that view, Ishmael, Esau, Pharaoh, and the vessels of wrath would seem to play no part in Paul's argument. Why then are they mentioned at all?

but begins his narrative sequence (vv. 6-18) by introducing a more restrictive definition of "Israel":

> Not all who are of Israel *are* Israel. And not all who are Abraham's children are his seed, but "in Isaac shall your seed be called." (9:6-7)

Here, the double οὐ . . . πάντες clearly serves to demarcate an Israel *within* Israel, a seed of Abraham *within* Abraham's children. While Paul has previously argued at length that Abraham's seed includes Gentiles (4:9-17), that is not the point here. The reference is to Jewish Christians — those whom God called ἐξ Ἰουδαίων (9:24), the "remnant" (9:27; 11:5).[18] Nowhere in Romans 9–11 is "Israel" said to include Gentiles: in all nine subsequent usages, the distinction from the Gentiles is absolutely clear.[19] Paul appeals to the story of Abraham's two sons as a precedent for the existence of a remnant within Israel. Not all Israelites are truly Israel, just as not all Abraham's children are his promised seed: otherwise the true people of God would be descended not only from Isaac but also from Ishmael and indeed from Zimran, Jokshan, Medan, Midian, Ishbak, and Shuah (Gen. 25:2). Had the divine electing purpose treated the sons of Abraham as the sons of Jacob were later to be treated, these eight figures would have become patriarchs, taking precedence (with their three mothers) over the twelve sons of Jacob (with their four mothers). Yet, in the case of Abraham's sons, the divine electing purpose operated selectively — anticipating the existence "at the present time" of "a remnant according to the election of grace" (11:5). Paul here at last gives substance to the claim that salvation in Christ is "for the Jew first" (1:16), giving priority to the Jewish Christian remnant as he attempts to state a scriptural doctrine of election that makes sense of the divine turning from Jews to Gentiles. In a move calculated to appeal to Roman Jewish Christian readers, Paul argues that the turning is not complete: God has turned from the majority in Israel, but not from the Israel within Israel.[20]

In *B* (9:10-13), it is less clear that the Jewish Christian remnant is in mind. While "Jacob" (9:13) is later a synonym for Israel (11:26), Paul applies *B2* (the Malachi text) not to the people of Jacob but to Jacob as an individual. Here, the emphasis is no longer on the restriction or demarcation signaled by the

---

18. Against L. Gaston, who claims that "[n]owhere in these chapters does Paul refer to Jewish Christians as such" (*Paul and the Torah*, 148).

19. Rom. 9:27 [× 2], 31; 10:19, 21; 11:2, 7, 25, 26.

20. That 9:6-9 has to do with Israel and the remnant (and not Gentiles) is noted by Käsemann, *Commentary on Romans*, 263; Fitzmyer, *Romans*, 560; Keck, *Romans*, 231; also K. Barth, *CD* II/2, 215-17.

"not all" statements. Paul might have used the story of the sons of Isaac and Rebecca merely to repeat what he has said about the story of Abraham's sons, but he does not do so. The scriptural text itself suggests a different treatment. Here, the relationship between the named pair is still closer than in *A* or *C*. Rebecca had conceived children "from one man, Isaac our father" (9:10), in contrast to Abraham, who produced sons by two (or three) women. Unlike Isaac and Ishmael, or Moses and Pharaoh, Jacob and Esau have both parents in common. Because they are twins, a single ante-natal oracle determines the destinies of them both. Yet, in spite of their common origin, their destinies diverge. Contrary to the established order of things, the older is to be subordinated to the younger *(B1):* for the younger is beloved by God whereas the older is hated *(B2)*. Why? Paul learns from *B1* that "the electing purpose of God" was already operative "when they were not yet born and had done nothing either good or bad" (9:11).[21] The rationale for the divine election is to be found not in "works" but solely in the divine call, articulated here in the oracle addressed to Rebecca *(B1)*. Paul appeals to this scriptural story primarily to exclude the obvious rationale for election, which is that it is determined by conduct. Those whom God chooses are the doers of the good; those whom God rejects are evildoers — or so one would think. And yet Paul learns from *B1* (and no doubt from the rest of the story of Jacob and Esau) that there is no such correlation between human conduct and the divine decision. There cannot be, for the divine decision is announced even before the twins' birth. If later Jewish piety portrays Jacob as zealous for the law and Esau as an apostate, Paul finds this distinction wholly lacking in the plain sense of the Genesis text.[22]

How does *B* further the task of restating the scriptural doctrine of election to accommodate the divine turning from Jews to Gentiles? The exclusion of any correlation between conduct and election is precisely the point of the references to the election of Gentiles and rejection of Jews with which Romans 9 concludes:

---

21. This seems to exclude the view of N. T. Wright that, according to Romans 9:6-29, "[i]t is not God who has failed, but Israel" (*The Climax of the Covenant*, 239).

22. In *Jubilees*, the prenatal oracle is omitted, and the biblical characterizations of Jacob and Esau (Gen. 25:27) are supplemented by references to their moral qualities: Jacob is not only "smooth" but also "righteous," and Esau is not only "hairy" but also "violent" — to such an extent that "all his works were violent" (*Jub.* 19:13-14). It follows that election corresponds closely to character: "Abraham saw what Esau did and he realized that it was through Jacob that his promised heirs would come, and he called Rebecca and gave instructions about Jacob, for he saw that she loved Jacob much more than Esau" (19:16). On this, see John C. Endres, S.J., *Biblical Interpretation in the Book of Jubilees*, 22-28.

> Gentiles who did not pursue righteousness have found righteousness, the righteousness which is by faith. Yet Israel, pursuing a law of righteousness, did not attain the law. Why? Because they pursued it not by faith but as if it were by works. (9:30-32a)

Here, too, the divine electing purpose subordinates the older to the younger. It takes no account of the good things done by Jews, in their "zeal for God" and for "the righteousness that is from the law" (cf. 10:2, 5), or of the bad things done by Gentiles, in their indifference to the demands of righteousness (cf. 1:18-32). The divine turning from Jews to Gentiles is not conditioned by or conditional on prior conduct. God's electing purpose is sovereign. It is not attracted to the good or repelled by the wicked. That is not to say that it is arbitrary or capricious, however, for in its sovereignty it is true to its own nature as disclosed in scripture. The existence of a Gentile Christian community in which righteousness has been attained instantly and unexpectedly, by faith, and of a Jewish community that has not found the righteousness it arduously sought in the law, is fully consistent with Rebecca's oracle. The scriptural oracle enables Paul *both* to acknowledge a sharp distinction between the prior conduct of Jews and Gentiles (in spite of arguments to the contrary earlier in the letter), *and* to deny that this distinction is relevant for the divine electing purpose.[23]

In *C* (9:14-18), Paul's narrative sequence concludes with the third pairing, that of Moses and Pharaoh. Here it might seem that conduct prior to the divine utterances *(C1,2)* is a significant factor, in contrast to *B*. Unlike *B1* (Rebecca's oracle), *C1* and *C2* occur at points in the scriptural narrative where the characters of Moses and Pharaoh are already well established. Yet — like *B1* and, indeed, *A1* — *C1* and *C2* speak comprehensively of the total life story of the individual concerned. The life of Pharaoh is the life of one who has been raised up to manifest divine power. The life of Moses is the life of one who is the object of divine compassion and mercy. In neither case does the divine utterance announce a decision conditioned by prior conduct — whether Pharaoh's hardness of heart or Moses' unparalleled faithfulness (cf. Num. 12:7 LXX). The divine decision may or may not *produce* a difference of this kind: Moses and Pharaoh represent opposite poles in this respect, but the same cannot be said of Jacob and Esau or of Isaac and Ishmael. In none of these cases, however, is the divine decision contingent upon an already-existing difference. Whether the divine decision is announced in advance of the respective life stories *(B)*, or soon after their begin-

---

23. The link between 9:10-13 and 9:29-30 is noted by Stephen Westerholm, "Paul and the Law in Romans 9–11," 223-24. Westerholm suggests that "behind Paul's claim that Israel's pursuit of (specific) 'works' was misguided" (9:29) is the general principle that "God achieves his purposes without reference to human activity" (9:11-12).

ning *(A)*, or when they are already well established *(C)*, it is the life story in its entirety whose determination is thereby revealed.

Paul, however, is not interested in these individual life stories per se, but in the scriptural precedents they establish for a divine electing purpose that takes *communal* form.[24] Within the narrative sequence, the communal dimension of election is best illustrated by *A*, where Ishmael and Isaac may readily be seen as types of the "children of the flesh" and the "children of the promise" — that is, of "Israel" in its broader and narrower forms. In *B*, the Malachi citation *(B2)* might have been understood communally rather than individually, but it is not. As we have seen, Jacob can represent the Gentile Christians whom Paul here has in mind only as an individual and not as a people (cf. 11:26). The passing reference to "Isaac our father" (9:10) will be plausible to Jewish Christians but not to Gentiles. It is, however, in the "prophetic sequence" that follows (9:19-29) that the communal orientation of Paul's scriptural exegesis becomes fully explicit. His argument is that the divine turn from Jews to Gentiles is consonant with the scriptural account of God's electing purpose, rather than flatly contradicting it (as his critics claim). Essentially, his strategy is to derive typological anticipations of the divine turn from Genesis and Exodus, but direct announcements from Hosea and Isaiah.[25] The law and the prophets vindicate the divine righteousness and refute the suspicion that there is "unrighteousness with God" (9:14) — or rather, with Paul's God.

The prophetic sequence opens with an anticipated question: "You will say to me then, 'Why does he still find fault? For who can oppose his will?'" (v. 19). Here as in v. 14, Paul addresses himself to a *resistant* reader who must be persuaded to accept conclusions that he or she initially finds unacceptable. The questioner is given short shrift, however, in language that echoes well-known prophetic imagery about the divine potter and the human clay (vv. 20-21).[26] Paul's initial point is merely to assert the potter's right to make vessels for honorable and dishonorable purposes from the same lump of clay (v. 22). Yet, as the argument moves beyond typology and imagery to explicit

---

24. I therefore disagree fundamentally with Douglas Moo's claim that Paul sees Jacob and Esau "in terms of their own personal relationship to the promise of God" (*Romans*, 585-86) — that is, in terms of a "double predestination" in which God decides, on the sole basis of his own sovereign pleasure, to save some individuals and to damn others (598). This is one point where the familiar plea for a historically informed exegesis, unfettered by the constraints of church dogma, seems not unreasonable.

25. As C. Müller rightly notes, vv. 6-21 are subordinate to vv. 22-29, where the problem underlying the earlier passage is finally made explicit (*Gottes Gerechtigkeit und Gottes Volk*, 32).

26. On the scriptural background to the potter imagery, see R. Wagner, *Heralds of the Good News*, 56-71.

statements about God's activity in the present, the image of the potter is significantly modified. Initially, there is a straightforward symmetry between the "vessel for honor" and the "vessel for dishonor" (v. 21). In the sequel, however, equivalence is replaced by teleology: God endures the vessels for dishonor with great patience, *in order* to show his mercy to the vessels for honor (vv. 22-23).[27] The vessels for honor — or rather, the "vessels of mercy that he prepared beforehand for glory" (v. 23) — are identified as "us whom he called not only from Jews but also from Gentiles" (vv. 22-24).

This shift from symmetry to teleology will prove crucially important in chapter 11, and it is inspired by the divine word to Pharaoh *(C2)*. Indeed, Romans 9:21-24 is simply an extended paraphrase of Exodus 9:16, as is indicated by common terminology, themes, and syntax.[28] The Exodus text contains five elements, each of which is preserved in the Pauline paraphrase:

(1) εἰς αὐτὸ τοῦτο (2) ἐξήγειρά σε (3) ὅπως ἐνδείξωμαι ἐν σοὶ τὴν δυναμίν μου (4) καὶ ὅπως διαγγελῇ τὸ ὄνομά μου (5) ἐν πάσῃ τῇ γῇ

(1) An indication of intent is followed by (2) a main verb signifying a divine action corresponding to the intent, which is specified in two distinct purpose clauses relating to disclosures of (3) the divine power and (4) the divine name, (5) the second disclosure being universal in scope. Each of these five elements has its equivalent in the Pauline paraphrase:

(1a) εἰς αὐτὸ τοῦτο
(1b) [εἰ δὲ] θέλων ὁ θεὸς . . .

While the citation is divine discourse in the first-person singular, the paraphrase is naturally in the third-person singular. It is signaled at the outset that

27. Here, "[t]here is no question of an equilibrium between God's will to show His wrath and God's will to manifest the riches of His glory on the vessels of mercy, as though He sometimes willed the one thing and sometimes the other. . . . The ἵνα clause indicates the one ultimate gracious purpose of God, for the sake of which He also wills to show His wrath" (Cranfield, *Romans*, 2:496). Compare Karl Barth: "In vv. 22-24 it is quite unambiguous that Paul is not speaking of a content of God's will which is to be interpreted as an abstract duality, but of God's way on which in execution of his one purpose he wills and executes in a determined sequence and order this twofold operation. The harsh appearance that can descend on the preceding passage if vv. 22-24 are not taken into account in advance — as if God's mercy and hardening, the existence of 'vessels of honour' and of 'dishonour', were the two goals of two different ways of God — is now finally dispelled" (*CD* II/2, 225).

28. Cf. R. Wagner, *Heralds of the Good News*, 71-75; the relationship to chapter 11 is also noted (75-78). Wagner puts more emphasis than I would on the significance of the wider context within Exodus.

the emphasis will lie not on the divine action that is to be specified in the main verb but on what is intended in it and beyond it.

(2a) ἐξήγειρά σε

(2b) . . . ἤνεγκεν ἐν πολλῇ μακροθυμίᾳ σκεύη ὀργῆς κατηρτισμένα εἰς ἀπώλειαν

God "raised up" Pharaoh, whereas he "endured with great patience" the vessels of wrath. Yet the difference is more apparent than real. The vessels of wrath have been created by the divine potter, just as Pharaoh was (cf. vv. 20-21). And God presumably endured Pharaoh with great patience. In conjunction with (1), we learn from (2) that the potter did not create the vessel of wrath for itself but with another end in view.

(3a) ὅπως ἐνδείξωμαι ἐν σοὶ τὴν δυναμίν μου

(3b) . . . ἐνδείξασθαι τὴν ὀργὴν καὶ γνωρίσαι τὸ δυνατὸν αὐτοῦ

This is the first of the two clauses identifying the intent underlying the action signified in the main verb. At this point, there are clear verbal connections between the citation and the paraphrase. The paraphrase doubles the single disclosure of the divine power by adding a reference to wrath. The aim is probably to indicate that the power to be disclosed is the power of God's wrath: thus, ἐνδείξασθαι τὴν ὀργήν is equivalent to γνωρίσαι τὸ δυνατὸν αὐτοῦ. Thus far, it would appear that God has created the vessels of wrath for the sole purpose of revealing his power by destroying them. Yet there is a further, more constructive dimension to the divine purpose.

(4a) καὶ ὅπως διαγγελῇ τὸ ὄνομά μου

(4b) καὶ ἵνα γνωρίσῃ τὸν πλοῦτον τῆς δόξης αὐτοῦ

In the Exodus text, the two purpose clauses (3) and (4) might be understood as closely connected. For God to show his power is to cause his name to be proclaimed. Yet the Pauline paraphrase finds here a contrast between the two disclosures, one of which reveals God's power/wrath, the other God's grace.

(5a) ἐν πάσῃ τῇ γῇ

(5b) ἐπὶ σκεύη ἐλέους ἃ προητοίμασεν εἰς δόξαν, οὓς καὶ ἐκάλεσεν ἡμᾶς οὐ μόνον ἐξ Ἰουδαίων ἀλλὰ καὶ ἐξ ἐθνῶν

In contrast to the vagueness of the citation, the paraphrase provides an exact specification of the beneficiaries of the second divine disclosure. "In all the earth" is understood as a reference to those called from among Jews and

Gentiles and destined for glory. At the very end of the paraphrase, Paul's language at last becomes fully concrete. A text that had originally applied to Pharaoh is now heard to speak of the rejection of the majority within Israel, which occurs *with a view to* the salvation not only of the "remnant" but also of Gentiles. By their trespass salvation has come to the Gentiles; their rejection means the world's reconciliation (cf. 11:11, 15). Also echoed here is the first Exodus text, which spoke of the sovereignty of the divine mercy (Exod. 33:19; Rom. 9:15). The vessels of mercy, prepared beforehand for glory and called in the gospel, are those of whom it was said, "I will have mercy on whom I have mercy, and I will have compassion on whom I have compassion." Here a paraphrase of C_1 is incorporated into the paraphrase of C_2.

Paul's Exodus paraphrase serves two main functions in his argument. First, following the citation, it adds a crucial teleological element to his account of the divine election/rejection, which has otherwise implied a mere equivalence between the children of the flesh and the children of the promise, those who are hardened and those who receive mercy, the vessels for dishonor and the vessels for honor. Second, it marks the transition to the concretion of the "prophetic sequence" (9:19-29), where scriptural texts speak directly of Israel and the Gentiles, in contrast to the anticipations and types of the "narrative sequence" (9:6-18).[29]

As we have seen, the narrative sequence consists of three pairings. The first of these uses the example of Abraham's sons to justify a distinction between Israel and the remnant *(A)*. The second finds in Rebecca's oracle a testimony to a sovereign and unconditioned election/rejection, independent of desert; Paul has Gentile inclusion primarily in view here *(B)*. The third creates a less obvious pairing from divine utterances addressed to Moses and Pharaoh, respectively representing the objects of the divine mercy and hardening *(C)*. As we shall now see, the prophetic sequence is a mirror image of this construction. The difference between the two sequences consists not just in their scriptural sources — Genesis and Exodus in one case, Hosea and Isaiah in the other — but also and above all in their modes of argumentation. The first deals in types, the second in their realization. Paul's paraphrase of Exodus 9:16 therefore belongs in the second sequence rather than in the first, for it is at this point that types and images give way to concrete communal realities. Since the citation belonged to *C* within the narrative sequence, we may

29. This way of relating narrative to prophetic material may be contrasted with the salvation-historical reading of N. T. Wright, for whom Romans 9:6-29 tells "the story of Israel, from Abraham to the exile and beyond" (*Romans*, 634). Here we read "of Israel's patriarchal foundation (vv. 6-13), then of the exodus (vv. 14-18), and then of God's judgment that led to exile and, through it, to the fulfillment of God's worldwide promise to Abraham (vv. 19-29)" (635).

designate the paraphrase as *C'*. Similarly, the Hosea citation *(B')* corresponds to *B*, and the double citation from Isaiah *(A')* to *A*. The entire scriptural argument forms an artful chiasmus, at the same time preserving scriptural sequence:

Narrative sequence

A	Israel within Israel	(Gen. 21:12; 18:14)
B	The divine call	(Gen. 25:23; Mal. 1:2-3)
C	Objects of mercy and hardening	(Exod. 33:19; 9:16)

Prophetic sequence

C'	Vessels of wrath and mercy	(Exod. 9:16; 33:19)
B'	The divine call	(Hos. 2:25, 1)
A'	The remnant within Israel	(Isa. 10:22-23; 1:9)

Both sequences are concerned with the election not of individuals but of communities. One community is "Israel" (Rom. 9:27, 31), another is "the Gentiles" (9:24, 30), and between the two and overlapping with both is the Israel within Israel (9:6), the "remnant" (9:27), those who are called ἐξ Ἰουδαίων (9:24). Each pairing *(A-A', B-B', C-C')* speaks of one community in relation to another. *A-A'* speaks of Israel in the comprehensive sense, in relation to the remnant. *B-B'* is concerned with the election of Gentiles at the expense of Jews. *C-C'* is concerned with the vessels of mercy (Jewish and Gentile Christians) over against the vessels of wrath (non-Christian Jews). Thus, the remnant is initially presented as a subset within Israel, without reference to Gentiles *(A-A')*. The elected Gentiles are initially contrasted with rejected Israel, without reference to the remnant *(B-B')*. Finally — or rather, at the heart of the argument — the elect remnant and the elect Gentiles stand together over against Israel *(C-C')*.

Once again, this intricately constructed argument has a pragmatic function. At this point, Paul's intended readership includes Jewish as well as Gentile Christians, and he associates himself with the former in speaking of "Isaac our father" (9:10) and with both parties in speaking of "us whom he called, not only from Jews but also from Gentiles" (9:24).[30] The remnant theology of *A-A'* is to be seen as an attempt to accommodate the self-understanding of the Roman Jewish Christian community, oriented primar-

---

30. The significance of "Isaac our father" is invariably missed by those who envisage an exclusively Gentile readership for the letter. It is only "Israelites" of whom it may be said, "Theirs are the fathers" (9:4-5).

ily towards "Israel," the majority Jewish community that has thus far rejected its claim that the Messiah has come in the person of Jesus. The theology of Gentile salvation *(B-B')* is distinctively Pauline in its emphasis on the sovereign divine call and on the exclusion of works (cf. 9:12). It speaks of God's creation of communities of Gentile believers, including the Roman Gentile Christians. Paul will later emphasize the part he himself has played in this divine creative work, by virtue of his calling as "apostle of the Gentiles" (11:13; cf. 15:15-21). Both Christian communities in Rome can trace their existence back to a divine electing word — the word of promise in the one case *(A1)*, the call to those without works on the other *(B1)*. They must recognize that they *together* constitute God's "vessels of mercy" *(C-C')* and that their primary orientation must be towards each other. When Paul identifies the called as deriving "not only from Jews but also from Gentiles" (9:24), he encourages Jewish Christian readers to move beyond A, accepting the existing reality represented by *B-B'* (cf. 14:1-12) and the future reality of full communion represented by *C-C'* (cf. 15:5-6). At the same time, Gentile Christian readers must accept the reality and authenticity of *A*, the existence of a remnant within Israel (cf. 11:1-10). They must not conclude that *all* Jews have been excised from the olive tree in order to make room for Gentiles (cf. 11:17-20). The shared reality of the "vessels of mercy, prepared beforehand for glory" *(C')* requires a change of perception on the part of Gentiles as well as of Jews.

B' (Hosea) and *A'* (Isaiah) are in need of further investigation at this point, to confirm that Paul's prophetic texts really do correspond to *B* and *A* in the narrative sequence.

B-B': Paul's Hosea citation conflates two passages, reversing their order. In their Septuagintal and Pauline forms, the passages are as follows:

1a (1) καὶ ἐλεήσω (2) τὴν οὐκ ἠλεημένην (3) καὶ ἐρῶ τῷ οὐ λαῷ μου λαός μου εἶ σύ. (Hos. 2:25)

1b (1) καλέσω (3) τὸν οὐ λαόν μου λαόν μου (2) καὶ τὴν οὐκ ἠγαπημένην ἠγαπημένην. (Rom. 9:25)

2a καὶ ἔσται ἐν τῷ τόπῳ οὗ ἐρρέθη οὐ λαός μου ὑμεῖς ἐκεῖ κληθήσονται υἱοὶ θεοῦ ζῶντος. (Hos. 2:1)

2b καὶ ἔσται ἐν τῷ τόπῳ οὗ ἐρρέθη οὐ λαὸς μου ὑμεῖς ἐκεῖ κληθήσονται υἱοὶ θεοῦ ζῶντος. (Rom. 9:26)[31]

---

31. Compare the fuller analysis of R. Wagner, *Heralds of the Good News*, 79-85, which adopts divergent textual variants in Romans 9:26 and Hosea 2:1 LXX.

Had Paul cited Hosea 2:25 in its Septuagintal form *(1a)*, it would have recalled Exodus 33:15 (ἐλεήσω ὃν ἂν ἐλεῶ), cited in Romans 9:15 *(C1)*. If he is himself responsible for the three most significant modifications *(1b)*, all of them serve to detach this text from *C* and to connect it to *B*.[32]

(i) The verb (καλέσω for the similar-sounding καὶ ἐλεήσω) is linked not only to ἐκάλεσεν (v. 24) and κληθήσονται (v. 26) but also to *B*, where God is "the one who calls" (9:12).

(ii) The reversal of (2) and (3) gives greater prominence to the transformation of "not my people" into "my people." This is confirmed by Paul's linking of *1a* with *2a*, which (by reversing their scriptural order) turns *2a* into a gloss on "I will call not my people my people." For Paul, "not my people" refers to the initial non-election of Gentiles, in contrast to the "Israelites," whose covenantal privileges are listed in vv. 4-5. Like Jacob in *B*, the Gentiles who are here said to become "my people" have absolutely no prior claim on God and show especially clearly the unconditioned nature of the divine election.

(iii) The substitution of ἠγαπημένην for ἠλεημένην detaches *1b* from *C* and creates a connection with *B2*, where it is said, τὸν Ἰακὼβ ἠγάπησα (v. 13).

Paul interprets the Hosea passages as a statement about the unconditioned divine calling of Gentiles.[33] The same is true of his interpretation of Rebecca's oracle, and the verbal and thematic links between the two passages are close enough to show that the second was intended to correspond to the first.

A-A': Isaiah is said to "cry out on behalf of Israel," and the passage cited from Isaiah 10:22-23 contrasts the "number of the sons of Israel," which is "as the sand of the sea," with the minority that will be saved (Rom. 9:27-28). This corresponds precisely to v. 6b: "Not all who are of Israel are Israel." The "sons of Israel" in the Isaiah citation correspond to οἱ ἐξ Ἰσραήλ, the "remnant" to Ἰσραήλ. A second Isaiah citation is, as Paul notes, from an earlier passage, where it is said: "If the Lord of hosts had not left us seed (σπέρμα), we would have become as Sodom, and would have resembled Gomorrah" (Isa. 1:29;

32. Cf. Wagner, *Heralds of the Good News*, 81-83.

33. C. Stanley envisages that biblically literate members of Paul's (exclusively Gentile) audience "would have referred to the original Hosean contexts" and concluded that both Hosea and Paul have *Israel* in mind (*Arguing with Scripture*, 158). Yet it is anachronistic to suppose that first-century readers necessarily held the same assumptions about the "literal sense" of a text as we do.

Rom. 9:29).[34] Similarly, in v. 7 the distinction within Israel is followed by a distinction between Abraham's children (the comprehensive category) and Abraham's "seed" (the category limited by the fact that only "*in Isaac* shall seed be called to you"). Thus the two Isaiah citations of vv. 27-28 and 29 correspond closely to vv. 6b and 7 respectively. There are further Abrahamic echoes in the Isaianic references to the innumerability of the sons of Israel (cf. Gen. 15:5), to the sand of the sea (cf. Gen. 22:17), and to Sodom and Gomorrah — whose destruction represents a threat to Abraham's family.

Thus, in Paul's prophetic sequence, Hosea has spoken of the Gentiles, who were "not my people" and are now "my people," passing from exclusion to inclusion. In contrast, Isaiah speaks of Israel's passing from inclusion to exclusion, through the "word that concludes and cuts short" (λόγον συντελῶν καὶ συντέμνων), which is evidently the reverse side of the divine word or "call" addressed to the Gentiles (n.b. καλέσω, v. 25). This exclusion would have been total, were it not for the preservation of the "seed," of which Isaiah also speaks (v. 29).[35] For Paul, that "seed" or "remnant" is identified with Jewish Christians, including the Jewish Christians of Rome, who may be spoken of both in their relation to "Israel" (vv. 27-29) and as recipients of the same divine call as Gentiles (v. 24). Paul encourages the Roman Jewish Christians to see a single divine electing purpose at work *both* in their own existence as the remnant *and* in the existence of "sons of the living God" in the "place" previously occupied by those who were "not my people" (cf. v. 26). That transformation of "place" has also occurred in the city of Rome. Astonishingly, the prophets speak of a reversal in which "not my people" become "my people," and "my people" become "not my people." The remnant at the center is invited to contemplate a revolution of 180 degrees, in which the peoples on the right and on the left exchange places. That, according to Paul, is the true scriptural teaching about the divine electing purpose that is now being realized. This account might be labeled as "supersessionist," so long as the pivotal position of the remnant is borne in mind.[36]

---

34. Isaiah 10:22-23 LXX is cited with minor deviations (one apparently derived from Hosea 2:1a); Isaiah 1:9 is cited verbatim. For detailed analysis, see R. Wagner, *Heralds of the Good News*, 92-100.

35. R. Hays argues that the reference to the "seed" in v. 27 is positive and that the explanatory "only" often inserted in translation (". . . *only* a remnant shall be saved") should be omitted (*Echoes of Scripture*, 68; see also S. Stowers, *A Rereading of Romans*, 302). This would seem to underplay the seriousness of the "word that concludes and cuts short" and the apparent contrast between the many and the few.

36. I am less worried by Pauline "supersessionism" than some recent interpreters, for three main reasons: (1) it expresses an alienation from the parent religious community integral to the

As the argument further unfolds in the following chapters, this initial account of the scriptural doctrine of election will be set within a broader context and will be significantly modified as a result. Yet it is important to understand Romans 9 on its own terms and not to force it into harmony with Romans 11 in one's anxiety to exonerate Paul of the "heresy" of supersessionism.[37] Forcible harmonizing is no more plausible here than in the case of Romans 2 and 3, where it is again some supposed "heresy" that is at issue. Harmonizers fail to note that, in this letter and elsewhere, Paul is engaged in an *ongoing process of theologizing*, rather than merely repeating and reporting theological positions that have long since become fixed and intransigent. "Pauline theology" exists only in the act of composition. As Paul embarks on his long discussion of Israel's election, he himself does not know exactly where the argument will take him. It is *as he writes* that he receives insight into "the depth of the riches and wisdom and knowledge of God" (11:33), enabling his audience to accompany him on the journey of faith seeking understanding.[38]

3. The Dynamics of Election (Romans 9:30–10:21)

In Romans 9:30–10:13, Paul reverts to the terminology familiar to his readers from chapters 3–4. Again we read of a "righteousness" that is "by faith" (9:30; 10:6) rather than "by works" (9:32), a "righteousness of God" (10:3) that is "for everyone who believes" (10:4) and that thereby removes the soteriological "distinction" between Jew and Greek (10:12). Yet it would be quite wrong to conclude that Paul here leaves the topic of election, asserting "Israel's responsibility" in order to counterbalance the predestinarian language

---

sect model employed in this work; (2) religious professionals are constantly seeking to supersede views held within interpretative communities other than their own; (3) nothing that Paul says on any topic should be taken as a *direct* mandate for contemporary theology or practice.

37. Even in our enlightened times, the charge of "heresy" continues to impair the practice of exegetical debate: see, for example, Douglas Harink's polemic against the "supersessionism" of N. T. Wright (Harink, *Paul among the Postliberals*, 153-84). Harink does, however, stop short of calling for Wright to be deprived of ecclesiastical office.

38. Contrast Harink's harmonizing account: "Throughout the sustained argument of Romans 9–11 Paul has kept a single thesis in view. God may harden and show mercy, now towards the nations, now toward a portion of Israel, as he wills . . . , but God will never reject his chosen fleshly people or allow them to fail in the race of salvation" (*Paul among the Postliberals*, 174). No such "single thesis" presides harmoniously over these chapters as a whole. The suggestion that "God has rejected his people," repudiated in 11:1, arises out of Paul's own argument thus far.

of 9:6-29.[39] Paul is still speaking on largely scriptural terrain of the divine electing purpose that has resulted in the exclusion of Jews and the inclusion of Gentiles. Thus, the argument is still dominated by scriptural quotations through which Paul seeks to legitimate his understanding of God's activity and its social consequences. Scriptural utterances such as Isaiah 28:16 (cited in Rom. 9:33 and 10:11) are not simply disclosures of a *prior* divine decision to elect and/or reject. Rather, they *are* that decision. The "predestination" of Israel or of Gentiles is identical to the pre-announcement of their respective destinies that occurs in the prophetic scriptures. Thus, scripture speaks of a "stone" established by God so that some may stumble on it whereas others will believe:

(1) ἰδοὺ τίθημι ἐν Σιὼν λίθον (2a) προσκόμματος καὶ πέτραν σκανδάλου, (3) καὶ ὁ πιστεύων ἐπ᾽ αὐτῷ οὐ καταισχυνθήσεται. (Rom. 9:33)

Paul's citation both abbreviates the original and substitutes words drawn from elsewhere in Isaiah:

(1) ἰδοὺ ἐγὼ ἐμβαλῶ εἰς τὰ θεμέλια Σιὼν λίθον (2b) πολυτελῆ ἐκλεκτὸν ἀκρογωνιαῖον ἔντιμον εἰς τὰ θεμέλια αὐτῆς, (3) καὶ ὁ πιστεύων ἐπ᾽ αὐτῷ οὐ μὴ καταισχυνθῇ. (Isa. 28:16 LXX)

καὶ ἐὰν ἐπ᾽ αὐτῷ πεποιθὼς ᾖς, ἔσται σοι εἰς ἁγίασμα καὶ οὐχ ὡς (2a) λίθου προσκόμματι συναντήσεσθε αὐτῷ οὐδὲ ὡς πέτρας πτώματι. (Isa. 8:14 LXX)

Paul's conflation replaces the stone that is "costly and chosen, a precious cornerstone" (2b) with "a stone for stumbling . . . , a rock for falling" (2a), which he presumably understands as the same stone seen from opposing perspectives. This is confirmed by the fact that the stone of Isaiah 8:14 will *not* be for stumbling or falling "if you put your trust in him," which Paul will have connected with "the one who believes in him" in 28:16. He thereby creates a text that announces a forthcoming divine act with two contrasting outcomes. Those who stumble are shamed thereby, whereas those who believe will not be put to shame. It is scripture itself that predestines some to fall and others to believe.

To "believe in him" is presumably to believe in Christ.[40] It is the citation

39. The view of Barrett, "Romans 9.30–10.21: Fall and Responsibility of Israel," *passim;* E. Dinkler, "Prädestination bei Paulus," 254; Dodd, *Romans,* 173; Käsemann, *Commentary on Romans,* 276. However, N. T. Wright, "The Messiah and the People of God," 212, regards this as an "alien theological theme."

40. This is denied by Lloyd Gaston (*Paul and the Torah,* 129) and others who wish to minimize the connection between Israel and Christ in Paul's theology. Gaston understands the stone

that has generated the recurrence of the faith terminology: for Paul understands ὁ πιστεύων ἐπ' αὐτῷ οὐ καταισχυνθήσεται (Rom. 9:33) to speak of a righteousness that is ἐκ πίστεως (9:30, 32), just as he understands "stumbling" as occasioned by the pursuit of righteousness "by works" (9:32). This antithetical rewriting of Isaiah 28:16 enables Paul to bring into focus the concrete form of the divine decision both to make "my people" out of "not my people" and to address a corresponding word that concludes and cuts short to the innumerable sons of Israel (9:25-29). Neither of his other two righteousness-by-faith texts (Hab. 2:4; Gen. 15:6) takes into account the possibility of non-faith as well as of faith, and this makes Isaiah 28:16 (+ 8:14) peculiarly suited to a context in which Paul is speaking of the non-realization of Israel's election as well as of the Gentiles. In the concluding paragraph of Romans 9, the rewritten Isaianic text can thus generate the following chiastic structure:

Present reality
- A   Faith leads to righteousness for the Gentiles (9:30)
- B   Israel fails to attain righteousness through the law (9:31-32a)

Scriptural foreordination
- B'   Israel is to stumble over the stone of stumbling, laid down by God (9:32b-33a)
- A'   Believers are to find in that stone the basis for their eternal well-being (9:33b)

We note in passing that ὁ πιστεύων ἐπ' αὐτῷ makes it difficult to refer ἐκ πίστεως (vv. 30, 32) to the faithfulness of Christ. We also note that "works" here refers exclusively to the practice of the Jewish law, which (Paul here argues) does *not* serve as an expression of Israel's elect status. On the contrary, God has foreordained in scripture that precisely this practice will cause Israel to stumble over the stone of stumbling and the rock of offense. Here, the sheer strangeness of the great reversal between the elected and the rejected (9:25-29) comes most clearly into focus. Israel has not been rejected on account of persistent and flagrant transgression, as in most later forms of Christian supersessionism, but *in spite of* zealous law observance (cf. 10:2). There is nothing inherently wrong with such law observance. Indeed, the contrast with Gentile indifference to righteousness makes it seem thoroughly

---

as "the gospel contained in Torah, the gospel of the inclusion of Gentiles," as announced to Abraham, identified in Isaiah 51:1 as "the rock from which you were hewn." This interpretation will not fit the partial repetition of the citation from Isaiah 28:16 in Romans 10:11, where the christological reference is inescapable.

admirable (cf. 9:30-31). It is simply that God has decreed both that righteousness shall be by faith and that this will prove unacceptable to those who pursue the law's works.[41] And this means that those who hunger and thirst for righteousness have no advantage over the indifferent and ignorant, as God re-creates the people of God in its new messianic form. Paul does not speculate as to why this act of re-creation has taken the form it has but is content to appeal to its sheer actuality as foreordained in scripture. Even the "exclusion of boasting" motif (3:27) is absent here. The section as a whole (9:30–10:21) continues to reflect on the strange reversal and its scriptural basis, and also begins to uncover grounds for suspecting that *the reversal may not be final.*

In its antithetical Pauline rewriting, Isaiah 28:16 creates a chiastic structure within Romans 9:30-33 but also inaugurates a second "prophetic sequence" that is itself chiastically structured (9:30–10:21). As in the first sequence, texts from Isaiah are supplemented by other prophetic texts: Joel 3:5 (Rom. 10:13), Psalm 18:5 (Rom. 10:18), and Deuteronomy 32:21 (Rom. 10:19). Yet it is the Isaianic texts that bear the weight of the argument, as their presentation in their scriptural order already implies. Paul has cited Isaiah 10:22-23 and 1:9 at the conclusion of the first sequence and has indicated the reversal of the scriptural order in the distinction between Ἠσαιας δὲ κράζει (v. 27) and καθὼς προείρηκεν Ἠσαιας (v. 29):

> *Isaiah 10:22-23:* "If the number of the sons of Israel is as the sand of the sea, only the remnant will be saved. For a word that concludes and cuts short shall the Lord perform upon the earth." (Rom. 9:27-28)

> *Isaiah 1:9:* "If the Lord Sabaoth had not left us seed, we would have become as Sodom and be like Gomorra." (Rom. 9:29)

In the second prophetic sequence, there are no further departures from the Isaianic order:

> *Isaiah 28:16 (+ 8:14):* "Behold, I lay in Sion a stone of stumbling and a rock of offense, and the one who believes in him will not be ashamed." (Rom. 9:33)

> *Isaiah 28:16* (partial repetition): "Everyone who believes in him will not be ashamed." (Rom. 10:11)

---

41. According to Paul's reading of scripture in Romans 9–11, Israel's failure to attain God's righteousness is actually decreed by God — as is rightly emphasized by M. Theobald, *Studien zum Römerbrief,* 374-78. In contrast, Richard Bell finds a "reason" for Israel's hardening or stumbling in the fact "that Israel assumed salvation had to be by works" (*The Irrevocable Call of God,* 223). Seeking any such reason for the divine predestination is excluded by 9:11.

Isaiah 52:7: "How beautiful are the feet of those who preach good things." (Rom. 10:15)

Isaiah 53:1: "Lord, who believed our message?" (Rom. 10:16)

Isaiah 65:1-2: "I was found by those who did not seek me, I was manifest to those who did not ask for me. All day long I stretched forth my hands to a disobedient and contrary people." (Rom. 10:20-21)

Within this sequence texts from Joel, the Psalter, and Deuteronomy are interspersed. Indeed, in Romans 9–10 as a whole scriptural order is generally maintained, from Genesis 18 to Isaiah 65, especially if Paul envisaged Hosea as belonging to a "Book of the Twelve" that preceded Isaiah in the canonical order (cf. Rom. 9:25-26).

These Isaianic texts play a crucial role within the chiastic structuring of the second prophetic sequence:

> A Gentiles chosen at Israel's expense (Rom. 9:30-33; Isa. 28:16)
> B The conversion of Israel: faith (Rom. 10:1-13; Isa. 28:16; Joel 3:5)
> C Salvation for the Gentiles: preaching the word (Rom. 10:14-17: Isa. 52:7; 53:1)
> C′ Salvation for the Gentiles: the universal proclamation (Rom. 10:18; Ps. 18:5)
> B′ The conversion of Israel: jealousy (Rom. 10:19; Deut. 32:21)
> A′ Gentiles chosen at Israel's expense (Rom. 10:20-21; Isa. 65:1-2)

B is formally differentiated from *A* by the direct address to the readers as ἀδελφοί and the return of first-person singular discourse for the first time since 9:1-3. *B* is characterized by a concern with "salvation" (10:1, 9, 10, 13) and by the use of second- and third-person singular discourse evidently arising from the term ἄνθρωπος in the Leviticus citation in 10:5. *C* opens with a series of three rhetorical questions introduced by πῶς and forming a chain construction in which each term ("invoke," "believe," "hear," "proclaim," "sent") is traced back to its origin in the next term in the series (vv. 14-15; cf. v. 17). The *C′-B′-A′* series is only a quarter of the length of the *A-B-C* series and consists in a group of citations with interrelated introductory formulae (vv. 18-21). In *C′* and *B′*, citations from Psalm 18:5 and Deuteronomy 32:21 are both introduced with the phrase ἀλλὰ λέγω, μή ... (vv. 18, 19). In *B′*, the term "Israel" is reintroduced for the first time since 9:31. The second half of the introductory formula (πρῶτος Μωϋσῆς λέγει) is linked to that of *A′* (Ἡσαΐας δὲ ἀποτολμᾷ καὶ λέγει). *A′* clearly differentiates between the Gentiles and Israel, and the relationship to *A* is especially close. The analysis suggested here is confirmed by formal as well as thematic features.

A-A': Isaiah 65:1-2 LXX reads as follows (bold = Pauline transpositions):

1a **ἐμφανὴς ἐγενόμην** τοῖς ἐμὲ μὴ ζητοῦσιν, 1b **εὑρέθην** τοῖς ἐμὲ μὴ ἐπερωτῶσιν. [εἶπα Ἰδού εἰμι τῷ ἔθνει οἳ ουκ ἐκαλέσαν μου τὸ ὄνομα.] *2* ἐξεπέτασα τὰς χεῖρας μου **ὅλην τὴν ημέραν** πρὸς λαὸν ἀπειθοῦντα καὶ αντιλέγοντα . . .

Paul's citation keeps close to the Septuagintal wording, apart from a couple of transpositions, which serve to correlate seeking with finding and to emphasize the divine constancy:

1a **εὑρέθην** ἐν τοῖς ἐμὲ μὴ ζητοῦσιν, *1b* **ἐμφανὴς ἐγενόμην** τοῖς ἐμὲ μὴ ἐπερωτῶσιν . . .
2 **ὅλην τὴν ημέραν** ἐξεπέτασα τὰς χειρὰς μου πρὸς λαὸν απειθοῦντα καὶ ἀντιλέγοντα.

Much more significant than the transpositions is the fact that (for Paul) Isaiah "dares to speak" of Gentiles in *1*, whereas in *2* he addresses Israel. What Isaiah daringly says about Gentiles is exactly what Paul himself had said in 9:30, where he recounted how "Gentiles who did not pursue righteousness attained righteousness — righteousness by faith." It is these same Gentiles who did not seek God and yet were found by God. Still more strikingly, Paul's treatment of Isaiah 65:1-2 closely resembles his earlier treatment of 28:16. In both cases, Paul finds an antithesis in the Isaianic text. In the first case, he does so by importing words from elsewhere (λίθον προσκόμματος καὶ πέτραν σκανδάλου, Isa. 8:14). As we have seen, there is some basis in Isaiah 8:14 for the assumption that the stone that was precious to some was an offense to others. In the later case, the disjunction is occasioned by the fact that in *1* God is said to have been "found" or "made manifest," whereas in *2* God's outstretched hands are taken to mean that God has not yet been found or made manifest. Thus *1* is read as a positive statement about the Gentiles, *2* as a negative statement about Israel. Paul marks the disjunction by providing *2* with a separate introductory formula indicating a change of addressee (πρὸς δὲ τὸν Ἰσραὴλ λέγει, Rom. 10:21).[42] The analogy with his earlier reworking of Isaiah 28:16 is striking.

---

42. See the detailed discussion of this passage in R. Wagner, *Heralds of the Good News*, 205-17.

B-B': In 10:1-13 and again in 10:19, Paul speaks of Israel's possible conversion, which can come only by way of an acknowledgment of the salvation of the Gentiles. In 10:1 Paul again expresses his longing and his prayer for his people's "salvation," and the recurrence of the noun in v. 10 and the cognate verb in vv. 9 and 13 suggests the thematic unity of this passage.

Paul longs for his people's salvation, and he does so on the basis of their "zeal for God" (10:2). While he does not go so far as to suggest that he prays for them to be saved because they deserve to be saved, his language is remarkably positive and hopeful. *It seems that the divine decision to elect Gentiles at the expense of Jews may not be final.* The decision is in force in the present, but it lacks eschatological finality: for "prayer to God" indicates that the future is open and not closed, and that a vessel of wrath fitted for destruction can become a vessel of mercy prepared for glory (cf. 9:22-23). If prayer is appropriate at all, then Ishmael may yet share the inheritance of Isaac, and Esau that of Jacob; even Pharaoh might cease to be an object of divine hardening and become an object of mercy like Moses, his *alter ego*. If in 9:3 Paul refers to a despairing earlier prayer to be anathema for the sake of his Jewish kin, the renewed possibility of prayer in 10:1 represents a remarkable step forward in the argument.

Yet the reference to prayer also serves a didactic purpose, introducing a passage in which Paul instructs those he addresses as ἀδελφοί as to what it would require for members of Israel to make the transition to faith and salvation. At present, they are ignorant of the righteousness of God, seeking to establish their own (10:3). That is, they are unaware that righteousness is for everyone who believes and that Christ is the τέλος of the law (10:4), the divine λόγος συντελῶν καὶ συντέμνων (9:28).[43] When in v. 3 Paul speaks of ἡ τοῦ θεοῦ δικαιοσύνη (or ἡ δικαιοσύνη τοῦ θεοῦ), this is synonymous with δικαιοσύνη παντὶ τῷ πιστεύοντι (v. 4) and ἡ ἐκ πίστεως δικαιοσύνη (v. 6). Similarly, when Paul speaks of Israel as "pursuing a law of righteousness" (9:31), of their doing so "by works" (9:32), of their "seeking to establish their own righteousness" (10:3), and of "the righteousness that is by the law," which Moses wrote (10:5), these are again synonymous expressions, referring to the practice of law observance, individually and communally, on the understanding that the law defines the divinely appointed way to "righteousness" — conduct approved by God.[44] Painstaking attempts to differentiate "one's own"

43. τέλος (10:4) appears to derive from συντελῶν (9:28): for the end of the law is also the word of judgment that decrees the non-salvation of the majority of the "sons of Israel." This would make redundant the usual laborious discussions about whether the term means "end" or "goal" or both (e.g., Moo, *Romans*, 638-43).

44. The claim that the Torah here represents a "charter of racial privilege" (N. T. Wright,

righteousness from righteousness that is "by the law," or "the righteousness of God" from "the righteousness of faith," or "faith" from "believing" should be subjected to the discipline of Ockham's razor. Paul has in mind here the two communal patterns of life that he finds in Isaiah 28:16, one characterized by believing, the other by the refusal of belief, and it is this simple dichotomy that he further elaborates in the passage following the citation. In particular, he is concerned to describe the transition from "stumbling" or "offense" to "believing in him" (Christ), on the assumption that the transition *can* be made.[45]

From a Jewish Christian standpoint, the most significant element in Paul's theoretical account of Jewish conversion to Christ is the fact that this requires a transformation of one's view of the law. Again, it is the Isaiah text that enables Paul to make this point. The stone of stumbling and rock of offense is, in the first instance, the crucified and risen Christ. Yet for Paul the σκάνδαλον is not Christ as such but Christ as the total embodiment of the divine gift of righteousness, received through faith and therefore not through observance of the law. In other words, the σκάνδαλον is occasioned not by the stone or rock per se but by the fact that "the one who *believes* in him will not be ashamed." What use would one have for a righteousness by faith when righteousness is defined once for all in the precepts and prohibitions of the law of Moses? According to Paul, Jewish conversion is to a Christ who is "the end of the law" and who inaugurates in its place a "righteousness for everyone who believes" (10:4).

How might such a conversion occur? Paul cites Moses' authoritative articulation of the righteousness that is by the law: "The person [ἄνθρωπος]

The *Climax of the Covenant*, 241) overlooks the emphasis on *conduct* (9:32; 10:5) as the means whereby Jews "seek to establish their own righteousness" and so miss "the righteousness of God" (10:3). "Privilege" is an appropriate term for the items listed in 9:4-5, but in 9:30–10:5 the emphasis is on the *praxis* that corresponds to the "privilege" of the νομοθεσία (9:4).

45. The concept of Jewish conversion to Christ is, of course, anathema to some recent North American scholarship. It is held that, "[f]rom his own account, Paul never tried to convert Jews" (L. Gaston, *Paul and the Torah*, 149); thus there is no interest in these chapters in "individual Jews converting to faith in Christ" (148). In Romans 9–11, "Israel's salvation, while not unrelated to the redemption of the Gentiles through Christ, does not take the form of embracing Christ" (J. G. Gager, in his aptly named *Reinventing Paul*, 142). While such a reading can exploit the lack of explicit christological references in the latter part of Romans 11, it can offer no coherent explanation of Romans 10:1-13 in its relation to the prayer for Jewish salvation in v. 1. Indeed, it becomes incomprehensible how Paul could ever have prayed such a prayer. Disparaging remarks about individual Jews coming to faith in Christ (see Harink, *Paul among the Postliberals*, 182) are disrespectful of the fact that, now as then, individual Jews do become Christians, just as individual Christians do become Jews.

who does these things shall live by them" (10:5). He then brings this person to life, making him or her the object of the second-person singular address of a personified Righteousness-of-faith, who uses well-known Mosaic language with insidiously Christian intent (10:6-10). The law-observant are characterized by an arduous quest: their "zeal for God" leads them to "pursue" and to "seek" righteousness. Yet Righteousness-of-faith counsels us not to indulge in such heroics, undertaking perilous heavenly or abysmal journeys in quest of righteousness, as though Christ had not already come down from heaven and been raised from the dead (10:6-7). If the "heart" has such aspirations to the heights or depths, it is out of touch with reality. It has a zeal for God that is not according to knowledge (v. 3). Rather, the "heart" should attend to a word that is not self-generated but that comes to it from the outside: that is, "the word of faith that we proclaim" (v. 8).[46] That way salvation lies — not just for the Jew but also for the Gentile, as Paul now begins to emphasize, adding a πᾶς to his repetition of the second line of the Isaiah citation: πᾶς ὁ πιστεύων ἐπ' αὐτῷ οὐ καταισχυνθήσεται (v. 11). The Jew, in fact, is to be saved in just the same way as the Greek. Owing to the overflowing divine generosity, there is no distinction (v. 12).[47]

This salvation is still "for the Jew first, and also for the Greek" (cf. 1:16). Yet Greeks (Gentiles) have attained righteousness, whereas Jews (Israel) have not (cf. 9:30-31), and this suggests that the order might have to be reversed: to the Greek first, and then to the Jew. This is the prospect that Paul finds in the citation from the Song of Moses that completes the B-B' stage of our chiasmus:

> But I say, did Israel not know? First, Moses says: "I will make you jealous of a no-nation [ἐπ' οὐκ ἔθνει], I will make you enraged at a senseless nation." (Rom. 10:19, citing Deut. 32:21)

If Israel is to be jealous of a "no-nation," then this presupposes that "not my people" has been transformed into "my people" (Rom. 9:25-26). Developing this thought in 11:13-14, Paul tells how he exercises his ministry to the Gentiles

46. I here assume an *antithetical* relationship between the "righteousness by law" articulated by the Leviticus text and the "righteousness by faith" that speaks in the reworked Deuteronomy text (see my *PHF*, 329-41). Attempts to deny the antithesis here (e.g., N. T. Wright, *Romans*, 658-63) leave Israel's pursuit of righteousness by the law without scriptural foundation and will therefore tend to shift the focus from the sovereign divine agency to the dubious category of "Israel's fault" (654-55).

47. Romans 10:1-13 is overwhelmingly positive in tenor and does not argue that "Israel is . . . guilty of a kind of meta-sin, the attempt to confine grace to one race," an "idolatry of national privilege" (the view of N. T. Wright, *The Climax of the Covenant*, 240).

in such a way as to make his own people jealous, and thus to secure the salvation of some of them. When he is preaching to Gentiles Paul has his own people in mind just as when he is praying for Jews (10:1). In spite of the reversal outlined in chapter 9, neither Paul nor his God has turned his back on Jews in turning toward Gentiles.

C-C': At the heart of Paul's second scriptural chiasmus (Rom. 9:30–10:21) lies a conjunction of passages in which Paul affirms the legitimacy of the mission to Gentiles. In this chiasmus, the brief *C'-B'-A'* sequence consists entirely in scriptural citations relating to Gentile mission (Ps. 18:5/Rom. 10:18), Jewish jealousy as a first step towards salvation (Deut. 32:21/Rom. 10:19), and the antithetical divine address to Gentiles and to Jews (Isa. 65:1-2/Rom. 10:20-21). *C'* is formally differentiated from *C* by the intrusion of a question introduced by ἀλλὰ λέγω μή . . . (v. 18), a format repeated in v. 19. The question "Did they not hear . . . ?" relates to the "sound" or "words" that have gone out "into all the earth" and that have therefore been heard by all the earth's inhabitants, i.e., Gentiles (v. 18). It follows that the preceding section (vv. 14-17 = *C*) also refers to the worldwide proclamation to Gentiles.

On the erroneous view that the theme of Romans 9:30–10:21 is "Israel's responsibility," 10:14-17 is generally interpreted as a reference to the mission to the Jews: Israel has no excuse because the gospel was duly preached to her.[48] But if Paul is seeking to justify his view of election and rejection by reference to scripture, this passage is more likely to be a defense from scriptural texts of his own Gentile mission. Exegesis confirms this. Verse 14 (πῶς οὖν ἐπικαλέσωνται) follows on directly from v. 13 (πᾶς γὰρ ὃς ἂν ἐπικαλέσηται κτλ), and, as the emphasis in vv. 11-13 is on the universality of salvation, it is hard to see how v. 14 can be confined to the mission to the Jews.[49] Its form is dictated by the polemical situation. Paul is addressing the Jewish Christian who rejects the idea of salvation for Gentiles and Paul's mission to them; this accounts for the argumentative style of vv. 14-18 and the frequent use of scriptural citations. Paul's argument runs: scripture says that "everyone who calls on the name of the Lord will be saved." But how is this possible unless they hear and believe the gospel preached to them by Christ's messengers (vv. 13-15a)? These messengers are spoken of in scripture (v. 15b). It is true that not all Gentiles have believed; but this too was predicted, by Isaiah, using words that also confirm the neces-

---

48. So Cranfield, *Romans,* 2:533; Dodd, *Romans,* 179; Käsemann, *Commentary on Romans,* 294; Leenhardt, *Romans,* 273; Schlier, *Der Römerbrief,* 316; Fitzmyer, *Romans,* 595; Moo, *Romans,* 664.

49. So N. T. Wright, "The Messiah and the People of God," 178-79, to whose arguments the following section is indebted. See also P. Richardson, *Israel,* 134; J. D. G. Dunn, *Romans,* 2:620.

sity of preaching (vv. 16-17).[50] But the Gentiles have *heard*, even if they have not all believed (v. 18). Israel should have known from her own scriptures that the Gentiles would enter her heritage while she was rejected, for both Moses and Isaiah spoke of this (vv. 19-21).

This interpretation, according to which Paul in 10:14-18 defends his mission against anticipated Jewish Christian objections, fits his language much better than the view that the section is concerned with the mission to the Jews. As we have seen, the link between vv. 13 and 14 favors this interpretation. The conventional view also finds vv. 18-21 hard to explain. According to v. 18, "they" have heard the gospel, for, as scripture says, it has been preached throughout the world.[51] This fits the Gentile mission much better than the mission to Jews. The gloss ". . . and therefore cannot be supposed not to have been heard by the generality of Jews" is cumbersome and unnatural.[52] Similarly, in v. 19 Paul claims that Israel should have known, because scripture (Moses and Isaiah) speaks of the salvation of the Gentiles and the rejection of the Jews (vv. 20-21). The natural interpretation is: Israel should have known about God's intention to save the Gentiles at the expense of the Jews. The conventional view requires another unnatural gloss: "If Gentiles, who, in relation to the knowledge of God, are, compared with Israel, but no-peoples, foolish nations, have come to know, then it certainly cannot be supposed that Israel has not known."[53] But if Paul's point is simply to prove that Israel has heard the gospel, he has made it in a very roundabout way: the Gentiles have heard it, so Israel must also have heard it. It is better to understand the theme of 10:14-18 as the Gentile mission, in its necessity (vv. 14-15, 17), its only partial effectiveness (v. 16), and its worldwide scope (v. 18); and the Gentile mission is therefore presupposed in the following statements that concern Israel (vv. 19-21).[54]

Paul's second scriptural chiasm (9:30–10:21) has to do with the concrete form of the divine foreordination whose general outline is traced in the first one

---

50. Verse 17 is unnecessarily rejected as a gloss by Bultmann, "Glossen," 199.

51. The assumption that "they" here means "Israel" (e.g., Barrett, *Romans*, 205) ignores the contrast between "they" in v. 18 and "Israel" in v. 19.

52. Cranfield, *Romans*, 2:537. Cf. Wilckens, *Der Brief an die Römer*, 2:230.

53. Cranfield, *Romans*, 2:539. Cf. Dodd, *Romans*, 181; Kuss, *Der Römerbrief*, 779.

54. As Christopher Stanley points out, the "rhetorically stylized mode of expression" appears to presuppose an audience that "either does not recognize or is unconcerned about the vital necessity of sending out preachers. . . . Paul's questions seem designed to motivate the Romans to lend more support to Christian missionary efforts (including his own, 15:23-24)" (*Arguing with Scripture*, 161n).

(9:6-29). It has nothing whatever to do with any attempt to "balance" the predestinarianism of the preceding passage with an emphasis on human freedom and responsibility. It is not concerned to identify "Israel's fault."[55] Rather, the scriptural focus and the maintenance of scriptural sequence ensure a single, gradually unfolding argument in which the apparent rigidity of the image of the potter (9:19-21) gives way to a more dynamic account of the relation between the vessels of mercy and the vessels of wrath. It here transpires that the rejected are rejected on account of their zealous pursuit of righteousness as defined by the law — a righteousness that God chooses not to accept *in order that* another way of righteousness may be opened to the hopelessly unrighteous Gentiles. Thus rejection is *teleologically* related to election. The stone that leads some to faith will inevitably cause others to stumble, and the offense of the one is a necessary precondition of the faith of the other. Yet rejection, stumbling, and offense need not be permanent. Paul reports his prayer for unbelieving Israel's salvation, which already indicates that the vessels of wrath and of mercy do not represent preordained, fixed categories. Having served its purpose as such, the vessel of wrath can *become* a vessel of mercy. Such a transformation will entail an acknowledgment of God's definitive saving action — both its content (the incarnation and resurrection of Jesus) and its worldwide, comprehensive scope. Israel's "jealousy" of the non-nation of the Gentile Christians might even be a first step towards such a transformation.

Thus, Paul's scriptural argumentation does not simply legitimate a status quo in which Gentile Christians and unbelieving Israel are set over against one another, with a remnant of Israel ambiguously positioned between them. He can and does defend that status quo on scriptural grounds (9:6-29); but this is not the end of the argument. Scripture is written not only to instruct but also to generate hope (cf. 15:4), and in 9:30–10:21 a scripturally based hope for future transformation begins to dawn. If Roman Jewish Christians do as Paul wishes and begin to work towards unity with Christian Gentiles, they will not be consigning their non-Christian fellow Jews to everlasting condemnation. The divine electing purpose is not a fixed order but a dynamic and unfolding agency whose goal is human salvation. If Israel is still defined as "a disobedient and contrary people" (10:21), the disobedience and contrariness is to a divine electing action whose scope would seem to be universal.

55. Dunn's section heading for 9:30–10:4 ("Israel Has Misunderstood God's Righteousness," 2:578) shows the continuing influence of the predestination/responsibility schema that generations of commentators have imposed on Romans 9–10. In this respect, it makes no difference whether Israel is blamed for attempting to earn salvation or for assuming a privileged covenant status (cf. 2:587).

4. The Scriptural Hope (Romans 11:1-36)

As he reflects on his selected scriptural material from Genesis and Exodus, Hosea and Isaiah, Paul discovers a pattern of reversal within the unfolding divine electing action — a reversal typologically foreshadowed in scriptural narrative, explicitly announced in the prophetic texts, and now realized in the existence of a community of Gentile as well as Jewish Christians over against the unbelieving majority in Israel (Rom. 9:6-29). It might seem that such an argument would suffice for Paul's pragmatic purposes, aligning the Jewish Christian remnant alongside Christian Gentiles and detaching them from the non-Christian Jewish community. Yet Paul reads on, from Isaiah 10 to Isaiah 28 and beyond, taking in supplementary scriptural material along the way, until he arrives at Isaiah 65 (Rom. 9:30–10:21). Further scriptural texts are cited in the concluding section of Paul's argument (Rom. 11:1-36), again derived from the Psalter, Deuteronomy, and Isaiah, together with the Elijah narrative. Yet scriptural citations are not so fundamental to the argument of Romans 11 as in chapters 9–10. Rather, Paul is here drawing conclusions of his own about the future of God's electing activity, conclusions suggested by the intense scriptural engagement in the preceding chapters. It is in chapter 11 that the dynamic nature of the preceding argument comes most clearly to light. Its unfolding logic takes him far beyond his starting point in chapter 9. Romans 9–11 may be seen as a single argument,[56] but — as at other points in the letter — its dynamic character precludes any straightforward harmonizing of what is said in its later stages with what is said earlier. Its conclusion arises out of its beginning, but could not have been predicted at the beginning. In retracing Paul's journey through the scriptural testimony to election, our task is to identify the moments in its earlier stages that retrospectively take on a new significance as he turns to consider the future of God's electing agency.[57]

(1) In 11:1-10, the Jewish Christian remnant is seen as a sign that God has not rejected his people, Israel, as a whole.[58] In 11:1-2, "his people" (τὸν λαὸν αὐτοῦ) refers to the present generation of Jews, and Paul as representative of them

---

56. Rightly emphasized by Cranfield, *Romans*, 2:447-48.

57. In *PJG¹*, 168-74, the analysis of Romans 11 similarly drew attention to the differences between Paul's argument there and in chapter 9. The emphasis here on the ongoing role of the scriptural citations in shaping the developing argument is new.

58. There is no indication here that Paul has Jewish preachers to Gentiles in mind, rather than Jewish Christians in general (the view of L. Gaston, *Paul and the Torah*, 142). "Seven thousand" (v. 4) seems disproportionate to the likely number of Jewish missionaries.

describes himself as "of the seed of Abraham." This contrasts with the situation in 9:6-29. In 9:25, λαόν μου refers to Gentile Christians: "Those who are not my people I will call 'my people.'" In 9:6-9, Paul distinguishes sharply between the fleshly descendants of Abraham and his true "seed," Isaac, as representing "the children of the promise." On this distinction Paul ventures nothing less than the dependability of the divine word (cf. 9:6a). In 9:6-29, a clear and coherent argument gradually unfolds, to the effect that the salvation of Gentiles and rejection of Jews coheres with God's purpose of election as revealed in scripture. Yet in 11:1-2 and indeed throughout this chapter, Paul reverts to a view of the people of God that he had previously seemed to reject — a view in which descent from the patriarchs bestows a privileged standing before God.[59] In chapter 9, the "remnant" (ὑπόλειμμα, v. 27) represents the minority within Israel who survive the catastrophe that has befallen the people as a whole (cf. 9:27-28, citing Isa. 10:22-23). In chapter 11, the remnant (λεῖμμα, v. 5) is the sign not of divine judgment but of divine grace — that "God has not abandoned his people whom he foreknew" (11:2). What has happened to the earlier insistence that Israel be differentiated from Israel, Abraham's seed from Abraham's children — a point laboriously elaborated and defended as far back as chapter 4 of this letter?

Paul's use of the scriptural term "Israel" may suggest an answer. He has stated that "not all who are of Israel are Israel" (9:6), appearing to confine the designation "Israel" to the remnant (i.e., Christian Jews) and to deny it to the unbelieving majority. And yet, even here it is acknowledged that this majority is ἐξ Ἰσραήλ. Indeed, he has previously acknowledged that "they are Israelites, to whom belong the sonship and the glory and the covenants and the law-giving and the worship and the promises . . . ," not to mention the patriarchs and the Christ himself (vv. 4-5). In such a context, the differentiation that follows between "those who are of Israel" and "Israel" (v. 6) is inevitably muted. Thus no terminological distinction between a "fleshly" and a "spiritual" Israel is to be found here. In spite of v. 6, Paul in Romans 9–11 consistently uses "Israel" to refer to the Jewish people as a whole and not to the remnant, let alone to the Gentile church. "Isaiah," we are told, "cries out on behalf of Israel . . ." (9:27), an introductory formulation no doubt influenced by the reference to "the number of the sons of Israel" in the citation itself. Thereafter, it is "Israel" that seeks righteousness through the law (9:31; cf. 11:7) and that is addressed by God in further scriptural texts (10:19, 21). "Israel" may contain "the elect" (ἡ ἐκλογή) and "the rest" (11:7), but "the rest" still belong

---

59. Cf. Dodd, *Romans,* 192; Wilckens, *Der Brief an die Römer,* 2:185, 197; C. Müller, *Gerechtigkeit,* 27, 38, 92-93; D. Zeller, *Juden und Heiden,* 115.

to Israel even in their temporary "hardened" state (11:25). Ultimately it is "all Israel" that will be saved (11:26).

It is, then, Paul's adherence to the plain sense of scripture that compels him to retain the identification of "Israel" with the Jewish people, rather than systematizing a distinction between a "fleshly" and a "spiritual" Israel. In Romans 11, it is scriptural usage that compels Paul to accommodate the Gentiles and the Gentile mission *within* the sphere of God's covenant with Israel, "his people." Insofar as Romans 9 is based on the *non*-equation of "those who are of Israel" and "Israel," it is destined to be surpassed in the further unfolding of Paul's scriptural argumentation. The texts marshaled in Romans 9 give a provisional, penultimate account of the divine electing purpose. They are not the last word.

(2) In Romans 11, a positive salvific role is repeatedly ascribed to Israel's failure to believe the gospel: "By their trespass salvation has come to the Gentiles" (v. 11; cf. vv. 12, 15, 17, 28, 30). In Romans 9, in contrast, the rejection of Jews and the salvation of Gentiles are generally set alongside one another as independent and equivalent events. Nowhere else in Paul or in the New Testament is there anything approaching this positive estimate of the value of Israel's failure to believe the gospel. In an earlier writing, Paul is bitterly critical of "the Jews" for "driving us out and displeasing God and opposing all people by preventing us from speaking to the Gentiles so that they may be saved," thereby "filling up" the predestined measure of their sins (1 Thess. 2:15-16). In Romans 11, this same violent hostility to the gospel is again seen as a mark of the divine rejection, but is now placed almost on a par with the saving act of Christ. When it is said in 11:15 that Israel's rejection (ἀποβολή) issues in the reconciliation (καταλλαγή) of the world, the christological analogy is unmistakable (cf. 5:10). It was suggested in Chapter 2 of this work that these passages from Romans 11 provide valuable historical information about the ideological origins of the Gentile mission, for which widespread Jewish rejection of the gospel appears to have been a precondition. This historical circumstance is given a simple and perhaps primitive theological explanation in vv. 17 and 19 (an explanation that Paul proceeds to qualify). Branches were broken off the olive tree in order that Gentiles might be grafted in instead; in other words, Israel's failure was needed in order to create space for Gentiles. In spite of this historical background, however, the way in which Israel is here virtually set alongside Christ as the bringer of salvation to the Gentiles is remarkable and requires explanation.

This point appears to derive from the conjunction of two of Paul's citations from chapter 9. In Exodus 9:16, it is said that Pharaoh is raised up "so that I may reveal my power in you and so that my name may be proclaimed in all the earth" (cited in Rom. 9:17).[60] As we have seen, Paul proceeds to establish a teleological relationship between rejection and election on the basis of this text (9:22-24), indicating that what is true of Pharaoh is true of the "vessels of wrath" in general. The precise mechanism by which Israel is rejected for the sake of Gentiles is established by the citation in 9:33 of Isaiah 28:16 (+ 8:14). In Jesus' death and resurrection God establishes a way of righteousness open to all, in spite of the inevitable offense to the people of Israel, zealous as they are for the righteousness defined by the law. It is in that sense that God lays in Zion a stone of stumbling and rock of offense: God rejects Israel by establishing a gospel that a people zealous for the law will inevitably reject.[61] Israel is cast away in order that the Gentiles may be saved. If it seems strange that Israel should unknowingly play a Christ-like salvific role in the very act of rejecting the gospel of Christ, we recall that Israel and the Christ are of the same flesh and blood (cf. 9:5).[62]

(3) The final goal of the Gentile mission is the salvation of the Jews, according to 11:11-16, 25-32. As 11:11 puts it, the purpose of the Gentile mission is that Israel should become jealous and so be saved. Paul expects this to happen to some extent within his own ministry: he preaches to the Gentiles "in order to make my fellow Jews jealous, and thus save some of them" (11:13-14). It will happen ultimately to τὸ πλήρωμα αὐτῶν (v. 12), which will mean ζωή ἐκ νεκρῶν for the world (v. 15). The salvation of "all Israel" (v. 26) will take place "by the mercy shown *to you*" (v. 31) — that is, to you Gentiles. The ultimate purpose of Paul's Gentile mission is thus not the salvation of Gentiles alone but also the salvation of Jews.[63] The Gentiles become the means to an end.

---

60. As Wright notes, Israel's hardening "relates to Gentile salvation somewhat as Pharaoh's hardening relates to the exodus" (*Romans*, 680).

61. So Michael Theobald, *Studien zum Römerbrief*, 377.

62. This parallel between Israel and Christ lies at the heart of N. T. Wright's unpublished thesis, "The Messiah and the People of God." According to Wright, "[t]he Messiah, the anointed one of Israel, represents his people, and sums them up in himself, so that what is true of him is true of them" (3). Thus, Romans 9–11 is to be read christologically (173): Israel must follow the pattern of Christ's death and resurrection, being cast away for the world's salvation as the people of the Messiah according to the flesh (181). "Insofar as Israel is a people κατὰ σάρκα, she acts out Adam's fall. Insofar as she remains the Messiah's people, that fall is of redemptive value for the world" (182). Paul rejects Israel's claim to "national privilege" because this has been put to an end by the crucified Messiah: Christ is the end of the law (Rom. 10:4) in the sense that "a crucified Messiah means a crucified Israel" (93-94). Wright's Christ/Israel parallel seems broadly correct to me and is easily detachable from the dubious "national privilege" concept.

63. C. Plag argues unpersuasively that the problem of Romans 9–11 is not the tension between chapters 9 and 11, but between chapters 9–11 as a whole and 11:25-27; he therefore regards

Nowhere else does Paul claim that he preaches to Gentiles in order to secure the salvation of Jews. Elsewhere, the salvation of the Gentiles, together with the Jewish remnant, is itself seen as the ultimate goal of God's purposes (cf. 4:16-17; 9:24-29). Here, however, the Jew-Gentile relationship is understood by way of a double teleology: as Israel is initially sacrificed for the sake of Gentile salvation, so Gentile salvation has Israel's salvation as its final goal (11:30-32). The teleology in which some are rejected so as to realize the election of others is succeeded by a second teleology, in which the election of others secures the final re-election of the rejected.

If the first teleology derives from Exodus 9:16 and Isaiah 28:16, the second derives initially from Deuteronomy 32:21:

> But I say, did Israel not know? First, Moses says: "I will make you jealous of that which is not a nation, with a senseless nation I will provoke you to anger." (Rom. 10:19)

Paul develops this jealousy motif in Romans 11. Israel's stumbling over the rock of offense is not final and irrevocable, because "by their mis-step [παράπτωμα] salvation has come to the Gentiles *in order to make them jealous*" (v. 11). Paul makes no secret of his Gentile mission so that "somehow I may make my own flesh jealous and so save some of them" (v. 14).[64] Thus it is the Gentile mission that brings about the salvation of Jews here and now, thereby anticipating the time when "the fullness of the Gentiles" issues in the salvation of "all Israel" (vv. 25-26). Admittedly, the jealousy motif is more clearly related to the Gentile mission of the present than to the eschaton. The new hope for Israel's final salvation has its grounding elsewhere.

(4) It is in fact the promises to the patriarchs that guarantee the salvation of the Jewish people as a whole (11:28-29).[65] It is because "as regards election they are beloved for the sake of their forefathers" and because "the gifts and call of God are irrevocable" that Paul can be so confident that "all Israel will be saved"

11:25-27 as a gloss (*Israels Wege zum Heil*, 41-42). Plag claims that two different ways of salvation for Israel are set forth in Romans 11: salvation through the Gentile mission (vv. 11-24) and an independent eschatological salvation (vv. 25-27). Yet this distinction is untenable, for in vv. 11-24 Paul speaks not only of the salvation of some Jews through the Gentile mission (vv. 13-14) but also of the final eschatological salvation of the whole people (vv. 12, 15).

64. As Richard Bell points out, "[t]he term παραζηλοῦν here takes on a positive meaning in the sense of provoke to emulation" (*The Irrevocable Call of God*, 249).

65. Against C. Müller, *Gerechtigkeit*, 99-100, who thinks that the salvation of Israel is here grounded in the promise of a new creation; as he puts it, "Gottesvolksgedanke" is "Schöpfungsgedanke" (99).

(v. 26). In v. 16, Paul has grounded his belief in the salvation of Israel (v. 15) in the principle that, "if the root is holy, so are the branches," a probable reference to the patriarchs.[66] Although he acknowledges in vv. 17-22 that some of the branches have been broken off in order to make room for the Gentiles, he expresses his hope in vv. 23-24 that God will graft them back in again. Admittedly, there is a proviso in v. 23 (". . . if they do not persist in their unbelief"); but this is no longer evident in vv. 25-32. In contrast, Paul has seemed to argue in Romans 4 and 9 that the promise to Abraham and his seed applies not to the Jewish people as such but to the new people called by God from among Jews and Gentiles. In Romans 11, however, the promise to the patriarchs has no direct application to the Gentiles and instead provides the basis for Paul's confidence in the salvation of the Jews. The point will later be repeated in 15:8, where it is said that "Christ became a servant to the circumcision because of the truthfulness of God, so as to confirm the promises made to the patriarchs, and so that the Gentiles might praise God for his mercy." Is salvation for Jews guaranteed by virtue of the promises to the fathers, whereas Gentiles lack any such guarantee and can only appeal to the divine mercy?

In Romans 11 both Jews and Gentiles are objects of the divine mercy, although in different yet symmetrical ways. Having singled out the election of the patriarchs as the guarantee for Israel's hope of salvation, Paul proceeds to ground this in a comprehensive divine mercy that encompasses Gentiles and Jews alike. Continuing to address Gentiles (cf. v. 13), he writes:

> For just as *you* were once disobedient to God but have now received mercy through their disobedience, so *they* are disobedient now (for the sake of your mercy), so that they too may receive mercy. For God confined everyone in disobedience so that he might have mercy on everyone. (11:30-32)

Arguably, it is this conviction of the all-encompassing divine mercy that makes it possible for Paul to reassert the link between the patriarchs and Israel (rather than the Gentiles). God's mercy ensures that the lack of a direct relation to the patriarchs will not prove to be a soteriological disadvantage. Indeed, the patriarchs themselves are the enduring sign of the inexhaustible divine mercy towards Israel. If Gentiles have no equivalent sign to which to appeal, this is not a problem: for Christ embodies both the divine faithfulness to the promises to Israel and the divine mercy to Gentiles, and ultimately God's faithfulness and God's mercy are one and the same.[67]

---

66. So, e.g., Schlier, *Der Römerbrief,* 332, who also identifies the "root" with the "first-fruits."

67. Also to be noted in vv. 30-32 is the fact that "not only the mercy but also the disobedience are seen from the perspective of their source in God" (L. Gaston, *Paul and the Torah,* 144).

It is, then, the theme of the divine mercy that concludes the remarkable account of the scriptural doctrine of election that Paul unfolds in Romans 9–11. At this point, argument gives way to doxology (11:33-36). Once again, it is the earlier scriptural citations that account for the argument of chapter 11. God said to Moses: "I will have mercy on whom I have mercy, and I will have compassion on whom I have compassion" (Rom. 9:15, citing Exod. 33:19). Paul's initial conclusion from this text (in conjunction with Exod. 9:16) was that God "has mercy on whom he wills and hardens whom he wills." By the conclusion of his argument, he has shown that the hardening is temporary (cf. 11:7, 25) and the mercy final and all-encompassing.

We may summarize the distinctiveness of Romans 11 by saying that, whereas elsewhere Paul sets his view of the salvation of the Gentiles *in polemical opposition* to Jewish covenant theology, in Romans 11 he seeks to show that the salvation of the Gentiles may be *incorporated* into a Jewish covenantal framework. The problem is often minimized by those who wish to stress Paul's continuity with Judaism at the expense of discontinuity, but it must be recognized that in Romans 11 Paul ends his extended reflection on Israel's election in a different place from the one he set out from in Romans 9. We may identify *internal* and *external* factors that have occasioned this shift. The external factors concern Paul's relationship with his Roman Christian addressees — a point to which we will shortly return. The factors internal to Paul's argument are to be found primarily in scriptural citations that serve an initial role in chapters 9 and 10 but that take on an additional role in chapter 11. They are not cited a second time, but they continue to shape the argument as it unfolds. The relevant passages have already been noted and are as follows:

(i) They are Israelites, to whom belong the sonship and the glory and the covenants and the lawgiving and the worship and the promises. (Rom. 9:4)

(ii) I will have mercy on whom I have mercy, and compassion on whom I have compassion. (Exod. 33:19 = Rom. 9:15)

(iii) For this purpose I raised you up, so that I might show in you my power and so that my name might be proclaimed in all the earth. (Exod. 9:16 = Rom. 9:17)

(iv) Behold I lay in Zion a stone of stumbling and a rock of offense, and the one who believes in him will not be put to shame. (Isa. 28:16 [+ 8:14] = Rom. 9:33)

(v) I will make you jealous of what is not a nation, with a senseless nation I will provoke you to anger. (Deut. 32:21 = Rom. 10:19)

In (i), Paul's initial reference to his fellow Jews is followed by the claim that "not all who are of Israel are Israel," which appears to cancel out "They are Israelites. . . ." Yet the exclusion proves to be only temporary. Those excised from the olive tree will in due course be grafted back in. The scriptural identification of the Jewish people with "Israel," the people of God, proves too strong for a sectarian redefinition of "Israel" to be able to take root.

In (ii), mercy is identified as a divine prerogative, but so too is hardening: God has mercy on whom he wills, but also hardens whom he wills (9:18). In chapter 11, however, the divine hardening is seen as partial and temporary (11:25; cf. vv. 7-10), the divine mercy as universal and final (11:30-32). The implication of equivalence, with mercy and hardening representing the two possible outcomes of an inscrutable divine predestining intent, has given way to a teleology in which hardening serves the final triumph of the divine mercy.

It is in (iii) that this teleology first comes to light. Pharaoh initially exemplifies the fact that God hardens whom he wills, yet the text cited speaks not of this hardening per se but of its rationale in the universal disclosure of God's power and God's name. This makes it possible for Paul in Romans 11 to find positive soteriological significance in Israel's rejection of the gospel, by way of (iv), in which the specific mechanism of rejection and salvation is identified.

In (v) Paul initially finds confirmation that scripture made Israel aware of God's surprising intention to bestow his favor on Gentiles. The "jealousy" in question arises from the fact of being supplanted and excluded. In chapter 11, on the other hand, the awakening of jealousy is the first step towards re-inclusion and salvation (vv. 11-14).

At each point, Paul's scriptural citation determines not only the initial direction of his meditation on Israel's election but also its unexpected ongoing development. Yet scripture is not read here in a vacuum but in the context of the act of communication between Paul and the Roman Christians that constitutes this letter. It is this "external" conditioning of the scriptural argumentation that must now be brought to light. We recall how, in 9:1-5, Paul's emphatic statements about his grief at Jewish rejection of the gospel seem to anticipate a Jewish Christian concern that Paul's Gentile mission presupposes that God has abandoned his covenant with Israel. An initial scriptural demonstration that God is free to reject Jews and to elect Gentiles (chapters 9–10) is in chapter 11 relocated within a new framework, in which the Pauline concern for the salvation of Gentiles is reconciled with Jewish Christian concern for the salvation of Israel.

In Romans 11:13-32, Paul directly and explicitly addresses the Gentile Christians in Rome. As 14:1–15:13 indicates, the union between Jewish and Gentile Christians there will require a change of heart on both sides: "Let not the one who eats despise the one who abstains, and let not the one who abstains pass judgment on the one who eats" (14:3). In Romans 11:17-24 Paul emphatically opposes the tendency among Gentile Christians to despise the Jewish community, on the grounds (1) that they (the Gentiles) are supported by the Jewish "root" (v. 18); (2) that the removal of certain branches because of unbelief ought to serve as a solemn warning and not as a reason for boasting (vv. 19-22); and (3) that God has the power to graft the excised branches back into the tree (vv. 23-24). The "mystery" of the salvation of Israel is recounted in vv. 25-32 "lest you be wise in your own conceits" (v. 25). Here again, it is the Gentiles who are being addressed (cf. vv. 28-31). The whole chapter may be seen as an attempt to diminish the hostility of the Gentile Christians towards the Jewish Christians, in order to bring the prospect of unity nearer.[68]

This is surely correct as far as it goes, but it is insufficient as an explanation of Romans 11. In Romans as a whole, Paul is more concerned to persuade Jewish Christians to accept the legitimacy of his own standpoint (and thus the legitimacy of the Pauline Gentile congregation in Rome) than to persuade his own followers to accept the legitimacy of the Jewish congregation. Romans 11 must therefore have some message for the Jewish Christians. Ostensibly addressed to Gentiles, it is intended to be overheard by Jews — just as chapter 7 is ostensibly addressed to Jews but is intended to be overheard by Gentiles.

What would Romans 11 mean for the Roman Jewish Christians? Elsewhere in the letter Paul has produced one argument after another to justify their union with the law-free Gentile congregation, together with the further ideological breach with the synagogue that this will entail. The question is whether the new theological position which Paul reaches in Romans 11 corresponds to a different social function. Does Paul perhaps advocate here something other than sectarian separation from the Jewish community? The answer is that, *from the point of view of its social function, Romans 11 is no different from the rest of Romans.* There is no change of mind here on the question of the law, the way of life of the Jewish community. In 11:5-6 Paul explicitly says that the remnant (among whom the Roman Jewish Christians would number themselves) is chosen by grace, and that "works" are irrelevant to this. In other words, continued observance of the law and membership of the Jewish community are inessential to the identity of Jewish Christians, who should rather regard themselves as chosen by grace just as the Gentiles are.[69] Although in vv. 17-24 Paul seems to speak of the Gentile Christians as proselytes who have been incorpo-

---

68. Cf. Cranfield, *Romans*, 2:568 — contra Schlier, *Der Römerbrief,* 333, who rejects the idea that Gentile Christian anti-Judaism is implied here. Opposition to a Gentile anti-Jewish tendency should not be read into Romans 9–11 as a whole, however, let alone into the entire letter.

69. Thus, "works" here should not be paraphrased as "their own meritorious achievement" (against Cranfield, *Romans*, 2:547).

rated into Israel, there is never any suggestion that they should submit themselves to the law as practiced within the Jewish community. The point is that, as Gentile Christians who do not observe the law, they are incorporated into the olive tree of God's people in spite of their alienation from the Jewish community; it is the Jewish community, and not the Gentile Christians, who have temporarily been excised from the olive tree in their unbelief.[70] For all its acknowledgment of the Jewish Christian concern for the final salvation of Israel, Romans 11 makes no concessions at all on the level of social consequences. The non-necessity of law observance in the united Roman Christian community continues to represent a "sectarian" stance vis-à-vis the majority Jewish community, although this has been harmonized to some degree with the continuing engagement with that community represented by the "reform movement." In principle, Roman Gentile and Jewish Christians will be able to meet on the terrain of this chapter, where theology is at one with ecclesial politics.

This completes our discussion of the social context and function of Paul's letter to the Romans. It has not been possible to demonstrate a single consistent and rationally coherent argument. When different passages are set alongside one another and compared, tensions and anomalies abound. Nevertheless, it has been argued that Romans is a highly coherent piece of writing when considered from a pragmatic standpoint. Virtually every part of it contributes in some way or other to Paul's attempt to persuade the Roman Jewish and Gentile Christians to unite with one another, to foster a common Christian identity, and to accept the ideological breach with the synagogue that this will entail. Paul argues for this outcome from a number of points of view, anticipating and answering a range of objections and correcting misunderstandings. The various sections of the argument of Romans 1–11 all contribute in different ways to the same pragmatic goal. The fact that Romans apparently contains so much more theoretical discussion than other Pauline letters should not blind us to its thoroughly practical intention. The "theory" is necessary not because Paul wishes here to expound his gospel in a universally applicable way, without regard for concrete circumstances, but because extensive theological argumentation is necessary in order to demonstrate how and why Roman Jewish and Gentile Christians should set aside their differences and reconstitute themselves as a single integrated community. The future community will be oriented towards one who is "Lord of all," who "bestows his riches on all who call upon him" — Jew and Gentile alike.

70. Gaston's suggestion that Paul has no interest in the broken-off branches is untenable (*Paul and the Torah*, 146-47).

CHAPTER 10

Conclusion

The present work has attempted to account for Paul's view of Judaism, the law, and the Gentiles in a number of relatively novel ways. The argument has inevitably been complex, and a concluding summary is therefore in order.

(1) We have attempted *to uncover the social reality underlying Paul's statements about Judaism, the law, and the Gentiles.* On the basis of various Pauline texts, it proved possible to reconstruct the historical circumstances that led Paul to his conviction that Gentiles could be saved apart from the law. He began his Christian career as a missionary to Jews and encountered Gentiles primarily in the context of Diaspora synagogues in which the non-circumcision of Gentiles was a recognized (if sometimes controversial) possibility. The transition to an ideologically self-conscious Gentile mission was occasioned by missionary experiences in which Paul's gospel met with a more favorable response from Gentiles than from Jews. This led to the formation of largely (not exclusively) Gentile communities, independent of the synagogue, in which the law was not observed.

Thus what had started out as a "reform movement" within the majority Jewish community became a "sect" in response to the opposition it encountered. This sociological process is also exemplified by the Qumran and Johannine communities. The problem for Paul was that other Christians did not accept his solution to the problem of Jewish unbelief, maintaining that the church should continue to exist as a reform movement within the Jewish community and to adhere to its way of life. From a sociological perspective, what was debated between Paul and his fellow Christians in Antioch, Galatia, and Rome was *the social location of the Christian community.* If one assumes that for Paul the law was largely a theoretical problem, unconditioned by concrete social circumstances, one will inevitably misunderstand what he has to say on the subject.

(2) Paul's discussions of such themes as law and works, grace and faith, election and promise are thus to be regarded as *an attempt to legitimate the social reality of sectarian Gentile Christian communities in which the law was not observed.* Paul sought to construct a theoretical rationale for separation. Any sectarian group must carefully define its relationship to the religious community from which it has separated itself, and this self-definition tends to take three forms: denunciation, antithesis, and reinterpretation. Members of the parent religious community are denounced for moral, ritual, or theological faults. Antitheses (e.g., between light and darkness, truth and error) express the absolute nature of the gulf that the sect perceives between itself and the community as a whole. Through reinterpretation, religious traditions are reapplied to the sect itself and denied to the wider community. These features are prominent in the ideologies of the Qumran and Johannine communities; and they are also prominent in Paul, especially in Galatians, Philippians, and Romans. It is therefore vitally important for the interpreter to bear in mind the social function of what Paul is saying.

(3) The application of this principle has important results in actual exegesis. This is the case above all with Romans, for so long regarded as the one letter in which Paul does *not* address himself to concrete circumstances in the church to which he is writing but expounds his gospel in a universally valid way. Exegesis of Romans 14–16 suggested that Paul understood there to be two main Christian groupings in Rome: Jewish Christians who constituted the remnant of the original Roman Christian congregation, and Pauline Gentile or Gentile-oriented Christians. Paul's aim was to persuade the two groupings to recognize and accept one another, with a view to the construction of a shared communal identity expressed in common worship. This interpretation of Romans 14–16 was then applied systematically to the argument of Romans 1–11, and it was found that the hypothesis about the social situation in the Roman church as perceived by Paul consistently shed light on his text.

(4) Attention to the social context and function of Paul's arguments produces an interpretation of Paul in some respects very different from one stemming from the Lutheran tradition. For example, it has been shown that the fundamental antithesis between faith and works is not to be understood as an ab-

stract theological contrast between receiving salvation as a free gift and earning it by one's own efforts, but as an attempt to demarcate two different modes of communal practice. "Faith" sums up the way of life of a Pauline congregation, marked by the abandonment of certain of the norms and beliefs of the surrounding society and the adoption of new norms and beliefs. "Works" sums up the way of life of the Jewish community, which seeks to live in conformity with the law of Moses. The two are incompatible not because one stresses grace and the other achievement, but because the law is not observed in the Pauline congregations and because, as a result, the primary orientation towards Jesus in one community and Moses in the other makes the two communities simply incommensurable. If one compares the abstract relationship between divine grace and human obedience in the two communities, the contrast is not as absolute as is often supposed. Paul frequently indicates that, in Judaism as he understands it, "works of law" are practiced within a covenantal context. His own soteriology involves a more dynamic view of grace, since the pattern of religion he advocates is conversionist rather than traditional; yet it is clear that, for Paul too, the responsive human obedience evoked by divine grace is a necessary precondition of salvation. The Reformational assumption that Pauline theology is summed up in the phrase *sola gratia* should be treated with considerable caution.

(5) Yet it is important at this point not to set up a new antithesis of our own, between "Lutheran" and "New Perspective" readings of Paul. The "Lutheran" insistence on the centrality and radicality of divine grace is not wholly in error. In spite of the emphasis here on the concrete nature of Pauline antithesis, we have seen that Paul is *also* capable of a degree of abstraction — when, for example, "boasting" of status is seen as possible within one communal context but not the other (Rom. 3:27). Conversely, if one seeks to understand Pauline antithesis as concerned purely with the *scope* of salvation (that is, with the exclusion or inclusion of Gentiles), and not at all with the contrasting roles assigned to the *divine agent* of salvation, this will result in a one-sidedness no more persuasive than the one it criticizes. Repeated often enough, the claim that "Judaism is a religion of grace" will prove to be at least as misleading as the older language of "legalism" or "works righteousness." While there should be no reversion to the Lutheran Paul of the "old" perspective, one does not read Paul aright merely by criticizing Luther and emphasizing Gentile inclusion.

What are the theological implications of this construal of Paul's texts? Does preoccupation with their socio-historical context undermine their canonical role as a resource for theological construction? Twenty years ago, at the conclusion of the first edition of this book, I argued that theological value could not be taken for granted. One would have to *work* to demonstrate it, rather than simply assuming it. The point was not that historical and theological perspectives were necessarily at odds with one another. While the book had used a "sociological approach" to criticize a specific theological appropriation of Paul, stemming from Martin Luther and impressively restated in twentieth-century idiom by Rudolf Bultmann, that did not amount to a criticism of theological appropriation of Paul as such. At no stage was it intended or expected that the "sociological approach" developed in this book would simply *supplant* theology. As practiced here, the sociological approach is simply ecclesiology in mildly secularized form. In the book's penultimate paragraph, I wrote:

> This negative estimate of the Reformation tradition's view of Paul is not intended to imply that, as a general principle, theological concerns are incompatible with the historical study of the New Testament. In practice, it can often be demonstrated that theological concerns *have* led to misunderstanding of the New Testament; but that is not a sufficient reason for a reductionist denial of the legitimacy of all such concerns in New Testament study, since in other cases it is at least arguable that they have led to levels of insight denied to more historically-minded scholarship. The demand for a complete separation between New Testament studies and theology is both narrow-minded and question-begging.[1]

There is no trace of an "anti-theological agenda" here. Yet, even if historical and theological perspectives were compatible in principle, I did not know how to bring them together in practice. The book concluded with a question, deliberately formulated in as sharp a form as possible. I wrote:

> [I]f the interpretation of Paul offered here is accepted, it is important to face the question: Can a Paul who devotes his energies to the creation and maintaining of sectarian groups hostile to all non-members, and especially to the Jewish community from which in fact they derived, still be seen as the bearer of a message with profound universal significance? Facing this question will mean that the permanent, normative value of Paul's theology will not simply be *assumed,* as is often the case at present. It must instead be *discussed* — and with genuine arguments, not with mere rhetorical appeals to the authority of the canon, the Reformers, or an *a priori* Christology. Should Paul's thought still be a major source of inspiration for contempo-

1. *PJG¹*, 180.

347

rary theological discussion? Or should it be rejected as a cul-de-sac, and should one seek inspiration elsewhere?[2]

These questions about future theological directions now seem to me to be poorly formulated. They take it for granted that "sectarian" identity is to be assessed negatively, overlooking the distinctive communal identity — grounded in a faith, hope, and love oriented towards Jesus Christ — that "sectarian" separation makes possible. They do not differentiate appropriate appeals to the canon or christology from the inappropriate ones that are dismissed with a mere gesture. They imply too rigid and legalistic a contrast between ascribing "permanent, normative value" to Paul's letters, on the one hand, and rejecting them "as a cul-de-sac," on the other.

Yet, poorly formulated or not, for me these were open and urgent questions. In my years as a graduate student, I had been deeply affected by Bultmann's theology, which I had found both disturbing and exhilarating. The dawning realization that it was subject to serious weaknesses was also a moment of disillusionment. As a result, the first edition of this book had something of the character of a ground-clearing exercise. It led directly to an engagement with hermeneutics, in the hope that this would offer a way back into theology; as indeed it did.

In principle, the book might have led to further studies in the relation between early Christian texts and their social contexts. No such ventures were even contemplated, however. It was the open questions about theology and theological hermeneutics that preoccupied me after the book had been completed. Initially, this preoccupation expressed itself in repeated attempts to come to terms no longer with Bultmann but with Luther himself. Was there perhaps a hermeneutical issue at stake here, and not just an exegetical one? In an unpublished paper dating from 1989, three years after the book's publication, I argued

> that Luther's reflections are at their best the product of an *extension* of the [Pauline] text, and therefore inseparable from it, and that they are not the result of an *imposition* upon the text of wholly alien thoughts. Where extension occurs, both text and interpreter are active in generating the new reading; where imposition occurs, the text is suppressed, overpowered by an interpreter who is simply using it as a vehicle for his or her own autonomous thoughts. Within the historical-critical tradition, however, the goal of exegesis is understood as *repetition,* in which the interpreter is in principle wholly subservient to the historical author and aspires never to stray

2. *PJG[1]*, 180-81.

beyond the immediate, historical limits of the texts. The only alternative to this apparent self-abnegation is supposed to be "imposition," suppressing a text's autonomy and denying its integrity by foisting upon it our own concerns and prejudices. Thus Luther is said to "impose" his own perception of late medieval Roman Catholicism upon Paul's texts, an act of interpretative violence whose effects we must now strive to undo. But repetition and imposition are not the only alternatives, and the possibility remains that, at least at certain points, Paul's text plays an active part in generating a reading which nevertheless does not remain confined within the original limits but establishes new horizons of its own. Where repetition is the interpretative goal, the text is understood as *closed,* focused upon itself in all its narrow particularity. Where the possibility of the extension of the text by the interpreter is taken seriously, the text is conceived as *open* to subsequent reflection and appropriation.

What is evident here is the attempt to answer the fundamental hermeneutical question that my own book put to me. Historically oriented interpretation (including and especially my own) had proved incapable of generating theologically interesting readings of the biblical texts: hence the turn to hermeneutics, in order to see what other kinds of interpretation might be available to us. Historical interpretation has its own integrity, but it cannot straightforwardly be used to undermine pre-modern readings such as Luther's or Augustine's, since these operate within different and incommensurable hermeneutical frameworks. In my book I had argued that "the Reformation tradition's approach to Paul is fundamentally wrong."[3] This blunt claim was justified insofar as its real target was a twentieth-century exegetical tradition in which key themes of Lutheran theology were surreptitiously imported into an interpretative paradigm oriented towards the first century rather than the sixteenth. But Luther's own theological interpretation of scripture could not so easily be dismissed.

I would now be less pessimistic about the theological potential of historically oriented readings of Paul. In reality, there is no singular, monolithic "historical approach," doomed to theological irrelevance. There are many ways of practicing history, just as there are many ways of practicing theology, and many ways of practicing each in the light of the other. The outstanding contributions to post-Sanders Pauline scholarship are outstanding precisely because they open up new ways for historical and theological concerns to engage with one another. (I refer, for example, to Richard Hays's *Echoes of Scrip-*

---

3. *PJG¹*, 1.

ture [1989], Daniel Boyarin's *A Radical Jew* [1994], and the Galatians commentary of J. Louis Martyn [1997] — all of them indebted to Sanders.) Even untheological exegesis can provide resources for constructive theological use. Indeed, if it is well executed and genuinely illuminates the sense of the text, biblical exegesis *cannot* lack theological potential.

In presenting *Paul, Judaism, and the Gentiles* in its new guise, I have not attempted to convert it retrospectively into an exercise in theological exegesis.[4] In spite of sometimes drastic rewriting, it is still what it was: an argument about "the Paul of history" rather than "the apostle of faith." That is its limitation, but also perhaps its strength. Of all the canonical scriptures of both Testaments, it is the Pauline letters that most explicitly demand that their own historicity be taken into account. Here, uniquely perhaps, history and theology are interconnected. If the argument about the historical Paul is broadly correct, it will not be lacking in theological potential.

4. But see the 1993 study reprinted as an Appendix to this volume.

APPENDIX

Christ, Law, and Freedom:
A Plea for the Sensus Literalis

It is a fundamental thesis of Pauline theology that Christ has freed us from the law; and it is a fundamental assumption of Pauline interpreters that something of great theological significance is being said here, and that the task of exegesis is to penetrate the surface of the texts in order to discover, concealed in the depths, the reality that here comes to expression. On the surface, however, what is said is simply that the Jewish law is not binding upon Christians. (There is, of course, an overlap between Jewish and early Christian ethical teaching, but Paul rarely appeals to the law to support an ethical imperative.) Thus, Paul admonishes the Galatians: "For freedom Christ has set us free; stand fast, therefore, and do not submit again to a yoke of slavery" (Gal. 5:1). What does he mean? Simply that his readers are not to submit themselves to circumcision or to the other ordinances of the law that follow from it (Gal. 5:2-3; 4:21): for the Galatians have been freed from the enslaving yoke of the law. We might describe this as the "literal" interpretation of the Pauline thesis that Christ has freed us from the law.

But why does Paul assume that Christ and law are mutually exclusive? This question cannot adequately be answered by referring to texts in which the law is presented in a negative light, as the bringer of "condemnation" (2 Cor. 3:9) or a "curse" (Gal. 3:10), for this would merely raise the further question why

---

This paper was presented at a conference at King's College London in 1993 and published in a volume entitled *God and Freedom,* edited by Colin Gunton. I have changed the original title, but otherwise alterations have been kept to a minimum. The paper attempts to answer the theological question posed at the end of *PJG¹*, drawing on Frei, Lindbeck, Gadamer, and my own work on the concept of the Christian "Old Testament."

Paul chooses to define the law in these negative terms. One possible way to proceed is to remove the limitations imposed by the concretion of the terms "Christ" and "law." As a concrete particular, "Christ" refers to the life, death, and resurrection of Jesus, who, as the Christ, remains the focal point of a new communal life; and "law" refers to a series of texts regarded as normative for the practice and beliefs of another, older form of communal life. In order to explain why this "Christ" and this "law" exclude one another, it is thought necessary to ask what broader realities underlie the two particularities and are represented by them. "Law" may be held to represent the broader category of a "legal" religion in which everyday conduct is subjected to a mass of rules and prohibitions. "Christ" will then represent the antithesis of this: a religion in which one is freed from legal burdens in order to enter into a personal relationship with God.[1] Or, another way of putting it, "law" may be said to represent an autonomous human striving to obtain God's favor on the basis of what one is and achieves, in which case "Christ" will represent the divine acceptance bestowed upon us irrespective of personal qualities and achievements.[2] This might be described as the "symbolic" interpretation of the thesis that Christ has freed us from the law, for its interest lies not in the particularity of the entities designated "Christ" and "law" but in their power to symbolize universal, symmetrically opposed truth claims about the divine-human relation.

Recent exegesis has made out a strong case for the literal as opposed to the symbolic (or allegorical) interpretation of Paul's claim that Christ has freed us from the law. It is probably true that at some points Paul's texts suggest more universal concerns, in which case the symbolic interpretation has a genuine exegetical basis to which to appeal. But the literal interpretation does not have to claim that Paul *never* sees beyond the opposition of two particularities, only that his language is in the first instance highly concrete. The following exegetical conclusions would now be widely accepted:

1. On this view, to be justified by faith is to "enter the world of a gracious God, out of which the old hard legal requirements, with the old hard boundaries of our personality and the old self-regarding claim of rights, have disappeared, a world which is the household of our Father where order and power and ultimate reality are of love and not of law" (John Oman, *Grace and Personality*, 213).

2. R. Bultmann writes: "A specifically human striving has merely taken on its culturally and, in point of time, individually distinct form in Judaism. For it is, in fact, a striving common to all men, to gain recognition of one's achievement; and this generates pride" ("Christ the End of the Law," 45). Christ, as the end of the law, is "the end of a life which, sustained by the need for recognition (implying secret dread and hatred of God), seeks to establish its own righteousness; . . . he is the means of access to the way of salvation through grace for the true believer, that is, for the man who gives up his own righteousness and surrenders himself completely to the God who leads man from death into life" (54).

(1) In developing his doctrine of freedom from the law, Paul does not engage in a systematic, general theorizing about the divine-human relationship. His theorizing reflects the concrete historical setting of his mission to the Gentiles.[3]

(2) As Apostle to the Gentiles, Paul established largely Gentile Christian communities in which the Jewish law — most notably the commandments regarding circumcision, the food laws, and the sabbath — was not observed. His denial of the normative status of the law as the code of conduct for the Christian community asserts the distinctiveness of his congregations over against the wider Jewish community. Among other things, the doctrine of justification by faith of Christ and not by works of the law entails a contrast between two different modes of communal life.

(3) For the Jew, observance of the law is a response to the disclosure of the will of God at Sinai. This disclosure does not take the form of sheer demand but is the culmination of an unfolding salvation history that includes the election of the patriarchs and the deliverance from Egypt. The obligation to observe the law is grounded in the election of Israel.[4]

(4) Paul opposes the circumcision of his Gentile converts because circumcision is the rite of entry into the Jewish people, and not because it is an example of a "good work" that helps to establish merit.[5] Thus in Galatians the issue between Paul and his opponents is not whether and how far one must perform good works in order to be saved, but whether access to the saving work of the Jewish Messiah is or is not to be found through membership of the Jewish community and practice of its way of life.

(5) If the opposition of "faith" to "works" relates in the first instance to the distinction between the Christian and the Jewish communities, then this opposition is compatible with passages that assert that a reorientation of

3. The fact that Paul's thinking derives from his experience as a missionary does not mean that he cannot be regarded as a theologian (the view of H. Räisänen, *Paul and the Law,* 267). As N. T. Wright comments: "Paul's qualification to be called a 'theologian' is not . . . that he wrote 'systematic theology'. Obviously he did not. His qualification lies in the way he went about obeying his vocation. His sense of purpose, call and mission demand to be understood in terms of a worldview which can only be called 'theological'" (*The Climax of the Covenant,* 262).

4. Sanders's criticism of the pejorative view of Judaism as a religion of legalistic works-righteousness is well known (see his *Paul and Palestinian Judaism,* esp. 33-59). Sanders argues that the expression "covenantal nomism" does more justice to the character of Palestinian Judaism (419-28), and he can cite Paul as a witness to this (*Paul, the Law and the Jewish People,* 46).

5. This point is made, in opposition to Bultmann, in *PJG¹,* 69. One corollary is that, "if it was no longer circumcision but baptism which was the primary rite of initiation, then women became full members of the people of God with the same rights and duties" (E. Schüssler Fiorenza, *In Memory of Her,* 210).

conduct in response to the gospel is indispensable for salvation.[6] This re-orientation can occur only within an ecclesial context.

It is assumed on both sides of the exegetical debate that an emphasis on particularities is characteristic of a primarily historical orientation, whereas a theological orientation will wish to emphasize the broader significance of those particularities. Either the text is studied as a historical document deriving from a context quite different from our own; or its contemporary theological relevance is asserted on the basis of its broader implications. The question whether non-Jewish Christians should submit to the Jewish law was once of vital concern, but it is so no longer — unless it can be shown that something more fundamental is at stake here than what appears on the surface. Yet the assumption that particularities are as such theologically uninteresting is obviously problematic. The assumption might be justified if we knew in advance that Christian faith is concerned with the necessary truths of reason rather than the contingent truths of history. A rationalist hermeneutic along these lines would dissolve all contingencies into generalities in its attempt to establish a "religion within the limits of reason alone." But Christian faith has preferred to believe that certain contingencies are supremely important. While it is obviously not the case that every particularity referred to in the New Testament is theologically significant, it is worth asking whether the Pauline thesis that Christ frees us from the law might be theologically significant precisely *in* its particularity, and not in spite of it.[7]

1. The Prejudice against Particularity

The tension between symbolic and literal interpretations of Paul's doctrine of freedom from the law is not a purely modern one, but stems from the unprecedented importance Luther assigned to this doctrine by installing it at the center of his reordering of Christian faith. It will be instructive to trace in Luther's position the antecedents of the modern hermeneutical assumptions I have outlined.

What does Paul mean when he asserts that Christ has set us free (Gal. 5:1)? In his Galatians commentary of 1535, Luther argues that "Christ has set

6. Cf. Sanders, *Paul, the Law and the Jewish People*, 105-6.

7. The hermeneutical and theological significance of the literal sense in its irreducible particularity is emphasized especially by Hans Frei (see his *Eclipse of Biblical Narrative* and *The Identity of Jesus Christ*). On Frei, see my *Text, Church and World: Biblical Interpretation in Theological Perspective,* chapter l.

us free, not for a political freedom or a freedom of the flesh but for a theological or spiritual freedom, that is, to make our conscience free and joyful, unafraid of the wrath to come."[8] Yet in this text Paul speaks not of freedom in general but of freedom from the yoke of slavery, and in the following verse he appears to identify that yoke not with fear of the wrath of God but with circumcision: "Now I, Paul, say to you that if you receive circumcision Christ will be of no advantage to you." According to Luther, the explanation is that

> Paul is not discussing the actual deed in itself, which has nothing wrong in it if there is no trust in it or presumption of righteousness. Rather, he is discussing how the deed is used, that is, the trust and the righteousness that are attached to the deed.[9]

Thus, Paul's reference to circumcision is stripped of its particularity — any other pious deed might have been referred to — and interpreted as representing the general disposition that typically comes to expression through such pious deeds: the disposition to trust that one's own actions are the way to acquire righteousness before God. To trust in one's own righteousness is to expose oneself to the wrath of God, and it is only in being freed from the law and the self-righteousness that it generates that the conscience becomes joyful and fearless. For Luther, it is essential that circumcision should be able to represent not only "ceremonial" but also "moral" works. Although

> it is easier to recognize a false reliance on righteousness in ceremonial works than it is in the moral works of the Decalogue, [yet] righteousness must not be sought through these works either, but through faith in Christ. I mention this lest someone get the impression from what I am saying that the apostle is opposing only the ceremonial features of the law.[10]

Thus, the thesis that Christ frees us from the law means that Christ frees us from the attempt to attain righteousness before God by performing the actions that the law requires, whether ceremonial or moral. Luther must presuppose the capacity of circumcision to symbolize moral as well as (Christian) ceremonial deeds oriented towards righteousness, if the promise of freedom from the law is to remain existentially relevant for his hearers and readers. If it represented only the ceremonial deeds distinctive to Judaism, it would have a merely historical interest for them. Justification by faith in Christ and not by works of the law would then mean simply that it is we

8. *LW,* 27:4.
9. *LW,* 27:10.
10. *LW,* 27:327.

355

Christians who are righteous before God, rather than non-Christian Jews: a point that it may have been necessary to emphasize in the early days of the church, but which is of no particular concern to Luther's contemporaries. If the Pauline gospel is to have any force, it must apply directly to us, announcing our freedom from the false disposition underlying our own ethical and ecclesial practices.

Luther is well aware that exegetes have traditionally confined Paul's polemic against works of the law to distinctively Jewish "ceremonies"; and, in his view, it is impossible to exaggerate the significance of this fundamental exegetical error, for which Jerome is largely to blame. Opposition to Jerome on this point is already signaled in the 1519 commentary on Galatians. With reference to Galatians 3 — "Did you receive the Spirit by works of the law, or by hearing with faith?" — Luther writes:

> I surely do not believe it when in this passage St Jerome distinguishes the works of the law from good works and thinks that Cornelius received the Spirit on the basis of works; for it is clear that the Holy Spirit descended on them at Peter's preaching, that is, when they heard with faith, as he says here. . . . The apostle is referring not only to the ceremonial law but to absolutely every law; for since it is faith alone that justifies and does good works, it follows that absolutely no works of any law justify, and that the works of no law are good, but that only the works of faith are good.[11]

Jerome had cited the example of Cornelius (cf. Acts 10:2, 35) to prove that the faith with which the Spirit is received is not without "good works," the pattern of behavior approved by God; thus the "works of the law" that are contrasted with "faith" must refer only to Jewish ceremonies. Luther rejects this restriction, and his whole doctrine of justification hangs on this point.

In *De Servo Arbitrio* (1525), the opposition to Jerome is still more implacable. The claim that "works of the law" refers only to Jewish ceremonies incompatible with Christian faith is, Luther tells us,

> the ignorant error of Jerome, which, in spite of Augustine's strenuous resistance . . . has spread out into the world and has persisted to the present day. It has consequently become impossible to understand Paul, and the knowledge of Christ has been inevitably obscured. Even if there had never been any other error in the church, this one alone was pestilent and potent enough to make havoc of the gospel.[12]

11. *LW*, 27:247, 248.
12. *LW*, 33:258.

Jerome's narrowing of the scope of "works" prevailed over Augustine's comprehensive view, and this is the fundamental apostasy of church history. Jerome's original sin, like Adam's, is inspired by Satan and infects generation after generation of his theological descendants. A mistake over this single word has made the true Pauline gospel unintelligible for centuries. As Christ comes to reverse the effects of Adam's fall, so Luther comes to reverse the effects of Jerome's misreading — and church history re-enacts the history of the world's salvation.

The "misreading" of Galatians or Romans will depict the apostle as engaging in controversy with Judaism or Jewish Christianity. He is convinced — rightly, as later Christian orthodoxy believes — that Christ has abolished the ceremonies of the Jewish law. The opposition between "faith of Christ" and "works of law" is therefore an appeal to Jews and Jewish Christians not to insist on the continuing necessity of those ceremonies, and to Gentile Christians to resist those who seek to impose ceremonies on them. Christ is the divinely appointed way to salvation, not Judaism. Thus Jerome represents an embryonic "literal-historical" reading of Paul, sensitive to the particularities to which the apostle addresses himself. Luther's assumption is that this concern with first-century particularities conceals the crucially important theological claims of the texts. Jerome's view is still concerned with theological truth: the truth that Jesus Christ does not require us to submit to the Jewish law. But for Luther it is only insofar as the conscience hears itself addressed by the judging and comforting word of God that one can speak of theological truth. A truth that exists outside the conscience in the world of objective history is at best a piece of scaffolding, radically subordinate to the encounter in which I hear myself addressed by the word of God. If this word is to be based in holy scripture, then the scriptural word must relate to our ultimate concern and not merely to past contingencies.

Operating here, it seems, is a *prejudice against historical particularity.* It is assumed that the historically particular is in itself theologically irrelevant, only becoming theologically relevant insofar as it symbolizes the general and ultimate concern of the conscience here and now.[13] True theological signifi-

---

13. Compare the hermeneutic of Immanuel Kant, in which the prejudice against particularity takes a still more extreme form. According to Kant, "[i]t is possible to explain how an historical account is to be put to a moral use without deciding whether this is the intention of the author or merely our interpretation, provided this meaning is true in itself, apart from all historical proof, and is moreover the only way in which we can derive something conducive to our betterment from a passage which otherwise would be only an unfruitful addition to our historical knowledge" (*Religion within the Limits of Reason Alone* [1793], 39n). On this, see H. Frei, *The Eclipse of Biblical Narrative*, 262-64.

cance is not to be found within the literal-historical sense of a text, but only beyond it. Whatever space is conceded to the literal-historical sense, the orientation will always be away from the merely particular towards the universal and ultimate concern of the conscience. In an article entitled "Reflections on the Doctrine of the Law" (1958), Gerhard Ebeling notes that in Luther "the concepts law and gospel are largely stripped of the concrete historical references they bear in Paul and are turned into fundamental theological concepts, so that they find a more universal application than in Paul."[14] We must proceed more cautiously, for "certain essential elements in the Pauline concept of *nomos* appear to oppose the extension of the concept of law which takes place in the theology of the Reformers."[15] Despite this concession, however, Ebeling argues that the way from particular to universal can claim some support from the Pauline texts. For example, Romans and 1 Corinthians suggest a concern with the problem of the law even among Gentile readers:

> Paul obviously did not merely expect the Gentiles to be interested in the problem of the Jewish law, but apparently also believed that they would discover in these discussions of it something which directly concerned themselves.[16]

On the one hand, Paul's texts refer to historical particularities; on the other hand, they imply that those particularities represent realities theologically relevant to those who are not concerned about the church's relation to Judaism. Theological relevance occurs not *in* historical particularity but *in spite of* it.

These exegetical claims serve to justify an existentialist interpretation of the Pauline language. A characteristic example is to be found in a later work dating from 1981, where Ebeling interprets Paul's faith/works antithesis as follows:

> What matters is what I live by, what I rely upon, what I take as the ground of my existence, what I understand to be my purpose with respect to God: is it faith, and therefore God himself in his grace, or is it my own demonstrable reality, and therefore I myself in what I achieve and represent?[17]

"Works" here represents not the practice of the Torah but a life based on my own status and achievements in the sphere of everyday reality; a non-literal, allegorical interpretation very similar to Luther's, despite the difference of id-

---

14. Ebeling, "Reflections on the Doctrine of the Law," 261.
15. Ebeling, "Reflections on the Doctrine of the Law," 275.
16. Ebeling, "Reflections on the Doctrine of the Law," 274.
17. Ebeling, *The Truth of the Gospel*, 176-77.

iom, and equally opposed to any attempt to find theological significance in the obvious primary reference to the practice of Judaism. Christ frees us from the law, but the reference to the concrete practice of Judaism has been supplanted by a reflection on a general human orientation from which we are freed by the word of the gospel.

Who is the "I" addressed by the divine word in the gospel? On Ebeling's view, the "I" is the person disposed to live on the basis of a demonstrable, empirical, social reality in which he or she occupies a certain position and fulfills certain roles. The word of the gospel exposes the questionableness of this attempt at an autonomous existence, disclosing that the only true ground of our existence is God himself. In this account, the gospel radically individualizes the socialized self, momentarily isolating it from the complex networks of fallen relationships in which it is entangled and confronting it with the foundational reality of an I-Thou relationship with the Creator. It is held that the biblical texts are to be interpreted in such a way that their witness to this fundamental encounter is made clear, in conformity with their appointed role as the vehicle of this encounter. Interpretation cannot itself bring about this event, but it can try to ensure that understanding conforms to faith.

All this may perhaps be open to criticism on theological grounds. As interpretation of Pauline language, however, Ebeling's comments should not be too quickly rejected. Unlike Luther, Ebeling is aware that the move from the particular to the universal will involve some loss of focus. An "existentialist" interpretation will not try to maintain the close adherence to the letter of the text that is appropriate to a more "literal" interpretation, for their purposes are different: on the one hand, to draw out theological implications that transcend particularity; on the other hand, to render the individual text with the greatest possible clarity and precision. At a certain level of abstraction, it is true that, in antithesis to "faith," the term "works" can stand for "my own demonstrable reality," "I myself in what I achieve and represent." Even at the literal level, "faith" for Paul is indeed a response called forth by God's grace in Christ, and it is therefore bound far more closely to prevenient divine action than are the (Jewish) "works," which allow correspondingly greater scope for semi-autonomous human agency. The theological claim that we are justified by God's grace and not by our own actions remains firmly grounded in the Pauline texts. Even the literal sense of the text may sometimes hint at implications transcending the particular issue under discussion, and it would be wrong to forbid attempts to follow up those implications. A hermeneutic that rejected every kind of distinction between what is said and what is meant would soon prove rigid and oppressive.

On the other hand, where an interpretative tradition has long concealed or overlooked particularity in its concern for the universal, an emphasis on particularity may be necessary in order to redress the balance. An interpretation oriented towards the universal inevitably reorders and unbalances the complex of interrelated particulars that constitutes the surface of the text, assigning theological potential to some while relegating others to the margins. Literal-historical interpretation can be of theological value in restoring the original interrelatedness and thereby enabling quite different kinds of theological exploration. On the basis of recent literal-historical interpretation, I shall argue that the Pauline theme of freedom from the law has to do with the laying down of permanent foundations for subsequent Christian communal identity.

2. The Elements of Christian Grammar

Recent exegesis of Galatians and Romans has achieved a certain clarity of focus in emphasizing the extent to which Paul's thinking is dominated by the ecclesial question of the relationship between Jews and Gentiles. However, it has largely failed to develop its insights in a theological direction, with the result that an interpretation along the lines laid down by Luther may still seem compelling if it is theological engagement rather than historical clarification that one is seeking.[18] The question is whether a literal-historical reading is capable of serving as the basis for a theological interpretation of these texts.

Why is it often assumed that the modern literal-historical interpretation of the Pauline theme of freedom from the law is of little direct theological value? The effect of this interpretation, it is said, is to show the extent to which Paul's theological horizons are dominated by a first-century issue that is irrelevant to "our own concerns."[19] A biblical text will be "relevant" when it says something that can be placed at the disposal of one or other of these concerns of ours. According to this hermeneutic, many texts fail to meet our criterion of relevance, and integrity demands that they be left outside the informal canon within the canon established by the way we construe our own

18. Thus John Ziesler argues that the "new perspective" is exegetically justified but that Luther's interpretation is still appropriate theologically, if it is regarded as exposition rather than exegesis ("Justification by Faith in the Light of the 'New Perspective' on Paul," 188-94).

19. The notion of "relevance to our own concerns," as discussed here, implies the possibility of a *positive* theological evaluation of a text. It is of course possible for a text to be highly "relevant" for *negative* reasons: thus E. Schüssler Fiorenza advocates a mode of biblical interpretation that seeks "to critically comprehend how the Bible functions in the oppression of women or the poor and thus to prevent its misuse for further oppression" (*Bread Not Stone: The Challenge of Feminist Biblical Interpretation*, 57).

concerns. The rejected alternative against which this approach defines itself is the claim that every part of the Bible is relevant to us, that its concerns must dictate and determine our own, and that what it says is to be directly identified with what God says. If one rejects a biblicism of this kind, one is bound to accept that the theological significance of some parts of the Bible may not be readily apparent. Yet it would be strange if this applied to texts at the heart of the Pauline corpus, considering their immense and varied impact on the subsequent history of Christian theology. No doubt classic texts can and do "die," losing their ability to speak to the present and thus their classic status. But the rumor of the death of these particular classics may be premature.

On the literal-historical reading, it is said, the texts are irrelevant to our own concerns; we become aware of a gulf separating our own world from their first-century world. These hermeneutical claims originate in a purely synchronic criterion of relevance that construes "our own time" as an autonomous, self-contained sphere out of which certain "concerns" arise, bearing with them a normative claim to exclusive attention.[20] It is not simply that we *choose* to adopt one contemporary concern or another; for these concerns are normative, imposing themselves upon us and demanding the right to reorder our interpretative priorities. It is implied that to refuse such a reordering is to be morally culpable as well as intellectually deficient.

Is there an alternative construal of "our own concerns" to this impoverished and dictatorial model? To be concerned about the theological significance of biblical texts is to locate oneself within a communal context that predisposes one to believe that the texts do actually possess such a significance — to a greater or lesser extent, in some way or other. This expectation of theological significance does not have to look for a fortuitous hermeneutical miracle in which the empty letter of the text is suddenly transformed into living address through the spontaneous activity of the Spirit. The expectation of theological significance in present and future derives from the fact that Christian communal identity has already been shaped and reshaped by precisely these texts, and from the conviction that no breach in tradition has occurred that is sufficiently serious to prevent their continuing to fulfill this role in the future.[21] We

20. For an example of this, see Sallie McFague, *Models of God: Theology for an Ecological, Nuclear Age*, 3-6.

21. This emphasis on an expectation grounded in tradition is broadly compatible with the "functionalist" understanding of scripture advocated by David Kelsey, who argues that "to call a set of texts 'scripture' is to say that it ought to be used in certain ways in the church's common life so as to nurture and preserve her communal self-identity" (*The Uses of Scripture in Modern Theology*, 147). But to call a set of texts "scripture" is to see them as somehow *foundational* to communal identity, and not just in terms of a prescribed "use."

do not possess the texts in the form of bare words on a page, but only as transmitted through the medium of an ongoing tradition, a *Wirkungsgeschichte* in which we too participate and which counterbalances our synchronic relation to our own limited time and place with a diachronic relation to a historic community of faith. If that is the case, then the criterion of relevance to our own concerns will have to be extended: for "our own concerns" include not only the normative demands of our own time and place but also the concerns integral to the diachronic life of the Christian community, which are our concerns, too, insofar as we participate in that life.

These concerns integral to the Christian community are, in large part, to do with communal identity. What is the Christian church, and what is it for? By what criteria are claims to be the Christian church assessed? How is the need for identity to adapt to changing circumstances compatible with the need for identity to be preserved if it is not simply to be lost and replaced with a new identity? Is there a relative stability of communal identity to which we must conform? Or is communal identity what each succeeding generation declares it to be, so that any attempt to assess the church's faithfulness to its own fundamental identity is ruled out? Questions such as these arise out of the entire range of activities in which the Christian church is engaged, from its preaching and sacramental life to the manner of its sociopolitical involvements. Among other things, they inquire about the language that is to be employed in the maintenance and development of communal identity and self-definition.[22]

In the Pauline texts, too, we find a preoccupation with the maintenance and development of communal identity. Recent literal-historical reading has served to highlight the irreducibly communal and ecclesial nature of these texts' fundamental concerns. But such texts do not merely offer interesting analogies or historical precedents to contemporary struggles over ecclesial self-definition. These are canonical texts that have already proved their effectiveness in determining some, if not all, of the directions in which communal identity subsequently developed. In accepting certain of the positions argued in the Pauline texts, the Christian community definitively excluded some possibilities of self-definition and gave normative status to others. Decisions taken by Paul and the early church remain foundational to the identity of the Christian community, and *insofar as this is the case Paul's texts cannot be regarded as irrelevant*. There is no yawning historical gulf separating these texts from our

---

22. Communal identity is not produced and maintained only by way of narratives, and it is therefore misleading to speak of "the narrative identity of the Christian community" (G. W. Stroup, *The Promise of Narrative Theology*, 170).

own present; for the apparent gulf is filled with the tradition that these texts helped to generate, within which they have continued to fulfill certain essential roles in the maintenance and development of Christian identity.[23]

It is not necessary to ascribe to an individual canonical text a distinctive role in the establishing of Christian communal identity. In general, it will not be possible to distinguish elements of communal identity that derive from one text rather than another. What is important is that all canonical texts participate in one way or another in the process of identity formation. With this proviso in mind, the significance of this analysis for theological interpretation can be further explored by taking Paul's letter to the Galatians as a test case.

In Galatians 5:1 it is said: "For freedom Christ has set us free; stand fast therefore, and do not submit again to a yoke of slavery." The context is not a debate with another religion (i.e., Judaism) but an inner-Christian debate about Christian identity; the question at issue is whether we have to be or become Jews in order to be Christians. Paul answers this question with an emphatic negative: for a Gentile Christian to adopt the Jewish way of life as defined in the Torah would be to submit to "a yoke of slavery." It is not that this can be shown to be the case by empirical demonstration — by appealing, for example, to the burdens that the law might be thought to impose upon the conscience. This negative assessment of the law appeals instead to a complex allegory in which the slave girl Hagar represents the law (4:21-31), and to an identification of the law (or the angelic authors of the law) with the enslaving elemental spirits of the universe (4:1-10).

As arguments, subsequent tradition has not judged these claims to be especially compelling. The assessment of the law seems too negative and does not give enough emphasis to the fact that the traditions relating to Mount Sinai bear witness to an authentic moment of divine disclosure. As regards allegory, the usefulness of this interpretative device for establishing doctrinal conclusions has often been questioned. And yet the fundamental thesis, that Christ has set us free from the yoke of the law, has nevertheless been accepted. The limitations of the supporting arguments challenge Christian theology to find better arguments (including arguments that try to do justice to the greatness of Judaism), but the conclusion itself is rapidly established in most areas as a fundamental component of subsequent Christian identity. In general,

---

23. "The important thing is to recognise the distance in time as a positive and productive possibility of understanding. It is not a yawning abyss, but is filled with the continuity of custom and tradition, in the light of which all that is handed down presents itself to us" (H.-G. Gadamer, *Truth and Method*, 264-65).

Christians do not submit to circumcision, dietary laws, sabbaths, or scriptural feasts, despite the fact that these observances are enjoined in texts that they, too, hold to be authoritative. It proves to be a complex balancing act to maintain the God-given authority of Jewish scripture while denying the normative character of many of its most characteristic ordinances. Yet, whatever the difficulties, it was soon clear to Christian thinkers that this particular balancing act was necessary, as it came to be established as a basic grammatical rule for Christian discourse that Christ has freed us from the yoke of the law.[24]

As this rule establishes itself, Paul's opponents' account of Christian identity is rejected. According to the rejected account, Jesus is the Messiah sent to fulfill the divine promises made through the prophets, and the question is, Who are the people for whom Jesus accomplishes his saving work? Clearly they are people who believe in him; those who disbelieve cut themselves off from God's saving action and are in danger of excluding themselves from his people. But is belief enough? Why should it be thought that Jesus does away with Moses, as though the two were enemies rather than fellow servants of God? There is, indeed, much in the law of Moses that seems strange to Gentile inquirers. But in the last resort, it should be enough that God has commanded certain actions and prohibited others. Our calling is not to fathom the depths of the divine wisdom, but to obey — as Jesus did, setting an example of faithfulness to the divine will that his followers of both Jewish and Gentile origin must imitate. For this reason, God raised him from the dead, as he will raise us if we reject ungodly passions and take upon ourselves the gentle yoke of the Torah.

Some such position as this appears to have been asserted as an appropriate foundation for Christian identity, over against the Pauline view. It can appeal more persuasively to scriptural warrants than can Paul, for it accepts the commonsense principle that "scriptural authority" means that clear, explicit divine commandments remain normative for present-day practice. Its claim that what is said about Jesus should not conflict with what is said about Moses might also seem to have the potential to become a normative rule of Christian grammar. Of course, this position is in fact "inadequate" as a foundation for Christian identity. But how do we know this to be the case, despite

24. For the interpretation of doctrines as grammatical rules, see G. A. Lindbeck, *The Nature of Doctrine: Religion and Theology in a Postliberal Age*, 79-82. Use of this rule model of doctrine need not entail the conclusion that "doctrines qua doctrines are not first-order propositions" (80), since it is possible to maintain *both* that doctrines are first-order propositions *and* that they also function as grammatical rules for Christian discourse. "Grammatical rule" is in this context a metaphor, which should not be pressed beyond its proper application.

the strong counter-arguments to which the Pauline view seems vulnerable? The answer is that we know this because we live in the aftermath of the fact that Paul's account was accepted while his opponents' account was rejected. That is not to say that we must trace Christian communal identity back to an arbitrary decision that has perhaps distorted the truth of its subject matter. On the contrary, Christian communal identity rests on the presupposition that the decision in favor of the Pauline view and against his opponents represents a true discernment of the significance of Jesus Christ. There are, of course, no neutral, uncontested criteria available that would enable us to get behind the texts to check which view conforms most closely to the truth.

Yet Christian communal identity is not bound by the decisions of the early church, which in some cases are revised on the assumption that communal identity must develop and is not a mere given. So it is possible in principle to imagine that the decision to set Christian communal identity at a distance from Jewish communal identity could be reversed. One cannot rule out *a priori* the legitimacy of advocating some such reversal or revision. So far, however, it has been such a fundamental component of Christian communal identity to maintain its distinctiveness over against Judaism that it is hard to see how it could be surrendered without jeopardizing the basic truth-claim that God was in Christ reconciling the world to himself. The view that Christian distinctiveness over against Judaism is inherently anti-Semitic, and that the Christian community is therefore morally obligated to abandon or diminish this distinctiveness, overlooks the possibility that conflicting truth-claims may be fully compatible with ethical responsibility towards the other.[25]

Freedom from the yoke of the law of Moses has as its positive corollary a view of Jesus Christ as the ultimate and universal enactment of the divine self-disclosure. The terms "ultimacy" and "universality" refer to truth-claims about Jesus Christ that are at the same time grammatical rules of Christian discourse. He is *ultimate* in the sense that the narrative of God's self-

25. For the view rejected here, compare the following statements: "The roots of Christian antisemitism need be traced no further than Christianity itself; Christians have been antisemitic because they have been Christians. . . . We must learn, I think, to live with the unpleasant fact that antisemitism is part of what it has meant historically to be a Christian, and is still part of what it means to be Christian" (R. L. Wilken, *The Myth of Christian Beginnings,* 197). "How is it possible to construe and proclaim the resurrection of Jesus other than in supersessionist and triumphalist ways? . . . For is it not God who through a special sacred-historical act vindicates the Christian faith in the face of its denial by Jews? . . . Are we driven to conclude, then, that at its very center the Christian faith is deprived, or acts to deprive itself, of moral credibility?" (A. R. Eckardt, "Salient Christian-Jewish Issues of Today," 162-63).

disclosure to the people of Israel reaches its goal and conclusion in him. Although history and divine self-disclosure continue, this ongoing divine self-disclosure occurs through the mediation of the community, texts, and sacraments that bear witness to Jesus Christ, so that a supplementary narrative of further divine self-disclosure is ruled out. His significance is *universal* in the sense that the hermeneutical horizon within which he is to be located is not the Jewish community whose Messiah he is, but the world, into which he enters as God's incarnate Son (cf. Gal. 4:1-5). As a rule of Christian discourse, the truth-claim that his significance is "universal" excludes the possible claim that independent, equally valid divine self-disclosures must occur elsewhere in the world, since Jesus Christ is too culture-bound and limited a symbol to possess a more than local significance.[26] The basic grammatical rules of Christian discourse that refer us to Jesus' ultimate and universal significance are already implicit in Paul's text, which sees in his opponents' proclamation a threat to that ultimacy and universality.[27]

The ongoing effect of this decision by Paul and the early Christian community can be seen in the basic shape of the Christian canon, which is far more than a mere list of authoritative books divided into two collections.[28] In the Jewish canon, however unclear its boundaries may still have been, the undisputed center is occupied by the five books that constitute the law of Moses; the rest is necessary supplementation, elaboration, and commentary. The Christian canon might have been closely modeled on this Jewish paradigm, in which case Christian and Jewish communal identities would have remained in closer proximity to one another. There do not appear to be any necessary limits to the canonical process in which the law of Moses is supplemented by additional books; an increasing number of supplementary books need not pose a threat to the centrality of the law. Thus, distinctively Christian books (including gospels and letters) could have been added to the existing three-fold canon comprising law, prophets, and writings, in such a way that the pri-

---

26. The view classically articulated by Ernst Troeltsch in *The Absoluteness of Christianity.*

27. This reading would be disputed by Sidney G. Hall III, who claims that "Paul equips Gentiles with a christology that allows Christians — the modern-day heirs of the Gentiles — to experience Christ as their decisive re-presentation of God's love, while also allowing Jews, with different faith communities, to experience righteousness through other decisive representations of God's love" (*Christian Anti-Semitism in Paul's Theology,* 133). The implausibility of this interpretation of Paul should not detract from the more important question whether a "Christology after Auschwitz" (133) is really obliged to take this general form.

28. James Barr's attempt to confine the meaning of "canon" to "list" is unconvincing (*Holy Scripture: Canon, Authority and Criticism,* 49). The Christian "Old Testament" may contain exactly the same books as the holy scripture of the Jewish community, but yet be a quite different entity.

macy of the Torah was maintained. Had Paul's opponents' account of Christian identity been accepted, a canonical structuring of this kind would have been a logical consequence.

On the other hand, Paul's assumption of the ultimate and universal significance of Jesus Christ has as its logical consequence a rejection of the foundational status of the law of Moses and its replacement by Jesus Christ as the center of the Christian canon. Thus the "New Testament" is not a fourth element added to the threefold Jewish canon founded on the Torah, but a new foundation that entails a radical restructuring of the Jewish canon so that it becomes a new, unheard-of entity, the Christian "Old Testament." This canonical restructuring is foundational for Christian identity. It is difficult to imagine how the decision could be reversed, reducing the Gospels to the status of secondary elaborations of the Torah, because it is difficult to imagine how such a revision could possibly be regarded within the Christian community as adequate to the ultimacy and universality of the truth-claim it hears within the Gospels. Paul's decision on this point is taken up into a canonical process whose effects have proved to be enduring.

The existence of a Christian "Old Testament" is arguably as fundamental to Christian identity as the existence of a "New Testament." Here, too, the theological decisions that Paul takes in writing to the Galatians help to establish basic rules of Christian discourse. Again, a possible alternative account of Christian identity is definitively excluded: an account in which the Jewish scriptures are handed back to the non-Christian Jewish community, so that Christians are left with a canon consisting solely of Christian writings. Why should Paul not have taken his dichotomy between Moses and Christ to what might seem its logical (proto-Marcionite) conclusion, a denial of the normative status of the Jewish scriptures within the Christian community?[29] Would this have made his argument for the sole authority of Jesus Christ more persuasive for his readers? Do his apparent equivocations about the divine origin of the law (Gal. 3:15-20; 4:1-10) indicate that he was tempted to take this route?

Be that as it may, Paul in fact rejected the possibility of *excluding* Jewish scripture from any role in the creation of Christian communal identity; and he rejected this possibility as decisively as he rejected the opposite possibility of conceding to Jewish scripture the role of *determining* Christian communal identity. Jewish scripture does not control the interpretation of Jesus Christ

---

29. Had Marcion been the historical winner of the debate about divine identity, then the (expurgated) Pauline texts would presumably still be basic to Christian communal identity but would prescribe different rules for Christian discourse.

but is reinterpreted in the event of its testimony to him. In the light of Christ, the potential universality of the promises to Abraham is highlighted (Gal. 3:6-9, 15-18, 29), the exodus is passed over without comment despite the language of slavery and freedom, the non-narrative parts of the Pentateuch are drastically subordinated (3:12, 19-25), and the prophets become witnesses to Christ rather than commentators on the Torah (3:11; 4:27).

The details of this fundamental restructuring of Jewish scripture did not necessarily prove persuasive. (Even Paul abandons in Romans 4 the claim of Galatians 3:16 that "Abraham's seed" refers to "Christ.") Far more important than the cogency of the details is to note the magnitude of what is here undertaken: the beginning of a restructuring of Jewish scripture that will lead to the creation of a new entity, the Christian "Old Testament," whose outlines are already discernible here in embryonic form. Once again, it is the fundamental shape of subsequent Christian communal identity that is here being determined — although the historic role of these arguments becomes clear only in retrospect. A reversal or revision of the Pauline and early Christian decision here is, indeed, imaginable. The Christian community might come to accept the claim that the Christian "Old Testament" represents an illegitimate and violent seizure of Jewish scripture from the community to which it rightfully belongs. Yet it is more likely that the "Old Testament" will endure, oriented not towards careful observance of the details of the Pentateuchal legislation but towards the ultimate divine self-disclosure in Jesus Christ — the external focal point that offers criteria for assessing the varied literary material that is to be found within this collection.

The Pauline outline of a Christian "Old Testament" invites further, more nuanced and careful elaboration. Indeed, it is characteristic of all the fundamental grammatical rules that this Pauline text helps to establish that they invite a theological elaboration that goes beyond the bounds of the canonical texts themselves. Thus, in Galatians, the single passing reference to Jesus Christ as God's Son (4:4) does not as yet provide an adequately worked out basis for the assumption of his ultimate and universal significance; and since this is also true of other New Testament texts, a theological elaboration is required at this point that remains in conformity with these texts while proceeding beyond them. Similarly, there is in Galatians no attempt to relate the universal significance of Jesus Christ to the universal horizon of the creation (contrast Col. 1:15-20), and this relative deficiency in the Pauline outline of an "Old Testament" must later be remedied — for example, in the theology that arises out of resistance to Marcion and the Gnostics. The theological relevance of a Pauline text derives in part from its invitation to participate in the theological reflection that it initiated and whose basic grammatical rules it helped to establish. Where it is assumed that Pauline and other canonical texts are theologically sufficient and final, this risks transferring the ultimacy of Jesus Christ to a text that, however significant in establishing the foundations of Christian communal identity, does not in itself constitute an ultimate and absolute norm.

In this interpretation of certain aspects of Paul's letter to the Galatians, an attempt has been made to preserve the sharp focus of the literal-historical sense on the assumption that precisely this sharp focus might also be relevant theologically. This necessitated a criticism of the view that the significance of the biblical texts can emerge only when their historical particularities are dissolved, and are replaced by a generality comprehensive enough to encompass a readership whose situation is quite different from the one envisaged by the biblical author. In some cases an anti-particularist hermeneutic may be entirely appropriate. In the case of the Pauline text, however, it seemed worthwhile to try the experiment of dispensing with this hermeneutic, reading certain of the particularities of this text on the assumption that they remain foundational for Christian communal identity. If this theological appropriation of the literal-historical sense proves to be persuasive, then the "relevance" of Paul's text to "our own concerns" is clear.

Bibliography

Primary Sources

The Apocrypha and Pseudepigrapha of the Old Testament in English: With Introductions and Critical and Explanatory Notes to the Several Books. 2 vols., ed. R. H. Charles. Oxford: Clarendon, 1913.

The Apocryphal Old Testament, ed. H. F. D. Sparks. Oxford: Clarendon, 1984.

The Dead Sea Scrolls: Study Edition, 2 vols., ed. F. García Martínez and E. J. C. Tigchelaar. Leiden: Brill; Grand Rapids: Eerdmans, 1997-98.

Discoveries in the Judean Desert, vol. 10, ed. E. Qimron and J. Strugnell. Oxford: Clarendon, 1994.

Greek and Latin Authors on Jews and Judaism, 2 vols., ed. M. Stern. Jerusalem: Israel Academy of Sciences and Humanities, 1974-80.

Josephus, LCL, 10 vols., ed. H. St. J. Thackeray et al. London: Heinemann; Cambridge, Mass.: Harvard University Press, 1926-65.

Kommentar zum neuen Testament aus Talmud und Midrasch, 6 vols., ed. H. L. Strack and P. Billerbeck. Munich: C. H. Beck, 1922-61.

The Old Testament Pseudepigrapha, 2 vols., ed. James H. Charlesworth. London: Darton, Longman and Todd, 1983-85.

Philo, LCL, 10 vols. and 2 supps., ed. F. H. Colson et al. London: Heinemann; Cambridge, Mass.: Harvard University Press, 1929-62.

Select Papyri II. Non-Literary Papyri: Public Documents, LCL, ed. A. S. Hunt and C. C. Edgar. London: Heinemann; Cambridge, Mass.: Harvard University Press, 1977.

Die Texte aus Qumran: Hebräisch und Deutsch, ed. E. Lohse. Munich: Kösel-Verlag, 1981³.

Bibliography

Secondary Literature

Althaus, P. *Paulus und Luther über den Menschen*. Gütersloh: Bertelsmann, 1950.

―――. *The Theology of Martin Luther*. English trans. Philadelphia: Fortress, 1966.

Bammel, E., C. K. Barrett, and W. D. Davies, eds. *Donum Gentilicium: New Testament Studies in Honour of David Daube*. Oxford: Clarendon, 1978.

Bandstra, A. J. *The Law and the Elements of the World: An Exegetical Study in Aspects of Paul's Theology*. Kampen: J. H. Kok, 1964.

Barclay, John M. G. *Obeying the Truth: A Study of Paul's Ethics in Galatians*. SNTW. Edinburgh: T&T Clark, 1988.

―――. *Jews in the Mediterranean Diaspora from Alexander to Trajan (323 BCE-117 CE)*. Edinburgh: T&T Clark, 1996.

―――. "'Do We Undermine the Law?' A Study of Romans 14.1–15.6." In *Paul and the Mosaic Law: The Third Durham-Tübingen Research Symposium on Earliest Christianity and Judaism (Durham, September 1994)*, ed. J. D. G. Dunn, 287-308. WUNT. Tübingen: Mohr Siebeck, 1996.

Barnard, L. "St. Stephen and Early Alexandrian Christianity." *NTS* 7 (1960-61): 31-45.

Barr, James. *Holy Scripture: Canon, Authority, Criticism*. Oxford: Clarendon, 1983.

Barrett, C. K. *A Commentary on the Epistle to the Romans*. BNTC. London: A. & C. Black, 1957.

―――. *The Gospel according to St John*. London: SPCK, 1958.

―――. *A Commentary on the First Epistle to the Corinthians*. BNTC. London: A. & C. Black, 1971².

―――. *A Commentary on the Second Epistle to the Corinthians*. BNTC. London: A. & C. Black, 1973².

―――. *Essays on Paul*. London: SPCK, 1982. Essays include: "Cephas and Corinth," 28-39; "Things Sacrificed to Idols," 40-59; "Paul's Opponents in 2 Corinthians," 60-86; "ΨΕΥΔΑΠΟΣΤΟΛΟΙ (2 Cor. 11.13)," 87-107; "Romans 9.30–10.21: Fall and Responsibility of Israel," 132-53; "The Allegory of Abraham, Sarah, and Hagar in the Argument of Galatians," 154-70.

―――. *The Acts of the Apostles*. 2 vols. ICC. Edinburgh: T&T Clark, 1994-98.

Barth, K. *The Epistle to the Romans*. English trans. London: Oxford University Press, 1933.

―――. *A Shorter Commentary on Romans*. English trans. London: SCM, 1959.

Barth, M. "Jews and Gentiles: The Social Character of Justification." *JES* 5 (1968): 241-61.

―――. *The People of God*. JSNTSup 5. Sheffield: Sheffield Academic Press, 1983.

Bassler, J. M. "Divine Impartiality in Paul's Letter to the Romans." *NovT* 26 (1984): 43-58.

Bauckham, Richard. "For Whom Were Gospels Written?" In *The Gospel for All Christians: Rethinking the Gospel Audiences*, ed. R. Bauckham, 9-48. Grand Rapids: Eerdmans, 1998.

Baur, F. C. "Über Zweck und Veranlassung des Römerbriefs und die damit zusammenhängenden Verhältnisse der römischen Gemeinde." *Tübinger Zeitschrift für Theologie*, 1836, Heft 3, 59-178; repr. in *Ausgewählte Werke in Einzelausgaben. 1*.

Historisch-kritische Untersuchungen zum Neuen Testament. Stuttgart: Bad Cannstatt, 1963.

————. "Über Zweck und Gedankengang des Römerbriefs, nebst einer Erörterung einiger paulinische Begriffe, mit besonderer Rücksicht auf die Kommentare von Tholuck und Philippi." *Theologisches Jahrbuch* 16 (Tübingen, 1857): 60-108, 184-208.

————. *Paul the Apostle of Jesus Christ.* English trans. London/Edinburgh: Williams & Norgate, 1873.

————. *The Church History of the First Three Centuries.* English trans. Vol. 1. London/Edinburgh: Williams & Norgate, 1875.

Beare, F. W. *The Epistle to the Philippians.* BNTC. London: A. & C. Black, 1959.

Becker, Jürgen. *Paul: Apostle to the Gentiles.* English trans. Louisville: Westminster John Knox, 1993.

Becker, J., H. Conzelmann, and G. Friedrich. *Die Briefe an die Galater, Epheser, Philipper, Kolosser, Thessalonicher, und Philemon.* NTD 8. Göttingen: Vandenhoeck & Ruprecht, 1976.

Beker, J. C. *Paul the Apostle: The Triumph of God in Life and Thought.* Edinburgh: T&T Clark, 1980.

Bell, Richard H. *No One Seeks for God: An Exegetical and Theological Study of Romans 1.18–3.20.* WUNT. Tübingen: Mohr Siebeck, 1998.

————. *The Irrevocable Call of God,* WUNT. Tübingen: Mohr Siebeck, 2005.

Berger, Peter, and Thomas Luckmann. *The Social Construction of Reality: A Treatise in the Sociology of Knowledge.* London: Pelican, 1967.

Betz, Hans Dieter. *Galatians: A Commentary on Paul's Letter to the Churches in Galatia.* Hermeneia. Philadelphia: Fortress, 1979.

Betz, O., "The Qumran Halakhic Text Miqsat Maʿasê Ha-Tôrah (4QMMT) and Sadducean, Essene, and Early Pharisaic Tradition." In *The Aramaic Bible: Targums in Their Historical Context,* ed. D. R. G. Beattie and M. J. McNamara, 176-202. JSOTSup. Sheffield: Sheffield Academic Press, 1994.

Betz, O., M. Hengel, and P. Schmidt, eds. *Abraham unser Vater* (Festschrift for O. Michel). Leiden/Köln: Brill, 1963.

Bläser, P. *Das Gesetz bei Paulus.* Münster: Aschendorff, 1941.

Blass, F., R. Debrunner, and R. W. Funk. *A Greek Grammar of the New Testament and Other Early Christian Literature.* Chicago: University of Chicago Press, 1961.

Boccaccini, Gabriele. *Beyond the Essene Hypothesis: The Parting of the Ways between Qumran and Enochic Judaism.* Grand Rapids: Eerdmans, 1998.

Bockmuehl, Markus. *The Epistle to the Philippians.* BNTC. London: A. & C. Black, 1997.

Borgen, P. "Paul Preaches Circumcision and Pleases Men." In *Paul and Paulinism,* ed. M. D. Hooker and S. G. Wilson, 37-46. London: SPCK, 1982.

Bornkamm, G. *Das Ende des Gesetzes: Paulusstudien.* BevTh 16. Munich: Chr. Kaiser, 1966. See especially "Paulinische Anakoluthe im Römerbrief," 76-92.

————. *Early Christian Experience.* London: SCM, 1969. See especially "The Revelation of God's Wrath," 47-70; "Sin, Law and Death: An Exegetical Study of Romans 7," 87-104.

————. "Gesetz und Natur (Röm 2,14-16)." In *Studien zu Antike und Urchristentum*, 93-118. BevTh 28. Munich: Chr. Kaiser, 1970.

————. *Geschichte und Glaube 2.* BevTh 53. Munich: Chr. Kaiser, 1971. See especially "Wandlungen im alt- und neutestamentlichen Gesetzesverständnis," 72-119.

————. *Paul.* English trans. London: Hodder & Stoughton, 1971.

————. "The Letter to the Romans as Paul's Last Will and Testament." In *The Romans Debate*, ed. K. P. Donfried, 17-31. Minneapolis: Augsburg, 1977[1].

Boyarin, Daniel. *A Radical Jew: Paul and the Politics of Identity.* Berkeley: University of California Press, 1994.

Bring, R. *Commentary on Galatians.* English trans. Philadelphia: Muhlenberg, 1961.

Brown, R. E., *The Gospel according to John.* AB (2 vols.). London: Geoffrey Chapman, 1966-70.

————. *The Community of the Beloved Disciple.* London: Geoffrey Chapman, 1979.

Bruce, F. F. *Romans: An Introduction and Commentary.* TNTC. London: IVP, 1963.

————. "Galatian Problems: 1. Autobiographical Data." *BJRL* 53 (1968-69): 292-309.

————. *Paul: Apostle of the Free Spirit.* Exeter: Paternoster, 1977.

————. *The Epistle of Paul to the Galatians: A Commentary on the Greek Text.* NIGTC. Exeter: Paternoster, 1982.

Bultmann, Rudolf. *Theology of the New Testament.* 2 vols. English trans. London: SCM, 1952-55.

————. "New Testament and Mythology." In *Kerygma and Myth: A Theological Debate*, ed. Hans Werner Bartsch, 1-44. English trans. London: SCM Press, 1954.

————. "History and Eschatology in the New Testament." *NTS* 1 (1954-55): 5-16.

————. "Christ the End of the Law." In *Essays Philosophical and Theological*, 36-66. English trans. London: SCM, 1955.

————. *Existence and Faith.* London: SCM, 1961. See especially "Paul," 111-46; "Romans 7 and the Anthropology of Paul," 147-57.

————. "Adam and Christ according to Romans 5." In *Current Issues in New Testament Interpretation*, ed. W. Klassen and G. F. Snyder, 143-65. London: SCM, 1962.

————. "ΔΙΚΑΙΟΣΥΝΗ ΘΕΟΥ." *JBL* 83 (1964): 12-16.

————. *Exegetica.* Tübingen: J. C. B. Mohr (Paul Siebeck), 1967. See especially "Glossen im Römerbrief," 278-84; "Zur Auslegung von Galater 2, 15-18," 394-99.

————. "Liberal Theology and the Latest Theological Movement." In *Faith and Understanding*, vol. 1, 28-52. London: SCM, 1969.

————. "Das Problem der Ethik bei Paulus." Repr. in *Das Paulusbild in der neueren Deutschen Forschung*, ed. K. H. Rengstorf, 179-99. Darmstadt: Wissenschaftliche Buchgesellschaft, 1969.

————. "Zur Geschichte der Paulus Forschung." In *Das Paulusbild in der neueren Deutschen Forschung*, ed. K. H. Rengstorf, 304-37. Darmstadt: Wissenschaftliche Buchgesellschaft, 1969.

————. *The Gospel of John.* English trans. Oxford: Blackwell, 1971.

————. *Der Zweite Brief an die Korinther.* KEKNT. Göttingen: Vandenhoeck & Ruprecht, 1976.

———. *Exegetische Probleme des zweiten Korintherbriefes.* SBU 9. Uppsala: Wretmans, 1947.

Burton, E. de W. *A Critical and Exegetical Commentary on the Epistle to the Galatians.* ICC. Edinburgh: T&T Clark, 1921.

Byrne, B., *"Sons of God" — "Seed of Abraham."* AnBib 83. Rome: Biblica Institute, 1979.

———. *Romans.* SP. Collegeville: Liturgical, 1996.

Cadbury, H. J. "The Hellenists." In *The Beginnings of Christianity,* ed. F. J. Foakes-Jackson and K. Lake, pt. 1, vol. 5, 59-74. London: Macmillan, 1933.

Caird, George B. *Paul's Letters from Prison.* Oxford: Oxford University Press, 1976.

———. "Review of E. P. Sanders, *Paul and Palestinian Judaism." JTS* 29 (1978): 538-43.

Campbell, Douglas A. *The Rhetoric of Righteousness in Romans 3.21-26.* JSNTSup. Sheffield: Sheffield Academic Press, 1992.

———. "The Meaning of ΠΙΣΤΙΣ and ΝΟΜΟΣ in Paul: A Linguistic and Structural Perspective." *JBL* 111 (1992): 91-103.

———. *The Quest for Paul's Gospel: A Suggested Strategy.* London and New York: T&T Clark International, 2005.

———. "An Evangelical Paul: A Response to Francis Watson's *Paul and the Hermeneutics of Faith." JSNT* 28 (2006): 337-51.

Carleton Paget, James. "Jewish Proselytism at the Time of Christian Origins: Chimera or Reality?" *JSNT* 62 (1996): 65-103.

Carson, D. A., Peter T. O'Brien, and Mark A. Seifrid, eds. *Justification and Variegated Nomism.* Volume 1: *The Complexities of Second Temple Judaism.* Tübingen: Mohr Siebeck; Grand Rapids: Baker, 2001.

———. *Justification and Variegated Nomism.* Volume 2: *The Paradoxes of Paul.* Tübingen: Mohr Siebeck; Grand Rapids: Baker, 2005.

Collange, J. F. *Énigmes de la Deuxième Épître de Paul aux Corinthiens.* SNTSMS 18. Cambridge: Cambridge University Press, 1972.

Collins, John J., *Seers, Sibyls and Sages in Hellenistic-Roman Judaism.* Leiden: Brill, 2001.

Conzelmann, H. "Die Rechtfertigungslehre des Paulus: Theologie oder Anthropologie?" *EvTh* 28 (1968): 389-404.

———. *An Outline of the Theology of the New Testament.* English trans. London: SCM, 1969.

———. "Current Problems in New Testament Research." In *New Testament Issues,* ed. R. Batey. London: SCM, 1970.

———. *1 Corinthians.* Hermeneia. Philadelphia: Fortress, 1975.

Cranfield, C. E. B. "St. Paul and the Law." *SJT* 17 (1964): 43-68.

———. *A Critical and Exegetical Commentary on the Epistle to the Romans.* ICC. 2 vols. Edinburgh: T&T Clark, 1975-79.

Cullmann, O. *The Johannine Circle.* Philadelphia: Westminster, 1976.

Dahl, N. A. *Studies in Paul.* Minneapolis: Augsburg, 1977. Essays include: "The Missionary Theology in the Epistle to the Romans," 70-94; "The Doctrine of Justification: Its Social Function and Implications," 95-120; "The One God of Jews and Gentiles (Rom. 3:29-30)," 178-91.

Das, A. Andrew. *Paul, the Law, and the Covenant*. Grand Rapids: Hendrickson, 2001.

Davies, W. D. *Paul and Rabbinic Judaism: Some Rabbinic Elements in Pauline Theology*. London: SPCK, 1970³.

———. "The Apostolic Age and the Life of Paul," in *Peake's Commentary on the Bible*, 870-81. London: Thomas Nelson & Sons, 1977.

———. "Paul and the People of Israel," *NTS* 24 (1977-78): 4-39.

———. "Paul and the Law: Reflections on Pitfalls in Interpretation." In *Paul and Paulinism*, ed. M. D. Hooker and S. G. Wilson. London: SPCK, 1982.

Deines, Roland. "The Pharisees between 'Judaisms' and 'Common Judaism.'" In *Justification and Variegated Nomism*. Volume 1: *The Complexities of Second Temple Judaism*, ed. D. A. Carson, Peter T. O'Brien, and Mark A. Seifrid, 443-504. Tübingen: Mohr Siebeck; Grand Rapids: Baker, 2001.

Dibelius, M. "The Conversion of Cornelius." In his *Studies in the Acts of the Apostles*, ed. H. Greeven, 109-22. London: SCM, 1956.

Dinkler, Erich. "Prädestination bei Paulus — Exegetische Bemerkungen zum Römerbrief." In *Signum Crucis: Aufsätze zum Neuen Testament und zur christlichen Archäologie*, 241-69. Tübingen: J. C. B. Mohr (Paul Siebeck), 1967.

Dodd, C. H. "The Mind of Paul, II." In *New Testament Studies*, 83-128. Manchester: Manchester University Press, 1953.

———. *The Epistle to the Romans*. MNTC. 1932; London: Hodder & Stoughton, 1959.

Donaldson, Terence L. *Paul and the Gentiles: Remapping the Apostle's Convictional World*. Minneapolis: Fortress, 1997.

Donfried, K. P. "Justification and Last Judgment in Paul." *ZNW* 67 (1976): 90-110.

———, ed. *The Romans Debate*. Minneapolis: Augsburg, 1977¹. See especially: "The Nature and Scope of the Romans Debate," ix-xvii; "A Short Note on Romans 16," 50-60; "False Presuppositions in the Study of Romans," 120-48.

Doughty, D. J. "The Priority of 'ΧΑΡΙΣ.'" *NTS* 19 (1972-73): 163-80.

Dülmen, A. van. *Die Theologie des Gesetzes bei Paulus*. SBM. Stuttgart: Katholisches Bibelwerk, 1968.

Duncan, G. S. *St. Paul's Ephesian Ministry: A Reconstruction with Special Reference to the Ephesian Origin of the Imprisonment Epistles*. London: Hodder & Stoughton, 1929.

———. *The Epistle of Paul to the Galatians*. MNTC. London: Hodder & Stoughton, 1934.

Dunn, J. D. G. "Rom. 7,14-25 in the Theology of Paul." *TZ* 31 (1975): 257-73.

———. "The New Perspective on Paul." *BJRL* 65 (1982-83): 95-122; repr. in *Jesus, Paul and the Law: Studies in Paul and Galatians*, 183-206. Louisville: Westminster John Knox, 1990.

———. "The Incident at Antioch (Gal. 2.11-18)." *JSNT* 18 (1983): 3-57.

———. *Romans*. WBC. 2 vols. Dallas: Word Books, 1988.

———, ed. *Paul and the Mosaic Law: The Third Durham-Tübingen Research Symposium on Earliest Christianity and Judaism (Durham, September 1994)*. WUNT. Tübingen: Mohr Siebeck, 1996.

————— "Once More ΠΙΣΤΙΣ ΧΡΙΣΤΟΥ." In *Pauline Theology*, vol. IV, ed. E. Elizabeth Johnson and David M. Hay, 61-81. Atlanta: Scholars, 1997.

—————. *The New Perspective on Paul.* WUNT. Tübingen: Mohr Siebeck, 2005.

Ebeling, G. *Word and Faith.* English trans. London, 1963. See especially "On the Doctrine of the Triplex Usus Legis in the Theology of the Reformation," 62-78; "Reflections on the Doctrine of the Law," 247-81.

—————. *Luther: An Introduction to His Thought.* English trans. London: Collins, 1970.

—————. *Die Wahrheit des Evangeliums: Eine Lesehilfe zum Galaterbrief.* Tübingen: J. C. B. Mohr (Paul Siebeck), 1981. English trans.: *The Truth of the Gospel: An Exposition of Galatians.* Philadelphia: Fortress, 1985.

Eckardt, A. R. "Salient Christian-Jewish Issues of Today." In *Jews and Christians: Exploring the Past, Present and Future,* ed. J. H. Charlesworth, 150-77. New York: Crossroad, 1990.

Eckert, J. *Die Urchristliche Verkündigung im Streit zwischen Paulus und seinen Gegnern nach dem Galaterbrief.* Munich: Chr. Kaiser, 1971.

Eichholz, G. *Die Theologie des Paulus im Umriss.* Neukirchen-Vluyn: Neukirchener Verlag, 1977².

Elliott, J. H. *A Home for the Homeless: A Sociological Exegesis of 1 Peter, Its Situation and Strategy.* London: SCM, 1982.

Endres, John C. *Biblical Interpretation in the Book of Jubilees.* CBQMS. Washington, D.C.: Catholic Biblical Association of America, 1987.

Engberg-Pedersen, Troels. *Paul and the Stoics.* Edinburgh: T&T Clark, 2000.

—————. "Once More a Lutheran Paul?" *SJT* 59 (2006): 439-60.

Esler, Philip F. *Community and Gospel in Luke-Acts: The Social and Political Motivations of Lucan Theology.* SNTSMS. Cambridge: Cambridge University Press, 1987.

—————. *Galatians.* London: Routledge, 1998.

—————. *Conflict and Identity in Romans: The Social Setting of Paul's Letter.* Minneapolis: Fortress, 2003.

Fitzmyer, Joseph A. *Romans: A New Translation with Introduction and Commentary.* AB. New York: Doubleday, 1992.

Flückiger, F. "Die Werke des Gesetzes bei den Heiden (nach Röm. 2,14ff)." *TZ* 8 (1952): 17-42.

Foakes-Jackson, F. J., and K. Lake, eds. *The Beginnings of Christianity,* part 1, vol. 5. London: Macmillan, 1933.

Franzmann, M. H. *Romans.* CC. St. Louis: Concordia, 1968.

Frei, Hans. *The Eclipse of Biblical Narrative: A Study in Eighteenth and Nineteenth Century Hermeneutics.* New Haven and London: Yale University Press, 1974.

—————. *The Identity of Jesus Christ: The Hermeneutical Bases of Dogmatic Theology.* Philadelphia: Fortress, 1975.

Friedrich, G. "Die Gegner des Paulus im 2. Korintherbrief." In *Abraham unser Vater,* ed. O. Betz, M. Hengel, and P. Schmidt, 181-215. Leiden/Köln: Brill, 1963.

—————. "Der Brief an die Philipper." In J. Becker, H. Conzelmann, and G. Friedrich, *Die*

Briefe an die Galater, Epheser, Philipper, Kolosser, Thessalonicher und Philemon. NTD 8. Göttingen: Vandenhoeck & Ruprecht, 1976.

Fuchs, E. *Die Freiheit des Glaubens: Römer 5-8 augelegt.* Munich: Chr. Kaiser, 1949.

Furnish, V. P. *Theology and Ethics in Paul.* Nashville: Abingdon, 1968.

Gadamer, Hans-Georg. *Truth and Method.* English trans. London: Sheed & Ward, 1979[2].

Gager, J. G. *Kingdom and Community: The Social World of Early Christianity.* Englewood Cliffs, N.J.: Prentice-Hall, 1975.

―――. *Reinventing Paul.* New York: Oxford University Press, 2000.

Gasque, W. W. *A History of the Criticism of the Acts of the Apostles.* Tübingen: J. C. B. Mohr (Paul Siebeck), 1975.

Gaston, Lloyd. *Paul and the Torah.* Vancouver: University of British Columbia, 1987.

Gathercole, Simon J. *Where Is Boasting? Early Jewish Soteriology and Paul's Response in Romans 1-5.* Grand Rapids: Eerdmans, 2002.

―――. "A Law unto Themselves: The Gentiles in Romans 2.14-15 Revisited." *JSNT* 85 (2002): 27-49.

Georgi, D. *The Opponents of Paul in Second Corinthians.* English trans. SNTW. Edinburgh: T&T Clark, 1987.

―――. *Die Geschichte der Kollekte des Paulus für Jerusalem.* Hamburg: Reich, 1965.

Gnilka, J. *Der Philipperbrief.* HTKNT. Freiburg/Basel/Vienna: Herder, 1968.

Goodman, Martin. "Jewish Proselytizing in the First Century." In *Jews among Pagans and Christians in the Roman Empire,* ed. J. Lieu, J. North, and T. Rajak, 53-78. London: Routledge, 1992.

Grieb, A. Katherine. *The Story of Romans: A Narrative Defense of God's Righteousness.* Louisville: Westminster John Knox, 2002.

Gundry, R. H. "The Moral Frustration of Paul before His Conversion: Sexual Lust in Romans 7:7-25." In *Pauline Studies,* ed. D. A. Hagner and M. J. Harris, 228-45. Exeter: Paternoster, 1980.

Gunton, Colin E., ed. *God and Freedom.* Edinburgh: T&T Clark, 1995.

Guthrie, D. *New Testament Introduction.* London: Inter-Varsity Press, 1970[3].

―――. *Galatians.* NCBC. London: Marshall, Morgan and Scott, 1973.

Haenchen, E. "The Book of Acts as Source Material for the History of Early Christianity." In *Studies in Luke-Acts,* ed. L. E. Keck and J. L. Martyn, 258-78. London: SPCK, 1968.

―――. *The Acts of the Apostles: A Commentary.* English trans. Oxford: Blackwell, 1971.

Hagner, D. A., and M. J. Harris, eds. *Pauline Studies: Essays Presented to F. F. Bruce on His 70th Birthday.* Exeter: Paternoster, 1980.

Hahn, F. *Mission in the New Testament.* SBT 47. English trans. London: SCM, 1965.

―――. "Das Gesetzesverständnis im Römer- und Galaterbrief." *ZNW* 67 (1976): 29-63.

―――. "Zum Verständnis von Römer 11,26a: '. . . und so wird ganz Israel gerettet werden.'" In *Paul and Paulinism,* ed. M. D. Hooker and S. G. Wilson, 221-36. London: SPCK, 1982.

Hall, D. R. "Romans 3.1-8 Reconsidered." *NTS* 29 (1982-83): 183-97.

Hall, Sidney G. *Christian Anti-Semitism and Paul's Theology.* Philadelphia: Fortress, 1993.

Hammond, N. G. L., and H. H. Scullard, eds. *The Oxford Classical Dictionary.* Oxford: Oxford University Press, 1970[2].

Harink, Douglas. *Paul among the Postliberals: Pauline Theology beyond Christendom and Modernity.* Grand Rapids: Brazos, 2003.

Hays, David M., and E. Elizabeth Johnson, eds. *Pauline Theology,* Volume III: *Romans.* Minneapolis: Fortress, 1995.

Hays, Richard B. "'Have We Found Abraham to Be Our Forefather According to the Flesh?' A Reconsideration of Rom. 4:1." *NovT* 27 (1985): 76-98.

———. *Echoes of Scripture in the Letters of Paul.* New Haven and London: Yale University Press, 1989.

———. *The Faith of Jesus Christ: The Narrative Substructure of Galatians 3:1–4:11.* Grand Rapids: Eerdmans, 2002[2].

Hengel, Martin. "Die Ursprünge der christlichen Mission." *NTS* 18 (1971-72): 15-38.

———. "Zwischen Jesus und Paulus: Die 'Hellenisten', die 'Sieben' und Stephanus." *ZTK* 72 (1975): 151-206.

———. *Acts and the History of Earliest Christianity.* English trans. London: SCM, 1979.

———. *The Pre-Christian Paul.* English trans. London: SCM, 1991.

———. "The Attitude of Paul to the Law in the Unknown Years between Damascus and Antioch." In *Paul and the Mosaic Law,* ed. J. D. G. Dunn, 25-51. Grand Rapids: Eerdmans, 2001.

Hester, J. D. "The Rhetorical Structure of Galatians 1:11–2:14." *JBL* 103 (1984): 223-33.

Holmberg, B. *Paul and Power: The Structure of Authority in the Primitive Church as Reflected in the Pauline Epistles.* CB. Lund: Almqvist & Wiksell, 1978.

Hooker, M. D. "Beyond the Things That Are Written? St. Paul's Use of Scripture." *NTS* 27 (1980-81): 295-309.

———. "Paul and 'Covenantal Nomism.'" In *From Adam to Christ: Essays on Paul,* 155-64. Cambridge: Cambridge University Press, 1990.

———, and S. G. Wilson, eds. *Paul and Paulinism: Essays in Honour of C. K. Barrett.* London: SPCK, 1982.

Horrell, David. *The Social Ethos of the Corinthian Correspondence: Interests and Ideology from 1 Corinthians to 1 Clement.* SNTW. Edinburgh: T&T Clark, 1996.

Howard, George. *Paul: Crisis in Galatia.* SNTSMS. Cambridge: Cambridge University Press, 1979.

Hübner, H. *Das Gesetz bei Paulus: Ein Beitrag zum Werden der paulinischen Theologie.* FRLANT. Göttingen: Vandenhoeck & Ruprecht, 1978. English trans.: *Law in Paul's Thought.* SNTW. Edinburgh: T&T Clark, 1984.

———. "Pauli Theologiae Proprium." *NTS* 26 (1979-80): 445-73.

Hughes, P. E. *Paul's Second Epistle to the Corinthians.* NLC. London: Marshall, Morgan & Scott, 1962.

Jervell, J. *Luke and the People of God: A New Look at Luke-Acts.* Minneapolis: Augsburg, 1972.

————. "The Letter to Jerusalem." In *The Romans Debate*, ed. K. P. Donfried. Minneapolis: Augsburg, 1977[1].

Jervis, L. Ann. *The Purpose of Romans: A Comparative Letter Structure Investigation.* JSNTSup. Sheffield: Sheffield Academic Press, 1991.

Jewett, Robert. "Conflicting Movements in the Early Church as Reflected in Philippians." *NovT* 12 (1970): 362-90.

————. "The Agitators and the Galatian Congregations." *NTS* 17 (1971): 198-212.

————. *Dating Paul's Life.* London: SCM, 1979.

————. "Major Impulses in the Theological Interpretation of Romans since Barth." *Int.* 34 (1980): 17-31.

Johnson, E. Elizabeth. "Romans 9–11: The Faithfulness and Impartiality of God." In *Pauline Theology*, Volume III: *Romans,* ed. David M. Hays and E. Elizabeth Johnson, 211-39. Minneapolis: Fortress, 1995.

Johnson, Luke Timothy. "Rom 3:21-26 and the Faith of Jesus." *CBQ* 44 (1982): 77-90.

Jüngel, E. "Das Gesetz zwischen Adam und Christus: Eine theologische Studie zu Röm 5, 12-21." *ZTK* 60 (1963): 42-74.

Kant, Immanuel. *Religion within the Limits of Reason Alone.* English trans. New York: Harper & Row, 1960.

Karris, R. J. "Romans 14:1–15:13 and the Occasion of Romans." In *The Romans Debate,* ed. K. P. Donfried, 75-99. Minneapolis: Augsburg, 1977[1].

Käsemann, E. "Die Legitimität des Apostels." *ZNW* 41 (1942): 33-71.

————. *New Testament Question of Today.* English trans. London: SCM, 1969. See especially "'The Righteousness of God' in Paul," 168-82; "Paul and Israel," 183-87; "Paul and Early Catholicism," 236-51.

————. *Exegetische Versuche und Besinnungen,* vol. 1. Göttingen: Vandenhoeck & Ruprecht, 1970[6]. See especially "Zum Verständnis von Römer 3, 24-26," 96-100.

————. *Perspectives on Paul.* English trans. Philadelphia: Fortress, 1971. See especially "Justification and Salvation-History in the Epistle to the Romans," 60-78; "The Faith of Abraham in Romans 4," 79-101; "The Spirit and the Letter," 138-68.

————. *Commentary on Romans.* English trans. London: SCM, 1980.

Kaye, B. N. *The Thought Structure of Romans with Special Reference to Chapter 6.* Austin, Tex.: Scholars Press, 1979.

Keck, Leander E. "Justification of the Ungodly and Ethics." In *Rechtfertigung,* ed. J. Friedrich, W. Pöhlmann, and P. Stuhlmacher, 199-209. Tübingen: J. C. B. Mohr (Paul Siebeck); Göttingen: Vandenhoeck & Ruprecht, 1976.

————. *Romans.* ANTC. Nashville: Abingdon, 2005.

————, and J. L. Martyn, eds. *Studies in Luke-Acts.* London: SPCK, 1968.

Ker, Donald P. "Paul and Apollos — Colleagues or Rivals?" *JSNT* 77 (2000): 75-97.

Kertelge, K. *"Rechtfertigung" bei Paulus: Studien zum Struktur und zum Bedeutungsgehalt des paulinischen Rechtfertigungsbegriffs.* Münster: Aschendorff, 1967.

————. "Gesetz und Freiheit im Galaterbrief." *NTS* 30 (1983-84): 382-94.

Kettunen, M. *Der Abfassungszweck des Römerbriefes.* Helsinki: Suomalainen Tiedeakatemia, 1979.

Kim, S. *The Origin of Paul's Gospel.* WUNT. Tübingen: J. C. B. Mohr (Paul Siebeck), 1981.

Klein, C. *Anti-Judaism in Christian Theology.* English trans. London: SPCK, 1978.

Klein, G. *Rekonstruktion und Interpretation: Gesammelte Aufsätze zum Neuen Testament.* Munich: Chr. Kaiser, 1969. See especially "Galater 2,6-9 und die Geschichte der Jerusalem Urgemeinde," 99-128; "Römer 4 und die Idee der Heilsgeschichte," 145-46.

———. "Präliminarien zum Thema 'Paulus und die Juden.'" In *Rechtfertigung,* ed. J. Friedrich, W. Pöhlmann, and P. Stuhlmacher, 229-43. Tübingen: J. C. B. Mohr (Paul Siebeck); Göttingen: Vandenhoeck & Ruprecht, 1976.

———. "Paul's Purpose in Writing the Epistle to the Romans." In *The Romans Debate,* ed. K. P. Donfried, 32-49. Minneapolis: Augsburg, 1977[1].

Klijn, A. F. J. "Paul's Opponents in Philippians III." *NovT* 7 (1964-65): 278-84.

Knox, J. *Chapters in a Life of Paul.* London: A. & C. Black, 1954.

Koester, H. "The Purpose of the Polemic of a Pauline Fragment (Philippians III)." *NTS* 8 (1961-62): 317-32.

Kuhr, F. "Römer 2,14f und die Verheissung bei Jeremia 31,31ff." *ZNW* 55 (1964): 243-61.

Kümmel, W. G. *The New Testament: The History of the Investigation of Its Problems.* English trans. London: SCM, 1973.

———. *Römer 7 und die Bekehrung des Paulus.* Leipzig: J. C. Hinrichs, 1929; repr. in *Römer 7 und das Bild des Menschen: Zwei Studien.* Munich: Chr. Kaiser, 1974.

———. *Introduction to the New Testament.* English trans. London: SCM, 1975.

Kuss, O. *Der Römerbrief übersetzt und erklärt.* 3 vols. Regensburg: Pustet, 1957-78.

Lampe, Peter. *From Paul to Valentinus: Christians at Rome in the First Two Centuries.* English trans. Minneapolis: Fortress, 2003.

Leenhardt, F. J. *The Epistle to the Romans.* English trans. London: Lutterworth, 1961.

Lightfoot, J. B. *St Paul's Epistle to the Galatians.* Cambridge/London: Macmillan, 1865.

———. *St. Paul's to the Philippians: A Revised Text with Introduction, Notes, and Dissertations.* London and Cambridge: Macmillan, 1873.

Lindbeck, George. *The Nature of Doctrine: Religion and Theology in a Postliberal Age.* London: SPCK, 1984.

Locke, John. *Paraphrases and Notes on the Epistles of St Paul to the Galatians, 1 and 2 Corinthians, Romans, Ephesians.* 2 vols. Ed. A. W. Wainwright. Oxford: Clarendon, 1987.

Lohmeyer, E. *Der Brief an die Philipper.* KEKNT. Göttingen: Vandenhoeck & Ruprecht, 1928.

Lüdemann, G. *Paul, Apostle to the Gentiles: Studies in Chronology.* English trans. London, 1984.

———. *Paulus, de Heidenapostel, Band II. Antipaulinismus im frühen Christentum.* Göttingen: Vandenhoeck & Ruprecht, 1983.

Lührmann, D. *Der Brief an die Galater.* ZBK. Zurich: Theologische Verlag, 1978.

Luther, Martin. *Lectures on Romans.* (1516). LW 25. St. Louis: Concordia, 1972.

———. *Lectures on Galatians Chapters 1-4.* (1535). LW 26. St. Louis: Concordia, 1963.

———. *Lectures on Galatians.* (1519). LW 27. St. Louis: Concordia, 1963.

———. *The Freedom of a Christian.* (1520). LW 31. St. Louis: Concordia, 1957.

Bibliography

————. *De Servo Arbitrio.* (1525). *LW* 33. St. Louis: Concordia, 1972.

————. *Word and Sacrament I. LW* 35. Philadelphia: Concordia, 1960.

Luz, U. *Das Geschichtsverständnis des Paulus.* BevTh 49. Munich: Chr. Kaiser, 1968.

Lyonnet, S. J. "Gratuité de la Justification et Gratuité du Salut." In AnBib 17-18, I, 95-110. Rome: Biblica Institute, 1963.

Kelsey, David H. *The Use of Scripture in Modern Theology.* London: SCM, 1975.

Manson, T. W. "St. Paul's Letter to the Romans — and Others." *BJRL* 31 (1948): 3-19.

Manson, W. *The Epistle to the Hebrews.* London: Hodder & Stoughton, 1951.

Marshall, I. Howard. *The Gospel of Luke: A Commentary on the Greek Text.* NIGTC. Exeter: Paternoster, 1978.

————. *Acts: An Introduction and Commentary.* TNTC. Leicester: Inter-Varsity Press, 1980.

Martin, Ralph P. *Philippians: An Introduction and Commentary.* TNTC. London: Tyndale, 1959.

Martyn, J. Louis. *History and Theology in the Fourth Gospel.* Nashville: Abingdon, 1968.

————. "Events in Galatia: Modified Covenantal Nomism Versus God's Invasion of the Cosmos in the Singular Gospel: A Response to J. D. G. Dunn and Beverly Gaventa." In *Pauline Theology,* vol. 1, ed. Jouette M. Bassler, 160-79. Minneapolis: Fortress, 1991.

————. *Galatians: A New Translation with Introduction and Commentary.* AB. New York: Doubleday, 1997.

————. *Theological Issues in the Letters of Paul.* SNTW. Edinburgh: T&T Clark, 1997.

————. "*Nomos* plus Genitive Noun in Paul: The History of God's Law." In *Early Christianity and Classical Culture: Comparative Studies in Honor of Abraham J. Malherbe,* ed. J. T. Fitzgerald, T. H. Olbricht, and L. M. White. Leiden: Brill, 2003.

Marxsen, W. *Introduction to the New Testament.* English trans. Philadelphia: Fortress, 1974.

Matlock, R. Barry. "Detheologizing the ΠΙΣΤΙΣ ΧΡΙΣΤΟΥ Debate: Cautionary Remarks from a Lexical Semantic Perspective." *NovT* 42 (1999): 1-23.

————. "Almost Cultural Studies? Reflections on the 'New Perspective' on Paul." In *Biblical/Cultural Studies: The Third Sheffield Colloquium,* ed. J. C. Exum and S. D. Moore, 144-83. Sheffield: Sheffield Academic Press, 1998.

Mauser, U. "Galater III.20: Die Universalität des Heils." *NTS* 13 (1966-67): 258-70.

McDonald, Patricia M. "Romans 5.1-11 as a Rhetorical Bridge." *JSNT* 40 (1990): 81-96.

McEleney, N. J. "Conversion, Circumcision and the Law." *NTS* 20 (1973-74): 319-41.

McFague, Sallie. *Metaphorical Theology: Theology for an Ecological, Nuclear Age.* London: SCM, 1987.

Meeks, W. "The Man from Heaven in Johannine Sectarianism." *JBL* 91 (1972): 44-72.

————. *The First Urban Christians: The Social World of the Apostle Paul.* New Haven and London: Yale University Press, 1983.

Michael, J. H. *The Epistle of Paul to the Philippians.* MNTC. London: Hodder & Stoughton, 1928.

Michel, O. *Der Brief an die Römer.* KEKNT. Göttingen: Vandenhoeck & Ruprecht, 1955.

Minear, P. S. *The Obedience of Faith*. SBT 2nd Series. London: SCM, 1971.

Moltmann, Jürgen, ed. *Anfänge der dialektischen Theologie, Teil I.* Munich: Chr. Kaiser, 1974.

Moo, Douglas J. "Israel and Paul in Romans 7.7-12." *NTS* 32 (1986): 122-35.

———. *The Epistle to the Romans*. NICNT. Grand Rapids: Eerdmans, 1996.

Moore, George Foot. "Christian Writers on Judaism." *HTR* 14 (1921): 197-254.

Morgan, R. "The Significance of 'Paulinism.'" In *Paul and Paulinism*, ed. M. D. Hooker and S. G. Wilson, 320-38. London: SPCK, 1982.

Moxnes, H. *Theology in Conflict: Studies of Paul's Understanding of God in Romans.* NovTSup LIII. Leiden: Brill, 1980.

Müller, C. *Gottes Gerechtigkeit und Gottes Volk: Eine Untersuchung zu Römer 9–11.* FRLANT. Göttingen: Vandenhoeck & Ruprecht, 1964.

Munck, J. *Paul and the Salvation of Mankind.* English trans. London: SCM, 1959.

Mundle, W. *Der Glaubensbegriff des Paulus.* Leipzig: Heinsius, 1932.

———. "Zur Auslegung von Röm 2,13ff." *TB* 13 (1934): 249-56.

Müssner, F. *Der Galaterbrief.* HTKNT. Freiburg/Basel/Vienna: Herder & Herder, 1974.

Nanos, Mark D. *The Mystery of Romans: The Jewish Context of Paul's Letter.* Minneapolis: Fortress, 1996.

———. *The Irony of Galatians: Paul's Letter in First-Century Context.* Minneapolis: Fortress, 2002.

Neill, S. C. *The Interpretation of the New Testament 1861-1961.* London: Oxford University Press, 1964.

Nolland, John. "Uncircumcised Proselytes?" *JSJ* 1 (1981): 173-94.

Nygren, A. *A Commentary on Romans.* English trans. London: SCM, 1952.

Oepke, A. *Der Brief des Paulus an die Galater.* THKNT. Berlin: Evangelische Verlagsanstalt, 1955².

Oman, John. *Grace and Personality.* Cambridge: Cambridge University Press, 1931⁴.

O'Neill, J. C. *The Theology of Acts in Its Historical Setting.* London: SPCK, 1966.

Packer, J. I. "The 'Wretched Man' in Romans 7." *StEv* 2 (1964): 621-27.

Pedersen, S., ed. *Die Paulinische Literatur und Theologie.* Göttingen: Vandenhoeck & Ruprecht, 1980.

Plag, C. *Israels Wege zum Heil: Eine Untersuchung zu Römer 9 bis 11.* Stuttgart: Calwer Verlag, 1969.

Plummer, A. *A Critical and Exegetical Commentary on the Second Epistle of St Paul to the Corinthians.* ICC. Edinburgh: T&T Clark, 1915.

Pregeant, R. "Grace and Recompense: Reflections on a Pauline Paradox." *JAAR* 47 (1979): 73-96.

Pucci Ben Zeev, Miriam. *Jewish Rights in the Roman World: The Greek and Roman Documents Quoted by Flavius Josephus.* TSAJ. Tübingen: Mohr Siebeck, 1998.

Räisänen, H. "Paul's Theological Difficulties with the Law." *StBib* 3 (1978): 301-15.

———. "Zum Gebrauch von ΕΠΙΘΥΜΙΑ und ΕΠΙΘΥΜΕΙΝ bei Paulus." *StTh* 33 (1979): 85-99.

———. "Legalism and Salvation by the Law: Paul's Portrayal of the Jewish Religion as a

Historical and Theological Problem." In *Die Paulinische Literatur und Theologie,* ed
S. Pedersen, 63-83. Göttingen: Vandenhoeck & Ruprecht, 1980.

———. *Paul and the Law.* WUNT 29. Tübingen: J. C. B. Mohr (Paul Siebeck), 1983; repr.
Philadelphia: Fortress, 1986.

Reicke, B. "Der geschichtliche Hintergrund des Apostelkonzils und der Antiochia-
Episode." In *Studia Paulina,* ed. J. N. Sevenster and W. C. van Unnik, 172-87.
Haarlem: E. F. Bohn, 1953.

Rhyne, C. T. *Faith Establishes the Law.* SBL Diss. Series 55. Chico: Scholars Press, 1981.

Richardson, P. *Israel in the Apostolic Church.* SNTSMS 10. Cambridge: Cambridge University Press, 1969.

Ridderbos, H. *Paul: An Outline of His Theology.* English trans. Grand Rapids: Eerdmans,
1975.

Riedl, J. "Die Auslegung von R2,14-16 in Vergangenheit und Gegenwart." AnBib 17-18, I,
271-81.

Rissi, M. *Studien zum zweiten Korintherbrief.* AThANT 56. Zurich: Zwingli Verlag, 1969.

Robertson, A., and A. Plummer. *A Critical and Exegetical Commentary on the First Epistle of St Paul to the Corinthians.* ICC. Edinburgh: T&T Clark, 1911.

Robinson, J. A. T. *Redating the New Testament.* London: SCM, 1976.

———. *Wrestling with Romans.* London: SCM, 1979.

Ropes, J. H. *The Singular Problem of the Epistle to the Galatians.* Cambridge, Mass.: Harvard University Press, 1929.

Sanday, W., and A. C. Headlam. *A Critical and Exegetical Commentary on the Epistle to
the Romans.* ICC. Edinburgh: T&T Clark, 1902[5].

Sanders, E. P. "The Covenant as a Soteriological Category and the Nature of Salvation in
Palestinian and Hellenistic Judaism." In *Jews, Greeks and Christians, Religious Cultures in Late Antiquity: Essays in Honour of W. D. Davies,* ed. R. Hamerton-Kelly
and R. Scroggs, 11-44. Leiden: Brill, 1976.

———. *Paul and Palestinian Judaism: A Comparison of Patterns of Religion.* London:
SCM, 1977.

———. "On the Question of Fulfilling the Law in Paul and Rabbinic Judaism." In
Donum Gentilicium: New Testament Studies in Honour of David Daube, ed.
E. Bammel, C. K. Barrett, and W. D. Davies, 103-26. Oxford: Clarendon, 1978.

———. *Paul, the Law and the Jewish People.* Philadelphia: Fortress, 1983.

———. *Jesus and Judaism.* London: SCM, 1985.

Sanders, J. T. "Paul's 'Autobiographical' Statements in Galatians 1–2." *JBL* 85 (1966): 335-
43.

———. *The Jews in Luke-Acts.* London: SCM, 1987.

Schaff, Philip, ed. *Creeds of Christendom,* Volume 3: *The Creeds of the Evangelical
Protestant Churches,* repr. Grand Rapids: Baker, 1977.

Scharlemann, M. H. *Stephen: A Singular Saint.* AnBib. Rome: Pontifical Biblical Institute, 1968.

Schiffman, Lawrence. "The New Halakhic Letter (4QMMT) and the Origins of the
Dead Sea Sect." *Biblical Archaeologist* 53 (1990): 64-73.

Schlatter, A. *Gottes Gerechtigkeit: Ein Kommentar zum Römerbrief.* Stuttgart: Calwer Verlag, 1935.

Schlier, H. *Der Brief an die Galater.* KEKNT. Göttingen: Vandenhoeck & Ruprecht, 1949[1].

———. *Der Römerbrief.* HTKNT. Freiburg/Basel/Vienna: Herder & Herder, 1979[2].

Schlueter, Carol J. *Filling up the Measure: Polemical Hyperbole in 1 Thessalonians 2.14-16.* JSNTSup. Sheffield: Sheffield Academic Press, 1994.

Schürer, Emil, *The History of the Jewish People in the Age of Jesus Christ,* rev. G. Vermes, F. Millar, and M. Black. 3 vols. Edinburgh: T&T Clark, 1973-87.

Schmithals, W. *Paul and James.* English trans. SBT 46. London: SCM, 1965.

———. *Paul and the Gnostics.* English trans. Nashville: Abingdon, 1972.

Schnackenburg, R. *The Gospel according to St John.* 3 vols. English trans. Tunbridge Wells: Burns & Oates, 1968-82.

Schoeps, H. J. *Theologie und Geschichte des Judenchristentums.* Tübingen: J. C. B. Mohr (Paul Siebeck), 1949.

———. *Paul: The Theology of the Apostle in the Light of Jewish Religious History.* English trans. London: Lutterworth, 1961.

Schüssler Fiorenza, E. *In Memory of Her: A Feminist Theological Reconstruction of Christian Origins.* London: SCM, 1983.

———. *Bread Not Stone: The Challenge of Feminist Biblical Interpretation.* Edinburgh: T&T Clark, 1990.

Schütz, J. H. *Paul and the Anatomy of Apostolic Authority.* SNTSMS 26. Cambridge: Cambridge University Press, 1975.

Schweitzer, A. *Paul and His Interpreters.* English trans. London: A. & C. Black, 1912.

———. *The Mysticism of Paul the Apostle.* English trans. London: A. & C. Black, 1931.

Scroggs, R. "Paul and the Eschatological Woman." *JAAR* 40 (1972): 283-303.

———. "The Earliest Christian Communities as Sectarian Movement." In *Christianity, Judaism and Other Greco-Romans Cults.* Leiden: Brill, 1975.

———. "Paul as Rhetorician: Two Homilies in Romans 1–11." In *Jews, Greeks and Christians, Religious Cultures in Late Antiquity: Essays in Honour of W. D. Davies,* ed. R. Hamerton-Kelly and R. Scroggs, 271-98. Leiden: Brill, 1976.

Seifrid, Mark A. "Unrighteous by Faith: Apostolic Proclamation in Romans 1:18–3:20." In *Justification and Variegated Nomism:* Volume 2 — *The Paradoxes of Paul,* ed. D. A. Carson et al., 105-45. Tübingen: Mohr Siebeck; Grand Rapids: Baker, 2005.

Sevenster, J. N., and W. C. van Unnik, eds. *Studia Paulina in Honorem J. de Zwaan.* Haarlem: E. F. Bohn, 1953.

Shaw, Graham. *The Cost of Authority.* London: SCM, 1983.

Simon, M. *St Stephen and the Hellenists in the Primitive Church.* London: Longman, 1958.

Slee, Michelle. *The Church in Antioch in the First Century C.E.* JSNTSup. London: T&T Clark International, 2003.

Smallwood, E. M. *The Jews under Roman Rule.* Leiden: Brill, 1976.

Staab, K. *Die Thessalonicherbriefe, Die Gefangenschaftsbriefe.* Regensburger NT. Regensburg: Friedrich Pustet, 1969[5].

Stanley, Christopher. *Arguing with Scripture: The Rhetoric of Quotations in the Letters of Paul.* London: T&T Clark, 2004.

Stanton, G. N. "Stephen in Lucan Perspective." *StBib* 3 (1978): 345-60.

———. "The Gospel of Matthew and Judaism." *BJRL* 66 (1984): 264-84.

Stendahl, K. "The Apostle Paul and the Introspective Conscience of the West." *HTR* 56 (1963): 199-215.

———. *Paul among Jews and Gentiles and Other Essays.* London: SCM, 1977.

Stowers, Stanley K. *The Diatribe and Paul's Letter to the Romans.* SBL Diss. Ann Arbor: Scholars, 1981.

———. "Friends and Enemies in the Politics of Heaven." In *Pauline Theology,* Volume 1, ed. Jouette M. Bassler, 105-21. Minneapolis: Fortress, 1991.

———. *A Rereading of Romans: Justice, Jews, and Gentiles.* New Haven and London: Yale University Press, 1994.

Stroup, George W. *The Promise of Narrative Theology.* London: SCM, 1984.

Stuhlmacher, P. *Gottes Gerechtigkeit bei Paulus.* FRLANT. Göttingen: Vandenhoeck & Ruprecht, 1965.

———. "'Das Ende des Gesetzes': Über Ursprung und Ansatz der paulinischen Theologie." *ZTK* 67 (1970): 14-39.

Sumney, Jerry L. *'Servants of Satan', 'False Brothers' and Other Opponents of Paul.* JSNTSup. Sheffield: Sheffield Academic Press, 1999.

Talbert, C. H., ed. "Again: Paul's Visits to Jerusalem." *NovT* 9 (1967): 26-40.

Theissen, G. *The First Followers of Jesus: A Sociological Analysis of the Earliest Christianity.* English trans. London: SCM, 1978.

———. *The Social Setting of Pauline Christianity.* English trans. Edinburgh: T&T Clark, 1982. See especially "Legitimation and Subsistence: An Essay on the Sociology of Early Christian Missionaries," 27-67; "The Sociological Interpretation of Religious Traditions," 175-200.

———. *Social Reality and the Early Christians: Theology, Ethics, and the World of the New Testament.* English trans. Minneapolis: Augsburg Fortress; Edinburgh: T&T Clark, 1992.

Theobald, Michael. *Studien zum Römerbrief.* WUNT. Tübingen: Mohr Siebeck, 2001.

Thorsteinsson, Runar M. *Paul's Interlocutor in Romans 2: Function and Identity in the Context of Ancient Epistolography.* CB. Stockholm: Almquist & Wiksell, 2003.

Thrall, M. E. *The Second Epistle to the Corinthians.* 2 vols. ICC. Edinburgh: T&T Clark, 1994-2000.

Troeltsch, Ernst. *The Absoluteness of Christianity and the History of Religions.* English trans. London: SCM, 1972.

Tyson, J. B. "Paul's Opponents in Galatia." *NovT* 10 (1968): 241-54.

Wagner, J. Ross. *Heralds of the Good News: Isaiah and Paul "in Concert" in the Letter to the Romans.* NovTSup. Leiden: Brill, 2002.

Walaskay, P. W. *"And So We Came to Rome."* SNTSMS. Cambridge: Cambridge University Press, 1983.

Walker, R. "Die Heiden und das Gericht." *EvTh* 20 (1960): 302-14.

Watson, Francis B. "2 Cor. x–xiii and Paul's Painful Letter to the Corinthians." *JTS* 35 (1984): 324-46.

————. "The Social Function of Mark's Secrecy Theme." *JSNT* 24 (1985): 49-69.

————. *Paul, Judaism and the Gentiles: A Sociological Approach.* SNTSMS. Cambridge: Cambridge University Press, 1986[1].

————. *Text, Church and World: Biblical Interpretation in Theological Perspective.* Edinburgh: T&T Clark; Grand Rapids: Eerdmans, 1994.

————. *Text and Truth: Redefining Biblical Theology.* Edinburgh: T&T Clark; Grand Rapids: Eerdmans, 1997.

————. *Agape, Eros, Gender: Towards a Pauline Sexual Ethic.* Cambridge: Cambridge University Press, 2000.

————. "The Triune Divinity Identity: Reflections on Pauline God-language, in Disagreement with J. D. G. Dunn." *JSNT* 80 (2000): 99-124.

————. *Paul and the Hermeneutics of Faith.* London and New York: T&T Clark, 2004.

Watson, N. M. "Justified by Faith, Judged by Works — An Antinomy?" *NTS* 29 (1982-83): 209-21.

Webster, John. *Barth's Ethics of Reconciliation.* Cambridge: Cambridge University Press, 1995.

Wedderburn, A. J. M. *The Reasons for Romans.* Edinburgh: T&T Clark, 1991.

Welborn, L. L. "The Identification of 2 Corinthians 10–13 with the 'Letter of Tears.'" *NovT* 37 (1995): 138-53.

Westerholm, Stephen. "Paul and the Law in Romans 9–11." In *Paul and the Mosaic Law: The Third Durham-Tübingen Research Symposium on Earliest Christianity and Judaism (Durham, September 1994)*, ed. J. D. G. Dunn, 215-37. WUNT. Tübingen: Mohr Siebeck, 1996.

————. *Perspectives Old and New on Paul: The "Lutheran" Paul and His Critics.* Grand Rapids: Eerdmans, 2004.

Wiefel, W. "The Jewish Community in Ancient Rome and the Origins of Roman Christianity." In *The Romans Debate*, ed. K. P. Donfried. Minneapolis: Augsburg, 1977[1].

Wilckens, U. *Rechtfertigung als Freiheit.* Neukirchen: Neukirchener Verlag, 1974. See especially "Die Bekehrung des Paulus als religionsgeschichtliches Problem," 11-32; "Die Rechtfertigung Abrahams nach Römer 4," 33-49; "Was heiss bei Paulus: 'Aus Werken des Gesetzes wird kein Mensch gerecht'?" 77-109; "Über Abfassungszweck und Aufbau des Römerbriefs," 110-70.

————. *Der Brief an die Römer.* 3 vols. EKKNT. Zurich/Neukirchen: Benziger, 1978-82.

————. "Zur Entwicklung des paulinischen Gesetzesverständnisses." *NTS* 28 (1981-82): 154-90.

Wilken, Robert. *The Myth of Christian Beginnings: History's Impact on Belief.* New York: Doubleday, 1972.

Williams, M. H. "The Expulsion of the Jews from Rome in AD 19." *Latomus* 48 (1989): 767-68.

Wilson, S. G. *The Gentiles and the Gentile Mission in Luke-Acts*. SNTSMS. Cambridge: Cambridge University Press, 1973.

―――. *Luke and the Law*. SNTSMS. Cambridge: Cambridge University Press, 1983.

Windisch, H. *Der zweite Korintherbrief*. KEKNT. Göttingen: Vandenhoeck & Ruprecht, 1924.

Wright, N. T. "The Messiah and the People of God." Unpublished D.Phil. thesis, Oxford, 1980.

―――. *The Climax of the Covenant: Christ and the Law in Pauline Theology*. Edinburgh: T&T Clark, 1991.

―――. "The Law in Romans 2." In *Paul and the Mosaic Law: The Third Durham-Tübingen Research Symposium on Earliest Christianity and Judaism (Durham, September 1994)*, ed. J. D. G. Dunn, 131-50. WUNT. Tübingen: Mohr Siebeck, 1996.

―――. "The Letter to the Romans: Introduction, Commentary, and Reflections." In *The New Interpreter's Bible*, vol. 10, 393-770. Nashville: Abingdon, 2002.

Yinger, Kent L. *Paul, Judaism, and Judgment According to Deeds*. SNTSMS. Cambridge: Cambridge University Press, 1999.

Zahn, T. *Der Brief des Paulus an die Römer*. Leipzig: Deichert, 1910.

Zeller, D. *Juden und Heiden in der Mission des Paulus: Studien zum Römerbrief*. Stuttgart: Verlag Katholischer Bibelwerk, 1973.

Ziesler, J. A. *The Meaning of Righteousness in Paul: A Linguistic and Theological Inquiry*. SNTSMS. Cambridge: Cambridge University Press, 1972.

―――. "Justification by Faith in the Light of the 'New Perspective' on Paul." *Theology* 94 (1991): 188-94.

Index of Authors

Althaus, P., 31, 32, 40

Bandstra, A. J., 299
Barclay, J., 122, 130, 167, 168, 171, 173, 174, 176, 180, 186, 196
Barnard, L., 85
Barr, J., 366
Barrett, C. K., 65-69, 80, 94, 111, 131, 151-58, 175-76, 178, 183, 189, 197, 200-202, 205, 249, 258, 271, 305, 323, 332
Barth, K., 5, 6, 11, 16, 33, 51, 210, 214, 270, 302, 311, 315
Barth, M., 4, 5, 50, 128, 302
Bassler, J. M., 175
Bauckham, R., 89
Baur, F. C., 4, 28, 37-38, 40-45, 53, 55, 163, 165-66, 177, 278
Beare F. W., 146, 147
Becker, J., 153
Beker, J. C., 157, 167, 287
Bell, R., 208, 218, 219, 325, 338
Berger, P., 10
Betz, H.-D., 101, 103, 104, 106, 107, 111, 114, 119
Betz, O., 91
Bläser, P., 278, 281
Boccaccini, G., 91
Bockmuehl, M., 137

Borgen, P., 76
Bornkamm, G., 39, 66, 125, 150, 158, 166, 175, 182, 195, 198, 207, 277, 281
Boyarin, D., 24, 39, 255, 284, 292, 293, 350
Bring, R., 123
Brown, R., 94, 95
Bruce, F. F., 85, 104, 106, 109, 114, 116, 289
Bultmann, R., 5, 28, 31-52, 71, 94-95, 125, 130, 158, 208, 212, 214, 221, 253, 267, 270-71, 281, 289, 294, 332, 347-48, 352, 353
Burton, E., 106, 114, 116, 123, 127
Byrne, B., 123, 176, 250, 265, 293, 304, 308

Cadbury, H. J., 68
Caird, G. B., 2, 7, 143, 146
Campbell, D., 25, 122, 233, 235, 240, 241, 243, 244, 245
Carleton-Paget, J., 74, 77
Collange, J.-F., 158
Collins, J., 196
Conzelmann, H., 34, 39, 47, 84, 152, 154, 155, 193, 202, 260, 281
Cranfield, C. E. B., 49, 157, 176, 178, 183, 185-86, 189, 199, 208, 210-11, 219, 221, 223, 260, 267-68, 271, 277, 281, 289-90, 302, 304, 315, 331-32, 334, 342
Cullmann, O., 69

Index of Subjects

Acts, historicity of, 60-66, 69, 71, 73-75, 82, 108

agency, divine, 15-19, 125-26, 129-30, 148-50, 212-14, 238, 252, 264-65

Antioch, church of, 64-69, 85-86, 103-8, 113

boasting, 246-52

canon, 366-69

Christology, 8, 35-36, 48-49, 54-55, 254-56, 269-70, 273-75, 337, 351, 365-67

chronology, Pauline, 108-12, 137-43, 150-51

circumcision, 64, 74-84, 102-3, 105-7, 112-15, 119, 130-31, 143-46, 201, 209, 267, 355

collection, Paul's, 111-12, 191

covenantal nomism, 3, 7, 12-15, 17, 125, 148, 201-2

Damascus Road, 59-60, 70-71

diatribe, 178-79, 262

faith, 30, 35-36, 121-30, 134-35, 148-50, 182, 212-14, 231-45, 330

food laws, 62-64, 84-86, 175-77

Gentile mission, 59-69, 70-74, 79-82, 184-85, 331-32

God-fearers, 65, 73-79

Hellenists, 64-69, 173, 184-86

Holy Spirit, 238-39, 273, 296-97, 300

identity, Christian, 180-81, 189, 229, 259-60, 265, 268, 277, 287, 298, 301, 303-4, 362-69

ideology, 21, 52, 88-89, 181

Jerusalem, church of, 69-70, 71, 78-79, 82, 102-6, 113, 115-16

Judaism, Second Temple, xii, 6-7, 13, 15-19, 22-24, 46-47, 54, 136

judgment by works, 205-9, 213-14

law, Paul's view of the, 59-61, 69, 83-86, 98-99, 129-34, 156-59, 182, 214-15, 219-31, 256-58, 276-300, 351-69

Lutheran interpretation, xii-xiii, 2-3, 5-6, 21, 25-26, 27-40, 53, 55-56, 101, 134-35, 147, 166-67, 197, 202, 211, 214, 216, 229-30, 235, 246, 278, 302, 345-49, 354-60

"New Perspective on Paul," xii-xiii, 2-26, 248-49, 254-56, 352-54, 360

north Galatian theory, 108-10

Index of Scripture and Other Ancient Texts